# CROSS-CULTURAL SAMPLES AND CODES

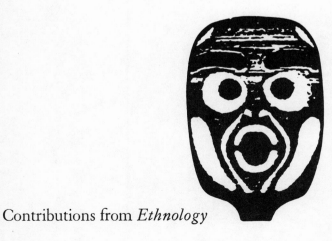

Contributions from *Ethnology*

# CROSS-CULTURAL SAMPLES and CODES

*Herbert Barry III and Alice Schlegel, Editors*

UNIVERSITY OF PITTSBURGH PRESS

in cooperation with *Ethnology*

Published by the University of Pittsburgh Press, Pittsburgh, Pa. 15260
Feffer and Simons, Inc., London
Manufactured in the United States of America

The studies in this volume are reprinted by arrangement with the editors of *Ethnology* and have appeared in the following issues of that journal: "Standard Cross-Cultural Sample," vol. 8 (October 1969): 329–69; "Subsistence Economy and Supportive Practices," vol. 9 (July 1970): 302–30; "Settlement Patterns and Community Organization," vol. 11 (July 1972): 254–95; "Political Organization," vol. 11 (October 1972): 436–64; "Measurement of Cultural Complexity," vol. 12 (October 1973): 379–92; "Infancy and Early Childhood," vol. 10 (October 1971): 466–508; "Traits Inculcated in Childhood," vol. 15 (January 1976): 83–114; "Agents and Techniques for Child Training," vol. 16 (April 1977): 191–230; "Adolescent Initiation Ceremonies," vol. 18 (April 1979): 199–210; "Factors in the Division of Labor by Sex," vol. 12 (April 1973): 203–25; "Cross-Cultural Codes on Twenty Sexual Attitudes and Practices," vol. 15 (October 1976): 409–29; "Cross-Cultural Codes Dealing with the Relative Status of Women," vol. 17 (April 1978): 211–37; "Patterns of Sibling Terminology," vol. 7 (January 1968): 1–24; "Kin Term Patterns and Their Distribution," vol. 9 (April 1970): 165–207; "Cross-Sex Patterns of Kin Behavior," vol. 10 (July 1971): 359–68.

## Library of Congress Cataloging in Publication Data

Main entry under title:

Cross-cultural samples and codes.

Bibliographies
   1.   Cross-cultural studies.   2.   Information storage and retrieval systems—Ethnology—Code words.   I.   Barry, Herbert, 1930–   II.   Schlegel, Alice.
GN345.7.C76        306        79-3878
ISBN 0-8229-3417-5
ISBN 0-8229-5317-X pbk.

# Contents

# Introduction

*Herbert Barry III* and *Alice Schlegel*

From its beginning *Ethnology* has strongly supported cross-cultural research. The first issue contained the initial installment of the Ethnographic Atlas (*Ethnology* 1962: 113–134), and the second carried the first cross-cultural article, "Child Training and Game Involvement" by J. M. Roberts and B. Sutton-Smith (1962: 166–185). Many additional articles using the cross-cultural method have been published in subsequent issues. This support reflects the interests of the journal's founder and first editor, George Peter Murdock, and the continuing commitment to cross-cultural research by the Department of Anthropology of the University of Pittsburgh, the publisher of *Ethnology*.

Between January 1962 and April 1967, *Ethnology* published twenty-one installments of the Ethnographic Atlas, the result of many years of research by Murdock on cultures around the world. These articles were designed to provide codes on specific variables for societies selected by world region. Beginning with nine variables and 100 societies, the Atlas eventually contained codings on nineteen variables for most societies with adequate ethnographic coverage to merit inclusion. The collated edition of the Ethnographic Atlas, containing codings on 863 societies, was published as the April 1967 issue of *Ethnology* (vol. 6, no. 2) and reprinted in a hardcover edition (now out of print) by the University of Pittsburgh Press in the same year. From 1967 to 1971, *Ethnology* published five supplements to the Ethnographic Atlas, containing ninety-four additional societies and correcting prior material.

In 1968 the Cross-Cultural Cumulative Coding Center was established at the University of Pittsburgh under the direction of Murdock and was supported until 1974 by the National Science Foundation. The first research result of the Center was the Standard Cross-Cultural Sample (Murdock and White 1969: 329-369), which was the culmination of years of Murdock's work on the development of such a sample. These 186 societies sample the universe of reported preindustrial cultures.

One of the features of the sample is the pinpointing of each cultural unit to a specific time and to the smallest identifiable subgroup of the society, generally a single community. Thus to some degree it is a sample of representative communities rather than of total tribes or nations. The temporal and geographical pinpointing enhances the accuracy of correlations between traits, because their presence or absence must coexist at the same time and place in order to be meaningful. This sample was used for subsequent coding and analysis by the Center's staff; the article presenting it is reprinted as chapter 1 of this book.

Chapters 2 through 8 and chapter 10 were completed through the Center. In each case the senior author was a member of the Department of Anthropology at the University of Pittsburgh, and the junior author or authors were members of the Center's staff. Each of these articles presents a new set of codes on the Standard Cross-Cultural Sample developed by, or under the direction of, the senior author. In most cases, each society was coded independently by two people. Sources and page numbers for each coding decision were recorded by the coders, thus ensuring that the codes could be checked for accuracy. The process was facilitated greatly by the availability of a set of the Human Relations Area Files at Hillman Library at the University of Pittsburgh. Although the sample is not drawn from the files, over half the societies are also contained in them. After each code set was completed, the data were transferred to computer cards and analyzed with the help of computer programs, principally the Statistical Package for the Social Sciences. Decks of cards for these codes are available from Human Relations Area Files, Inc., New Haven, Connecticut 06520.

The three sets of codes on the Standard Cross-Cultural Sample reprinted in chapters 9, 11, and 12 were not done through the Center. They are included here because they present new codes on the same sample of societies and can be cross-tabulated with the codes developed through the Center. Schlegel and Barry in chapter 9 and Broude and Greene in chapter 11 employ the entire sample, while Whyte in chapter 12 uses half the sample, ninety-three societies selected alternately from a listing by geographical area and thus a representative subsample of the larger sample.

We have divided the articles on the Standard Cross-Cultural Codes in Part I into three categories, each reflecting strong interests of Murdock and his colleagues at the Center: Herbert Barry III, John M. Roberts, Alice Schlegel, Arthur Tuden, and Douglas R. White. Since the Center developed codes derived from Murdock's *Social Structure* (1949), it is understandable that a body of research at the Center focused on various measures of the organization of society. Articles specifically related to this have been grouped under the heading "Cultural Elements" (chapters 2–5). The earliest of these, "Subsistence Economy and Supportive Practices: Cross-Cultural Codes 1" by Murdock and Morrow, gives detailed codes of subsistence practices and money and credit. While subsistence economy was coded for the Ethnographic Atlas, the new codes comprise a more detailed and accurate set of data for the Standard Cross-Cultural Sample. They have proven to be useful and basic to later studies of both social organization and levels of cultural complexity. The second article is directly related to social organization: "Settlement Patterns and Community Organization: Cross-Cultural Codes 3" by Murdock and Wilson includes codes on descent, residence, family form, and features of community life. "Political Organization: Cross-Cultural Codes 4" by Tuden and Marshall considers executive, legislative, and judicial features of political organization and levels of administrative hierarchy. Measures from these studies and others were adapted to construct the codes in the final article of this section, "Measurements of Cultural Complexity" by Murdock and Provost, which permit a scaling of societies by cultural and organizational features.

Three of the articles in the next section, "Socialization" (chapters 6–9), have as senior author Herbert Barry III. They reflect his training as a psychologist and are developed from earlier work done with psychologists Irwin L. Child and Margaret K. Bacon. "Infancy and Early Childhood: Cross-Cultural Codes 2" by Barry and Paxson deals with the treatment of infants and young children up to age four or five. "Traits Inculcated in Childhood: Cross-Cultural Codes 5" by Barry et al. quantitatively measures personality traits instilled in children from about age four or five. A distinction is made between early and late childhood and between boys and girls for each of those two stages. In "Agents and Techniques for Child Training: Cross-Cultural Codes 6" by Barry et al., the same age and sex groups as in the preceding article are coded for the principal socializers and what techniques they use. The final article in this section, "Adolescent Initiation Ceremonies: A Cross-Cultural Code" by Schlegel and Barry, covers the common but not universal ceremony that formally moves children out of childhood into adolescence. Like the two preceding papers, it contains separate codings for boys and girls.

A feature fundamental to the organization of all societies, and to socialization at least beyond infancy, is the social differentiation of the sexes; articles related to this topic appear under "Sex Differentiation" (chapters 10–12). In "Factors in the Division of Labor by Sex: A Cross-Cultural Analysis" by Murdock and Provost, sex roles in production are coded for the sample. The sexual features of social reproduction have been coded in "Cross-Cultural Codes on Twenty Sexual Attitudes and Practices" by Broude and Greene. In "Cross-Cultural Codes Dealing with the Relative Status of Women" by Whyte, a set of measures gives information on the social position of women (and thereby, of course, of men).

Part II of this book consists of three articles on kinship by Murdock which use samples drawn from the Ethnographic Atlas. "Patterns of Sibling Terminology" classifies sibling terms into seven basic types. With data on 800 societies from the EA, Murdock shows that sibling term patterns are related both to language family and to descent systems. A somewhat smaller sample of 566 societies was drawn for "Kin Term Patterns and Their Distribution," which presents a set of codes of term patterns for grandparents, grandchildren, uncles, aunts, nephews and nieces, siblings, cross-cousins, and siblings-in-law. In "Cross-Sex Patterns of Kin Behavior" material is drawn from a sample of eighty-nine societies assessing cross-sex kin behavior between nine pairs of relatives, including both consanguineal and affinal kin. The behavior patterns range in a continuum from avoidance to sexual license. The diverse topics of linguistics, social organization, and family relationships are integrated in these studies of kinship terms.

The purpose of the Cross-Cultural Cumulative Coding Center, as implied by its name, was to build up a collection of codes that could be cross-tabulated, thus increasing exponentially the utility of each code. The appendix, "Studies

Using the Standard Cross-Cultural Sample," contains both a list and a discussion of articles appearing from 1970 to 1978 which cite any of the articles reprinted here as chapters 1 through 12, thus indicating that the purpose of the Center is being fulfilled over time. These publications were identified mainly with the help of the Social Sciences Citation Index, an annual compilation of reference lists in a wide variety of scientific journals.

An especially important aspect of this list is that it indicates those publications which report new codes on the same sample of societies used in the standard sample. As each new code appears, it becomes possible to conduct an increasing number of tests of distribution and association, thus expanding our knowledge of functional relationships and the patterning of cultural features. We expect that the existing codes will be refined and expanded and that new codes will be developed concomitant with new theoretical orientations in anthropology. Work with the Standard Cross-Cultural Sample continues to be done at the Cross-Cultural Research Center of the Department of Anthropology at the University of Pittsburgh, and elsewhere.

The publications that have cited the Standard Cross-Cultural Sample reveal other ways in which the articles reprinted here have already been influential. Several important theories have been formulated or tested with the use of available codes on this sample or on portions of the sample. Several of the publications discuss the superiority of this standard sample as a method for minimizing Galton's problem of lack of independence of cases in a world sample of societies.

Cross-cultural research has proven to be a highly effective method to develop and test hypotheses. It produces studies that stand on their own merit and also those which provide comparisons with findings obtained by other methods, such as investigations of a single culture (our own or another), controlled comparisons, or experimental manipulations in laboratory settings. Not to be overlooked in these days of dwindling resources, cross-cultural research is economical in time and money when compared with some other methods. We believe that the collection of these papers in a single volume will be helpful to those who already use the method and that it will encourage others to add it to their research tools.

# I. The Standard Cross-Cultural Sample and Its Codes

# Standard Cross-Cultural Sample

*George P. Murdock and Douglas R. White*

This paper presents the first research results of the Cross-Cultural Cumulative Coding Center (CCCCC), a unit established at the University of Pittsburgh in May, 1968, with support from the National Science Foundation. It offers to scholars a representative sample of the world's known and well described cultures, 186 in number, each "pinpointed" to the smallest identifiable subgroup of the society in question at a specific point in time.

### PINPOINTING

The basic assumption underlying cross-cultural research is that the elements of any culture tend over time to become functionally integrated or reciprocally adjusted to one another. As new elements are invented or borrowed they are gradually fitted into the pre-existing cultural matrix, and the latter is modified to accommodate them. If such adaptations were instantaneous, cultures would at all times exhibit perfect integration, and, as British social anthropologists following Radcliffe-Brown have often rashly assumed, functional relationships among the elements of a culture or social system would readily become manifest through observation and analysis. If such were the case, valid scientific generalizations could be reached by the intensive study of individual cultures, and cross-cultural research would be unnecessary (a common corollary assumption among the same group of scholars).

Unfortunately, the integrative process is much more complex. New and introduced elements of culture require time—often the passage of generations—before they become adapted to the cultural matrix and it to them. Ogburn (1922: 200-280) coined the apt term "cultural lag" for this necessary interval. Because of the delay in adjustment, cultures never reveal perfect integration but only what Sumner (1906: 5-6) called a "strain toward consistency," in which innumerable adaptive processes are continually being interrupted by innovations and other events before they have fully run their course. Thus any culture at any time exhibits relationships among its constituent elements which are in part completely integrated functionally and in part still unadjusted or only imperfectly adjusted to each other. It is impossible for ethnographic analysis to identify these except by conjecture—and the conjectures of anthropologists who investigate functional relationships are not notably superior to those of anthropologists who attempt to reconstruct culture history.

When faced with problems of this sort, scientists resort to statistics. Distrustful of *ad hoc* interpretations of single instances, they examine a large and representative number of cases to determine whether the postulated relationships among relevant variables are quantitatively substantiated. This is precisely the rationale of cross-cultural research. Since some of the relationships among cultural elements are surely functional whereas others are not, statistics offers the only dependable technique for segregating them and thus arriving at scientifically valid generalizations.

By definition, cultural elements can be considered functionally interrelated only if they occur together at the same time among the same culture-bearing group. Elements occurring in the same society at different time periods, or in culturally variant subgroups, cannot be assumed to be functionally related, even though in some cases they may still reflect an earlier functional congruence. Methodologically, it is just as crucial to establish the actual concurrence of elements as to employ appropriate sampling and other statistical techniques to the analysis of their association. Unfortunately, previous cross-cultural research has commonly been as defective with respect to the former as to the latter requirement. The Human Relations Area Files assembles materials under the name of a society regardless of the date of the ethnographic observations and of whether the name embraces subgroups with marked cultural differences, and few researchers have sought a sharper focus, even though HRAF normally supplies the necessary information. All too frequently, therefore, assumed associations or their negation are invalidated by differences of time or place between the elements compared.

The authors have made a strenuous effort to correct this defect. They have "pinpointed" every society in the standard sample to a specific date and a specific locality, typically the local community where the principal authority conducted his most intensive field research, and they have eliminated from the sample all societies for which the sources do not permit reasonably accurate pinpointing. It is often possible, of course, for coders to make fairly reliable inferences by extrapolation from data on neighboring local groups with closely similar subcultures or from observations at somewhat earlier or later dates, but they should be instructed to use great caution in so doing and to specify their reasons. Focusing attention on a specific pinpointed date and locality should, it is believed, substantially enhance the accuracy of cross-cultural research.

Appendix A summarizes the data on the pinpointing sheets prepared by the Cross-Cultural Cumulative Coding Center for the guidance of its coders. The appendix specifies for each society of the standard sample its geographical focus with the name and coordinates of the pinpointed subgroup, its temporal focus with a specific date, and some indication of the reasons for the selection of both. It also names, for the guidance of researchers, the authority or authorities adjudged most dependable or useful, indicates whether or not HRAF has a file on the society (giving its identifying number) and whether such a file is of excellent, good, or marginal quality (i.e., the extent to which supplementation by library research may be necessary), and presents in abbreviated form the information on linguistic affiliation, type of subsistence economy, level of political integration, and prevailing rule of descent used below in estimating the relative strength of historical and integrative factors in producing cultural similarities. Bibliographical references to the principal sources on most of the societies may be found in the Ethnographic Atlas of this journal by means of the identifying numbers of the societies as given in the Appendix. Supplementary information will appear in future installments of the Atlas.

## SAMPLING

Another major but vexing problem of cross-cultural research is that of sampling, i.e., the selection for comparison of a number of societies that will adequately represent the entire range of known cultural variation and at the same time eliminate as far as possible the number of cases where similarities are presumably due to the historical influences of diffusion or common derivation. Five methods of coping with "Galton's problem," as this is called, have been advanced by Naroll (1961, 1964; Naroll and D'Andrade 1963), several of which the present authors have found useful.

Since his first major work utilizing a large cross-cultural sample (Murdock 1949), the senior author has proposed a series of improved and expanded world samples (Murdock 1957, 1963, 1968) and has discussed the problem of sampling from a theoretical point of view (Murdock 1966, 1968). The standard cross-cultural sample presented herewith represents the culmination of these efforts. It is designed specifically to correct a serious shortcoming of previous cross-cultural research. In general, each scholar has worked with a sample of his own choosing. Most of these have been small and selected in a relatively haphazard fashion with only casual reference to sampling principles. The selections have varied with each researcher, and the overlap between them has been small, so that it has rarely been possible to intercorrelate the findings of different studies. The progress of cross-cultural research has consequently been slow, and merely additive rather than multiplicative. What is needed to correct this situation is a large world sample, constructed with strict regard to ethnographic distributions and sophisticated sampling procedures, which can be used in different studies, so that the results of each can be intercorrelated with one another and the progress of comparative research thus lifted from an arithmetic to a geometric rate.

The establishment of such a sample has depended on three arduous but necessary preliminary research activities: (1) the analysis of more than 1,250 societies (in the Ethnographic Atlas of this journal), a very high proportion of all those whose cultures have been adequately described, to identify those with the fullest ethnographic coverage and to make certain that no major cultural variant has been overlooked; (2) the classification of all the cultures assessed into "clusters" (Murdock 1967), i.e., groups of contiguous societies with cultures so similar, owing either to diffusion or to recent common origin, that no world sample should include more than one of them; (3) the grouping of clusters, usually but not always adjacent, into "sampling provinces" (Murdock 1968) where linguistic and cultural evidence reveals similarities of a lesser order but still sufficient to raise the presumption of historical connections in violation of Galton's objections.

In general, one society was selected from each of the 200 world sampling provinces distinguished by Murdock (1968). However, for two of these provinces—Ancient Egypt (50) and Tasmania (110)—pinpointing to a particular locality and date proved impossible, and they are therefore unrepresented in the standard sample. Two other provinces (56 and 159) have been split in half and a representative selected from each. In fourteen other instances (Provinces 16, 26, 29, 33, 47, 71, 74, 87, 125, 147, 148, 157, 175, and 181) no representative was selected because the province was adjudged to resemble another too closely to warrant representation of both. In view of these changes and of the numerical reordering of the provinces for reasons to be presented later, the revised provinces from which the 186 sample societies are drawn will be designated hereinafter as "distinctive world areas" (or simply "areas") to distinguish them from the original "world sampling provinces."

The 186 societies included in the standard sample are distributed relatively equally among the six major regions of the world, as follows:

| | | |
|---|---|---|
| A | (Sub-Saharan Africa) | 28 |
| C | (Circum-Mediterranean) | 28 |
| E | (East Eurasia) | 34 |
| I | (Insular Pacific) | 31 |
| N | (North America) | 33 |
| S | (South and Central America) | 32 |

If Africa appears slightly underrepresented, the reader should note that the sample also includes two Negro societies in South America as well as several on the Sudan fringe of the Circum-Mediterranean.

The selection of the particular society to represent an area was based in most cases on the adjudged superiority of its ethnographic coverage. Sometimes, however, the overriding criterion was its distinctiveness in world perspective as regards either language (as in Areas 50 and 64), economy (as in 9 and 93), political organization (as in 31 and 54), or descent (as in 4 and 101). Oftentimes, too, the choice was determined by the availability of information in the Human Relations Area Files (as in Areas 55, 80, 81, 89, and 140). The standard sample thus constructed will naturally be modified in detail as superior ethnographies become available and as historical relationships within and between the sampling provinces are clarified by future research. For the time being, however, it represents the best selection of which the authors are capable. Comparison of our standard sample with previous samples of comparable or larger size (see Table 1) reveals, it is believed, its definite superiority in range, exhaustiveness, and relative independence of cases.

The sample of 250 societies used in *Social Structure* (Murdock 1949), when judged by current standards, was so obviously defective in several important respects that it can be excused only as a pioneer effort. The societies were not pinpointed in time or space. Two of the great world regions —the Circum-Mediterranean and South America—were seriously under-

TABLE 1. STANDARD SAMPLE (with Comparisons)

| Societies of the Standard Sample | Major Region | Sampling Province | Representation in Other Samples SS (250) | Textor (400) | HRAF (220) |
|---|---|---|---|---|---|
| 1. Nama Hottentot | A | 1 | 1 | 2 | 1 |
| 2. Kung Bushmen | A | 2 | 0 | 1 | 1 |
| 3. Thonga | A | 3 | 6 | 3 | 3 |
| 4. Lozi | A | 4 | 3 | 3 | 0 |
| 5. Mbundu | A | 5 | 2 | 3 | 1 |
| 6. Suku | A | 6 | 1 | 4 | 0 |
| 7. Bemba | A | 7 | 5 | 4 | 3 |
| 8. Nyakyusa | A | 9 | 1 | 2 | 1 |
| 9. Hadza | A | 10 | 0 | 3 | 0 |
| 10. Luguru | A | 11 | 0 | 1 | 0 |
| 11. Kikuyu | A | 12 | 0 | 2 | 2 |
| 12. Ganda | A | 13 | 5 | 4 | 2 |
| 13. Mbuti Pygmies | A | 15 | 0 | 1 | 0 |
| 14. Nkundo Mongo | A | 14 & 16 | 0 | 5 | 2 |
| 15. Banen | A | 17 | 0 | 3 | 0 |
| 16. Tiv | A | 29 & 30 | 6 | 5 | 2 |
| 17. Ibo | A | 18 | 3 | 1 | 0 |
| 18. Fon | A | 19 | 1 | 3 | 2 |
| 19. Ashanti | A | 20 | 2 | 1 | 1 |
| 20. Mende | A | 21 | 5 | 3 | 1 |
| 21. Wolof | C | 22 | 0 | 2 | 1 |
| 22. Bambara | A | 24 | 2 | 2 | 1 |
| 23. Tallensi | A | 26 & 27 | 3 | 4 | 2 |
| 24. Songhai | C | 25 | 0 | 1 | 0 |
| 25. Fulani | C | 23 | 0 | 1 | 0 |
| 26. Hausa | C | 28 | 3 | 2 | 2 |
| 27. Massa | A | 31 | 2 | 3 | 0 |
| 28. Azande | A | 33 & 34 | 1 | 4 | 1 |
| 29. Fur | C | 32 | 0 | 0 | 0 |
| 30. Otoro Nuba | A | 35 | 1 | 2 | 0 |
| 31. Shilluk | A | 37 | 3 | 4 | 2 |
| 32. Mao | A | 36 | 1 | 1 | 0 |
| 33. Kafa | C | 39 | 0 | 0 | 0 |
| 34. Masai | A | 38 | 6 | 6 | 2 |
| 35. Konso | C | 40 | 0 | 1 | 0 |
| 36. Somali | C | 41 | 0 | 1 | 1 |
| 37. Amhara | C | 42 | 0 | 1 | 1 |
| 38. Bogo | C | 43 | 0 | 1 | 0 |
| 39. Nubians | C | 44 | 0 | 1 | 0 |
| 40. Teda | C | 45 | 0 | 1 | 0 |
| 41. Tuareg | C | 46 | 0 | 0 | 1 |
| 42. Riffians | C | 47 & 48 | 0 | 5 | 2 |
| 43. Egyptians | C | 49 & 50 | 1 | 3 | 1 |
| 44. Hebrews | C | 51 | 0 | 1 | 0 |
| 45. Babylonians | C | 53 | 0 | 0 | 0 |
| 46. Rwala Bedouin | C | 52 | 0 | 2 | 6 |
| 47. Turks | C | 54 | 0 | 0 | 1 |
| 48. Gheg Albanians | C | 55 | 1 | 3 | 3 |
| 49. Romans | C | 56 (east) | 0 | 1 | 1 |
| 50. Basques | C | 56 (west) | 0 | 3 | 0 |
| 51. Irish | C | 57 | 1 | 7 | 3 |
| 52. Lapps | C | 58 | 1 | 1 | 1 |

TABLE 1   (*continued*)

| Societies of the Standard Sample | Major Region | Sampling Province | Representation in Other Samples | | |
|---|---|---|---|---|---|
| | | | SS (250) | Textor (400) | HRAF (220) |
| 53. Yurak Samoyed | E | 73 | 0 | 2 | 1 |
| 54. Russians | C | 59 | 1 | 3 | 2 |
| 55. Abkhaz | C | 60 | 1 | 2 | 1 |
| 56. Armenians | C | 61 | 0 | 1 | 0 |
| 57. Kurd | C | 62 | 1 | 0 | 2 |
| 58. Basseri | E | 63 | 0 | 1 | 0 |
| 59. Punjabi | E | 64 | 0 | 1 | 1 |
| 60. Gond | E | 67 | 4 | 5 | 2 |
| 61. Toda | E | 65 | 2 | 2 | 2 |
| 62. Santal | E | 68 | 3 | 5 | 1 |
| 63. Uttar Pradesh | E | 69 | 1 | 3 | 3 |
| 64. Burusho | E | 70 & 71 | 0 | 6 | 4 |
| 65. Kazak | E | 72 | 0 | 2 | 1 |
| 66. Khalka Mongols | E | 82 | 0 | 5 | 2 |
| 67. Lolo | E | 84 | 0 | 4 | 2 |
| 68. Lepcha | E | 85 | 1 | 3 | 2 |
| 69. Garo | E | 86 | 0 | 2 | 1 |
| 70. Lakher | E | 87 & 88 | 8 | 4 | 1 |
| 71. Burmese | E | 89 | 0 | 2 | 1 |
| 72. Lamet | E | 90 | 0 | 1 | 0 |
| 73. Vietnamese | E | 97 | 0 | 1 | 1 |
| 74. Rhade | E | 96 | 0 | 1 | 0 |
| 75. Khmer | E | 95 | 0 | 1 | 1 |
| 76. Siamese | E | 91 | 0 | 1 | 0 |
| 77. Semang | E | 94 | 1 | 1 | 1 |
| 78. Nicobarese | E | 93 | 0 | 1 | 0 |
| 79. Andamanese | E | 92 | 1 | 1 | 1 |
| 80. Vedda | E | 66 | 1 | 2 | 1 |
| 81. Tanala | E | 8 | 1 | 2 | 1 |
| 82. Negri Sembilan | E | 102 | 3 | 4 | 2 |
| 83. Javanese | I | 103 | 0 | 1 | 0 |
| 84. Balinese | I | 104 | 1 | 1 | 1 |
| 85. Iban | I | 101 | 0 | 2 | 1 |
| 86. Badjau | I | 100 | 0 | 1 | 0 |
| 87. Toradja | I | 105 | 0 | 2 | 1 |
| 88. Tobelorese | I | 106 | 0 | 0 | 0 |
| 89. Alorese | I | 107 | 0 | 3 | 1 |
| 90. Tiwi | I | 108 | 1 | 4 | 2 |
| 91. Aranda | I | 109 & 110 | 4 | 3 | 2 |
| 92. Orokaiva | I | 111 | 3 | 2 | 1 |
| 93. Kimam | I | 112 | 4 | 1 | 0 |
| 94. Kapauku | I | 114 | 0 | 2 | 1 |
| 95. Kwoma | I | 113 | 7 | 3 | 1 |
| 96. Manus | I | 120 | 1 | 1 | 1 |
| 97. New Ireland | I | 121 | 2 | 2 | 1 |
| 98. Trobrianders | I | 122 | 3 | 2 | 1 |
| 99. Siuai | I | 123 | 6 | 3 | 1 |
| 100. Tikopia | I | 124 & Tikopia | 2 | 2 | 2 |
| 101. Pentecost | I | 125 & 126 | 9 | 3 | 2 |
| 102. Mbau Fijians | I | 128 | 1 | 3 | 1 |
| 103. Ajie | I | 127 | 0 | 2 | 0 |
| 104. Maori | I | 130 | 1 | 1 | 1 |

TABLE 1 (*continued*)

| Societies of the Standard Sample | Major Region | Sampling Province | Representation in Other Samples | | |
|---|---|---|---|---|---|
| | | | SS (250) | Textor (400) | HRAF (220) |
| 105. Marquesans | I | 131 | 3 | 6 | 2 |
| 106. Samoans | I | 129 | 5 | 4 | 2 |
| 107. Gilbertese | I | 119 | 0 | 1 | 0 |
| 108. Marshallese | I | 118 | 2 | 1 | 1 |
| 109. Trukese | I | 117 | 1 | 3 | 2 |
| 110. Yapese | I | 116 | 0 | 1 | 1 |
| 111. Palauans | I | 115 | 0 | 1 | 0 |
| 112. Ifugao | I | 99 | 1 | 5 | 3 |
| 113. Atayal | I | 98 | 0 | 2 | 1 |
| 114. Chinese | E | 83 | 1 | 1 | 4 |
| 115. Manchu | E | 81 | 1 | 1 | 1 |
| 116. Koreans | E | 80 | 0 | 1 | 1 |
| 117. Japanese | E | 79 | 0 | 2 | 1 |
| 118. Ainu | E | 78 | 0 | 1 | 1 |
| 119. Gilyak | E | 77 | 1 | 1 | 1 |
| 120. Yukaghir | E | 74 & 75 | 1 | 2 | 1 |
| 121. Chukchee | E | 76 | 2 | 2 | 3 |
| 122. Ingalik | N | 135 | 1 | 1 | 0 |
| 123. Aleut | N | 132 | 0 | 1 | 1 |
| 124. Copper Eskimo | N | 133 | 2 | 2 | 1 |
| 125. Montagnais | N | 151 | 1 | 2 | 2 |
| 126. Micmac | N | 152 | 1 | 1 | 1 |
| 127. Saulteaux | N | 153 | 1 | 1 | 3 |
| 128. Slave | N | 134 | 1 | 0 | 0 |
| 129. Kaska | N | 138 | 2 | 1 | 1 |
| 130. Eyak | N | 136 | 1 | 2 | 0 |
| 131. Haida | N | 137 | 3 | 2 | 1 |
| 132. Bellacoola | N | 139 | 1 | 1 | 2 |
| 133. Twana | N | 140 | 2 | 1 | 0 |
| 134. Yurok | N | 141 | 2 | 2 | 1 |
| 135. Pomo | N | 143 | 1 | 2 | 1 |
| 136. Yokuts | N | 144 | 3 | 3 | 2 |
| 137. Paiute | N | 146 & 147 | 2 | 2 | 3 |
| 138. Klamath | N | 142 & 148 | 7 | 3 | 0 |
| 139. Kutenai | N | 149 | 3 | 2 | 3 |
| 140. Gros Ventre | N | 150 | 2 | 3 | 1 |
| 141. Hidatsa | N | 154 | 2 | 2 | 2 |
| 142. Pawnee | N | 159 less Natchez | 2 | 3 | 1 |
| 143. Omaha | N | 155 | 4 | 4 | 4 |
| 144. Huron | N | 156 | 1 | 2 | 2 |
| 145. Creek | N | 157 & 158 | 4 | 4 | 1 |
| 146. Natchez | N | 159 (Natchez) | 1 | 1 | 0 |
| 147. Comanche | N | 160 | 4 | 3 | 1 |
| 148. Chiricahua | N | 161 | 3 | 2 | 1 |
| 149. Zuni | N | 162 | 6 | 5 | 2 |
| 150. Havasupai | N | 145 | 4 | 3 | 3 |
| 151. Papago | N | 163 | 2 | 3 | 3 |
| 152. Huichol | N | 164 | 0 | 1 | 0 |
| 153. Aztec | N | 165 | 0 | 3 | 3 |
| 154. Popoluca | N | 166 | 0 | 2 | 0 |
| 155. Quiche | S | 167 | 1 | 4 | 1 |
| 156. Miskito | S | 168 | 0 | 1 | 1 |

TABLE 1    (*continued*)

| Societies of the Standard Sample | Major Region | Sampling Province | Representation in Other Samples SS (250) | Textor (400) | HRAF (220) |
|---|---|---|---|---|---|
| 157. Bribri | S | 169 | 0 | 1 | 1 |
| 158. Cuna | S | 170 | 1 | 2 | 1 |
| 159. Goajiro | S | 172 | 0 | 4 | 2 |
| 160. Haitians | S | 174 | 0 | 0 | 2 |
| 161. Callinago | S | 173 | 1 | 2 | 1 |
| 162. Warrau | S | 175 & 176 | 1 | 3 | 2 |
| 163. Yanomamo | S | 177 | 0 | 2 | 0 |
| 164. Carib | S | 178 | 3 | 3 | 1 |
| 165. Saramacca | S | 179 | 0 | 1 | 1 |
| 166. Mundurucu | S | 180 & 181 | 0 | 2 | 1 |
| 167. Cubeo | S | 182 | 1 | 4 | 1 |
| 168. Cayapa | S | 171 | 1 | 4 | 2 |
| 169. Jivaro | S | 183 | 0 | 1 | 1 |
| 170. Amahuaca | S | 184 | 0 | 0 | 0 |
| 171. Inca | S | 185 | 1 | 1 | 1 |
| 172. Aymara | S | 186 | 1 | 1 | 2 |
| 173. Siriono | S | 187 | 1 | 3 | 2 |
| 174. Nambicuara | S | 188 | 1 | 1 | 1 |
| 175. Trumai | S | 189 | 0 | 4 | 2 |
| 176. Timbira | S | 190 | 2 | 2 | 1 |
| 177. Tupinamba | S | 191 | 1 | 3 | 2 |
| 178. Botocudo | S | 192 | 0 | 1 | 0 |
| 179. Shavante | S | 193 | 1 | 2 | 1 |
| 180. Aweikoma | S | 194 | 1 | 1 | 1 |
| 181. Cayua | S | 195 | 0 | 0 | 0 |
| 182. Lengua | S | 196 & Lengua | 0 | 3 | 0 |
| 183. Abipon | S | 197 less Lengua | 1 | 3 | 2 |
| 184. Mapuche | S | 198 | 1 | 1 | 1 |
| 185. Tehuelche | S | 199 | 1 | 2 | 1 |
| 186. Yahgan | S | 200 | 1 | 2 | 1 |

represented, as were complex societies in general. No examples were included from the past civilizations that are adequately described in contemporary documents. For the present sample the authors made a special search for such cases and were able to include three—the Babylonians at the end of Hammurabi's reign (Area 45), the Hebrews at the time of the promulgation of the Deuteronomic code (Area 44), and the Romans of the early imperial period (Area 49), for whom the Athenians of the Periclean Age might well have been substituted. Several other possibilities were rejected as inadequately described or incapable of exact pinpointing as to date or locality, notably the Carthaginians, Egyptians (of either the Middle Kingdom or the New Empire), Indo-Aryans, Persians, Scythians, and Sumerians, although an early dynastic period in China could probably have been used if the authors had been able to control the Chinese language and literature.

The numerous gaps and duplications of the SS sample constitute an even more serious fault. Of the 186 areas represented by one case each in the present sample, 75 (or 41 per cent) had no representatives in the earlier sample, whereas 34 (or 18 per cent) were heavily overrepresented, i.e., by three or more cases each. Fortunately it is possible to profit by one's own past errors.

The sample of 400 societies used by Textor (1967), derived from the Ethnographic Atlas (Murdock 1963), reveals a marked improvement. Of the 186 areas of our standard sample, only eleven (or 6 per cent) are completely unrepresented and 28 (or 15 per cent) are seriously overrepresented. Textor's correlations can therefore be accepted with only modest reservations. The chief lesson to be learned from Textor's work, however, is that samples of such large size are unnecessary. Our own research indicates that a carefully drawn sample of around 200 cases essentially exhausts the universe of known and adequately described culture types.

The files of good (or at least fair) quality produced to date by the Human Relations Area Files constitute a third large world sample—and one deserving special analysis because of their enormous potential utility in cross-cultural research. From an examination of the set at the University of Pittsburgh the authors have estimated that the files on 220 societies are usable, though in some cases only marginally so. They are analyzed in Table 2 with regard to their distribution by major regions and distinctive world areas, by their use and availability for the societies of our standard sample, and by the relative quality of those available.

TABLE 2.   DISTRIBUTION OF HRAF FILES BY REGIONS, AREAS, QUALITY, AND USE

| Major Region | Number of HRAF Files | Areas Represented By | | | | Sample Societies Using HRAF Files | | Societies Not Using Available HRAF Files |
|---|---|---|---|---|---|---|---|---|
| | | No Files | One File | Two Files | 3–6 Files | Adequate | Marginal | |
| A | 30 | 10 | 8 | 8 | 2 | 16 | 1 | 1 |
| C | 29 | 12 | 9 | 4 | 3 | 13 | 2 | 1 |
| E | 47 | 4 | 19 | 7 | 4 | 17 | 8 | 5 |
| I | 32 | 7 | 16 | 7 | 1 | 14 | 5 | 5 |
| N | 46 | 8 | 12 | 6 | 7 | 19 | 2 | 4 |
| S | 36 | 5 | 18 | 9 | 0 | 22 | 1 | 4 |
| Total | 220 | 46 | 82 | 41 | 17 | 101 | 19 | 20 |

In the adequacy of its distribution the HRAF sample stands about midway between the SS and Textor samples. It lacks any representative for 46 (25 per cent) of our 186 distinctive areas, ranging from a maximum of 12 (43 per cent) of those of the Circum-Mediterranean to a minimum of 4 in East Eurasia. Of the societies in our standard sample, 120 (or 64 per cent) are represented by HRAF files; 19 of these, however, are adjudged only marginally useful for the pinpointed subgroup, i.e., requiring supplementation by library research. In 20 instances in which a HRAF file exists for a particular area, another society, not represented in HRAF, was selected as more suitable. Hence researchers may, without departing from strict sampling principles, substitute any of the following HRAF files for the alternative selections in the standard sample: Yoruba for Fon in Area 18, Maltese for

Romans in 49, Kol for Santal in 62, Khasi for Garo in 69, Kachin for Lakher in 70, Macassarese for Toradja in 87, Wogeo for Kwoma in 95, Kurtatchi (Buka) for Siuai in 99, Malekula or Santa Cruz for Pentecost in 101, Lau Fijians for Mbau Fijians in 102, Okinawans for Japanese in 117, Yakut for Yukaghir in 120, Tlingit for Haida in 131, Mandan for Hidatsa in 141, Iroquois for Huron in 144, Tewa for Chiricahua in 148, Yucatec Maya for Quiche in 155, Tucuna for Cubeo in 167, Bacairi or Bororo for Trumai in 175, Caraja for Shavante in 179. They must, however, resort to library research for any society in the 46 areas not represented in HRAF; failure to do so would result in sampling distortion and consequent reduction in the reliability of findings.

Cross-cultural researchers, in short, though they will find HRAF of invaluable assistance, cannot depend exclusively on this resource if they wish to adhere to sophisticated sampling procedures. Little improvement in this respect can be envisaged for the future. The so-called "blue ribbon" enrichment sample of fifteen societies on which the HRAF staff is currently working, for example, will fill only three of the 46 areas now unrepresented: 27 (Kanuri), 50 (Bahia Brazilians), and 181 (Guarani). Four other cases are improvements of already existing files: Somali of Area 36, Serbs of 48, Khasi of 69, and Siamese of 76. The remaining eight will merely produce new files on areas already represented, adding the Dogon to the Mossi and Tallensi in Area 33, the Santal to the Kol in 62, the Garo to the Khasi in 69, the Sinhalese to the Vedda in 80, the Toradja to the Macassarese in 97, the Taiwan Chinese to four existing Chinese files in 114, the Tzeltal to the Yucatec Maya in 155, and the Tucano to the Tucuna in 167.

Most cross-cultural samples reveal a definite bias in favor of sources in the English language. In compiling our standard sample the authors have specifically sought to discount this bias and to select the best described societies irrespective of the nationality or native language of the ethnographers. To be sure, speakers of English (Americans, Australians, British, Canadians, New Zealanders, and South Africans) have made a preponderant contribution to world ethnography, and it is not surprising that they include the principal authorities on 62 per cent of the societies in the standard sample. However, the contributions from other nationals have been far from negligible. We estimate the number of societies in our sample for which the principal authority is (or was) a native speaker of a language other than English, regardless of the language in which his description may have been written or published, as follows:

| | | | |
|---|---|---|---|
| 4 | Arabic or other Semitic | 2 | Italian or Latin |
| 2 | Bantu or other African | 2 | Japanese |
| 3 | Chinese | 6 | North Germanic or Scandinavian |
| 4 | Dutch | 9 | Russian or other Slavic |
| 16 | French | 5 | Spanish |
| 16 | German | 1 | Turkish |

Excluded from the above count, of course, are authors who emigrated in childhood or youth from one language area to another.

In the effort to achieve diversity and relative historical independence among the societies of the standard sample, we selected a single society from each of 51 independent linguistic families (not necessarily independent phyla) and also one as the sole representative of each of 34 linguistic subfamilies where other subfamilies of the same family were represented. Since the speakers of distinct subfamilies have normally been separated for well over 2,000 years, the cultures of these 85 societies, constituting 43 per cent of the total sample, may be considered exempt or nearly so from historical influences stemming from common origins. The remaining 101 societies, not thus exempt, have been chosen from linguistic subfamilies having other representatives in the sample, as follows:

2 from the Berber, 2 from the Chadic, 4 from the Cushitic, and 5 from the Semitic subfamilies of Afro-Asiatic or Hamito-Semitic;
4 from Algonkian;
2 from the Turkic subfamily of Altaic;
3 from the Northern subfamily of Athapaskan;
2 from Australian;
2 from Cariban;
2 from the Eastern subfamily of Chari-Nile or Macro-Sudanic;
2 from Chibchan (as well as a third from a different subfamily);
2 from Dravidian;
2 from Ge (as well as a third from a distinct subfamily);
3 from the Indic, 2 from the Iranian, and 3 from the Italic or Romance subfamilies of Indo-European;
2 from the Southern subfamily of Khoisan;
4 from the Carolinian, 11 from the Hesperonesian, 6 from the Melanesian, and 4 from the Polynesian subfamilies of Malayo-Polynesian;
2 from Nahuatlan or Mexicano;
2 from the Atlantic, 13 from the Bantoid or Central, 3 from the Kwa, and 2 from the Mande subfamilies of Niger-Congo;
2 from Salishan;
2 from Shoshonean;
2 from Siouan;
4 from Tupi-Guarani.

Such linguistic duplication is impossible to avoid in Africa, the Circum-Mediterranean, and the Insular Pacific because of the preponderance of very large families and subfamilies in these regions, and especial attention was therefore paid to cultural differentiation in selecting samples from these linguistic groups.

The distribution of other cultural features in the sample probably approximates that in the world as a whole. The major types of subsistence economy in the sample societies are classified as follows:

141 food-producing economies: 126 agricultural and 15 pastoral. In Appendix A, the agricultural economies are further differentiated into advanced agriculture (56), horticulture (19), and simple or swidden agriculture (51).
45 food-collecting economies: 13 primarily gathering, 14 primarily hunting (including 4 societies of equestrian hunters), and 18 primarily fishing (including one which depends for food more on trade than on direct subsistence activities). The great majority of the food-collecting societies are located in North and South America.

The complexity of political organization (see Table 3) is greatest in the Circum-Mediterranean, intermediate in Africa and East Eurasia, and rel-

TABLE 3.   RELATIVE POLITICAL COMPLEXITY BY MAJOR WORLD REGIONS

| Major Region | Stateless Societies | Societies With Minimal States | Societies With Small States | Societies With Large States | Total |
|---|---|---|---|---|---|
| A | 8 | 9 | 6 | 5 | 28 |
| C | 1 | 8 | 5 | 14 | 28 |
| E | 11 | 10 | 2 | 11 | 34 |
| I | 13 | 11 | 6 | 1 | 31 |
| N | 23 | 7 | 2 | 1 | 33 |
| S | 23 | 5 | 2 | 2 | 32 |
| Total | 79 | 50 | 23 | 34 | 186 |

atively slight in the Insular Pacific and the Americas. The several societies which form an integral part of a large state dominated by another society are classed as having the level of political integration of their rulers (i.e., with three or more levels above that of the local community).

The major types of social organization, as represented by the prevailing rule of descent, reveal a fairly even distribution among the regions of the earth (see Table 4), despite some preponderance of patrilineal forms in the Old World and of bilateral forms in the New World. In Table 4, quasi-patrilineal descent (three cases) is grouped with bilaterality, and double descent is classified as matrilineal (one case) or patrilineal (six cases) depending upon the prevailing rule of marital residence.

In selecting the dates for which the societies of the sample are pinpointed, the authors have in general chosen the earliest period for which satisfactory ethnographic data are available or can be reconstructed, though we have sometimes used a later date for which the descriptive materials are appreciably richer. The reason, of course, is to avoid insofar as possible the acculturative effects of contacts with Europeans, which in recent centuries have exerted a convergent influence on all the cultures of the world. To further offset this influence, we have excluded from our sample the great colonizing and imperialistic societies of Europe—the Belgians, Dutch, English, French, Germans, Italians, Portuguese, and Spaniards—since their cultures are assumed to be reflected to some degree in those of the peoples they have governed or missionized. Table 5 shows the range of the pinpointed dates for the societies of the sample, classified by major regions as

TABLE 4.   RULES OF DESCENT BY MAJOR REGIONS

| Region | Ambilineal | Bilateral | Matrilineal | Patrilineal | Total |
|---|---|---|---|---|---|
| A | 2 | 3 | 4 | 19 | 28 |
| C | 0 | 9 | 2 | 17 | 28 |
| E | 0 | 9 | 5 | 20 | 34 |
| I | 6 | 7 | 7 | 11 | 31 |
| N | 2 | 20 | 8 | 3 | 33 |
| S | 0 | 21 | 5 | 6 | 32 |
| Total | 10 | 69 | 31 | 76 | 186 |

TABLE 5.  RANGE OF PINPOINTED DATES FOR THE SAMPLE SOCIETIES

| Time Period | A | C | E | I | N | S | Total |
|---|---|---|---|---|---|---|---|
| 1750 to 1 B.C. | 0 | 2 | 0 | 0 | 0 | 0 | 2 |
| A.D. 1 to 1500 | 0 | 1 | 1 | 0 | 0 | 0 | 2 |
| A.D. 1501 to 1600 | 0 | 0 | 0 | 0 | 1 | 2 | 3 |
| A.D. 1601 to 1700 | 0 | 0 | 0 | 0 | 2 | 1 | 3 |
| A.D. 1701 to 1800 | 0 | 0 | 0 | 1 | 3 | 1 | 5 |
| A.D. 1801 to 1850 | 0 | 1 | 0 | 4 | 4 | 2 | 11 |
| A.D. 1851 to 1900 | 9 | 7 | 11 | 4 | 16 | 5 | 52 |
| A.D. 1901 to 1950 | 19 | 13 | 17 | 16 | 7 | 19 | 91 |
| A.D. 1951 to 1965 | 0 | 4 | 5 | 6 | 0 | 2 | 17 |
| Total | 28 | 28 | 34 | 31 | 33 | 32 | 186 |

well as time periods. The earliest dates, of course, are for the Old World, whereas the New World shows a preponderance of the intermediate dates. The heaviest concentration naturally falls in the century from 1851 to 1950, the heyday of professional anthropology.

## MAPS

Six maps, each constructed to a similar scale on equal-area projections, locate the pinpointed focus of 184 of the sample societies; only the Marquesans and Samoans of Polynesia could not be accommodated. The authors acknowledge with gratitude the assistance rendered by Professor Hibberd V. B. Kline, Jr., and Mr. Howard N. Ziegler of the Department of Geography, University of Pittsburgh, in preparing these maps. They give a graphic picture of the geographic distribution of the sample societies. The areas where such societies are sparsely represented are in most cases either those which are largely uninhabited (like much of the Sahara Desert and of Arctic Canada), those whose indigenous cultures mainly disappeared before they were recorded (like the eastern seaboards of Brazil and the United States), or those where essentially similar cultures cover extensive territories (as in China and aboriginal Australia). In general, only inhabited islands are indicated (outlined or suggested by dots), others being completely omitted, and in no case are areas shown in one map duplicated in any other. The maps correspond only roughly to our six major world regions (A, C, E, I, N, and S), the discrepancies being noted beneath each map.

The numerical order in which the 186 societies (and areas) of the sample have been arranged (see Table 1 and Appendix A) can be readily followed on the maps by observing their numbers sequentially. The ordering, though it may appear arbitrary at first glance, was designed to place each area, insofar as possible, between the two others to which it is geographically most contiguous and culturally most similar. The alignment thus zigzags across the maps, guided by the restraints imposed by major geographic, linguistic, and ethnic boundaries, and crosses from one region to another where they are most contiguous.

MAP I: AFRICA

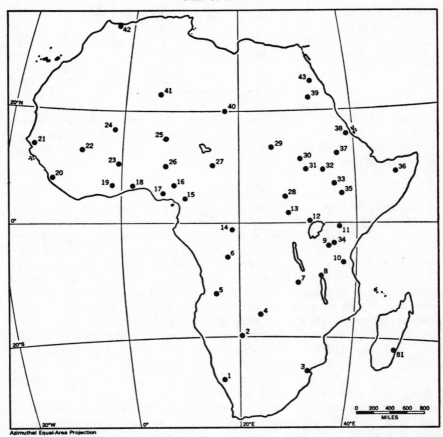

This map locates all 28 of the sample societies in Sub-Saharan Africa (A), fifteen of those in the Circum-Mediterranean region (C), and one in Madagascar, which is included in East Eurasia (E).

MAP 2: WEST EURASIA

**This map locates thirteen of the sample societies of the Circum-Mediterranean region (C) and five of those in East Eurasia (E).**

MAP 3: EAST EURASIA

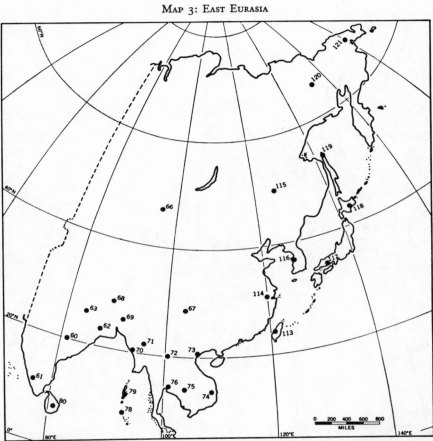

**This map locates 25 of the sample societies from the world region of East Eurasia (E) and one from the Insular Pacific (I).**

MAP 4: INSULAR PACIFIC

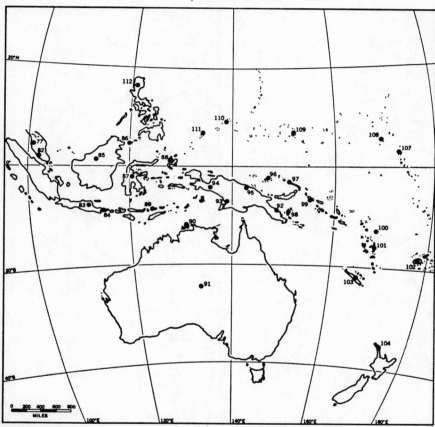

This map locates two of the sample societies from the East Eurasian region (E) and 28 of those from the Insular Pacific region (I).

MAP 5: NORTH AMERICA

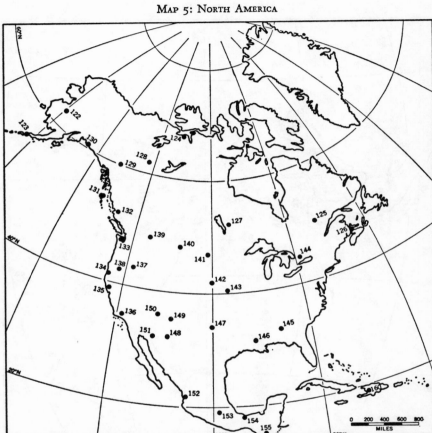

This map locates all 33 of the sample societies of the North American region (N) and two of those from the South American region (S).

MAP 6: SOUTH AMERICA

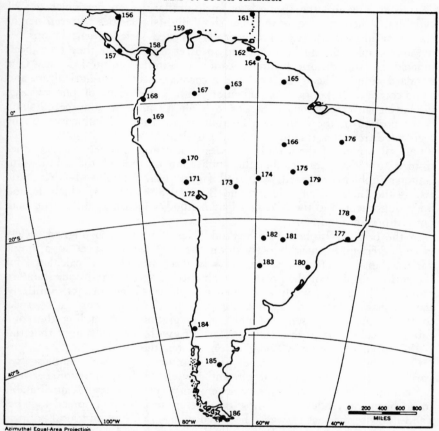

This map locates 30 of the 32 societies from the South American region (S).

## Measurement of Historical Influences

The delimitation of distinctive world areas as sampling strata can at best minimize, but cannot eliminate, the cultural similarities between neighboring areas which result from the historical influences of common origin and cultural diffusion. The most effective way of meeting Galton's objections is to measure the strength of such similarities on particular sets of variables. Where particular variables show high similarities between neighboring or historically (e.g., linguistically) related societies, correlations between variables should be examined to ascertain whether they have been inflated by the historical multiplication of similar cultural forms. Our standard sample reveals, for example, a correlation between agriculture and supra-community political organization with a coefficient of phi $= .457$. For any such correlation, a solution to Galton's problem may be obtained if the portion of the correlation attributable to historical influences can be segregated from that due to functional parallelism.

Our alignment of the sample societies in a continuous geo-cultural series from 1 to 186 makes possible the application of four of the solutions to Galton's problem proposed by Naroll (1961, 1964; Naroll and D'Andrade 1963)—the Linked Pair, Cluster, and Bimodal Sift methods, which depend upon alignment, and the Matched Pair method, which may utilize but does not require an alignment.

In the original Linked Pair method (Naroll 1964) each aligned society is compared to its neighbor (next on the list) with respect to a single variable, and a coefficient of similarity between neighbors is calculated for the entire sample. For the presence or absence of agriculture in our standard sample, for example, we have calculated a phi coefficient of .351. Similarly, the correlation between neighboring pairs in the alignment with respect to the presence or absence of political integration transcending the community level yields a phi coefficient of .316, with the probability that this is due to chance being $< .0001$ or one in ten thousand.

Given the high correlations between alignment neighbors on these two variables, it is likely that a significant portion of the correlation between agriculture and supra-community sovereignty (phi $= .457$) is attributable to an historical tendency for these two factors to diffuse or spread together (and likewise for that between the absence of agriculture and local political autonomy). The Matched Pair method of Naroll and D'Andrade (1963) can be used to estimate the relative strengths of the hypothesis of historical influence *versus* that of functional integration. This test, however, merely indicates whether one hypothesis is superior, equal, or inferior to the other. In the case of agriculture and supra-community sovereignty, the two hypotheses come out equally. The obvious weakness of this method is that it does not provide an estimate of what the functional correlation between the two variables would be if historical influences could be factored out; one does not know whether the residual functional correlation would be statistically significant or not. One of the solutions of Naroll and D'Andrade (1963), which would answer this question, is the Interval Sift method, in which the independent variable (e.g., economic type) is examined to ascertain the size of the "patches" of greater-than-random similarities (reflecting historical influences) between contiguous societies and to choose a subsample from representatives of distinct patches. The present authors have found it useful to examine successively more distant pairs along the alignment to determine at what interval the similarities between pairs fall within the acceptable probabilities of a random model. This interval then becomes the criterion of the size of the "patches" of historical relatedness from which a subsample can be drawn which is free of noticeable historical effects.

In developing this modification of the Linked Pair method, we have employed an index of similarity between pairs instead of using Naroll's technique of calculating the correlation between pairs on a single attribute. This index of similarity can yield a valid measure of average similarities within regions, whereas the correlation method is unsuited for such comparison; for example, if agriculture is the dominant economic mode in a region, a correlation of the presence of agriculture between neighbors does not reflect this homogeneity. In constructing our index of similarity we have utilized the information presented in Appendix A on linguistic affiliation, subsistence economy, level of political integration, and rule of descent, and have assigned weights of 0, 1, or 2 to likenesses in each of these categories, as follows:

0   for essential identity, e.g., for membership in the same linguistic subfamily, for having economies of the same major type and subtype, for exhibiting the same number of levels of political integration, and for adhering to an identical rule of descent.
1   for partial similarity, e.g., for membership in different subfamilies of the same linguistic family, for having different subtypes of an agricultural or other major type of economy, for exhibiting a difference of only one in the number of levels of political integration, and for such relatively minor differences in descent as those between double and either matrilineal or patrilineal descent.
2   for maximal dissimilarity, e.g., for membership in independent linguistic families, for having different major types of subsistence economy, for exhibiting a difference of two or more in the number of levels of political integration, and for adhering to entirely different rules of descent.

Given the frequencies of each attribute for each of the four variables, a random model for the percentage of 0's, 1's, and 2's in a pairwise sample can be calculated for each variable by multiplying the co-occurrence probabilities of all possible permutations. These calculations revealed the following expected frequencies for the random model: 1.94 (standard error .05) for language, 1.32 (s.e. .09) for subsistence economy, 1.06 (s.e. .08), for political integration, and 1.48 (s.e. .07) for descent, or a total of 5.80 (s.e. .20).

The actual observed similarities between adjacent pairs in the alignment show a predictably marked divergence from the random model—$p < .01$ for political integration, $p < .00005$ for economy and rule of descent, $p < .0000001$ for language. The degree of similarity is strong between adjacent pairs, as might be expected in practically any cross-cultural sample.

The alignment also makes it possible to evaluate successively more distant pairs (i.e., at intervals of 2, 3, etc.) to ascertain at precisely what interval, for a given variable, historical influences cease to operate, i.e., at that where the pairwise similarities are reduced to values within the expectations of the random model. Accordingly intervals of 2 and 3 were tested for the entire sample, and intervals of 4, 5, 7, 9, 10, 20, 30, and 100 for subsamples of 10 to 20 per cent, with the results shown in Table 6.

Table 6 shows that, for the variables of political integration and subsistence economy, marked differences from randomness decrease linearly to within 1.96 standard deviations of the expected random mean [this is just the reverse of the $p < .05$ significance test of departure from the null hypothesis, since we are here interested in the first acceptable approximation to randomness] at the intervals of 3 and 4, respectively, whereas for language and descent the decrease in similarity, also approximately linear, continues to successively

TABLE 6.   Observed Frequencies in the Measure of Similarity
Between Linked Pairs at Various Intervals

| Intervals | Language | Economy | Pol. Integ. | Descent | Total |
|---|---|---|---|---|---|
| 1 (adjacent) | 1.37 | .87 | .84 | 1.10 | 4.18 |
| 2 (alternate) | 1.50 | .97 | .84 | 1.07 | 4.38 |
| 3 | 1.59 | 1.10 | *.98 | 1.21 | 4.88 |
| 4 | 1.50 | *1.20 | 1.08 | 1.30 | 5.08 |
| 5 | 1.58 | 1.26 | .84 | 1.26 | 4.94 |
| 7 | 1.78 | 1.30 | .81 | 1.27 | 5.16 |
| 9 | *1.89 | 1.45 | 1.05 | 1.33 | *5.72 |
| 10 | 1.89 | 1.44 | 1.10 | *1.50 | 5.93 |
| 20 | 1.94 | 1.59 | 1.06 | 1.29 | 5.88 |
| 30 | 2.00 | 1.55 | .90 | 1.45 | 5.90 |
| 100 | 2.00 | 1.48 | 1.38 | 1.30 | 6.16 |
| Random | 1.94 | 1.32 | 1.06 | 1.48 | 5.80 |

* First approximation to the random model where $p > .05$ that the value could have come from a random distribution.

more distant pairs, with differences from the random model that are statistically significant ($p < .01$) up to the interval of 9. (Political integration, which deviates from randomness at the intervals of 5 and 7, returns to a second approximation thereof at the same interval of 9). This means that, for sampling considerations, the construction of an Interval Sift sample (Naroll 1961) entirely free from historical influences on language, social organization, and possibly also political complexity would require a world subsample of no more than about 20 societies (one-ninth of 186)—a number too small to yield statistically reliable correlations. Any larger sample would presumably yield correlations between the independent and dependent variables that would be in at least some measure inflated by historical influences.

Treating economic type as the independent variable and political type as the dependent variable, an Interval Sift sample presumably free of historical influences affecting the independent variable could include all societies in the alignment at intervals of 4, or a total size of about 46 societies. Taking societies 1, 5, 9, etc. in the alignment, the correlation between neighbors with respect to agriculture is phi = .13 (p > .40 or nonsignificant), while the correlation between agriculture and supra-community sovereignty is phi = .36 (p < .02). Using a modification of the Interval Sift method on a sample of 53 societies in which the correlation between the presence of agriculture among neighboring societies is phi = −.05, we have calculated a phi of .32 (p < .01) for the relation between agriculture and supra-community sovereignty. The true functional correlation between the two variables probably lies between .32 and .36, still statistically significant after a reduction from the original correlation by about 30 per cent, the portion of the correlation due to historical influences in the sample.

The method formulated by the authors might be called the Successive Pairs test to determine the size of patches of historical relatedness, or a sixth solution to Galton's problem. The general results of the method, as applied to four variables in Table 6, would seem to indicate that most previous cross-cultural studies, if the variables of descent, political complexity, and economy are any indication, probably embody statistically significant effects of historical influence which would tend to inflate the functional correlations. Cross-cultural researchers, with the exception of Naroll, Driver (1956), and a few other recent commentators (Barry 1968; Sawyer and LeVine 1966) have ignored historical influences, assuming that some kind of cross-cultural sampling would take care of them. What is perhaps most surprising is the large size of the interval at which we have found historical effects to be operative, leaving only about 20 large subcontinental tracts from which cases truly independent of historical influences can be drawn. Extension of the techniques for getting at historical and functional influences from continuous distributions has been carried out by Driver (1966) for North America, and by White (1967, 1969) in his discussion of large culture tracts or subcontinental regions in North America and Africa.

For cross-cultural research, these results support the conclusion of the authors that, instead of seeking a specially drawn "random" or Interval Sift sample in which historical contamination is assumed to be negligible, it is safer to use one of the methods of measuring historical influences and to design the sample as the best possible representation of the world's culture types. Even for a randomly drawn sample of 20 societies, the lack of systematic intervals between them would probably introduce statistically significant historical effects with respect to such a variable as social organization. Interval Sift samples are likely to be too small for statistically reliable results. The present standard sample of 186, although not free from historical effects, allows the best of both worlds by the use of the alignment methods. Not only can the Linked Pair test (Naroll 1964) be used, along with the Successive Pairs method of the present authors, but the Cluster method (Naroll 1961, using the Wald-Wolfowitz runs test) and the Matched Pair method are also suitable for use with the alignment. The same alignment can also be used for substitute or additional societies, since it is the distinctive world areas or sampling provinces that have been aligned and substitute societies can always be assigned to a specific area or province in the sample (Murdock 1968).

The superiority of our standard world sample in minimizing historical influences can be demonstrated by direct comparison with other samples, when these are arranged in the same geographical alignment. For the 220 usable societies of the HRAF sample, selected because of its nearly equivalent size, calculation of the similarities between neighboring pairs on the alignment showed a total index of similarity of 3.28, as compared with 4.18 for our standard sample and 5.80 for purely random comparisons (see Table 6). This substantial reduction in historical similarities in our sample, as compared to that of HRAF, was greatest in language, followed by descent, economy, and political integration in this order. From the magnitude of these differences it is estimated that the true value of a funcional correlation, such as in our example of that between agriculture and supra-community sovereignty, might frequently be doubled for the HRAF sample owing to its much stronger reflection of historical influences.

### CONCLUSION

Cross-cultural researchers who use our standard sample (or a close approximation thereto) in future studies can reap a number of advantages from so doing:

1. From our pinpointing specifications they can make certain that all elements compared actually coexisted in the same subgroup at the same point in time;

2. They can intercorrelate their findings with those of other users of the sample, including the Cross-Cultural Cumulative Coding Center at the University of Pittsburgh, which is currently engaged in coding information on all the societies of the sample and a substantial number of alternates for three sets of codes—on infancy and the transition to childhood, on subsistence economy and the local community, and on settlement pattern and community organization;

3. They need not use all the 186 societies of the standard sample but may conveniently work with smaller subsamples of 83 (half of the standard sample consisting of every alternate society in it) or 62 (a third of the standard sample consisting of every third society), either being equally representative of the world's known and well described cultures as well as exhibiting slightly less contamination from historical influences;

4. By using the same geo-cultural alignment they can employ the same methods of measuring or controlling for historical influences;

5. They may for any good reason substitute other societies from the same distinctive areas or sampling provinces without sacrificing any of the advantages except possibly that of intercorrelation with the results of other studies.

### APPENDIX A: SPECIFIC DATA ON EACH SAMPLE SOCIETY

In the following summary of the pinpointing data and other relevant information on the 186 societies of the standard sample, after the ordinal number of each society in the adopted alignment there is recorded: (1) its name or names, followed in parentheses by its identifying number in the Ethnographic Atlas; (2) the number of the world sampling province (Murdock 1968) in which it is included, followed in parentheses by the (occasionally altered) name of the province; (3) the linguistic family to which it belongs, often followed in parentheses by the name of the subfamily; (4) a symbol characterizing its type of subsistence economy; (5) two symbols characterizing respectively the level of its political integration and its prevailing rule of descent; (6) a definition of its focus, i.e., the pinpointed local group and date recommended for the coding of cultural data; (7) the availability (with identifying number) or nonavailability of a HRAF file on the society, followed in parentheses by a symbol estimating the relative usefulness of the particular file for cross-cultural research involving the focal group; and (8) the names of one or more of its most dependable or helpful ethnographic authorities. The symbols used in the listing are defined below, with the frequencies of each type or subtype in parentheses.

*For the type of subsistence economy:*

A   Advanced agriculture (56), employing irrigation, fertilization, crop rotation, or other techniques which largely eliminate fallowing.

B   Horticulture (19), i.e., semi-intensive agriculture limited mainly to vegetable gardens and/or groves of fruit trees rather than the cultivation of field crops.

C   Simple or shifting cultivation (51), as where new fields are cleared annually, cultivated for a year or two, and then allowed to revert to forest or brush for a long fallow period.

D   Domestic animals (15), where their products provide a major source of subsistence, as in a pastoral economy.

E   An exchange economy (1), in which food products are largely obtained through trade rather than by subsistence techniques.

F   Fishing (17), including shellfishing and/or the pursuit of large aquatic animals, where these activities provide a major source of subsistence.

G   Gathering (13), where wild plants and/or small land fauna provide a major source of subsistence.

H   Hunting (14), including trapping and fowling, where these activities provide a major source of subsistence.

Capital letters indicate the dominant mode of subsistence; lower-case letters an important subsidiary or auxiliary mode, normally where it provides more than 25 per cent of the food supply. Examples: Ae for advanced agriculture supplemented by the substantial importation of food products; Fb for fishing supplemented by horticulture; Hd for mounted or equestrian hunters. Frequencies treated as intermediate in comparison with the reverse symbols in the Linked Pair test: Fg (3), Fh (8), Gf (1), Gh (12), Hf (4), Hg (4).

*For the level of political integration:*

I   Independent local communities (79), i.e., a stateless society.

J   A single level of political integration transcending the local community (50), e.g., a petty paramount chiefdom.

K   Two levels of supra-community integration (23), e.g., a small state organized into districts.

L   Three or more levels of supra-community integration (34), e.g., a large state subdivided into provinces and districts.

*For the prevailing rule of descent:*

M   Matrilineal (24), with any rule of residence other than avunculocal. Treated for the Linked Pair test as partially similar to N, Np, and Pm.

N   Matrilineal (6, plus one case of Np), with a predominantly avunculocal rule of residence.

O   Nonlineal or bilateral (66), i.e., without lineages though often with personal kindreds.

P   Patrilineal (70, plus 6 cases of Pm).

Q   Quasi-patrilineal (3), i.e., with incipient or decadent patrilineages. Treated for the Linked Pair test as partially similar to both O and P.

R   Ambilineal (10), e.g., with nonunilineal ramages.

For intermediate cases a double symbol is used, i.e., Pm for double descent where the patrilineal rule is dominant and the matrilineal rule subordinate and Np where the reverse obtains.

*For the adequacy of the corresponding HRAF file:*

a   Satisfactory (74), i.e., containing a good selection of the source materials, including all the major sources.

b   Useful (25), i.e., including the major sources but an incomplete selection of other important ones and thus adjudged adequate for most cross-cultural research but requiring supplementation by library research on particular subjects.

c   Inadequate (19), i.e., lacking at least one of the major sources or several important ones and thus to be used in cross-cultural research only with caution and preferably with supplementation by library research.

\* \* \*

1. Nama or Namaqua (Aa3: 102) of Province 1 (Hottentots). Language: Khoisan (Southern). Economy: D. Organization: J, P. Focus: The Gei//Khauan tribe (27°30′S, 17°E) reconstructed for 1860, just prior to their decimation and loss of independence in the Herero War. HRAF: FX13 (a). Authorities: Schultze, Schapera (secondary).

2. Kung (Aa1: 1) of Province 2 (Bushmen). Language: Khoisan (Southern). Economy: Gh. Organization: I, O. Focus: The Agau Kung of the Nyae Nyae region (19°50′S, 20°35′E) in 1950, when the Marshalls began their study of this still unacculturated group. HRAF: FX10 (a). Authority: L. Marshall.

3. Thonga or Bathonga (Ab4: 104) of Province 3 (Southeastern Bantu). Language: Niger-Congo (Bantoid). Economy: Cd. Organization: K, P. Focus: The Ronga subtribe around Lourenço Marques (25°50′S, 32°20′E) in 1895, at the beginning of Junod's missionary field work. HRAF: FT6 (a). Authority: Junod.

4. Lozi or Barotse (Ab3: 103) of Province 4 (Sotho). Language: Niger-Congo (Bantoid). Economy: Ad. Organization: L, R. Focus: The ruling Luyana (14° to 18°20′S, 22° to 25°E) in 1900, at the height of Barotse political expansion. HRAF: No file. Authority: Gluckman.

5. Mbundu or Ovimbundu (Ab5: 203) of Province 5 (Southwestern Bantu). Language: Niger-Congo (Bantoid). Economy: C. Organization: K, Pm. Focus: Bailundo subtribe (12°15′S, 16°30′E) in 1890, just prior to Portuguese conquest and missionization. HRAF: FP13 (a). Authority: Childs.

6. Suku or Pindi (Ac17: 731) of Province 6 (Western Central Bantu). Language: Niger-Congo (Bantoid). Economy: C. Organization: L, N. Focus: The Suku of Feshi Territory (6°S, 18°E) in 1920, just prior to their loss of independence. HRAF: No file. Authorities: Kopytoff, Torday & Joyce.

7. Bemba or Awemba (Ac3: 105) of Province 7 (Eastern Central Bantu). Language: Niger-Congo (Bantoid). Economy: C. Organization: L, M. Focus: The Bemba of Zambia (9° to 12°S, 29° to 32°E) in 1897, just prior to the advent of British administration. HRAF: FQ5 (b). Authority: Richards.

8. Nyakyusa (Ad6: 208) of Province 9 (Interior Tanzania). Language: Niger-Congo (Bantoid). Economy: Ad. Organization: K, P. Focus: The Nyakyusa around the towns of Mwaya (9°35′S, 34°10′E) and Masoko (9°20′S, 34°E) in 1934, at the beginning of the Wilsons' field work. HRAF: FN17 (b). Authority M. Wilson.

9. Hadza or Kindiga (Aa9: 726) of Province 10 (Rift). Language: Khoisan (Northern). Economy: Hg. Organization: I, O. Focus: The small Hadza tribe as a whole (3°20′ to 4°10′S, 34°40′ to 35°25′E) in 1930, when still unacculturated. HRAF: No file. Authorities: Kohl-Larsen, Woodburn.

10. Luguru or Waluguru (Ad14: 704) of Province 11 (Northeast Coastal Bantu).

Language: Niger-Congo (Bantoid). Economy: C. Organization: I, M. Focus: The Luguru of west central Morogoro District (6°25′ to 7°25′S, 37°20′ to 38°E) in 1925, the last date of the traditional political organization. HRAF: No file. Authorities: Beidelman, Scheerder & Tastevin.

11. Kikuyu or Akikuyu (Ad4: 108) of Province 12 (Kenya Highland Bantu). Language: Niger-Congo (Bantoid). Economy: Ad. Organization: I, P. Focus: The Kikuyu of the Metume or Fort Hall district (0°40′S, 37°10′E) in 1920, prior to intensive acculturation. HRAF: FL10 (a). Authorities: Kenyatta, Leakey.

12. Ganda or Baganda (Ad7: 306) of Province 13 (Lacustrine Bantu). Language: Niger-Congo (Bantoid). Economy: B. Organization: L, P. Focus: The Ganda of Kyaddondo district (0°20′N, 32°30′E) in 1875, just prior to the founding of Kampala and the initiation of significant administrative changes. HRAF: FK7 (a). Authorities: Roscoe, Mair.

13. Mbuti or Bambuti (Aa5: 202) of Province 15 (Pygmies). Language: Niger-Congo (Bantoid). Economy: Gh. Organization: I, O. Focus: The Epulu net-hunters of the Ituri Forest (1°30′ to 2°N, 28°15′ to 28°25′E) in 1950, just prior to Turnbull's field work. HRAF: No file. Authorities: Turnbull, Schebesta.

14. Nkundo Mongo (Ae4: 110) of combined Provinces 14 and 16 (Equatorial Bantu). Language: Niger-Congo (Bantoid). Economy: C. Organization: K, P. Focus: The Mongo of the Ilanga subtribe (0°15′ to 1°15′S, 18°35′ to 19°45′E) in 1930, the approximate date of Hulstaert's description. HRAF: FO32 (a). Authority: Hulstaert.

15. Banen or Banyin (Ae51: 830) of Province 17 (Cameroon Bantu). Language: Niger-Congo (Bantoid). Economy: C. Organization: I, P. Focus: The Ndiki subtribe (4°35′ to 4°45′N, 10°35′ to 11°E) in 1935, at the beginning of Dugast's field work. HRAF: No file. Authority: Dugast.

16. Tiv or Munshi (Ah3: 116) of combined Provinces 29 and 30 (Nigerian Plateau). Language: Niger-Congo (Bantoid). Economy: C. Organization: J, R. Focus: The Tiv of Benue Province (6°30′ to 8°N, 8° to 10°E) in 1920, prior to extensive organizational changes wrought by the British. HRAF: FF57 (a). Authorities: Bohannan, East.

17. Ibo or Igbo (Af10: 643 of Province 18 (Southeastern Nigeria). Language: Niger-Congo (Kwa). Economy: C. Organization: J, P. Focus: The Eastern and Peripheral subgroups of the Isu-Ama division of the Southern or Owerri Ibo (5°20′ to 5°40′N, 7°10′ to 7°30′E) in 1935, near the beginning of Green's field work. HRAF: No file. Authorities: Green, Uchendu.

18. Fon or Dahomeans (Af1: 10) of Province 19 (Slave Coast). Language: Niger-Congo (Kwa). Economy: C. Organization: L, P. Focus: The Fon in the vicinity of Abomey (7°12′N, 1°56′E) in 1890, prior to the conquest of the Dahomean kingdom by the French. HRAF: No file. Authorities: Herskovits, Le Herissé.

19. Ashanti (Af3: 111) of Province 20 (Akan). Language: Niger-Congo (Kwa). Economy: C. Organization: K, Np. Focus: The Ashanti of the state of Kumasi (6° to 8°N, 0° to 3°W) in 1895, just prior to British conquest. HRAF: FE12 (a). Authorities: Rattray, Fortes.

20. Mende (Af5: 211) of Province 21 (Grain Coast). Language: Niger-Congo (Mande). Economy: C. Organization: J, P. Focus: The central Mende around the town of Bo (7°50′N, 12°W) in 1945, at the beginning of Little's field work. HRAF: FC7 (a). Authority: Little.

21. Wolof or Ouolof (Cb2: 21) of Province 22 (Senegambians). Language: Niger-Congo (Atlantic). Economy: Cd. Organization: K, Pm. Focus: The Wolof of Upper and Lower Salum in the Gambia (centering on 13°45′N, 15°20′W) in 1950, the date of the field work of Ames. HRAF: MS30 (a). Authorities: Ames, Gamble.

22. Bambara or Banmana (Ag1: 12) of Province 24 (Mande). Language: Niger-Congo (Mande). Economy: A. Organization: J. P. Focus: The Bambara along the Niger River from Segou to Bamako (12°30′ to 13°N, 6° to 8°W) in 1902,

at approximately the beginning of Henry's field experience as a missionary and Monteil's as an administrator. HRAF: FA8 (a). Authorities: Monteil, Henry, Pacques (secondary).

23. Tallensi (Ag4: 114) of combined Provinces 26 and 27 (Voltaic Peoples). Language: Niger-Congo (Voltaic or Gur). Economy: A. Organization: I, P. Focus: The small Tallensi tribe as a whole (10°30′ to 10°45′N, 0°30′ to 0°50′W) in 1934, at the beginning of the field work of Fortes. HRAF: FE11 (a). Authority: Fortes.

24. Songhai (Cb3: 122) of Province 25 (Songhai). Language: Songhaic. Economy: Ad. Organization: L, P. Focus: The Songhai of the Bamba or central division (16° to 17°15′N, 0°10′E to 3°10′W) in 1940, at approximately the beginning of the field work of Rouch and Miner. HRAF: No file. Authorities: Rouch, Miner.

25. Fulani (Cb24: 1082) of Province 23 (Fulani). Language: Niger-Congo (Atlantic). Economy: D. Organization: J, P. Focus: The Alijam and Degeriji subgroups of Wodaabe Fulani around Adan and Damergou in Niger (13° to 17°N, 5° to 10°E) in 1951, at the beginning of the field work of Dupire and Stenning. HRAF: No file. Authorities: Dupire, Stenning.

26. Hausa (Cb26: 1084) of Province 28 (Hausa). Language: Afroasiatic or Hamito-Semitic (Chadic). Economy: Ad. Organization: L, P. Focus: The Zazzagawa Hausa (9°30′ to 11°30′N, 6° to 9°E) in 1900, just prior to the advent of British rule. HRAF: MS12 (b). Authority: Smith.

27. Massa or Bana (Ai9: 646) of Province 31 (Lake Chad Region). Language: Afroasiatic (Chadic). Economy: Af. Organization: I, P. Focus: The Cameroon Massa around Yagoua (10°20′N, 15°15′E) in 1910, the approximate date of the early field work by von Hagen. HRAF: No file. Authorities: de Garine, von Hagen.

28. Azande or Niam-Niam (Ai3: 117) of combined Provinces 33 and 34 (North Equatoria). Language: Niger-Congo (Eastern). Economy: C. Organization: K, P. Focus: The Azande of the Yambio chiefdom (4°20′ to 5°50′N, 27°40′ to 28°50′E). in 1905, just prior to British conquest and the collapse of the Avongara political system. HRAF: FO7 (a). Authority: Evans-Pritchard.

29. Fur or For (Cb17: 875) of Province 32 (Wadai and Darfur). Language: Furian. Economy: Ad. Organization: L, M. Focus: The Fur of western Darfur around Jebel Marra (13°30′N, 25°30′E) in 1880, prior to effective Egyptian subjugation. HRAF: No file. Authorities: Felkin, Beaton.

30. Otoro (Ai10: 647) of Province 35 (Nuba). Language: Kordofanian. Economy: A. Organization: J, P. Focus: The Otoro of the Nuba Hills (11°20′N, 30°40′E) in 1930, prior to substantial migration into the plains. HRAF: No file. Authority: Nadel.

31. Shilluk (Ai6: 218) of Province 37 (Northern Nilotes). Language: Chari-Nile or Sudanic (Eastern). Economy: C. Organization: J, P. Focus: The politically unified Shilluk as a whole (9° to 10°30′N, 31° to 32°E) in 1910, the date of the field work by Westermann and the Seligmans. HRAF: FJ23 (a). Authorities: C. & B. Seligman, Westermann.

32. Mao (Ai47: 1062) of Province 36 (Prenilotes). Language: Koman. Economy: C. Organization: J, P. Focus: The Northern Mao (9°5′ to 9°35′N, 34°30′ to 34°50′E) in 1939, the date of Grottanelli's field work. HRAF: No file. Authority: Grottanelli.

33. Kafa or Kafficho (Ca30: 860) of Province 39 (Western Cushites). Language: Afroasiatic (Western Cushitic). Economy: A. Organization: L, P. Focus: The politically unified Kafa as a whole (6°50′ to 7°45′N, 35°30′ to 37°E) in 1905, the date of Bieber's field work. HRAF: No file. Authority: Bieber.

34. Masai (Aj2: 119) of Province 38 (Southern Nilotes). Language: Chari-Nile (Eastern). Economy: D. Organization: J, P. Focus: The Kisonko or Southern Masai of Tanzania (1°30′ to 5°30′S, 35° to 37°30′E) in 1900, about the time of Merker's field work. HRAF: FL12 (c). Authorities: Merker, Jacobs.

35. Konso (Ca1: 18) of Province 40 (Galla-Konso). Language: Afroasiatic (Eastern Cushitic). Economy: Ad. Organization: J, P. Focus: The Konso of the town of Buso (5°15′N, 37°30′E) in 1935, the date of Jensen's field work. HRAF: No file. Authorities: Hallpike, Jensen.

36. Somali (Ca2: 19) of Province 41 (Horn). Language: Afroasiatic (Eastern Cushitic). Economy: D. Organization: K, P. Focus: The Dolbahanta subtribe (7° to 11°N, 45°30′ to 49°E) in 1900, subsequent to the earliest descriptions but prior to the later and fuller accounts. HRAF: MO4 (c). Authority: Lewis.

37. Amhara (Ca7: 679) of Province 42 (Central Ethiopia). Language: Afroasiatic (Semitic). Economy: Ad. Organization: L, O. Focus: The Amhara of the Gondar district (11° to 14°N, 36° to 38°30′E) in 1953, at the beginning of Messing's field work. HRAF: MP5 (a). Authority: Messing.

38. Bogo or Belen (Ca37: 867) of Province 43 (Central and Northern Cushites). Language: Afroasiatic (Central Cushitic). Economy: D. Organization: J, P. Focus: The small Bogo tribe as a whole (15°45′N, 38°45′E) in 1855, the approximate date of Munzinger's field work. HRAF: No file. Authority: Munzinger.

39. Nubians (Cd1: 24) of Province 44 (Nubians). Language: Chari-Nile (Nubian). Economy: Ad. Organization: Integrated in the large Egyptian state, P. Focus: The Kenuzi or northernmost branch of the Barabra or Nile Nubians (22° to 24°N, 32° to 33°E) in 1900, just prior to their displacement by the first Aswan dam. HRAF: No file. Authority: Herzog.

40. Teda (Cc2: 23) of Province 45 (Tebu). Language: Kanuric or Central Saharan. Economy: Ad. Organization: J, P. Focus: The Teda of Tibesti (19° to 22°N, 16° to 19°E) in 1950, the approximate date of Chapelle's field work. HRAF: No file. Authorities: Chapelle, Le Coeur.

41. Tuareg (Cc9: 880) of Province 46 (Tuareg). Language: Afroasiatic (Berber). Economy: Da. Organization: J, N. Focus: The Ahaggaren or Tuareg of Ahaggar (21° to 25°N, 4° to 9°E) in 1900, prior to the French military occupation of the Sahara. HRAF: MS25 (a). Authorities: Nicolaisen, Lhote.

42. Riffians (Cd3: 125) of combined Provinces 47 and 48 (Berbers of the Maghreb). Language: Afroasiatic (Berber). Economy: Ad. Organization: J, P. Focus: The Riffians as a whole (34°20′ to 35°30′N, 2°30′ to 4°W) in 1926, at the beginning of Coon's field work. HRAF: MX3 (b). Authority: Coon.

43. Egyptians (Cd2: 124) of Province 49 (Arabs of North Africa). Language: Afroasiatic (Semitic). Economy: Ad. Organization: L, P. Focus: The town and environs of Silwa (24°45′N, 33°E) in 1950, the approximate date of Ammar's field work. HRAF: MR13 (a). Authorities: Ammar, Wilber (secondary).

44. Hebrews (Cj3: 230) of Province 51 (Jews). Language: Afroasiatic (Semitic). Economy: Ad. Organization: K, P. Focus: The kingdom of Judah (30°30′ to 31°55′N, 34°20′ to 35°30′E) in 621 B.C., the date of promulgation of the Deuteronomic laws. HRAF: No file. Authorities: Old Testament, DeVaux (secondary).

45. Babylonians (Cj4: 413) of Province 53 (Ancient Mesopotamia). Language: Afroasiatic (Semitic). Economy: A. Organization: L, O. Focus: The city and environs of Babylon (32°35′N, 44°45′E) in 1750 B.C., at the end of the reign of Hammurabi. HRAF: No file. Authorities: Pritchard (translation of Hammurabi's law code), Saggs (secondary).

46. Rwala (Cj2: 132) of Province 52 (Arabs of Arabia and the Levant). Language: Afroasiatic (Semitic). Economy: D. Organization: J, P. Focus: The Rwala Bedouin of south central Syria and northeastern Jordan (31° to 35°30′, 36° to 41°E) in 1913, early in the periods of field work of Musil and Raswan. HRAF: MD4 and MJ1 (a). Authorities: Musil, Raswan.

47. Turks (Ci5: 653) of Province 54 (Turkey). Language: Altaic (Turkic). Economy: Ad. Organization: L, O. Focus: The Turks of the northern Anatolian plateau (38°40′ to 40°N, 32°40′ to 35°50′E) in 1950, during the periods of field work of Stirling and Makal. HRAF: MB1 (b). Authorities: Stirling, Makal.

48. Gheg (Ce1: 25) of Province 55 (Balkans). Language: Indo-European (Albanian). Economy: Ad. Organization: K, P. Focus: The Mountain Gheg of northern Albania (41°20' to 42°N, 19°30' to 20°31'E) in 1910, just prior to the expulsion of the Turks in the two Balkan Wars. HRAF: EG1 (a). Authorities: Coon, Durham.

49. Romans (Ce3: 126) of eastern Province 56 (Greece and Italy). Language: Indo-European (Italic). Economy: Ae. Organization: L, O. Focus: The Romans of the city and environs of Rome (41°50'N, 13°30'E) in A.D. 110, the twelfth year of Trajan's reign at the approximate zenith of the imperial period. HRAF: No file. Authorities: Pliny the Younger, Carcopino (secondary), Friedländer (secondary).

50. Basques (Ce4: 225) of western Province 56 (Southwestern Europeans). Language: Basque. Economy: Ad. Organization: Integrated in the large Spanish state, O. Focus: The mountain village of Vera de Bidasoa (43°18'N, 1°40'W) in 1934 the date of the field work by Caro Baroja. HRAF: No file. Authority: Caro Baroja.

51. Irish (Cg3: 128) of Province 57 (Northwestern Europeans). Language: Indo-European (Celtic). Economy: Ad. Organization: K, O. Focus: The Irish of County Clare (52°40' to 53°10'N, 8°20' to 10°W) in 1932, at the time of the field work by Arensberg and Kimball. HRAF: ER6 (a). Authorities: Arensberg & Kimball, Cresswell.

52. Lapps (Cg4: 129) of Province 58 (Lapps). Language: Uralic (Finnic). Economy: D. Organization: I, O. Focus: The Konkama Lapps of Karesuando parish in northern Sweden (68°20' to 69°5' N, 20°5' to 23°E) in 1950, during the period of Pehrson's field work. HRAF: EP4 (a). Authorities: Pehrson, Whitaker.

53. Yurak Samoyed or Nenets (Ec4: 136) of Province 73 (Ostyak and Samoyed). Language: Uralic (Samoyedic). Economy: Df. Organization: I, P. Focus: The Tundra Yurak (65° to 71°N, 41° to 62°E) in 1894, during the periods of observation by Englehardt and Jackson. HRAF: RU4 (a). Authorities: Jackson, Englehardt.

54. Russians (not in EA) of Province 59 (Northeastern Europe). Language: Indo-European (Slavic). Economy: A. Organization: L, O. Focus: The Great Russians of the peasant village of Viriatino (52°40'N, 41°20'E) in 1955, the date of the field work by Kushner. HRAF: RF1 (c). Authorities: Kushner, Dunn & Dunn (secondary).

55. Abkhaz (not in EA) of Province 60 (Caucasus). Language: Abasgo-Kerketian. Economy: Ad. Organization: J, P. Focus: The small Abkhaz tribe as a whole (42°50' to 43°25'N, 40° to 41°35'E) in 1880, at about the time of Dzhanashvili's field work. HRAF: RI3 (b). Authority: Dzhanashvili.

56. Armenians (Ci10: 912) of Province 61 (Armenia and Azerbaijan). Language: Indo-European (Armenian). Economy: Ad. Organization: L, O. Focus: The Armenians in the vicinity of Erevan (40°N, 44°30'E) in 1843, the date of the field observations by Haxthausen. HRAF: RJ1 and RJ3 (not included in tabulation). Authority: Haxthausen.

57. Kurd (Ci11: 913) of Province 62 (North Iran). Language: Indo-European (Iranian). Economy: Ad. Organization: K, P. Focus: The Kurd of the town and environs of Rowanduz (36°30'N, 44°30'E) in 1951, the date of the field work by Masters. HRAF: MA11 (c). Authorities: Masters, Leach.

58. Basseri (Ea6: 358) of Province 63 (South Iran). Language: Indo-European (Iranian). Economy: D. Organization: J, P. Focus: The nomadic Basseri (27° to 31°N, 53° to 54°E) in 1958, during the period of Barth's field work. HRAF: No file. Authority: Barth.

59. Punjabi (not in EA) of Province 64 (Indus Valley). Language: Indo-European (Indic). Economy: A. Organization: L, P. Focus: The western Punjabi of the village of Mohla (32°30'N, 74°E) in 1950, during the period of Eglar's field work. HRAF: AW6 (c). Authority: Eglar.

60. Gond (Eg3: 142) of Province 67 (Southeast India). Language: Dravidian.

Economy: C. Organization: J, P. Focus: The Hill Maria Gond (19°15′ to 20°N, 80°30′ to 81°20′E) in 1938, during the period of Grigson's field observations. HRAF: AW32 (a). Authority: Grigson.

61. Toda (Eg4: 143) of Province 65 (Southwest India). Language: Dravidian. Economy: D. Organization: J, Pm. Focus: The small Toda tribe as a whole (11° to 12°N, 76° to 77°E) in 1900, just prior to the field work of Rivers. HRAF: AW60 (a). Authority: Rivers.

62. Santal (Ef1: 42) of Province 68 (Munda). Language: Mon-Khmer (Munda). Economy: A. Organization: J, P. Focus: The Santal of the Bankura and Birbhum districts of Bengal (23° to 24°N, 86°50′ to 87°30′E) in 1940, during the period of Culshaw's field work. HRAF: No file (but one in process). Authorities: Culshaw, Datta-Majumder.

63. Uttar Pradesh (not in EA) of Province 69 (North India). Language: Indo-European (Indic). Economy: A. Organization: K, P. Focus: The village of Senapur in the small kingdom of Dobhi Taluka (25°55′N, 83°E) in 1945, prior to a major shift in the traditional power base. HRAF: AW19 (c). Authorities: Cohn, Opler & Singh.

64. Burusho (Ee2: 139) of combined Provinces 70 and 71 (Afghanistan and Dardistan). Language: Burushaski. Economy: Ad. Organization: J, P. Focus: The Burusho of Hunza state (36°20′ to 36°30′N, 74°30′ to 74°40′E) in 1934, during the period of the Lorimers' field work. HRAF: AV7 (a). Authorities: D. and E. Lorimer.

65. Kazak (Eb1: 35) of Province 72 (Turkestan). Language: Altaic (Turkic). Economy: D. Organization: L, P. Focus: The Kazak of the Great Horde (37° to 48°N, 68° to 81°E) in 1885, the approximate time of Grodekov's field work. HRAF: RQ2 (b). Authorities: Grodekov, Hudson.

66. Khalka Mongols (Eb3: 134) of Province 82 (Mongols). Language: Altaic (Mongolic). Economy: D. Organization: L, P. Focus: The Khalka of the Narobanchin temple territory (47° to 47°20′N, 95°10′ to 97°E) in 1920, the approximate date of Vreeland's reconstruction. HRAF: AH7 (b). Authority: Vreeland.

67. Lolo or Nosu (Ed2: 40) of Province 84 (Southwest China). Language: Tibeto-Burman (Akha-Lahu-Lisu-Lolo subfamily). Economy: Ad. Organization: I, P. Focus: The independent and relatively unacculturated Lolo of the Taliang Shan mountains (26° to 29°N, 103° to 104°E) in 1910, the approximate date of the field work by D'Ollone. HRAF: AE4 (c). Authorities: D'Ollone, Lin.

68. Lepcha or Rong (Ee3: 140) of Province 85 (Tibet). Language: Tibeto-Burman (Tibetan). Economy: Ad. Organization: J, P. Focus: The Lepcha in the vicinity of Lingthem in Sikkim (27° to 28°N, 89°E) in 1937, the date of Gorer's field work. HRAF: AK5 (a). Authorities: Gorer, Morris.

69. Garo (Ei1: 47) of Province 87 (Garo-Khasi). Language: Tibeto-Burman (Garo). Economy: C. Organization: J, M. Focus: The Garo of Rengsanggri and neighboring intermarrying villages (26°N, 91°E) in 1955, during the period of Burling's field work. HRAF: No file (but one in process). Authority: Burling.

70. Lakher or Mara (Ei4: 147) of combined Provinces 87 and 88 (North Burma and South Assam). Language: Tibeto-Burman (Kuki-Chin). Economy: C. Organization: J, P. Focus: The small Lakher tribe as a whole (22°20′N, 93°E) in 1930, the approximate date of Parry's field work. HRAF: no file. Authority: Parry.

71. Burmese (Ei3: 146) of Province 89 (South Burma). Language: Tibeto-Burman (Burman). Economy: A. Organization: L, O. Focus: The village of Nondwin in Upper Burma (22°N, 95°40′E) in 1965, during the period of Nash's field work. HRAF: AP1 (c). Authorities: Nash, Scott.

72. Lamet (Ej1: 49) of Province 90 (Palaung-Wa). Language: Tibeto-Burman (Palaung-Wa). Economy: C. Organization: I, P. Focus: The small Lamet tribe as a whole (20°N, 100°40′E) in 1940, the approximate date of the field work by Izikowitz. HRAF: No file. Authority: Izikowitz.

73. Vietnamese (Ej4: 149) of Province 97 (Vietnam and Hainan). Language: Annam-Muong. Economy: A. Organization: L, P. Focus: The Tonkinese or North Vietnamese of the delta of the Red River (20° to 21°N, 105°30′ to 107°E) in 1930, during Gourou's period of field work. HRAF: AM11 (a). Authority: Gourou.

74. Rhade (Ej10: 456) of Province 96 (Montagnards). Language: Malayo-Polynesian (Hesperonesian). Economy: C. Organization: I, M. Focus: The Rhade of the village of Ko-sier on the Darlac plateau (13°N, 108°E) in 1962, the date of Donoghue's field work. HRAF: No file. Authorities: Donoghue *et al.*

75. Khmer or Cambodians (Ej5: 248) of Province 95 (Cambodia). Language: Mon-Khmer (Khmer). Economy: A. Organization: L, O. Focus: The city of Angkor (13°30′N, 103°50′E), the capital of the old Khmer kingdom at its height, in 1292, the date of the visit and description by Chou. HRAF: AM4 (c). Authorities: Chou Ta-Kuan, Groslier, Aymonier.

76. Siamese or Central Thai (Ej9: 367) of Province 91 (Thai). Language: Thai-Kadai. Economy: A. Organization: L, O. Focus: The Central Thai village of Bang Chan (14°N, 100°50′E) about 1955, the midpoint of the Cornell University research project. HRAF: AO1 (c). Authorities: Sharp, L. & J. Hanks.

77. Semang (Ej3: 148) of Province 94 (Semang-Sakai). Language: Mon-Khmer (Semang-Sakai). Economy: Gh. Organization: I, O. Focus: The Jahai subtribe (4°30′ to 5°30′N, 101° to 101°30′E) in 1925, at the approximate beginning of Schebesta's field work. HRAF: AN6 (b). Authorities: Schebesta, Evans.

78. Nicobarese (Eh5: 244) of Province 93 (Nicobar Islands). Language: Mon-Khmer (Khasi-Nicobarese). Economy: B. Organization: I, O. Focus: The Nicobarese of the northern islands of Car Nicobar, Chowra, Teressa, and Bompoka (8°15′ to 9°15′N, 92°40′ to 93°E) in 1870, near the beginning of Man's administrative experience. HRAF: No file. Authorities: Man, Whitehead.

79. Andamanese (Eh1: 45) of Province 92 (Andaman Islands). Language: Anda-manese. Economy: Fg. Organization: I, O. Focus: The Aka-Bea tribe of South Andaman (11°45′ to 12°N, 93° to 93°10′E) in 1860, prior to significant acculturation and depopulation. HRAF: AZ2 (a). Authorities: Man, Radcliffe-Brown.

80. Vedda (Eh4: 145) of Province 66 (Ceylon). Language: Indo-European (Indic). Economy: Gh. Organization: I, M. Focus: The Danigala group of Forest Vedda (7°30′ to 8°N, 81° to 81°30′E) in 1860, the date of the observations by Bailey made prior to intensive acculturation. HRAF: AX5 (a). Authorities: C. and B. Seligmann, Bailey.

81. Tanala (Eh3: 144) of Province 8 (Madagascar). Language: Malayo-Polynesian (Hesperonesian). Economy: A. Organization: J, P. Focus: The Menabe sub-tribe (22°S, 48°E) in 1925, just prior to Linton's field work. HRAF: FY8 (b). Authority: Linton.

82. Negri Sembilan (not in EA) of Province 102 (Malaya and Sumatra). Language: Malayo-Polynesian (Hesperonesian). Economy: A. Organization: K, M. Focus: The district of Inas (2°30′ to 2°40′N, 102°10′ to 102°20′E), in 1958, the date of Lewis' field work. HRAF: AN5 (b). Authority: Lewis.

83. Javanese (Ib2: 54) of Province 103 (Java). Language: Malayo-Polynesian (Hes-peronesian). Economy: A. Organization: L, O. Focus: The town and environs of Pare in central Java (7°43′S, 112°13′E) in 1954, during the period of field work of the Geertzes. HRAF: No file. Authorities: C. and H. Geertz.

84. Balinese (Ib3: 152) of Province 104 (Western Lesser Sundas). Language: Malayo-Polynesian (Hesperonesian). Economy: Ad. Organization: K, R. Focus: The village of Tihingan in the district of Klunghung (8°30′S, 105°20′E) in 1958, the date of the field work of the Geertzes. HRAF: OF7 (c). Authorities: C. and H. Geertz.

85. Iban or Sea Dayak (Ib1: 53) of Province 101 (Borneo). Language: Malayo-Polynesian (Hesperonesian). Economy: C. Organization: I, O. Focus: The Iban

of the Ulu Ai group (2°N, 112°30′ to 113°30′E) in 1950, near the beginning of Freeman's field work. HRAF: OC6 (a). Authority: Freeman.

86. Badjau (Ia13: 1099) of Province 100 (Badjau or Sea Gypsies). Language: Malayo-Polynesian (Hesperonesian). Economy: F. Organization: I, O. Focus: The Badjau of southwestern Tawi-Tawi and adjacent islands of the Sulu Archipelago (5°N, 120°E) in 1963, the date of Nimmo's field work. HRAF: No file. Authority: Nimmo.

87. Toradja (Ic5: 254) of Province 105 (Celebes). Language: Malayo-Polynesian (Hesperonesian). Economy: C. Organization: J, O. Focus: The Bare'e subgroup of eastern Toradja (2°S, 121°E) in 1910, the approximate date of the completion of the field work by Adriani and Kruijt. HRAF: No file (but one in process). Authorities: Adriani & Kruijt.

88. Tobelorese or Tobelo (Ic10: 1118) of Province 106 (Moluccas). Language: Papuan (distinct family). Economy: C. Organization: K, O. Focus: The Tobelorese as a whole (2°N, 128°E) in 1900, just prior to the missionary field work of Hueting. HRAF: No file. Authorities: Hueting, Riedel.

89. Alorese or Abui (Ic2: 154) of Province 107 (Southeastern Indonesia). Language: Malayo-Polynesian (Moluccan). Economy: C. Organization: K, P. Focus: The village complex of Atimelang in north central Alor (8°20′S, 124°40′E) in 1938, at the beginning of the field work by DuBois. HRAF: OF5 (a). Authority: DuBois.

90. Tiwi (Id3: 157) of Province 108 (Tropical Australia). Language: Australian. Economy: Gh. Organization: I, M. Focus: The Tiwi of Bathurst and Melville Islands as a whole (11° to 11°45′S, 130° to 132°E) in 1929, the date of Hart's field work. HRAF: OI20 (a). Authorities: Hart & Pilling, Goodale.

91. Aranda or Arunta (Id1: 56) of Province 109 (Central and Southern Australia). Language: Australian. Economy: Gh. Organization: I, Pm. Focus: The Arunta Mbainda of Alice Springs (23°30′ to 25°S, 132°30′ to 134°20′E) in 1896, the date of the early field work by Spencer and Gillen. HRAF: OI8 (a). Authorities: Spencer & Gillen, Strehlow.

92. Orokaiva (Ie9: 457) of Province 111 (Southeastern New Guinea). Language: Papuan (distinct family). Economy: B. Organization: I, P. Focus: The Aiga subtribe (8°20′ to 8°40′S, 147°50′ to 148°10′E) in 1925, at the end of the second period of field work by Williams. HRAF: OJ23 (a). Authority: Williams.

93. Kimam (Ie18: 1101) of Province 112 (Southern New Guinea). Language: Papuan (Kiwai family). Economy: A. Organization: I, O. Focus: The village of Bamol in northeast central Frederick Hendrik Island or Kolekom (7°30′S, 138°30′E) in 1960, at the beginning of Serpenti's field work. HRAF: No file. Authority: Serpenti.

94. Kapauku (Ie1: 57) of Province 114 (Northwestern New Guinea). Language: Papuan (distinct family). Economy: C. Organization: J, P. Focus: The village of Botukebo in the Kamu Valley (c.4°S, 36°E) in 1955, the date of Pospisil's first field trip. HRAF: OJ29 (c). Authority: Pospisil.

95. Kwoma (Ie12: 655) of Province 113 (Northeastern New Guinea). Language: Papuan (Middle Sepik family). Economy: Bg. Organization: I, P. Focus: The Hongwam subtribe (4°10′S, 142°40′E) in 1937, at the conclusion of Whiting's field work. HRAF: No file. Authority: J. Whiting.

96. Manus (Ig9: 373) of Province 120 (Admiralty and Western Islands). Language: Malayo-Polynesian (Melanesian). Economy: Ef. Organization: I, Pm. Focus: The village of Peri (2°10′S, 147°E) in 1929, the date of Mead's first field trip. HRAF: OM6 (a). Authority: Mead.

97. New Ireland (Ig4: 163) of Province 121 (New Britain and New Ireland). Language: Malayo-Polynesian (Melanesian). Economy: Bf. Organization: I, M. Focus: The village of Lesu (2°30′S, 151°E) in 1930, at the time of Powdermaker's field work. HRAF: OM10 (a). Authority: Powdermaker.

98. Trobrianders (Ig2: 62) of Province 122 (Massim). Language: Malayo-Polynesian

(Melanesian). Economy: B. Organization: J, M. Focus: The island of Kiriwina (8°38′S, 151°4′E) in 1914, at the beginning of Malinowski's field work. HRAF: OL6 (a). Authority: Malinowski.

99. Siuai or Motuna (Ig1: 61) of Province 123 (Solomon Islands). Language: Papuan (distinct family). Economy: B. Organization: I, M. Focus: The northeastern Siuai of southern Bougainville (7°S, 155°20′E) in 1939, at the conclusion of Oliver's field work. HRAF: No file. Authority: Oliver.

100. Tikopia (Ii2: 66) of Province 124 (Polynesian Outliers). Language: Malayo-Polynesian (Polynesian). Economy: Bf. Organization: J, P. Focus: The small island of Tikopia as a whole (12°30′S, 168°30′E) in 1930, at the conclusion of Firth's first field trip. HRAF: OT11 (a). Authority: Firth.

101. Pentecost (Ih3: 164) of combined Provinces 125 and 126 (New Hebrides and Banks Islands). Language: Malayo-Polynesian (Melanesian). Economy: B. Organization: I, P. Focus: The village of Bunlap and neighboring intermarrying pagan villages in southeastern Pentecost Island (16°S, 168°E) in 1953, the date of the first field trip by the Lanes. HRAF: No file. Authorities: R. and B. Lane.

102. Mbau Fijians (not in EA) of Province 128 (Fiji and Rotuma). Language: Malayo-Polynesian (Melanesian). Economy: Bf. Organization: K, P. Focus: The island of Mbau off the east coast of Viti Levu (18°S, 178°35′E) in 1840, the approximate date of the best early descriptions. HRAF: No file. authorities: Tonganivalu, Waterhouse.

103. Ajie (Ih5: 263) of Province 127 (New Caledonia and Loyalty Islands). Language: Malayo-Polynesian (Melanesian). Economy: A. Organization: J, P. Focus: The petty chiefdom of Neje (21°20′S, 165°40′E), reconstructed for 1845, prior to strong European influence. HRAF: no file. Authorities: Leenhardt, Guiart.

104. Maori (Ij2: 167) of Province 130 (Southern Polynesia). Language: Malayo-Polynesian (Polynesian). Economy: B. Organization: J, R. Focus: The Nga Puhi tribe of the nothern isthmus (35°10′ to 35°30′S, 174° to 174°20′E) in 1820, prior to European settlement and missionization. HRAF: OZ4 (c). Authorities: Earle, Clarke.

105. Marquesans (Ij3: 168) of Province 131 (Eastern Polynesia). Language: Malayo-Polynesian (Polynesian). Economy: Bf. Organization: J, R. Focus: The Te-i'i chiefdom of southwestern Nuku Hiva Island (8°55′S, 140°10′W) about 1800, at about the time of the earliest reliable descriptions. HRAF: OX6 (c). Authorities: Fleurieu, Forster, Langsdorff.

106. Samoans (Ii1: 65) of Province 129 (Western Polynesia). Language: Malayo-Polynesian (Polynesian). Economy: Bf. Organization: K, R. Focus: The kingdom of Aana in western Upolu Island (13°48′ to 14°S, 171°54′ to 172°3′W) in 1829, prior to the military defeat of Aana and the beginning of intensive European contact. HRAF: OU8 (b). Authorities: Turner, Stair.

107. Gilbertese (If14: 633) of Province 119 (Gilbert Islands). Language: Malayo-Polynesian (Carolinian). Economy: Bf. Organization: J, R. Focus: The northern Gilbertese of Makin and Butiritari islands (3°30′N, 172°20′E), reconstructed for about 1890. HRAF: No file. Authority: Lambert.

108. Marshallese (If3: 160) of Province 118 (Marshall Islands and Nauru). Language: Malayo-Polynesian (Carolinian). Economy: Bf. Organization: J, M. Focus: The atoll of Jaluit (6°N, 165°30′E) in 1900, the mean date of the early German ethnographers. HRAF: OR11 (a). Authorities: Erdland, Krämer & Nevermann.

109. Trukese (If2: 60) of Province 117 (Central and Eastern Carolines). Language: Malayo-Polynesian (Carolinian). Economy: Bf. Organization: I, M. Focus: The island of Romonum or Ulalu (7°24′N, 151°40′E) in 1947, the date of the Yale field expedition to Truk. HRAF: OR19 (b). Authorities: Goodenough, LeBar, Gladwin & Sarason.

110. Yapese (If6: 260) of Province 116 (Yap). Language: Malayo-Polynesian (Carolinian). Economy: Bf. Organization: J, Pm. Focus: The island of Yap as a

whole (9°30′N, 138°10′E) in 1910, at the close of Müller's period of field work. HRAF: OR22 (a). Authorities: Müller, Schneider.

111. Palauans (If1: 59) of Province 115 (Palau and Marianas). Language: Malayo-Polynesian (Hesperonesian). Economy: Bf. Organization: K, N. Focus: The village of Ulimang in northern Babelthuap Island (7°30′N, 134°35′E) in 1947, the date of Barnett's field work. HRAF: No file. Authorities: Barnett, Krämer.

112. Ifugao (Ia3: 150) of Province 99 (Philippines). Language: Malayo-Polynesian (Hesperonesian). Economy: A. Organization: I, O. Focus: The Central and Kiangan Ifugao (16°50′N, 121°10′E) in 1910, near the beginning of Barton's field work. HRAF: OA19 (b). Authorities: Barton, Lambrecht.

113. Atayal (Ia1: 51) of Province 98 (Formosa). Language: Malayo-Polynesian (Hesperonesian). Economy: C. Organization: J, R. Focus: The Atayal proper (excluding the Sedeq) as a whole (23°50′ to 24°50′N, 120°20′ to 120°50′E) about 1930, when the aboriginal culture was still relatively intact. HRAF: AD4 (c). Authorities: Okada, Li.

114. Chinese (not in EA) of Province 83 (Chinese). Language: Sinitic (Wu dialect). Economy: Ad. Organization: L, P. Focus: The village of Kaihsienkung in northern Chekiang (31°N, 120°5′E) in 1936, the date of Fei's field work. HRAF: AF1 (a). Authority: Fei.

115. Manchu (Ed3: 137) of Province 81 (Tungusic Peoples). Language: Altaic (Tungusic). Economy: Ad. Organization: Incorporated in the large Chinese state, P. Focus: The Aigun district of northern Manchuria (50°N, 125°30′E) in 1915, the date of the beginning of Shirokogoroff's field work. HRAF: AG1 (a). Authority: Shirokogoroff.

116. Koreans (Ed1: 39) of Province 80 (Korea). Language: Korean. Economy: Ad. Organization: L, P. Focus: The village of Sondup'o and town of Samku Li on Kanghwa Island (37°37′N, 126°25′E) in 1947, the date of Osgood's field work. HRAF: AA1 (a). Authority: Osgood.

117. Japanese (Ed5: 237) of Province 79 (Japan). Language: Japano-Ryukyuan. Economy: Ae. Organization: L, O. Focus: The village of Niiike in Okayama prefecture (34°40′N, 133°48′E) in 1950, at the beginning of the University of Michigan Japanese Project. HRAF: No file. Authorities: Beardsley, DeVos & Wagatsuma.

118. Ainu (Ec7: 325) of Province 78 (Ainu). Language: Ainu. Economy: Fh. Organization: J, M. Focus: The Ainu of the basins of the Tokapchi and Saru rivers in southeastern Hokkaido (42°40′ to 43°30′N, 142° to 144°E), reconstructed for about 1880. HRAF: AB6 (c). Authorities: Watanabe, Munro, Batchelor.

119. Gilyak (Ec1: 37) of Province 77 (Lower Amur). Language: Gilyak. Economy: Fh. Organization: I, P. Focus: The Gilyak of Sakhalin Island (53°30′ to 54°30′N, 141°50′ to 143°10′E) in 1890, at the beginning of Shternberg's field work. HRAF: RX2 (a). Authority: Shternberg.

120. Yukaghir (Ec6: 236) of combined Provinces 74 and 75 (Northern Siberia). Language: Yukaghir. Economy: Hf. Organization: I, O. Focus: The Yukaghir of the Upper Kolyma River (63°30′ to 66°N, 150° to 157°E) in 1850, prior to marked depopulation. HRAF: No file. Authority: Jochelson.

121. Chukchee (Ec3: 135) of Province 76 (Paleo-Siberians). Language: Luorawetlan. Economy: Df. Organization: I, O. Focus: The Reindeer Chukchee (63° to 70°N, 171°W to 171°E) in 1900, the date of the beginning of the field work by Bogoras. HRAF: RY2 (a). Authority: Bogoras.

122. Ingalik or Tinneh (Na8: 377) of Province 135 (Yukon). Language: Athapaskan (Northern). Economy: Fh. Organization: I, O. Focus: The village of Shageluk 62°30′N, 159°30′W), reconstructed for 1885, just prior to missionization. HRAF: No file. Authority: Osgood.

123. Aleut (Na9: 458) of Province 132 (Western Eskimo). Language: Eskimauan (Aleut). Economy: F. Organization: I, Q. Focus: The Unalaska branch of the Aleut (53° to 57°30′N, 158° to 170°W) about 1800, prior to intensive acculturation. HRAF: NA6 (a). Authorities: Veniaminov, Sarytschew.

124. Copper Eskimo (Na3: 169) of Province 133 (Central and Eastern Eskimo). Language: Eskimauan (Eskimo). Economy: Fh. Organization: I, O. Focus: The Copper Eskimo of the Arctic mainland (66°40′ to 69°20′N, 108° to 117°W) in 1915, during the period of field work by Jenness. HRAF: ND8 (a). Authorities: Jenness, Rasmussen.

125. Montagnais (Na32: 495) of Province 151 (Cree-Montagnais). Language: Algonkian. Economy: H. Organization: I, O. Focus: The Montagnais of the Lake St. John and Mistassini bands (48° to 52°N, 73° to 75°W) in 1910, near the beginning of Speck's field work. HRAF: NH6 (a). Authorities: Speck, Lips.

126. Micmac or Souriquois (Na41: 504) of Province 152 (Maritime Algonkians). Language: Algonkian. Economy: Hf. Organization: J, O. Focus: The Micmac of the mainland (43°30′ to 50°N, 60° to 66°W) in 1650, midway in the governorship of Denys. HRAF: NJ5 (b). Authorities: Denys, Le Clercq.

127. Saulteaux (Na33: 496) of Province 153 (Ojibwa). Language: Algonkian. Economy: Hf. Organization: I, P. Focus: The Northern Saulteaux of the Berens River band (52°N, 95°30′W) in 1930, at the beginning of Hallowell's field work. HRAF: NG6 (b). Authority: Hallowell.

128. Slave or Etchareottine (Na17: 466) of Province 134 (Northeastern Athapaskans). Language: Athapaskan (Northern). Economy: Hf. Organization: I, O. Focus: The Slave in the vicinity of Fort Simpson (62°N, 122°W) in 1940, just prior to the heavy acculturation following World War II. HRAF: No file. Authorities: Helm (MacNeish), Honigmann.

129. Kaska or Eastern Nahani (Na4: 170) of Province 138 (Carrier-Nahani). Language: Athapaskan (Northern). Economy: Fh. Organization: I, M. Focus: The Kaska of the Upper Liard River (60°N, 131°W), reconstructed for 1900, just prior to intensive missionization. HRAF: ND12 (a). Authority: Honigmann.

130. Eyak (Nb5: 270) of Province 136 (South Central Alaska). Language: Eyak. Economy: F. Organization: J, N. Focus: The small Eyak tribe as a whole (60° to 61°N, 144° to 146°W) in 1890, prior to full acculturation. HRAF: No file. Authorities: Birket-Smith & de Laguna.

131. Haida (Nb1: 70) of Province 137 (Northern Northwest Coast). Language: Skittagetan. Economy: F. Organization: I, N. Focus: The village of Masset (54°N, 132°30′W), reconstructed for 1875, immediately prior to missionization. HRAF: No file. Authorities: Swanton, Murdock.

132. Bellacoola or Bilqula (Nb9: 471) of Province 139 (Wakashan-Bellacoola). Language: Salishan. Economy: F. Organization: I, R. Focus: The central Bellacoola along the lower Bella Coola River (52°20′N, 126° to 127°W) in 1880, shortly prior to the early field work of Boas. HRAF: NE6 (a). Authorities: McIlwraith, Boas.

133. Twana (Nb2: 71) of Province 140 (Coast Salish). Language: Salishan. Economy: Fh. Organization: I, O. Focus: The small Twana tribe as a whole (47°20′ to 47°30′N, 123°10′ to 123°20′W), reconstructed for 1860, prior to missionization. HRAF: No file. Authorities: Elmendorf, Eells.

134. Yurok (Nb4: 172) of Province 141 (Central Pacific Coast). Language: Ritwan. Economy: Fg. Organization: I, O. Focus: The village of Tsurai (41°30′N, 124°W) in 1850, the date of the arrival of Loeffelholz, the earliest ethnographer. HRAF: NS31 (b). Authorities: Kroeber, Heizer & Mills.

135. Pomo (Nc18: 533) of Province 143 (Central California). Language: Hokan (Kulanapan). Economy: Gh. Organization: I, O. Focus: The Eastern Pomo of Clear Lake (39°N, 123°W) in 1850, prior to the inrush of European settlers. HRAF: NS18 (a). Authorities: Gifford, Barrett, Loeb.

136. Yokuts (Nc24: 539) of Province 144 (Southern California). Language: Penutian (Mariposan). Economy: Gf. Organization: I, P. Focus: The Lake Yokuts (35°10′N, 119°20′W) in 1850, prior to the influx of settlers following the gold rush. HRAF: NS29 (a). Authority: Gayton.

137. Paiute (Nd22: 564) of combined Provinces 146 and 147 (Great Basin). Language: Shoshonean. Economy: Gh. Organization: I, O. Focus: The Wadadika or

Harney Valley band of Northern Paiute (43° to 44°N, 118° to 120°W), reconstructed for about 1870, just prior to the establishment of the reservation. HRAF: NR13 (a). Authority: B. Whiting.

138. Klamath (Nc8: 523) of combined Provinces 142 and 148 (Southern Plateau and Northeast California). Language: Sahaptin (Lutuamian). Economy: Fg. Organization: I, O. Focus: The Klamath tribe as a whole (42° ot 43°15′N, 121°20′ to 122°20′W) in 1860, prior to intensive acculturation. HRAF: No file. Authorities: Spier, Gatschet.

139. Kutenai or Kootenay (Nd7: 380) of Province 149 (Northern Plateau). Language: Kitunahan. Economy: Fh. Organization: J, O. Focus: The Lower Kutenai (48°40′ to 49°10′N, 116°40′W) in 1890, the date of Chamberlain's field work. HRAF: No file. Authorities: Turney-High, Chamberlain.

140. Gros Ventre or Atsina (Ne1: 75) of Province 150 (Northern Plains). Language: Algonkian. Economy: Hd. Organization: J, O. Focus: The homogeneous Gros Ventre as a whole (47° to 49°N, 106° to 110°W) in 1880, shortly prior to missionization and the disappearance of the buffalo. HRAF: NQ13 (a). Authorities: Flannery, Cooper.

141. Hidatsa or Minitari (Ne15: 662) of Province 154 (Upper Missouri). Language: Siouan. Economy: A. Organization: I, M. Focus: The village of Hidatsa (47°N, 101°W), reconstructed for 1836, prior to depopulation in a severe smallpox epidemic. HRAF: No file. Authorities: Bowers, Matthews.

142. Pawnee (Nf6: 342) of Province 159 (Caddoans). Language: Caddoan. Economy: Ch. Organization: J, M. Focus: The Skidi or Skiri Pawnee (42°N, 100°W), reconstructed for 1867. HRAF: NQ18 (c). Authorities: Weltfish, Dorsey & Murie.

143. Omaha (Nf3: 179) of Province 155 (Prairie). Language: Siouan. Economy: Ch. Organization: J, P. Focus: The Omaha tribe as a whole (41°10′ to 41°40′N, 96° to 97°W) in 1860, prior to the disappearance of the buffalo. HRAF: NQ12 (b). Authorities: Fletcher & LaFlesche, Dorsey.

144. Huron or Wendot (Ng1: 79) of Province 156 (Northeastern Woodlands). Language: Iroquoian. Economy: Cf. Organization: K, M. Focus: The Attignawantan (Bear People) and Attigneenongnahac (Cord People) tribes of the Huron Confederacy (44° to 45°N, 78° to 80°W) in 1634, the date of the beginning of Jesuit missionary activity. HRAF: No file. Authorities: Brébeuf, Sagard-Théodat, Tooker (secondary).

145. Creek or Muskogee (Ng3: 180) of Province 157 (Southeastern Woodlands). Language: Natchez-Muskogean (Muskogean). Economy: C. Organization: K, M. Focus: The Upper Creek of Alabama (32°30′ to 34°20′N, 85°30′ to 86°30′W) in 1800, prior to Tecumseh's rebellion and removal to Oklahoma. HRAF: NN11 (c). Authority: Swanton.

146. Natchez (Ng7: 385) of Province 158 (Lower Mississippi). Language: Natchez-Muskogean (Natchesan). Economy: Ch. Organization: J, O. Focus: The politically integrated Natchez as a whole (31°30′N, 91°25′W) in 1718, the date of the arrival of the first missionaries and ethnographers. HRAF: No file. Authorities: Dumont de Montigny, Le Page du Pratz, Swanton (secondary).

147. Comanche (Ne3: 177) of Province 160 (Southern Plains). Language: Shoshonean. Economy: Hd. Organization: I, O. Focus: The Comanche as a whole (30° to 38°N, 98° to 103°W) in 1870, just prior to pacification and removal to Oklahoma. HRAF: NO6 (a). Authority: Hoebel.

148. Chiricahua Apache (Nh1: 81) of Province 161 (Apache-Tanoan). Language: Athapaskan (Southern). Economy: Gh. Organization: I, O. Focus: The central band or Chiricahua proper (32°N, 109°30′W) in 1870, immediately prior to the reservation period. HRAF: No file. Authority: Opler.

149. Zuni (Nh4: 183) of Province 162 (Pueblo-Navaho). Language: Zunian. Economy: A. Organization: I, M. Focus: The village of Zuni (35° to 35°30′N, 108°30′ to 109°W) in 1880, approximately the beginning of the field work

of both Cushing and Stevenson. HRAF: NT23 (a). Authorities: Cushing, Stevenson.

150. Havasupai (Nd3: 175) of Province 145 (Yumans). Language: Hokan (Yuman). Economy: Ag. Organization: I, Q. Focus: The small Havasupai tribe as a whole (35°20′ to 36°20′N, 111°20′ to 113°W) in 1918, at the beginning of Spier's field work. HRAF: NT14 (a). Authority: Spier.

151. Papago (Ni2: 184) of Province 163 (Northwest Mexico). Language: Piman. Economy: Ag. Organization: I, O. Focus: The Archie Papago near Sells, Arizona (32°N, 112°W) in 1910, the date of the early observations by Lumholtz. HRAF: NU28 (a). Authorities: Underhill, Lumholtz.

152. Huichol (Ni3: 282) of Province 164 (Western Mexico). Language: Nahuatlan. Economy: C. Organization: I, O. Focus: The small Huichol tribe as a whole (22°N, 105°W) in 1890, at the beginning of Lumholz's field work. HRAF: No file. Authorities: Zingg, Lumholtz, J. & B. Grimes.

153. Aztec or Tenochca (Nj2: 185) of Province 165 (Central Mexico). Language: Nahuatlan. Economy: A. Organization: L, R. Focus: The city and environs of Tenochtitlan (19°N, 99°10′W) in 1520, the date of the arrival of the Spaniards. HRAF: NU7 (b). Authorities: Sahagun, Vaillant (secondary).

154. Popoluca (Nj3: 284) of Province 166 (Tehuantepec). Language: Mizocuavean. Economy: C. Organization: I, O. Focus: The Sierra Popoluca of the town and vicinity of Soteapan (18°15′N, 94°50′W) in 1940, the date of Foster's first period of field work. HRAF: No file. Authority: Foster.

155. Quiche (Sa13: 1166) of Province 167 (Maya), Language: Mayan. Economy: C. Organization: J, P. Focus: The town of Chichicastenango (15°N, 91°W) in 1930, the date when both Bunzel and Schultze-Jena began their field work. HRAF: No file. Authorities: Bunzel, Schultz-Jena.

156. Miskito or Mosquito (Sa9: 390) of Province 168 (Honduras and Nicaragua). Language: Misumalpan. Economy: C. Organization: J, O. Focus: The Miskito in the vicinity of Cape Gracias a Dios (15°N, 83°W) in 1921, the date of the field work by Conzemius. HRAF: SA15 (b). Authority: Conzemius.

157. Bribri (Sa5: 287) of Province 169 (Costa Rica). Language: Chibchan. Economy: C. Organization: I, M. Focus: The Bribri tribe of the Talamanca nation (9°N, 83°15′W) in 1917, the date of Skinner's field work. HRAF: Sa19 (a). Authorities: Stone, Skinner.

158. Cuna or Tule (Sa1: 85) of Province 170 (Panama). Language: Chibchan. Economy: Cf. Organization: J, O. Focus: The Cuna of the San Blas Archipelago (9° to 9°30′N, 78° to 79°W) in 1927, the date of Nordenskiöld's field work. HRAF: SB5 (a). Authorities: Nordenskiöld, Wafer, Stout.

159. Goajiro (Sb6: 391) of Province 172 (Northern Colombia and Venezuela). Language: Arawakan. Economy: D. Organization: I, M. Focus: The homogeneous Goajiro tribe as a whole (11°30′ to 12°20′N, 71° to 72°30′W) in 1947, the date of the field work by Gutierrez de Pineda. HRAF: SC13 (a). Authorities: Gutierrez de Pineda, Bolinder.

160. Haitians (Sb9: 1237) of Province 174 (Caribbean Negroes). Language: Indo-European (Romance). Economy: C. Organization: K, O. Focus: The Haitians of Mirebalais (18°50′N, 72°10′W) in 1935, the date of the field work by Herskovits. HRAF: SV3 (b). Authorities: Herskovits, Métraux.

161. Callinago or Island Carib (Sb1: 87) of Province 173 (Antillean Indigenes). Language: Cariban. Economy: Fa. Organization: I, M. Focus: The Callinago of the island of Dominica (15°30′N, 60°30′W), reconstructed for 1650, shortly prior to missionization. HRAF: ST13 (a). Authorities: Breton, Taylor.

162. Warrau or Guarauno (Sc1: 88) of combined Provinces 175 and 176 (Orinoco). Language: Warrauan. Economy: Gh. Organization: I, O. Focus: The Warrau of the Orinoco delta (8°30′ to 9°50′N, 60°40′ to 62°30′W) in 1935, early in the period of missionary field work by Turrado Moreno. HRAF: SS18 (a). Authorities: Turrado Moreno, Wilbert.

163. Yanomamo (not in EA) of Province 177 (Southern Venezuela). Language:

Yanoaman. Economy: C. Organization: I, P. Focus: The Shamatari subtribe around the village of Bisaasi-teri (2° to 2°45′N, 64°30′ to 65°30′W) in 1965, at the time of Chagnon's field work. HRAF: No file. Authority: Chagnon.

164. Carib (Sc3: 189) of Province 178 (Guiana). Language: Cariban. Economy: C. Organization: I, O. Focus: The Carib along the Barama River in British Guiana (7°10′ to 7°40′N, 59°20′ to 60°20′W) in 1932, at the beginning of Gillin's field work. HRAF: SR9 (a). Authority: Gillin.

165. Saramacca (Sc6: 392) of Province 179 (Bush Negroes). Language: Indo-European (creolized Romance). Economy: C. Organization: K, N. Focus: The Saramacca group of Bush Negroes in the upper basin of the Suriname River (3° to 4°N, 55°30′ to 56°W) in 1928, early in the periods of field work of Herskovits and Kahn. HRAF: SR8 (a). Authorities: Kahn, Herskovits.

166. Mundurucu (Sd1: 90) of combined Provinces 180 and 181 (Amazon). Language: Tupi-Guarani. Economy: Ch. Organization: I, P. Focus: The savanna-dwelling Mundurucu of the Rio de Tropas drainage (6° to 7°S, 56° to 57°W), reconstructed for about 1850, prior to the period of increasing assimilation. HRAF: SQ13 (b). Authorities: Murphy, Tocantins.

167. Cubeo (Se5: 293) of Province 182 (Northwest Amazonia). Language: Betoyan. Economy: Cf. Organization: I, P. Focus: The Cubeo of the Caduiari River (1° to 1°50′N, 70° to 71°W) in 1939, at the beginning of Goldman's field work. HRAF: No file. Authority: Goldman.

168. Cayapa (Sf3: 194) of Province 171 (Highland Colombia and Ecuador). Language: Chibchan (Paezan). Economy: H. Organization: I, O. Focus: The Cayapa in the drainage of the Rio Cayapas (0°40′ to 1°15′N, 78°45′ to 79°10′W) in 1908, at the beginning of Barrett's field work. HRAF: SD6 (a). Authorities: Barrett, Altschuler.

169. Jivaro or Xibaro (Se3: 191) of Province 183 (Eastern Ecuador). Language: Jivaran. Economy: C. Organization: I, O. Focus: The Jivaro proper (2° to 4°S, 77° to 79°W) in 1920, near the beginning of Karsten's field work. HRAF: SD9 (a). Authorities: Karsten, Stirling.

170. Amahuaca (Se8: 634) of Province 184 (Montaña). Language: Panoan. Economy: Ch. Organization: I, O. Focus: The Amahuaca on the upper Inuya River (10°10′ to 10°30′S, 72° to 72°30′W) in 1960, the date of the beginning of the field work by Carneiro and Dole. HRAF: No file. Authorities: Carneiro, Dole, Huxley & Capa.

171. Inca (Sf1: 93) of Province 185 (Highland Peru). Language: Kechumaran (Quechuan). Economy: A. Organization: L, O. Focus: The Quechua-speaking Indians in the vicinity of Cuzco (13°30′S, 72°W) in 1530, immediately prior to the Spanish conquest. HRAF: SE13 (b). Authorities: Cobo, Cieza de Leon, Rowe (secondary).

172. Aymara (Sf2: 193) of Province 186 (Highland Bolivia). Language: Kechumaran (Aymaran). Economy: Cd. Organization: incorporated in the large Peruvian state, P. Focus: The Aymara of the community of Chucuito in Peru (16°S, 70°W) in 1940, at the beginning of Tschopik's field work. HRAF: SF5 (a). Authority: Tschopik.

173. Siriono (Se1: 91) of Province 187 (Lowland Bolivia). Language: Tupi-Guarani. Economy: Hg. Organization: I, O. Focus: The Siriono in the forests near the Rio Blanco (14° to 15°S, 63° to 64°W) in 1942, during the period of Holmberg's field work. HRAF: SF21 (a). Authority: Holmberg.

174. Nambicuara (Si4: 198) of Province 188 (Western Mato Grosso). Language: Nambicuaran. Economy: Gh. Organization: I, O. Focus: The Cocozu or eastern Nambicuara (12°30′ to 13°30′S, 58°30, to 59°W) in 1940, shortly prior to the field work of Lévi-Strauss. HRAF: SP17 (a). Authority: Lévi-Strauss.

175. Trumai (Si2: 98) of Province 189 (Upper Xingu). Language: Trumaian. Economy: Cf. Organization: I, Q. Focus: The single surviving Trumai village (11°50′S, 53°40′W) in 1938, the date of Quain's field work. HRAF: No file. Authorities: Murphy & Quain.

176. Timbira (Sj4: 200) of Province 190 (Northern Ge). Language: Ge. Economy: Ch. Organization: I, M. Focus: The Ramcocamecra or Eastern Timbira (6° to 7°S, 45° to 46°W) in 1915, near the beginning of Nimuendajú's field work. HRAF: SO8 (b). Authorities: Nimuendajú, Crocker.
177. Tupinamba (Sj8: 400) of Province 191 (Tupi). Language: Tupi-Guarani. Economy: C. Organization: J, O. Focus: The Tupinamba near Rio de Janeiro (22°30' to 23°S, 42° to 44°30'W) in 1550, at the time of Staden's captivity. HRAF: SO9 (a). Authorities: Staden, Thevet.
178. Botocudo or Aimore (Sj5: 299) of Province 192 (East Brazilian Highlands). Language: Botocudan. Economy: Hg. Organization: I, O. Focus: The Naknenuk subtribe in the basin of the Rio Doce (18° to 20°S, 41°30' to 43°30'W) in 1884, the date of Ehrenreich's field work. HRAF: No file. Authority: Ehrenreich.
179. Shavante (Sj11: 1184) of Province 193 (Upper Araguaya and Tocantins). Language: Ge. Economy: Gh. Organization: I, P. Focus: The Akwe-Shavante in the vicinity of São Domingos (13°30'S, 51°30'W) in 1958, the date of the first field work by Maybury-Lewis. HRAF: No file. Authority: Maybury-Lewis.
180. Aweikoma or Shokleng (Sj3: 199) of Province 194 (Caingang). Language: Ge (Caingang). Economy: Hg. Organization: I, O. Focus: The Aweikoma of the Duque de Caxias Reservation (38°S, 50°W) in 1932, at the beginning of Henry's field work. HRAF: No file. Authority: Henry.
181. Cayua or Caingua (Sj10: 1170) of Province 195 (Guarani). Language: Tupi-Guarani. Economy: C. Organization: I, O. Focus: The Cayua of southern Mato Grosso, Brazil (23° to 24°S, 54° to 56°W) in 1890, the approximate period of the earlier good descriptions. HRAF: No file. Authorities: Watson, Müller.
182. Lengua (Sh9: 1168) of Province 196 (Paraguayan Chaco). Language: Mascoian. Economy: H. Organization: I, O. Focus: The Lengua in contact with the Anglican mission (23° to 24°S, 58° to 59°W) in 1889, the date of the founding of the mission. HRAF: No file. Authority: Grubb.
183. Abipon or Mepene (Sh3: 196) of Province 197 (Argentine Chaco). Language: Guaycuran. Economy: Hd. Organization: I, O. Focus: The Apipon in contact with the Jesuit mission (27° to 29°S, 59° to 60°W) in 1750, at the beginning of Dobrizhoffer's missionary field work. HRAF: SI4 (a). Authority: Dobrizhoffer.
184. Mapuche (Sg2: 195) of Province 198 (Araucanians). Language: Araucanian. Economy: A. Organization: I, P. Focus: The Mapuche in the vicinity of Temuco (38°30'S, 72°35'W) in 1950, just prior to Faron's field work. HRAF: SG4 (c). Authorities: Faron, Hilger, Titiev.
185. Tehuelche or Patagon (Sg4: 349) of Province 199 (Patagonians). Language Tehuelchean. Economy: Hd. Organization: I, O. Focus: The equestrian Tehuelche (40° to 50°S, 64° to 72°W) in 1870, during the period of field work by Musters. HRAF: SH5 (a). Authority: Musters.
186. Yahgan or Yamana (Sg1: 94) of Province 200 (Fuegians). Language: Yahgan. Economy: F. Organization: I, O. Focus: The eastern and central Yaghan (54°30' to 55°30'S, 67° to 70°W), reconstructed for 1865, early in the period of missionary field work by Bridges. HRAF: SH6 (b). Authorities: Gusinde, Bridges, Lothrop.

## BIBLIOGRAPHY

Barry, H., III. 1968. Regional and Worldwide Variations in Culture. Ethnology 7: 207-217.
Driver, H. E. 1956. An Integration of Functional, Evolutionary, and Historical Theory by Means of Correlations. Indiana University Publication in Anthropology and Linguistics, Memoir 12.
———— 1966. Geographical *versus* Psycho-Functional Explanations of Kin Avoidances. Current Anthropology 7: 131-182.
Murdock, G. P. 1949. Social Structure. New York.
———— 1957. World Ethnographic Sample. American Anthropologist 59: 664-687.
———— 1963. Ethnographic Atlas (fifth installment). Ethnology 2: 109-110.

———— 1966. Cross-Cultural Sampling. Ethnology 5: 97-114.

———— 1967. Ethnographic Atlas: A Summary. Ethnology 6: 109-236.

———— 1968. World Sampling Provinces. Ethnology 7: 305-326.

Naroll, R. 1961. Two Solutions to Galton's Problem. Philosophy of Science 28: 15-39.

———— 1964. A Fifth Solution to Galton's Problem. American Anthropologist 66: 863-867.

———— 1965. Galton's Problem: The Logic of Cross-Cultural Analysis. Social Research 32: 428-451.

Naroll, R., and R. G. D'Andrade. 1963. Two Further Solutions to Galton's Problem. American Anthropologist 65: 1053-1067.

Ogburn, W. F. 1922. Social Change. New York.

Sawyer, J., and R. A. LeVine. 1966. Cultural Dimensions: A Factor Analysis of the World Ethnographic Sample. American Anthropologist 68: 708-731.

Sumner, W. G. 1906. Folkways. Boston.

Textor, R. B. 1967. A Cross-Cultural Summary. New Haven.

White, D. R. 1967. Concomitant Variation in Kinship Structures. M. A. thesis, University of Minnesota.

———— 1969. Decision-making in Equestrian Indian Societies: An Essay in Comparative Pragmatics. Ph.D. dissertation, University of Minnesota.

# 2

# Subsistence Economy and Supportive Practices: Cross-Cultural Codes 1

*George P. Murdock* and *Diana O. Morrow*

This paper presents a set of codes and a body of coded cultural data pertaining to the derivation, transportation, preservation, and storage of food in a typical (or focal) community in each of the 186 societies selected by Murdock and White (*Ethnology* 8:329-369) as a representative sample of the world's known cultures. Comparable materials are being prepared on other topics by the Cross-Cultural Cumulative Coding Center (CCCCC) at the University of Pittsburgh, a research program supported by the National Science Foundation, and will be published in this journal when completed. Data are also presented herewith on a few additional societies, which will be supplemented in the future (1) to provide alternatives which may be substituted for societies of the standard sample and (2) to form special samples for particular purposes.

The reader who uses the coded materials in Table 1 should bear in mind two warnings. First, since the data for each society have been assessed or "pinpointed" with reference to a particular local group at a particular date, the codes may or may not hold true for the larger society as a whole. For such complex and diversified cultures as those of the Burmese, Chinese, Egyptians, Japanese, Russians, Turks, and Vietnamese, for example, the indicated absence of such traits as banks, fishing, improved highways, markets, and motorized land and water transport, however valid for the pinpointed locality, may actually be misrepresentative of the total society. Second, since the data were coded primarily with reference to food or subsistence, the reader should not assume that the codes adequately reflect the actual importance of such activities as trade, animal husbandry, or transportation in the total culture. Column 3, for example, assesses only the contribution of animal husbandry to the food supply and ignores its importance in other respects, e.g., as a source of prestige or of products other than food.

## Definition of Codes

Twenty items of information for each society are summarized in Table 1 in ten columns of two symbols each—a capital and a lower-case letter. In cases of doubt as to which symbol to employ, the coders gave precedence to the last one listed in the definitions. Anomalous cases are indicated in the table by an asterisk and are discussed briefly in notes. A dot ( · ) indicates the absence of available information. Inferences unless very strong, are indicated by the enclosure of symbols in parentheses.

### Column 1: Intercommunity Trade

O   Trade with other communities does not occur.

N   Intercommunity trade occurs but does not contribute to the local food supply.

M   Minerals which enter into the diet, such as salt, are obtained by trade but no significant amounts of other edible products.

U   Food products produced in other communities are imported through trade, tribute, or other forms of exchange but in an amount constituting less than 10 per cent of the food consumed locally.

S   Intercommunity trade contributes more than 10 per cent of the food consumed but less than the amount produced locally by one or more of the extractive techniques.

I   Intercommunity trade contributes more to the local food supply than any single extractive technique but less than half of the total food consumption.

D   Intercommunity trade contributes more of the food consumed locally than all the extractive techniques combined.

One of the following lower-case symbols appears after any capital letter other than O or N.

b   Imported food is obtained primarily by barter, purchase, or direct ceremonial exchange with individuals of other communities.

i   Imported food is obtained primarily by indirect exchange with members of other communities, e.g., through ceremonial gifts, ritual contributions of food by kinsmen, or tribute.

m   Imported food is distributed primarily through markets in the same or nearby communities.

s   Imported food is distributed primarily through shops or other specialized middlemen.

v   Imported food is distributed by three or four of the above methods, no one of which preponderates.

### Column 2: Agriculture

O   Agriculture is not practiced (not followed by a lower-case symbol).

N   Agriculture is practiced but is confined to non-food crops.

U   Agriculture is unimportant, yielding less than 10 per cent of the local food supply.

S   Agriculture is significant, yielding more than 10 per cent of the local food supply but less than the amount contributed by one or more other subsistence techniques (including trade).

I   Agriculture contributes more of the local food supply than any other subsistence technique but less than half of the total food consumption.

D   Agriculture contributes more to the local food supply than all other subsistence techniques combined.

n   The principal local agricultural products are non-food crops, e.g., cotton, indigo, opium, or tobacco.

v   The pricipal local crops are vegetables, e.g., greens, legumes, or cucurbits.

t   The principal local crops are tree or vine products, e.g., bananas, coconuts, dates, or grapes.

r   The principal local crops are roots or tubers, e.g., manioc, potatoes, or yams.

c   The principal local crops are cereal grains, e.g., maize, millet, rice, or wheat.

### Column 3: Animal Husbandry

O   No domestic animals are kept (not followed by a lower-case symbol).

N   Some domestic animals (at least dogs) are kept, but they do not contribute to the local food supply, e.g., are not eaten or milked.

U   Domestic animals are kept and contribute to the local food supply but in an amount constituting less than 10 per cent of the total food consumed.
F   Domestic animals are kept and contribute more than 10 per cent of the local food supply, especially in the form of flesh or meat, but less than one or more other subsistence techniques.
M   Domestic animals are kept and contribute more than 10 per cent of the local food supply, especially in the form of milk or dairy products, but less than one or more other subsistence techniques.
H   Domestic animals contribute more than 10 per cent of the local food supply, mainly in the form of honey rather than milk or meat.
P   The subsistence economy is primarily pastoral, with animal husbandry contributing more to the local food supply than any other subsistence technique. The use of dairy products is assumed in the absence of an asterisked note to the contrary.
s   The principal domestic animals kept locally are small species, e.g., bees, cats, dogs, fowl, or guinea pigs.
p   The principal domestic animals are pigs.
o   The principal domestic animals are ovide species, e.g., sheep and/or goats.
e   The principal domestic animals are equine species, e.g., horses or donkeys, regardless of the importance of their contribution to the local food supply.
d   The principal domestic animals are reindeer, regardless of their contribution to the local food supply.
c   The principal domestic animals are camels or related species, e.g., llamas.
b   The principal domestic animals, especially with reference to their contribution to the local food supply, are bovine species, e.g., cattle, mithun, water buffaloes, or yaks.

## Column 4: Fishing

O   Fishing is not practiced, at least for food (not followed by a lower-case symbol).
U   Fishing contributes to the local food supply but in an amount constituting less than 10 per cent of the total food consumed.
S   Fishing contributes more than 10 per cent of the local food supply but less than the amount contributed by one or more other subsistence techniques.
I   Fishing contributes more to the local food supply than any other subsistence technique but less than half of the total food consumed.
D   Fishing contributes more to the local food supply than all other subsistence techniques combined.
s   Fishing consists predominantly in the collecting of shellfish or other small aquatic fauna.
f   Fishing consists predominantly in the catching of true fish.
a   Fishing consists predominantly in the capture of large aquatic animals.
v   Fishing assumes two or more of the above forms, no one of which preponderates.

## Column 5: Hunting

O   Hunting is not practiced in any form (not followed by a lower-case symbol).
N   Hunting is practiced, e.g., for furs or hides, but does not contribute to the local food supply.
U   Hunting contributes to the local food supply but in an amount constituting less than 10 per cent of the total food consumed.
S   Hunting contributes more than 10 per cent of the local food supply but less than the amount contributed by one or more other subsistence techniques.
I   Hunting contributes more to the local food supply than any other subsistence technique but less than half of the total food consumed.
D   Hunting contributes more to the local food supply than all other subsistence techniques combined.
f   Hunting consists predominantly of the snaring, netting, or shooting of waterfowl or other birds.

s   Hunting consists predominantly of the trapping, netting, or shooting of small mammals.
l   Hunting consists predominantly of the killing of large game, e.g., buffalo, deer, guanaco, or kangaroos.
v   Hunting assumes two or more of the above forms, no one of which preponderates.

*Column 6: Gathering*

O   Gathering is not practiced or makes no appreciable contribution to the local food supply (not followed by a lower-case symbol).
U   Gathering contributes to the local food supply but in an amount constituting less than 10 per cent of the total food consumed.
S   Gathering contributes more than 10 per cent of the local food supply but less than the amount contributed by one or more of the other subsistence techniques.
I   Gathering contributes more of the local food supply than any other subsistence technique but less than half of the total food consumed.
D   Gathering contributes more to the local food supply than all other subsistence techniques combined.
a   Gathering consists predominantly in the collecting of wild animal products, e.g., eggs, honey, insects, or lizards.
h   Gathering consists predominantly in the collecting of wild herbs, leaves, edible blossoms, or the like.
p   Gathering consists predominantly in the extraction of edible pith from tree trunks, e.g., sago.
r   Gathering consists predominantly in the digging of wild roots or tubers.
s   Gathering consists predominantly in the collecting of wild seeds, berries, fruits, or nuts.
v   Gathering assumes two or more of the above forms, no one of which preponderates.

*Column 7: Land Transport* (with special but not exclusive reference to the transportation of food products from their sources to the place of consumption)

H   Land transport is done exclusively by human carriers, with at most the aid of a tumpline, a carrying pole, or the like.
A   Land transport is done to at least an appreciable extent by animal carriers, e.g., pack animals.
S   Land transport is done to a considerable extent by means of draft animals dragging a sled, travois, or other vehicle without wheels.
W   Land transport is done to a considerable extent by means of animal-drawn wheeled vehicles, e.g., carts or wagons.
M   Land transport is done to a considerable extent by means of motorized vehicles, e.g., railroads, trucks.
t   Routes of land transport consist exclusively (or almost so) of unimproved trails or footpaths.
p   Routes of land transport consist in considerable measure of improved paths, leveled or widened to accommodate human porters or beasts of burden.
r   Routes of land transport between communities consist in considerable measure of improved but unpaved roads capable of accommodating wheeled vehicles.
h   Routes of land transport between communities consist in considerable measure of paved highways or railroads.

*Column 8: Water Transport*

O   Water craft are not made or used despite the suitability of the environment to them (not followed by a lower-case symbol).
N   Water craft are not used, the environment being unsuited to them (not followed by a lower-case symbol).
F   Water craft consist exclusively of floats or rafts rather than boats.

B    Water craft consist predominantly of boats, e.g., dugout or bark canoes, coracles, or plank boats, propelled mainly by human power with the aid of paddles, oars, or poles.

S    Water craft consist, at least in part, of vessels propelled by sails.

M    Water craft consist, at least in part, of vessels propelled by motors, e.g., by steam or internal combustion engines. But S rather than M is indicated if sailing craft preponderate.

s    Water craft are exclusively small, capable of carrying only light loads or a very few people for relatively short distances.

m    At least some of the water craft used are capable of carrying at least ten people and/or loads of comparable size over considerable distances, e.g., across broad rivers, lakes, estuaries, or short stretches of sea.

l    At least some of the water craft used are capable of carrying at least forty people and/or comparable amounts of freight over the sea to destinations hundreds of miles away.

*Column 9: Money and Credit* (with special but not exclusive reference to the facilitation of intercommunity trade for food)

O    No money or other medium of exchange was in use at the designated time period, mercantile transactions being conducted exclusively through the direct or indirect exchange of goods.

D    Domestically usable articles, e.g., salt, grain, livestock, tobacco, furs, tools, or ornaments circulated freely as a medium of exchange in intercommunity trade, true money being absent.

T    Articles of token or conventional value, not domestically usable at least in quantity, such as cowrie shells, wampum, imitation tools or weapons, feathers, or bars of metal, circulated freely in intercommunity exchange as an elementary form of money.

A    The currency of an alien people circulated freely as money.

C    An indigenous currency in the form of metal coins of standard weight and fineness, and/or their equivalents in paper currency, circulated freely as money in intercommunity exchange.

o    There are no formal mechanisms for the extension of credit, which occurs only in the form of personal loans between relatives or friends.

i    There are individual members of the society who specialize in the extension of credit, e.g., money lenders, brokers, or entrepreneurs who seek power and wealth by financing marriage transactions, engaging in potlatches, or the like.

e    Comparable individuals who are external to the society, e.g., traders or factors, engage in the extension of credit.

b    There are banks or comparable institutions, such as wealthy mercantile houses or in some cases temples, which specialize in the financing of business enterprises.

*Column 10: Preservation and Storage of Food*

Techniques of food preservation (e.g., drying, smoking, salting, refrigeration) and the prevalence and types of food storage depend so heavily upon ecological variables that they are likely to be useful in cross-cultural comparisons only when related to particular configurations of ecological and technological conditions. Five such configurations are defined below together with types of adjustment to each.

Condition 1: The food resources utilized by the society are notably constant from year to year, season to season, and day to day, so that an adequate supply for daily needs is regularly available by the expenditure of a reasonable amount of effort. This condition normally prevails in pastoral societies, where reserves of food are always at hand on the hoof; in fishing societies where the supply of aquatic products varies little from season to season; in agricultural and gathering societies where plant foods ripen and can be harvested throughout the year; and in particularly favored hunting societies where large game is regularly available in abundance. Under Condition 1 the ecology creates no urgent need for preservation and storage.

A   The society exemplifies Condition 1 and lacks significant techniques for the preservation and storage of food.

B   The society exemplifies Condition 1 and has a few simple techniques of food preservation and/or storage which provide adequate insurance against all food shortages not caused by natural calamities.

C   The society exemplifies Condition 1 but possesses significant techniques for food preservation and/or storage which are adapted to the accumulation of substantial surpluses for other than subsistence purposes, especially for later consumption in potlatches, elaborate feasts, or lavish sacrifices.

Condition 2: The food resources are constant from year to year and from season to season, but there is substantial diurnal variation in the available supply owing to chance factors such as the success or failure of hunters on particular days. Under Condition 2 the principal need for preservation and storage is to even out the diurnal differences in the food supply and prevent the succession of brief periods of glut and shortage.

E   The society exemplifies Condition 2 and lacks significant techniques for the preservation and storage of food.

F   The society exemplifies Condition 2 and has a few simple techniques of food preservation and/or storage sufficient to even out diurnal variations in the food supply.

G   The society exemplifies Condition 2 but possesses techniques of food preservation and/or storage for the accumulation of substantial surpluses for other than subsistence purposes.

Condition 3: The food resources, though relatively constant from year to year, vary markedly from season to season depending upon such climatic and ecological factors as sharp contrasts between hot and cold or wet and dry seasons and great differences in the seasonal availability of plant and/or animal foods. This condition prevails commonly in agricultural and hunting societies, especially outside the tropics. Under Condition 3 the urgent problem in preservation and storage is to accumulate reserves in seasons of abundance to provide subsistence during the ensuing lean seasons.

I   The society exemplifies Condition 3 and has at best techniques of food preservation and/or storage barely adequate to carry it safely through seasons of food shortage. There may often be an annual period of deprivation and semi-starvation at the end of the season of shortest supply.

J   The society exemplifies Condition 3 and has techniques of food preservation and/or storage fully adequate to tide over seasons of shortage without discomfort.

K   The society exemplifies Condition 3 and has techniques of food preservation and storage by which it not only tides over seasons of short supply but accumulates substantial surpluses for other than subsistence purposes.

Condition 4: The food resources, whatever their diurnal and seasonal variation, are markedly variable from year to year owing to extreme annual differences in rainfall or other recurrent but unpredictable climatic vicissitudes. This condition is especially common in agricultural societies without irrigation techniques living in semi-arid environments with irregular precipitation. Under Condition 4 the primary problem in preservation and storage is to accumulate surpluses well above normal needs in years of abundance as an insurance against possible lean years to follow. Such surpluses, of course, also protect against diurnal and seasonal shortages.

O   The society exemplifies Condition 4 and has techniques of food preservation and storage barely adequate to carry it through a single lean year. There is likely to be a "tightening of belts" every lean year and actual famine in a second successive lean year.

P    The society exemplifies Condition 4 and has techniques of food preservation and/or storage fully adequate for tiding over at least one lean year without discomfort.

Q    The society exemplifies Condition 4 and has techniques of food preservation and storage that enable it not only to survive lean years without difficulty but to accumulate substantial surpluses for other than subsistence purposes.

Condition 5: This condition is most likely to prevail in advanced agricultural or mercantile societies which depend for their food supply largely on trade and especially on imports from a distance. The system of land and water transport must be adequate to assure the distribution of food in normal and even lean years, but it may break down in the face of calamities, such as devastating floods, serious epidemics of plant or animal diseases, or destructive wars, causing a severe shortage of food and widespread starvation. Under Condition 5 the most urgent problem is not that of the accumulation and storage of food reserves but the adequacy of the distribution system to cope with unpredictable emergencies.

U    The society exemplifies Condition 5 and has a transportation system adequate for the distribution of food in normal or lean years but inadequate, at least in particular regions, to prevent severe shortage and famine during periods of major calamities.

V    The society exemplifies Condition 5 and has a distribution system adequate to prevent famine even in the case of severe disasters.

Lower-case symbols which follow the capital letter are defined as follows.

o    There is no significant storage of food supplies.

h    Food reserves are stored mainly in individual households, e.g., in dwellings, adjacent granaries or other outbuildings, or private caches located elsewhere.

c    Food reserves are stored largely in communal warehouses or other facilities under the control of representatives of the community as a whole, or of its major segments (e.g., clans), or of its principal wielders of power.

s    Food reserves are stored largely in repositories controlled by a supra-community political organization or state.

d    Food reserves are stored largely in repositories of a distribution system not directly under political control, e.g., in shops, in the warehouses of middlemen or large producers, or in transit in the transportation system.

## CODED MATERIAL

The ethnographic data, coded in accordance with the foregoing definitions, are presented in the ten columns of Table 1. Asterisks refer to brief qualifying notes which follow the table. The societies of the sample are ordered according to the numbers of the sampling provinces to which they belong. The additional or alternative societies, most of which were analyzed in pretesting the codes, appear at the end of the table.

TABLE 1
Coded Data on Subsistence Economy and Supportive Practices

|   | Society | 1 | 2 | 3 | 4 | 5 | 6 | 7 | 8 | 9 | 10 |
|---|---|---|---|---|---|---|---|---|---|---|---|
| 1 | Nama Hottentot | Ub | O | Mb | O | Sl | Sa | At | N | Oo | Ao |
| 2 | Kung Bushmen | N | O | O | O | Sl | Dv | Ht | N | Oo | Ao |
| 3 | Thonga | Ub | Dc | Uo | Uf | Ul | Us | Hp | Bs | A(o) | Ih |
| 4 | Lozi | Ub | Ic | Fb | Sf | Uv | Us | Ht | Bs | Oo | Qh |
| 5 | Mbundu | . | Dc | Fb | Uf | Us | Us | Ht | Bm | To | Ih |
| 6 | Suku | Um | Dr | Us | Uf | Uv | Sv | (Ht) | (O) | T(o) | Bh |
| 7 | Bemba | O | Ic | Us | Sf | Sl | Sv | Hp | B(s) | Oo | Ih |

TABLE 1. *Continued*

| | Society | 1 | 2 | 3 | 4 | 5 | 6 | 7 | 8 | 9 | 10 |
|---|---|---|---|---|---|---|---|---|---|---|---|
| 8 | Nyakyusa | N | Dc | Fb | Uf | Uf | Us | Ht | B. | D. | Ao |
| 9 | Hadza | N | O | Ns | O | Sl | Dv | Ht | N | Oo | Ao |
| 10 | Luguru | Um | Dc | Uo | Uf | Us | (Ua) | Ht | N | (Do) | Jh |
| 11 | Kikuyu | Ub | Dc | Fb | O | Us | . | Ht | O | Do | Kh |
| 12 | Ganda | Um | Dt | Fo | Sf | Sl | Uv | Hp | Bm | T. | Bo |
| 13 | Mbuti | Ub | O | Ns | Uv | Sv | Iv | Ht | N | Oo | Ao |
| 14 | Nkundo Mongo | Ui | Dr | Us | Uf | Us | Uv | Ht | Bl | C. | Ao |
| 15 | Banen | Mm | Dr | Us | Uf | Uv | Uh | Ht | N | (Ao) | Bh |
| 16 | Tiv | Sm | Dr | Us | Uf | Ul | Us | Ht | Bs | Oo | Ih |
| 17 | Ibo | Sm | Dr | Ub | (Uf) | (O) | Uv | Hp | (O) | Ti | Ih |
| 18 | Fon | Sm | Ic | Fp | O | Sl | Us | Hp | (N) | To | Jh |
| 19 | Ashanti | Ub | Dr | Fo | Uf | Ss | Us | Ht | (N) | T(i) | Jh |
| 20 | Mende | Ss | Dc | Uo | Uf | Us | Us | Mh | (N) | A(o) | (Jh) |
| 21 | Wolof | Ss | Dc | Ub | Uf | Ul | Us | Mr | (O) | Ai | Oh |
| 22 | Bambara | U(b) | Dc | Mb | Uf | U(l) | Us | . | Bs | Ai | J(h) |
| 23 | Tallensi | Sm | Dc | Us | Uf | Us | Us | Ht | (N) | Ao | Ic |
| 24 | Songhai | Um | Ic | Mb | Uf | Ul | Uv | A. | B(m) | (Oo) | I. |
| 25 | Wodaabe Fulani | Sb | Uc | Pb | (O) | Uv | Uv | At | N | O(o)* | Bh |
| 26 | Hausa | Sm | Dc | Ue | Uf | Uf | Uv | Ap | N | Ai | K(d) |
| 27 | Massa | U. | Ic | Mb | Sf | Ul | Ua | Ht | (O) | Oo | Jh |
| 28 | Azande | N | Ic | Us | Uf | Sv | Sv | Ht | N | T(o) | Ih |
| 29 | Fur | Um | Ic | Mb | Sf | Sl | Uv | A(p) | N | Do | Jh |
| 30 | Otoro Nuba | Us | Dc | Fo | O | Us | O | Ht | N | Oo | Jh |
| 31 | Shilluk | Us | Dc | Mb | Sf | Sv | Us | Hp | Bs | Oo | Jh |
| 32 | Mao | Um | Dc | Uo | Sf | Sl | Ua | Hp | O | Ao | Jh |
| 33 | Kaffa | N | Dc | Fb | O | Ul | Ss | Ap | O | Do | Ch |
| 34 | Masai | Sb | O | Pb | O | O | Uv | At | N | Do | Ao |
| 35 | Konso | N | Dc | Mb | O | Ul | O | A(t) | N | Oe | Kh |
| 36 | Somali | Us | Uc | Pc | O | Ul | Us | At | N | Ao | Ah |
| 37 | Amhara | Sm | Ic | Mb | Uf | Ul | Ua | Ap | . | Ab | Jh |
| 38 | Bogo | Ui | Sc | Pb | (O) | Ul | Ua | Ap | N | A(o) | O(o) |
| 39 | Kenuzi Nubians | . | Dc | Fo | Uf | Ul | (O) | At | Ss | . | Ph |
| 40 | Teda | Sb | Ut | Pc | O | Ul | Us | At | N | Ae | B. |
| 41 | Tuareg | Sm | Sc | Po | O | Uv | Us | At | N | Do | Ph |
| 42 | Riffians | Um | Dt | Mb | Uf | Uv | Ss | At | Sm | C(o) | Jh |
| 43 | Egyptians | Ss | Dc | Ub | Uf | O | (O) | Ar | B. | Ci | Jh |
| 44 | Hebrews | (U)m | Ic | Mo | Uf | Sl | Uv | Ar | N | Cb | Ao |
| 45 | Babylonians | (N) | Dc | Mb | Sf | (Nl) | (O) | W(r) | Bl | Cb | Kc |
| 46 | Rwala Bedouin | Ss | O | Pc | O | Uv | Ua | At | N | A. | Ao |
| 47 | Turks | Us | Dc | Mo | O | O | Uh | Mh | N | Ci | Jh |
| 48 | Gheg Albanians | Us | Ic | Mb | Uf | Us | Uv | Ap* | B(s) | C. | Ih |
| 49 | Romans | Dv | St | Fo | Uf | O | O | Wh | Sl | Cb | Ud |
| 50 | Basques | Us | Dc | Mb | Uf | Us | Uh | Wr | N | Cb | Cd |
| 51 | Irish | Ss | Dr | Mb | Uf | (O) | O | Mh | . | Ci | Kd |
| 52 | Lapps | Us | Uc | Pd | Sf | Uv | Uv | At | N | (Oo) | Bh |
| 53 | Yurak Samoyed | Ub | Uc | Pd* | Sf | Ul | Us | St | (Bs) | Ae | Bh |
| 54 | Russians | Us | Dc | Mb | Uf | (O) | Uv | Mr | N | C. | Ks |
| 55 | Abkhaz | O | Sc | Pb | (Uf) | Ul | Uh | W(t) | N | Oo | Bh |
| 56 | Armenians | (U)s | Dc | Mb | . | . | . | A(r) | N | A. | Jh |
| 57 | Kurd | Ss | Ic | Mo | Uf | Uv | (O) | Ar | (O) | Ci | Jh |
| 58 | Basseri | Sb | Sc | Po | O | Ul | Uh | A(t) | N | Oi | Bh |
| 59 | West Punjabi | Ub | Dc | Mb | Uf | Uf | O | Ar | O | Ci | Oh |
| 60 | Gond | Um | Ic | Fb | Uf | Us | Sv | Hp | N | (To) | Kh |
| 61 | Toda | Sm | O | Pb | O | O | Ss | Ht | N | Ao | Ah |

TABLE 1. *Continued*

| | Society | 1 | 2 | 3 | 4 | 5 | 6 | 7 | 8 | 9 | 10 |
|---|---|---|---|---|---|---|---|---|---|---|---|
| 62 | Santal | Um | Dc | Ub | Uf | Us | Uv | Hr | (O) | Ae | Ih |
| 63 | Uttar Pradesh | Uv | Dc | Mb | Us | O | Ua | Mh | N | Ci | (J)h |
| 64 | Burusho | N | Dc | Mo | O | (O) | Uh | A. | N | Oo | Ih |
| 65 | Kazak | N | Nn | Pb | Uf | Us | (O) | At | N | Ai | Bh |
| 66 | Khalka Mongols | Ss | Uc | Po | Uf | Us | Uh | Wt | (Bs) | Ae | Bh |
| 67 | Lolo | N | Dc | Fo | Uf | Ul | . | Ap | N | T. | Ao |
| 68 | Lepcha | Us | Ic | Fb | Uf | Uv | Sr | Ht | N | Ae | Jh |
| 69 | Garo | Sm | Ic | Fo | (O) | . | Uv | Ht | B. | Ae | Kh |
| 70 | Lakher | N | Dc | Fb | Uf | Uv | Uv | Ht | N | D. | Jh |
| 71 | Burmese | Sb | Ic | Us* | Sf | Uv | Uv | Wp | N | Ci | Jh |
| 72 | Lamet | N | Ic | Fb | Uf | Sv | Uh | Ht | N | D(o) | Jh |
| 73 | Vietnamese | Um | Dc | Up | Sf | Us | Ua | Hp | Sm | Ai | Bh |
| 74 | Rhade | Uv | Dc | Fp | (Uf) | . | U. | Ht | . | Ao | (Bo) |
| 75 | Khmer | Ui | Dc | Up | Sf | Ul | Uv | Wr | Bl | Co | B. |
| 76 | Siamese | Us | Dc | Ub | Sf | O | Uh | Mr | Bm | Ci | Oh |
| 77 | Semang | Sb | Ur | Ns | Uv | Ss | Iv | Ht | Fs | Oe | Ao |
| 78 | Nicobarese | Us | Dt | Fp | Sf | Uv | Ua | Ht | Bm | Oo | Ah |
| 79 | Andamanese | N | O | O | Iv | Ss | Sv | Ht | Bm | Oo | Bo |
| 80 | Vedda | Ub | Uc | Ns | Uf | Il | Sa | Ht | O | Ao | Eh |
| 81 | Tanala | N | Dc | Us | Uf | Us | Ua | Ht | Bs | Oo | (J)h |
| 82 | Negri Sembilan | Us | Dc | Ub | Sf | Ns | Us | Wr | . | C(o) | Jh |
| 83 | Javanese | Ss | Dc | Ub | (O) | O | O | Mh | . | Cb | Cd |
| 84 | Balinese | Sb | Ic | Fb | Uf | U(s) | . | Mh | N | Cb | Jc |
| 85 | Iban | Us | Dc | Up | Uf | Uv | Up | Ht | B(m) | Oo | Oh |
| 86 | Badjau | Sb | Uc | O | Df | O | O | H* | Mm | Oo | Bh |
| 87 | Toradja | . | Dc | (Up) | Uf | Sl | Up | Ht | B. | . | (Jh) |
| 88 | Tobelorese | Ub | Dc | Up | Sv | Uv | Up | Ht | Sl | C. | Bh |
| 89 | Alorese | Um | Dc | Up | Us | Us | Us | Hp* | N | Ti | Kh |
| 90 | Tiwi | Ub | O | Ns | Sf | Sl | Ir | Ht | Bs | Oo | Ao |
| 91 | Aranda | N | O | Ns | Uf | Iv | Sv | Ht | N | Oo | Eo |
| 92 | Orokaiva | N | Dr | Up | Uf | Uv | Up | Ht | Bs | Oo | Ah |
| 93 | Kimam | O | Dr | Up | Uf | Ul | Sv | Ht | Bs | Oo | Ih |
| 94 | Kapauku | Sm | Ir | Fp | Us | Uv | Ua | Ht | B. | Ti | Ch |
| 95 | Kwoma | Um | Ir | Up | Uf | Us | Sp | Ht | O | T(o) | Ch |
| 96 | Manus | Dm | O | Up | Sf | O | Up | Ht | Sm | To | Ao |
| 97 | New Ireland | N | Ir | Up | Sf | Us | Sv | Hr | B. | T. | Ao |
| 98 | Trobrianders | Si | Dr | Up | Sf | Uf | Us | Ht | Sm | Oo | Kc |
| 99 | Siuai | Si | Dr | Fp | Uf | Us | Sv | Ht | Fs | T(o) | Ch |
| 100 | Tikopia | N | Dr | O | Sf | Uf | Us | Ht | Bs | Oo | Jh |
| 101 | Pentecost | N | Dr | Up | Uf | Uf | Sv | Ht | B. | A. | Ch |
| 102 | Mbau Fijians | N | Sr | Up | Dv | (O) | Uv | Ht | Sl | T(o) | Ch |
| 103 | Ajie | Sb | Ir | Up | Sv | Uv | Ur | Ht | Sm | T(o)* | Jh |
| 104 | Maori | Ub | Ir | Up | Sv | Sf | Ur | Ht | Sl | (Oo) | Jh |
| 105 | Marquesans | (N) | Dt | Up | Sv | Us | (Us) | Hp | Sm | Oo | Qc |
| 106 | Samoans | Ui | Dr | Up | Sv | Uf | Ur | Ht | Sm | O(o) | Bh· |
| 107 | Gilbertese | Ub | Dt | Ns | Sv | Uf | (O) | Ht | Sl | Ae | Bh |
| 108 | Marshallese | Ub | St | Up | Df | Uf | Us | Ht | Sl | A(o) | Jh |
| 109 | Trukese | Us | It | Up | Ss | Uf | Ua | Hp | Sm | Ai | Jh |
| 110 | Yapese | Us | Dr | Up | Sv | Uf | Uv | Hr* | Sl | C. | Ao |
| 111 | Palauans | Ui | Dr | Us | Sv | Uf | Uv | Ht | Bm | Ti | Ch |
| 112 | Ifugao | Us | Dr | Up | Uv | Uv | Us | (Ap) | N | D(o) | Jh |
| 113 | Atayal | Mb | Dc | Up | Uf | Ss | Ur | (Ht) | N | T(o) | Ih |
| 114 | Chinese | Ss | Dc | No | Sv | O | Uh | Mh | Sl | Ci | Ud |
| 115 | Manchu | (N) | Dc | Fp | Uf | U. | (O) | W(r) | (O) | . | (Jh) |

TABLE 1.   *Continued*

| Society | 1 | 2 | 3 | 4 | 5 | 6 | 7 | 8 | 9 | 10 |
|---|---|---|---|---|---|---|---|---|---|---|
| 116 Koreans | Sm | Dc | Ub | Uf | Ul | (O) | Wp | Sm | Ci | Ih |
| 117 Japanese | Sb | Dc | Us | (O) | O | Uh | Mh | N | Ci | Kh |
| 118 Ainu | Ub | Uc | Ns | If | Sl | Sv | Ht | Bm | Oo | Jh |
| 119 Gilyak | Ub | O | Ns | Df | Sl | Sv | St | Bs* | Ae | Ph |
| 120 Yukaghir | Ub | O | Ns | If | Sl | Us | St | Bs | Oe | Eh |
| 121 Chukchee | Ub | O | Pd | Uf | Sl | Uh | St | N | Oi | Ah |
| 122 Ingalik | N | O | Ns | Df | Sv | Us | Ht* | Bs | T(o) | Ch |
| 123 Aleut | N | O | O | Dv | Uf | Uv | (Ht) | Bm | Oo | Jh |
| 124 Copper Eskimo | N | O | Ns | Dv | Sl | Uv | St | Bs | Oo | Fh |
| 125 Montagnais | Ss* | O | Ns | Sf | Dl | Us | Ht | Bm | Oo | Ih |
| 126 Micmac | Us | O | Us | Sv | Dl | Us | Ht | B(m) | To | Io |
| 127 Saulteaux | Ss | Ur | Ns | If | Sv | Us | St | Bs | A(o) | Oo |
| 128 Slave | Ss | Ur | Ns | Sf | Il | Us | St | Ms | Ae | Fh |
| 129 Kaska | Us | O | Ns | If | Sv | Us | St | Bm | Oe | Ih |
| 130 Eyak | N | O | Ns | Dv | Ss | Uv | Ht* | Bm | (Oo) | Kh |
| 131 Haida | Ub | Nn | Ns | Df | Uv | Sv | Ht | Bm | De | Kh |
| 132 Bellacoola | N | O | Ns | Df | Sl | Ss | Ht | Bm | Ao | Kh |
| 133 Twana | Ub | O | Ns | Df | Sl | Sr | Ht | B(s) | To | Jh |
| 134 Yurok | Ub | O | Ns | If | Sl | Ss | Ht | Bs | Oo* | Bh |
| 135 Pomo | Ub | O | O | Sv | Sv | Iv | Ht | Fs | To | Bh |
| 136 Yokuts | Ub | O | Us | If | Sf | Ss | Ht | Fs | To | Bh |
| 137 Paiute | (N) | O | Ue | Sf | Sl | Is | Ht | Fs | Oo | Ih |
| 138 Klamath | Ub | O | Ne | Df | Ul | Ss | Ht | Bm | Oo | Ih |
| 139 Kutenai | Us | N | Ne | If | Sv | Sv | At | Bs | (Ae) | Kh |
| 140 Gros Ventre | Us | O | Ne | O | Dl | Sv | St | Fs | De | Bh |
| 141 Hidatsa | N | Dc | Ne | Uf | Sl | Sv | St | Bs | (Oe) | Jh |
| 142 Pawnee | Ub | Ic | Ne | Uf | Sl | Uv | St | Fs | Oe | Jh |
| 143 Omaha | N | Sc | Ne | Sf | Il | Uv | St | O | O(o) | Jh |
| 144 Huron | Ub | Ic | Us | Sf | Sl | Us | Ht* | Bs | Oe | Jh |
| 145 Creek | (N) | Ic | Ue | Sf | Sl | Uv | A. | B. | (Te) | Jc |
| 146 Natchez | Mb | Ic | Us | Sf | Sl | Us | Ht | Bs | (Oo) | Bh |
| 147 Comanche | Ub | O | Ne | Uf* | Dl | Ss | St | N | Oo | Jh |
| 148 Chiricahua | Ub | Uc | Ue | Uf | Sl | Iv | Ht | Fs | (Oo) | Jh |
| 149 Zuni | Ub | Dc | Fo | O | Ul | Ua | Wr | O | Ao | Ph |
| 150 Havasupai | N | Dc | Ne | O | Sl | Ss | At | N | Oo | Jh |
| 151 Papago | Si | Ic | Fb | O | Ul | Ss | At | N | Ao | Io |
| 152 Huichol | Ub | Ic | Fb | Uv | Sl | Ur | At | N | A(o) | Kh |
| 153 Aztec | Si | Ic | Fs | Uf | Sv | Uv | Hr | Bs | T(i) | Ps |
| 154 Popoluca | N | Dc | Fs | Uf | Uv | Us | Ht | N | A(o) | J. |
| 155 Quiche | Um | Dc | Uo | O | O | Uv | Ar | N | A. | Jh |
| 156 Miskito | N | Ir | Up | Sv | Ss | Us | Ht | Bm | Ao | Ao |
| 157 Bribri | (M)b | It | Up | Uf | Sv | Uv | Hp | N | Oo | Jh |
| 158 Cuna | Ub | Dt | Us | Sv | Ss | Ua | Hp | Sl | Ae | Ch |
| 159 Goajiro | (Ub) | Uc | Pb | Uv | Uv | Ss | At | N | Ae | Ch |
| 160 Haitians | Um | Dc | Fb | . | . | U. | Ar | B. | Ci | Bd |
| 161 Callinago | N | Ir | Ns | Ss | Ss | Ua | Ht | Sl | Oo | Ch |
| 162 Warrau | N | Ut | Us | If | Ss | Sp | Ht | Bs | Oo | E(o) |
| 163 Yanomamo | N | Dt | Ns | Uf | Us | Ss | Ht | Bs | Oo | Ao |
| 164 Carib | N | Sr | Ns | Iv | Sv | Uv | Ht | Bs | Oo | Ao |
| 165 Saramacca | N | Ir | Us | Sf | Sv | Us | Ht | Bs | Oo* | Bh |
| 166 Mundurucu | N | Ir | Ns | Sf | Sl | Us | Ht | Bm | Oo | Ao |
| 167 Cubeo | N | Ir | Us | Sf | Ss | Uv | (Ht) | Bm | (Oo) | Jh |
| 168 Cayapa | Ub | It | (U)p | Sv | Sv | Us | Ht | Bm | Oo | Ch |
| 169 Jivaro | N | Ir | Fp | Sf | Ss | Uh | Ht | B. | Oo | Ao |

TABLE 1.  *Continued*

| | Society | 1 | 2 | 3 | 4 | 5 | 6 | 7 | 8 | 9 | 10 |
|---|---|---|---|---|---|---|---|---|---|---|---|
| 170 | Amahuaca | O | Dc | Ns | Uf | Sv | Us | Ht | O | Oo | Bh |
| 171 | Inca | Si | Dc | Uc | Uf | Ul | Uh | Ar | Bs | Oo | Qs |
| 172 | Aymara | Ub | Ir | Fo | Sf | Uf | Uv | At | Fs | Oo | Ih |
| 173 | Siriono | N | Uc | O | Uf | Iv | Ss | Ht | O | Oo | Eo |
| 174 | Nambicuara | N | Sc | Us | Sf | Sv | Iv | Ht | (O) | Oo | Ah |
| 175 | Trumai | N | Ir | O | Sf | Ul | Ss | Hp | Bs | Oo | Bh |
| 176 | Timbira | N | Ir | Up | Uf | Sv | Ur | Hp | O | Oo | Ah |
| 177 | Tupinamba | N | Ir | Ns | Sv | Sv | Uv | Ht | Bl | Oo | Ah |
| 178 | Botocudo | N | O | Ns | Sf | Dv | Uv | Ht | N | Oo | Eo |
| 179 | Shavante | N | Uc | Ns | Uf | Ss | Dr | Ht | Bs | (Oo) | Ao |
| 180 | Aweikoma | O | O | Ns | Uf | Dl | Ss | Ht | O | Oo | Io |
| 181 | Cayua | N | Sc | Ns | Uf | Iv | Sv | Ht | Bs | Oo | Bc |
| 182 | Lengua | N | Sr | Ue | Sf | Iv | Sv | At | Bs | Oo | Eo |
| 183 | Abipon | O | O | Fb | Uf | Il | Sv | At | Fs | Oo | Ao |
| 184 | Mapuche | Us | Dc | Fo | Sv | Uf | Us | Wr | Bm | Ae | Ih |
| 185 | Tehuelche | Ub | O | Ue | Us | Dl | Ur | At | Bs | Oo | Eh |
| 186 | Yahgan | O | O | Ns | Dv | Uf | Uh | Ht | Bs | Oo | Ao |
| 11a | Chagga | N | Dc | Mb | O | Sl | Uv | Ht | N | Oo | Bh |
| 16a | Katab | U(m) | Dc | Fo | Uf | Us | Ss | Ht | N | (To) | (Jh) |
| 34a | Dorobo | Ub | Uc | Hs | O | Dl | Sv | Ht | O | Do | Eo |
| 46a | Lebanese | Is | St | Ub | Uv | O | (O) | Ar | N | Co | Ud |
| 60a | Chenchu | Us | Uc | Ub | Uf | Ul | Dr | Ht | Fs | Ae | Io |
| 95a | Wogeo | Sb | It | Up | Sf | Us | Uv | Ht | Sm | Oo | Cc |
| 106a | Pukapukans | O | It | O | Sv | Uf | . | Ht | Sm | Oo | Jc |
| 141a | Crow | Ub | Nn | Ne | O | Dl | Sv | St | Fs | Do | Bh |
| 175a | Bororo | . | Dc | O | Sf | Sv | Uv | Ht | Bs | Oo | Ao |
| 177a | Tenetehara | N | Dr | Us | Sf | Sl | Us | Ht | Bs | Ae | Ah |
| 179a | Caraja | Ub | Ir | Ns | Sf | Us | Us | Ht | Bm | Oo | Ao |

*Notes on Table 1*

25, column 9: But French currency is an object of barter.
48, column 7: But Wr in local flat areas.
53, column 3: But milk is not used.
71, column 3: Cattle and water buffaloes are kept but are not a source of food.
86, column 7: Transport is exclusively by water.
89, column 7: The colonial government required the construction of horse paths.
103, column 9: But food was obtained only by barter.
110, column 7: The colonial government required the building of roads.
119, column 8: But sails were occasionally used.
122, column 7: But man-drawn sleds were used in winter.
125, column 1: Transport services were paid for in food.
130, column 7: But man-drawn sleds were also used.
134, column 9: But minor use was made of shell money.
144, column 7: But man-drawn sleds were used in winter.
145, column 4: But fish were eaten only in times of scarcity.
165, column 9: But an alien currency is used to a limited extent.

## CODING PROCEDURES AND PROBLEMS

The codes and their definitions were prepared primarily by the senior author. The sample societies were coded in their alphabetical rather than geographical order. For each society the coders were provided with a "pinpointing sheet" specifying the precise local group and date for which information was to be sought, summarizing the pertinent geographical and historical background data, and listing the relevant bibliographical sources ordered according to their overall quality and presumed usefulness. The coders read the sources in this order, taking notes on each in the form of direct quotations with page references. After all the listed sources had been assessed, or the principal sources were found to contain essentially all the data required, a master code sheet for the society was prepared; if necessary the coder returned to the sources to fill gaps or resolve discrepancies.

Of the 197 societies covered herein—the standard sample of 186 plus eleven additional ones—119 were coded primarily by the junior author, 42 by Diana Obrinsky, 32 by Richmond Morrow, and two each by the senior author and Douglas R. White. In addition, Edith Lauer assisted other coders in handling sources in the German language on eleven of the same societies, and Richmond Morrow independently coded twelve of the societies coded by others as a check on coding reliability. Discrepancies were found to be gratifyingly few—less frequent indeed than purely clerical errors. Finally, the two authors together reviewed all the code sheets, checked the findings with comparable entries for 150 of the same socieites in the Ethnographic Atlas, and arrived at a joint decision on all cases of doubt or disagreement.

A number of problems were repeatedly encountered by the coders, and an indication of their nature and of the manner in which they were resolved may contribute to an understanding of the coded data. The first such problem is that of the exceptional or sporadic incidence of the cultural datum in question. For example, the Kimam (93), who ordinarily do not obtain food by trade from other communities, are reported to do so in times of famine. They are coded as O in Column 1 on the principle that codes should reflect the normal rather than the exceptional practice. Where the incidence of an item is sporadic, occurring in some subgroups of the society but not in others, it is the situation in the focal or pinpointed local group that is coded. As previously noted, this may sometimes misrepresent the situation in the society at large, especially in complex societies.

A second problem is that of conflicting evidence. When two sources were found in disagreement upon a particular point, further sources were consulted in an attempt to resolve the issue. If no consensus emerged, coders followed the source adjudged superior on the basis of length of time in the field, fullness of description, internal consistency, and comparable criteria. Contradictory statements within the same source, though occasionally encountered, were rare in the more dependable sources and usually relatively easy to resolve.

A more difficult problem is that of insufficient evidence, where the coder is compelled to depend to some extent upon inference in reaching a decision. Several types of inference were distinguished by the coders, but only one is retained in Table 1, where parentheses indicate a really substantial doubt. Especially vexing is the question of determining when failure to mention an item can be interpreted as indicating its absence in the culture rather than an oversight on the part of the ethnographer. Relative fullness in treating the general subject often suggests the former. In several instances, careful scanning of photographs revealed the presence of an item unmentioned in the text. Knowledge or examination of ethnographic distributions often provided the decisive clue, e.g., for entering an S in Column 7 on Plains Indian tribes for which the sources consulted did not happen to note the use of the travois.

A fifth problem is the frequent necessity for temporal extrapolation. The best information on a particular subject may relate to a period considerably prior or subsequent to the pinpointed date. In such cases the coder sought to determine the direction and amount of cultural change over the entire time span and to estimate the situation prevailing at the indicated date. In doubtful instances, preference in coding was given to the earlier situation. The sources on the Abkhaz (55), for example, record a shift from a predominantly pastoral to a predominantly agricultural economy after the Crimean War (1853-56). Since, however, they do not indicate whether the transition had been completed by 1880, the pinpointed date, the symbols in Columns 2 and 3 assume the earlier rather than the later subsistence balance.

A sixth problem arises from the fact that the symbols as defined, having been devised for cross-cultural application, do not always mirror accurately the situation in particular societies. Careful pretesting of the codes on eleven societies not included in the standard sample resulted in improved definitions but could not eliminate all misfits and ambiguities. Where these are deemed particularly serious, an asterisk in Table 1 refers the reader to a clarifying note.

A special definitional problem relates to Column 1, where it was necessary to define the local community for each society before selecting a symbol appropriate to the prevailing incidence and character of intercommunity trade. In the case of the Pukapukans (106a), for example, the entire small island was treated as a single community, and the symbol O indicates that there was no off-island trade; it does not deny the existence of trade between different villages on the island, which was in fact considerable. For complex urbanized societies like the Aztecs, Babylonians, Hebrews, and Romans, where the capital city was selected as the focal area, the community was defined as the city plus its agricultural environs. Only thus did it seem possible to preserve a workable distinction between intra-community and intercommunity trade in foodstuffs, i.e., between imports from within and those from without the metropolitan area.

## IDENTIFICATION AND BIBLIOGRAPHY

The societies analyzed in Table 1 are briefly identified below by their "pinpointed" localities and dates, and for each of them the sources found most useful by the coders are listed in the approximate order of the quantity of pertinent information on subsistence practices provided by them. Many important ethnographic works, omitted herewith because of a paucity of information on these matters, will be listed in subsequent publications concerned with other subjects.

1. Nama Hottentot of the Gei/ /Khauan tribe (27°30'S, 17°E) in 1860.
   Schultze, L.   1907.   Aus Namaland und Kalahari. Jena.
   Schapera, I.   1930.   The Khoisan Peoples. London.
2. Kung Bushmen of the Nyae Nyae region (19°50'S, 20°35'E) in 1950.
   Marshall, L.   1960.   !Kung Bushman Bands. Africa 30: 325-355.
   ———   1961.   Sharing, Talking, and Giving. Africa 31: 231-249.
3. Thonga of the Ronga subtribe (25°50'S, 32°20'E) in 1895.
   Junod, H. A.   1927.   The Life of a South African Tribe. 2d edit. 2v. London.
4. Lozi (14° to 18°S, 22° to 25°E) in 1900.
   Gluckman, M.   1941.   Economy of the Central Barotse Plain. Rhodes-Livingstone Papers 7.
   ———   1951.   The Lozi of Barotseland. Seven Tribes of British Central Africa, ed. E. Colson and M. Gluckman, pp. 1-93. London.
5. Mbundu of the Bailundo subtribe (12°15'S, 16°30'E) in 1890.
   Hambly, W. D.   1934.   The Ovimbundu of Angola. Field Museum Anthropological Series 21: 89-362.
   McCulloch, M.   1952.   The Ovimbundu of Angola. London.
   Childs, G. M.   1949.   Umbundu Kinship and Character. London.
6. Suku of Feshi Territory (6°S, 18°E) in 1920.
   Kopytoff, I.   1965.   The Suku of Southwestern Congo. Peoples of Africa, ed. J. L. Gibbs, Jr., pp. 441-477. New York.
   ———   1964.   Family and Lineage Among the Suku. The Family Estate in Africa, ed. R. F. Gray and P. H. Gulliver, pp. 83-116. Boston.
   Holemans, K.   1959.   Etudes sur l'alimentation en milieu coutumier du Kwango. Annales de la Société Belge de Médecine Tropicale 39: 361-374.
7. Bemba of Zambia (9° to 12°S, 29° to 32°E) in 1897.
   Richards, A. I.   1939.   Land, Labour and Diet in Northern Rhodesia. Oxford.
   ———   1940.   Bemba Marriage and Present Economic Conditions. Rhodes-Livingstone Papers 4.
   ———   1951.   The Bemba of North-eastern Rhodesia. Seven Tribes of British Central Africa, ed. E. Colson and M. Gluckman, pp. 164-191. London.
   Gouldsbury, C., and A. Sheane.   1911.   The Great Plateau of Northern Rhodesia. London.
8. Nyakyusa near Mwaya and Masoko (9°30'S, 34°E) in 1934.
   Wilson, M.   1951.   Good Company. London.
   Wilson, G.   1936.   An Introduction to Nyakyusa Society. Bantu Studies 10: 253-292.
9. Hadza (3°20' to 4°10'S, 34°40' to 35°25'E) in 1930.
   Kohl-Larsen, L.   1958.   Wildbeuter in Ostafrika. Berlin.
   Woodburn, J.   1968.   An Introduction to Hadza Ecology. Man the Hunter, ed. R. B. Lee and I. DeVore, pp. 49-55. Chicago.
10. Luguru around Morogoro (6°50'S, 37°40'E) in 1925.
    Beidelman, T. C.   1967.   The Matrilineal Peoples of Eastern Tanzania. London.
    Scheerder and Tastevin.   1950.   Les Wa lu guru. Anthropos 45: 241-286.
11. Kikuyu of the Fort Hall or Metume district (0°40'S, 37°10'E) in 1920.
    Kenyatta, J.   1939.   Facing Mount Kenya. London.
    Leakey, L. S. B.   1952.   Mau Mau and the Kikuyu. London.
    Lambert, H. E.   1950.   The Systems of Land Tenure in the Kikuyu Land Unit. Communications from the School of African Studies, n.s. 22:1-185.
    Middleton, J.   1953.   The Kikuyu and Kamba of Kenya. London.
12. Ganda of the Kyaddondo district (0°20'N, 32°30'E) in 1875.
    Roscoe, J.   1911.   The Baganda. London.
    Fallers, M. C.   1960.   The Eastern Lacustrine Bantu. London.

13. Mbuti Pygmies of the Epulu group (1°30′ to 2°N, 28°20′E) in 1950.
    Turnbull, C. N. 1961. The Forest People. New York.
    —— 1965. Wayward Servants. New York.
    Putnam, P. 1948. The Pygmies of the Ituri Forest. A Reader in General An-
    thropology, ed. C. S. Coon, pp. 322-342. New York.
14. Nkundo Mongo of the Ilanga group (0°15′ to 1°15′S, 18°35′ to 19°45′E) in 1930.
    Hulstaert, G. 1938. Le mariage des Nkundó. Mémoires de l'Institut Royal Co-
    lonial Belge 8: 1-520. Brussels.
    Gutersohn, T. 1920. Het economisch leven van den Mongo-neger. Congo 1:
    i, 92-105.
15. Banen of the Ndiki subtribe (4°35′ to 4°45′N, 10°35′ to 11°E) in 1935.
    Dugast, I. 1959. Monographie de la tribu des Ndiki. Travaux et Mémoires
    de l'Institut d'Ethnologie 58: ii, 1-635, Paris.
    McCulloch, M., M. Littlewood, and I. Dugast. 1954. Peoples of the Central
    Cameroons. London.
16. Tiv of Benue province (6°30′ to 8°N, 8° to 10°E) in 1920.
    Bohannan, P., and L. Bohannan. 1958. Three Source Notebooks in Tiv Eth-
    nography. New Haven.
    —— 1953. The Tiv of Central Nigeria. London.
    Bohannan, P. 1960. Tiv Trade and Markets. Ms.
    —— 1955. Some Principles of Exchange and Investment Among the Tiv.
    American Anthropologist 57: 60-70.
17. Ibo of the Isu-Ama division (5°20′ to 5°40′N, 7°10′ to 7°30′E) in 1935.
    Green, M. M. 1947. Ibo Village Affairs. London.
    Uchendu, V. C. 1965. The Igbo of Southeast Nigeria. New York.
18. Fon of the city and environs of Abomey (7°12′N, 1°56′E) in 1890.
    Herskovits, M. J. 1938. Dahomey. 2v. New York.
19. Ashanti of Kumasi state (6° to 8°N, 0° to 3°W) in 1895.
    Lystad, R. A. 1958. The Ashanti. New Brunswick.
    Busia, K. A. 1951. The Position of the Chief in the Modern Political Systems
    of Ashanti. London.
    Manoukian, M. 1950. Akan and Ga-Adangme Peoples of the Gold Coast. Lon-
    don.
20. Mende near the town of Bo (7°50′N, 12°W) in 1945.
    Little, K. L. 1951. The Mende of Sierra Leone. London.
    Staub, J. 1936. Beiträge zur Kenntnis der materiellen Kultur der Mendi. Solo-
    thurn.
    McCulloch, M. 1950. The Peoples of Sierra Leone Protectorate. London.
21. Wolof of Upper and Lower Salum in the Gambia (13°45′N, 15°20′W) in 1950.
    Gamble, D. P. 1957. The Wolof of Senegambia. London.
    Ames, D. W. 1953. Plural Marriage Among the Wolof in the Gambia. Ph.D.
    dissertation, Northwestern University.
    —— 1962. The Rural Wolof of the Gambia. Markets in Africa, ed. P. Bo-
    hannan and G. Dalton, pp. 29-60. Evanston.
    —— 1959. Wolof Co-operative Work Groups. Continuity and Change in
    African Cultures, ed. W. R. Bascom and M. J. Herskovits, pp. 224-237.
    Chicago.
22. Bambara between Segou and Bamako (12°30′N, 6° to 8°W) in 1902.
    Monteil, C. 1924. Les Bambara du Ségou et du Kaarta. Paris.
    Pacques, V. 1954. Les Bambara. Paris.
    Dieterlen, G. 1951. Essai sur la religion Bambara. Paris.
23. Tallensi (10°30′ to 10°45′N, 0°30′ to 0°40′W) in 1934.
    Fortes, M., and S. L. Fortes. 1936. Food in the Domestic Economy of the
    Tallensi. Africa 9: 237-276.
    Lynn, C. W. 1937. Agriculture in North Mamprusi. Bulletins of the Gold
    Coast Department of Agriculture 34: 1-93.

24. Songhai of the Bamba division (16° to 17°15′N, 0°10′E to 3°10′W) in 1940.
    Rouch, J. 1954. Les Songhay. Paris.
25. Wodaabe Fulani of Niger (13° to 17°N, 5° to 10°E) in 1951.
    Dupire, M. 1962. Peules nomades. Travaux et Mémoires de l'Institut d'Ethnologie 64: 1-327.
    ——— 1961. Trade and Markets in the Economy of the Nomadic Fulani of Niger. Markets in Africa, ed. P. Bohannan and G. Dalton, pp. 335-362. Evanston.
26. Hausa of Zaria or Zazzau (9°30′ to 11°30′N, 6° to 9°E) in 1900.
    Smith, M. G. 1965. The Hausa of Northern Nigeria. Peoples of Africa, ed. J. L. Gibbs, pp. 119-155. New York.
    ——— 1955. The Economy of Hausa Communities of Zaria. Colonial Office Research Studies 16: 1-264. London.
    ——— 1962. Exchange and Marketing Among the Hausa. Markets in Africa, ed. P. Bohannan and G. Dalton, pp. 69-81. Evanston.
    Prothero, R. M. 1957. Land Use at Soba. Economic Geography 33: 72-86.
27. Massa of Cameroon (10° to 11°N, 15° to 16°E) in 1910.
    Garine, I. de. 1964. Les Massa du Cameroun. Paris.
28. Azande of the Yambio chiefdom (4°20′ to 5°50′N, 27°40′ to 28°50′E) in 1905.
    De Schlippe, P. 1956. Shifting Cultivation in Africa. London.
    Schweinfurth, G. 1874. The Heart of Africa. 2v. New York.
    Larkin, G. M. 1926-27. An Account of the Azande. Sudan Notes and Records 9: 235-247; 10: 85-134.
29. Fur around Jebel Marra (13°30′N, 25°30′E) in 1880.
    Felkin, R. W. 1885. Notes on the Fur Tribe. Proceedings of the Royal Society of Edinburgh 13: 205-265.
30. Otoro of the Nuba Hills (11°20′N, 30°40′E) in 1930.
    Nadel, S. F. 1947. The Nuba. London.
31. Shilluk (9° to 10°30′N, 31° to 32°E) in 1910.
    Hofmayr, W. 1925. Die Schilluk. Wien.
    Westermann, D. 1912. The Shilluk People. Philadelphia.
    Seligman, C. G., and B. Z. Seligman. 1932. Pagan Tribes of the Nilotic Sudan. London.
    Dempsey, J. 1955. Mission on the Nile. London.
32. Northern Mao (9° to 9°35′N, 34°30′ to 34°50′E) in 1939.
    Grottanelli, V. L. 1940. I Mao. Missione Etnografica nel Uollaga Occidentale 1: 1-387. Roma.
33. Kaffa (6°50′ to 7°45′N, 35°30′ to 37°E) in 1905.
    Bieber, F. J. 1920-23. Kaffa. 2v. Münster.
34. Masai of Tanzania (1°30′ to 5°30′S, 35° to 37°30′E) in 1900.
    Merker, M. 1904. Die Masai. Berlin.
    Huntingford, G. W. B. 1953. The Southern Nilo-Hamites. London.
    Fosbrooke, H. A. 1948. An Administrative Survey of the Masai Social System. Tanganyika Notes and Records 26: 1-50.
35. Konso of the vicinity of Buso (5°15′N, 37°30′E) in 1935.
    Kluckhohn, R. 1962. The Konso Economy. Markets in Africa, ed. P. Bohannan and G. Dalton, pp. 409-428. Evanston.
    Hallpike, C. R. 1969. The Konso of Ethiopia. Ms.
36. Somali of the Dolbahanta subtribe (7° to 11°N, 45°30′ to 49°E) in 1900.
    Lewis, I. M. 1955. Peoples of the Horn. London.
    ——— 1965. The Northern Pastoral Somali. Peoples of Africa, ed. J. L. Gibbs, Jr., pp. 319-360. New York.
    ——— 1962. Trade and Markets in Northern Somaliland. Markets in Africa, ed. P. Bohannan and G. Dalton, pp. 365-385. Evanston.
    Puccioni, N. 1936. Antropologia e etnographia delle genti della Somalia. Bologna.
37. Amhara of the Gondar district (11° to 14°N, 36° to 38°30′E) in 1953.

Messing, S. D. 1957. The Highland-Plateau Amhara of Ethiopia. Ph.D. dissertation, University of Pennsylvania.
38. Bogo or Belen (15°45′N, 38°45′E) in 1855.
Munzinger, W. 1859. Ueber die Sitten und das Recht der Bogos. Winterthur.
39. Kenuzi Nubians (22° to 24°N, 32° to 33°E) in 1900.
Herzog, R. 1957. Die Nubier. Berlin.
40. Teda nomads of Tibesti (19° to 22°N, 16° to 19°E) in 1950.
Le Coeur, C. 1950. Dictionnaire ethnographique Teda. Mémoires de l'Institut Français d'Afrique Noire 9: 1-213.
Cline, W. 1950. The Teda of Tibesti, Borku and Kawar. General Series in Anthropology 12: 1-52.
Briggs, L. L. 1958. The Living Races of the Sahara Desert. Papers of the Peabody Museum, Harvard University 28: ii, 1-217.
Chapelle, J. 1957. Nomades noirs du Sahara. Paris.
41. Tuareg of Ahaggar (21° to 25°N, 4° to 9°E) in 1900.
Nicolaisen, J. 1963. Ecology and Culture of the Pastoral Tuareg. Nationalmuseets Skrifter, Etnografisk Raeke 9: 1-540. Copenhagen.
42. Riffians of northern Morocco (34°20′ to 35°30′N, 2°30′ to 4°W) in 1926.
Coon, C. S. 1931. Tribes of the Rif. Harvard African Studies 9: 1-417.
43. Egyptians of the town and environs of Silwa (24°45′N, 33°E) in 1950.
Ammar, H. 1954. Growing Up in an Egyptian Village. London.
Ayrout, H. H. 1945. The Fellaheen. Cairo.
44. Hebrews of the kingdom of Judah (30°30′ to 31°55′N, 34°20′ to 35°30′E) in 621 B.C.
Holy Bible. Old Testament.
Dalman, G. 1932. Arbeit und Sitte in Palestina. 8v. Gütersloh.
Noth, M. 1966. The Old Testament World. 4th edit. Philadelphia.
DeVaux, R. 1961. Ancient Israel. New York.
Balyn, D. 1957. The Geography of the Bible. New York.
45. Babylonians of the city and environs of Babylon (32°35′N, 44°45′E) in 1750 B.C.
Saggs, H. W. F. 1962. The Greatness that was Babylon. London.
Driver, G. R., and J. C. Miles. 1952-55. The Babylonian Laws. 2v. Oxford.
Gadd, C. J. 1965. Hammurabi and the End of His Dynasty. Cambridge Ancient History, rev. edit., fascicle 35. Cambridge.
Delaporte, L. J. 1925. Mesopotamia. New York.
46. Rwala Bedouin (31° to 35°30′N, 36° to 41°E) in 1913.
Musil, A. 1928. The Manners and Customs of the Rwala Bedouins. New York.
47. Turks of the Anatolian plateau (38°40′ to 40°N, 32°40′ to 35°50′E) in 1950.
Pierce, J. E. 1964. Life in a Turkish Village. New York.
Makal, M. 1954. A Village in Anatolia. London.
Yasa, I. 1957. Hasanoglan. Ankara.
Sterling, P. 1963. The Domestic Cycle and the Distribution of Power in a Turkish Village. Mediterranean Countrymen, ed. J. Pitt-Rivers, pp. 201-213. Paris.
48. Gheg Albanians (41°20′ to 42°40′N, 19°30′ to 20°30′E) in 1910.
Coon, C. S. 1950. The Mountain of Giants. Papers of the Peabody Museum of Archaeology and Ethnology, Harvard University 23: iii, 1-105.
49. Romans of the city and environs of Rome (41°50′N, 13°30′E) in A.D. 110.
Friedländer, L. 1908. Roman Life and Manners Under the Early Empire. London.
Carcopino, J. 1940. Daily Life in Ancient Rome, ed. H. T. Howell. New Haven.
Harrison, F., ed. 1913. Roman Farm Management: The Treatises of Cato and Varro. New York.
50. Basques of Vera de Bidasoa (43°12′ to 43°20′N, 1°35′ to 1°45′W) in 1940.
Caro Baroja, J. 1944. La vida rural en Vera de Bidasoa. Madrid.
——— 1958. Los Vascos. 2d edit. Madrid.
Douglass, W. A. 1969. Death in Murelaga. Seattle.

51. Irish of Kinvarra parish (53°5′N, 9°W) in 1955.
    Cresswell, R.   1969.   Une communauté rurale d'Irlande. Travaux et Mémoires
       de l'Institut d'Ethnologie 74: 1-571. Paris.
52. Lapps of Könkämä district (68°20′ to 69°5′N, 20°5′ to 23°E) in 1950.
    Pehrson, R. N.   1957.   The Bilateral Network of Social Relations in Könkämä
       Lapp District. Indiana University Publications, Slavic and East European
       Series 5: 1-128.
    Minn, E. K.   1955.   The Lapps. New Haven.
53. Yurak Samoyed (65° to 71°N, 41° to 62°E) in 1894.
    Englehardt, E. A.   1899.   A Russian Province of the North. Westminster.
    Jackson, F. G.   1895.   The Great Frozen Land. London.
    ———   1895.   Notes on the Samoyeds of the Great Tundra. Journal of the
       Royal Anthropological Institute 24: 388-410.
    Islavin, V.   1847.   Samoiedy v domashnem i obshchestvennom bytu. St. Peters-
       burg.
    Kopytoff, I.   1955.   The Samoyed. New Haven.
54. Russians of the peasant village of Viriatino (52°40′N, 41°20′E) in 1955.
    Dunn, S. P., and E. Dunn.   1967.   The Peasants of Central Russia. New York.
    ———   1963.   The Great Russian Peasant. Ethnology 2. 320-338.
55. Abkhaz (42°50′ to 43°25′N, 40° to 41°35′E) in 1880.
    Dzhanashvili, M. G.   1894.   Abkhaziya i Abkhaztsy. Zapiski Kavkazkago
       Otdiela Inperalorskago Russkago Geograficheskago Obshchestva 16: 1-59.
       Tiflis.
    Byhan, A.   1926.   Die kaukasischen Völker. Illustrierte Völkerkunde, ed. G.
       Buschan 2: ii, 749-844. Stuttgart.
56. Armenians in the vicinity of Erevan (40°N, 44°30′E) in 1843.
    Haxthausen, A. von.   1854.   Transcaucasia. London.
    Klidschian, A.   1911.   Das armenische Eherecht. Zeitschrift für Vergleichende
       Rechtswissenschaft 25: 257-377.
    Lynch, H. F. B.   1901.   Armenia, v.i. London.
57. Kurd in and near the town of Rowanduz (36°30′N, 44°30′E) in 1951.
    Masters, W. M.   1953.   Rowanduz. Ph.D. dissertation, University of Michigan.
58. Basseri of the nomadic branch (27° to 31°N, 53° to 54°E) in 1958.
    Barth, F. K.   1961.   Nomads of South Persia. London.
    ———   1964.   Capital, Investment and Social Structure of a Pastoral Nomadic
       Group. Capital, Saving and Credit in Peasant Societies, ed. R. Firth and
       B. S. Yamey, pp. 69-81. Chicago.
59. West Punjabi of the village of Mohla (32°30′N, 74°E) in 1950.
    Eglar, Z. S.   1960.   A Punjabi Village in Pakistan, New York.
    Dass, A.   1934.   An Economic Survey of Gajju Chak. Punjab Village Surveys
       6. Lahore.
    Wilbur, D, N.   1964.   Pakistan. New Haven.
60. Gond of the Hill Maria division (19°15′ to 20°N, 80°30′ to 81°20′E) in 1930.
    Grigson, W. V.   1938.   The Maria Gonds of Bastar. London.
61. Toda of the Nilgiri Hills (11° to 12°N, 76° to 77°E) in 1900.
    Rivers, W. H. R.   1906.   The Todas. London.
    Marshall, W. E.   1873.   A Phrenologist Amongst the Todas. London.
62. Santal of Bankura and Birbhum districts (23° to 24°N, 86°50′ to 87°30′E) in
       1940.
    Datta-Majumder, N.   1955.   The Santal. Memoirs of the Department of An-
       thropology, Government of India 2: 1-150.
    Culshaw, W. J.   1949.   Tribal Heritage. London.
63. Uttar Pradesh in and near Senapur village (25°55′N, 83°E) in 1945.
    Opler, M. E., and R. D. Singh.   1954.   The Division of Labor in an Indian
       Village. A Reader in General Anthropology, ed. C. S. Coon, pp. 464-496.
       New York.
    ———   1952.   Economic and Social Change in a Village of North Central India.
       Human Organization 11: 5-12.

Rowe, W. L. 1960. The Marriage Network and Structural Change in a North Indian Community. Southwestern Journal of Anthropology 16: 299-311.
64. Burusho of Hunza state (36°20′ to 36°30′N, 74°30′ to 74°40′S) in 1934.
Lorimer, E. O. 1938. The Burusho of Hunza. Antiquity 12: 5-15.
Lorimer, D. L. R. 1935. The Burushaski Language, v.l. Oslo.
Rodale, J. I. 1948. The Healthy Hunzas. Emmaus, Pa.
Clark, J. 1963. Hunza in the Himalayas. Natural History 72: 38-45.
65. Kazak of the Great Horde (37° to 48°N, 68° to 81°E) in 1885.
Grodekov, N. I. 1889. Kirghizy i Karakirgizy sur Dar'inskoi Oblasti. Tashkent.
Radloff, W. 1893. Aus Sibirien. 2v. Leipzig.
66. Khalka Mongols of Narobanchin territory (47° to 47°20′N, 95°10′ to 97°E) in 1920.
Vreeland, H. H. 1954. Mongol Community and Kinship Structure. New Haven.
67. Lolo of Taliang Shan mountains (26° to 29°N, 103° to 104°E) in 1910.
Lin, Y. H. 1961. The Lolo of Liang Shan. Shanghai.
D'Ollone, H. M. 1912. In Forbidden China. Boston.
Tseng, C. L. 1945. The Lolo District in Liang-Shan. Chungking.
68. Lepcha of Lingthem and vicinity (27° to 28°N, 89°E) in 1937.
Gorer, G. 1938. Himalayan Village. London.
69. Garo of Rengsanggri and neighboring villages (26°N, 91°E) in 1955.
Burling, R. 1963. Rengsanggri. Philadelphia.
Playfair, A. The Garos. London.
70. Lakher (22°20′N, 93°E) in 1930.
Parry, N. E. 1932. The Lakhers. London
71. Burmese of Nondwin village (22°N, 95°40′E) in 1960.
Nash, M. 1965. The Golden Road to Modernity. New York
LeBar, F. M., G. C. Hickey, and J. K. Musgrave. 1964. Ethnic Groups of Mainland Southeast Asia, pp. 38-44. New Haven.
Trager, F. N., ed. 1956. Burma. 3v. New Haven.
72. Lamet of northwestern Laos (20°N, 100°40′E) in 1940.
Izikowitz, K. G. 1951. Lamet. Etnologiska Studier 17: 1-375 Göteborg.
73. North Vietnamese of the Red River delta (20° to 21°N, 105°30′ to 107°E) in 1930.
Gourou, P. 1936. Les paysans du delta tonkinois. Paris.
——— 1954. Land Utilization in French Indochina. 3v. Washington.
74. Rhade of the village of Ko-sier (13°N, 108°E) in 1962.
Donoghue, J. D., D. D. Whitney, and I. Ishino. 1962. People in the Middle. East Lansing.
75. Khmer of Angkor (13°30′N and 103°50′E) in 1292.
Chou Ta-Kuan. 1902. Mémoires sur les coutumes du Cambodge, ed. P. Pelliot. Bulletin de l'Ecole Francaise d'Extrême-Orient 2: 123-177.
Aymonier, E. 1901. Le Cambodge, v. l. Paris.
Groslier, B. P. 1956. Angkor, hommes et pierres. Paris.
76. Siamese of the village of Bang Chan (14°N, 100°52′E) in 1955.
Sharp, R. L., H. M. Hauck, K. Janlekha, and R. B. Textor. 1954. Siamese Village. Bangkok.
Hauck, H. M. *et al.* 1958. Food Habits and Nutrient Intake in a Siamese Rice Village. Ithaca.
77. Semang of the Jahai subtribe (4°30′ to 5°30′N, 101° to 101°30′E) in 1925.
Schebesta, P. 1927. Among the Forest Dwarfs of Malaya. London.
Evans, I. H. N. 1937. The Negritos of Malaya. Cambridge.
78. Nicobarese of the northern islands (8°15′ to 9°15′N, 92°40′ to 93°E) in 1870.
Man, E. H. 1932. The Nicobar Islands and Their People. Guilford.
Whitehead, G. 1924. In the Nicobar Islands. London.
79. Andamanese of the Aka Bea tribe (11°45′ to 12°N, 93° to 93°10′E) in 1860.

Man, E. H. On the Aboriginal Inhabitants of the Andaman Islands. London.
Radcliffe-Brown, A. R. 1922. The Andaman Islanders. Cambridge.

80. Forest Vedda (7°30' to 8°N, 81° to 81°30'E) in 1860.
Bailey, J. 1863. An Account of the Wild Veddahs of Ceylon. Transactions of the Ethnological Society of London 2: 278-320.
Seligmann, C. G., and B. Z. Seligmann. 1911. The Veddas. Cambridge.

81. Tanala of the Menabe subtribe (20°S, 48°E) in 1925.
Linton, R. 1933. The Tanala. Field Museum of Natural History Anthropological Series 22: 1-334.

82. Negri Sembilan of Inas district (2°30' to 2°40'N, 102°10' to 102°20'E) in 1958.
Lewis, D. K. 1962. The Minangkabau Malay of Negri Sembilan. Ph.D. dissertation, Cornell University.

83. Javanese in the vicinity of Pare (7°43'S, 112°13'E) in 1955.
Dewey, A. G. 1962. Peasant Marketing in Java. New York.
Geertz, C. 1963. Peddlers and Princes. Chicago.
―――― 1965. The Social History of an Indonesian Town. Cambridge.
―――― 1960. The Religion of Java. Chicago.

84. Balinese of the village of Tihingan (8°30'S, 115°20'E) in 1958.
Geertz, C. 1963. Peddlers and Princes. Chicago.
―――― 1967. Tihingan. Villages in Indonesia, ed. Koentjaraningrat, pp. 210-243. Ithaca.
―――― 1959. Form and Variation in Balinese Village Structure. American Anthropologist 61: 991-1012.
Covarrubias, M. 1937. The Island of Bali. New York.

85. Iban of the Ulu Ai group (2°N, 112°30' to 113°30'E) in 1950.
Freeman, J. D. 1955. Iban Agriculture. Colonial Research Studies 18: 1-148.
―――― 1955. Report on the Iban of Sarawak. Kuching.

86. Badjau of Tawi-Tawi and adjacent islands (5°N, 120°E) in 1863.
Nimmo, H. A. 1964. Nomads of the Sulu Sea. Ph.D. dissertation, University of Hawaii.
―――― 1965. Social Organization of the Tawi-Tawi Badjaw. Ethnology 4: 421-439.
―――― 1968. Reflections on Bajau History. Philippine Studies 16: 32-59.

87. Toradja of the Bare'e subgroup (2°S, 121°E) in 1910.
Adriani, N., and A. C. Kruijt. 1912. De Bare'e-sprekende Toradja's. 3v. Batavia.

88. Tobelorese of Tobelo district (1°N, 128°30'E) in 1900.
Hueting, A. 1921. De Tobeloreezen in hun denken en doen. Bijdragen tot de Taal-, Land-, en Volkenkunde 77: 217-385; 78: 137-342.
Riedel, J. G. F. 1885. Galela und Tobeloresen. Zeitschrift für Ethnologie 17: 58-89.

89. Alorese of Atimelang (8°20'S, 124°40'E) in 1938.
DuBois, C. 1944. The People of Alor. Minneapolis.
―――― 1941. Attitudes Toward Food and Hunger in Alor. Language, Culture, and Personality, ed. L. Spier et al, pp. 272-281. Menasha.
―――― 1945. The Alorese. The Psychological Frontiers of Society, ed. A. Kardiner, pp. 101-145. New York.
―――― 1940. How They Pay Debts in Alor. Asia 40: 482-486.

90. Tiwi (11° to 11°45'S, 130° to 132°E) in 1929.
Hart, C. W. M., and A. R. Pilling. 1960. The Tiwi of North Australia. New York.
Basedow, H. 1913. Notes on the Natives of Bathurst Island. Journal of the Royal Anthropological Institute 48: 291-323.

91. Aranda of Alice Springs (23°30' to 25°S, 132°30' to 134°20 E) in 1896.
Spencer, B., and F. J. Gillen. 1927. The Arunta. 2v. London.
Murdock, G. P. 1934. Our Primitive Contemporaries, pp. 20-47. New York.

92. Orokaiva of the Aiga subtribe (8°20' to 8°40'S, 147°50' to 148°10'E) in 1925.
Williams, F. E. 1930. Orokaiva Society. London.

Waddell, E. W., and P. A. Krinks. 1968. The Organization of Production and Distribution Among the Orokaiva. New Guinea Research Bulletin 24.
93. Kimam of the village of Bamol (7°30′S, 38°30′E) in 1960.
Serpenti, L. M. 1965. Cultivators in the Swamps. Assen.
94. Kapauku of Botukebo village (4°S, 36°E) in 1955.
Pospisil, L. 1963. Kapauku Papuan Economy. Yale University Publications in Anthropology 67: 1-502.
──── 1960. The Kapauku Papuans and Their Kinship Organization. Oceania 30: 188-205.
──── 1958. Kapauku Papuans and Their Law. Yale University Publications in Anthropology 54: 1-296.
95. Kwoma of the Hongwam subtribe (4°10′S, 142°40′E) in 1937.
Whiting, J. W. M. 1941. Becoming a Kwoma. New Haven.
96. Manus of Peri village (2°10′S, 147°10′E) in 1929.
Mead, M. 1930. Growing Up in New Guinea. New York.
──── 1930. Melanesian Middlemen. Natural History 30: 115-130.
──── 1937. The Manus of the Admiralty Islands. Cooperation and Competition Among Primitive Peoples, ed. M. Mead, pp. 210-239.
97. New Irelanders of Lesu village (2°30′S, 151°E) in 1930.
Powdermaker, H. 1933. Life in Lesu. New York.
──── 1932. Feasts in New Ireland. American Anthropologist 34: 236-247.
98. Trobrianders of Kiriwina island (8°38′S, 151°4′E) in 1914.
Malinowski, B. 1935. Coral Gardens and Their Magic. 2v. New York.
──── 1921. The Primitive Economics of the Trobriand Islanders. Economic Journal 31: 1-16.
99. Siuai of the northeastern group (7°S, 155°20′E) in 1939.
Oliver, D. L. 1955. A Solomon Island Society. Cambridge.
──── 1949. Studies in the Anthropology of Bougainville. Papers of the Peabody Museum, Harvard University 29.
100. Tikopia (12°30′S, 168°30′E) in 1930.
Firth, R. 1939. A Primitive Polynesian Economy. London.
──── 1936. We the Tikopia. London.
101. Pentecost islanders of Bunlap village (16°S, 168°E) in 1953.
Lane, R. B. 1956. The Heathen Communities of Southeast Pentecost. Journal de la Société des Oceanistes 12: 139-180.
──── 1965. The Melanesians of South Pentecost. Gods, Ghosts and Men in Melanesia, ed. P. Lawrence and M. G. Meggitt, pp. 250-279. London.
Lane, R. B., and B. S. Lane. Various unpublished and undated manuscripts.
102. Fijians of Mbau island (18°S, 178°35′E) in 1840.
Williams, T. 1884. Fiji and the Fijians. Rev. edit. London.
Tippett, A. R. 1968. Fijian Material Culture. Bulletins of the Bernice P. Bishop Museum 232: 1-193.
103. Ajie of Neje chiefdom (21°20′S, 165°40′E) in 1845.
Barrau, J. 1956. L'agriculture vivrière autochtone. Noumea.
Leenhardt, M. 1930. Notes d'ethnologie néo-calédonienne. Travaux et Mémories de l'Institut d'Ethnologie 8: 1-340. Paris.
──── 1937. Gens de la Grand Terre, Nouvelle Calédonie. Paris.
104. Maori of the Nga Puhi tribe (35°10′ to 35°30′S, 174° to 174°20′E) in 1820.
Polack, J. S. 1838. New Zealand. 2v. London.
Best, E. 1924. The Maori. 2v. Wellington.
──── 1925. Maori Agriculture. Wellington.
Buck, P. 1949. The Coming of the Maori. Wellington.
Maning, F. E. 1876. Old New Zealand. London.
105. Marquesans of southwest Nuku Hiva (8°55′S, 140°10′W) in 1800.
Lisiansky, R. 1814. Voyage Round the World in the Years 1803-06. London.
Porter, D. 1823. A Voyage in the South Seas in the Years 1812-14. London.
La Barre, R. W. 1934. Marquesan Culture. Ms.

106. Samoans of western Upolu (13°48′ to 14°S, 172°W) in 1829.
 Turner, G.   1884.   Samoa. London.
 Stair, J. B.   1897.   Old Samoa. London.
 Buck, P. H.   1930.   Samoan Material Culture. Bulletins of the Bishop Museum 75: 1-724.
107. Gilbertese of Makin island (3°30′N, 172°20′E) in 1890.
 Lambert, B.   1968.   The Economic Activities of a Gilbertese Chief. Political Anthropology, ed. M. J. Schwartz *et al.*, pp. 155-172. Chicago.
 ——— 1970.   The Gilbert Islands. Land Tenure in the Pacific, ed. R. G. Crocombe (in press).
 ——— 1964.   Fosterage in the Northern Gilbert Islands. Ethnology 3: 232-258.
 Finsch, O.   1893.   Ethnologische Erfahrungen und Belegstücke aus der Südsee 3: 19-89. Wien.
 Krämer, A.   1906.   Hawaii, Ostmikronesien, und Samoa, pp. 253-315. Stuttgart.
108. Marshallese of Jaluit atoll (6°N, 169°15′E) in 1900.
 Krämer, A., and H. Nevermann.   1938.   Ralik-Ratak. Ergebnisse der Südsee-Expedition 1908-10, ed. G. Thilenius 2: xi, 1-438. Hamburg.
 Mason, L. E.   1947.   The Economic Organization of the Marshall Islands. Ms.
 Erdland, P. A.   1914.   Die Marshall-Insulaner. Anthropos Bibliothek Ethnological Monographs 2: 1-376 Münster i. Wien.
109. Trukese of Romonum island (7°24′N, 151°40′E) in 1947.
 LeBar, F. M.   1964.   The Material Culture of Truk. Yale University Publications in Anthropology 68: 1-185.
 Goodenough, W. H.   1949.   Property, Kin, and Community on Truk. Yale University Publications in Anthropology 46: 1-192.
110. Yapese (9°30′N, 138°10′E) in 1910.
 Müller, W.   1917.   Yap. Ergebnisse der Südsee-Expedition 1908-1910, ed. G. Thilenius 2: B, iii, 1-380. Hamburg.
 Salesius.   1906.   Die Karolineninsel Jap. Berlin.
 Hunt, E. E., Jr., D. M. Schneider, N. R. Kidder, and W. D. Stevens.   1949.   The Micronesians of Yap and Their Depopulation. Washington.
 Tetens, A., and J. Kubary.   1873.   Die Carolineninsel Yap. Journal des Museum Godeffroy 1: 84-120. Hamburg.
111. Palauans of Koror island (7°N, 134°30′E) in 1873.
 Keate, G.   1788.   An Account of the Pelew Islands. London.
 Force, R. W.   1960.   Leadership and Cultural Change in Palau. Fieldiana, Anthropology 50: 1-211.
 Murdock, G. P., C. S. Ford, and J. W. M. Whiting.   1944.   West Caroline Islands. Civil Affairs Handbook, OPNAV 50-E-7, pp. 1-222. Washington.
112. Ifugao of the Kiangan group (16°50′N, 121°10′E) in 1910.
 Barton, R. F.   1922.   Ifugao Economics. University of California Publications in American Archaeology and Ethnology 15: 385-446.
113. Atayal (23°50′ to 24°50′N, 120°20′ to 120°50′E) in 1930.
 Okada, Y.   1949.   The Social Structure of the Atayal Tribe. (Ms translated from Essays Presented to Teizo Toda, pp. 393-433). Tokyo.
 Ruey Yih-Fu.   1955.   Ethnographical Investigation of Some Aspects of the Atayal. Bulletin, Department of Archaeology and Anthropology, National Taiwan University 5: 113-127.
114. Chinese of Kaihsienkung village in north Chekiang (31°N, 120°5′E) in 1936.
 Fei, H.   1946.   Peasant Life in China. New York.
115. Manchu of the Aigun district (50°N, 125°30′E) in 1915.
 Shirokogoroff, S. M.   1924.   Social Organization of the Manchus. Royal Asiatic Society, North China Branch, Extra Volume 3: 1-196. Shanghai.
116. Koreans of Kanghwa island (37°37′N, 126°25′E) in 1950.
 Osgood, C.   1951.   The Koreans and Their Culture. New York.
117. Japanese of southern Okayama prefecture (34°30′ to 35°N, 133°40′E) in 1950.

Beardsley, R. K., J. W. Hall, and R. E. Ward. 1959. Village Japan. Chicago.
Norbeck, E. 1954. Takashima. Salt Lake City.
118. Ainu of the Tokapchi and Saru basins (42°40′ to 43°N, 142° to 144°E) in 1880.
Watanabe, H. 1964. The Ainu. Journal of the Faculty of Science, University of Tokyo, Anthropology 2: vi, 1-164.
Batchelor, J. 1927. Ainu Life and Lore. Tokyo.
119. Gilyak (53° to 54°30′N, 139° to 143°10′E) in 1880.
Seeland, N. 1882. Die Ghiliaken. Russische Revue 21: 97-130, 222-254.
Shternberg, L. 1933. Semya i rod u narodov severo-vostochnoi Azii. Leningrad.
120. Yukaghir of the upper Kolyma River (63°30′ to 66°N, 150° to 157°E) in 1900.
Jochelson, W. 1926. The Yukaghir and Yukaghirized Tungus. Memoirs of the American Museum of Natural History 13: 1-469.
121. Chukchee of the Reindeer group (63° to 70°N, 171°E to 171°W) in 1900.
Bogoras, W. 1904-09. The Chukchee. Memoirs of the American Museum of Natural History 11: 1-703.
Orlovshii, P. N. 1928. God Anadrysko-Chukotskoga olenevoda. Severnaia Aziia 2: 61-70. Moskva.
122. Ingalik of Shageluk village (62°30′N, 159°30′W) in 1885.
Osgood, C. 1940. Ingalik Material Culture. Yale University Publications in Anthropology 22: 1-500.
——— 1958. Ingalik Social Culture. Yale University Publications in Anthropology 55: 1-289.
123. Aleut of the Unalaska branch (53° to 57°30′N, 158° to 170°W) in 1778.
Cook, J. 1785. A Voyage to the Pacific Ocean. London.
Sarytschew, G. 1806. Account of a Voyage of Discovery, vol. 2. London.
Elliott, H. W. 1886. Our Arctic Province. New York.
124. Copper Eskimo of the mainland (66°40′ to 69°20′N, 108° to 117°W) in 1915.
Jenness, D. 1922. The Life of the Copper Eskimos. Report of the Canadian Arctic Expedition, 1913-18, 12: 5-227. Ottawa.
——— 1917. The Copper Eskimos. Geographical Review 4: 81-91.
Stefansson, V. 1914. The Stefansson-Anderson Arctic Expedition. Anthropological Papers of the American Museum of Natural History 14: i, 1-395.
125. Montagnais of the Lake St. John and Mistassini bands (48° to 52°N, 73° to 75°W) in 1910.
Lips, J. E. 1947. Notes on Montagnais-Naskapi Economy. Ethnos 12: 1-78.
Speck, F. G. 1935. Naskapi. Norman.
126. Micmac of the mainland (43°30′ to 50°N, 60° to 66°W) in 1650.
Le Clercq, C. 1910. New Relation of Gaspesia. Publications of the Champlain Society 5: 1-452.
Denys, N. 1908. The Description and Natural History of the Coasts of North America. Publications of the Champlain Society 2: 1-625.
Bock, P. K. 1966. The Micmac Indians of Restigouche. Bulletins of the National Museum of Canada 213: 1-95.
Speck, F. G., and R. W. Dexter. 1951. Utilization of Animals and Plants by the Micmac Indians. Journal of the Washington Academy of Sciences 41: 250-259.
127. Saulteaux of the Berens River, Little Grand Rapids, and Pekangekum bands (51°30′ to 52°30′N, 94° to 97°W) in 1930.
Dunning, R. W. 1959. Social and Economic Change Among the Northern Ojibwa. Toronto.
Hallowell, A. I. 1938. Notes on the Material Culture of the Island Lake Saulteaux. Journal de la Société des Américanistes, n.s., 30: 128-140.
128. Slave in the vicinity of Fort Simpson (62°N, 122°W) in 1940.
Helm, J. 1961. The Lynx Point People. Bulletin of the National Museum of Canada 176: 1-193.
Honigmann, J. J. 1946. Ethnography and Acculturation of the Fort Nelson Slave. Yale University Publications in Anthropology 33: 1-169.

129. Kaska of the upper Liard River (60°N, 131°W) in 1900.
Honigmann, J. J. 1954. The Kaska Indians. Yale University Publications in Anthropology 51: 1-163.
────── 1949. Culture and Ethos of Kaska Society. Yale University Publications in Anthropology 40: 1-368.

130. Eyak (60° to 61°N, 144° to 146°W) in 1890.
Birket-Smith, K., and F. de Laguna. 1938. The Eyak Indians. Copenhagen.

131. Haida of the village of Masset (54°N, 132°30'W) in 1875.
Murdock, G. P. 1934. Our Primitive Contemporaries, pp. 221-263. New York.
────── 1934. Kinship and Social Behavior Among the Haida. American Anthropologist 36: 355-385.

132. Bellacoola (52°20'N, 126° to 127°W) in 1880.
McIlwraith, T. F. 1948. The Bella Coola Indians. 2v. Toronto.

133. Twana (47°20' to 47°30'N, 123°10' to 123°20'W) in 1860.
Elmendorf, W. W. 1960. The Structure of Twana Culture. Washington State University Research Studies, Monographic Supplement 2: 1-576.

134. Yurok (41°30'N, 124°W) in 1850.
Heizer, R. F., and J. E. Mills. 1952. The Four Ages of Tsurai. Berkeley.
Kroeber, A. L. 1960. Comparative Notes on the Structure of Yurok Culture. Washington State University Research Studies, Monographic Supplement 2.

135. Eastern Pomo of Clear Lake (39°N, 123°W) in 1850.
Loeb, E. M. 1926. Pomo Folkways. University of California Publications in American Archaeology and Ethnology 19: 149-404.
Gifford, E. W. 1926. Clear Lake Pomo Society. University of California Publications in American Archaeology and Ethnology 18: 287-390.

136. Yokuts around Tulare Lake (35°10'N, 119°20'W) in 1850.
Gayton, A. H. 1948. Yokuts and Western Mono Ethnography. Anthropological Records 10: 1-301.
────── Estudillo Among the Yokuts. Essays in Anthropology presented to A. L. Kroeber, ed. R. H. Lowie, pp. 67-85. Berkeley.
Kroeber, A. L. 1925. Handbook of the Indians of California. Bulletins of the Bureau of American Ethnology 78: 474-543.

137. Wadadika Paiute of Harney Valley (43° to 44°N, 118° to 120°W) in 1870.
Whiting, B. B. 1950. Paiute Sorcery. Viking Fund Publications in Anthropology 15: 1-110.
Stewart, O. C. 1941. Northern Paiute. Anthropological Records. 4: 361-446.

138. Klamath (42° to 43°15'N, 121°20' to 122°20'W) in 1860.
Spier, L. 1930. Klamath Ethnography. University of California Publications in American Archaeology and Ethnology 30: 1-328.

139. Kutenai of the Lower or eastern branch (48°40' to 49°10'N, 116°40'W) in 1890.
Chamberlain, A. F. 1892. Report on the Kootenay Indians. Reports of the British Association for the Advancement of Science 62: 539-617.
Turney-High, H. H. 1941. Ethnography of the Kutenai. Memoirs of the American Anthropological Association 56: 1-202.

140. Gros Ventre (47° to 49°N, 106° to 110°W) in 1880.
Flannery, R. 1953. The Gros Ventres of Montana. Catholic University of America Anthropological Series 15: 1-221.
Kroeber, A. L. 1908 Ethnology of the Gros Ventre. Anthropological Papers of the American Museums of Natural History 1: 141-281.

141. Hidatsa of Hidatsa village (47°N, 101°W) in 1836.
Bowers, A. W. 1965. Hidatsa Social and Ceremonial Organization. Bulletins of the Bureau of American Ethnology 194: 1-528.
Matthews, W. 1877. Ethnography and Philology of the Hidatsa Indians. U. S. Geological and Geographical Survey Miscellaneous Publication 7: 1-239.
Wilson, G. L. 1917. Agriculture of the Hidatsa Indians. University of Minnesota Studies in the Social Sciences 4: 1-129.

142. Pawnee of the Skidi band (42°N, 100°W) in 1867.
    Weltfish, G. 1965. The Lost Universe. New York.
143. Omaha (41°10′ to 41°40′N, 96° to 97°W) in 1860.
    Fletcher, A. C., and F. LaFlesche. 1911. The Omaha Tribe. Annual Reports of the Bureau of Ethnology 27: 17-672.
    Mead, M. 1932. The Changing Culture of an Indian Tribe. Columbia University Contributions to Anthropolgy 15: 1-313.
144. Huron of the Attignawantan and Attigneenongnahac tribes (44° to 45°N, 78° to 80°W) in 1634.
    Tooker, E. 1964. An Ethnography of the Huron Indians. Bulletins of the Bureau of American Ethnology 190: 1-183.
    Kinietz, W. V. 1940. The Indians of the Western Great Lakes. Occasional Contributions from the Museum of Anthropology, University of Michigan 10: 1-427.
145. Creek of the Upper Creek division (32°30′ to 34°20′N, 85°30′ to 86°30′W) in 1800.
    Swanton, J. R. 1946. The Indians of the Southeastern United States. Bulletins of the Bureau of American Ethnology 137: 1-943.
    ———— 1928. Social Organization and Social Usages of the Creek Confederacy. Annual Reports of the Bureau of American Ethnology 42: 23-472, 859-900.
146. Natchez (31°30′N, 91°25′W) in 1718.
    Swanton, J. R. 1911. Indian Tribes of the Lower Mississippi Valley. Bulletins of the Bureau of American Ethnology 43: 1-387.
147. Comanche (30° to 38°N, 98° to 103°W) in 1870.
    Hoebel, E. A. 1940. The Political Organization and Law-Ways of the Comanche Indians. Memoirs of the American Anthropological Association 54: 1-149.
    Wallace, E., and E. A. Hoebel. 1952. The Comanches. Norman.
148. Chiricahua Apache of the Central band (32°N, 109°30′W) in 1870.
    Opler, M. E. 1941. An Apache Life-Way. Chicago.
149. Zuni (35° 50′ to 35°30′N, 108°30′ to 109°W) in 1880.
    Stevenson, M. C. 1904 The Zuni Indians. Annual Reports of the Bureau of American Ethnology 23: 1-634.
    Cushing, F. H. 1920. Zuni Breadstuffs. Indian Notes and Monographs 8: 1-673.
150. Havasupai (35°20′ to 36°20′N, 111°20′ to 113°W) in 1918.
    Spier, L. 1928. Havasupai Ethnography. Anthropological Papers of the American Museum of Natural History 24: 81-408.
151. Papago of the Archie division (32°N, 112°W) in 1910.
    Underhill, R. M. 1936. Social Organization of the Papago Indians. Columbia University Contributions to Anthropology 30: 1-280.
    ———— 1936. The Autobiography of a Papago Woman. Memoirs of the American Anthropological Association 46: 1-64.
    Lumholtz, C. 1912. New Trails in Mexico. New York.
    Castetter, E. F., and W. H. Bell. 1942. Pima and Papago Agriculture. University of New Mexico Inter-Americana Studies 1: 1-245.
152. Huichol (22°N, 105°W) in 1890.
    Zingg, R. M. 1938. The Huichols. University of Denver Contributions to Anthropology 1: 1-826.
    Lumholtz, C. 1898. The Huichol Indians. Bulletins of the American Museum of Natural History 5: x, 1-14.
    ———— 1902. Unknown Mexico, v. 2. London.
153. Aztec of the city and environs of Tenochtitlan (19°N, 99°10′W) in 1520.
    Vaillant, G. C. 1941. Aztecs of Mexico. New York.
    Soustelle, J. 1961. Daily Life of the Aztecs. New York.
154. Popoluca around the pueblo of Soteapan (18°15′N, 94°50′W) in 1940.
    Foster, G. M. 1940. Notes on the Popoluca of Veracruz. Publications del Instituto Panamericano de Geografía e Historia 51: 1-41.

―――― 1942. A Primitive Mexican Economy. Monographs of the American Ethnological Society 5: 1-115.

―――― 1943. The Geographical, and Linguistic, and Cultural Position of the Popoluca of Veracruz. American Anthropologist 45: 531-546.

155. Quiche of the town of Chichicastenango (15°N, 91°W) in 1930.

Bunzel, R. 1952. Chichicastenango. Publications of the American Ethnological Society 22: 1-438.

156. Miskito near Cape Gracias a Dios (15°N, 83°W) in 1921.

Conzemius, E. 1932. Ethnographic Survey of the Miskito and Sumu Indians. Bulletins of the Bureau of American Ethnology 106: 1-191.

157. Bribri tribe of Talamanca (9°N, 83°15'W) in 1917.

Stone, D. 1962. The Talamancan Tribes of Costa Rica. Papers of the Peabody Museum, Harvard University 43: ii, 1-108.

Skinner, A. 1920. Notes on the Bribri of Costa Rica. Indian Notes and Monographs 6: 37-106.

Johnson, F. 1948. The Caribbean Lowland Tribes: The Talamancan Division. Bulletins of the Bureau of American Ethnology 143: iv, 231-251.

Gabb, W. M. 1876. On the Indian Tribes and Languages of Costa Rica. Proceedings of the American Philosophical Society 14: 483-602.

158. Cuna of San Blas Archipelago (9° to 9°30'N, 78° to 79°W) in 1927.

Nordenskiöld, E. 1938. An Historical and Ethnological Survey of the Cuna Indians. Comparative Ethnographical Studies 10: 1-686. Göteborg.

Stout, D. C. 1947. San Blas Cuna Acculturation. Viking Fund Publications in Anthropology 9: 1-124.

Holmer, N. M. 1951. Cuna Chrestomathy. Etnologiska Studier 18: 1-191.

159. Goajiro (11°30' to 12°20'N, 71° to 72°30'W) in 1947.

Gutierrez de Pineda, V. 1948. Organizacion social en la Guajira. Revista del Instituto Etnologico Nacional 3: ii.1-255. Bogota.

Bolinder, G. 1957. Indians on Horseback. London.

Armstrong, J. M., and A. Métraux.1948. The Goajiro. Bulletins of the Bureau of American Ethnology 143: iv, 360-383.

Simons, F. A. A. 1885. An Exploration of the Goajira Peninsula. Proceedings of the Royal Geographical Society, n.s., 7: 781-796.

160. Haitians of Mirebalais (18°50'N, 72°10'W) in 1935.

Herskovits, M. J. 1937. Life in a Haitan Valley. New York.

Simpson, G. E. 1940. Haitian Peasant Economy. Journal of Negro History 25: 498-519.

Underwood, F. W. 1960. A Survey of Haitian Markets. Yale University Publications in Anthropology 60: 3-33.

Leyburn, J. G. 1941. The Haitian People. New Haven.

Mintz, S. W. 1963. The Employment of Capital by Market Women in Haiti. Capital, Saving and Credit in Peasant Societies, ed. R. Firth and B. S. Yamey, pp. 256-286. Chicago.

161. Callinago of Dominica (15°30'N, 60°30'W) in 1650.

Rouse, I. 1948. The Carib. Bulletins of the Bureau of American Ethnology 143: iv, 547-565.

Breton, R., and A. de la Paix. 1929. Relation de l'île de la Guadeloup, ed. J. Rennard. Histoire Coloniale 1: 45-74. Paris.

Taylor, D. 1938. The Caribs of Dominica. Bulletins of the Bureau of American Ethnology 119: 103-159.

―――― 1949. The Interpretation of Some Documentary Evidence on Carib Culture. Southwestern Journal of Anthropology 5: 379-392.

Bouton, J. 1640. Relation de l'establissement des Francois depuis l'an 1635 en l'isle de Martinique. Paris.

162. Warrau of the Orinoco delta (8°30' to 9°50'N, 60°40' to 62°30'W) in 1935.

Turrado Moreno, A. 1945. Etnographia de los Indios Guaraunos. Caracas.

Wilbert, J. 1958. Die soziale und politische Organisation der Warrau. Kölner Zeitschrift für Soziologie und Sozialpsychologie, n.s., 10: 272-291.
——— 1964. Warao Oral Literature. Caracas.
Kirchhoff, P. 1948. The Warrau. Bulletins of the Bureau of American Ethnology 143: iii, 869-881.
163. Yanomamo of the Shamatari tribe (2° to 2°45'N, 64°30' to 65°30'W) in 1965.
Chagnon, N. A. 1968. The Fierce People. New York.
——— 1968. Personal Fierceness and Headmen in Yanomamö Disputes. Ms.
——— 1967. Yanomamö Social Organization and Warfare. Ms.
164. Carib along the Barama River (7°10' to 7°40'N, 59°20' to 60°20'W) in 1932.
Gillin, J. 1936. The Barama River Caribs. Papers of the Peabody Museum, Harvard University 14. ii, 1-274.
——— 1948. Tribes of the Guianas. Bulletins of the Bureau of American Ethnology 143: iii, 799-860.
165. Saramacca of the upper Suriname River (3° to 4°N, 55°30' to 56°W) in 1928.
Kahn, M. C. 1931. Djuka: The Bush Negroes of Dutch Guiana. New York.
166. Mundurucu of Cabrua village (7°S, 57°W) in 1850.
Murphy, R. F. 1960. Headhunter's Heritage. Berkeley and Los Angeles.
——— 1956. Matrilocality and Patrilineality in Mundurucú Society. American Anthropologist 58: 414-434.
167. Cubeo of the Caduiari River (1° to 1°50'N, 70° to 71°W) in 1939.
Goldman, I. The Cubeo Indians. Illinois Studies in Anthropology 2: 1-305.
168. Cayapa of the Rio Cayapas drainage (0°40' to 1°15'N, 78°45' to 79°10'W) in 1908.
Barrett, S. A. 1925. The Cayapa Indians. Indian Notes and Monographs 40: 1-476.
Altschuler, M. 1965. The Cayapa. Ph.D. dissertation, University of Minnesota.
169. Jivaro (2° to 4°S, 77° to 79°W) in 1920.
Karsten, R. 1935. The Head-Hunters of Western Amazonas. Societas Scientiarum Fennica, Commentationes Humanarum Litterarum 7: 1-588.
170. Amahuaca of the upper Inuya River (10°10' to 10°30'S, 72° to 72°30'W) in 1960.
Carneiro, R. L. 1964. Shifting Cultivation Among the Amahuaca. Niedersächsisches Landesmuseum, Völkerkundliche Abhandlungen 1: 9-18. Hannover.
——— 1962. The Amahuaca Indians. Explorers Journal 40: iv, 28-37.
——— 1968. Hunting and Hunting Magic Among the Amahuaca. Ms.
171. Inca in the vicinity of Cuzco (13°30'S, 72°W) in 1530.
Rowe, J. H. 1946. Inca Culture at the Time of the Conquest. Bulletins of the Bureau of American Ethnology 143: ii, 183-330.
Cieza de León, P. de. 1554. Parte primera de la cronica del Perú. Antwerp.
Cobo, B. 1890-95. Historia del Nuevo Mundo. 4v. Seville.
172. Aymara of Chucuito (16°S, 65°45'W) in 1940.
Tschopik, H., Jr. 1951. The Aymara of Chucuito. Anthropological Papers of the American Museum of Natural History 44: 137-308.
——— 1946. The Aymara. Bulletins of the Bureau of American Ethnology 143: ii, 501-573.
173. Siriono near the Rio Blanco (14° to 15°S, 63° to 64°W) in 1942.
Holmberg, A. R. 1950. Nomads of the Long Bow. Publications of the Institute of Social Anthropology, Smithsonian Institution 10: 1-104.
174. Nambicuara of the Cocozu group (12°30' to 13°30'S, 58°30' to 59°W) in 1940.
Lévi-Strauss, L. 1948. The Nambicuara. Bulletins of the Bureau of American Ethnology 143: iii, 361-369.
——— 1948. La vie familiale et sociale des Indiens Nambikwara. Journal de la Société des Américanistes 37: 1-131. Paris.
175. Trumai (11°50'S, 53°40'W) in 1938.
Murphy, R. F., and B. Quain. 1955. The Trumai Indians. Monographs of the American Ethnological Society 24: 1-108.

176. Timbira of the Ramcocamecra subtribe (6° to 7°S, 45° to 46°W) in 1915.
    Nimuendajú, C. 1946. The Eastern Timbira. University of California Publications
        in American Archaeology and Ethnology 41: 1-357.
177. Tupinamba in vicinity of Rio de Janeiro (22°35′ to 23°S, 42° to 44°30′W) in
    1550.
    Métraux, A. 1948. The Tupinamba. Bulletins of the Bureau of American
        Ethnology 143: iii, 95-133.
    Thevet, A. 1878. Les singularitez de la France antarctique, ed. P. Gaffarel.
        Paris.
    Léry, J. de. 1880. Histoire d'un voyage faict en la terre du Brésil, ed. P. Gaf-
        farel. Paris.
    Staden, H. 1928. The True Story of His Captivity, ed. M. Lotts. London.
178. Botocudo of the Naknenuk subtribe (18° to 20°S, 41°30′ to 43°30′W) in 1884.
    Ehrenreich, P. 1887. Ueber die Botocudos. Zeitschrift für Ethnologie 19: 49-82.
    Métraux, A. 1946. The Botocudo. Bulletins of the Bureau of American
        Ethnology 143: i, 531-540.
179. Shavante in the vicinity of São Domingo (13°30′S, 51°30′W) in 1958.
    Maybury-Lewis, D. 1967. Akwẽ-Shavante Society. Oxford.
180. Aweikoma (28°S, 50°W) in 1932.
    Henry, J. 1941. Jungle People. New York.
    Métraux, A. 1946. The Caingang. Bulletins of the Bureau of American Ethnol-
        ogy 143: i, 445-475.
181. Cayua of southern Mato Grosso (23° to 24°S, 54° to 56°W) in 1890.
    Koenigswald, G. von. 1908. Die Cayuás. Globus 93: 376-381.
    Strelnikov, I. D. 1928. Les Kaa-iwuá de Paraguay. Proceedings of the Inter-
        national Congress of Americanists 22: ii, 333-366.
    Watson, J. B. 1952. Cayuá Culture Change. Memoirs of the American Anthro-
        pological Association 73: 1-144.
182. Lengua (23° to 24°S, 58° to 59°W) in 1889.
    Grubb, W. B. 1911. An Unknown People in an Unknown Land. London.
183. Abipon (27° to 29°S, 59° to 60°W) in 1750.
    Dobrizhoffer, M. 1822. An Account of the Abipones. 3v. London.
184. Mapuche in the vicinity of Temuco (38°30′S, 72°35′W) in 1950.
    Faron, L. C. 1968. The Mapuche Indians of Chile. New York.
    ――――― 1961. Mapuche Social Structure. Illinois Studies in Anthropology 1:
        1-247.
    Titiev, M. 1951. Araucanian Culture in Transition. Occasional Contributions
        from the Museum of Anthropology, University of Michigan 15: 1-164.
185. Tehuelche (40° to 50°S, 64° to 72°W) in 1870.
    Musters, G. C. 1871. At Home with the Patagonians. London.
186. Yahgan (54°30′ to 56°30′S, 67° to 72°W) in 1865.
    Gusinde, M. 1937. Die Feuerland-Indianer 2: Yamana. Mödling bei Wien.
    Cooper, J. M. 1917. An Analytical and Critical Bibliography of the Tribes
        of Tierra del Fuego. Bulletins of the Bureau of American Ethnology 63:
        1-243.
    ――――― 1946. The Yahgan. Bulletins of the Bureau of American Ethnology 143:
        i, 81-106.
11a. Chagga of Mt. Kilimanjaro (3° to 4°S, 37° to 38°E) in 1906.
    Gutmann, B. 1913. Feldbausitten und Wachstumsbräuche der Wadeschagga.
        Zeitschrift für Ethnologie 45: 475-511.
    ――――― 1926. Das Recht der Dschagga. Arbeiten zur Entwicklungspsychologie
        7: 1-733. München.
    Dundas, C. 1924. Kilimanjaro and Its Peoples. London.
    Abbott, W. R. 1892. Ethnological Collections. Reports of the U. S. National
        Museum, 1890-91, 381-428.
16a. Katab of the Jos plateau (10°N, 8°E) in 1925.
    Meek, C. K. 1931. Tribal Studies in Northern Nigeria, v.2. London.

Gunn, H. D. 1956. Pagan Peoples of the Central Area of Northern Nigeria. London.

34a. Dorobo of the North Tindiret Forest band (0°10′N, 35°30′E) in 1927.
Huntingford, G. W. B. 1955. The Economic Life of the Dorobo. Anthropos 50: 602-634.
—— 1953. The Southern Nilo-Hamites. London.
—— 1929. Modern Hunters. Journal of the Royal Anthropological Institute 59: 333-378.

46a. Lebanese of Al-Munsif village (34°25′N, 35°40′E) in 1950.
Gulick, J. 1955. Social Structure and Culture Change in a Lebanese Village. Viking Fund Publications in Anthropology 21: 1-118.
—— 1953. The Lebanese Village. American Anthropologist 55: 367-372.
—— 1956. Village Organization. The Republic of Lebanon, ed. R. Patai, 1: 136-209. New Haven.
Touma, T. 1958. Un village de montagne au Lebanon. Paris.
Tannous, A. I. 1949. The Village in the National Life of Lebanon. Middle East Journal 3: 151-163.

60a. Chenchu of the Forest group (16°15′N, 79°E) in 1940.
Fürer-Haimendorf, C. von. 1943. The Chenchus. London.

95a. Wogeo Islanders of Wonevaro district (3°S, 144°E) in 1930.
Hogbin, H. I. 1938. Tillage and Collection: A New Guinea Economy. Oceania 9: 127-151, 286-325.
—— 1935. Native Culture of Wogeo. Oceania 5: 308-337.
—— 1935. Trading Expedition in Northern New Guinea. Oceania 5: 375-407.

106a. Pukapukans of Danger Island (10°53′S, 165°50′W) in 1915.
Beaglehole, E., and P. Beaglehole. 1938. Ethnology of Pukapuka. Bulletins of the Bernice P. Bishop Museum 150: 1-419.

141a. Crow Indians (42°30′ to 47°N, 105° to 111°W) in 1870.
Lowie, R. H. 1935. The Crow Indians. New York.
—— 1919. The Tobacco Society of the Crow Indians. Anthropological Papers, American Museum of Natural History 21: 101-200.
—— 1922. The Material Culture of the Crow Indians. Anthropological Papers, American Museum of Natural History 21: 201-270.
Denig, E. T. 1961. Five Indian Tribes of the Upper Missouri. Norman.

175a. Bororo of the Rio Vermelho (15°30′ to 16°S, 54°30′ to 55°W) in 1936.
Lévi-Strauss, C. 1936. Contribution à l'étude de l'organisation sociale des Indiens Bororo. Journal de la Société des Américanistes 28: 269-304.
Frič, V. A., and P. Radin. 1906. Contributions to the Study of the Bororo Indians. Journal of the Royal Anthropological Institute 36: 382-406.
Steinen, K. von den. 1894. Unter den Naturvölkern Zentral-Brasiliens. Berlin.

177a. Tenetehara of the Guajajara subgroup (3° to 6°S, 44° to 46°W) in 1941.
Wagley, C. 1949. The Tenetehara Indians. Columbia University Contributions to Anthropology 35: 1-200.
Wagley, C., and E. Galvão. 1948. The Tenetehara. Bulletins of the Bureau of American Ethnology 143: iii, 137-148.

179a. Caraja along the west bank of the Araguaya River (10°12′ to 15°15′S, 50°25′ to 51°50′W) in 1908.
Krause, F. 1911. In den Wildnissen Brasiliens. Leipzig.
Lipkind, W. 1948. The Carajá. Bulletins of the Bureau of American Ethnology 143: iii, 179-191.
Ehrenreich, P. 1891. Beiträge zur Völkerkunde Brasiliens. Veröffentlichungen aus dem Königlichen Museum für Völkerkunde 2: 1-80. Leipzig.

# 3

# Settlement Patterns and Community Organization: Cross-Cultural Codes 3

*George P. Murdock* and *Suzanne F. Wilson*

This paper is the third in a series presenting coded ethnographic data on a representative sample of 186 of the world's societies. It follows comparable reports on subsistence economy (Murdock and Morrow 1970) and on infancy and early childhood (Barry and Paxson 1971). Similar studies are in progress or in preparation on political organization, childhood, expressive behavior, kinship, theories of illness, and technology and division of labor. Appreciation is extended to the National Science Foundation for generous support of this research at the Cross-Cultural Cumulative Coding Center (CCCCC) at the University of Pittsburgh.

The code definitions were originally phrased by the senior author, pretested by the junior author against a special sample of eleven societies (those added at the end of Table 1), and jointly revised by both authors. The actual work of assessing the ethnographic sources and assigning code symbols to the data was done by the junior author for 146 of the sample societies, by Mrs. Edith Lauer for 59 societies, and independently by Douglas R. White for 60 societies. The authors would like gratefully to acknowledge the assistance received in the coding of particular societies from the following ethnographers: Keith L. Brown, Ruth Bunzel, Ward H. Goodenough, Eileen Kane, Andre Köbben, Bernd Lambert, Triloki Pandey, John M. Roberts, and Alexander Spoehr. The senior author, who had coded most of the same societies for similar topics in compiling the Ethnographic Atlas (Murdock 1967), worked closely with the junior author and Mrs. Lauer in reviewing all coding results and resolving discrepancices. The authors are confident of the essential accuracy of the coding and have kept sufficiently full records of the problems encountered and of the reasons for all decisions that they are prepared to justify any item in Table 1 to any interested or skeptical reader.

Experience has engendered in the authors a sense of general satisfaction with the research design of the project and with its major distinctive features—the use of a single sample for a variety of studies to make possible the intercorrelation of all coded findings, the stratification of this sample through the selection of a single representative for each of 186 empirically established cultural provinces, the "pinpointing" of each sample society to a specific date and locality as a guide to extrapolations in time or space where such are necessary, and the ranking of the relative usefulness of the bibliographical sources used for each society and each set of codes for the guidance of subsequent researchers. On four of the sample societies—the Botocudo (#178), Bribri (#157), Kenuzi Nubians (#39), and Tobelorese (#88)—the information in the sources was found barely adequate for coding, but no alternative society with fuller coverage came to light for the same province. For a handful of other sample societies—most notably the Nkundo Mongo (#14) and the Rwala Bedouin (#46)—the sources were also found only marginally adequate, but an alternative society with superior coverage might have been found to represent the particular province.

## THE COMMUNITY

The concept of the community and its identification for each society is of crucial importance to this code. In using these coded materials it is essential that the researcher refer to the bibliography for the identification of the community since all of the items in Table 1 refer specifically to this unit of social interaction. We assume that there is and must be a unit of significant social interaction beyond the family. It follows that it is possible to identify this unit as the community for each society. The main criteria for determining the community are: (1) it is "the maximal number of people who normally reside together in face-to-face association" (Murdock *et al.* 1945); (2) the members interact with some regularity; (3) it is a significant focus of social identity for the members.

These criteria have a number of advantages for cross-cultural research. First, they focus on units of social interaction of the same order because the standards for the identification of the community have been the same for all the societies. Since these criteria are free from the strictures of size, political level, or economic function, they permit the comparison of groups of different technological levels, political development, and points in time. Second, since we want to investigate the social functions and cultural attributes of a specific type of social unit and compare these with those of like units, it would bias our findings to assume in advance that particular functions or attributes are necessarily inherent to its definition. This is not to deny the importance of particular types of social units in other contexts; it is only to say that tying the concept of community to one of these contexts would severely limit its usefulness for comparative purposes.

Other codes deal with social units tied to contexts that are relevant to the investigation of the specific problems with which they are concerned. For example, in the subsistence economy code (Murdock and Morrow 1970), it was necessary to define a local community for each society before coding intercommunity trade. This was of necessity primarily an economic unit and was therefore commonly not only different from, but also larger than, the community as defined in the present code. For example, the whole island of Pukapuka was treated as the local community for the purposes of the subsistence code, whereas the unit chosen for the present code was the village. In Pukapuka the villages were strung closely together along the shore, and their inhabitants interacted frequently with those of the neighboring villages. As oftentimes in areas of high population density, interaction was thus based more on proximity than on a sense of identity with the unit to which people felt they belonged.

The political code (Tuden and Marshall 1972) provides another example of the difference between a definition of the community that is specific to one of its functions and our more general criteria for the community. It was necessary to identify a local community as the lowest level of political integration before determining the number of levels of political integration. The difference between the definitions of the community in the present code and in that on political organization is that the latter must be a political unit whereas the former need not be. Political integration may begin at a level above that of the community, as in the case of the Irish, where the village is not a political unit, or it may begin at a lower level, as in the case of the political wards of the Fon. The degree to which the community in the present code can be regarded as a political unit is indicated in Column 15 of Table 1. If an "O" or an "X" appears in that column, the community can be regarded as having little political importance.

The importance of the community as a ceremonial unit is indicated in Column 13 of Table 1. If ceremonial activity occurs on a level below or above the community, this is indicated by a superscript "s" or "w" respectively. Thus, for the Shilluk $M^wp^s$ indicates that there is no significant ceremonial activity at the level of the community, the village cluster; rather it occurs at a higher ($M^w$) or lower ($p^s$) level.

The community is identified for each society in the bibliography. Here two types of community are differentiated: focal (F) and typical (T). A focal community is the specific community in which the ethnographer worked and/or for which he provides his principal information. The designation of a community as typical ordinarily implies that the ethnographer presents his material as applying to an area broader than a specific community. It was sometimes difficult to identify, among two or more alternatives, the level of social interaction most appropriate for selection as the community. In general, we chose the unit that seemed to be the focus of the most significant regular interaction and identification.

## DEFINITION OF CODES

The symbols used for the coding of data in the sixteen columns of Table 1 are defined below.

### Column 1: Fixity of Settlement

A capital letter indicates the degree to which the focal or typical community is migratory or sedentary. A postposited lower-case letter indicates an alternative pattern, whether due to local or seasonal variation.

B   Migratory or nomadic bands, occupying temporary camps for brief periods successively throughout the year.

S   Seminomadic communities, occupying temporary camps for much of the year but aggregated in a fixed settlement at some season or seasons, e.g., recurrently occupied winter quarters.

R   Rotating settlements, i.e., two or more permanent or semipermanent settlements occupied successively at different seasons.

T   Semisedentary settlements, occupied throughout the year by at least a nucleus of the community's population, but from which a substantial proportion of the population departs seasonally to occupy shifting camps, e.g., on extended hunting or fishing trips or during pastoral transhumance.

I   Impermanent settlements, occupied throughout the year but periodically moved for ecological reasons or because of untoward events like an epidemic or the death of a headman.

P   Permanent settlements, occupied throughout the year and for long or indefinite periods. P is used instead of I in default of specific evidence of impermanence.

## Column 2: Compactness of Settlement

A capital letter indicates the degree to which the focal or typical community is a dispersed or concentrated settlement. A postposited lower-case letter indicates an important alternative pattern, prevailing for a shorter season or in fewer instances.

C   Compact settlements, e.g., nucleated villages or concentrated camps, whether of circular, linear, or amorphous shape.

D   Dispersed settlements, e.g., neighborhoods of isolated family homesteads, bands whose members live in dispersed family camps, or villages with dwellings strung out at appreciable intervals along a highway, shore, or river bank.

H   Settlements composed of spatially separated subsettlements, e.g., sedentary hamlets or clusters containing two or three families of nomadic groups.

P   Partially dispersed settlements, e.g., a central village or town core with satellite hamlets or family homesteads.

## Column 3: Community Size

The population size of the focal or typical community is ranked by a numerical symbol in one of the following categories:

1   Fewer than 50 persons.
2   From 50 to 99 persons.
3   From 100 to 199 persons.
4   From 200 to 399 persons.
5   From 400 to 999 persons.
6   From 1,000 to 4,999 persons.
7   From 5,000 to 49,000 persons.
8   50,000 persons or more.

## Column 4: Density of Population

A capital letter indicates the density of population in the area exploited or controlled by the focal or typical community. A postposited minus sign (—) indicates that the density for the society at large is substantially less than that indicated for the focal community, as when distortion is produced by the presence of urban centers. Densities are ranked in one of the following categories:

A   Less than one person per five square miles.

B   From one person per square mile to one per five square miles.

C   From 1.1 to 5 persons per square mile.

D   From 5.1 to 25 persons per square mile.

E   From 26 to 100 persons per square mile.

F   From 101 to 500 persons per square mile.

G   Over 500 persons per square mile.

## Column 5: Type of Dwelling

A capital letter indicates the prevailing house type as defined below. A postposited lower-case letter indicates an important alternative type (exclusive of types resulting from recent acculturation).

The first class of dwellings (types B, C, and D) consists of structures with a circular or occasionally oval ground plan in which roof and walls are not distinct but grade imperceptibly into each other.

B   Dwellings of beehive shape with a pointed peak from which the roof (commonly but not necessarily of thatch) curves to the ground in all directions.

C   Conical dwellings with a pointed peak from which the roof slopes straight to the ground in all directions, e.g., tipis.

D   Dome-shaped or hemispherical dwellings lacking a pointed peak, usually roofed with thatch, brush, bark, mats, or hides, but sometimes with wood (hogans) or snow (igloos), and occasionally also with an outer layer of earth.

The second class of dwellings (types E and H) consists of structures with a rectangular or occasionally elliptical ground plan in which roof and walls merge, at least at the sides.

E   Dwellings with a wedge-shaped or two-slope roof extending from a ridgepole straight to the ground, as in a pup tent or an elongated tipi, regardless of the roofing material.

H   Dwellings shaped like a half barrel or horizontal semicylinder, regardless of the roofing material and of whether the end walls are rounded or straight.

The third class of dwellings (type A) consists of structures with a circular or occasionally polygonal ground plan and a clear distinction between walls and roof.

A   Cone-cylinder dwellings—with vertical cylindrical walls of adobe, wattle-and daub, wood, or other materials and a conical or occasionally dome-shaped or beehive-shaped roof (commonly but not necessarily of thatch).

The fourth class of dwellings (types F, P, Q, and R) consists of structures with a rectangular, quadrangular, or occasionally hexagonal ground plan and a clear distinction between walls and roof.

F   Dwellings with flat roofs (commonly of beaten earth) and substantial walls (commonly of adobe or stone masonry).

P   Rectangular dwellings raised on piles or posts with hip (4-sloped), gable (2-sloped), or shed (1-sloped) roofs, whatever the wall and roofing materials (commonly thatch, bamboo, mats, or wood). Pile dwellings of circular ground plan, which are rare, are otherwise classed (e.g., under A).

Q   Quadrangular or rectangular dwellings built on or close to the ground with hip, gable, or shed roofs (commonly of thatch) and walls of adobe, stone, brick, plaster, or other mineral materials.

R   Rectangular dwellings built on or close to the ground with hip, gable, or shed roofs and walls of wood, bamboo, wattle, mats, or other vegetal materials.

The fifth class of dwellings consists of several types (S, T, U, and Z) which are defined by criteria other than shape.

S   Semisubterranean dwellings in which the main floor (excluding cellars or smaller excavations) is constructed, at least in part, below the surface of the ground, without regard to the shape or materials of the roof.

T   Tents consisting of fabrics or hide stretched over a frame, especially if dismountable and portable, but exclusive of conical tipis (C) and dome-shaped shelters (D).

U   Partially unenclosed shelters, e.g., caves, rock shelters, half-enclosed sheds, or open-sided windbreaks.

Z   Miscellaneous house types that deviate in important respects from any of the above definitions.

## Column 6: Large or Impressive Structures

A capital letter indicates the presence of a particularly large or impressive structure or type of structure in the focal or typical community. A postposited lower-case letter indicates an additional important type of large or impressive structure.

O   There are no structures in the community that are appreciably larger or more impressive than the usual residential dwellings.

R   The most impressive structure (or type of structure) in the community is the residence of a category of influential individuals, e.g., a noble, a wealthy landowner, or the local headman.

A   The most impressive structure (or type of structure) is an assembly hall, men's house, or other essentially secular or public building.

T   The most impressive structure (or type of structure) is a temple, church, commemorative monument, or other essentially religious or ceremonial edifice.

F   The most impressive structure (or type of structure) is a fort, citadel, massive defensive wall, or other military installation.

E   The most impressive structure (or type of structure) is an economic or industrial edifice, e.g., a storehouse, factory, or office building.

## Column 7: Household Form

A capital letter indicates the prevailing form of household relative to its family composition and component dwelling units.

L   Longhouses or other large communal dwellings, the entire community residing in one or a very few such structures, each occupied by a social group larger than an extended family.

A   Apartment houses or other multi-family dwellings (exclusive of long-houses) whose residents do not constitute a familial group.

H   Family homesteads, in which a single family, whatever its composition, occupies a single residential structure in a cluster of structures which may also include important outbuildings (e.g., granaries or stables) and/or separate quarters for dependents (e.g., slaves, servants, or unmarried youths).

F   Family dwellings, in which each family, whatever its composition, occupies a single residential structure without important outbuildings.

C   Multi-dwelling households, in which a larger familial unit occupies a compound or cluster of residential structures, and each dwelling houses a component nuclear or polygamous family.

I   Multi-dwelling households, in which a larger familial unit occupies a compound or cluster of residential structures, and each dwelling is occupied by an individual married man or woman rather than by married pairs.

J   Multi-dwelling households, in which a larger familial unit occupies a compound or cluster of residential structures, and each dwelling is occupied by a married woman with her children, the husband residing with his wives in rotation.

M   Mother-child households, in which each married woman with her young children occupies a separate dwelling, the husband residing elsewhere, e.g., in a men's house.

## Column 8: Form of Family

A capital letter indicates the social composition of the predominant form of the family, regardless of its residential distribution. One symbol (M, N, P, Q) suffices if the predominant form is nuclear or polygamous. In the case of extended family forms (E, F, S), a post-posited lower-case symbol indicates whether marriage is preferentially monogamous (m) or polygamous (n, p, q).

E   The predominant form of family organization is a large extended family, i.e., one normally embracing the families of procreation of at least two siblings or cousins in each of two adjacent generations.

F   The predominant form of family organization is a small extended family, i.e., one normally embracing only one family of procreation in the senior generation but at least two in the next generation. Such families usually dissolve on the death of the head.

S   The predominant form of family organization is a "stem family," i.e., a minimal extended family consisting of only two related families of procreation (disregarding polygamous unions) of adjacent generations. But see "Q" below.

M   The predominant form of family organization is an independent monogamous family, polygyny being forbidden or disapproved.

N   The predominant form of family organization is an independent nuclear family, polygyny being permitted but having an incidence of less than 20 per cent.

P   The predominant form of family organization is an independent polygynous family, the incidence of polygyny being 20 per cent or higher. In cases of doubt about incidence, N rather than P is indicated.

Q   The predominant form of family organization is an independent polyandrous family or a stem family with polyandry.

*Column 9: Marital Residence*

A capital letter indicates the prevailing practice of residence after marriage. A postposited lower-case letter indicates an alternative but less frequent residential pattern or one confined to a particular phase of the developmental cycle.

A   Avunculocal residence, i.e., with or near the maternal uncle or other male matrilineal kinsmen of the husband, including cases where men preferentially and typically marry a MoBrDa and reside matrilocally.

B   Ambilocal residence, i.e., optionally with or near the parents of either the husband or wife depending upon personal choice or circumstances, where neither alternative exceeds the other in actual frequency by a ratio greater than two to one.

M   Matrilocal or uxorilocal residence, i.e., with or near the female matrilineal kinsmen of the wife.

N   Neolocal residence, i.e., where spouses establish a common household at a location not determined by the kin ties of either.

P   Patrilocal or virilocal residence, i.e., with or near the male patrilineal kinsmen of the husband.

*Column 10: Descent*

A capital letter indicates the prevailing rule of descent.

M   The principal consanguineal kin groups are based on matrilineal descent, e.g., matrilineages.

P   The principal consanguineal kin groups are based on patrilineal descent, e.g., patrilineages.

D   Double descent prevails, both matrilineal and patrilineal descent groups being present.

A   The principal consanguineal kin groups are based on ambilineal descent, e.g., ramages.

B   Descent is bilateral, i.e., ancestor-oriented descent groups are absent, and kinsmen are aggregated only by consanguineal and/or affinal ties between individuals, as in personal kindreds or kiths.

A postposited lower-case letter gives an indication of the extent to which the membership of descent groups is dispersed or concentrated. The symbol is based on the numerically largest kin group of the prevailing type in the focal or typical community and on its adult membership of the sex which shifts residence less frequently in marriage.

s     The majority of the adult members belonging to the less mobile sex reside outside the focal or typical community, as in the case of dispersed sibs.

c     The majority of the adult members belonging to the less mobile sex reside in the focal or typical community and comprise the majority of adults of that sex in the community, as in the case of clan-communities.

I     The majority of the adult members belonging to the less mobile sex reside in the focal or typical community and constitute a minority of all adults of that sex in the community, as in the case of small localized lineages.

## Column 11: Intercommunity Marriage

A capital letter indicates the extent to which the community as a whole forms an endogamous or exogamous unit.

A     The focal or typical community is agamous, marriages both within and outside the community being permitted and roughly equal in frequency, i.e., with frequencies of between 40 and 60 per cent.

B     The focal or typical community is agamous, but endogamous unions are in fact appreciably more common than intercommunity marriages, i.e., with a frequency of between 61 and 89 per cent.

C     The focal or typical community is agamous, but exogamous unions are in fact appreciably more common than marriages within the community, i.e., with a frequency of between 61 and 89 per cent.

N     Local endogamy is strictly enjoined or strongly preferred, marriages with members of other communities being rare or exceptional.

X     Local exogamy is strictly enjoined or strongly preferred, marriages with a member of the same community (at least with the exception of levirate and sororate unions) being rare or exceptional.

## Column 12: Community Integration

A capital letter indicates the predominant factor or factors contributing to the solidarity of the focal or typical community. A postposited lower-case symbol indicates an important auxiliary feature contributing to solidarity.

O     The focal or typical community is notably lacking in social integration, at least as compared with its constituent local segments or with some larger political unit of which it forms a part.

I     The focal or typical community is distinguished from other neighboring communities by a sense of common identity, e.g., a common dialect or subculture.

K     The focal or typical community is integrated by kin ties, whether these are consanguineal or affinal.

S     The focal or typical community is integrated primarily by common social or economic status, e.g., membership in a social class or participation in a common economic activity.

P   The focal or typical community is integrated primarily (not incidentally) by common political ties, e.g., through allegiance to a particular chief or by interdependence through patron-client relationships.

R   The focal or typical community is integrated primarily by a common cult or religious affiliation or by a civil-religious system of offices, the religious element in either case transcending in importance all other types of local bonds.

C   The focal or typical community is primarily integrated, not by common kinship, social status, worship, or political allegiance, but by the choice, fact, or accident of common residence.

## Column 13: Prominent Community Ceremonials

A capital letter indicates the most prominent type of ceremonial activity in which all or most members of the local community normally participate. A second capital letter indicates another almost equally prominent type. A postposited lower-case letter(s) indicates a less prominent but important additional type of ceremonial activity. A superscript letter indicates, in the case of s, that the particular ceremony is confined to a social unit smaller than that considered as the community; in the case of w, that it is normally participated in by members of more than one community.

C   The most prominent ceremonies are calendrical, being determined by the annual cycle of economic activities (e.g., first-fruits rites, harvest ceremonies), by astronomical observations (e.g., new-moon or solstice celebrations), or by a ritual calendar (e.g., saints' days).

P   The most prominent ceremonies are rites of passage performed for individuals at critical points in their life cycle but normally attended by all or most members of the community, e.g., naming ceremonies, puberty initiations, weddings, funerals.

M   The most prominent ceremonies are magical or religious rites performed on irregular occasions of individual or community concern, e.g., shamanistic curing performances, purification rituals, ceremonies before and after wars, or rites celebrating the installation of a chief, in which participation is normally by the community at large.

I   The most prominent ceremonies are individually sponsored rites other than rites of passage which are normally attended by the community at large, e.g., potlatches, "feasts of merit," votive sacrifices.

## Column 14: Ceremonial Elements

A capital letter indicates the feature or element that is most strongly emphasized in community-wide ceremonies. A second capital letter indicates another ceremonial element equally emphasized. A postposited lower-case letter indicates a less emphasized but important additional type of ceremonial element.

C   Cannibalism, human sacrifice, and/or the ceremonial killing of war captives, widows, or other victims.

D   Distribution or exchange of property other than food.
F   Feasting and/or drinking (other than cannibalistic), including the distribution of food for subsequent consumption.
M   Music, dancing, games, and/or dramatic performances.
S   Sacrifice (other than human), prayer, laudation, and/or other forms of propitiating spirits, deities, or ghosts of the dead, whatever their specific purpose (e.g., atonement, foretelling the future, pleas for help, thanksgiving).
T   Self-torture, self-mutilation, or comparable extreme masochistic behavior, not including fasting or other forms of self-abnegation.

## Column 15: Community Leadership

A capital letter indicates the form and complexity of political organization within the focal or typical community.

O   The focal or typical community lacks centralized leadership, political authority being dispersed among its component households or other segments, which remain essentially autonomous.
X   The focal or typical community lacks centralized leadership, but such leadership exists at a higher level of political integration.
H   The community has a single leader or headman but lacks other political offices other than, at most, an informal council of elders.
D   The community has dual or plural headmen with distinct but co-ordinate authority but lacks a complex system of subordinate political statuses.
F   The community has a single leader or headman with one or more functional assistants and/or a formal council or assembly, but lacks an elaborate or hierarchical political organization.
E   The community has a single leader or headman plus an elaborate or hierarchical system of subordinate political statuses.
C   The community lacks a single political head but is governed collectively by a committee, a council, an age-grade organization, or the like.
U   The political organization of the local community is too complex to be appropriately coded under any of the foregoing symbols, as when religious functionaries play important political roles.

## Column 16: Local Political Succession

A capital letter indicates the mode of succession to political leadership within the focal or typical community. A postposited lower-case letter indicates a necessary auxiliary qualification for succession.

O   There is no community headman or council.
A   Succession to the office of headman, if such or an approximate equivalent exists, is through appointment (not merely acquiescence) by some higher political authority.
S   Succession is based primarily upon seniority or age, as under gerontocracy.
D   Succession is based on divination, dreams, or the like.
I   Succession is not appointive or hereditary but is achieved primarily by informal consensus or the recognition of leadership qualities on the basis of the acquisition of personal influence, wealth, or prestige.

R    Succession is not appointive or hereditary but is achieved through some
     formal electoral process, e.g., selection by a council or body of electors.
P    Succession tends to be hereditary, by a son or other patrilineal kinsman
     of the predecessor.
M    Succession tends to be hereditary, by a sister's son or other matrilineal
     kinsman of the predecessor.
L    Succession tends to be hereditary, but passes not to a particular category
     of kinsman but to a member of a ruling lineage or other privileged
     group selected for his personal qualifications by some electoral or
     appointive procedure.

## CODED MATERIAL

The ethnographic material, coded in accordance with the foregoing
definitions, is presented in the sixteen columns of Table 1. Data on the
societies used for pretesting, but not forming part of the standard sample,
are included at the end of the table. A symbol enclosed in parentheses
indicates that the information is based on a weak and possibly erroneous
inference. A dot (•) indicates an absence of even inferential information.
An asterisk (*) refers to a qualifying note following the table.

## CODING PROCEDURES AND PROBLEMS

Among the difficulties encountered in coding, several were similar to
those reported by Murdock and Morrow (1970) for the codes on subsistence economy and were in general dealt with in the same manner.
These include the problems of insufficient or conflicting evidence and of
temporal extrapolation. Insufficient evidence was not a major problem for
the present code because most writers, whether missionaries, travelers, or
anthropologists, usually comment on the general features of  community
organization and settlement pattern. The problem of temporal extrapolation
was found to be rather more serious. It occurred particularly with respect
to such items as leadership and the extent of polygyny, both of which tend
to be especially sensitive to external influences which trigger cultural change.
In such cases, as elsewhere when the evidence was found insufficient or
inconclusive, the facts were clarified by resort to an unusual number of
additional sources.

A number of other problems were encountered which appeared particularly relevent to this set of codes. Among them was that of bias in the
sources. In addition to preconceived notions as to the nature of religion
or political organization, moral or theoretical prejudgments were not in-
frequently encountered, e.g., the notion that the Hebrews must always have
been monogamous or the assumption that the thought and behavior of
"savages" are necessarily simple and illogical. An excessive preoccupation
with particular subjects to the exclusion of others introduces a more
insidious form of bias by obscuring or distorting the relative importance of
data.

The choice of terminology frequently presented difficulty, especially in the
case of such terms as "clan" or "extended family." Different authors assign

## Table 1

### Settlement Pattern and Community Organization

| | 1 | 2 | 3 | 4 | 5 | 6 | 7 | 8 | 9 | 10 | 11 | 12 | 13 | 14 | 15 | 16 |
|---|---|---|---|---|---|---|---|---|---|---|---|---|---|---|---|---|
| 001 Nama | B | C | 3 | A | D | O | F | N | P | Ps | X | K | $C^Wp$ | SFm | F | Ps |
| 002 Kung | B | C | 1 | A | D | O | F | Fn | Bm | B | (C) | K | Mp | M | H | Ps |
| 003 Thonga | I | C | 1 | F | A | O | I | Ep | P | Ps | X | Kp | PcW | Sf | F | Ps |
| 004 Lozi | R | C | 5 | D | A | R | I | P | P | As | (A) | P | C | S | E | Pi |
| 005 Mbundu | P | C | 3 | D | A | A | J | P | P | Ds | X | K | P | M | F | Ps |
| 006 Suku | I | C | 2 | D | R | O | I | Fp | Pa | Ms | C | K | $P^W$ | M | F | Ms |
| 007 Bemba | I | C | 3 | C | A | E | C | Fn | Ma | Ms | C | K | $PM^W$ | Fms | H | M |
| 008 Nyakyusa | I | P | 3 | E | Ar | R | F | P | N | Ps | C | S | P | FM | H | R |
| 009 Hadza | B | C | 1 | B | Du | O | C | Fn | Mp | B | C | Ck | $C^Wp^W$ | Fm | O | O |
| 010 Luguru | P | H | 4 | G | Ra | O | F | N | Mp | Ms | X | K | Mp | Sf | H | Mi |
| 011 Kikuyu | P | D | 3 | F | A | O | I | P | P | Ps | X | K | $P^Wm$ | MFs | C | S |
| 012 Ganda | P | D | 3 | F | B | O | I | P | N | Ps | X | P | CWP | CSf | H | A |
| 013 Mbuti | B | C | 2 | B | D | O | F | N | Pm | B | X | C | P | M | O | O |
| 014 Nkundu | P | H | (3) | (C) | R | O | I | Ep | Pa | Pc | X | K | $I^Wp$ | MF | F | Ps |
| 015 Banen | P | D | 4 | D | R | O | I | P | P | Pc | X | K | P | MF | H | P |
| 016 Tiv | P | D | 5 | E | A | O | I | Ep | Pa | Ps | C | K | M | Cs | C | S |
| 017 Ibo | P | H | 6 | G | Q | O | I | Fp | P | P1 | A | RK | $Cp^s$ | Sf | O | O |
| 018 Fon | P | C | 7 | E- | Q | R | J | Ep | Pm | Ps | (B) | $P_R$ | $Mp^s$ | Cs | U | Ps |
| 019 Ashanti | P | C | (4) | E | Q | O | F | Fp | Ap | Ds | B | K | $C^Wp$ | CSm | F | L |
| 020 Mende | P | Ph | 3 | E | Ar | O | M | Fp | Pc | P(s) | A | Ks | CP | SF | F | Pi |
| 021 Wolof | P | C | 3 | F | A | R | I | Fp | P | D(s) | S | C | PC | FM | F | Ps |
| 022 Bambara | P | C | 5 | D | Af | O | C | Ep | P | Ps | (C) | Rk | Cp | Sm | F | Ps |
| 023 Tallensi | P | D | 5 | F | A | O | I | Fp | P | Ps | X | KR | $CWp$ | S | U | Ps |
| 024 Songhai | P | C | 5 | D | H | O | F | N | P | P1 | A | R | CP | Sm | F | P |
| 025 Wodaabe | B | D | 3 | C | Z* | O | J | P | P | Ps | N | K | C | SF | F | Pi |
| 026 Hausa | P | C | 6 | E | Af | Rt | I | Fp | P | P1 | A | P | Cp | SDf | E | A |
| 027 Massa | P | D | 4 | E | A | O | I | Fp | P | Ps | X | K | CP | SMf | H | • |
| 028 Azande | P | D | 3 | (C) | A | O | I | P | Pn | Ps | (A) | Pk | Pm | Mf | H | (P) |

|      |           | 1  | 2   | 3   | 4    | 5  | 6  | 7   | 8   | 9   | 10   | 11  | 12 | 13      | 14   | 15  | 16  |
|------|-----------|----|-----|-----|------|----|----|-----|-----|-----|------|-----|----|---------|------|-----|-----|
| 029  | Fur       | P  | C   | 3   | D    | A  | A  | I   | En  | M   | (M1) | C   | K  | $C^W$P  | Fm   | F   | P*  |
| 030  | Otoro     | P  | H   | (5) | D    | A  | .O | J   | P   | Pn  | Pl   | (B) | Ck | Pi      | Fms  | O   | O   |
| 031  | Shilluk   | P  | H   | 5   | E    | A  | O  | J   | P   | P   | Ps   | A   | P  | $M^W p^S$ | Sm | F   | L   |
| 032  | Mao       | P  | C   | 2   | D    | Ab | R  | H   | N   | P   | Pc   | X   | K  | $P^W$C  | SMf  | F   | Ps  |
| 033  | Kaffa     | P  | D   | 2   | (E)  | Az | R  | H   | P   | P   | Ps   | A   | O  | PI      | FM   | X   | O   |
| 034  | Masai     | B  | H   | 4   | C    | H  | O  | J   | P   | P   | Ps   | A   | g  | Pc      | Fm   | C   | R   |
| 035  | Konso     | P  | C   | 6   | F    | A  | Fa | H   | Sn  | Pn  | Ps   | A   | C  | Pc      | Fm   | C   | R   |
| 036  | Somali    | B  | H   | 5   | D    | D  | O  | (J) | P   | P   | Ps   | X   | K  | $M^W$c  | Fms  | C   | S   |
| 037  | Amhara    | P  | H   | 4   | (E)  | A  | O  | C   | Em  | P   | B    | (A) | Pc | Pc      | FM   | F   | Ap  |
| 038  | Bogo      | T  | (C) | 5   | C    | Dt | O  | F   | N   | P   | Ps   | (C) | Kc | P       | Fm   | X   | O   |
| 039  | Kenuzi    | P  | C   | 2   | •    | Fh | (A)| F   | N   | Pm  | Ps   | B   | C  | $Pc^W$  | FS   | X   | O   |
| 040  | Teda      | Bs | D   | 2   | A    | Ta | O  | F   | N   | Pm  | Ps   | C   | O  | PCm     | FSd  | O   | O   |
| 041  | Tuareg    | B  | Cd  | 1   | A    | Tu | R  | C   | (F)m| Ap  | Ms   | C   | K  | P       | M    | H   | L   |
| 042  | Riffians  | P  | D   | 5   | F    | Qf | T  | C   | En  | Pm  | Pl   | N   | O  | PC      | Sf   | C   | P   |
| 043  | Egyptians | P  | C   | 6   | G    | F  | T  | C   | Fn  | Pm  | Ps   | B   | K  | P       | F    | F   | Ri  |
| 044  | Hebrews   | P  | C   | 7   | G-   | F  | Tr | F   | Fn  | P   | Ps   | B   | R  | C       | Sf   | U   | Ps  |
| 045  | Babylonia | P  | C   | 8   | G    | F  | Tr | F   | N   | Pm  | B    | (B) | R  | C       | S    | U   | P   |
| 046  | Rwala     | B  | C   | (2) | B    | T  | O  | J   | P   | P   | Ps   | (A) | K  | Pm      | MF   | H   | •   |
| 047  | Turks     | P  | C   | 5   | E    | F  | Tr | F   | Fn  | P   | Pl   | B   | Kc | Pc      | FM   | F   | Ri  |
| 048  | Gheg      | T  | D   | (3) | E    | Rq | T  | F   | Fp  | P   | Ps   | C   | C  | $P^S$   | Fm   | F   | Rp  |
| 049  | Romans    | P  | C   | 8   | G    | F  | At | A   | M*  | P   | B    | B   | R  | CM      | SFM  | E   | (P) |
| 050  | Basques   | P  | P   | 6   | D    | Q  | T  | F   | Sm  | Pm  | B    | B   | O  | Cp      | Sm   | F   | R   |
| 051  | Irish     | P  | P   | 5   | E    | Q  | Et | H   | Sm  | Pn  | B    | B   | Ks | CP      | Sm   | X   | O   |
| 052  | Lapps     | B  | Dc  | 1   | C    | Ct | O  | F   | M   | Pm  | B    | C   | K  | Cp      | S    | H   | Pi  |
| 053  | Yurak     | B  | Cd  | 1   | A    | C  | O  | F   | Fn  | P   | Ps   | X   | Kr | M       | S    | H   | P   |
| 054  | Russians  | P  | P   | 6   | (D)  | Rq | A  | H   | M   | (N) | B    | A   | C  | CP      | MF   | F   | A   |
| 055  | Abkhaz    | P  | D   | (4) | E    | R  | O  | H   | En  | P   | Pc   | X   | K  | $Pm^S$  | Fs   | (F) | S   |
| 056  | Armenians | P  | C   | 5   | E    | Fq | Tr | H   | Em  | P   | Pl   | B   | IR | CP      | SF   | F   | R   |
| 057  | Kurd      | P  | P   | 6   | (F)  | F  | At | F   | Sn  | P   | Pl   | B   | C  | Cp      | FMs  | E   | A   |

| | 1 | 2 | 3 | 4 | 5 | 6 | 7 | 8 | 9 | 10 | 11 | 12 | 13 | 14 | 15 | 16 |
|---|---|---|---|---|---|---|---|---|---|---|---|---|---|---|---|---|
| 058 Basseri | B | Ch | 3 | C | T | O | F | N | Pn | Ps | B | K | Pc | F | H | P |
| 059 W Punjabi | P | C | 4 | F | F | At | F | Fm | P | Ps | C | R | CP | DF | F | Pi |
| 060 Gond | I | C | 2 | D | R | O | H | Fp | P | Ps | X | K | C | SFm | F | P |
| 061 Toda | R | C | 1 | E | H | O | F | Q | P | Ds | X | KR | CP | Sm | H | (P) |
| 062 Santal | P | C | 3 | F | Q | O | H | Fn | P | Ps | C | Rp | CP | SMf | F | Ps |
| 063 U Pradesh | P | P | 6 | G | Q | R | F | En | P | Pl | X | P | PC | SMd | F | L |
| 064 Burusho | P | C | 3 | C | F | F | F | Fn | P | Ps | A | (R) | C | Mf | F | A |
| 065 Kazak | S | Cd | 5 | C | Tf | O | C | Fp | P | Ps | X | K | P | MF | (F) | R |
| 066 Khalka | S | C | 1 | C | T | O | C | Sm | Pn | Ps | C | Ck | C<sup>w</sup>P | Fs | C | Ps |
| 067 Lolo | P | D | 3 | C | Qr | O | F | N | P | Ps | (C) | P | C | FS | H | L |
| 068 Lepcha | P | D | 3 | E | P | T | F | Fn | P | Ps | X | R | Cp | SF | F | Pr |
| 069 Garo | P | C | 4 | E | P | R | H | Sn | Ma | Ms | C | K | C | FMs | H | M |
| 070 Lakher | P | C | 4 | D | R | R | F | M | P | Ps | A | P | Pic | SFm | F | P |
| 071 Burmese | P | C | 5 | F | P | (T) | F | M | Mp | B | N | R | I | Df | F | Pr |
| 072 Lamet | T | C | 3 | A | P | A | H | P | Pm | Ps | A | R | CI | SF | F | P |
| 073 Vietnamese | P | Ch | 5 | G | Rq | T | H | Sn | P | P(s) | B | RI | C | SF | U | R |
| 074 Rhade | I | D | 5 | G | P | O | F | Fm | M | Ms | (B) | Ik | PC | SFm | F | (I) |
| 075 Khmer | P | C | 7 | E | P | Tr | F | N | (Nm) | B | (B) | Pr | Cp | MFd | U | Ps |
| 076 Siamese | P | C | 6 | F | Rp | T | F | N | M(n) | B | B | R | CP | Fd | F | I |
| 077 Semang | B | C | 1 | A | U | O | F | N | Pm | B | C | K | M | St | H | Si |
| 078 Nicobarese | P | H | 4 | E | B | A | F | N | Mp | B | A | R | P<sup>w</sup>m | MFs | F | I |
| 079 Andamanese | S | C | 1 | C | U | O | F | M | B | B | A | C | P | M | H | I |
| 080 Vedda | S | C | 1 | A | Ur | O | F | Fm | M | Ms | X | K | M | MS | O | O |
| 081 Tanala | Ri | C | 4 | (C) | P | A | C | Fn | P | Ps | C | R | Pm | Sfm | F | R |
| 082 N Sembilan | P | H | 6 | G | P | T | F | N | M | Ms | N | R | CP | DFs | F | R |
| 083 Javanese | P | C | 5 | G | Rq | R | F | N | Mp | B | C | Cr | PC | Fs | F | Rs |
| 084 Balinese | P | C | 5 | G | Q | At | H | Fm | P | Pl | B | R | C | Sm | C | R |
| 085 Iban | I | P | 2 | D | P | O | L | Sm | B | B | A | Cr | CP | Sf | F | I |
| 086 Badjau | B | C | 4 | A* | Z* | O | F | N | B | B | C | CK | Mp | Sm | H | Pi |

| | 1 | 2 | 3 | 4 | 5 | 6 | 7 | 8 | 9 | 10 | 11 | 12 | 13 | 14 | 15 | 16 |
|---|---|---|---|---|---|---|---|---|---|---|---|---|---|---|---|---|
| 087 Toradja | P | P | 3 | D | Pr | T | H | En | Mp | B | B | K | CP | FS | F | I |
| 088 Tobelorese | P | C | • | (D) | R | T | F | Fm | M | (B) | C | Ki | PM | DCf | F | • |
| 089 Alorese | P | Pc | 3 | G- | P | A | F | N | Pm | Ps | C | (C) | $P^{sc}$ | Sf | H | A |
| 090 Tiwi | B | D | 3 | B | U | O | F | P | Pm | Ds | A | K | P | Mf | O | O |
| 091 Aranda | B | D | 1 | B | U | O | F | P | P | Ds | X | R | $P^w_m$ | M | H | Ps |
| 092 Orokaiva | P | C | 2 | C | P | A | H | N | P | Pc | A | K | $P^w$ | FM | H | Ls |
| 093 Kimam | P | H | 5 | B | Rb | O | F | Fn | Pn | B | N | Ck | P | F | D | Ai |
| 094 Kapauku | P | D | 3 | F | R | R | F | Fp | P | Ps | X | K | I | FM | H | I |
| 095 Kwoma | P | H | 4 | E | R | T | H | P | P | Pl | B | Kr | Cpm | MF | C | Is |
| 096 Manus | P | C | 4 | E | P | (A) | F | N | Pm | Dl | B | Ks | P | Df | H | Is |
| 097 N Ireland | P | H | 4 | (D) | R | A | F | N | M | Ms | A | Kr | $P^w$ | Fm | F | Is |
| 098 Trobriands | P | C | 3 | E | E | Er | H | N | A | Ms | X | Pr | PCI | FDm | F | Ms |
| 099 Siuai | P | P | 2 | E | Rp | A | F | N | Ap | Ms | B | (K) | $Ip^s$ | Fd | F | Ai |
| 100 Tikopia | P | H | 5 | F | R | Tr | H | P | Pn | Ps | B | CI | $Cp^s$ | Fsd | D | Ps |
| 101 Pentecost | P | D | 2 | D | R | A | F | N | Pn | Ds | C | (K) | Pc | SF | C | S |
| 102 Fijians | P | C | 6 | G- | R | Tr | H | N | P | Ps | C | P | Mpc | CFs | U | Ps |
| 103 Ajie | P | C | 2 | C | Ar | A | M | P | P | Ps | X | KR | Mcp | SFm | F | Ps |
| 104 Maori | P | C | 3 | (B) | Rp | A | H | Fp | Pm | As | B | Ks | Mcp | Cfm | F | Ps |
| 105 Marquesans | P | D | 3 | E | R | Rf | H | Q | Nb | B | B | Ir | CMp | FCm | F | Pi |
| 106 Samoans | P | C | 4 | F | R* | A | C | En | Pm | B | C | Pr | MPc | Fmd | E | L |
| 107 Gilbertese | P | P | 4 | F | R | Ar | F | Fn | Pm | Al | A | Ck | $M^w p$ | FD | F | S |
| 108 Marshalls | P | D | 3 | F | R | R | C | En | M | Ms | (C) | Pk | P | M | E | M |
| 109 Trukese | P | H | 4 | G | Pr | A | C | En | Mp | Ms | B | K | Cm | Fm | D | Ms |
| 110 Yapese | P | P | 3 | E | Rp | A | H | Fn | Pa | Dl | A | S | $P^w$ | Dm | E | P |
| 111 Palauans | P | C | 2 | E | R | A | H | N | Ap | Ms | C | Pk | $I^w$ | Mfd | C | Ms |
| 112 Ifugao | P | H | 5 | F | P | O | F | N | B | B | A | Ck | Mic | Smf | O | O |
| 113 Atayal | I | Cd | 3 | D | R | O | H | Sm | Pn | As | A | Rk | MCp | SF | F | I |
| 114 Chinese | P | C | 6 | G | Q | E | F | Sm | P | Ps | C | Ik | $P^{sc^s}$ | Sf | D | I |
| 115 Manchu | P | C | 3 | (F) | Q | O | H | Fm | Pm | Ps | X | Kr | CMp | Sfm | F | R |

| | 1 | 2 | 3 | 4 | 5 | 6 | 7 | 8 | 9 | 10 | 11 | 12 | 13 | 14 | 15 | 16 |
|---|---|---|---|---|---|---|---|---|---|---|---|---|---|---|---|---|
| 116 Koreans | P | D | 3 | G | R | R | F | Sm | Pn | Pl | X | S | PC | Fsd | (D) | R |
| 117 Japanese | P | C | 3 | G | R | O | H | Sm | Pn | B | X | Sc | Cp | Fs | F | R |
| 118 Ainu | T | D | 1 | B | R | R | H | N | Pm | Ds | B | Kr | Mc | Sfm | H | Ps |
| 119 Gilyak | S | C | 2 | A | Sp | O | H | Sn | Pm | Ps | A | Rc | Ip | Sf | F | I |
| 120 Yukaghir | B | D | 2 | A | Cs | O | F | Sm | B | (B) | B | Kc | Mp | Sm | H | S |
| 121 Chuckchee | S | C | 1 | A | C | O | C | Fp | P | B | A | K | Cm | Sm | H | P |
| 122 Ingalik | R | Cd | 2 | A | Sre | A | A | N | Mp | B | A | Ir | Icp | DMf | C | S |
| 123 Aleut | T | C | 4 | D | S | O | F | Ep | Pm | P(s) | A | K | Cmp | Mf | H | (S) |
| 124 C Eskimo | S | Dc | 1 | A | Td | O | F | N | Nr | B | A | Kc | M | M | O | O |
| 125 Montagnais | S | Dc | 3 | A | C | O | F | En | Pm | B | B | Ki | Mp | FM | H | Pi |
| 126 Micmac | S | C | 1 | A | C | O | F | P | Nb | (B) | B | Cr | Mp | MFd | F | P |
| 127 Saulteaux | S | Dc | 3 | A | Drc | O | F | N | Pn | (Ps) | B | Ki | M | Ms | F | (Pi) |
| 128 Slave | Rt | C | 2 | B | Et | O | F | M | Pm | B | A | Ki | C | F | F | I |
| 129 Kaska | S | C | 1 | A | Ce | O | C | En | M | Ms | C | K | MPi | FDm | H | I |
| 130 Eyak | T | C | 1 | A | R | Ft | F | (F)p | A | Ms | A | (I) | Pm | Dfm | F | Mi |
| 131 Haida | T | C | 3 | B | R | O | F | En | A | Ms | X | K | Ipm | Dfm | H | Mi |
| 132 Bellacoola | P | C | 2 | (C) | Rp | R | F | Fn | Pm | Ac | B | KR | IFC | MDf | H | I |
| 133 Twana | S | Dc | 1 | E* | R | T | F | En | P | B | C | Ck | PIc | DFm | F | I |
| 134 Yurok | P | C | 1 | C | S | O | F | Fn | Pn | B | C | O | $C^{w}m$ | Mf | O | O |
| 135 E Pomo | T | D | 4 | C | D | T | A | Sn | B | B | A | Ik | PM | Mf | D | Mi |
| 136 Yokuts | T | Cd | 4 | D | Ec | R | L | (E)n | Pm | Ps | C | K | MP | M | D | Pi |
| 137 Wadadika | S | H | 3 | A | Cd | O | F | N | B | B | A | C | $Cm^{S}$ | M | H | I |
| 138 Klamath | S | D | 1 | B | Scd | R | H | Fn | Pm | B | A | Kc | M | M | H | I |
| 139 Kutenai | S | C | 3 | A | Ce | R | F | N | Mp | B | A | S | Mc | MSf | F | (D) |
| 140 G Ventre | B | C | 3 | A | C | O | F | N | Pm | B | X | Kr | I | SMf | H | I |
| 141 Hidatsa | T | C | 5 | A | Sc | O | F | Ep | Mp | Ms | N | Ks | I | Mst | C | I |
| 142 Pawnee | T | C | 4 | B | Sct | R | H | Ep | M | (B) | N | KR | Cm | FMc | F | Ps |
| 143 Omaha | T | C | 6 | C | Sc | O | F | N | B | Pl | (N) | RI | C | M | C | I |
| 144 Huron | Ti | C | 6 | E | H | A | F | Em | M | Ms | A | R | Mp | FMC | F | Mi |

| | 1 | 2 | 3 | 4 | 5 | 6 | 7 | 8 | 9 | 10 | 11 | 12 | 13 | 14 | 15 | 16 |
|---|---|---|---|---|---|---|---|---|---|---|---|---|---|---|---|---|
| 145 Creek | T | C | 4 | C | R | A | H | En | M | Ms | B | Ip | Cm | MFc | E | L |
| 146 Natchez | P | D | 5 | D | Q* | Tr | F | Ep | P | B | A | Rs | FWC | CFM | F | A |
| 147 Comanche | B | D | 4 | A | C | O | C | Ep | Pn | B | B | Cl | M | M | F | I |
| 148 Chiricahua | B | D | 2 | A | Dc | O | C | Fn | M | B | A | Cp | Pm | MF | F | I |
| 149 Zuni | P | P | 6 | C | F | O | F | Em | M | Ml | N | Ir | Cp | Ms | U | Mr |
| 150 Havasupai | S | Cd | 3 | A | D′ | O | C | Fn | Pm | B | N | IK | C | M | F | I |
| 151 Papago | R | Pd | 4 | E | Rd | A | F | Fn | P | B* | X | K | C^W pm | MDf | F | P |
| 152 Huichol | P | D | 4 | C | A | T | C | Fn | B | B | B | R | Cm | SFm | U | D |
| 153 Aztec | P | C | 8 | G | F | Tr | H | N | P | Al | B | Rp | Cm | CSm | U | L |
| 154 Popoluca | P | C. | 5 | E | R | T | H | P | Pm | B | • | Rs | Cip | Fms | F | R |
| 155 Quiche | P | P | 7 | (E) | Q | T | F | Fm | P | Pl | B | R | CP | SMf | E | R |
| 156 Miskito | P | C | 4 | (D) | Pr | O | H | Fn | M | B | A | R | P^Wc^W | FM | H | R |
| 157 Bribri | P | D | 2 | • | Cr | O | F | Fn | Mp | Ms | X | K | P | FM | H | I |
| 158 Cuna | P | C | 5 | E | R | A | H | En | M | B | B | Is | Pm | Fm | E | R |
| 159 Goajiro | B | H | 2 | B | R | O | C | Fp | Ma | Ms | A | Kc | Cpm | MF | H | Mi |
| 160 Haitians | P | P | 7 | F | Rq | T | C | Fn | Pn | B | B | Sr | M^S c | SM | F | A |
| 161 Callinago | I | C | 4 | D | E | A | I | Fp | Mp | B | C | K | MP | CFm | H | I |
| 162 Warrau | S. | C | 2 | B | Pr | O | F | Fn | M | B | B | Ik | Cp | MF | H | I |
| 163 Yanomamo | I | H | 3 | B | A | O | L | P | Pn | Ps | B | K | M^W | Fc | D | I |
| 164 Carib | I | D | 1 | A | R | R | H | N | Nm | B | A | Pk | Im | Fs | H | I |
| 165 Saramacca | P | C | 3 | D | R | O | J | P | Am | Ms | A | K | PC | SM | F | L |
| 166 Mundurucu | P | C | 3 | A | R | A | M | En | Mp | Ps | A | Is | M^W | Csm | H | P |
| 167 Cubeo | P | C | 1 | B | R | O | L | N | Pm | Ps | X | Kc | P^WI^W | FM | H | Ps |
| 168 Cayapa | P | P* | 5 | C | P | Rt | H | Fm | Bn | B | A | O | Cp | Fm | E | P |
| 169 Jivaro | I | D | 2 | B | R | O | F | Fp | Pm | B | B | Kc | Icp | fM | O | O |
| 170 Amahuaca | I | D | 1 | A | R | O | F | Sn | Pn | B | C | Kc | Pc | Cm | O | O |
| 171 Inca | P | C | (3) | D | Q | Fr | C | Fn | Pn | B | B | C | Cmp | Scm | F | P |
| 172 Aymara | P | (D) | 5 | F- | Q | O | C | Em | P | Pl | B | R | Cm^S | Sfm | H | I |
| 173 Siriono | S | Cd | 2 | A | Z*u | O | L | Ep | M | B | B | K | Pl | TMf | H | Ps |

| | 1 | 2 | 3 | 4 | 5 | 6 | 7 | 8 | 9 | 10 | 11 | 12 | 13 | 14 | 15 | 16 |
|---|---|---|---|---|---|---|---|---|---|---|---|---|---|---|---|---|
| 174 Nambicuara | S | Hc | 2 | B | Ub | O | F | P | Pm | B | B | K | Cpm | Mfs | H | I |
| 175 Trumai | P | C | 1 | A | H | O | A | En | P | B | B | I | C | M | H | P |
| 176 Timbira | I | C | 4 | C | Rb | O | F | Fm | M | Ms | N | Rk | Pc | Mf | C | R |
| 177 Tupinamba | I | C | 5 | B | H | O | L | .Ep | M | B | B | P | M$^w$p | Cfm | F | P |
| 178 Botocudo | B | D | 2 | A | Ud | O | F | Fn | • | B | X | (I) | M | (C)M | H | I |
| 179 Shavante | S | Ch | 4 | A | D | O | C | Fp | M | Ps | A | Kc | P | Mf | F | I |
| 180 Aweikoma | B | C | 1 | A | U | O | F | P* | B | B | B | C | P | MF | O | O |
| 181 Cayua | S | C | 1 | (B) | E | O | F | Fn | Pm | B | (A) | C | IP | Fm | H | I |
| 182 Lengua | B | C | 3 | A | U | O | F | Fn | Mp | B | A | R | PC | Mf | H | I |
| 183 Abipon | B | C | 4 | B | T | O | F | N | Nm | B | A | P | Mpc | MFt | H | Pi |
| 184 Mapuche | P | D | 2 | E | Qr | O | F | N* | Pm | Pl | C | Ir | Cmp | Sfm | H | P |
| 185 Tehuelche | B | C | 3 | A | T | O | F | Fn | P | B | A | P | Pm | Sfm | F | P |
| 186 Yahgan | B | D | 1 | B | C | O | F | N | Pm | B | X | K | P | Mf | H | Is |
| | | | | | | | | | | | | | | | | |
| 011a Chagga | P | D | 4 | D | B | O | J | P | P | Pc | X | K | P | Sf | H | I |
| 016a Katab | P | D | 5 | F | Z* | (T) | I | Fp | P | Ps | X | K | Cp | SFm | H | A |
| 034a Dorobo | B | D | 1 | C | D | O | F | N | P | Pc | X | K | P | F | C | S |
| 046a Lebanese | P | C | 5 | G | Fq | T | F | M | Pn | Pc | B | Kr | CP | Smf | F | R |
| 060a Chenchu | S | Cd | 1 | C | Ad | O | F | M | B | Ps | X | Kc | Cp | Sfm | F | Ip |
| 090a Murngin | B | Hc | 2 | A | Uh | O | F | P | Pm | Ds | X | RK | Pm | Mf | H | Ps |
| 106a Pukapuka | T | C | 3 | F | R | (O) | H | M | P | Dl | A | C | Mp | F | F | P |
| 141a Crow | S | C | 4 | A | C | O | F | P | P | Ms | B | C | Icm | Tsm | F | I |
| 175a Bororo | T | C | 3 | A | R | A | F | Fn | M | Ms | B | R | P | M | D | M |
| 179a Caraja | S | C | 1 | B | E | O | F | Fn | M | B | A | O | C$^w$p | MFt | H | P |
| 183a Mataco | B | C | 2 | B | D | O | F | Fn | Mp | B | A | C | Cpm | FM | H | R |

### Notes on Table 1

| | | |
|---|---|---|
| 025, | column 5: | Individual sleeping shelters. |
| 029, | column 15: | Ultimogeniture. |
| 049, | column 8: | Also concubines. |
| 106, | column 5: | But elliptical. |
| 133, | column 4: | Probably C in the pre-reservation period. |
| 146, | column 5: | But dome-shaped roof. |
| 151, | column 10: | But with nearly functionless patrilineal sibs and moieties. |
| 168, | column 2: | Village occupied only during festivals. |
| 173, | column 5: | But approaching E with four slopes. |
| 180, | column 8: | But also considerable polyandry. |
| 184, | column 8: | But substantial remnants of F |
| 016a, | column 5: | Modified from A. |

different meanings to such terms, and the same author even shifts inconsistently from one term to another in different portions of the same work. We have chosen to adhere rigorously to our own definitions regardless of the usage of the particular writer, for without consistent criteria comparison becomes impossible.

A third problem concerns the difference between ideal and actual behavior. For instance, the ideal family form may be a large extended family, but this may actually occur in only a small proportion of the population. In coding we consistently sought to isolate patterns of actual behavior rather than ideal norms. Statistics proved particularly useful in deciding such issues. In the absence of specific statistical evidence or strong verbal statements of frequency, the coders assumed, for example, a mere tendency toward exogamy, endogamy, or polygyny and avoided categorizing the society as fully exogamous, endogamous, or polygynous.

Some of the codes involved decisions regarding emphasis. For example, in coding community integration (Column 12 of Table 1), the emphasis was placed on the degree to which the particular item bound the members of the community to one another rather than on its social importance alone. Among the Bororo, for example, kinship, though prominent in the organization of the community, does not actually exert an integrating influence, while religion does. In coding for prominence of community ceremonials (Column 13 of Table 1), it was not the importance of the behavior for the individual but the prominence of the ceremony in the life of the community that received primary emphasis.

All of the above problems indicate the importance of complete ethnographies, with quantitative as well as descriptive data to provide an adequate basis for cross-cultural coding and theoretical generalizations. However great the theoretical interest of the subject, it does not lend itself to coding if such data are not available. The best solution to the problem of insufficient data is often to revise the codes in order to make them conform better to the kinds of data that ethnographers habitually report.

### SUBSTANTIVE FINDINGS

The coded data in Table 1 are capable of yielding a mass of intercorrelations, not only within the table but also in comparison with the coded data presented in other CCCCC publications, notably Murdock and Morrow (1970), Barry and Paxson (1971), and Tuden and Marshall (1972). Such intercorrelations will in general be reserved for a special volume, but a few interesting and suggestive examples are included herewith as a foretaste of what is to come.

As our first example we present in Table 2 an intercorrelation of the rules of descent and marital residence as tabulated in Columns 9 and 10 of Table 1.

Examination of Table 2 reveals that matrilineal descent is almost invariably found in association with either avunculocal or matrilocal (uxorilocal) residence, and that patrilocal (virilocal) residence regularly accompanies

**TABLE 2**

Intercorrelation of Rules of Descent and Residence

| Rule of Residence | Matrilineal Descent | Double Descent | Patrilineal Descent | Ambilineal Descent | Bilateral Descent | Total |
|---|---|---|---|---|---|---|
| Avunculocal | 7 | 1 | 0 | 0 | 0 | 8 |
| Matrilocal | 18 | 0 | 2 | 0 | 18 | 38 |
| Patrilocal | 1 | 9 | 70 | 6 | 32 | 118 |
| Ambilocal | 0 | 0 | 1 | 0 | 11 | 12 |
| Neolocal | 0 | 0 | 2 | 0 | 7 | 9 |
| Total | 26 | 10 | 75 | 6 | 68 | 185 |

patrilineal, ambilineal, and double descent (only six exceptions in 91 cases), whereas bilateral descent (more properly the absence of any rule affiliating an individual with the kin group or groups of an ancestor) coexists freely with all except the avunculocal rule of residence. Information is lacking only for marital residence among the Botocudo (#178). To the extent that the sample is representative of all known cultures—and it was expressly selected with this objective in mind—we may conclude that roughly 64 per cent of the peoples of the earth are patrilocal in residence, 21 per cent matrilocal, 6 per cent ambilocal, 5 per cent neolocal, and 4 per cent avunculocal. For descent, the comparable worldwide incidence is approximately 41 per cent patrilineal, 37 per cent bilateral, 14 per cent matrilineal, 5 per cent double (i.e., both patrilineal and matrilineal), and 3 per cent ambilineal.

In the nineteenth century, anthropologists and sociologists commonly agreed that forms of social organization could be arranged in an evolutionary sequence from a postulated original matrilineate, through a transition to patrilocal residence and patrilineal descent, to eventual cognatic descent with an equal recognition of kinship ties through both sexes. The senior author subjected this hypothesis to a statistical test in his first cross-cultural paper (Murdock 1937) and found it to be unacceptable. A more decisive test is now possible by correlating the coded data on descent in Column 10 of Table 1 with the data on subsistence economy assembled by Murdock and Morrow (1970).

The 186 societies of the sample are grouped by their prevailing rules of descent into three categories—Matrilineal, Patrilineal, and Cognatic. The Cognatic rubric combines the ambilineal and bilateral societies of Table 2. The societies with double descent are distributed between the Matrilineal and Patrilineal categories, being classed as matrilineal where residence is avunculocal, as patrilineal where residence is patrilocal. The same societies are classed by the prevailing mode of subsistence economy into the following categories:

Agricultural and/or Mercantile—where more than 50 per cent of the food supply is acquired by agriculture, intercommunity trade, or a combination of both.

Pastoral—where more of the food supply is derived from animal husbandry than from any other single subsistence technique.

Incipiently Agricultural—where more of the food supply is produced by agriculture than by any other subsistence technique but where its total amount is exceeded by that derived from the other techniques in combination.

Fishing—where more of the food supply is derived from fishing, including marine hunting and shellfishing, than from any other single subsistence technique. (Incidentally, the Tobelorese are now classified under this category since recoding of their subsistence economy indicates that it depends more strongly on fishing than on agriculture.)

Hunting and/or Gathering—where more of the food supply is derived from either hunting or gathering than from any other subsistence technique.

TABLE 3

Correlation of Descent with the Prevailing Subsistence Economy

| Subsistence Economy | Matrilineal Descent | Patrilineal Descent | Cognatic Descent | Total |
|---|---|---|---|---|
| Agricultural and/or Mercantile | 9 | 44 | 25 | 78 |
| Pastoral | 2 | 13 | 2 | 17 |
| Incipiently Agricultural | 10 | 16 | 16 | 42 |
| Fishing | 4 | 7 | 13 | 24 |
| Hunting and/or Gathering | 1 | 3 | 21 | 25 |
| Total | 26 | 83 | 77 | 186 |

The distribution of cases in Table 3 lends support to a number of evolutionary inferences. First, the fact that our sample reveals only a single instance of matrilineal descent among 25 societies of hunters and gatherers renders highly dubious the nineteenth century assumption of matrilineal priority. Second, the fact that 84 per cent of these societies (21 out of 25) are characterized by cognatic descent argues against the frequency, if not the existence, of any form of unilinear descent during the many millennia when men, in the absence of agriculture and animal husbandry, subsisted by food gathering alone. Third, matrilineal descent reaches its highest frequency at the intermediate evolutionary level of incipient agriculture and declines with the rise of food production to a dominant position. Fourth, patrilineal descent clearly reflects the domestication of large animals, as is shown by its occurrence among 77 per cent (13 out of 17) of the pastoral societies of our sample, as well as by the attested importance of large domesticated animals in the economies of 21 of the 44 agricultural-mercantile societies which are patrilineal.

A third example of our substantive findings contrasts with the second in confirming rather than negating a unilinear evolutionary sequence. Table 4 correlates the categories of subsistence economy defined for Table 3 with the data on population density presented in Column 4 of Table 1. With three of the sample societies omitted for insufficiency of evidence—the Kenuzi Nubians (#37), Tobelorese (#88), and Bribri (#157)—Table 4

TABLE 4

Correlation of Population Density with Type of Subsistence Economy

| Mean Population Density | Agric.-Mercant. | Incip. Agric. | Pastoral | Fishing | Hunting-Gathering | Total |
|---|---|---|---|---|---|---|
| More than 500 persons per square mile | 14 | 4 | 0 | 1 | 0 | 19 |
| 100 to 499 persons per square mile | 15 | 4 | 0 | 1 | 0 | 20 |
| 25 to 99 persons per square mile | 23 | 9 | 2 | 1 | 0 | 35 |
| 5 to 24.9 persons per square mile | 14 | 9 | 1 | 2 | 0 | 26 |
| One to 4.9 persons per square mile | 6 | 7 | 7 | 3 | 2 | 25 |
| Fewer than one per square mile to one per five square miles | 2 | 5 | 2 | 5 | 8 | 22 |
| Fewer than one person per five square miles | 3 | 3 | 5 | 10 | 15 | 36 |
| Total | 77 | 41 | 17 | 23 | 25 | 183 |

demonstrates a marked tendency for mean population density to increase in direct proportion to the complexity of the prevailing techniques of food acquisition or production.

Fourth, we should like to call attention to a striking anomaly in the world distribution of household forms. In presenting the data in Table 5 we have combined two subtypes of multi-family households distinguished in Column 7 of Table 1—longhouses (L) and apartment houses (A)—and have likewise combined three subtypes of mother-child households, namely, those in which married men reside in separate individual dwellings (I) or a special men's house (M) or else rotate among the houses of their plural wives (J). We have, however, retained the distinction between three subtypes of family households—single dwellings (F), homesteads (H), and compounds (C).

Although multi-family households are mainly confined to the New World, the most striking regional disparity is the concentration of mother-child households in Africa. This is clearly less a geographic than an ethnic phenomenon, for the mother-child family does not occur in the non-Negro societies of Africa (the Bushmen, Hottentot, Hadza, and Pygmies), is characteristic of 18 of the 24 Negro societies of that continent in the sample, extends to five Negro tribes in the immediately adjacent Circum-Mediterranean (the Fur, Hausa, Somali, Wodaabe Fulani, and Wolof), and is also reported for the Saramacca Bush Negroes of South America. In short, of the 28 occurrences of such households in our entire sample, 24 are among peoples who are specifically Negro in race.

The tendency toward the exclusion of the father in the several subtypes of mother-child households contributes toward lessening the father's role

TABLE 5
Distribution of Household Forms by World Regions

| World Region | Multi-Family Households | Family Households | | | Mother-Child Households | Total |
|---|---|---|---|---|---|---|
| | | Single Dwelling | Home-stead | Compound | | |
| Africa (sub-Saharan) | 0 | 6 | 1 | 3 | 18 | 28 |
| Circum-Mediterranean | 1 | 11 | 6 | 4 | 6 | 28 |
| East Eurasia | 0 | 21 | 9 | 4 | 0 | 34 |
| Insular Pacific | 1 | 14 | 12 | 3 | 1 | 31 |
| North America | 3 | 20 | 5 | 5 | 0 | 33 |
| South America | 5 | 15 | 4 | 5 | 3 | 32 |
| Total | 10 | 87 | 37 | 24 | 28 | 186 |

in the care and socialization of infants and young children. Barry and Paxson (1971: Table 1, Column 14) have coded the closeness of the father's relationship to the child in the early years of life for the societies of our sample under the following categories:

1. No close proximity.
2. Rare instances of close proximity.
3. Occasional or irregular close proximity.
4. Frequent close proximity.
5. Regular, close relationship or companionship.

Comparison of their findings (averaging their codes for infancy and early childhood) with our own classification of mother-child households as opposed to other household forms (from Table 5) yields the striking correlation presented in Table 6.

TABLE 6
Relationship of Father to Young Child in Societies with Mother-Child Households As Opposed to Other Household Types

| Relationship of Father to Young Child | In Societies with Mother-Child Households | In Societies with Other Types of Households |
|---|---|---|
| Remote (coded 1 or 1.5) | 6 | 3 |
| Rather remote (coded 2 or 2.5) | 7 | 19 |
| Intermediate (coded 3) | 9 | 36 |
| Rather close (coded 3.5) | 4 | 27 |
| Close (coded 4, 4.5, or 5) | 0 | 53 |
| Coding average per society | 2.5 | 3.35 |

Our startling and wholly unexpected discovery of a nearly exclusive association between mother-child households and societies that are Negro in race draws attention to the now extensive literature on the so-called "matrifocal family" among American Negroes, especially in the Caribbean area. Our data confirm the earlier view, e.g., of Herskovits, that the matrifocal family is basically an "Africanism" imported into the New World with the slave trade. Though doubtless perpetuated there by the conditions of slavery and low economic status, these cannot account for its origin, as various recent authors have maintained. The ultimate explanation must be sought in the social and economic conditions which gave rise to the mother-child household as the predominant indigenous form of family organization in Africa. Among these are the widespread occurrence of polygyny and slavery, both of which are appreciably more prevalent in Negro Africa than in any other major region of the world.

## REFERENCES CITED

Barry, H., III, and L. M. Paxson. 1971. Infancy and Early Childhood: Cross-Cultural Codes 2. Ethnology 10: 466-508.

Murdock, G. P. 1937. Correlations of Matrilineal and Patrilineal Institutions. Studies in the Science of Society, ed. G. P. Murdock, pp. 445-470. New Haven.

——— 1967. Ethnographic Atlas. Pittsburgh. (See also installments in Ethnology 1-10.

Murdock, G. P., C. S. Ford, A. E. Hudson, R. Kennedy, L. W. Simmons, and J. W. M. Whiting. 1945. Outline of Cultural Materials. New Haven.

Murdock, G. P., and D. O. Morrow. 1970. Subsistence Economy and Supportive Practices: Cross-Cultural Codes 1. Ethnology 9: 302-330.

Tuden, A., and C. Marshall. 1972. Political Organization: Cross-Cultural Codes 4. Ethnology 11 (forthcoming).

## IDENTIFICATION AND BIBLIOGRAPHY

The societies for which coded data were presented in Table 1 are listed below. Each is located (L) by its approximate geographical co-ordinates. The unit selected for analysis as the "community," whether focal (F) or typical (T), is identified or defined, with an indication of the date for which data were sought. For each society the bibliographical source listed first is that found to contain the fullest and most satisfactory information on the coded topics. Full citations are also given for other useful sources not cited in the previously published codes—Murdock and Morrow (1970), Barry and Paxson (1971)—arranged roughly in the order of their adjudged usefulness. If cited in either of these earlier works, additional sources are listed only in abbreviated form by author and date, with numbers inserted in parentheses, where necessary, to indicate their position in the adjudged rank order of usefulness. Omitted entirely are standard reference works consulted, such as atlases and encyclopedias, as well as all sources analyzed but found to contain little information not also available in the references cited.

1. Nama Hottentot. L: 27°30′S, 17°E. T: "clan" of the Gei //Khauan tribe in 1860.

Schapera, I. 1930. The Khoisan Peoples. London.

Hoernlé, A. W. 1925. The Social Organization of the Nama Hottentots. American Anthropologist 27: 1-24.

Murdock, G. P. 1934. Our Primitive Contemporaries, pp. 475-507. New York.
Schultze 1907 (4).

2. Kung Bushmen. L: 19°50'S, 20°35'E. T: band of the Nyae Nyae region in 1950.
Marshall, L. 1965. The !Kung Bushmen of the Kalahari Desert. Peoples of Africa, ed. J. L. Gibbs, Jr., pp. 241-278. New York.

3. Thonga. L: 25°50'S, 32°20'E. T: village of the Ronga subtribe in 1895.
Junod, H. A. The Life of a South African Tribe. 2d edit. 2v. London.

4. Lozi. L: 14° to 18°S, 22° to 25°E. T: "royal village" in 1900.
Gluckman, M. 1951. The Lozi of Barotseland. Seven Tribes of British Central Africa, ed. E. Colson and M. Gluckman, pp. 1-93. London.
Bertrand, A. 1899. The Kingdom of the Barotsi. London.

5. Mbundu. L: 12°15'S, 16°30'E. T: village of the Bailundo subtribe in 1890.
Childs, G. M. 1949. Umbundu Kinship and Character. London.
Edwards, A. C. 1962. The Ovimbundu Under Two Sovereignties. London.
Hambly 1934 (3).

6. Suku. L: 6°S, 18°E. T: "lineage center" in Feshi Territory in 1920.
Kopytoff, I. 1965. The Suku of Southwestern Congo. Peoples of Africa, ed. J. L. Gibbs, Jr., pp. 441-477. New York.
———— 1961. Extension of Conflict as a Method of Conflict Resolution Among the Suku of the Congo. Journal of Conflict Resolution 5: 61-69.
Kopytoff 1964 (2).

7. Bemba. L: 9° to 12°S, 29° to 32°E. T: village in Zambia in 1897.
Richards, A. I. 1951. The Bemba of North-eastern Rhodesia. Seven Tribes of British Central Africa, ed. E. Colson and M. Gluckman, pp. 164-191. London.
———— 1940. The Political System of the Bemba Tribe. African Political Systems, ed. M. Fortes and E. E. Evans-Pritchard, pp. 83-120. Oxford.
———— 1950. Some Types of Family Structure Amongst the Central Bantu. African Systems of Kinship and Marriage, ed. A. R. Radcliffe-Brown and D. Forde, pp. 206-251. London.
Delhaise, C. 1908. Chez les Wabemba. Bulletin de la Société Royale Belge de Géographie 32: 173-227, 261-283.
Gouldsbury and Sheane 1911 (3).

8. Nyakyusa. L: 9°30'S, 34°E. T: age village near Mwaya and Masoko in 1934.
Wilson, M. 1951. Good Company. London.
Wilson, G. 1951. The Nyakyusa of South-Western Tanganyika. Seven Tribes of British Central Africa, ed. E. Colson and M. Gluckman, pp. 253-201. Oxford.

9. Hadza. L: 3°20' to 4°10'S, 34°40' to 35°25'E. T: "camp" in 1930.
Woodburn, J. 1964. The Social Organization of the Hadza of North Tanzania. Ph.D. dissertation, University of Cambridge.
———— 1968. Stability and Flexibility in Hadza Residential Groupings. Man the Hunter, ed. R. B. Lee and I. DeVore, pp. 103-110. Chicago.
Kohl-Larsen 1958 (3).

10. Luguru. L: 6°50'S, 37°40'E. T: hamlet cluster around Morogoro in 1925.
Young, R., and H. Fosbrooke. 1960. Land and Politics Among the Luguru of Tanganyika. London.
Christensen, J. B. 1963. Utani: Joking, Sexual License and Social Obligations Among the Luguru. American Anthropologist 65: 1314-1327.
McVicar, J. n.d. Notes on the Waluguru. Ms.
Beidelman 1967 (2); Scheerder and Tastevin 1950 (4).

11. Kikuyu. L: 0°40'S, 37°10'E. T: *mbari* settlement in the Fort Hall district in 1920.
Middleton, J. 1953. The Kikuyu and Kamba of Kenya. London.
Lambert, H. E. 1956. Kikuyu Social and Political Institutions. London.
Kenyatta 1939 (2).

12. Ganda. L: 0°20′N, 32°30′E. T: neighborhood in the Kyaddondo district in 1875.
Southwold, M. 1965. The Ganda. Peoples of Africa, ed. J. L. Gibbs, Jr., pp. 81-118. New York.
Murdock, G. P. 1934. Our Primitive Contemporaries, pp. 508-550. New York.
Roscoe 1911 (2).
13. Mbuti Pygmies. L: 1°30′ to 2°N, 28°20′E. T: band of net-hunters in 1950.
Turnbull, C. N. 1965. Wayward Servants. New York.
14. Nkundo Mongo. L: 0°15′ to 1°15′S, 18°35′ to 19°45′E. T: village of the Ilanga group in 1930.
Hulstaert, G. 1938. Le mariage des Nkundó. Mémoires de l'Institut Royal Colonial Belge 8: 1-520. Brussels.
Boelaert, E. 1940. De Nkundu-maatschappij. Kongo-Overzee 6: 148-161.
Brepoels, H. 1930. Het familiehoofd bij de Nkundo negers. Congo 11: ii, 332-430.
15. Banen. L: 4°35′ to 4°45′N, 10°35′ to 11°E. T: clan territory of the Ndiki subtribe in 1935.
McCulloch, M., M. Littlewood, and I. Dugast. 1954. Peoples of the Central Cameroons. London.
16. Tiv. L: 6°30′ to 8°N, 8° to 10°E. T: *tar* of Benue province in 1920.
Bohannan, P., and L. Bohannan. 1953. The Tiv of Central Nigeria. London.
Bohannan, L. 1957. Political Aspects of Tiv Social Organization. Tribes Without Rulers, ed. J. Middleton and D. Tait, pp. 33-36. London.
17. Ibo. L: 5°30′N, 7°20′E. T: village group of the Isu-Ama division in 1935.
Green, M. M. 1947. Ibo Village Affairs. London.
Forde, D., and G. I. Jones. 1950. The Ibo and Ibibio-speaking Peoples. London.
Uchendu 1965 (2).
18. Fon. L: 7°12′N, 1°56′E. F: city and environs of Abomey in 1890.
Herskovits, M. J. 1938. Dahomey. 2v. New York.
Murdock, G. P. 1934. Our Primitive Contemporaries, pp. 551-595. New York.
Argyle, W. J. 1966. The Fon of Dahomey. London.
Herskovits, M. J. 1932. Some Aspects of Dahomean Ethnology. Africa 5: 266-296.
19. Ashanti. L: 6° to 8°N, 0° to 3°W. T: village of Kumasi state in 1895.
Rattray, R. S. 1923. Ashanti. Oxford.
Fortes, M., R. W. Steel, and P. Ady. 1947. Ashanti Survey, 1945-46. Geographical Journal 110: 149-179.
Fortes, M. 1949. Time and Social Structure: An Ashanti Case Study. Social Structure, ed. M. Fortes, pp. 54-84.
Fortes 1950 (2); Rattray 1927 (4); Rattray 1929 (5); Busia 1951 (6).
20. Mende. L: 7°50′N, 12°W. T: *kuwui* or "compound" near the town of Bo in 1945.
Little, K. L. 1951. The Mende of Sierra Leone. London.
―――― 1948. The Mende Farming Household. Sociological Review 40: 37-56.
McCulloch 1950 (3).
21. Wolof. L: 13°45′N, 15°20′E. T: village of Upper and Lower Salum in 1950.
Ames, D. W. 1953. Plural Marriage Among the Wolof in the Gambia. Ph.D. dissertation, Northwestern University.
Gamble 1957; Ames 1959; Ames 1962.
22. Bambara. L: 12°30′N, 6° to 8°W. T: village between Segou and Bamako in 1902.
Monteil, C. 1924. Les Bambara du Ségou et du Kaarta. Paris.
Pacques 1954.
23. Tallensi. L: 10°38′N, 0°35′W. T: neighborhood in 1934.
Fortes, M. 1945. The Dynamics of Clanship Among the Tallensi. London.
―――― 1949. The Web of Kinship Among the Tallensi. London.

———— 1940. The Political System of the Tallensi. African Political Systems, ed. M. Fortes, and E. E. Evans-Pritchard, pp. 239-271. London.

24. Songhai. L: 16° to 17°15′N, 0°10′ to 3°10′W. T: village in the Bamba division in 1940.
Rouch, J. 1954. Les Songhay. Paris.
Proust, A. 1954. Notes sur les Songhay. Bulletin de l'Institut Français de l'Afrique Noire, ser. 3, 16: 167-213.

25. Wodaabe Fulani. L: 13° to 17°N, 5° to 10°E. T: "fraction" in 1951.
Stenning, D. J. 1965. The Pastoral Fulani of Northern Nigeria. Peoples of Africa, ed. J. L. Gibbs, Jr., pp. 361-401. New York.
———— 1959. Savannah Nomads. London.
———— 1958. Household Variability Among the Pastoral Fulani. Cambridge Papers in Social Anthropology 1: 92-119.
Dupire 1962 (3).

26. Zazzagawa Hausa. L: 9°30′ to 11°30′N, 6° to 9°E. T: village in 1900.
Smith, M. G. 1965. The Hausa of Northern Nigeria. Peoples of Africa, ed. J. L. Gibbs, Jr., pp. 119-155. New York.
———— 1960. Government in Zazzau. London.
Dry, D. P. L. 1956. Some Aspects of Hausa Family Structure. Proceedings of the International West African Conference held at Ibadan, 1949, pp. 158-163.

27. Massa. L: 10° to 11°N, 15° to 16°E. T: neighborhood in Cameroon in 1910.
Hagen, F. von. 1912. Die Bana. Baessler-Archiv 2: 77-116.
De Garine 1964; Lembezat 1961.

28. Azande. L: 4°20′ to 5°50′N, 27°40′ to 28°50′E. T: district of the Yambio chiefdom in 1905.
Baxter, P. T. W., and A. Butt. 1954. The Azande and Related Peoples of the Anglo-Egyptian Sudan and Belgian Congo. London.
Evans-Pritchard 1937; Seligman and Seligman 1932; Larkin 1926-27.

29. Fur. L: 13°30′N, 25°30′E. T: village near Jebel Marra in 1880.
Beaton, A. C. 1948. The Fur. Sudan Notes and Records 29: 1-39.
Barth, F. 1967. Economic Spheres in Darfur. Themes in Economic Anthropology, ed. R. Firth. Association for Social Anthropology Monographs 6.
Felkin 1885 (2); Muhammad Ibn Umar, al-Tūnusi 1845 (3).

30. Otoro Nuba. L: 11°20′N, 30°40′E. T: "hill community" in 1930.
Nadel, S. F. 1947. The Nuba. London.

31. Shilluk. L: 9° to 10°30′N, 31° to 32°E. T: "village group" in 1910.
Seligman, C. G., and B. Z. Seligman. 1932. Pagan Tribes of the Nilotic Sudan. London.
Howell, P. P. 1941. The Shilluk Settlement. Sudan Notes and Records 24: 47-66.
Pumphrey, M. E. C. 1941. The Shilluk Tribe. Sudan Notes and Records 24: 1-45.
Butt, A. 1952. The Nilotes of the Anglo-Egyptian Sudan and Uganda. London.
Hofmayr 1925 (2).

32. Mao. L: 9° to 9°35′N, 34°30′ to 34°50′E. T: localized clan among the Northern Mao in 1939.
Grottanelli, V. L. 1940. I Mao. Missione Etnografica nel Uollaga Occidentale 1: 1-387. Rome.
Cerulli 1956.

33. Kaffa. L: 6°50′ to 7°45′N, 35°30′ to 37°30′E. T: neighborhood in 1905.
Bieber, F. J. 1920-23. Kaffa. 2v. Münster.
Huntingford, G. W. B. 1955. The Kingdoms of Kafa and Janjero. London.

34. Masai. L: 1°30′ to 5°30′S, 35° to 37°30′E. T: district in Tanzania in 1900.
Merker, M. 1904. Die Masai. Berlin.

Baumann, O. 1894. Durch Massailand zur Nilquelle. Berlin.
Huntingford 1953 (2).

35. Konso. L: 5°15'N, 37°30'E. F: town of Buso.
Hallpike, C. R. 1969. The Konso of Ethiopia. Ms.
Jensen 1936.

36. Somali. L: 7° to 11°N, 45°30' to 49°E. T: "encampment" of the Dolba-hanta subtribe in 1900.
Lewis, I. M. 1961. A Pastoral Democracy. London.
——— 1962. Marriage and the Family in Northern Somaliland. Kampala: East African Institute for Social and Economic Research.

37. Amhara. L: 11° to 14°N, 36° to 38°30'E. T: *mandar* of the Gondar district in 1953.
Messing, S. D. 1957. The Highland-Plateau Amhara of Ethiopia. Ph.D. dissertation, University of Pennsylvania.

38. Bogo. L: 15°45'N, 38°45'E. T: village in 1855.
Munzinger, W. 1859. Ueber die Sitten und das Recht der Bogos. Winterthur.

39. Kenuzi Nubians. L: 22° to 24°N, 38°45'E. T: village in Dahmit in 1900.
Fernea, R. A., ed. 1966. Contemporary Egyptian Nubia. 2v. New Haven.
Herzog 1957.

40. Teda. L: 19° to 22°N, 16° to 19°E. T: nomadic band in Tibesti in 1950.
Chapelle, J. 1957. Nomades noirs du Sahara. Paris.
Nachtigal, G. 1877. Sahara und Sudan 1: 377-464 Berlin.
Fuchs 1956 (2); Cline 1950 (3); Briggs 1958 (5).

41. Tuareg. L: 21° to 25°N, 4° to 9°E. T: "section" in Ahaggar in 1900.
Nicolaisen, J. 1963. Ecology and Culture of the Pastoral Tuareg. National-museets Skrifter, Etnografisk Raeke 9: 1-540. Copenhagen.
Lhote, H. 1944. Les Touaregs du Hoggar. Paris.
Briggs, L. L. 1958. The Living Races of the Sahara Desert. Papers of the Peabody Museum, Harvard University 28: ii, 1-217.

42. Riffians. L:34°20' to 35°30'N, 2°30' to 4°W. T: village in 1926.
Hart, D. M. 1954. An Ethnographic Survey of the Riffian Tribe of Aith Waryaghil Tamuda 1: 55-86. Tetuan.
Moulieras, A. 1895. Le Maroc inconnu, 1: Exploration du Rif. Paris.
Coon 1931 (2).

43. Egyptians. L: 24°45'N, 33°E. F: town and environs of Silwa in 1950.
Ammar, H. 1954. Growing Up in an Egyptian Village. London.
Ayrout 1945.

44. Hebrews. L: 30°30' to 31°55'N, 34°20' to 35°30'E. F: city of Jerusalem in 621 B.C.
DeVaux, R. 1961. Ancient Israel. New York.
Holy Bible; Dalman 1932; Patai 1961.

45. Babylonians. L: 32°35'N, 44°45'E. F: city and environs of Babylon in 1750 B.C.
Driver, G. R., and J. C. Miles. 1952-55. The Babylonian Laws. 2v. Oxford.
Thompson, R. C. 1923. The Golden Age of Hammurabi. Cambridge Ancient History 1: 494-551. New York.

46. Rwala. L: 31° to 35°30'N, 36° to 41°E. T: Bedouin camp in 1913.
Musil, A. 1928. The Manners and Customs of the Rwala Bedouin. New York.
Raswan, C. R. 1947. Black Tents of Arabia. New York.
Ashkenazi, T. 1948. The 'Anazah Tribes. Southwestern Journal of Anthropology 4: 222-239.

47. Turks. L: 38°40' to 40°N, 32°40' to 35°50'E. T: village in Anatolia in 1950.
Stirling, P. 1965. Turkish Village. London.
——— 1953. Social Ranking in a Turkish Village. British Journal of Sociology 4: 31-44.
Stirling 1963 (2)

48. Gheg Albanians. L: 41°20' to 42°40'N, 19°30' to 20°50'E. T: village in 1910.
Coon, C. S. 1950. The Mountain of Giants. Papers of the Peabody Museum, Harvard University 23: iii, 1-150.

Hasluck, M.   1954.   The Unwritten Law in Albania. Cambridge.
49. Romans.   L: 41°40'N, 13°30'E. F: city and environs of Rome in A.D. 110.
Carcopino, J.   1940.   Daily Life in Ancient Rome, ed. H. T. Howell. New Haven.
Abbott, F. F.   1917.   Common People of Ancient Rome. New York.
Friedländer 1908 (2).
50. Basques.   L: 43°15'N, 1°40'W. F: village of Vera de Bidasoa in Spain in 1940.
Caro Baroja, J.   1944.   La vida rural en Vera de Bidasoa. Madrid.
Caro Baroja 1944; Douglass 1969.
51. Irish.   L: 53°30'N, 10°W. F: village of Carraroe, County Galway, in 1970.
Kane, E.   1970.   An Analysis of the Cultural Factors Inimical to the Develop-
ment of the Nationalistic-Revivalistic Industrial Process of Rural Irish
Gaeltachts. Ph.D. dissertation, University of Pittsburgh.
———   1972.   Personal communication.
52. Lapps.   L: 68°20' to 69°5'N, 20°5' to 23°E. T: band in Könkämä district in 1950.
Pehrson, R. N.   1957.   The Bilateral Network of Social Relations in Könkämä
Lapp District. Indiana University Publications, Slavic and East European
Series 5: 1-128.
———   1954.   The Lappish Herding Leader. American Anthropologist 56:
1076-1080.
———   Reindeer Herding Among the Karesuando Lapps. American-Scandinavian
Review 39: 271-279.
Whitaker, I.   1955.   Social Relations in a Nomadic Lappish Community.
Uigitt af Norsk Folkmuseum 2: 1-178.
Haglund 1935 (5).
53. Yurak Samoyed.   L: 65° to 71°N, 41° to 62°E. T: nomadic camp in 1894.
Englehardt, E. A.   1899.   A Russian Province of the North. Westminster.
Hajdu, P.   1963.   Samoyed Peoples and Languages. Indiana University Publica-
cations, Uralic and Altaic Series 14: 1-114.
Castrén, M. A.   1853.   Reiseerrinnerungen aus den Jahren 1838-1844. St. Peters-
burg.
Rae, E.   1875.   The Land of the North Wind. London.
Islavin 1847 (2); Jackson 1895 (6).
54. Russians.   L: 52°40'N, 41°20'E. F: peasant village of Viriatino in 1955.
Dunn, S. P., and E. Dunn.   1967.   The Peasants of Central Russia. New York.
Dunn, E.   1971.   The Importance of Religion in the Soviet Rural Community.
The Soviet Rural Community, ed. J. R. Millar, pp. 346-375. Urbana.
Dunn, S. P., 1971 (2).
55. Abkhaz.   L: 42°50' to 43°25'N, 40° to 41°35'E. T: village in 1880.
Dzhanashvili, M. G.   1894.   Abkhaziya i Abkhaztsy. Zapiski Kavkazkago
Otdiela Inperalorskago Russkago Geograficheskago Obschestva 16: 1-59.
Tiflis.
Lotz, J.   1956.   The Caucasus. 2v. New Haven.
Byhan 1926 (3); Lutzbetak 1951 (4).
56. Armenians.   L: 40°N, 44°30'E. T: village in the vicinity of Erevan in 1843.
Haxthausen, A. von.   1854.   Transcaucasia. London.
Karst, J.   1906-07.   Grundriss der Geschichte des armenischen Rechtes.
Zeitschrift für Vergleichende Rechtswissenschaft 19: 313-422; 20: 14-112.
Lynch 1901 (2); Klidschian 1911 (3).
57. Kurd.   L: 36°30'N, 44°30'E. F: the town and environs of Rowanduz in 1951.
Masters, W. M.   1953.   Rowanduz. Ph.D. dissertation, University of Michigan.
58. Basseri.   L: 27° to 31°N, 53° to 54°E. T: nomadic camp in 1958.
Barth, F. K.   1961.   Nomads of South Persia. London.
59. West Punjabi.   L: 32°30'N, 74°E. F: village of Mohla in 1950.
Eglar, Z. S.   1960.   A Punjabi Village in Pakistan. New York.
60. Gond.   L: 19°15' to 20°N, 80°30' to 81°20'E. T: Hill Maria village in 1930.
Grigson, W. V.   1938.   The Maria Gonds of Bastar. London.
61. Toda.   L: 11° to 12°N, 76° to 77°E. T: village in 1900.
Rivers, W. H. R.   1906.   The Todas. London.

Murdock, G. P. 1934. Our Primitive Contemporaries, pp. 107-134. New York.

Emeneau, M. B. 1941. Language and Social Forms: A Study of Toda Kinship Terms and Double Descent. Language, Culture and Personality, ed. L. Spier *et al.,* pp. 158-179. Menasha.

62. Santal. L: 23° to 24°N, 86°50′ to 87°30′ E. T: village in 1940.

Datta-Majumder, N. 1956. The Santal. Memoirs of the Department of Anthropology, Government of India 2: 1-150.

Culshaw, W. J. 1949. Tribal Heritage. London.

63. Uttar Pradesh. L: 25°55′N, 83°E. F: village and environs of Senapur in 1945.

Luschinsky, M. S. 1963. The Life of Women in a Village of North India. Ph.D. dissertation, Cornell University.

Cohn, B. S. n.d. Chamar Family in a North Indian Village. Ms.

Opler, M. E. 1956. The Extensions of an Indian Village. Journal of Asian Studies 16: 5-10.

Cohn, B. S. 1958. Changing Traditions of a Low Caste. Journal of American Folklore 71: 412-421.

Opler and Singh 1954 (2); Opler and Singh 1952 (6).

64. Burusho. L: 36°25′N, 74°35′E. T: village in Hunza state in 1934.

Lorimer, E. O. 1939. Language Hunting in the Karakoram. London.

Tobe, J. H. 1960. Hunza: Adventures in a Land of Paradise. Emmaus.

Clark 1963 (3).

65. Kazak. L: 37° to 48°N, 68° to 81°E. T: winter settlement of the Great Horde in 1885.

Grodekov, N. I. 1889. Kirgizy i Karakirgizy Syr Dar'inskoi Oblasti. Tashkent.

Hudson 1938; Murdock 1934.

66. Khalka Mongols. L: 47° to 47°20′N, 95°10′ to 97°E. T: camp in Narobanchin territory in 1920.

Vreeland, H. H. 1954. Mongol Community and Kinship Structure. New Haven.

67. Lolo. L: 26° to 29°N, 103° to 104°E. T: village in Taliang Shan mountains in 1910.

Lin, Y. H. 1961. The Lolo of Liang Shan. Shanghai.

LeBar, F. M., G. C. Hickey, and J. K. Musgrave. 1964. Ethnic Groups of Mainland Southeast Asia, pp. 19-27. New Haven.

D'Ollone 1912 (3).

68. Lepcha. L: 27° to 28°N, 89°E. F: village and environs of Lingthem in 1937.

Gorer, G. 1938. Himalayan Village. London.

Das, A. K., and S. K. Banerjee. 1962. The Lepchas of Darjeeling District. Calcutta.

Morris 1938 (2).

69. Garo. L: 26°N, 91°E. F: village and environs of Rengsanggri in 1955.

Burling, R. 1963. Rengsanggri. Philadelphia.

70. Lakher. L: 22°20′N, 93°E. T: village in 1930.

Parry, N. E. 1932. The Lakhers. London.

71. Burmese. L: 22°N, 95°40′E. F: village of Nondwin in 1960.

Nash, M. 1965. The Golden Road to Modernity, New York.

———— 1963. Burmese Buddhism in Everyday Life. American Anthropologist 65: 285-295.

Brohm, J. 1963. Buddhism and Animism in a Burmese Village. Journal of Asian Studies 22: 155-167.

72. Lamet. L: 20°N, 100°40′E. F: village of Mokola Panghay in 1940.

Izikowitz, K. G. 1951. Lamet. Etnologiska Studier 17: 1-375. Göteborg.

73. Vietnamese. L: 20° to 21°N, 105°30′ to 107°E. T: village in the Red River delta in 1930.

Gourou, P. 1936. Les paysans du delta tonkinois. Paris.

Hickey 1964.

74. Rhade. L: 13°N, 108°E. F: hamlet of Ko-sier in 1962.

Donoghue, J. D., D. D. Whitney, and I. Ishino. 1962. People in the Middle. East Lansing.

75. **Khmer.** L: 13°N, 103°50′E. F: city of Angkor in 1292.
    Chou Ta-Kaun. 1902. Mémoires sur les coutumes du Cambodge, ed. P.
        Pelliot. Bulletin de l'Ecole Française d'Extrême-Orient 2: 123-177.
    Aymonier 1901; Steinberg 1959.
76. **Siamese.** L: 14°N, 100°52′E. F: "natural community" of Bang Chan in 1955.
    Sharp, R. L., H. M. Hauck, K. Janlekha, and R. B. Texor. 1954. Siamese
        Village. Bangkok.
    Sharp and Hanks n.d.
77. **Semang.** L: 4°30′ to 5°30′N, 101° to 101°30′E. T: band of the Jahai subtribe
        in 1925.
    Schebesta, P. 1952-57. Die Negrito Asiens. Studia Instituti Anthropos 6, i; 12,
        ii; 13, iii. Wien-Mödling.
    LeBar, F. M., G. C. Hickey, and J. K. Musgrave. 1964. Ethnic Groups
        of Mainland Southeast Asia. pp. 181-186.
    Murdock, G. P. 1934. Our Primitive Contemporaries, pp. 85-106. New Haven.
    Evans 1937 (4).
78. **Nicobarese.** L: 7°N, 93°45′E. T: village in Car Nicobar in 1870.
    Man, E. H. 1932. The Nicobar Islands and Their People. Guilford.
    ———— 1888. The Nicobar Islanders. Journal of the Royal Anthropologi-
        cal Institute 18: 354-394.
    Whitehead 1924 (3).
79. **Andamanese.** L: 11°45′N, 93°5′E. T: "local group" of the Aka Bea tribe in 1860.
    Radcliffe-Brown, A. R. 1922. The Andaman Islanders. Cambridge.
    Man 1932.
80. **Vedda.** L: 7°30′ to 8°N, 81° to 81°30′E. T: Danigala hunting group in 1860.
    Seligmann, C. G., and B. Z. Seligmann. 1911. The Veddas. Cambridge.
    Spittel, R. L. 1945. Wild Ceylon. 3rd edit. Colombo.
    Bailey 1863 (2).
81. **Tanala.** L: 20°S, 48°E. T: village of the Menabe subtribe in 1925.
    Linton, R. 1933. The Tanala. Field Museum of Natural History Anthro-
        pological Series 22: 1-334.
    Murdock, G. P. 1959. Africa, pp. 212-220. New York.
    Linton 1939 (2).
82. **Negri Sembilan.** L: 2°35′N, 102°15′E. F: district of Inas in 1958.
    Lewis, D. K. 1962. The Minangkabau Malay of Negri Sembilan. Ph.D.
        dissertation, Cornell University.
    Gullick, J. M. 1958. Indigenous Political Systems of Western Malaya. London
        School of Economics Monographs on Social Anthropology 17: 1-151.
83. **Javanese.** L: 7°43′S, 112°13′E. T: *desa* in the vicinity of Pare in 1955.
    Jay, R. R. 1969. Javanese Villagers. Cambridge, Mass.
    ———— 1963. Religion and Politics in Central Java. New Haven.
    Koentjaraningrat. Tjelapar: A Village in South Central Java. Villages in Indo-
        nesia, ed. Koentjaraningrat, pp. 244-280. Ithaca.
    Geertz 1963 (4).
84. **Balinese.** L: 8°30′S, 115°20′E. F: village of Tihingan in 1958.
    Geertz, C. 1967. Tihingan. Villages in Indonesia, ed. Koentjaraningrat, pp. 210-
        243. Ithaca.
    Geertz, C., and H. Geertz. 1959. The Balinese Kinship System. Ms.
    Geertz, C. 1959. Balinese Religion in Transition. Ms.
    Geertz 1959 (2); Belo 1936 (5); Covarrubias 1937 (6).
85. **Iban.** L: 2°N, 112°30′ to 113°30′E. T: "long house community" of the Ulu Ai
        group in 1950.
    Freeman, J. D. 1955. Report on the Iban of Sarawak. Kuching.
    ———— 1958. The Family System of the Iban. Cambridge Papers in Social
        Anthropology 1: 15-52.
    Freeman 1955 (2); Gomes 1911 (4).

86. Badjau. L: 5°N, 120°E. T: "boat village" of the Tawi-Tawi Badjau in 1963.
    Nimmo, H. A. 1969. The Structure of Bajau Society. Ph.D. dissertation,
    University of Hawaii.
87. Toradja. L: 2°S, 121°E. T: village of the Bare'e subgroup in 1910.
    Adriani, N., and A. C. Kruijt. 1912. De Bare'e-sprekende Toradja's. 3v. Batavia.
    Downs 1956.
88. Tobelorese. L: 1°N, 128°30'E. T: village of Tobelo district in 1900.
    Riedel, J. G. F. 1885. Galela und Tobeloresen. Zeitschrift für Ethnologie 17:
    58-89.
    Hueting, A. 1921. De Tobeloreezen in hun denken en doen. Bijdragen
    tot de Taal-, Land-, en Volkenkunde 77: 217-385; 78: 137-342.
89. Alorese. L: 8°20'S, 124°40'E. T: village in Atimelang in 1938.
    DuBois, C. 1944. The People of Alor. Minneapolis.
    DuBois 1945; DuBois 1940; DuBois 1944.
90. Tiwi. L: 11° to 11°45'S, 130° to 132°E. T: band in 1929.
    Hart, C. W. M., and A. R. Pilling. 1960. The Tiwi of North Australia. New
    York.
    Goodale, J. C. 1971. Tiwi Wives. Seattle.
    ——— 1962. Marriage Contracts Among the Tiwi. Ethnology 1: 452-466.
91. Aranda. L: 23°30' to 25°S, 132°30' to 134°30'E. T: "local group" near Alice
    Springs in 1896.
    Spencer, B., and F. J. Gillen. 1927. The Arunta. 2v. London.
    Murdock 1934.
92. Orokaiva. L: 8°30'S to 148°E. T: village of the Aiga subtribe in 1925.
    Williams, F. E. 1930. Orokaiva Society. London.
    Reay 1953.
93. Kimam. L: 7°30'S, 38°30'E. F: village of Bamol in 1960.
    Serpenti, L. M. 1965. Cultivators in the Swamps. Assen.
94. Kapauku. L: 4°S, 36°E. F: village of Botukebo in 1955.
    Pospisil, L. 1958. Kapauku Papuans and Their Law. Yale University
    Publications in Anthropology 54: 1-296.
    ——— 1963. The Kapauku Papuans of West New Guinea. New York.
    Pospisil 1963 (3).
95. Kwoma. L: 4°10'S, 142°40'E. F: Hongwam subtribe in 1937.
    Whiting, J. W. M. 1941. Becoming a Kwoma. New Haven.
    Whiting and Reed 1938.
96. Manus. L: 2°10'S, 147°10'E. F: village of Peri in 1929.
    Mead, M. 1930. Growing Up in New Guinea. New York.
    Mead 1969; Mead 1934.
97. New Irelanders. L: 2°30'S, 151°E. F: village of Lesu in 1930.
    Powdermaker, H. 1933. Life in Lesu. New York.
    ——— 1931. Mortuary Rites in New Ireland. Oceania 2: 26-43.
    ——— 1931. Vital Statistics in New Ireland. Human Biology 3: 351-375.
    Powdermaker 1932 (2).
98. Trobrianders. L: 8°38'S, 151°4'E. T: village on Kiriwina island in 1914.
    Malinowski, B. 1935. Coral Gardens and Their Magic. 2v. New York.
    ——— 1922. Argonauts of the West Pacific. London.
    ——— 1926. Crime and Custom in Savage Society. London.
    Fathauer, G. H. 1954. Kinship and Social Structure of the Trobriand
    Islands. Ms.
    Malinowski 1929 (2).
99. Siuai. L: 7°S, 155°20'E. T: village of the northeastern group in 1939.
    Oliver, D. L. 1955. A Solomon Island Society. Cambridge.
100. Tikopia. L: 12°30'S, 168°30'E. F: district of Ravenga in 1930.
    Firth, R. 1939. We the Tikopia. London.
    ——— 1940. Work of the Gods. London School of Economics Monographs
    on Social Anthropology 1-2.

―――― 1952. Conflict and Adjustment in Tikopia Religious Systems. Ms.
101. Pentecost. L: 16°S, 168°E. F: village of Bunlap in 1953.
Lane, R. B., and B. S. Lane. Various unpublished and undated Mss. and communications.
Lane 1956; Lane 1965.
102. Fijians. L: 18°S, 178°35′E. F: island of Mbau in 1840.
Williams, T. 1884. Fiji and the Fijians. Rev. edit. London.
Ross, G. K. 1953. Fijian Way of Life. Melbourne.
Waterhouse 1886 (2); Tippett 1968 (4); Toganivalu 1911 (5); Deane 1921 (6).
103. Ajie. L: 21°20′S, 165°40′E. T: village of Neje chiefdom in 1845.
Leenhardt, M. 1930. Notes d'ethnologie néo-calédonienne. Travaux et Mémoires de l'Institut d'Ethnologie 8: 1-340. Paris.
―――― 1937. Gens de la Grande Terre. Paris.
Guiart, J. 1956. L'organisation sociale et coutumière de la population autochtone. Noumea.
Barrau 1956 (4).
104. Maori. L: 35°10′ to 35°30′S, 174° to 174°20′E. T: village of the Nga Puhi tribe in 1820.
Best, E. 1924. The Maori. 2v. Wellington.
Firth, R. 1959. Economics of the New Zealand Maori. Wellington.
Hawthorn, H. 1944. The Maori.: A Study in Acculturation. Memoirs of the American Anthropological Association 64: 1-130.
Shortland, E. 1856. Traditions and Superstitions of the New Zealanders. London.
Earle 1932 (3); Buck 1949 (4).
105. Marquesans. L: 8°55′S, 140°10′W. T: "tribe" of southwest Nuku Hiva in 1800.
Handy, E. S. C. 1932. The Native Culture in the Marquesas. Bulletins of the Bernice P. Bishop Museum 9: 1-358.
Sheahan, G. M., ed. 1952. Marquesan Source Materials. Ms.
Miranda, P. 1964. Marquesan Social Structure. Ethnohistory 11: 301-379.
Tautain. 1896. Sur l'anthropophagie et les sacrifices humains aux Iles Marquises. L'Anthropologie 7: 443-452.
―――― 1897. Notes sur les constructions et monuments des Marquises. L'Anthropologie 8: 538-558.
La Barre 1934 (2).
106. Samoans. L: 13°48′ to 14°S, 172°W. T: "village community" of western Upolu in 1829.
Krämer, A. 1901-02. Die Samoa-Inseln. 2v. Stuttgart.
Grattan 1948; Murdock 1934; Stair 1897; Turner 1884; Buck 1930.
107. Gilbertese. L: 3°30′N, 172°20′E. T: village on Makin island in 1890.
Lambert, B. 1963. Rank and Ramage in the Northern Gilbert Islands. Ph.D. dissertation, University of California at Berkeley.
―――― n.d. Gilbert Islands. Adoption in Eastern Oceania, ed. V. Carroll. Honolulu.
Lambert 1970 (2); Lambert 1964 (3); Lambert 1968 (4); Finsch 1893 (6).
108. Marshallese. L: 6°N, 169°15′E. T: village of Jaluit atoll in 1900.
Spoehr, A. 1949. Majuro: A Village in the Marshall Islands. Fieldiana: Anthropology 39: 1-266.
Murdock, G. P., C. S. Ford, and J. W. M. Whiting. 1943. Marshall Islands. Military Government Handbook OPNAV 50E-1, 1-113. Washington.
Finsch, O. 1893. Ethnologische Erfahrungen und Belegstücke aus der Südsee 3: 119-383.
Krämer and Nevermann 1938 (2); Mason 1947 (3); Erdland 1914 (5).
109. Trukese. L: 7°24′N, 151°40′E. F: island of Romonum in 1947.
Goodenough, W. H. 1949. Property, Kin, and Community on Truk. Yale University Publications in Anthropology 46: 1-192.
LeBar 1964; Gladwin and Sarason 1953.

110. Yapese. L: 9°30′N, 138°10′E. T: village in 1910.
Müller, W. 1917. Yap. Ergebnisse der Südsee-Expedition 1908-1910, ed.
G. Thilenius 2: B, iii, 1-380. Hamburg.
Schneider, D. M. 1962. Double Descent on Yap. Journal of the Polynesian
Society 71: 1-24.
——— 1957. Political Organization, Supernatural Sanctions and the Punishment for Incest on Yap. American Anthropologist 59: 791-800.
Murdock, Ford, and Whiting 1944 (2).

111. Palauans. L: 7°N, 134°30′E. T: village on Koror island in 1873.
Krämer, A. 1929. Palau. Ergebnisse aus der Südsee-Expedition 1908-1910, ed.
G. Thilenius, 2, B, III. Hamburg.
Barnett 1960; Force 1960; Murdock, Ford, and Whiting 1944.

112. Ifugao. L: 16°50′N, 121°10′E. T: "home region" of the Kiangan group in 1910.
Barton, R. F. 1938. Philippine Pagans. London.
Barton 1930; Barton 1919; Barton 1946; Barton 1922.

113. Atayal. L: 23°50′ to 24°50′N, 120°20′ to 120°50′E. T: village of the Gaogaon
subtribe in 1930.
Okada, Y. 1949. The Social Structure of the Atayal Tribe. (Ms. translated from Essays Presented to Teizo Toda, pp. 393-433). Tokyo.
Mabuchi, T. 1960. The Aboriginal Peoples of Formosa. Viking Fund
Publications in Anthropology 29: 127-140.
Ruey Yih-Fu. n.d. The Atayal. Ms.
Ruey 1955 (3).

114. Chinese. L: 31°N, 120°5′E. F: village of Kaihsienkung in north Chekiang in
1936.
Fei, H. 1946. Peasant Life in China. New York.

115. Manchu. L: 50°N, 125°30′E. T: "ancient Manchu" *mokun* of the Aigun district
in 1915.
Shirokogoroff, S. M. 1924. Social Organization of the Manchus. Royal
Asiatic Society, North China Branch, Extra Volume 3: 1-196. Shanghai.

116. Koreans. L: 37°37′N, 126°25′E. F: village of Sondup'e on Kanghwa island in
1950.
Osgood, C. 1951. The Koreans and Their Culture. New York.
Rutt 1964.

117. Japanese. L: 34°30′N, 133°40′E. F: the *buraku* of Niiike in 1950.
Beardsley, R. K., J. W. Hall, and R. E. Ward. 1959. Village Japan. Chicago.

118. Ainu. L: 42°40′ to 43°N, 142° to 144°E. T: "local group" of the Tokapchi and
Saru basins in 1880.
Watanabe, H. 1964. The Ainu. Journal of the Faculty of Science, University of
Tokyo, Anthropology 2: vi, 1-164.
Sugiura, S., and H. Befu. 1962. Kinship Organization of the Saru Ainu.
Ethnology 1: 287-298.
Munro 1962 (2); Batchelor 1927 (4).

119. Gilyak. L: 53° to 54°30′N, 139° to 143°10′E. T: village in 1880.
Shternberg, L. Semya i rod u narodov severo-vostochnoi Azii Leningrad.
Schrenck, L. von. 1881. Reisen und Forschungen im Amur-Lande 3:
Die Völker des Amur-Landes. St. Petersburg.
Hawes, C. H. 1903. In the Uttermost East. London.
Ivanov, S. V., M. G. Levin, and A. V. Smolyak. n.d. The Nevkhi. The
People of Siberia, ed. M. G. Levin and L. P. Potapuv, pp. 767-785. Chicago.

120. Yukaghir. L: 63° to 70°N, 150° to 157°E. T: local group of the upper Kolyma
River in 1900.
Jochelson, W. 1926. The Yukaghir and Yukaghirized Tungus. Memoirs
of the American Museum of Natural History 13: 1-469.

121. Chukchee. L: 63° to 70°N, 150° to 157°E. T: camp group of the Reindeer
Chukchee in 1900.

Bogoras, W.  1904-09.  The Chukchee.  Memoirs of the American Museum of Natural History 11: 1-703.
—— 1901.  The Chukchee of Northeastern Asia.  American Anthropologist 3: 80-108.

122. Ingalik.  L: 62°30′N, 159°30′W.  F: village of Shageluk in 1885.
Osgood, C.  1958.  Ingalik Social Culture.  Yale University Publications in Anthropology 55: 1-289.
—— 1959.  Ingalik Mental Culture.  Yale University Publications in Anthropology 56: 1-195.
Osgood 1940 (2).

123. Aleut.  L: 53° to 57°30′N, 158° to 170°W.  T: village of the Unalaska division in 1778.
Veniaminov, I. E. P.  1840.  Zapiski ob ostrovakh unalashkinskago otdela.  St. Petersburg.
Lantis, M.  1970.  Ethnohistory in Southwestern Alaska and the Southern Yukon.  Lexington, Ky.
Sarytschew 1806 (3).

124. Copper Eskimo.  L: 66°40′ to 69°20′N, 108° to 117°W.  T: *miut* group in 1915.
Jenness, D.  1922.  The Life of the Copper Eskimos.  Report of the Canadian Arctic Expedition, 1913-18, 12: 5-227.  Ottawa.
—— 1928.  People of the Twilight.  New York.
Jenness 1917 (3).

125. Montagnais.  L: 48° to 52°N, 73° to 75°W.  T: Lake St. John or Mistassini band in 1910.
Lips, J. E.  1947.  Notes on Montagnais-Naskapi Economy.  Ethnos 12: 1-78.
Speck, F. G.  1931.  Montagnais-Naskapi Bands and Early Eskimo Distributions in the Labrador Peninsula.  American Anthropologist 33: 557-600.
Leacock, E.  1969.  The Montagnais-Naskapi Band.  Bulletins of the National Museum of Canada 228: 1-20.
Speck 1935 (2).

126. Micmac.  L: 43°30′ to 50°N, 60° to 66°W.  T: band on the mainland in 1650.
Denys, N.  1908.  The Description and Natural History of the Coasts of North America.  Publications of the Champlain Society 2: 1-625.
Wallis and Wallis 1955; Le Clercq 1910; Bock 1966.

127. Saulteaux.  L: 51°30′ to 52°30′N, 94° to 97°W.  T: Berens River, Little Grand Rapids, or Pekangekum band in 1930.
Hallowell, A. I.  1955.  Culture and Experience.  Philadelphia.
Dunning 1959; Hallowell 1938.

128. Slave.  L: 62°N, 122°W.  F: Lynx Point band in 1940.
Helm, J.  1961.  The Lynx Point People.  Bulletin of the National Museum of Canada 176:1-193.

129. Kaska.  L: 60°N, 131°W.  T: band on the upper Liard River in 1900.
Honigmann, J. J.  1954.  The Kaska Indians.  Yale University Publications in Anthropology 51: 1-163.
Honigmann 1949; Teit 1956.

130. Eyak.  L: 60° to 61°N, 144° to 146°W.  T: village in 1890.
Birket-Smith, K., and F. de Laguna.  1938.  The Eyak Indians.  Copenhagen.

131. Haida.  L: 54°N, 132°30′W.  T: village of the Masset division in 1875.
Murdock, G. P.  1934.  Our Primitive Contemporaries, pp. 221-263.  New York.
Swanton, J. R.  1909.  Contributions to the Ethnology of the Haida.  Memoirs of the American Museum of Natural History 8: 1-300.
Murdock 1931 (3).

132. Bellacoola.  L: 52°20′N, 126° to 127°W.  T: village in 1880.
McIlwaith, T. F.  1948.  The Bella Coola Indians.  2v.  Toronto.

133. Twana.  L: 47°25′N, 123°15′W.  T: village in 1860.

Elmendorf, W. W. 1960. The Structure of Twana Culture. Washington State University Research Studies, Monographic Supplement 2: 1-576.

Eells, M. 1877. Twana Indians of the Skokomish Reservation. Bulletins of the U.S. Geographical and Geological Survey of the Territories 3: 57-114.

134. Yurok. L: 41°30′N, 124°W. T: village in 1850.

Kroeber, A. L. 1925. Handbook of the Indians of California. Bulletins of the Bureau of American Ethnology 78: 1-97.

Loeffelholz, K. von, ed. 1893. Die Zoreisch-Indianer der Trinidad-Bai. Mitteilungen der Anthropologischen Gesellschaft in Wien 23: 101-123.

Waterman, T. T., and A. L. Kroeber. Yurok Marriages. University of California Publications in American Archaeology and Ethnology 35: 1-14.

Kroeber 1960 (2); Heizer and Mills 1952 (4).

135. Eastern Pomo. L: 39°N, 123°W. F: village of Cigom in 1850.

Gifford, E. W. 1926. Clear Lake Pomo Society. University of California Publications in American Archaeology and Ethnology 18: 287-390.

Barrett, S. A. 1917. Ceremonies of the Pomo Indians. University of California Publications in American Archaeology and Ethnology 12: 397-441.

———— 1916. Pomo Buildings. Holmes Anniversary Volume, pp. 1-17. Washington.

Loeb 1926 (2).

136. Lake Yokuts. L: 35°N, 119°20′W. T: village in 1850.

Gayton, A. H. 1948. Yokuts and Western Mono Ethnography. Anthropological Records 10: 1-301.

Beals, R. L., and J. A. Hester. 1958. A Lacustrine Economy in California. Miscellanea Paul Rivet Octogenario Dictata 1: 211-217. Mexico.

Kroeber, 1925 (2); Latta 1949 (4).

137. Wadadika Paiute. L: 43° to 44°N, 118° to 120°W. F: Wada band in 1870.

Whiting, B. B. 1950. Paiute Sorcery. Viking Fund Publications in Anthropology 15: 1-110.

Stewart 1941.

138. Klamath. L: 42° to 43°15′N, 121°20′ to 122°20′W. T: village in 1860.

Spier, L. 1930. Klamath Ethnography. University of California Publications in American Archaeology and Ethnology 30: 1-328.

Gatschet, A. S. 1890. The Klamath Indians of Southwestern Oregon. U.S. Geographical and Geological Survey of the Rocky Mountain Region, Contributions to North American Ethnology 2. 2v. Washington.

Stern 1965 (2); Voegelin 1942 (3).

139. Kutenai. L: 49°N, 116°40′W. T: band of the Lower or eastern branch in 1890.

Turney-High, H. H. 1941. Ethnography of the Kutenai. Memoirs of the American Anthropological Association 56: 1-202.

Chamberlain 1892.

140. Gros Ventre. L: 47° to 49°N, 106° to 110°W. T: band in 1880.

Flannery, R. 1953. The Gros Ventres of Montana. Catholic University of America Anthropological Series 15: 1-221.

Cooper 1956; Kroeber 1908.

141. Hidatsa. L: 47°N, 101°W. F: Hidatsa proper village in 1836.

Bowers, A. W. 1965. Hidatsa Social and Ceremonial Organization. Bulletins of the Bureau of American Ethnology 194: 1-528.

Matthews 1877.

142. Pawnee. L: 42°N, 100°W. T: village of the Skidi division in 1867.

Weltfish, G. 1965. The Lost Universe. New York.

Dorsey and Murie 1940.

143. Omaha. L: 41°10′ to 41°41′N, 96° to 97°W. F: the Omaha tribe in 1854.

Fletcher, A. C., and F. LaFlesche. 1911. The Omaha Tribe. Annual Reports of the Bureau of Ethnology 27: 17-672.

Dorsey 1884.

144. Huron. L: 44° to 45°N, 78° to 80°W. T: village of the Attignawantan and Attigneenongnahac tribes in 1634.

Trigger, B. G.   1969.   The Huron. New York.
Tooker 1964; Kinietz 1940.
145. Creek.   L: 32°30′ to 34°20′N, 85°30′ to 86°30′W. T: Upper Creek town in 1800.
Swanton, J. R.   1928.   Social Organization and Social Usages of the Creek Confederacy. Annual Reports of the Bureau of American Ethnology 42: 23-472, 859-900.
Murdock, G. P.   1956.   Political Moieties. The State of the Social Sciences, ed. L. D. White, pp. 133-147. Chicago.
Swanton 1946 (3).
146. Natchez.   L: 31°30′N, 91°25′W. T: village in 1718.
Swanton, J. R.   1946.   Indian Tribes of the Lower Mississippi Valley. Bulletins of the Bureau of American Ethnology 43: 1-387.
147. Comanche.   L: 30° to 38°N, 98° to 103°W. T: band in 1870.
Hoebel, E. A.   1940.   The Political Organization and Law-Ways of the Comanche Indians. Memoirs of the American Anthropological Association 54: 1-149.
Wallace and Hoebel 1952.
148. Chiricahua.   L: 32°N, 109°30′W. T: "local group" of the Central band in 1870.
Opler, M. E.   1941.   An Apache Life-Way. Chicago.
────── 1955.   An Outline of Chiricahua Apache Social Organization. Social Organization of North American Tribes, ed. F. Eggan, pp. 173-242. Chicago.
149. Zuni.   L: 35°40′N, 108°45′W. F: Zuni pueblo in 1880.
Stevenson, M. C.   1904.   The Zuni Indians. Annual Reports of the Bureau of American Ethnology 23: 1-634.
Kroeber, A. L.   1917.   Zuni Kin and Clan. Anthropological Papers of the American Museum of Natural History 18: ii, 39-204.
Bunzel, R.   1930.   Zuni Katcinas. Annual Reports of the Bureau of American Ethnology 47: 837-1086.
────── 1932.   Introduction to Zuni Ceremonialism. Annual Reports of the Bureau of American Ethnology 47: 467-544.
Smith, W., and J. M. Roberts.   1954.   Zuni Law. Papers of the Peabody Museum, Harvard University 43: i, 1-175.
Leighton and Adair 1966 (2); Roberts 1956 (6).
150. Havasupai.   L: 35°20′ to 36°20′N, 111°20′ to 113°W. F: Havasupai tribe in 1918.
Spier, L.   1928.   Havasupai Ethnography. Anthropological Papers of the American Museum of Natural History 24: 81-408.
151. Papago.   L: 32°N, 112°W. T: village of the Archie division in 1910.
Underhill, R. M.   1936.   Social Organization of the Papago Indians. Columbia University Contributions to Anthropology 30: 1-280.
Underhill 1936; Lumholt 1912.
152. Huichol.   L: 22°N, 105°W. T: district in 1890.
Zingg, R. M.   1938.   The Huichols. University of Denver Contributions to Anthropology 1: 1-826.
Lumholtz 1902; Klineberg 1934; Lumholtz 1898.
153. Aztec.   L: 19°N, 99°10′W. F: city and environs of Tenochtitlan in 1520.
Soustelle, J.   1961.   Daily Life of the Aztecs. New York.
Murdock 1934; Sahagun 1950-57.
154. Popoluca.   L: 18°15′N, 94°50′W. F: town and environs of Soteapan in 1940.
Foster, G. M.   1942.   A Primitive Mexican Economy. Monographs of the American Ethnological Society 5: 1-115.
────── 1945.   Sierra Popoluca Folklore and Beliefs. University of California Publications in American Archaeology and Ethnology 42: 177-250.
Foster 1940 (2).
155. Quiche.   L: 15°N, 91°W. F: town of Chichicastenango in 1930.
Bunzel, R.   1952.   Chichicastenango. Publications of the American Ethnological Society 22: 1-438.
Schultze-Jena 1933.
156. Miskito.   L: 15°N, 91°W. T: village near Cape Gracias a Dios in 1921.

Conzemius, E. 1932. Ethnographic Survey of the Miskito and Sumu Indians. Bulletins of the Bureau of American Ethnology 106: 1-191.
Kirchhoff, P. 1948. The Caribbean Lowland Tribes. Bureau of American Ethnology 143: iv, 219-229.
Pijoan, M. 1946. The Health and Customs of the Miskito Indians. México: Instituto Indigenista Interamericano.
Helms 1971 (2).
157. Bribri. L: 9°N, 83°W. T: clan neighborhood in 1917.
Stone, D. 1962. The Talamancan Tribes of Costa Rica. Papers of the Peabody Museum, Harvard University 43: ii, 1-108.
Gabb 1876; Skinner 1920.
158. Cuna. L: 9° to 9°30′N, 78° to 79°W. T: island community in 1927.
Stout, D. C. 1947. San Blas Acculturation. Viking Fund Publications in Anthropology 9: 1-124.
Nordenskiöld 1938.
159. Goajiro. L: 11°30′ to 12°20′N, 71° to 72°30′W. T: local group in 1947.
Gutierrez de Pineda, V. 1948. Organizacion social en la Guajira. Revista del Instituto Etnologico Nacional 3: ii, 1-255. Bogota.
Pineda Giraldo, R. 1950. Aspectos de la magia en la Goajira. Revista del Instituto Etnologico Nacional 3: i, 1-164. Bogota.
Armstrong and Métraux 1948 (2); Bolinder 1957 (3).
160. Haitians. L: 18°50′N, 72°10′W. T: "rural section" of Mirebalais in 1935.
Herskovits, M. J. 1937. Life in a Haitian Valley. New York.
Bastien 1951; Romain 1955.
161. Callinago. L: 15°30′N, 60°30′W. T: village on Dominica in 1650.
Breton, R. 1665. Observations of the Island Carib. Auxerre.
Breton and de la Paix 1929; Du Tertre 1667; Taylor 1946; Rouse 1948.
162. Warrau. L: 8°30′ to 9°50′N, 60°40′ to 62°30′W. T: "rancheria" in 1935.
Turrado Moreno, A. 1945. Etnographia de los Indios Guaraunos. Caracas.
Wilbert 1958; Hill *et al.* 1962.
163. Yanomamo. L: 2°25′N, 65°W. F: village of Bisaasi-Teri in 1965.
Chagnon, N. A. 1968. The Fierce People. New York.
164. Carib. L: 7°25′N, 60°10′W. F: settlement of Sawari.
Gillin, J. 1936. The Barama River Caribs. Papers of the Peabody Museum, Harvard University 14: ii, 1-274.
165. Saramacca. L: 3° to 4°N, 55°30′ to 56°W. T: village in 1932.
Price, R. 1972. Saramaka Social Strutcure. Caribbean Monograph Series, University of Puerto Rico (forthcoming).
Neumann, P. 1967. Wirtschaft und materielle Kultur der Buschneger Surinames. Abhandlungen und Berichte des Staatlichen Museums für Völkerkunde Dresden 25: 1-181.
Herskovits and Herkovits 1935 (3).
166. Mundurucu. L: 7°S, 57°W. F: village of Cabrua in 1850.
Murphy, R. F. 1960. Headhunter's Heritage. Berkeley and Los Angeles.
———— 1958. Mundurucu Religion. University of California Publications in American Archaeology and Ethnology 48: 1-154.
———— 1957. Intergroup Hostility and Social Cohesion. American Anthropologist 59: 1018-1035.
Murphy 1956 (3).
167. Cubeo. L: 1° to 1°50′S, 70° to 71°W. T: village on the Caduiari river in 1939.
Goldman, I. 1963. The Cubeo Indians. Illinois Studies in Anthropology 2: 1-305.
168. Cayapa. L: 1°N, 79°W. F: district of Punta Venado in 1908.
Barrett, S. A. 1925. The Cayapa Indians. Indian Notes and Monographs 40: 1-476.
Heimann, M. 1932. Die Cayapa-Indianer. Zeitschrift für Ethnologie 63: 281-287.
Altschuler 1965 (2).

114 *Cultural Elements*

169. Jivaro. L: 2° to 4°S, 77° to 79°W. T: "subtribe" in 1920.
Karsten, R. 1935. The Head-Hunters of Western Amazonas. Societas Scientiarum Fennica, Commentationes Humanarum Litterarum 7: 1-588.
Rivet, P. 1907-08. Les Indiens Jibáros. L'Anthropologie 18: 333-368, 583-618; 19: 68-87, 235-259.
Stirling 1938 (2); Harner 1960 (3).

170. Amahauca. L: 10°20'S, 72°15'W. T: "local group" on the upper Inuya river in 1960.
Huxley, M., and C. Capa. 1964. Farewell to Eden. New York.
Dole, G. E. 1962. Endocannibalism Among the Amahuaca Indians. Transactions of the New York Academy of Sciences, ser. 2, 24: 567-573.
Carneiro 1962 (2); Carneiro 1968 (3).

171. Inca. L: 13°30'S, 72°W. T: *ayllu* in the vicinity of Cuzco in 1530.
Rowe, J. H. 1946. Inca Culture at the Time of the Conquest. Bulletins of the Bureau of American Ethnology 143: ii, 183-330.
Mason, J. A. 1957. The Ancient Civilizations of Peru. London.
Cobo 1890-95 (2); Murdock 1934 (4).

172. Aymara. L: 16°S, 65°45'W. T: *ayllu* near Chucuito in 1940.
Tschopik, H., Jr. 1951. The Aymara of Chucuito. Anthropological Papers of the American Museum of Natural History 44: 137-308.
Tschopik 1946; LaBarre 1948.

173. Siriono. L: 14° to 15°S, 63° to 64°W. T: band near the Rio Blanco in 1942.
Holmberg, A. R. 1950. Nomads of the Long Bow. Publications of the Institute of Social Anthropology, Smithsonian Institution 10: 1-104.

174. Nambicuara. L: 12°30' to 13°30'S, 58°30' to 59°W. T: "group" of Cocozu Nambicuara in 1940.
Lévi-Strauss, C. 1948. La vie familiale et sociale des Indiens Nambikwara. Journal de la Société des Américanistes 37: 1-131.
———— 1955. Tristes tropiques, pp. 235-310. Paris.
———— 1944. The Social and Psychological Aspects of Chieftainship in a Primitive Tribe. Transactions of the New York Academy of Sciences, ser. 2, 7: 16-42.
Oberg 1953 (4).

175. Trumai. L: 11°50'S, 53°40'W. F: the sole surviving village in 1938.
Murphy, R. F., and B. Quain. 1955. The Trumai Indians. Monographs of the American Ethnological Society 24: 1-108.

176. Timbira. L: 6° to 7°S, 45° to 46°W. F: village of Ponto in 1915.
Nimuendajú, C. 1946. The Eastern Timbira. University of California Publications in American Archaeology and Ethnology 41: 1-357.

177. Tupinamba. L: 22°35' to 23°S, 42° to 44°30'S. T: village in the vicinity of Rio de Janeiro in 1550.
Staden, H. 1928. The True Story of His Captivity, ed. M. Lotts. London.
Métraux 1946; Soares de Souza 1951.

178. Botocudo. L: 18° to 20°S, 41°30' to 43°30'W. T: band of the Naknenuk subtribe in 1884.
Ehrenreich, P. 1887. Ueber die Botocudos. Zeitschrift für Ethnologie 19: 49-82.
Saint-Hilaire, A. 1930-33. Voyages dans l'intérieur du Brésil. Paris.
Métraux 1946 (2).

179. Shavante. L: 13°30'S, 51°30'W. F: settlement of São Domingos in 1958.
Maybury-Lewis, D. 1967. Akwē-Shavante Society. Oxford.

180. Aweikoma. L: 28°S, 50°W. T: band in 1913.
Henry, J. 1941. Jungle People. New York.
Paula, J. M. de. 1924. Memoria sobre os Botocudos do Paraná e Santa Catharina. Proceedings of the International Congress of Americanists 20: i, 117 138.
Métraux 1946 (3).

181. Cayua. L: 23° to 24°S, 54° to 56°W. T: local group in 1890.

Rengger, J. R. 1835. Reise nach Paraguay in den Jahre 1818 bis 1828. Aarau. Koenigswald 1908; Watson 1952; Strelnikov 1928.
182. Lengua. L: 23° to 24°S, 58° to 59°W. T: band in 1889.
Grubb, W. B. 1911. An Unknown People in an Unknown Land. London.
Hawtrey, S. H. C. 1901. The Lengua Indians of the Paraguayan Chaco. Journal of the Royal Anthropological Institute 31: 280-299.
183. Abipon. L: 27° to 29°S, 59° to 60°W. T: band in 1750.
Dobrizhoffer, M. 1822. An Account of the Abipones. 3v. London.
184. Mapuche. L: 38°30'S, 72°35'W. T: neighborhood in the vicinity of Temuco in 1950.
Faron, L. C. 1961. Mapuche Social Structure. Illinois Studies in Anthropology 1: 1-247.
——— 1964. Hawks of the Sun. Pittsburgh.
Faron 1968 (2); Titiev 1951 (4).
185. Tehuelche. L: 40° to 50°S, 64° to 72°W. T: band in 1870.
Viedma, A. de. 1837. Descripción de la costa meridional del sur. Colección de obras y documentos relativos a la historia antigua y moderna de la provincias del Rio de la Plata, ed. P. de Angelis 6: 63-81. Buenos Aires.
Cooper, J. M. 1946. The Patagonian and Pampean Hunters. Bulletins of the Bureau of American Ethnology 143: i, 127-168.
Musters 1873 (2); Bourne 1874 (4).
186. Yahgan. L: 54°30' to 56°30'S, 67° to 72°W. T: "local group" in 1865.
Gusinde, M. 1937. Die Feuerland-Indianer 2: Yamana. Mödling bei Wien.
Cooper 1946.
11a. Chagga. L: 3° to 4°S, 37° to 38°E. T: neighborhood in 1906.
Gutmann, B. 1926. Das Recht der Dschagga. Arbeiten zur Entwicklungspsychologie 7: 1-733. München.
——— 1932. Die Stammeslehren der Dschagga. Arbeiten zur Entwicklungspsychologie 12: 1-671.
Dundas 1924 (3); Abbott 1892 (3).
16a. Katab. L: 10°N, 8°E. T: village in 1925.
Meek, C. K. 1931. Tribal Studies in Northern Nigeria, v. 2. London.
——— 1928-29. The Katab and Their Neighbors. Journal of the African Society 27-28.
34a. Dorobo. L: 0°10'N, 35°30'E. T: "clan" of the North Tindiret Forest band in 1927.
Huntingford, G. W. B. 1951. The Social Institutions of the Dorobo. Anthropos 46: 1-48.
——— 1942. The Social Organization of the Dorobo. African Studies 1: 183-200.
——— 1954. The Political Organization of the Dorobo. Anthropos 49: 123-148.
Huntingford 1953 (3); Huntingford 1929 (5).
46a. Lebanese. L: 34°25'N, 35°40'E. F: village of Al-Munsif in 1950.
Gulick, J. 1955. Social Structure and Culture Change in a Lebanese Village. Viking Fund Publications in Anthropology 21: 1-118.
60a. Chenchu. L: 16°15'N, 79°E. T: "village community" of the Forest Chenchu in 1940.
Fürer-Haimendorf, C. von. 1943. The Chenchus. London.
90a. Murngin. L: 4°45' to 12°35'S, 136°10' to 137°E. T: clan community of the eastern Murngin in 1930.
Warner, W. L. 1937. A Black Civilization. New York.
Elkin, A. 1950. The Complexity of Social Organization in Arnhem Land. Southwestern Journal of Anthropology 6: 1-20.
Thompson 1949 (3).
106a. Pukapukans. L: 10°53'S, 165°50'W. T: village in 1915.
Beaglehole, E., and P. Beaglehole. 1938. Ethnology of Pukapuka. Bulletins of the Bernice P. Bishop Museum 150: 1-419.

141a. Crow.   L: 42°30′ to 47°N, 105° to 111°W. T: band in 1870.
   Lowie, R. H.   1935.   The Crow Indians. New York.
   Denig, E. T.   1953.   Of the Crow Nation, ed. J. C. Ewers. Bulletins of the
      Bureau of American Ethnology 151: 1-74.
   Lowie   1912   (2); Lowie   1919   (3); Murdock   1934   (4).
175a. Bororo.   L: 15°30′ to 16°S, 54°30′ to 55°W. F: village of Kejara in 1936.
   Lévi-Strauss, C.   1936.   Contribution à l'étude de l'organisation sociale des In-
      diens Bororo. Journal de la Société des Américanistes 28: 269-304.
   ———   1955.   Tristes tropiques, pp. 181-232. Paris.
   Lowie   1954   (3); Steinen   1894   (4).
179a. Caraja.   L: 10°12′ to 15°15′S, 50°25′ to 51°50′N. T: "settlement" on the west
      bank of the Araguaya River in 1908.
   Krause, F.   1911.   In den Wildnissen Brasiliens. Leipzig.
   Lipkind   1948; Ehrenreich   1891.
183a. Mataco.   L: 22° to 24°S, 62° to 64°W. T: band of the Guisnay and Vejó divi-
      sions in Argentina in 1875.
   Pelleschi, J.   1896.   Los Indios Mataco y su lengua. Boletin del Instituto Geo-
      grafico Argentina 17: 559-662; 18: 173-350.
   Karsten   1932; Métraux   1944.

# 4

# Political Organization:
# Cross-Cultural Codes 4

*Arthur Tuden* and *Catherine Marshall*

This paper, the fourth in a series prepared at the Cross-Cultural Cumulative Coding Center, University of Pittsburgh, presents a set of codes and a body of coded data pertaining to the political organization of the societies of the standard world sample selected by Murdock and White (1969). Of the 186 societies in this sample, two—the Abkhaz (No. 55) and the Tobelorese (No. 88)—were found lacking in pertinent data. Arthur Tuden is largely responsible for the hypotheses and theoretical orientation of this paper. Catherine Marshall, the principal coder, is responsible for the data analysis and the preparation of the text.

The codes were designed to provide raw data on a large sample of literate and preliterate societies which will facilitate further research into political structure and behavior. Coded material has been published on many aspects of human behavior, but a detailed and basic description of political behavior has been significantly absent. With the present interest in comparative analysis and explanations of political change, valid documentary materials of political systems are needed. This paper differs from previous cross-cultural work on political organization because (1) the codes are applied to a representative sample of all rather than part of the world's cultures, and (2) because they utilize a wider range of political variables. The coding of political behavior by Hobhouse, Wheeler, and Ginsberg (1915) was limited to a sample of "simpler peoples"; others have studied stateless societies (Middleton and Tait 1958; Schapera 1956), or single-community societies (Carneiro 1967). Use of the standard sample permits an examination of the full range of political organization and the approximate distribution of its major forms. Other studies have been limited to a single political variable, that of political complexity as measured by levels of integration. Notable exceptions are Freeman and Winch (1957), who, in proposing a sequence of societal development, coded presence or absence of full and part-time bureaucrats in 48 societies as one measure of social complexity, and Schwartz and Miller (1964), who rated presence or absence of legal counsel, mediation, and police in a sample of 51 societies.

In the present paper, no attempt is made to measure or analyze political change, or to present any major theoretical position. Our intention is to provide social scientists with data on the distribution and varieties of political systems. Since there has been little previous analysis, the major concern of the paper is with the definition and presentation of the coded variables, but some consideration is also given to the world distribution of the variables and to the internal relationships among them.

## DEFINITION OF CODES

The thirteen variables used are described below, and the coded material is presented in Table 1. As in previous codes, parentheses are used to indicate ratings which are doubtful or based on inference; brackets indicate unresolvable contradictions; a period indicates that no information was available; and an asterisk refers to notes following the Table. The use of two letters in Column 7 refers to a bicameral legislature. In the remaining columns, a second letter indicates a secondary but significant quality. Among the Riffians, for example, subordinate officials achieve their positions primarily through informal recognition, but there is a strong tendency toward patrilineal selection, hence Column 12: ip.

*Column 1: Political Autonomy*

The following symbols indicate the degree of political independence of the society or its pinpointed subgroup at the pinpointed date.

D The society is politically dependent, being governed directly by functionaries of a dominant society of alien culture, e.g., through direct rule.

S The society is politically semi-autonomous, being governed by another society with an alien culture which operates largely through the indigenous political institutions, e.g., through indirect rule, but which requires conformity on major issues such as refraining from war, headhunting, or cannibalism.

T The society pays tribute (or its equivalent) to another society with a different culture in return for which it enjoys essential autonomy in its internal affairs.

U The society is theoretically subject to another society with an alien culture, e.g., to a colonial power, but is in fact essentially unadministered by the latter and thus enjoys *de facto* autonomy.

I The society is politically integrated with others in a pluralistic state within which it enjoys theoretically equal status. In subsequent codes in this set, this political system is to be treated as that of the society itself, whereas in other cases the codes pertain to the society's own indigenous political system.

A The society or its relevant subgroup is (or was) fully autonomous politically.

*Column 2: Trend in Autonomy*

The following symbols indicate the trend over the quarter to half century prior to the pinpointed date with respect to the degree of political autonomy enjoyed by the society.

d Declining autonomy, i.e., an increase in the political control exerted by another society of alien culture.

f A state of relative equilibrium with respect to autonomy but a decline in the territory or population politically controlled.

e A state of relatively stable equilibrium with respect to the degree of autonomy and the extent of territorial control.

g A state of relative equilibrium with respect to autonomy but an expansion in the territory or population politically controlled.

i Increasing autonomy, i.e., a trend toward greater independence from a formerly dominant society of alien culture.

## Column 3: Levels of Sovereignty

The symbols below indicate the level of effective sovereignty, defined as the highest level of indigenous political integration at which functionaries have and commonly exercise the power to enforce important decisions at subordinate levels in the political structure—notably to compel participation in warfare, to collect taxes or tribute, and/or to exact sanctions for major delicts. Unless at least one of these powers is found at a particular level, a lack of effective sovereignty is assumed for that level.

A Absence of effective sovereignty at any level transcending that of the local community, i.e., a stateless society.

B Effective sovereignty occurs at the first (but no higher) level of political integration above the local community, as in the case of a petty paramount chief ruling a district composed of a number of local communities.

C Effective sovereignty occurs at the second (but no higher) level of political integration above the local community, as in the case of a small state comprising a number of administrative districts under subordinate functionaries.

D Effective sovereignty is found at the third (or higher) level of political integration above the local community, as in the case of a large state divided into administrative provinces which are further subdivided into lesser administrative districts.

## Column 4: Higher Political Organization

The following symbols indicate the existence of some form of political organization, but one lacking effective sovereignty, at a higher level than that specified in Column 3.

o Absence of any political organization at a higher level.

p A peace group, based on such factors as common descent, a common cult, trade or connubium, which encourages peaceful relations, arbitration of disputes, or other forms of voluntary co-operation but cannot compel or enforce them.

a Alliances, whether enduring or transitory, between two or more political units with effective sovereignty which, though they may facilitate voluntary participation in war, payment of tribute or taxes, or execution of punitive sanctions, are powerless to enforce them.

c Confederation, i.e., the formal union of two or more political units possessing effective sovereignty where the confederate unit can expect comparable voluntary co-operation from its component parts.

i   An international organization of soverign states, e.g., the Holy Roman Empire or the United Nations, which can similarly recommend but cannot enforce co-operation.

## Column 5: Executive

The following symbols indicate the political status or statuses in which are vested the primary decision-making powers at the level of effective sovereignty.

O   Absence of effective sovereignty, and consequently of executive functionaries, at any level above that of the local community. Regularly accompanies A in Column 3.

C   Supreme decision-making authority is vested in a council, assembly, or other deliberative body with no single executive other than at best a presiding officer.

S   Supreme decision-making authority is shared more or less equally by a single (or plural) executive and a deliberative body, e.g., a king, president, or prime minister and a supreme council or parliament.

P   Supreme decision-making authority is vested in a plural executive, e.g., a committee, dual executives, or a triumvirate.

L   Supreme decision-making authority is concentrated in a single authoritative leader, e.g., a paramount chief, king, or dictator, however much he may in fact be influenced by advisors.

## Column 6: Selection of Executive

The following symbols indicate the mode of selection of supreme executive functionaries other than members of an authoritative council or deliberative body.

o   Absence of effective sovereignty, and consequently of executive functionaries at any level above that of the local community. Regularly accompanies O in Column 5.

p   Succession is hereditary and patrilineal, normally from father to son.

q   The same except that a brother takes precedence over a son.

m   Succession is hereditary and matrilineal, normally from MoBr to SiSo.

n   The same except that a brother takes precedence over a nephew.

f   Succession is hereditary within a ruling family (or group of families), the choice among potential heirs being made by the family, the predecessor, a council, or special functionaries with electoral powers.

l   Succession is nonhereditary and is determined by a body of limited size, e.g., a ruling clique, a particular political party, or a small body of designated electors. This symbol is to be used instead of e when elections are merely a stereotyped confirmation of the decision of a limited power group.

c   The single (or plural) executive is elected or otherwise chosen by a council or other deliberative body. In the absence of such an executive, the same symbol can be employed for the presiding officer of the supreme council.

i Succession is through informal recognition on the basis of personal qualifications.

e Succession is nonhereditary by a formal electoral procedure which is participated in by a substantial proportion of the free citizenry.

a The single (or plural) executive is an appointee of a dominant alien society, e.g., a colonial power.

s The succession is determined primarily by supernatural means, e.g., divination.

## Column 7: Deliberative and Consultative Bodies

The following symbols indicate the composition of a deliberative body which exercises or shares supreme decision-making authority at the level of effective sovereignty, as indicated by C or S in Column 5. A bicameral legislature with different modes of selection is indicated by two letters.

O Absence of a supreme deliberative body. Regularly accompanies O, L, or P in Column 5.

A An aristocratic deliberative body whose membership is hereditary or otherwise confined to ascribed statuses and is representative primarily of a ruling class or classes, e.g., a council of nobles.

C A deliberative council whose members are appointed by, but are relatively independent of, the chief executive, a ruling clique or party, or particularly designated electors at the same level of political integration, e.g., a supreme soviet.

R A deliberative body representative of several or all of the state's major class or ethnic components.

E An elective legislature or parliament chosen independently by the franchise of a substantial proportion of the free citizenry.

## Column 8: Advisory Bodies

The following symbols indicate the composition of political bodies or groups at the same level which have important advisory or consultative functions but do not have independent or co-ordinate decision-making powers.

o Absence of effective sovereignty at any level above that of the local community. Regularly accompanies A in Column 3.

n Absence of a separate consultative body.

r The principal advisors of the supreme executive (or of the more influential members of the supreme council where C is indicated in Column 5) are his (or their) close relatives, e.g., members of the royal family or lineage.

f The principal advisors are a coterie of personal favorites of the supreme executive (or of influential council members), among whom neither close relatives nor sodality mates predominate, e.g., royal courtiers, a "kitchen cabinet."

s The principal advisors are members of a secret society, cult group, age-grade, or other sodality.

y The advisory body is composed of representatives of subordinate groups.

z The consultative body is otherwise constituted, e.g., composed of individuals with hereditary status.

a  The principal advisors are administrative functionaries, e.g., the heads of administrative departments, a president's or prime minister's cabinet.

## Column 9: Judiciary

The following symbols indicate the locus of supreme judicial jurisdiction (normally appellate) at the level of effective sovereignty.

O  Supreme judicial authority is lacking at any level above that of the local community.

L  Supreme judicial authority exists at a level above that of the local community but below that of effective sovereignty.

E  Supreme judicial authority is exercised by the supreme executive, e.g., the king is also the supreme judge, the council is also the supreme court.

I  Supreme judicial authority is vested in a functionary or functionaries who are appointed by the supreme executive and/or the supreme deliberative body but are at least relatively independent of the appointing authority.

P  Supreme judicial authority is independent of the political system and is vested in a priesthood or other primarily religious functionaries.

H  Supreme judicial authority is exercised by independent hereditary functionaries.

## Column 10: Police

The following symbols indicate the degree of specialization and institutionalization of police functions.

o  Police functions are not specialized or institutionalized at any level of political integration, the maintenance of law and order being left exclusively to informal mechanisms of social control, to private retaliation, or to sorcery.

i  There is only incipient specialization, as when groups with other functions are assigned police functions in emergencies, e.g., military societies at a Plains Indian annual sun dance and buffalo hunt.

r  Police functions are assumed by the retainers of chiefs.

m  Police functions are assumed by the military organization.

s  Police functions are specialized and institutionalized on at least some level or levels of political integration.

## Column 11: Administrative Hierarchy

The following symbols indicate the type of subordinate functionaries who occupy the most influential statuses at the level of political integration immediately below that characterized by effective sovereignty, and the relationship of these functionaries to the supreme executive. Note that when Sovereignty is rated B in Column 3, the level indicated in this column is that of the local community.

A  Absence of effective sovereignty at any level above that of the local community. Regularly accompanies A in Column 3.

P  The principal subordinate functionaries are popular assemblies, councils of notables, or other plural (rather than individual) statuses which represent their constituencies and enjoy a substantial measure of independence *vis-à-vis* the supreme executive.

K The principal subordinate functionaries are heads of component kin groups rather than of territorial divisions of the state, and owe their positions primarily to kinship principles.

D The principal subordinate functionaries are heads of territorial divisions of the state who enjoy a substantial degree of decentralized independence *vis-à-vis* the supreme executive.

S The principal subordinate functionaries are heads of territorial divisions of the state who are closely supervised by the supreme executive and form part of a centralized administrative system.

+ A plus following a letter indicates the presence of a deliberative body which shares authority at this level.

## Column 12: Selection of Subordinate Officials

The following symbols indicate the prevailing mode of succession to the statuses of the principal subordinate administrative functionaries.

o Absence of effective sovereignty at any level above that of the local community. Regularly accompanies A in Column 3.

p Patrilineal succession.

m Matrilineal succession.

h Hereditary succession within a ruling lineage or other privileged group, the particular individual choice being determined by some special elective or appointive procedure.

s Succession is based primarily on seniority or age.

i Informal recognition on the basis of personal influence, prestige, or wealth.

e Formal election by their constituencies.

a Appointment by the supreme executive.

## Column 13: Sources of Political Power

In this column are listed in the approximate descending order of their importance, the symbols for any of the following sources of power, wealth, and/or influence which contribute substantially (not marginally) to the status of the politically dominant class or classes in the society. In the case of stateless or classless societies, the same symbols are employed for the categories of individuals who enjoy the highest social prestige.

D Direct subsistence production, i.e., the production of food and/or artifacts for use by the producer and his own family or household. This symbol is to be used only by itself and only when even the most prestigious members of the society derive their support mainly from their own direct subsistence activities.

W Plunder, trophies, and/or captives acquired in warfare.

T Tribute or taxes levied against conquered or subject people.

S Labor of and products produced by slaves or other unfree dependents (except serfs bound to the land).

F Contributions, taxes, and/or labor of free citizens.

L Rents and/or other income derived from large landholdings, including production by serfs or peons who are bound to the land.

O Perquisites from the holding of political office, including salaries, fees, commissions, special privileges, gifts, and bribes.

E Income and profits derived from foreign commerce, including shipping and caravan trade.

C Income and profits received from investments in industry, business, or other capitalistic enterprises within the society.

P Payments, privileges, and/or contributions received in return for priestly and/or shamanistic services.

## CODING PROCEDURES AND PROBLEMS

The present codes were designed by Frances Gaver, George P. Murdock, and Arthur Tuden. The coding procedure is essentially the same as that described by Barry and Paxson (1971). All societies in the standard sample were coded by Catherine Marshall; 27 of them were independently coded by Alice Fry Bauman, 16 by Frances Gaver. Sources in German, Italian, and Dutch were read by Edith Lauer, Caterina F. Provost, and Josephine Stanton, respectively, who then discussed the material orally with the principal coder. The codes were prepared for computer analysis by Alice Fry Bauman and Catherine Marshall in consultation with Herbert Barry III. The IBM 360 and IBM 7090 digital computers at the University of Pittsburgh Computer Center were used for cross-tabulation and statistical analysis of the data.

Of the thirteen variables, Autonomy, Sovereignty, and Executive posed the most problems. The coding of autonomy influenced some choices in the remaining codes; particular attention was therefore paid to this variable, especially with regard to colonial societies. Where the pinpointed date coincides with the beginning of colonial administration or the establishment of a reservation, the code reflects the indigenous structure on the assumption that administrative changes had not yet taken effect (e.g. 27 Massa, 133 Twana). Where colonial rule was long established, the coding was based on such factors as the presence of colonial administrators and the extent of their involvement in decision-making. In the autonomy code, therefore, a colonial society was coded U or T if it had no formal contact with agents of the dominant power, or contact only once a year for payment of tax or receipt of government subsidy. If agents or district officers were in residence and had assumed some of the functions formerly exercised by natives, the society was coded S. Other criteria for use of S were: alteration of behavior through fear of police retaliation; alteration of settlement patterns (natives moved from dispersed dwellings into compact villages); changes in economic activities through restriction of hunting territory, encouragement of settled agriculture, or participation in a money economy such as temporary plantation labor. Societies were coded D when colonial officials were regularly in contact with small native communities and had assumed all ultimate decision-making functions.

It should be noted, however, that the D societies may exhibit a wide range of political behavior as indicated by the remaining variables. Al-

TABLE 1

Coded Data on Political Organization

| | 1 | 2 | 3 | 4 | 5 | 6 | 7 | 8 | 9 | 10 | 11 | 12 | 13 |
|---|---|---|---|---|---|---|---|---|---|---|---|---|---|
| 001 Nama Hottentot | U | f | B | o | C | p | R | n | E | o | K | p | D |
| 002 Kung Bushmen | U | e | A | o | O | o | O | o | O | o | A | o | D |
| 003 Thonga | S | e | C | a | L | q | O | r | E | o | D | a | F P |
| 004 Lozi | U | d | C | o | S | f | (C) | n | E | o | Z* | a | L T W |
| 005 Mbundu | U | e | B | c | S | f | . | n | E | o | D | o | E T |
| 006 Suku | A | e | D | o | L | (m) | O | r | E | r | D | . | (F) |
| 007 Bemba | U | e | D | o | L | n | O | za | E | s | S | h | F W E |
| 008 Nyakyusa | S | d | C | (c) | S | p | AR | n | E | o | D | o | D |
| 009 Hadza | U | e | A | o | O | o | O | o | O | o | A | o | D |
| 010 Luguru | D | g | A | o | O | o | O | o | O | o | A | o | D |
| 011 Kikuyu | D | d | (A) | o | O | o | O | o | O | o | A | o | D |
| 012 Ganda | A | e | D | o | L | f | O | a | E | o | S | a | F S O W |
| 013 Mbuti | U | e | A | o | O | o | O | o | O | o | A | o | D |
| 014 Nkundo Mongo | D | f | A | o | O | o | O | o | O | o | A | o | S |
| 015 Banen | S | d | B | o | L | p | O | . | E | o | D | p | D |
| 016 Tiv | U | d | A | p | O | o | O | o | O | o | A | o | D |
| 017 Ibo | S | g | A | p | O | o | O | o | O | o* | A | o | D |
| 018 Fon | A | g | C | o | L | f | O | a | E | (s)* | S | a | W F S O E |
| 019 Ashanti | U | d | D | o | S | f | R | r | E | o | D | h | F S E |
| 020 Mende | S | g | D | o | S | f | R | n | E | o | D | h | L F O |
| 021 Wolof | D | e | B | o | L | a | O | n | E | s | D | (e) | C S O |
| 022 Bambara | S | d | B | o | L | f | O | (yr) | . | . | D | o | D |
| 023 Tallensi | S | d | B | o | L | f | O | r | E | o | D | a | F O |
| 024 Songhai | (D) | d | A | o | O | o | O | o | O | o | A | o | E S |
| 025 Wodaabe Fulani | T | d | B | o | (L) | a | (C) | (n) | E | o | K | p | O |

|                       | 1   | 2   | 3   | 4 | 5 | 6   | 7  | 8   | 9   | 10 | 11  | 12   | 13          |
|-----------------------|-----|-----|-----|---|---|-----|----|-----|-----|----|-----|------|-------------|
| 026 Hausa             | I   | e   | D   | c | L | f   | O  | r   | I   | s  | S   | a    | S T W F O E |
| 027 Massa             | U   | d   | A   | a | O | o   | O  | o   | O   | o  | A   | e    | D           |
| 028 Azande            | U   | g   | D   | o | L | p   | O  | (y) | E   | m  | D   | a    | T F W       |
| 029 Fur               | A   | d   | D   | o | L | p   | O  | (f) | E   | m  | D   | .    | L F         |
| 030 Otoro Nuba        | U   | e   | A   | a | O | o   | O  | o   | O   | o  | A   | o    | W S         |
| 031 Shilluk           | S   | e   | D   | o | L | f   | O  | y   | E   | o  | S   | a    | S F         |
| 032 Mao               | U   | f   | A   | o | O | o   | O  | o   | O   | o  | A   | o    | D           |
| 033 Kaffa             | A   | e   | D   | c | L | f   | O  | a   | E   | .  | S   | (h)  | F O S W     |
| 034 Masai             | U   | d   | A   | o | O | o   | O  | o   | O   | o  | A   | o    | D           |
| 035 Konso             | U   | d   | B   | a | P | e   | O  | n   | (O) | m  | P   | e    | (D)         |
| 036 Somali            | S   | e   | A   | p | O | o   | O  | o   | P   | o  | A   | o    | D           |
| 037 Amhara            | I   | e   | D   | i | L | p   | O  | r   | I   | s  | S   | a    | L O E C     |
| 038 Bogo              | T   | e   | (B) | o | . | .   | .  | .   | (L) | o  | .   | .    | S W         |
| 039 Kenuzi Nubians    | (S) | (e) | A   | o | O | o   | O  | o   | O   | o  | A   | o    | .           |
| 040 Teda              | S   | d   | A   | o | O | o   | O  | o   | O   | o  | A   | o    | S E         |
| 041 Tuareg            | A   | f   | D   | o | L | f   | O  | y   | E   | o  | D   | h    | F S W E     |
| 042 Riffians          | U   | d   | C   | p | P | *   | O  | n   | E   | o  | P   | ip   | (D)         |
| 043 Egyptians         | A   | i   | D   | i | S | p   | E  | a   | L   | s  | S   | (a)  | L E C       |
| 044 Hebrews           | A   | i   | B   | a | L | p   | O  | .   | E   | s  | P*  | .    | F E S       |
| 045 Babylonians       | A   | g   | (D) | a | L | p   | O  | n   | E   | m  | S   | a    | F E         |
| 046 Awala Bedouin     | U   | e   | B   | a | L | (f) | O  | (y) | H   | o  | K   | p    | T S         |
| 047 Turks             | A   | f   | D   | a | S | c   | E  | a   | (I) | s  | S+  | (a)  | C E O       |
| 048 Gheg Albanians    | U   | g   | C   | a | C | p   | Ř  | n   | E   | o  | D   | p    | D           |
| 049 Romans            | A   | g   | D   | a | L | f   | O  | rfz | E   | s  | S   | a    | L C E O S T |
| 050 Basques           | I   | d   | C   | a | L | .   | O  | a   | I   | s  | S   | a    | O C         |
| 051 Irish             | A   | i   | C   | i | S | c   | CE | a   | I   | s  | S+  | e    | C E O       |
| 052 Lapps             | D   | e   | A   | o | O | o   | O  | o   | O   | o  | A   | o    | D           |
| 053 Yurak Samoyed     | T   | f   | B   | o | L | e   | O  | n   | E   | o  | D   | .    | O P         |
| 054 Russians          | I   | g   | D   | i | L | c   | O  | a   | L   | s  | S+  | e    | O           |

| | 1 | 2 | 3 | 4 | 5 | 6 | 7 | 8 | 9 | 10 | 11 | 12 | 13 |
|---|---|---|---|---|---|---|---|---|---|---|---|---|---|
| 055 Abkhaz | . | . | . | . | . | . | . | . | . | . | . | . | . |
| 056 Armenians | I | g | D | a | L | f | O | f | E | s | (S) | a | L |
| 057 Kurd | I | i | D | i | S | p | AE | a | L | s | S | a | F L O |
| 058 Basseri | S | d | C | o | L | fi | O | n | E | o | D | p | F L E |
| 059 West Punjabi | A | i | D | i | S | * | E | a | I | s | D‡ | ah | L C O |
| 060 Gond | S | i | B | o | C | (p) | * | n | E | o | P | (p) | D |
| 061 Toda | (S) | e | B | o | C | (p) | R | n | E | o | K | (s) | D |
| 062 Santal | I | g | D | i | S | a | CE* | a | I | s | (D)‡ | ah | E C O |
| 063 Uttar Pradesh | I | g | D | i | S | a | CE* | a | I | s | (D)‡ | ah | E C O |
| 064 Burusho | S | g | B | o | L | p | O | (r) | E | o | S | a | F L |
| 065 Kazak | S | d | A | o | O | o | O | o | O | o | A | o | D |
| 066 Khalka Mongols | U | i | (D) | o | S | s | A | a | (L) | . | D | (e) | S |
| 067 Lolo | U | e | A | a | O | o | O | o | O | o | A | o | S W |
| 068 Lepcha | S | f | B | o | L | p | O | n | E | s | D | p | D |
| 069 Garo | I | i | D | i | S | c | E | a | I | s | D‡ | a | C E L O |
| 070 Lakher | S. | d | A | a | O | o | O | o | O | o | A | o | D |
| 071 Burmese | I | i | D | i | S | c | RE | a | I | s | D | e | C E |
| 072 Lamet | D | e | A | o | O | o | O | o | O | o | A | o | D |
| 073 Vietnamese | D | g | D | o | S | (p) | (A) | n | (L) | s | S | (a) | L O |
| 074 Rhade | D | d | A | o | O | o | O | o | O | o | A | o | D |
| 075 Khmer | A | (e) | D | a | L | f | O | (r) | E | (s) | S | a | S F E T |
| 076 Siamese | A | e | D | i | L | * | O | a | I | s | S | a* | O E |
| 077 Semang | U | d | A | o | O | o | O | o | O | o | A | o | D |
| 078 Nicobarese | S | e | A | p | O | o | O | o | O | o | A | o | D |
| 079 Andamanese | U | e | A | p | O | o | O | o | O | o | A | o | D |
| 080 Vedda | U | f | A | p | O | o | O | o | O | o | A | o | D |
| 081 Tanala | (U) | d | B | o | L | f | O | n | E | o | P | i | W S |
| 082 Negri Sembilan | I | i | D | i | S | c | CE | a | I | s | (S)‡ | (h) | E C |

| | 1 | 2 | 3 | 4 | 5 | 6 | 7 | 8 | 9 | 10 | 11 | 12 | 13 |
|---|---|---|---|---|---|---|---|---|---|---|---|---|---|
| 083 Javanese | I | i | D | i | L | c | O | y | I | s | S | a | O E C |
| 084 Balinese | I | i | D | i | L | c | O | y | I | s | S | a | O E C |
| 085 Iban | S | d | A | o | O | o | O | o | O | o | A | o | D |
| 086 Badjau | U | e | A | o | O | o | O | o | O | o | A | o | D |
| 087 Toradja | S | d | A | p | O | o | O | o | O | o | A | o | S |
| 088 Tobelorese | . | . | . | . | . | . | . | . | . | . | . | . | . |
| 089 Alorese | D | d | D | o | L | a | O | (n) | E | s | S | a | F |
| 090 Tiwi | U | e | A | p | O | o | O | o | O | o | A | o | D |
| 091 Aranda | U | e | A | p | O | o | O | o | O | o | A | o | D |
| 092 Orokaiva | S | d | A | p | O | o | O | o | O | o | A | o | D |
| 093 Kimam | D | d | A | p | O | o | O | o | O | o | A | o | D |
| 094 Kapauka | U | g | C | a | L | i | O | y | E | o | D | i | C E P O |
| 095 Kwoma | S | d | A | ap | O | o | O | o | O | o | A | o | D |
| 096 Manus | S | d | A | o | O | o | O | o | O | o | A | o | D |
| 097 New Ireland | S | e | A | o | O | o | O | o | O | o | A | o | D |
| 098 Trobrianders | S | e | A | a | O | o | O | o | O | o | A | o | F E P |
| 099 Siuai | D | d | A | o | O | o | O | o | O | o | A | o | D |
| 100 Tikopia | U | e | B | p | L | p | O | r | E | r | K | p | O |
| 101 Pentecost | U | f | A | o | O | o | O | o | O | o | A | o | D |
| 102 Mbau Fijians | A | f | D | a | L | q | O | y | E | o | D | h | F T W |
| 103 Ajie | A | e | B | a | C | f | R | n | (O) | (o) | K | . | F O |
| 104 Maori | A | f | A | a | O | o | O | o | O | o | A | o | D |
| 105 Marquesans | A | f | A | a | O | o | O | o | O | o | A | o | S P |
| 106 Samoans | A | e | B | a | S | f | A | z | E | s | P | h | D |
| 107 Gilbertese | A | e | B | o | (L) | p | O | y | O | o | D | p | F O |
| 108 Marshallese | S | d | B | a | L | m | O | y | E | o | K | m | F |
| 109 Trukese | S | d | A | o | O | o | O | o | O | o* | A | o | D |
| 110 Yapese | S | d | B | o | L | p | O | n . | E | o | P | p | S L E O P |

|  | 1 | 2 | 3 | 4 | 5 | 6 | 7 | 8 | 9 | 10 | 11 | 12 | 13 |
|---|---|---|---|---|---|---|---|---|---|---|---|---|---|
| 111 Paluans | A | f | D | a | C | c | (R) | n | E | i | D | (h) | T W O F |
| 112 Ifugao | D | e | A | o | O | o | O | o | O | o | A | o | D |
| 113 Atayal | S | d | A | a | O | o | O | o | O | o | A | o | D |
| 114 Chinese | A | i | D | i | L | c | O | s | (I) | s | S* | a | C L O E |
| 115 Manchu | S | d | A | o | O | o | O | o | O | o | A | o | S |
| 116 Koreans | A | i | D | i | L | c | O | a | (I) | s | S | (a) | C E O |
| 117 Japanese | S | d | D | o | S | c | E | a | I | s | D | e | C E O |
| 118 Ainu | S | d | A | p | O | o | O | o | O | o | A | o | D |
| 119 Gilyak | S | d | A | o | O | o | O | o | O | o | A | o | D |
| 120 Yukaghir | D | f | A | o | O | o | O | o | O | o | A | o | D |
| 121 Chukchee | T | g | A | p | O | o | O | o | O | o | A | o | D |
| 122 Ingalik | U | f | A | o | O | o | O | o | O | o | A | o | D |
| 123 Aleut | U | d | B | o | L | f | O | y | (E) | o | D | s | W O S |
| 124 Copper Eskimo | U | e | A | p | O | o | O | o | O | o | A | o | D |
| 125 Montagnais | U | g | A | p | O | o | O | o | O | o | A | o | D |
| 126 Micmac | U | d | A | p | O | o | O | o | O | o | A | o | D |
| 127 Saulteaux | U | g | A | o | O | o | O | o | O | o | A | o | P |
| 128 Slave | U | f | A | c | O | o, | O | o | O | o | A | o | D |
| 129 Kaska | U | d | A | p | O | o | O | o | O | o | A | o | D |
| 130 Eyak | U | f | B | o | L | q | O | n | O | o | D | p | O P W S |
| 131 Haida | U | f | A | ap | O | o | O | o | O | o | A | o | W S E |
| 132 Bellacoola | U | f | A | o | O | o | O | o | O | o | A' | o | D |
| 133 Twana | U | f | A | a | O | o | O | o | O | o | A | o | D |
| 134 Yurok | U | e | A | a | O | o | O | o | O | o | A | o | P S E |
| 135 Pomo | U | e | A | p | O | o | O | o | O | o | A | o | O P |
| 136 Yokuts | U | f | B | a | L | p | O | n | E | (o) | D | p | E |
| 137 Paiute | U | f | A | p | O | o | O | o | O | o | A | o | D |
| 138 Klamath | U | f | A | a | O | o | O | o | O | o | A | o | D |
| 139 Kutenai | U | d | A | a | O | o | O | o | O | o | A | o | D |

| | 1 | 2 | 3 | 4 | 5 | 6 | 7 | 8 | 9 | 10 | 11 | 12 | 13 |
|---|---|---|---|---|---|---|---|---|---|---|---|---|---|
| 140 Gros Ventre | U | d | A | p | O | o | O | o | O | i | A | o | W |
| 141 Hidatsa | A | f | A | c | O | o | O | o | O | s | A | o | D |
| 142 Pawnee | U | d | A | p | O | o | O | o | O | i | A | o | P |
| 143 Omaha | U | f | A | a | O | o | O | o | O | i | A | o | O W |
| 144 Huron | U | f | C | a | C | f | R | n | E | o | D | h | O E |
| 145 Creek | U | d | A | c | O | o | O | o | O | s | A | o | O s |
| 146 Natchez | U | d | B | a | L | m | O | r | (E) | r | [DS] | (h) | F |
| 147 Comanche | U | f | A | a | O | o | O | o | O | o | A | o | W |
| 148 Chiricahua | U | d | B | o | L | i | O | (y) | O | o | D | i | W P |
| 149 Zuni | U | d | A | o | O | o | O | o | O | m | A | o | D |
| 150 Havasupai | U | d | A | p | O | o | O | o | O | o | A | o | D |
| 151 Papago | U | f | A | p | O | o | O | o | O | o | A | o | D |
| 152 Huichol | S | f | A | p | O | o | O | o | O | s | A | o | D |
| 153 Aztec | A | g | C | c | (L) | f | O | ry | I | s | D | (h) | L F T W S |
| 154 Popoluca | I | g | D | a | S | e | E | a | I | s | D+ | e | C E O |
| 155 Quiche | I | e | C | a | S | e | E | a | I | s | S | a | L E C O |
| 156 Miskito | D | d | A | o | O | o | O | o | O | o | A | o | D |
| 157 Bribri | (U) | (f) | A | o | O | o | O | o | O | o | A | o | D |
| 158 Cuna | A | i | B | . | L | e | O | n | O | s | D | e | D |
| 159 Goajiro | U | f | (B) | p | L | m | O | n | E | o | (K) | (m) | S |
| 160 Haitians | A | i | D | o | L | l | O | a | I | m | S | (a) | O E |
| 161 Callinago | U | (f) | A | a | O | o | O | o | O | o | A | o | W |
| 162 Warrau | U | e | B | o | L | [pm] | O | n | E | r | S | . | D |
| 163 Yanomamo | U | e | A | a | O | o | O | o | O | o | A | o | D |
| 164 Carib | S | (e) | A | o | O | o | O | a | O | o | A | o | D |
| 165 Saramacca | U | g | O | o | L | [ma] | O | y | E | (s) | D | (e) | D |
| 166 Mundurucu | S | f | A | p | O | o | O | o | O | o | A | o | D |
| 167 Cubeo | S | (e) | A | a | O | o | O | o | O | o | A | o | D |

| | 1 | 2 | 3 | 4 | 5 | 6 | 7 | 8 | 9 | 10 | 11 | 12 | 13 |
|---|---|---|---|---|---|---|---|---|---|---|---|---|---|
| 168 Cayapa | S | f | A | o | O | o | O | o | O | s | A | o | (D) |
| 169 Jivaro | U | f | A | o | O | o | O | o | O | o | A | o | D |
| 170 Amahuaca | U | f | A | o | O | o | O | o | O | o | A | o | D |
| 171 Inca | A | g | D | o | L | f | O | r | I | s | S | a | L |
| 172 Aymara | (D) | e | A | o | O | o | O | o | O | o | A | o | D |
| 173 Siriono | U | f | A | o | O | o | O | o | O | o | A | o | D |
| 174 Nambicuara | U | f | A | o | O | o | O | o | O | o | A | o | D |
| 175 Trumai | U | f | A | o | O | o | O | o | O | o | A | o | D |
| 176 Timbira | S | d | A | a | O | o | O | o | O | o | A | o | D |
| 177 Tupinamba | U | e | A | a | O | o | O | o | O | o | A | o | W S |
| 178 Botocudo | U | d | (A) | o | O | o | O | o | O | o | A | o | D |
| 179 Shavante | U | f | A | o | O | o | O | o | O | o | A | o | D |
| 180 Aweikoma | (S) | d | A | o | O | o | O | o | O | o | A | o | D |
| 181 Cayua | U | (e) | A | o | O | o | O | o | O | o | A | o | D |
| 182 Lengua | U | e | A | a | O | o | O | o | O | o | A | o | D |
| 183 Abipon | U | f | A | a | O | o | O | o | O | o | A | o | W |
| 184 Mapuche | I | f* | D | i | S | e | E | a | I | s | (S) | (a) | C O |
| 185 Tehuelche | U | f | A | a | O | o | O | o | O | o | A | o | D |
| 186 Yahgan | U | e | A | o | O | o | O | o | O | o | A | o | D |
| | | | | | | | | | | | | | |
| 11a Chagga | S | d | B | a | L | p | O | s | E | r | K | p | F W |
| 34a Dorobo | U | d | B | o | C | c | R | n | E | o | P | s | D |
| 46a Lebanese | A | i | D | i | S | c | E | a | I | s | S | a | C L O F |
| 60a Chenchu | S | d | B | o | C | p | R | n | E | o | D | p | (D) |
| 68a Sherpa | I | i | C | o | L | f | O | r | E | s | (S) | a | F |
| 90a Murngin | U | f | A | p | O | o | O | o | O | o | A | o | D |
| 95a Wogeo | S | d | A | o | O | o | O | o | O | o | A | o | D |
| 106a Pukapukans | S | d | B | o | L | p | O | y | E | o | D | p | D |
| 138a Washo | U | d | A | a | O | o | O | o | O | o | A | o | (D) |

| | 1 | 2 | 3 | 4 | 5 | 6 | 7 | 8 | 9 | 10 | 11 | 12 | 13 |
|---|---|---|---|---|---|---|---|---|---|---|---|---|---|
| 141a Crow | U | d | A | p | 0 | o | 0 | o | 0 | i | A | o | W 0 |
| 149a Navaho | S | d | A | o | 0 | o | 0 | o | 0 | o | A | o | (D) |
| 175a Bororo | S | d | (B) | o | L | (m) | 0 | y | 0 | o | . | . | D |
| 179a Caraja | U | f | A | o | 0 | o | 0 | o | 0 | o | A | o | 0 |
| 183a Mataco | U | d | B | o | L | c | 0 | y | 0 | o | D | i | (D) |

## NOTES ON TABLE 1

4, column 11: All people were assigned to nonterritorial sectors headed by an appointed councilor resident in the capital. Each sector was responsible for justice, tribute collection, public works, and mobilization.

17, column 10: Youths in age-grades may collect levies or guard property.

18, column 10: Co-operative work groups perform some police functions.

42, column  6: Executive tribal council consists of all councilors and moderators of administrative subdivisions; no presiding officer.

44, column 11: Capital city had an appointed governor.

59, column  6: Not clear whether to code Governor-general or Prime Minister.

60, column  7: Pargana headman shares authority with a panchayat of 4 headmen chosen yearly by assembled headmen of villages of the pargana.

62, column  7: Both chambers have appointed as well as elected members.

63, column  7: Both chambers have appointed as well as elected members.

76, column  6: Prime Minister installed by coup.

76, column 12: Appointed by Minister of Interior.

109, column 10: But some r.

114, column 11: Plural functionaries at this level.

184, column  2: Decline in territory but increase in population.

though many have no political organization beyond the local community, it is possible to combine direct rule with several levels of sovereignty as in a society where the dominant power has created or retained indigenous political structures, exercising close supervision over their operations (73 Vietnamese, 89 Alorese, 21 Wolof). The coding of autonomy thus significantly affects the strength of the remaining variables: the single authoritative leader or the chief judicial functionary of a semiautonomous state has less power than in an autonomous or unadministered state, but more power than in one directly ruled. That is, the kinds of political or judicial decisions which a leader is empowered to make may depend on the degree of autonomy the society enjoys.

It should be stressed that this set of codes applies specifically to political structure above the level of the local community but, with the exception of societies coded B (one level beyond the local community), does not assume that the local community, as defined in Murdock and Wilson (1972), has political authority. The local community was not defined as the smallest unit possessing sovereign powers as this could have resulted in coding of individual families. Rather, the local community was regarded as either a social unit into which executive powers may penetrate or as a social unit which may lie below the lowest level at which sovereign functions are performed.

Where sovereignty levels vary geographically within the area controlled by the society, the rating reflects the typical number of levels (35 Konso, 95a Wogeo, 105 Marquesan, 144 Huron). In those societies where sovereignty level depends upon the personal ability of the executive (106 Samoans, 148 Apache) the coders have analyzed the sources to determine whether the achievement of effective sovereignty at the highest level was customary or atypical and have coded the typical number of levels, using lower case a or c to indicate the occasional existence of a higher level. Finally, there are a few societies where kinship ties are strong and hierarchical but the kin group is not localized in a clear geographic area. In Tikopia and Goajiro, authority lies in the lineage and clan, but it appears that a clan chief has authority over his neighbors regardless of clan.

The coding of both Sovereignty and Executive involved careful analysis of terminology in order to evaluate the extent to which the person holding office did in fact exercise executive authority. The coding was based on concrete examples of political decision-making to ensure consistent coding where chiefs had been created to serve colonial interests and enjoyed no real power or prestige (23 Tallensi, 67 Lolo, 96 Manus, 101 Pentecost, 128 Slave, 140 Gros Ventre, 175a Bororo), or where constitutional limitations on executive power were at variance with political practice at the pinpointed date (37 Amhara, 54 Russians, 114 Chinese, 116 Koreans). For those societies which have both an hereditary ruler (e.g., king) and a popularly chosen leader (e.g., prime minister), the coders again relied on concrete examples to decide which exercises executive authority.

In a number of societies, the sovereign functions as defined in the code—warfare, taxation, judiciary—are of less interest than matters such as religion or land use. The executive of such a society may have some control over the exercise of sovereign authority, but other types of functionaries wield more authority on a daily basis (Tallensi tendaana, Ajie kavu). Similarly, many societies lacking permanent executive functionaries according to the code have temporary leaders with absolute power in time of war or during communal hunts.

## DISCUSSION

### Coder Reliability and Validity

To test the reliability of the coding, the independent ratings of the coders for the 39 societies that were coded by more than one person were subjected to computer analysis. The fourteen alternate societies used for pretesting were included in the reliability study but were omitted from subsequent cross-tabulations. Parentheses were dropped, and in cases of contradiction, the first rating was used. The highest correlations were obtained for variables 1, 3, 9, 10, 12, and 13. Correlations were low for variables 2, 5, 7, and 8. The remaining variables showed intermediate levels of correlation.

As indicated in the discussion of coding problems, variable 5, Executive, was particularly difficult. Rulers of large estates invariably have advisors; whether they constitute a formal body with their own area of jurisdiction is a question which the ethnographer or historian rarely answers. Montezuma, for example, was regarded by the early Spaniards as a single authoritative leader (L) whereas later students of the Aztecs have regarded the leadership as more oligarchic (P) or even shared (S). The advent of written constitutions has not significantly clarified the issue, for, despite constitutional guarantees of separation of powers, a society may in fact have a single authoritative leader. The difficulty of evaluating the degree of control exercised by a political leader, while allowing for the biases of the authors involved, may in part account for the variations in coding. In addition wherever the coders differed on Levels of Sovereignty they would also differ on Executive since they would not be coding the same statuses. The low level of coder reliability on the executive is reflected in variables 7 and 8 which are to some extent dependent on variable 5.

Too little independent coding of political variables has been done to permit extensive testing of the validity of the present ratings. The Ethnographic Atlas (Murdock 1967), however, presents coding of supracommunity levels for 182 of the societies. Despite minor differences in code definitions, there was a high degree of correlation between the two ratings ($r = .71$, $p < .01$).

## Regional Distribution and Percentages

There is significant regional distribution of the thirteen political variables. Of the 184 coded societies, 98 had no political organization beyond the community level; 60 per cent of these stateless societies are found in North and South America, while East Eurasia and Circum-Mediterranean account for the majority of complex states, 61 per cent. As one would expect, unadministered societies nominally controlled by a colonial power occur primarily in North America (36.3 per cent), South America (24.6 per cent), and in Africa (18.1 per cent). These findings are confirmed by the dates of our sample societies, 130 of which fall in the century of colonial expansion, 1850-1945. The further influence of colonialism can be seen in the distribution of variable 2, Trend in Autonomy. Societies with declining autonomy appear in areas with the most exploitative type of colonialism: Insular Pacific (21.8 per cent), North America (21.8 per cent), Africa (18.1 per cent), and East Eurasia (18.1 per cent).

One unanticipated combination was the high incidence of concentrated executive and judicial power: 29 per cent of the sample had single authoritative leaders, and 26.34 per cent had executives who were also chief judicial functionaries. The proportion is even higher if we exclude the 98 stateless societies. Of the remaining 86 societies, 62.7 per cent had single executives, and 57.4 per cent had executives with judicial power. This type of executive and judicial officer occurs primarily in African and Circum-Mediterranean societies, while the shared executive and independent judiciary are more common in East Eurasia.

One striking pattern within the code is the bimodal distribution of levels of authority. The great bulk of the societies are clearly noncentralized, and lack elaborate political superstructures; only a small percentage of the coded societies are intermediate. An evolutionary conclusion can be drawn from the materials. Once societies begin to grow more complex they rapidly develop elaborate centralized systems. If they do not begin to emerge as centralized systems they remain low-level and local in terms of the structure of political behavior. The small number of societies with one or two supra-community levels reflects an unstable political system reminiscent of Highland Burma (Leach 1954), where the political system vacillates between centralization and decentralization. Political systems appear to have a take-off point: once they pass a given level of centralization they continue to develop more complex structures.

*Analysis*

Cross-tabulation of the codes revealed a number of statistically significant findings concerning the economic basis of leadership, methods of state expansion, and recruitment of political officials. Although the intent of this paper is not to present detailed analyses, a brief discussion of these findings is presented here.

The analysis correlated the level of political integration with methods of recruitment. One hypothesis is that high levels of integration will be characterized by bureaucratic models of recruitment.

The code for Selection of Executive can be roughly divided into hereditary (p, q, m, n, f) and nonhereditary (l, c, i, e, a, s). It should be noted that f stands at the borderline since, while choice is limited to a family, the actual number of possible heirs may be large and the final choice open to influence of various sorts. Table 2 corroborates the hypothesis that the method of selection is significant.

TABLE 2

Cross-Tabulation of Variables 3 and 6

| Selection of Executive | Levels | |
| --- | --- | --- |
| | B and C | D |
| Hereditary | 20 | 10 |
| Ruling Family | 13 | 11 |
| Nonhereditary | 9 | 18 |
| $\chi^2 = 10.86$, df $= 2$, p $< .01$ | | |

Furthermore, 57 per cent of the patrilineal executives are in B-level societies while 91 per cent of the council-chosen executives are in D-level societies.

If we consider the type of advisors to the executive, Table 3 shows that examples of relatives occur only where the executive is hereditary, including ruling families, while 75 per cent of the administrative officials occur where the executive is nonhereditary.

TABLE 3

Cross-Tabulation of Variables 6 and 8

| Selection of Executive | Advisors | |
|---|---|---|
| | Relatives | Administrators |
| Hereditary | 6 | 2 |
| Ruling Family | 8 | 3 |
| Nonhereditary | 0 | 15 |

$\chi^2 = 18.8$, df $= 2$, p $< .001$

Of the 41 D-level societies coded, 58.5 per cent had no deliberative or consultative bodies, indicating that the executive was either L (a single authoritative leader) or P (a plural executive). There were fourteen instances of elected bodies: twelve at D level, the other two at C level. Hereditary bodies occurred only five times: three at D level, one each at B and C. Only 27 societies had a deliberative or consultative body; 154 had none, and for five no information was available.

The low number of cases for coding variable 7 reflects the dominant pattern of authoritative executive (L). Of the societies with political organization beyond the community level, 63 per cent have a single authoritative executive. These are found in 76.6 per cent of the B-level, 50 per cent of the C-level, and 58.5 per cent of the D-level societies.

Advisory bodies are most likely to assume an administrative function at higher levels of political integration. Table 4 shows that 50 per cent of the instances of relatives forming the advisory body occur at D level, but, as we have seen, this occurs only where the executive is also hereditary.

Selection of subordinate officials in D-level societies is never strictly hereditary although it may occur within a lineage or privileged group (h). As shown in Table 5, 66 per cent of such cases occur in D-level societies. But as noted above with regard to f in variable 6, this category is midway between hereditary and nonhereditary. More significant is the fact that 50 per cent of elected subordinate officials and 78.78 per cent of the officials appointed by the chief executive occur in D-level societies.

A further characteristic of complex societies is revealed by a correlation

TABLE 4

Cross-Tabulation of Variables 3 and 8

| Advisory Bodies | Levels | | |
|---|---|---|---|
| | B | C | D |
| None | 17 | 6 | 5 |
| Relatives | 5 | 2 | 7 |
| Administrative | 0 | 4 | 19 |

$\chi^2 = 25.17$, df $= 4$, p $< .001$

## TABLE 5
### Cross-Tabulation of Variables 3 and 12

| Selection of Subordinates | Levels | | |
|---|---|---|---|
| | B | C | D |
| Hereditary | 15 | 3 | 0 |
| Lineage | 2 | 2 | 8 |
| Elected | 3 | 2 | 5 |
| Appointed | 2 | 5 | 26 |

$\chi^2 = 38.09$, df = 6, p < .001

between Levels of Sovereignty and Trend in Autonomy. Of the 41 societies with three or more levels, 78 per cent were rated as stable, expanding, or increasing in autonomy during the 25 years preceding the pinpointed date. Conversely 66.3 per cent of the stateless societies were declining in autonomy, population, or territory. Of the fifteen societies with increasing autonomy, only four had an hereditary executive, while in eight cases the executive was selected by a council.

### REFERENCES CITED

Barry, H., and L. M. Paxson. 1971. Infancy and Early Childhood. Ethnology 10: 466-508.

Carneiro, R. L. 1967. On the Relationship between Size of Population and Complexity of Social Organization. Southwest Journal of Anthropology 23: 234-243.

Freeman, L. C., and R. F. Winch. 1957. Societal Complexity: An Empirical Test of a Typology of Societies. American Journal of Sociology 62: 461-466.

Hobhouse, L. T., G. C. Wheeler, and M. Ginsberg. 1915. The Material Culture and Social Institutions of the Simpler Peoples: An Essay in Correlation. London.

Leach, E. R. 1954. Political Systems of Highland Burma. London.

Middleton, J., and D. Tait, eds. 1958. Tribes Without Rulers. London.

Murdock, G. P. 1967. Ethnographic Atlas. Pittsburgh. (Also contained in installments in Ethnology, v. 1-10, 1962-71.)

Murdock, G. P., and D. O. Morrow. 1970. Subsistence Economy and Supportive Practices. Ethnology 9: 302-330.

Murdock, G. P., and D. R. White. 1969. Standard Cross-Cultural Sample. Ethnology 8: 329-369.

Murdock, G. P., and S. Wilson. 1972. Settlement Patterns and Community Organization. Ethnology 11: 254-295.

Schapera, I. 1956. Government and Politics in Tribal Societies. London.

Schwartz, R. D., and J. C. Miller. 1964. Legal Evolution and Societal Complexity. American Journal of Sociology 70: 159-169.

### IDENTIFICATION AND SUPPLEMENTARY BIBLIOGRAPHY

Each society is briefly identified by name, geographical coordinates, and date. The dates are especially significant for this set of codes and should be carefully noted in each case. The coders have attempted to conform precisely to the dates of the Standard Cross-Cultural Sample in order to facilitate intercorrelation, but in some cases this proved impossible. The dates have been altered by no more than 7 years, in order to code a stable and clearly described indigenous system as free as possible from the effects of alien domination or violent upheaval.

The great majority of the sources used in coding are identical with those assessed and published in the previous codes by Murdock and Morrow (1970), Barry and Paxson (1971), and Murdock and Wilson (1972), and the references are therefore omitted below. All additional references used for the present code, however, are listed except for such standard encyclopedic sources as the Statesman's Yearbook.

1. Nama Hottentot of the Gei/ /Khauan tribe (27°30′S, 17°E) in 1860.
2. Kung Bushmen of the Nyae Nyae region (19°50′S, 20°35′E) in 1950.
   Marshall, Lawrence, and Lorna Marshall. 1956. !Kung Bushmen of South West Africa. South West Africa Annual 1956: 11-23.
3. Thonga of the Ronga subtribe (25°50′S, 32°20′E) in 1895.
4. Lozi (14° to 18°S, 22° to 25°E) in 1900.
5. Mbundu of the Bailundo subtribe (12°15′S, 16°30′E) in 1890.
   Duffy, J. 1959. Portuguese Africa. Cambridge, Mass.
6. Suku of Feshi Territory (6°S, 18°E) in 1920.
7. Bemba of Zambia (9° to 12°S, 29° to 32°E) in 1897.
8. Nyakyusa near Mwaya and Masoko (9°30′S, 34°E) in 1934.
9. Hadza (3°20′ to 4°10′S, 34°40′ to 35°25′E) in 1930.
10. Luguru around Morogoro (6°50′S, 37°40′E) in 1925.
11. Kikuyu of the Fort Hall or Metume district (0°40′S, 37°10′E) in 1920.
    Hailey, W. M. H. 1950. Native Administration in the British African Territories, pt. 1. London.
    MacPhee, A. M. 1968. Kenya. New York.
    Ross, W. M. 1968. Kenya from Within: A Short Political History. London.
12. Ganda of the Kyaddondo district (0°20′N, 32°30′E) in 1875.
13. Mbuti Pygmies of the Epulu group (1°30′ to 2°N, 28°20′E) in 1950.
14. Nkundo Mongo of the Ilanga group (0°15′ to 1°15′S, 18°35′ to 19°45′E) in 1930.
    Schebesta, P. 1936. My Pygmy and Negro Hosts. London.
15. Banen of the Ndiki subtribe (4°35′ to 4°45′N, 10°35′ to 11°E) in 1935.
16. Tiv of Benue Province (6°30′ to 8°N, 8° to 10°E) in 1920.
17. Ibo of the Isu-Ama division (5°20′ to 5°40′N, 7°10′ to 7°30′E) in 1935.
18. Fon of the city and environs of Abomey (7°12′N, 1°56′E) in 1890.
19. Ashanti of Kumasi state (6° to 8°N, 0° to 3°W) in 1895.
20. Mende near the town of Bo (7°50′N, 12°W) in 1945.
    Little, K. L. 1947. Mende Political Institutions in Transition. Africa 17: 8-23.
21. Wolof of Upper and Lower Salum in the Gambia (13°45′N, 15°20′W) in 1950.
    Gailey, H. A. 1965. A History of the Gambia. New York.
    Gray, J. M. 1966. A History of the Gambia. New York.
22. Bambara between Segou and Bamako (12°30′N, 6° to 8°W) in 1902.
23. Tallensi (10°30′ to 10°45′N, 0°30′ to 0°40′W) in 1934.
    Rattray, R. S. 1932. Tribes of the Ashanti Hinterland. Oxford.
24. Songhai of the Bamba division (16° to 17°15′N, 0°10′E to 3°10′W) in 1940.
25. Wodaabe Fulani of Niger (13° to 17°N, 5° to 10°E) in 1951.
26. Hausa of Zaria or Zazzau (9°30′ to 11°30′N, 6° to 9°E) in 1900.
    Smith, M. G. 1960. Government in Zazzau. London.
27. Massa of Cameroon (10° to 11°N, 15° to 16°E) in 1910.
28. Azande of the Yambio chiefdom (4°20′ to 5°50′N, 27°40′ to 28°50′E) in 1905.
    Evans-Pritchard, E. E. 1956. A History of the Kingdom of Gbudwe. Zaire 10: 451-491; 675-710; 815-860.
    ———— 1957. The Zande Royal Court. Zaire 11: 361-389; 493-511; 687-713.

———— 1960. The Organization of a Zande Kingdom. Cahiers d'Etudes Africaines 4: 5-37.
29. Fur around Jebel Marra (13°30′N, 25°30′E) in 1880.
MacMichael, H. A. 1967. A History of the Arabs in the Sudan. New York.
30. Otoro of the Nuba Hills (11°20′N, 30°40′E) in 1930.
31. Shilluk (9° to 10°30′N, 31° to 32°E) in 1910.
32. Northern Mao (9° to 9°35′N, 34°30′ to 34°50′E) in 1939.
33. Kaffa (6°50′ to 7°45′N, 35°30′ to 37°E) in 1896.
34. Masai of Tanzania (1°30′ to 5°30′S, 35° to 37°30′E) in 1900.
Sandford, G. R. 1918. An Administrative and Political History of the Masai Reserve. London.
35. Konso of the vicinity of Buso (5°15′N, 37°30′E) in 1935.
36. Somali of the Dolbahanta subtribe (7° to 11°N, 45°30′ to 49°E) in 1900.
Lewis, I. M. 1957. The Somali Lineage System and the Total Genealogy: A General Introduction to Basic Principles of Somali Political Institutions. Hargeisa.
37. Amhara of the Gondar district (11° to 14°N, 36° to 38°30′E) in 1953.
38. Bogo or Belen (15°45′N, 38°45′E) in 1855.
39. Kenuzi Nubians (22° to 24°N, 32° to 33°E) in 1900.
40. Teda nomads of Tibesti (19° to 22°N, 16° to 19°E) in 1950.
41. Tuareg of Ahaggar (21° to 25°N, 4° to 9°E) in 1900.
Nicolaisen, J. 1959. Political Systems of Pastoral Tuareg in Air and Ahaggar. Folk 1: 67-131.
———— 1963. Ecology and Culture of the Pastoral Tuareg. Nationalmuseets Skrifter, Etnografisk Raekke 9: 1-540. Copenhagen.
42. Riffians of northern Morocco (34°20′ to 35°30′N, 2°30′ to 4°W) in 1926.
43. Egyptians of the town and environs of Silwa (24°45′N, 33°E) in 1950.
Harris, G. L., ed. 1957. Egypt. New Haven.
44. Hebrews of the kingdom of Judah (30°30′ to 31°55′N, 34°20′ to 35°30′E) in 621 B.C.
Bright, J. 1959. A History of Israel. Philadelphia.
45. Babylonians of the city and environs of Babylon (32°35′N, 44°45′E) in 1750 B.C.
46. Rwala Bedouin (31° to 35°30′N, 36° to 41°E) in 1913.
47. Turks of the Anatolian plateau (38°40′ to 40°N, 32°40′ to 35°50′E) in 1950.
Lerner, D. 1958. The Passing of Traditional Society. New York.
48. Gheg Albanians (41°20′ to 42°40′N, 19°30′ to 20°30′E) in 1910.
49. Romans of the city and environs of Rome (41°50′N, 13°30′E) in A.D. 110.
Grant, M. 1960. The World of Rome. London.
Pliny. 1969. Letters and Panegyricus, 2v., trans. B. Radice. Cambridge.
Rostovtzeff, M. I. 1945. A History of the Ancient World, trans. J. D. Duff. Oxford.
50. Basques of Vera de Bidasoa (43°12′ to 43°20′N, 1°35′ to 1°45′W) in 1940.
Madariaga, S. de. 1940. Spain. New York.
51. Irish of Kinvarra parish (53°5′N, 9°W) in 1955.
52. Lapps of Könkämä district (68°20′ to 69°5′N, 20°5′ to 23°E) in 1950.
Manker, E. 1953. The Nomadism of the Swedish Mountain Lapps. Nordiska Museet: Acta Lapponica 7: 1-261.
53. Yurak Samoyed (65° to 71°N, 41° to 62°E) in 1894.
54. Russians of the peasant village of Viriatino (52°40′N, 41°20′E) in 1952.
Fainsod, M. 1958. How Russia is Ruled. Cambridge.
Schapiro, L. 1960. The Communist Party of the Soviet Union. London.
55. Abkhaz (42°50′ to 43°25′N, 40° to 41°35′E) in 1880.
56. Armenians in the vicinity of Erevan (40°N, 44°30′E) in 1843.
Seton-Watson, H. 1967. The Russian Empire. Oxford.
57. Kurd in and near the town of Rowanduz (36°30′N, 44°30′E) in 1951.
Leach, E. R. 1940. Social and Economic Organization of the Rowanduz Kurds. London School of Economics, Monographs on Social Anthropology 3: 1-74.
Longrigg, S. H. 1953. 'Iraq, 1900-1950. London.

58. Basseri of the nomadic branch (27° to 31°N, 53° to 54°E) in 1958.
59. West Punjabi of the village of Mohla (32°30'N, 74°E) in 1950.
    Callard, K., and R. S. Wheeler. 1963. Pakistan. Major Governments of Asia, ed. G. McT. Kahin, pp. 419-532. Ithaca.
    Palmer, N. D. 1961. The Indian Political System. Boston.
    Symonds, R. 1950. The Making of Pakistan. London.
60. Gond of the Hill Maria division (19°15' to 20°N, 80°30' to 81°20'E) in 1932.
    Grigson, W. V. 1949. The Maria Gonds of Bastar. Rev. edit. London.
61. Toda of the Nilgiri Hills (11° to 12°N, 76° to 77°E) in 1900.
    Fox, R. G. 1963. Caste Dominance and Coercion in the Nilgiris. Papers of the Michigan Academy of Science, Arts, and Letters 48: 493-512.
62. Santal of Bankura and Birbhum districts (23° to 24°N, 86°50' to 87°30'E) in 1940.
63. Uttar Pradesh in and near Senapur village (25°55'N, 83°E) in 1945.
64. Burusho of Hunza state (36°20' to 36°30'N, 74°30' to 74°40'E) in 1934.
    Lorimer, D. L. R. 1935. The Burushaski Language, v.i. Olso.
65. Kazak of the Great Horde (37° to 48°N, 68° to 81°E) in 1885.
    Sedel'nikov, A. N., A. N. Bukeikhanov, and S. D. Chadov. 1903. Kirgizskii Krai. Polnoe Geograficheskoe Opisanie Nashego Otechestva, ed. V. P. Semenov, v. 18, pp. 138-222. St.-Peterburg.
66. Khalka Mongols of Narobanchin territory (47° to 47°20'N, 95°10' to 97°E) in 1915-19.
    Friters, G. M. 1949. Outer Mongolia and Its International Position. Baltimore.
    Rupen, R. A. 1956. General Character of the Society. Mongolian People's Republic, ed. W. M. Ballis, v. 1, pp. 1-48. New Haven.
67. Lolo of Taliang Shan mountains (26° to 29°N, 103° to 104°E) in 1910.
    Liétard, A. 1913. Au Yun-nan: Les Lo-Lo P'o. Anthropos 1: 1-272.
68. Lepcha of Lingthem and vicinity (27° to 28°N, 89°E) in 1937.
69. Garo of Rengsanggri and neighboring villages (26°N, 91°E) in 1955.
70. Lakher (22°20'N, 93°E) in 1930.
71. Burmese of Nondwin village (22°N, 95°40'E) in 1960.
    Somit, A., and J. Welsh. 1956. The Constitution and Government. Burma, ed. F. N. Trager, v. 2, pp. 899-958. New Haven.
72. Lamet of northwestern Laos (20°N, 100°40'E) in 1940.
73. North Vietnamese of the Red River delta (20° to 21°N, 105°30' to 107°E) in 1930.
    Gourou, P. 1955. Peasants of Tonkin Delta, a Study of Human Geography. New Haven.
    Linton, A. n.d. Summary of Vietnameses culture prepared for HRAF. Ms.
74. Rhade of the village of Ko-sier (13°N, 108°E) in 1962.
75. Khmer of Angkor (13°30'N, 103°50'E) in 1292.
    Coedès, G. 1968. The Indianized States of Southeast Asia, ed. W. F. Vella. Honolulu.
76. Siamese of the village of Bang Chan (14°N, 100°52'E) in 1955.
    Busch, N. F. 1964. Thailand: An Introduction to Modern Siam. Princeton.
    Insor, D. 1963. Thailand, a Political, Social, and Economic Analysis. New York.
    Ninth Pacific Science Conference. 1957. Thailand Past and Present. Bangkok.
77. Semang of the Jahai subtribe (4°30' to 5°30'N, 101° to 101°30'E) in 1925.
78. Nicobarese of the northern islands (8°15' to 9°15'N, 92°40' to 93°E) in 1870.
79. Andamanese of the Aka Bea tribe (11°45' to 12°N, 93° to 93°10'E) in 1860.
80. Forest Vedda (7°30' to 8°N, 81° to 81°30'E) in 1860.
81. Tanala of the Menabe subtribe (20°S, 48°E) in 1925.
82. Negri Sembilan of Inas district (2°30' to 2°40'N, 102°10' to 102°20'E) in 1958.
    Parmer, J. N. 1959. Malaya and Singapore. Government and Politics of Southeast Asia, ed. G. McT. Kahin, pp. 241-312. Ithaca.
83. Javanese in the vicinity of Pare (7°43'S, 112°13'E) in 1960.
    Grant, B. 1964. Indonesia. Melbourne.

Kahin, G. McT. 1963. Indonesia. Major Governments of Asia, ed. G. McT. Kahin, pp. 535-688. Ithaca.
84. Balinese of the village of Tihingan (8°30'S, 115°20'E) in 1960.
Grant, B. 1964. Indonesia. Melbourne.
Kahin, G. McT. 1963. Indonesia. Major Governments of Asia, ed. G. McT. Kahin, pp. 535-688. Ithaca.
85. Iban of the Ulu Ai group (2°N, 112°30' to 113°30'E) in 1950.
Roberts, C. F., and I. Kaplan, eds. 1956. North Borneo, Brunei, Sarawak. New Haven.
86. Badjan of Tawi-Tawi and adjacent islands (5°N, 120°E) in 1863.
87. Toradja of the Bare'e subgroup (2°S, 121°E) in 1910.
88. Tobelorese of Tobelo district (1°N, 128°30'E) in 1900.
89. Alorese of Atimelang (8°20'S, 124°40'E) in 1938.
90. Tiwi (11° to 11°45'S, 130° to 132°E) in 1929.
91. Aranda of Alice Springs (23°30' to 25°S, 132°30' to 134°20'E) in 1896.
92. Orokaiva of the Aiga subtribe (8°20' to 8°40'S, 147°50' to 148°10'E) in 1925.
93. Kimam of the village of Bamol (7°30'S, 38°30'E) in 1960.
94. Kapauku of Botukebo village (4°S, 36°E) in 1955.
95. Kwoma of the Hongwam subtribe (4°10'S, 142°40'E) in 1937.
96. Manus of Peri village (2°10'S, 147°10'E) in 1929.
97. New Irelanders of Lesu village (2°30'S, 151°E) in 1930.
98. Trobrianders of Kiriwina island (8°38'S, 151°4'E) in 1914.
Powell, H. A. 1960. Competitive Leadership in Trobriand Political Organization. Journal of the Royal Anthropological Institute 90: 118-145.
Uburoi, J. P. S. 1962. Politics of the Kula Ring. New York.
99. Siuai of the northeastern group (7°S, 155°20'E) in 1939.
100. Tikopia (12°30'S, 168°30'E) in 1930.
Firth, R. 1960. Succession to Chieftainship in Tikopia. Oceania 30: 161-180.
101. Pentecost islanders of Bunlap village (16°S, 168°E) in 1953.
102. Fijians of Mbau island (18°S, 178°35'E) in 1840.
103. Ajie of Neje chiefdom (21°20'S, 165°40'E) in 1845.
Guiart, J. 1963. Structure de la chefferie en Mélanésie du Sud. Travaux et Mémoires de l'Institut d'Ethnologie 66: 1-688.
104. Maori of the Nga Puhi tribe (35°10' to 35°30'S, 174° to 174°20'E) in 1820.
Best, E. 1952. The Maori as He Was. Wellington.
Wright, H. M. 1959. New Zealand, 1769-1840: Early Years of Western Contact. Cambridge.
105. Marquesans of southwest Nuku Hiva (8°55'S, 140°10'W) in 1800.
Forster, J. G. A. 1777. A Voyage Round the World in His Britannic Majesty's Sloop Resolution, Commanded by Captain J. Cook, During the Years 1772, 3, 4, and 5. London.
106. Samoans of western Upolu (13°48' to 14°S, 172°W) in 1829.
Bülow, W. von. 1897. Der Stammbaum der Könige von Samoa. Globus 71.
Davidson, J. W. 1948. Political Development in Western Samoa. Pacific Affairs 21: 136-149.
Ember, M. 1962. Political Authority and the Structure of Kinship in Aboriginal Samoa. American Anthropologist 64: 964-971.
Keesing, F. M. 1934. Modern Samoa: Its Government and Changing Life. London.
Krämer, A. 1906. Hawaii, Ostmikronesien, Samoa. Stuttgart.
Panoff, M. 1964. L'ancienne organisation cérémonielle et politique des Samoa occidentales. L'Homme, v. 4, no. 2: 63-83.
107. Gilbertese of Makin island (3°30'N, 172°20'E) in 1890.
108. Marshallese of Jaluit atoll (6°N, 169°15'E) in 1900.
Senfft, A. 1903. Die Marshall-Insulaner. Rechtsverhältnisse von eingeborenen Völkern in Afrika und Ozeanien, ed. S. R. Steinmetz, pp. 425-455. Berlin.

109. Trukese of Romonum island (7°24′N, 151°40′E) in 1947.
     Goodenough, W. H. 1951. Property, Kin, and Community on Truk. Yale University Publications in Anthropology 46: 1-192.
     —— 1969. Changing Social Organization on Romonum, Truk: 1947-1965. Unpublished ms.
110. Yapese (9°30′N, 138°10′E) in 1910.
     Schneider, D. M. 1953. Yap Kinship Terminology and Kin Groups. American Anthropologist 55: 215-236.
     Senfft, A. 1903. Ethnographische Beiträge über die Carolineninsel Yap. Petermanns Mitteilungen 49: 46-60, 83-87.
111. Palauans of Koror island (7°N, 134°30′E) in 1873.
     Kubary, J. S. 1873. Die Palau-Inseln in der Südsee. Journal des Museum Godeffroy 1: 181-238. Hamburg.
     —— 1900. Die Verbrechen und das Strafverfahren auf den Pelau-Inseln. Die mikronesischen Kolonien aus ethnologischen Gesichtspunkten, ed. A. Bastian, 2: 1-36. Berlin.
     Semper, K. 1873. Die Palau-Inseln im Stillen Ozean. Leipzig.
112. Ifugao of the Kiangan group (16°50′N, 121°10′E) in 1910.
113. Atayal (23°50′ to 24°50′N, 120°20′ to 120°50′E) in 1930.
     Ferrell, R. 1969. Taiwan Aboriginal Groups: Problems in Cultural and Linguistic Classification. Institute of Ethnology Academia Sinica, Monograph 17.
114. Chinese of Kaihsienkung village in north Chekiang (31°N, 120°5′E) in 1936.
     Ch'ien, Tuan-sheng. 1967. The Government and Politics of China. Cambridge.
     Linebarger, P. M. A., D. Chu, and A. W. Burks. 1956. Far Eastern Governments and Politics: China and Japan. Princeton.
115. Manchu of the Aigun district (50°N, 125°30′E) in 1915.
116. Koreans of Kanghwa island (37°37′N, 126°25′E) in 1950.
117. Japanese of southern Okayama prefecture (34°30′ to 35°N, 133°40′E) in 1950.
     Buck, P. W., and J. W. Masland. 1950. The Governments of Foreign Powers, pp. 591-710. New York.
118. Ainu of the Tokapchi and Saru basins (42°40′ to 43°N, 142° to 144°E) in 1880.
     Cornell, J. B. 1964. Ainu Assimilation and Cultural Extinction: Acculturation Policy in Hokkaido. Ethnology 3: 287-304.
119. Gilyak (53° to 54°30′N, 139° to 143°10′E) in 1880.
120. Yukaghir of the upper Kolyma River (63°30′ to 66°N, 150° to 157°E) in 1900.
121. Chukchee of the Reindeer group (63° to 70°N, 171°E to 171°W) in 1900.
122. Ingalik of Shageluk village (62°30′N, 159°30′W) in 1885.
123. Aleut of the Unalaska branch (53° to 57°30′N, 158° to 170°W) in 1778.
     Sauer, M. 1802. An Account of a Geographical and Astronomical Expedition to the Northern Parts of Russia. London.
124. Copper Eskimo of the mainland (66°40′ to 69°20′N, 108° to 117°W) in 1915.
125. Montagnais of the Lake St. John and Mistassini bands (48° to 52°N, 73° to 75°W) in 1910.
126. Micmac of the mainland (43°30′ to 50°N, 60° to 66°W) in 1650.
127. Saulteaux of the Berens River, Little Grand Rapids, and Pekangekum bands (51°30′ to 52°30′N, 94° to 97°W) in 1930.
128. Slave in the vicinity of Fort Simpson (62°N, 122°W) in 1940.
     Helm, J., and E. Leacock. n.d. The Hunting Tribes of Subarctic Canada. Unpublished ms.
129. Kaska of the upper Liard River (60°N, 131°W) in 1900.
130. Eyak (60° to 61°N, 144° to 146°W) in 1890.
131. Haida of the village of Masset (54°N, 132°30′W) in 1875.
132. Bellacoola (52°20′N, 126° to 127°W) in 1880.
133. Twana (47°20′ to 47°30′N, 123°10′ to 123°20′W) in 1860.
134. Yurok (41°30′N, 124°W) in 1850.
135. Eastern Pomo of Clear Lake (39°N, 123°W) in 1850.

Aginsky, B. W., and E. G. Aginsky. 1967. Deep Valley. New York.

Barrett, S. A. 1908. The Ethno-Geography of the Pomo and Neighboring Indians. University of California Publications in American Archaeology and Ethnology 6: 1-332.

Gifford, E. W., and A. L. Kroeber. 1937. Culture Element Distributions: IV, Pomo. University of California Publications in American Archaeology and Ethnography 37: 117-254.

136. Yokuts around Tulare Lake (35°10′N, 119°20′W) in 1850.

Cook, S. F. 1955. The Aboriginal Population of the San Joaquin Valley. Anthropological Records 16: 31-81.

Gayton, A. H. 1936. Estudillo Among the Yokuts: 1819. Essays in Anthropology presented to A. L. Kroeber, ed. R. H. Lowie, pp. 67-85. Berkeley.

Powers, S. 1877. Tribes of California. Contributions to North American Ethnology 3: 369-392.

137. Wadadika Paiute of Harney Valley (43° to 44°N, 118° to 120°W) in 1870.
138. Klamath (42° to 43°15′N, 121°20′ to 122°20′W) in 1860.
139. Kutenai of the Lower or eastern branch (48°40′ to 49°10′N, 116°40′W) in 1890.
140. Gros Ventre (47° to 49°N, 106° to 110°W) in 1880.
141. Hidatsa of Hidatsa village (47°N, 101°W) in 1836.
142. Pawnee of the Skidi band (42°N, 100°W) in 1867.
143. Omaha (41°10′ to 41°40′N, 96° to 97°W) in 1854.
144. Huron of the Attignawantan and Attigneenongnahac tribes (44° to 45°N, 78° to 80°W) in 1634.
145. Creek of the Upper Creek division (32°30′ to 34°20′N, 85°30′ to 86°30′W) in 1800.
146. Natchez (31°30′N, 91°25′W) in 1718.

MacLeod, W. C. 1924. Natchez Political Evolution. American Anthropologist 26: 201-229.

147. Comanche (30° to 38°N, 98° to 103°W) in 1870.
148. Chiricahua Apache of the Central band (32°N, 109°30′W) in 1870.

Opler, M. E. 1937. An Outline of Chiricahua Apache Social Organization. Social Anthropology of North American Tribes, ed. F. Eggan, pp. 173-239. Chicago.

149. Zuni (35°50′ to 35°30′N, 108°30′ to 109°W) in 1880.

Eggan, F. 1950. Social Organization of the Western Pueblos. Chicago.

150. Havasupai (35°20′ to 36°20′N, 111°20′ to 113°W) in 1918.
151. Papago of the Archie division (32°N, 112°W) in 1910.

Underhill, R. M. 1939. Social Organization of the Papago Indians. Columbia University Contributions to Anthropology 30: 1-280.

152. Huichol (22°N, 105°W) in 1890.
153. Aztec of the city and environs of Tenochtitlan (19°N, 99°10′W) in 1520.

Prescott, W. H. 1922. The Conquest of Mexico. 2v. New York.

154. Popoluca around the Pueblo of Soteapan (18°15′N, 94°50′W) in 1940.
155. Quiche of the town of Chichicastenango (15°N, 91°W) in 1930.
156. Miskito near Cape Gracias a Dios (15°N, 83°W) in 1921.

Helms, M. W. 1969. The Cultural Ecology of a Colonial Tribe. Ethnology 8: 76-84.

157. Bribri tribe of Talamanca (9°N, 83°15′W) in 1917.
158. Cuna of San Blas Archipelago (9° to 9°30′N, 78° to 79°W) in 1927.

Holloman, R. 1969. Acculturation and the Cuna. Field Museum of Natural History Bulletin 40: 7, 4-9.

159. Goajiro (11°30′ to 12°20′N, 71° to 72°30′W) in 1947.

Santa Cruz, A. 1960. Acquiring Status in Goajiro Society. Anthropological Quarterly 33: 115-127.

160. Haitians of Mirebalais (18°50′N, 72°10′W) in 1935.
161. Callinago of Dominica (15°30′N, 60°30′W) in 1650.
162. Warrau of the Orinoco delta (8°30′ to 9°50′N, 60°40′ to 62°30′W) in 1935.

163. Yanomamo of the Shamatari tribe (2° to 2°45′N, 64°30′ to 65°30′W) in 1965.
164. Carib along the Barama River (7°10′ to 7°40′N, 59°20′ to 60°20′W) in 1932.
165. Saramacca of the upper Suriname River (3° to 4°N, 55°30′ to 56°W) in 1928.
166. Mundurucu of Cabrua village (7°S, 57°W) in 1850.
167. Cubeo of the Caduiari River (1° to 1°50′N, 70° to 71°W) in 1939.
168. Cayapa of the Rio Cayapas drainage (0°40′ to 1°15′N, 78°45′ to 79°10′W) in 1908.
169. Jivaro (2° to 4°S, 77° to 79°W) in 1920.
170. Amahuaca of the upper Inuya River (10°10′ to 10°30′S, 72° to 72°30′W) in 1960.
171. Inca in the vicinity of Cuzco (13°30′S, 72°W) in 1530.
     Brundage, B. C. 1963. Empire of the Inca. Norman.
172. Aymara of Chucuito (16°S, 65°45′W) in 1940.
173. Siriono near the Rio Blanco (14° to 15°S, 63° to 64°W) in 1942.
174. Nambicuara of the Cocozu group (12°30′ to 13°30′S, 58°30′ to 59°W) in 1940.
175. Trumai (11°50′S, 53°40′W) in 1938.
176. Timbira of the Ramcocamecra subtribe (6° to 7°S, 45° to 46°W) in 1915.
177. Tupinamba in the vicinity of Rio de Janeiro (22°35′ to 23°S, 42° to 44°30′W) in 1550.
     Magalhaes de Gandavo, P. de. 1922. History of the Province of Santa Cruz. Documents and Narratives Concerning the Discovery and Conquest of Latin America: The Histories of Brazil 2: 11-121. New York.
178. Botocudo of the Naknenuk subtribe (18° to 20°S, 41°30′ to 43°30′W) in 1884.
     Wied-Neuwied, M. zu. 1820-21. Reise nach Brasilien in den Jahren 1815 bis 1817, v.2. Frankfurt am main.
179. Shavante in the vicinity of São Domingo (13°30′S, 51°30′W) in 1958.
180. Aweikoma (28°S, 50°W) in 1932.
181. Cayua of southern Mato Grosso (23° to 24°S, 54° to 56°W) in 1890.
182. Lengua (23° to 24°S, 58° to 59°W) in 1889.
183. Abipon (27° to 29°S, 59° to 60°W) in 1750.
184. Mapuche in the vicinity of Temuco (38°30′S, 72°35′W) in 1950.
185. Tehuelche (40° to 50°S, 64° to 72°W) in 1870.
186. Yahgan (54°30′ to 56°30′S, 67° to 72°W) in 1865.
11a. Chagga of Mt. Kilimanjaro (3° to 4°S, 37° to 38°E) in 1906.
     Dundas, C. 1924. Kilimanjaro and Its People. London.
34a. Dorobo of the North Tindiret Forest band (0°10′N, 35°30′E) in 1927.
46a. Lebanese of Al-Munsif village (34°25′N, 35°40′E) in 1950.
     Patai, R., ed. 1956. The Republic of Lebanon. New Haven.
60a. Chenchu of the Forest group (16°15′N, 79°E) in 1940.
68a. Sherpa of the Khumbu region (86°40′ to 86°50′E, 17°48′ to 27°54′N) about 1950.
     Bishop, R. N. W. 1952. Unknown Nepal, ed. J. E. Cunningham. London.
     Vamśávali. 1958. History of Nepal, ed. D. Wright. Calcutta.
90a. Northeastern Murngin of Capes Arnhem and Wilburforce (136°10′ to 137°E, 11°45′ to 12°35′S) about 1930.
     Berndt, R. M. 1955. 'Murngin' (Wulamba) Social Organization. American Anthropologist 57: 84-106.
     Berndt, R. M., and C. H. Berndt. 1954. Arnhem Land: Its History and Its People. Melbourne.
95a. Wogeo Islanders of Wonevaro district (3°S, 144°E) in 1930.
     Hogbin, H. I. 1938. Social Reaction to Crime: Law and Morals in the Schouten Island, New Guinea. Journal of the Royal Anthropological Institute of Great Britain and Ireland 68: 223-262.
     ———— 1939. Native Land Tenure in New Guinea. Oceania 10: 113-165.
106a. Pukapukans of Danger Island (10°53′S, 165°50′W) in 1915.
138a. Washo around Lake Tahoe and Washoe Lake in Southwestern Nevada and

the Californian border (38°20′ to 40°10′N, 119°30′ to 120°15′W) about 1860.
141a. Crow Indians (42°30′ to 47°N, 105° to 111°W) in 1870.
Wildschut, W., and J. C. Ewers. 1960. Crow Indian Medicine Bundles. Contributions from the Museum of the American Indian 17: 1-178.
149a. Ramah Navaho, centered around the town of Ramah (35°N, 108°30′W) in 1940.
175a. Bororo of the Rio Vermelho (15°30′ to 16°S, 54°30′ to 55°W) in 1936.
Lévi-Strauss, C. 1961. World on the Wane. New York.
179a. Caraja along the west bank of the Araguaya River (10°12′ to 15°15′S, 50°25′ to 51°50′W) in 1908.
183a. Mataco of the Guisnay and Vejó divisions in Argentina (22° to 24°S, 62° to 64°W) in 1875.
Métraux, A. 1946. Ethnography of the Chaco. Bulletins of the Bureau of American Ethnology 143: i, 197-370.

# 5

# Measurement of Cultural Complexity

*George P. Murdock* and *Caterina Provost*

When anthropologists differentiate cultures in terms of their relative complexity, they do not use the term "complex" in its ordinary, literal, or dictionary sense. What they imply, rather, is their status *vis-à-vis* one another with reference to one or more classificatory criteria which have been postulated to correlate with different levels or stages in cultural development. Examples are legion, e.g., literate as opposed to preliterate societies, food producers *vs.* food gatherers, sedentary *vs.* nomadic populations, state builders *vs.* stateless societies, workers in stone, bronze, and iron, Morgan's levels of savagery, barbarism, and civilization. Though frequently illustrated, such classificatory categories or sequences have rarely been established, much less tested, by quantitative scientific methods.

A noteworthy exception is the scalogram analysis by Carneiro (1970), in which the incidence of several hundred traits was noted for 100 societies, which were ranked according to Guttman's technique in terms of the number of traits reported for each. The present authors have been stimulated by this study to test its results by different methods with the data on 186 sample societies assembled by the Cross-Cultural Cumulative Coding Center at the University of Pittsburgh. Instead of examining the incidence of individual traits, we have chosen to assess ten groups of comparable traits, each ordered according to a five-point scale of relative complexity.

## The Scales and Their Definition

The ten scales and the five points on each are defined below.

### Scale 1: Writing and Records

This scale was devised to take account of the widely recognized distinction between literate and nonliterate (or preliterate) societies. It assigns higher scores to writing and lower ones to nonwritten records and mnemonic devices.

4 The society has an indigenous system of true writing and possesses written records of at least modest significance.

3 The society has an indigenous system of writing but lacks any significant accumulation of written records, or alternatively has long used the script of alien people.

2 The society lacks true writing but possesses significant nonwritten records in the form of picture writing, quipus, pictorial inscriptions, or the like.

1 Writing and significant records are lacking but the people employ mnemonic devices, e.g., simple tallies.
0 Writing, records, and mnemonic devices in any form are lacking or unreported.

## Scale 2: Fixity of Residence

This scale is designed to indicate the extent to which the mode of life is sedentary or nomadic, cultural complexity having frequently been found to be correlated with settled life. It is adapted from Column 1 in Murdock and Wilson (1972).
4 Settlements are sedentary and relatively permanent.
3 Settlements are sedentary but impermanent.
2 The pattern of settlement is semisedentary.
1 The pattern of settlement is seminomadic.
0 The pattern of settlement is fully nomadic.

## Scale 3: Agriculture

This scale, indicating the degree of dependence upon agriculture for subsistence and the intensity with which it is practiced, is intended to provide a measure of the extent to which the society subsists by food production as opposed to food gathering. It is adapted from Column 2 in Murdock and Morrow (1970) with additional information from Murdock and Provost (1973) and Murdock (1967).
4 Agriculture contributes more to the society's food supply than does any other subsistence activity and is conducted by intensive techniques such as irrigation, plowing, or artificial fertilization.
3 Agriculture contributes more to the food supply than does any other subsistence activity but is not conducted by intensive techniques.
2 Agriculture yields more than 10 per cent of the society's food supply but not as much as does some other subsistence activity.
1 Agriculture is practiced but yields less than 10 per cent of the food supply.
0 Agriculture is not practiced or is confined to nonfood crops.

## Scale 4: Urbanization

This scale, indicating the average population of local communities, is designed to measure the degree of urbanization of the society, large concentrations of population having frequently been found to be correlated with cultural complexity. It is adapted from Column 3 in Murdock and Wilson (1972).
4 The population of local communities averages in excess of 1,000 persons.
3 The population of local communities averages between 400 and 999 persons.
2 The population of local communities averages between 200 and 399 persons.
1 The population of local communities averages between 100 and 199 persons.
0 The population of local communities averages fewer than 100 persons.

## Scale 5: Technological Specialization

This scale is designed to measure the degree of complexity and specialization in technological crafts. It is adapted from data in Murdock and Provost (1973).

4 The society is reported to have a variety of craft specialists, including at least smiths, weavers, and potters.

3 The society is reported to have specialized metalworkers or smiths but to lack loom weaving and/or pottery.

2 Loom weaving is practiced but metalworking is absent or unreported.

1 Pottery is made but metalworking and loom weaving are absent or unreported.

0 Metalworking, loom weaving, and potterymaking are all absent or unreported.

## Scale 6: Land Transport

This scale is designed to measure the degree of complexity in the means of land transportation and thus presumably indirectly the extent of intergroup trade. It is adapted from Column 7 in Murdock and Morrow (1970).

4 Automotive vehicles, e.g., railroads and trucks, are employed extensively in land transport. Since these have commonly been introduced by foreigners in formerly colonial areas they are indicated only where they were thoroughly integrated into the indigenous economy at the pinpointed date.

3 Animal-drawn wheeled vehicles are employed in land transport but motorized vehicles are seldom or never used.

2 Land transport is conducted to a considerable extent by means of draft animals dragging a sled, travois, or other vehicle without wheels.

1 Land transport is effected mainly by pack rather than draft animals.

0 Land transport is effected exclusively by human carriers.

## Scale 7: Money

This scale is designed to measure the degree of complexity with respect to media of exchange and thus indirectly the level of economic organization. It is adapted from Column 9 in Murdock and Morrow (1970).

4 The society uses an indigenous currency in the form of metal coins of standard weight and fineness and/or their equivalent in paper currency.

3 The society uses indigenous articles of token or conventional value, such as cowrie shells, wampum, or imitation tools, as an elementary form of money.

2 The society lacks any form of indigenous money but has long used the currency of an alien people, e.g., that of its colonial rulers.

1 True money is lacking but the society employs domestically usable articles, such as salt, grain, livestock, or ornaments, as a medium of exchange.

0 The society lacks any recognized medium of exchange, conducting mercantile transactions through the direct or indirect exchange of goods, e.g., barter.

## Scale 8: Density of Population

This scale, which indicates the mean density of population in the territory controlled or exploited by the society, is designed to provide an indirect measure of cultural complexity, which is commonly considered to correlate with population density. It is adapted from Column 4 in Murdock and Wilson (1972).

4 The mean density of population exceeds 100 persons per square mile.

3 The density of population averages between 26 and 100 persons per square mile.

2 The density of population averages between 5.1 and 25 persons per square mile.

1 The density of population averages between one and five persons per square mile.

0 The density of population averages fewer than one person per square mile.

## Scale 9: Level of Political Integration

This scale indicates the complexity of political organization in terms of the number of distinct jurisdictional levels recognizable in the society. It is adapted from Columns 1 and 3 in Tuden and Marshall (1972), Column 15 in Murdock and Wilson (1972), and Column 32 in Murdock (1967).

4 Three or more administrative levels are recognized above that of the local community, as in the case of a large state organized into provinces which are subdivided into districts.

3 Two administrative levels are recognized above that of the local community, as in the case of a small state divided into administrative districts.

2 One administrative level is recognized above that of the local community, as in the case of a petty state with a paramount chief ruling over a number of local communities. Societies which are politically completely dependent, lacking any political organization of their own and wholly absorbed into the political system of a dominant society of alien culture, are likewise coded as 2.

1 The society is stateless but is composed of politically organized autonomous local communities.

0 The society is stateless, and political authority is not centralized even on the local level but is dispersed among households or other small component units.

## Scale 10: Social Stratification

This scale is designed to indicate the relative complexity of graded status distinctions within the society. It is adapted from Columns 67, 69, and 71 in Murdock (1967).

4 The society exhibits a complex stratification into three or more distinct classes or castes regardless of the presence or absence of slavery.

3 The society is stratified into two social classes of freemen, e.g., nobles and

commoners or a propertied elite and a propertyless proletariat, plus hereditary slavery and/or recognized caste divisions.

2 The society is stratified into two social classes of freemen but lacks both caste distinctions and hereditary slavery.

1 Formal class distinctions are lacking among freemen, but hereditary slavery prevails and/or there are important status differences based on the possession or distribution of wealth.

0 The society is essentially egalitarian, lacking social classes, castes, hereditary slavery, and important wealth distinctions.

## Coded Data

The coded data are presented in Table 1, where the 186 sample societies are listed in order of their identifying numbers, followed by their names and a symbol indicating the world region in which they are located (A for Africa, C for Circum-Mediterranean, E for East Eurasia, I for Insular Pacific, N for North America, and S for South America). The numbered columns present the ratings for each society on Scales 1 through 10, and the final column gives the sum of these ratings.

The authors followed a conservative policy in coding. Thus a cultural element not mentioned in any of the sources consulted was ordinarily coded as absent. On Scales 4 and 8, however, it was considered preferable to make an educated guess, and on Scale 5 an item recently lost was counted as present. For societies like the Basques, Chinese, Irish, and Japanese, where a focal rather than a typical community was pinpointed, a symbol representative of the society at large was selected in preference to one applying exclusively to the particular community.

## Individual and Composite Scales

The ten scales were selected, largely on the basis of suggestions in the literature, as potential indicators of cultural complexity. Although obviously intended to measure different phenomena, there were no *a priori* grounds for assuming in advance that particular scales would prove better indicators than others. Actually, when the coded results were compared, the ten scales revealed both a fairly even scatter and a satisfying degree of consistency. The closest correlation was found between the results for Scales 2 and 3 (Fixity of Residence and Agriculture). The only negative correlations occurred between these two scales and that for Land Transport (Scale 6). This discrepancy is clearly attributable to the fact that Scales 2 and 3 stress immobility whereas Scale 6 stresses mobility. That the use of Land Transport as an indicator is not thereby negated is demonstrated, for example, by the fact that its results correlate more strongly with those for Writing and Records (Scale 1) than do those of any other scale. In general, Scale 9 (Level of Political Integration) comes closest to occupying a median position inasmuch as its results show the highest average correlation with all other scales. In view of these facts the authors have deemed it advisable not to depend on the individual scales but rather to combine them in a single com-

## TABLE 1
### Indices of Cultural Complexity

| Society | Region | 1 | 2 | 3 | 4 | 5 | 6 | 7 | 8 | 9 | 10 | Total |
|---|---|---|---|---|---|---|---|---|---|---|---|---|
| 001 Nama Hottentot | A | 0 | 0 | 0 | 1 | 3 | 1 | 0 | 0 | 2 | 1 | 8 |
| 002 Kung Bushmen | A | 1 | 0 | 0 | 0 | 0 | 0 | 0 | 0 | 1 | 0 | 2 |
| 003 Thonga | A | 0 | 3 | 3 | 0 | 3 | 0 | 2 | 4 | 3 | 2 | 20 |
| 004 Lozi | A | 0 | 2 | 4 | 3 | 2 | 0 | 0 | 2 | 4 | 3 | 20 |
| 005 Mbundu | A | 0 | 4 | 3 | 1 | 3 | 0 | 3 | 2 | 3 | 3 | 22 |
| 006 Suku | A | 0 | 3 | 3 | 0 | 3 | 0 | 3 | 2 | 4 | 2 | 20 |
| 007 Bemba | A | 1 | 3 | 3 | 1 | 3 | 0 | 0 | 1 | 4 | 2 | 18 |
| 008 Nyakyusa | A | 0 | 3 | 4 | 1 | 3 | 0 | 1 | 3 | 3 | 0 | 18 |
| 009 Hadza | A | 0 | 0 | 0 | 0 | 0 | 0 | 0 | 0 | 0 | 0 | 0 |
| 010 Luguru | A | 0 | 4 | 3 | 2 | 3 | 0 | 1 | 4 | 1 | 1 | 19 |
| 011 Kikuyu | A | 0 | 4 | 4 | 1 | 3 | 0 | 1 | 4 | 1 | 1 | 19 |
| 012 Ganda | A | 1 | 4 | 4 | 1 | 3 | 0 | 3 | 4 | 4 | 3 | 27 |
| 013 Mbuti Pygmies | A | 0 | 0 | 0 | 0 | 0 | 0 | 0 | 0 | 0 | 0 | 0 |
| 014 Nkundo Mongo | A | 0 | 4 | 3 | 1 | 3 | 0 | 4 | 1 | 2 | 2 | 20 |
| 015 Banen | A | 0 | 4 | 3 | 2 | 3 | 0 | 2 | 2 | 2 | 1 | 19 |
| 016 Tiv | A | 0 | 4 | 3 | 3 | 3 | 0 | 0 | 3 | 2 | 1 | 19 |
| 017 Ibo | A | 0 | 4 | 3 | 4 | 3 | 0 | 3 | 4 | 2 | 1 | 24 |
| 018 Fon | A | 2 | 4 | 3 | 4 | 4 | 0 | 3 | 3 | 4 | 3 | 30 |
| 019 Ashanti | A | 0 | 4 | 3 | 2 | 3 | 0 | 3 | 3 | 4 | 2 | 24 |
| 020 Mende | A | 0 | 4 | 3 | 1 | 4 | 0 | 2 | 3 | 2 | 3 | 22 |
| 021 Wolof | C | 3 | 4 | 3 | 1 | 4 | 1 | 2 | 4 | 3 | 4 | 29 |
| 022 Bambara | A | 2 | 4 | 4 | 3 | 4 | 2 | 2 | 2 | 2 | 3 | 28 |
| 023 Tallensi | A | 0 | 4 | 4 | 3 | 3 | 0 | 2 | 4 | 1 | 1 | 22 |
| 024 Songhai | C | 3 | 4 | 4 | 3 | 3 | 1 | 0 | 2 | 2 | 4 | 26 |
| 025 Wodaabe Fulani | C | 0 | 0 | 1 | 1 | 0 | 1 | 0 | 1 | 2 | 0 | 6 |
| 026 Zazzagawa Hausa | C | 4 | 4 | 4 | 4 | 3 | 1 | 2 | 3 | 4 | 4 | 33 |
| 027 Massa | A | 0 | 4 | 4 | 2 | 3 | 0 | 0 | 3 | 1 | 0 | 17 |
| 028 Azande | A | 1 | 4 | 3 | 1 | 3 | 0 | 3 | 1 | 3 | 2 | 21 |
| 029 Fur | C | 4 | 4 | 4 | 1 | 4 | 1 | 1 | 2 | 4 | 2 | 27 |
| 030 Otoro Nuba | A | 1 | 4 | 4 | 3 | 3 | 0 | 0 | 2 | 0 | 1 | 18 |
| 031 Shilluk | A | 0 | 4 | 3 | 3 | 3 | 0 | 0 | 3 | 2 | 4 | 22 |
| 032 Northern Mao | A | 0 | 4 | 3 | 0 | 3 | 0 | 2 | 2 | 1 | 0 | 15 |
| 033 Kaffa | C | 1 | 4 | 4 | 0 | 4 | 1 | 1 | 3 | 4 | 3 | 25 |
| 034 Masai | A | 0 | 0 | 0 | 2 | 3 | 1 | 1 | 1 | 1 | 0 | 9 |
| 035 Konso | C | 0 | 4 | 4 | 4 | 4 | 1 | 0 | 4 | 2 | 1 | 24 |
| 036 Somali | C | 3 | 0 | 1 | 3 | 3 | 1 | 2 | 2 | 2 | 1 | 18 |
| 037 Amhara | C | 4 | 4 | 4 | 2 | 4 | 1 | 2 | 3 | 4 | 4 | 32 |
| 038 Bogo | C | 0 | 2 | 2 | 3 | 1 | 1 | 2 | 1 | 2 | 3 | 17 |
| 039 Kenuzi Nubians | C | 4 | 4 | 4 | 0 | 2 | 1 | 4 | 3 | 1 | 1 | 24 |
| 040 Teda | C | 1 | 0 | 1 | 0 | 3 | 1 | 2 | 0 | 1 | 2 | 11 |
| 041 Ahaggaren Tuareg | C | 3 | 0 | 2 | 0 | 3 | 1 | 1 | 0 | 3 | 3 | 16 |
| 042 Riffians | C | 4 | 4 | 4 | 3 | 4 | 1 | 4 | 4 | 3 | 1 | 32 |
| 043 Egyptians | C | 4 | 4 | 4 | 4 | 4 | 1 | 4 | 4 | 4 | 4 | 37 |
| 044 Hebrews | C | 4 | 4 | 4 | 4 | 4 | 1 | 4 | 4 | 3 | 4 | 36 |
| 045 Babylonians | C | 4 | 4 | 4 | 4 | 4 | 3 | 4 | 4 | 4 | 4 | 39 |
| 046 Rwala Bedouin | C | 4 | 0 | 0 | 0 | 3 | 1 | 2 | 0 | 2 | 1 | 13 |
| 047 Turks | C | 4 | 4 | 4 | 3 | 4 | 4 | 4 | 3 | 4 | 4 | 38 |
| 048 Gheg Albanians | C | 4 | 2 | 4 | 1 | 3 | 1 | 4 | 3 | 3 | 1 | 26 |
| 049 Romans | C | 4 | 4 | 4 | 4 | 4 | 3 | 4 | 4 | 4 | 4 | 39 |
| 050 Spanish Basques | C | 4 | 4 | 4 | 4 | 4 | 4 | 4 | 2 | 3 | 4 | 37 |
| 051 Irish | C | 4 | 4 | 4 | 3 | 4 | 4 | 4 | 3 | 3 | 4 | 37 |
| 052 Könkämä Lapps | C | 1 | 0 | 1 | 0 | 2 | 1 | 0 | 1 | 1 | 1 | 8 |
| 053 Yurak Samoyed | C | 1 | 0 | 1 | 0 | 0 | 2 | 2 | 0 | 1 | 1 | 8 |

TABLE 1 *Continued*

| Society | Region | 1 | 2 | 3 | 4 | 5 | 6 | 7 | 8 | 9 | 10 | Total |
|---|---|---|---|---|---|---|---|---|---|---|---|---|
| 054 Russians | C | 4 | 4 | 4 | 4 | 4 | 4 | 4 | 2 | 4 | 4 | 38 |
| 055 Abkhaz | C | 3 | 4 | 2 | 2 | 3 | 3 | 0 | 3 | 2 | 4 | 26 |
| 056 Armenians | C | 4 | 4 | 4 | 3 | 4 | 1 | 2 | 3 | 4 | 4 | 33 |
| 057 Kurd | C | 3 | 4 | 4 | 4 | 4 | 1 | 4 | 4 | 3 | 2 | 33 |
| 058 Basseri | E | 3 | 0 | 2 | 1 | 3 | 1 | 0 | 1 | 3 | 1 | 15 |
| 059 West Punjabi | E | 4 | 4 | 4 | 2 | 4 | 1 | 4 | 4 | 4 | 4 | 35 |
| 060 Maria Gond | E | 0 | 3 | 3 | 0 | 3 | 0 | 3 | 2 | 2 | 1 | 17 |
| 061 Toda | E | 0 | 2 | 0 | 0 | 0 | 0 | 2 | 3 | 2 | 0 | 9 |
| 062 Santal | E | 1 | 4 | 4 | 1 | 2 | 0 | 2 | 4 | 3 | 0 | 21 |
| 063 Uttar Pradesh | E | 4 | 4 | 4 | 4 | 4 | 4 | 4 | 4 | 4 | 4 | 40 |
| 064 Burusho | E | 3 | 4 | 4 | 1 | 3 | 1 | 0 | 1 | 2 | 4 | 23 |
| 065 Kazak | E | 3 | 1 | 0 | 3 | 3 | 1 | 2 | 1 | 3 | 3 | 20 |
| 066 Khalkha Mongols | E | 4 | 1 | 1 | 0 | 3 | 3 | 2 | 1 | 4 | 3 | 22 |
| 067 Lolo | E | 4 | 4 | 4 | 1 | 3 | 1 | 3 | 1 | 1 | 3 | 25 |
| 068 Lepcha | E | 3 | 4 | 4 | 1 | 2 | 0 | 2 | 3 | 2 | 1 | 22 |
| 069 Garo | E | 0 | 4 | 3 | 2 | 3 | 0 | 2 | 3 | 3 | 1 | 21 |
| 070 Lakher | E | 1 | 4 | 3 | 2 | 3 | 0 | 1 | 2 | 2 | 3 | 21 |
| 071 Burmese | E | 4 | 4 | 4 | 3 | 4 | 3 | 4 | 4 | 4 | 4 | 38 |
| 072 Lamet | E | 0 | 2 | 3 | 1 | 0 | 0 | 1 | 0 | 1 | 1 | 9 |
| 073 North Vietnamese | E | 4 | 4 | 4 | 3 | 4 | 4 | 2 | 4 | 4 | 4 | 37 |
| 074 Rhade | E | 0 | 3 | 3 | 3 | 2 | 0 | 2 | 4 | 1 | 1 | 19 |
| 075 Khmer | E | 2 | 4 | 4 | 4 | 4 | 3 | 4 | 3 | 4 | 4 | 36 |
| 076 Siamese | E | 4 | 4 | 4 | 4 | 4 | 4 | 4 | 4 | 4 | 4 | 40 |
| 077 Semang | E | 0 | 0 | 1 | 0 | 0 | 0 | 0 | 0 | 1 | 0 | 2 |
| 078 Nicobarese | E | 1 | 4 | 3 | 2 | 3 | 0 | 0 | 3 | 1 | 0 | 17 |
| 079 Andamanese | E | 0 | 1 | 0 | 0 | 1 | 0 | 0 | 1 | 1 | 0 | 4 |
| 080 Forest Vedda | E | 1 | 1 | 1 | 0 | 1 | 0 | 2 | 0 | 0 | 0 | 6 |
| 081 Menabe Tanala | E | 0 | 2 | 4 | 2 | 3 | 0 | 1 | 2 | 3 | 3 | 17 |
| 082 Negri Sembilan | I | 4 | 4 | 4 | 4 | 3 | 3 | 4 | 4 | 3 | 2 | 35 |
| 083 Javanese | I | 4 | 4 | 4 | 3 | 4 | 4 | 4 | 4 | 4 | 4 | 39 |
| 084 Balinese | I | 4 | 4 | 4 | 3 | 4 | 4 | 4 | 4 | 3 | 4 | 38 |
| 085 Iban | I | 0 | 3 | 3 | 0 | 3 | 0 | 0 | 2 | 1 | 1 | 13 |
| 086 Tawi-Tawi Badjau | I | 0 | 0 | 1 | 2 | 0 | 0 | 0 | 0 | 1 | 1 | 5 |
| 087 Toradja | I | 1 | 4 | 3 | 1 | 3 | 0 | 1 | 2 | 2 | 1 | 18 |
| 088 Tobelorese | I | 1 | 4 | 3 | 2 | 3 | 0 | 2 | 2 | 3 | 1 | 21 |
| 089 Alorese | I | 1 | 4 | 3 | 1 | 0 | 0 | 3 | 4 | 3 | 1 | 20 |
| 090 Tiwi | I | 1 | 0 | 0 | 1 | 0 | 0 | 0 | 0 | 0 | 0 | 2 |
| 091 Aranda | I | 2 | 0 | 0 | 0 | 0 | 0 | 0 | 0 | 1 | 0 | 3 |
| 092 Orokaiva | I | 0 | 4 | 3 | 0 | 1 | 0 | 0 | 1 | 1 | 0 | 10 |
| 093 Kimam | I | 0 | 4 | 4 | 3 | 0 | 0 | 0 | 0 | 1 | 0 | 12 |
| 094 Kapauku | I | 1 | 4 | 3 | 1 | 0 | 0 | 3 | 4 | 2 | 1 | 19 |
| 095 Kwoma | I | 1 | 4 | 3 | 2 | 1 | 0 | 3 | 3 | 1 | 0 | 18 |
| 096 Manus | I | 1 | 4 | 0 | 2 | 1 | 0 | 3 | 3 | 1 | 1 | 16 |
| 097 Lesu | I | 1 | 4 | 3 | 2 | 0 | 0 | 3 | 2 | 1 | 0 | 16 |
| 098 Trobrianders | I | 0 | 4 | 3 | 1 | 1 | 0 | 0 | 3 | 2 | 2 | 16 |
| 099 Siuai | I | 1 | 4 | 3 | 0 | 1 | 0 | 3 | 3 | 1 | 1 | 17 |
| 100 Tikopia | I | 0 | 4 | 3 | 3 | 0 | 0 | 0 | 4 | 2 | 2 | 18 |
| 101 Bunlap | I | 0 | 4 | 3 | 0 | 0 | 0 | 2 | 2 | 1 | 1 | 13 |
| 102 Mbau Fijians | I | 0 | 4 | 2 | 4 | 1 | 0 | 3 | 4 | 3 | 1 | 22 |
| 103 Ajie | I | 1 | 4 | 4 | 0 | 1 | 0 | 3 | 1 | 2 | 0 | 16 |
| 104 Maori | I | 2 | 4 | 3 | 1 | 0 | 0 | 0 | 0 | 2 | 2 | 14 |
| 105 Marquesans | I | 2 | 4 | 3 | 1 | 0 | 0 | 0 | 3 | 2 | 2 | 17 |
| 106 Samoans | I | 0 | 4 | 3 | 2 | 0 | 0 | 0 | 4 | 3 | 2 | 18 |
| 107 Makin Gilbertese | I | 0 | 4 | 3 | 2 | 0 | 0 | 2 | 4 | 2 | 2 | 19 |

TABLE 1 *Continued*

| Society | Region | 1 | 2 | 3 | 4 | 5 | 6 | 7 | 8 | 9 | 10 | Total |
|---|---|---|---|---|---|---|---|---|---|---|---|---|
| 108 Jaluit Marshallese | I | 2 | 4 | 2 | 1 | 0 | 0 | 2 | 4 | 2 | 2 | 19 |
| 109 Trukese | I | 0 | 4 | 3 | 2 | 2 | 0 | 2 | 4 | 1 | 0 | 18 |
| 110 Yapese | I | 1 | 4 | 3 | 1 | 2 | 0 | 3 | 3 | 2 | 3 | 22 |
| 111 Palauans | I | 0 | 4 | 3 | 0 | 1 | 0 | 3 | 3 | 3 | 2 | 19 |
| 112 Ifugao | I | 0 | 4 | 4 | 3 | 3 | 1 | 1 | 4 | 0 | 1 | 21 |
| 113 Atayal | I | 0 | 3 | 3 | 1 | 3 | 0 | 3 | 2 | 2 | 0 | 17 |
| 114 Chekiang Chinese | E | 4 | 4 | 4 | 4 | 4 | 4 | 4 | 4 | 4 | 4 | 40 |
| 115 Aigun Manchu | E | 3 | 4 | 4 | 1 | 3 | 3 | 1 | 4 | 2 | 1 | 26 |
| 116 Koreans | E | 4 | 4 | 4 | 3 | 4 | 3 | 4 | 4 | 4 | 4 | 38 |
| 117 Japanese | E | 4 | 4 | 4 | 4 | 4 | 4 | 4 | 4 | 4 | 4 | 40 |
| 118 Saru Ainu | E | 1 | 2 | 1 | 0 | 2 | 0 | 0 | 0 | 1 | 0 | 7 |
| 119 Gilyak | E | 0 | 1 | 0 | 0 | 3 | 2 | 2 | 0 | 1 | 0 | 9 |
| 120 Yukaghir | E | 1 | 0 | 0 | 0 | 3 | 2 | 0 | 0 | 1 | 0 | 7 |
| 121 Reindeer Chukchee | E | 0 | 1 | 0 | 0 | 3 | 2 | 0 | 0 | 1 | 1 | 8 |
| 122 Ingalik | N | 1 | 2 | 0 | 0 | 1 | 0 | 3 | 0 | 1 | 1 | 9 |
| 123 Aleut | N | 0 | 2 | 0 | 2 | 0 | 0 | 0 | 2 | 2 | 3 | 11 |
| 124 Copper Eskimo | N | 0 | 1 | 0 | 0 | 3 | 2 | 0 | 0 | 0 | 0 | 6 |
| 125 Montagnais | N | 2 | 1 | 0 | 1 | 0 | 0 | 0 | 0 | 1 | 0 | 5 |
| 126 Micmac | N | 2 | 1 | 0 | 0 | 0 | 0 | 3 | 0 | 1 | 0 | 7 |
| 127 Northern Saulteaux | N | 2 | 1 | 1 | 1 | 0 | 2 | 2 | 0 | 1 | 0 | 10 |
| 128 Slave | N | 0 | 2 | 1 | 0 | 0 | 2 | 2 | 0 | 1 | 0 | 8 |
| 129 Kaska | N | 0 | 1 | 0 | 0 | 0 | 2 | 0 | 0 | 1 | 0 | 4 |
| 130 Eyak | N | 0 | 2 | 0 | 0 | 1 | 0 | 0 | 0 | 2 | 1 | 6 |
| 131 Masset Haida | N | 2 | 2 | 0 | 1 | 3 | 0 | 1 | 0 | 1 | 3 | 13 |
| 132 Bellacoola | N | 1 | 4 | 0 | 0 | 0 | 0 | 2 | 1 | 1 | 3 | 12 |
| 133 Twana | N | 1 | 1 | 0 | 0 | 2 | 0 | 3 | 3 | 1 | 1 | 12 |
| 134 Yurok | N | 2 | 4 | 0 | 0 | 0 | 0 | 0 | 1 | 0 | 1 | 8 |
| 135 Eastern Pomo | N | 2 | 2 | 0 | 2 | 0 | 0 | 3 | 1 | 1 | 1 | 12 |
| 136 Lake Yokuts | N | 0 | 2 | 0 | 2 | 0 | 0 | 3 | 2 | 1 | 1 | 11 |
| 137 Wadadika Paiute | N | 1 | 1 | 0 | 1 | 0 | 0 | 0 | 0 | 1 | 0 | 4 |
| 138 Klamath | N | 1 | 1 | 0 | 0 | 0 | 0 | 0 | 0 | 1 | 1 | 4 |
| 139 Lower Kutenai | N | 1 | 1 | 0 | 1 | 1 | 1 | 2 | 0 | 1 | 0 | 8 |
| 140 Gros Ventre | N | 1 | 0 | 0 | 1 | 1 | 2 | 1 | 0 | 2 | 0 | 8 |
| 141 Hidatsa | N | 1 | 2 | 4 | 3 | 1 | 2 | 0 | 0 | 1 | 0 | 14 |
| 142 Skidi Pawnee | N | 1 | 2 | 3 | 2 | 1 | 2 | 0 | 0 | 2 | 2 | 15 |
| 143 Omaha | N | 1 | 2 | 2 | 4 | 1 | 2 | 0 | 1 | 2 | 0 | 15 |
| 144 Huron | N | 1 | 2 | 3 | 4 | 1 | 0 | 0 | 3 | 3 | 1 | 18 |
| 145 Upper Creek | N | 2 | 2 | 3 | 2 | 2 | 1 | 3 | 1 | 3 | 0 | 19 |
| 146 Natchez | N | 2 | 4 | 3 | 3 | 2 | 0 | 0 | 2 | 3 | 3 | 22 |
| 147 Comanche | N | 2 | 0 | 0 | 2 | 0 | 2 | 0 | 0 | 1 | 0 | 7 |
| 148 Chiricahua Apache | N | 1 | 0 | 1 | 0 | 1 | 0 | 0 | 0 | 2 | 0 | 5 |
| 149 Zuni | N | 2 | 4 | 4 | 4 | 4 | 3 | 2 | 1 | 1 | 0 | 25 |
| 150 Havasupai | N | 1 | 1 | 4 | 1 | 1 | 1 | 0 | 0 | 1 | 0 | 10 |
| 151 Papago | N | 1 | 2 | 4 | 2 | 1 | 1 | 2 | 3 | 1 | 0 | 17 |
| 152 Huichol | N | 1 | 4 | 3 | 2 | 2 | 1 | 2 | 1 | 1 | 1 | 18 |
| 153 Aztec | N | 4 | 4 | 4 | 4 | 4 | 0 | 3 | 4 | 3 | 4 | 34 |
| 154 Sierra Popoluca | N | 0 | 4 | 3 | 3 | 2 | 0 | 2 | 3 | 2 | 0 | 19 |
| 155 Quiche | S | 3 | 4 | 3 | 4 | 2 | 1 | 2 | 3 | 2 | 1 | 25 |
| 156 Miskito | S | 0 | 4 | 3 | 2 | 2 | 0 | 2 | 2 | 2 | 0 | 17 |
| 157 Bribri Talamanca | S | 1 | 4 | 3 | 0 | 2 | 0 | 0 | 2 | 1 | 0 | 13 |
| 158 Cuna | S | 2 | 4 | 3 | 3 | 3 | 0 | 2 | 3 | 2 | 1 | 23 |
| 159 Goajiro | S | 1 | 0 | 1 | 0 | 2 | 1 | 2 | 0 | 2 | 1 | 10 |
| 160 Haitians | S | 4 | 4 | 3 | 4 | 3 | 1 | 4 | 4 | 4 | 4 | 35 |
| 161 Callinago | S | 1 | 3 | 4 | 2 | 2 | 0 | 0 | 2 | 1 | 1 | 16 |

TABLE 1 *Continued*

| Society | Region | 1 | 2 | 3 | 4 | 5 | 6 | 7 | 8 | 9 | 10 | Total |
|---|---|---|---|---|---|---|---|---|---|---|---|---|
| 162 Warrau | S | 1 | 1 | 1 | 0 | 2 | 0 | 0 | 0 | 1 | 0 | 6 |
| 163 Yanomamo | S | 0 | 3 | 3 | 1 | 0 | 0 | 0 | 0 | 1 | 0 | 8 |
| 164 Barama Carib | S | 1 | 3 | 2 | 0 | 1 | 0 | 0 | 0 | 1 | 0 | 8 |
| 165 Saramacca | S | 2 | 4 | 3 | 1 | 1 | 0 | 0 | 2 | 3 | 0 | 16 |
| 166 Mundurucu | S | 0 | 4 | 3 | 1 | 2 | 0 | 0 | 0 | 1 | 0 | 11 |
| 167 Cubeo | S | 0 | 4 | 3 | 0 | 1 | 0 | 0 | 0 | 1 | 1 | 10 |
| 168 Cayapa | S | 0 | 4 | 3 | 3 | 2 | 0 | 0 | 1 | 1 | 0 | 14 |
| 169 Jivaro | S | 0 | 3 | 3 | 0 | 2 | 0 | 0 | 0 | 0 | 0 | 8 |
| 170 Amahuaca | S | 0 | 3 | 3 | 0 | 2 | 0 | 0 | 0 | 0 | 0 | 8 |
| 171 Inca | S | 2 | 4 | 4 | 1 | 4 | 1 | 0 | 2 | 4 | 4 | 26 |
| 172 Aymara | S | 2 | 4 | 4 | 3 | 3 | 1 | 0 | 4 | 2 | 1 | 24 |
| 173 Siriono | S | 0 | 1 | 1 | 0 | 1 | 0 | 0 | 0 | 1 | 0 | 4 |
| 174 Nambicuara | S | 0 | 1 | 2 | 0 | 2 | 0 | 0 | 0 | 1 | 0 | 6 |
| 175 Trumai | S | 0 | 4 | 3 | 0 | 2 | 0 | 0 | 0 | 1 | 0 | 10 |
| 176 Ramcocamecra Timbira | S | 1 | 3 | 3 | 2 | 2 | 0 | 0 | 1 | 1 | 0 | 13 |
| 177 Tupinamba | S | 0 | 3 | 3 | 3 | 2 | 0 | 0 | 0 | 2 | 1 | 14 |
| 178 Botocudo | S | 0 | 0 | 0 | 0 | 0 | 0 | 0 | 0 | 1 | 0 | 1 |
| 179 Shavante | S | 0 | 1 | 1 | 2 | 0 | 0 | 0 | 0 | 1 | 0 | 5 |
| 180 Aweikoma | S | 0 | 0 | 0 | 0 | 1 | 0 | 0 | 0 | 0 | 0 | 1 |
| 181 Cayua | S | 0 | 1 | 2 | 0 | 2 | 0 | 0 | 0 | 1 | 0 | 6 |
| 182 Lengua | S | 1 | 0 | 2 | 1 | 2 | 1 | 0 | 0 | 1 | 0 | 8 |
| 183 Abipon | S | 0 | 0 | 0 | 2 | 2 | 1 | 0 | 0 | 1 | 3 | 9 |
| 184 Mapuche Araucanians | S | 1 | 4 | 4 | 0 | 3 | 3 | 2 | 3 | 2 | 1 | 23 |
| 185 Tehuelche | S | 0 | 0 | 0 | 1 | 3 | 1 | 0 | 0 | 1 | 0 | 6 |
| 186 Yahgan | S | 0 | 0 | 0 | 0 | 0 | 0 | 0 | 0 | 1 | 0 | 1 |

posite scale. For this purpose we employ the sums of the ratings on the ten individual scales as presented in the last column of Table 1.

## REGIONAL DIFFERENCES IN COMPLEXITY

When analyzed by regions, the composite indices of cultural complexity revealed, as expected, rather substantial differences in magnitude. The mean rating on all ten scales was 2.6 for the societies of the Circum-Mediterranean, 2.2 for those of East Eurasia, 1.8 for both Africa and the Insular Pacific, and 1.2 for both continents of the New World. In the case of East Eurasia, the average was lowered by the inclusion of a number of Paleo-Siberian societies in the north and of several Negrito and Veddoid hunting groups in the south, without which it would not have differed significantly from the Circum-Mediterranean.

When the individual scores are segregated, as is done in Table 2, the regional differences are more pronounced. Particularly noteworthy are the discrepancies in the indices of complexity for Africa, which fall far below those of all other regions on Scales 1 and 6 yet compare favorably with those of East Eurasia, and are not notably lower than those of the Circum-Mediterranean, on the other scales. The fact that the cultures of one region can rank at the top according to some measures of complexity and at the very bottom according to other measures casts serious doubt on the assumption, accepted by Carneiro, that cultural development is essentially unilinear.

TABLE 2

Mean Indices of Cultural Complexity by Region

| Scale | Africa | Circum-Medit. | East Eurasia | Insular Pacific | North America | South America |
|---|---|---|---|---|---|---|
| 1.  Writing & Records | 0.2 | 3.3 | 2.0 | 1.0 | 1.2 | 0.7 |
| 2.  Fixity of Residence | 3.1 | 3.4 | 2.7 | 3.6 | 1.9 | 2.0 |
| 3.  Agriculture | 2.8 | 3.0 | 2.6 | 2.8 | 1.3 | 2.3 |
| 4.  Urbanization | 1.6 | 2.2 | 1.6 | 1.5 | 1.5 | 1.1 |
| 5.  Techn.. Specialization | 2.7 | 3.2 | 2.7 | 1.2 | 1.0 | 1.8 |
| 6.  Land Transport | 0.1 | 1.6 | 1.5 | 0.5 | 0.8 | 0.3 |
| 7.  Money | 1.5 | 2.4 | 1.9 | 1.8 | 1.2 | 0.4 |
| 8.  Population Density | 2.3 | 2.6 | 2.2 | 2.6 | 0.9 | 0.9 |
| 9.  Polit. Integration | 2.1 | 2.5 | 2.4 | 1.8 | 1.2 | 1.4 |
| 10.  Soc. Stratification | 1.5 | 2.7 | 2.0 | 1.3 | 0.8 | 0.6 |

COMPARATIVE RANKING OF CULTURAL COMPLEXITY

That we cannot accept Carneiro's theoretical conclusion by no means implies disagreement with his assessment of the facts. Using his scalogram method of analysis he has been able to arrange the societies he has examined in a linear rank order of cultural complexity. Though our method of scoring is entirely different from his, we can achieve a comparable rank order of our 186 societies by rearranging them according to the magnitude of the figures in the last column of Table 1, which represent the sums of the scores on the ten individual scales and can be considered as constituting overall or composite indices of cultural complexity. This is done in Table 3, where the sample societies are arranged in ascending rank order from the minimum total score of zero (the lowest possible rating on all ten scales) to a maximum of 40 (the highest possible rating on every scale).

The indices in Table 3 should not be taken as exact measures of cultural complexity in the sense used by anthropologists, but only as close approximations thereto. Leeway of a few points must be allowed for what are essentially accidental factors. For example, the contemporary Russians, who certainly do not yield to any other society in the sample with respect to actual complexity, fall two points below the maximum rating by virtue only of the fact that they receive a median rather than a high score on population density (Scale 8). Again only a factor of time prevents a maximum rating for the Babylonians of 1750 B.C. and the Romans of 110 A. D., who score only 3 points on Scale 6 since automotive wheeled vehicles had not yet been invented.

That our indices of cultural complexity have a substantial measure of validity is indicated by the degree of agreement in rank order between the ratings by Carneiro (1970: 846) and ourselves for the societies included in both studies. Table 4 presents this comparison. There are differences, to be sure, especially in the middle of the two lists, but they are less than might reasonably be expected in view of the utterly distinct methodologies employed.

CONCLUSIONS

The fact that independent measures of cultural complexity largely con-

TABLE 3

The Sample Societies in Rank Order of Overall Cultural Complexity

0 Hadza (9), Mbuti Pygmies (13).
1 Botocudo (178), Aweikoma (180), Yahgan (186).
2 Kung Bushmen (2), Semang (77), Tiwi (90).
3 Aranda (91).
4 Andamanese (79), Kaska (129), Wadadika Paiute (137), Klamath (138), Siriono (173).
5 Badjau (86), Montagnais (125), Chiricahua Apache (148), Shavante (179).
6 Wodaabe Fulani (25), Vedda (80), Copper Eskimo (124), Eyak (130), Warrau (162), Nambicuara (174), Cayua (181), Tehuelche (185).
7 Ainu (118), Yukaghir (120), Micmac (126), Comanche (147).
8 Nama Hottentot (1), Lapps (52), Yurak Samoyed (53), Chukchee (121), Slave (128), Yurok (134), Kutenai (139), Gros Ventre (140), Yanomamo (163), Barama Carib (164), Jivaro (169), Amahuaca (170), Lengua (182).
9 Masai (34), Toda (61), Lamet (72), Gilyak (119), Ingalik (122), Abipon (183).
10 Orokaiva (92), Saulteaux (127), Havasupai (150), Goajiro (159), Cubeo (167), Trumai (175).
11 Teda (40), Aleut (123), Yokuts (136), Mundurucu (166).
12 Kimam (93), Bellacoola (132), Twana (133), Eastern Pomo (135).
13 Rwala Bedouin (46), Iban (85), Bunlap (101), Haida (131), Bribri (157) Timbira (176).
14 Maori (104), Hidatsa (141), Cayapa (168), Tupinamba (177).
15 Northern Mao (32), Basseri (58), Pawnee (142), Omaha (143).
16 Ahaggaren Tuareg (41), Manus (96), Lesu (97), Trobrianders (98), Ajie (103), Callinago (161), Saramacca (165).
17 Massa (27), Bogo (38), Maria Gond (60), Nicobarese (78), Tanala (81), Siuai (99), Marquesans (105), Atayal (113), Papago (151), Miskito (156).
18 Bemba (7), Nyakyusa (8), Otoro Nuba (30), Somali (36), Toradja (87), Kwoma (95), Tikopia (100), Samoans (106), Trukese (109), Huron (144), Huichol (152).
19 Luguru (10), Kikuyu (11), Banen (15), Tiv (16), Rhade (74), Kapauku (94), Makin Gilbertese (107), Marshallese (108), Palauans (111), Creek (145), Popoluca (154).
20 Thonga (3), Lozi (4), Suku (6), Nkundo Mongo (14), Kazak (65), Alorese (89).
21 Azande (28), Santal (62), Garo (69), Lakher (70), Tobelorese (88), Ifugao (112).
22 Mbundu (5), Mende (20), Tallensi (23), Shilluk (31), Khalka Mongols (66), Lepcha (68), Mbau Fijians (102), Yapese (110), Natchez (146).
23 Burusho (64), Cuna (158), Mapuche (184).
24 Ibo (17), Ashanti (19), Konso (35), Kenuzi Nubians (39), Aymara (172).
25 Kaffa (33), Lolo (67), Zuni (149), Quiche (155).
26 Songhai (24), Gheg Albanians (48), Abkhaz (55), Manchu (115), Inca (171).
27 Ganda (12), Fur (29).
28 Bambara (22).
29 Wolof (21).
30 Fon (18).
31 (No cases).
32 Amhara (37), Riffians (42).
33 Zazzagawa Hausa (26), Armenians (56), Kurd (57).
34 Aztec (153).
35 West Punjabi (59), Negri Sembilan (82), Haitians (160).
36 Hebrews (44), Khmer (75).
37 Egyptians (43), Basques (50), Irish (51), North Vietnamese (73).
38 Turks (47), Russians (54), Burmese (71), Balinese (84), Koreans (116).
39 Babylonians (45), Romans (49), Javanese (83).
40 Uttar Pradesh (63), Siamese (76), Chinese (114), Japanese (117).

TABLE 4

Rank Order on Scales of Complexity of the Societies
Rated in Both Carneiro's Study and the Present One

| Ordinal Position | In Carneiro | In This Study |
|---|---|---|
| 1 | Romans | Chinese |
| 2 | Aztec | Romans |
| 3 | Chinese | Aztec |
| 4 | Inca | Fon |
| 5 | Fon | Ganda |
| 6 | Ashanti | Inca |
| 7 | Ganda | Ashanti |
| 8 | Marquesans | Fijians |
| 9 | Fijians | Suku |
| 10 | Bemba | Thonga |
| 11 | Suku | Creek |
| 12 | Tanala | Bemba |
| 13 | Maori | Marquesans |
| 14 | Rwala Bedouin | Tanala |
| 15 | Creek | Siuai |
| 16 | Tuareg | Tuareg |
| 17 | Thonga | Omaha |
| 18 | Omaha | Maori |
| 19 | Nama Hottentot | Tupinamba |
| 20 | Tupinamba | Rwala Bedouin |
| 21 | Siuai | Timbira |
| 22 | Toda | Mundurucu |
| 23 | Lapps | Havasupai |
| 24 | Yukaghir | Cubeo |
| 25 | Comanche | Toda |
| 26 | Havasupai | Nama Hottentot |
| 27 | Timbira | Lapps |
| 28 | Warrau | Jivaro |
| 29 | Jivaro | Gros Ventre |
| 30 | Tehuelche | Barama Carib |
| 31 | Mundurucu | Amahuaca |
| 32 | Gros Ventre | Lengua |
| 33 | Barama Carib | Yukaghir |
| 34 | Cubeo | Comanche |
| 35 | Amahuaca | Warrau |
| 36 | Copper Eskimo | Tehuelche |
| 37 | Andamanese | Copper Eskimo |
| 38 | Lengua | Vedda |
| 39 | Siriono | Andamanese |
| 40 | Vedda | Siriono |
| 41 | Kaska | Kaska |
| 42 | Bushmen | Bushmen |
| 43 | Yahgan | Semang |
| 44 | Semang | Yahgan |
| 45 | Mbuti Pygmies | Mbuti Pygmies |

firm one another provides evidence of their validity but has no bearing on their utility. The usefulness of a scale or other measure, and hence its scientific value, depends exclusively on whether its application generates new knowledge. We have therefore subjected our overall scale of cultural complexity to one such test, choosing for this purpose an example from the field of social organization, which has proved particularly resistant to developmental hypotheses since the general rejection of nineteenth century evolutionism. Specifically we have selected rules of descent, which occupied a central position in early assumptions of the "priority of mother-right."

The prevailing rule of descent has been assessed by Murdock and Wilson (1972: Column 13) for all the societies surveyed in the present study, and the results can readily be correlated with the ratings for cultural complexity presented herewith. This is done in Table 5, where the sample societies are classified by cultural complexity into four quartiles:

(1) Low complexity, i.e., with scores from 0 to 9;
(2) Lower middle complexity, with scores from 10 to 19;
(3) Upper middle complexity, with scores from 20 to 29;
(4) High complexity, with scores from 30 to 40.

Their rules of descent are classified in terms of the modern categories of bilateral, ambilineal, matrilineal, patrilineal, and double descent.

Scrutiny of Table 5 leads to the following conclusions:

1. The cases of ambilineal and double descent are too few for reliable generalizations, though their distribution most clearly resembles that of patrilineal descent in the former instance and matrilineal descent in the latter.
2. Matrilineal descent is heavily concentrated in the Lower Middle range with only a relatively negligible number of cases at other levels. This is totally inconsistent with the allegations of the priority of matrilineal descent by the unilineal evolutionists of the nineteenth century.
3. Patrilineal descent is common throughout the middle and higher levels and is especially prevalent in the Upper Middle range, where its incidence is 73 per cent.
4. Bilateral descent strongly predominates at the level of Low Complexity, where its incidence approaches 70 per cent, suggesting that it may well predate other rules of descent in the culture history of mankind. Its incidence declines in the middle ranges, especially sharply at the Upper Middle level, but rises to nearly 50 per cent among the cultures of

TABLE 5
Complexity Rating and Rules of Descent

| Descent | Low Complexity | Lower Middle Complexity | Upper Middle Complexity | High Complexity | Mean Complexity | Number of Societies |
|---|---|---|---|---|---|---|
| Bilateral | 34 | 18 | 5 | 12 | 14.7 | 69 |
| Ambilineal | 0 | 4 | 1 | 1 | 19.3 | 6 |
| Matrilineal | 3 | 18 | 4 | 1 | 16.8 | 26 |
| Patrilineal | 8 | 25 | 28 | 14 | 21.3 | 75 |
| Double | 4 | 2 | 4 | 0 | 14.7 | 10 |
| Totals | 49 | 67 | 42 | 28 | 17.8 | 186 |

highest complexity. This essentially bimodal or curvilinear distribution is inconsistent with any unilinear interpretation of social development.

The above conclusions, though by no means entirely novel, nevertheless demonstrate that features of social organization are in fact related to cultural complexity, provide a solid basis for reassessing this relationship, and indicate that measures such as the one we have devised may possess scientific utility as well as validity.

### BIBLIOGRAPHY

The references listed below cover only sources cited in the text. They include (see especially Murdock and Wilson 1972) identifications of the precise locations and dates for each of the societies of our sample and complete listings of ethnographic sources from which data were assembled.

Carneiro, R. L. 1970. Scale Analysis, Evolutionary Sequences, and the Rating of Cultures. A Handbook of Method in Cultural Anthropology, ed. R. Naroll and R. Cohen, pp. 834-871. Garden City.

Murdock, G. P. 1967. Ethnographic Atlas. Pittsburgh.

Murdock, G. P., and D. O. Morrow. 1970. Subsistence Economy and Supportive Practices. Ethnology 9: 302-330.

Murdock, G. P., and C. Provost. 1973. Factors in the Division of Labor by Sex. Ethnology 12: 203-225.

Murdock, G. P., and S. F. Wilson. 1972. Settlement Patterns and Community Organization. Ethnology 11: 254-295.

Tuden, A., and C. Marshall. 1972. Political Organization. Ethnology 11: 436-464.

# 6

# Infancy and Early Childhood:
# Cross-Cultural Codes 2

*Herbert Barry III* and *Leonora M. Paxson*

This article presents a new set of codes on a world sample of 186 societies, selected by Murdock and White (1969). A previous article by Murdock and Morrow (1970) has reported on codes of subsistence economy and supportive practices.

Infancy may be of special interest to some analysts of culture and personality because of the widely accepted belief that experiences early in life have important influences on the development of adult character. Numerically coded measures of infancy and childhood have previously been reported by Barry, Bacon, and Child (1967) and by Whiting and Child (1953) for smaller samples of societies. Relationships of these variables with others have been reported in a number of publications reviewed by Barry (1969b) and by Naroll (1970). A compilation by Textor (1967) shows many relationships between these measures and other cultural variables. However, the samples in these studies were not truly representative, being selected preponderantly from preliterate, "primitive" societies, many of which were closely related to each other, and omitting large areas of the world. The majority of the codes were concerned with childhood rather than infancy, although the earlier stage of development may be especially important in personality formation. The ethnographic accounts used for many of the societies contain scanty information on children.

The present study was designed to correct many of the deficiencies in previous research. In comparison with the samples used by Whiting and Child (1953) and by Barry, Bacon, and Child (1967), the present sample is larger and carefully selected to provide a single representative in each of 186 differentiated culture areas (Murdock and White 1969). Thereby all the major known cultural types in the world are represented, with maximal independence of the societies from each other. Since quality of ethnographic information was the principal criterion for selection of the society representing each culture area, adequate information on infancy and childhood was available for a large proportion of these societies. The new codes presented herewith were designed to provide measures of a wide range of variables. Limitation of the codes to infancy and early childhood enabled greater detail and variety in the information coded on this early stage of development.

The principal purpose of the present article is to provide the information needed for researchers to use the new codes on infancy and early childhood, in particular relating them with other features of culture. The new codes are defined and discussed, and the scores listed (in Table 1) on the selected representative for each of the 186 culture areas plus an alternate society for fifteen of these areas. This article also reports on a few interrelationships of the codes with each other and with measures of social organization in the Ethnographic Atlas (Murdock 1967) and subsistence economy (Murdock and Morrow 1970). Reliability and validity of some of the new codes is assessed by correlations with similarly defined, independently coded measures of infancy and childhood previously reported by Barry, Bacon, and Child (1967) and by Whiting and Child (1953).

## DEFINITION OF CODES

This article presents 34 numerical codes, most of which are defined according to a quantitative scale from 1 to 5. In Table 1, they are grouped into 16 columns. These codes were applied to the same sample of societies as in Murdock and Morrow (1970), and to fifteen societies listed at the end of Table 1.

In Table 1, Columns 1-5 are limited to the stage described as infancy or babyhood by the society. This begins at birth and continues until the substantial change in treatment or care which marks the transition to early childhood, usually after the age of one year. Columns 6-9 include both infancy and the following stage of early childhood to the age of approximately four or five years. Columns 10-12 apply to the transition to childhood, beginning at approximately the age of 12-18 months, when the child begins walking. Columns 13-16 provide comparisons of infancy with early childhood, applying the same or similar criteria to both stages. All the codes are based on the typical cultural practices for male, middle-born children.

### Column 1: Sleeping Proximity

The nighttime sleeping proximity of mother and father to infant is coded as follows.

1  Mother and father both sleep in a different room.
2-4 Mother sleeps in the same room but in a different bed.
2  Father sleeps in a different room or building.
3  Father's proximity not specified.
4  Father sleeps in same room but different bed.
5  Mother and father sleep in same room; bed not specified.
6-9 Mother sleeps in same bed.
6  Father sleeps in a different room or building.
7  Father's proximity not specified.
8  Father sleeps in same room but different bed.
9  Father sleeps in same bed.

### Column 2: Bodily Restrictiveness

This refers to the type of physical restraint generally applied while the infant is not being carried, fed, or otherwise attended to. Separate codes are made for two stages: (a) early period, the first few months after birth; (b) later infancy, usually beginning when the baby first crawls, at approximately nine months of age.

   1 No physical restriction except in emergency situations.
   2 Infant is loosely confined, with freedom of bodily movement within a restricted radius, e.g., on a tether or in a playpen.
   3 Infant is confined in a limited space, such as a bed or hammock.
   4 Body movement is limited by swaddling, heavy blankets, or a small cradle.
   5 Infant is bound much of the time in a cradle board or other mechanism for restricting movement of the limbs as well as the body

## Column 3: Bodily Contact

This measures the proportion of the day when the baby is held or carried by any caretakers. Two stages (a, early period; b, later infancy) are defined as in Column 2.

   1 Limited to routine and precautionary care.
   2 Only occasionally.
   3 Up to half of the time.
   4 More than half of the time.
   5 Almost constantly.

## Column 4: Carrying Technique

The usual method of transporting the infant is designated by the following two codes.

(a) *Carrying Devices*
   1 None, with skin contact between infant and carrier.
   2 None, with clothing or a blanket.
   3 Sling or flexible pouch.
   4 Basket.
   5 Rigid cradleboard.

(b) *Carrying Position*
   1 Back.
   2 Side.
   3 Front.
   4 Other.

This code is followed by the letter a, if the infant faces away from the carrier or b, if toward the carrier, when this additional information is available.

## Column 5: Crying

Two codes are differentiated, both for the entire infancy period.

(a) *Reward.* This is defined as the caretaker's attempts to gratify the infant's needs expressed by crying.
   1 Prevalently indifferent or punitive response.
   2 Slow or perfunctory nurturant response.
   3 Prevalently but inconsistently a speedy, nurturant response.
   4 Generally speedy, nurturant response.
   5 Always a speedy and highly nurturant response.

(b) *Amount.* This is based on both frequency and duration of crying by the infant.
   1 Very infrequent and brief.
   2 Occasional but for short periods.

3 Infrequent occasions of prolonged crying.
4 Frequent.
5 Both frequent and prolonged.

## Column 6: Pain Infliction

This includes rough handling, painful punishments, cold baths, hardening procedures, ear-piercing, depilation, and bodily mutilations.

1 Absence of inflicted pain.
2 Only neonatally or very mild pain.
3 Occasional mild pain.
4 Frequent mild pain or infrequent severe pain.
5 Greater frequency of pain.
6 Great severity of pain infliction.

## Column 7: Post-Partum Sex Taboo

This is the duration of abstinence from sexual intercourse by the mother after birth, described as the cultural norm. The coding categories 2-7 correspond closely to categories 0-5 in Column 36 of the Ethnographic Atlas (Murdock 1967). Enclosure of the code in parentheses signifies an inference based on the interval until termination of the mother's confinement and return of her husband. The letter e, following the code, signifies that it was obtained from the Ethnographic Atlas in cases when the present coders felt unable to make a rating on the basis of their examination of the sources.

1 Intercourse expected soon after birth.
2 No taboo.
3 One month or less.
4 No more than six months.
5 No more than one year.
6 No more than two years.
7 More than two years.

## Column 8: Special Procedures

(a) *Ceremonialism.* This refers only to formal, social rituals or communications beyond the nuclear family, centered around the child. Examples are naming and baptism ceremonies and festivals or public announcements to commemorate developmental stages such as first smile, first tooth, or walking.

1 None.
2 Only within the first two months after birth.
3 One ceremonial occasion at later age.
4 Two or more ceremonies.
5 Marked concern with ceremonies.

(b) *Magical Protectiveness.* This includes symbolic actions, rituals, and restrictions applied to the parents as well as to the child.

1 None or very slight.
2 Limited to the neonatal period, e.g., couvade.
3 Slight efforts both neonatally and later.
4 Moderate efforts both neonatally and later.
5 Exaggerated efforts both neonatally and later.

(c) *Physical Protectiveness.* This includes all physical efforts to alleviate or prevent illness and discomfort.

1 No special effort.

2 Slight or sporadic protective measures.
3 Moderate effort, such as regular baths.
4 Some exceptional techniques, such as special food, medicines, ointments, diapers or bedding.
5 Strong emphasis on a variety of exceptional techniques, e.g., regular use of modern medical personnel and techniques.

## Column 9: New Foods

Age and gradualness at which foods (other than milk or water) are first given. Liquids given only in the first few days after birth are not counted as new foods.

1 Before one month.
2 1-6 months.
3 7-12 months, including solid foods.
4 7-12 months, only liquids or premasticated.
5 After 12 months.

## Column 10: Code for Five Aspects of Development

Earliness and severity are measured by the following scales for five aspects of the transition from infancy to childhood.

*Weaning (W).* This refers to the termination of sucking milk from breast or bottle and thus reliance on supplemental or substitute foods. The distinction between gentle and severe weaning takes into account the abruptness of weaning and the degree of similarity of the supplementary or substitute food. Thus a shift to premasticated food is an example of gentle weaning.

1 Completion of weaning is late (after two years or the establishment of fully independent walking) and gentle.
2 Weaning is late and severe.
3 Weaning is intermediate (after one year or the first independent steps) and gentle.
4 Weaning is intermediate and severe.
5 Weaning is early (after six months or the onset of crawling) and gentle.
6 Weaning is early and severe.
7 Weaning is very early (before six months) and gentle.
8 Weaning is very early and severe.

*Motor Skills (M).* This refers to the encouragement, rewarding, and guiding of the child's motor skills and activity, involving use of the limbs, crawling, grasping, standing, walking, and exploratory behavior.

1 Discouragement or punishment of early development of motor skills.
2 Ignoring the child's motor development.
3 Attention and encouragement given for motor skills, but child proceeds at own pace, with no active assistance or guidance.
4 Definite but inconsistent rewards, encouragement, and attention to child's motor accomplishments.
5 Strong, persistent attempts to encourage and train motor accomplishments.

*Autonomy (A).* This refers to the development of activities either alone or with the children's play group and thus becoming independent of the caretakers of the infancy period.

1 Autonomy is late (after 4 years of age), incomplete (not achieved completely until after 4-5 years of age), and gradual.
2 Autonomy is late but somewhat abrupt.
3 Autonomy is fairly early (at 2-4 years) but gradual.
4 Autonomy is fairly early and abrupt, or very early (before two years of age) but gradual.
5 Autonomy is very early and abrupt.

*Elimination Control (E).* This refers to the initiation of training the child to refrain from urination and defecation except for specified places and times. Both forms of elimination were taken into account, with more weight given to reports on control of defecation, because this is a more universal necessity for cultural control.

0 None during infancy or transition period.
1 Very late, between three and five years of age.
2 Late, after 18 months or the establishment of steady, independent walking.
3 Intermediate, after one year or the first independent steps.
4 Early, after six months or the onset of crawling.
5 Very early, before six months.

*Covering Genitals (C).* Training in modesty is assumed to begin at the age when the genitals are first covered.

0 Even adults go uncovered or naked.
1 Very late; covering is not assumed until after the transition period.
2 Late; covering of the genitals begins late in the transition period, i.e., after fully independent walking is achieved.
3 Intermediate; clothing is assumed after one year of age or the first steps but before fully independent walking.
4 Early; clothing or covering of the genitals is assumed after about six months or the onset of crawling but before the first steps are taken.
5 Very early; clothing or covering of the genitals begins at or shortly after birth, even when the infant is in the home.

## Column 11: Age of Weaning

This designates the usual age in months at the onset of weaning as defined in Column 10 above. The highest age shown is 72 months; a plus symbol (+) after the age means that weaning begins later than the specified age. For some societies, a range of usual ages is indicated by specifying two ages for the onset of weaning.

## Column 12: Ranking of Age for Five Aspects of Development

Each aspect of development (WMAEC) defined in Column 10 is ranked for earliness of onset relative to the other aspects. A rank of 1 is given for the code with the youngest age of onset and a rank of 5 for the one with the oldest age of onset. Tied codes are given the same rank, following immediately after any lower ranks, but any higher ranks are based on the number of lower-ranking codes. For example, tied ranks of 2-3 are both ranked 2 and the next code is ranked 4. Codes with insufficient information, designated by a dot (.), are excluded and the number of ranks for the society is correspondingly decreased.

## Column 13: Non-Maternal Relationships

This specifies the importance of the role of caretakers and companions other than the mother.

*(a) Infancy.*

1 Almost exclusively the mother.
2 Principally mother, others have minor roles.
3 Principally mother, others have important roles.
4 Mother provides half or less of the care.
5 Mother's role is significant but less than all others combined.

6 Most care except nursing is by others.
7 Practically all care, including nursing, is by others.

*(b) Early Childhood.*

1 Almost exclusively the mother.
2 Principally the mother, but others have important roles.
3 Child spends half or less of the time with mother.
4 Majority of time is spent away from mother.
5 Practically all the time is spent away from mother.

## Column 14: Role of Father

This code excludes other adult males unless they are classified by the society as equivalents of the father in their relationship to the child. The same scale is used for (a) Infancy and (b) Early childhood.

1 No close proximity.
2 Rare instances of close proximity.
3 Occasional or irregular close proximity.
4 Frequent close proximity.
5 Regular, close relationship or companionship.

## Column 15: Principal Relationships

The principal caretakers and companions are classified according to the following categories.

*(a) Infancy Caretakers.*

1 Children (female only).
2 Children (sex unspecified).
3 Children (both sexes).
4 Adult family members (female only).
5 Adult family members (sex unspecified).
6 Adult family members (both sexes).
7 Others, including employees (female only).
8 Others, including employees (sex unspecified).
9 Others, including employees (both sexes).

*(b) Early Childhood Companions or Caretakers.*

1 Peer group (single sex).
2 Peer group (sex unspecified).
3 Peer group (both sexes).
4 Older children (single sex).
5 Older children (sex unspecified).
6 Older children (both sexes).
7 Adults (single sex)
8 Adults (sex unspecified).
9 Adults (both sexes).

Designation of a single sex (1, 4, or 7) is followed by a letter, f designating Female or s designating Same sex as the child.

## Column 16: General Indulgence

This takes into account all relevant aspects of treatment and care, in particular expressions of affection and permissiveness, and the consistency and effectiveness of nurturance and care. The information on reward for crying (Column 5a) and pain infliction (Column 6) are among the important criteria.

*(a) Infancy.*

1 Severe or neglectful treatment.
2 Lesser degree of severity and deprivation.
3 Usually affectionate, but occasional harshness or deprivation.
4 Greater degree of indulgence.
5 Highly affectionate and nurturant with consistent, immediate response to demands.

*(b) Early Childhood.*

1 Harshness, including severe or persistent punishments.
2 Lesser degree of severity.
3 Generally permissive but occasional punishment or disapproval.
4 Greater degree of lenience.
5 Consistently lenient and indulgent.

For both (a) and (b), the numerical score is followed by a letter, H for the High portion of the scale category, M for the Middle portion, and L for the Low portion. This provides an optional means for differentiating the large number of societies grouped together in some of the scale categories.

## CODED MATERIAL

Table 1 summarizes in pairs of pages (left-hand and right-hand) the information obtained on 186 world area representatives and 15 alternate societies. The area number, name of society, and Columns 1-8 are on the left-hand pages; the area number and Columns 9-16 are on the right-hand pages.

Enclosure of the code by parentheses indicates a rating which is somewhat doubtful or a strong inference, when the information is substantial but ambiguous or not directly pertinent to the code. Brackets enclose highly doubtful or uncertain ratings, when the information is meager or contradictory or when the code is based on a single instance or a weak inference. A dot (.) indicates that information is lacking or excessively meager or conflicting.

The adequacy of ethnographic information shows variation both among the 186 societies of the sample and among the 34 numerical codes in the 16 columns of Table 1. In general, most of the societies were given numerical scores on most of the codes. The highest percentage of societies (96 per cent) were coded on Ceremonialism (Column 8a); other codes with more than 90 per cent were Sleeping Proximity (Column 1), Magical Protectiveness (Column 8b), and rank-order for Motor Activity (Column 12M). The lowest percentage of societies (25 per cent) were coded on Frequency of Crying (Column 5b); the only others with scores for less than half the sample were New Foods (Column 9), Motor Activity and Elimination Control (Column 10M, E), and the rank-order for Elimination Control (Column 12E). For all the codes, the majority of numerical scores were confident, without enclosure in parentheses or brackets; among the doubtful scores, the majority were generally given the relatively higher degree of confidence indicated by parentheses.

## CODING PROCEDURES

The codes were devised principally by the senior author, with helpful contributions from several colleagues, in particular George P. Murdock,

Douglas R. White, Frances Gaver, and John W. M. Whiting. Most of the fifteen alternate societies were used as a pretesting sample for earlier versions of the codes and for training the coders for the final version.

Most of the societies were coded by two people working independently with the same pinpointing sheets and bibliographic sources. After they completed their codings, they conferred and agreed on a set of consensus codes. Some societies were coded by only one person, generally because the information was judged to be insufficient to justify the duplicate effort or because important sources were in a foreign language which could be read with facility by only one coder. In some cases a second person used the notes of the first person in making an independent set of codes, followed by conference and consensus. A few societies were coded by three people.

The total of 201 societies were coded by four people. The junior author coded 176 of them, Frances Gaver 65, Margaret A. M. Pexton 54, and Diana Obrinsky 43. In addition, pretest coding of some of the alternate societies was done by the senior author and by Frank Lounsbury with a preliminary version of the codes. The bibliography of ethnographic sources, listed near the end of this article, was compiled by the junior author with help from Edith Lauer and Alice Fry Bauman.

Most of the coding was done in alphabetical sequence of the society names, beginning with A, but several societies, for which sources subsequently became available, were coded or recoded later than others in adjacent alphabetical positions.

The sources listed in the pinpointing sheets were examined thoroughly for material pertaining to treatment and responses of children. Even when a book contained a chapter on infancy and childhood, other portions of the text often contained useful information. Pictures often provided usable information for some codes, especially on carrying techniques and ages of developmental changes. When the Human Relations Area Files were used, the coder examined the text in page sequence rather than the pages rearranged according to topical categories.

The coding sheet grouped the variables into three categories: (a) Infancy, (b) Infancy and Transition, (c) Transition. Thus, for example, Columns 13-16 in Table 1 were divided between the first and third categories. With these exceptions, the sequence of variables in Table 1 follows closely the sequence on the coding sheet. The coders were not required to fill out the sheet in the sequence given, but they generally found it convenient to fill out the three main categories of codes in the same sequence as on the sheet. The user of Table 1 will generally find more convenient the grouping together of closely related variables, even when they pertain to different stages of development.

In some cases, the definitions given in the instructions to the coders are revised in the present article, to eliminate redundant or unnecessarily detailed material and to incorporate a few modifications or elaborations developed by the coders. For Column 16b, the original scale was reversed so that increasing magnitudes would signify increasing indulgence, as in Column 16a, instead of increasing severity.

TABLE 1
Coded Data on Infancy and Early Childhood

| Area | Society | 1 | 2(a) | 2(b) | 3(a) | 3(b) | 4(a) | 4(b) | 5(a) | 5(b) | 6 | 7 | 8(a) | 8(b) | 8(c) |
|---|---|---|---|---|---|---|---|---|---|---|---|---|---|---|---|
| 1 | Nama Hottentot | 5 | [4] | [1] | 4 | 4 | 3 | 1b | . | . | (3) | 4e | 2 | 3 | 4 |
| 2 | Kung Bushmen | 8 | [1] | [1] | 5 | (5) | 3 | 2b | 5 | . | 1 | 4e | (2) | 1 | (2) |
| 3 | Thonga | (6) | (1) | (1) | (4) | (3) | 3 | 1b | 4 | 4 | 4 | 5 | 4 | 4 | 4 |
| 4 | Lozi | . | . | . | . | . | . | . | . | . | . | . | 2 | (4) | . |
| 5 | Mbundu | 9 | 1 | 1 | 5 | 5 | 3 | 1b | 4 | . | 2 | . | (2) | (3) | 4 |
| 6 | Suku | (6) | . | . | . | . | (1) | 2b | . | . | . | 6 | 3 | 3 | (2) |
| 7 | Bemba | 5 | . | . | 5 | (5) | 3 | 1b | 4 | 2 | 3 | 7 | 3 | 4 | 4 |
| 8 | Nyakyusa | (2) | . | . | [4] | [4] | 3 | 1b | . | . | . | 6 | 2 | (3) | 4 |
| 9 | Hadza | 5 | . | . | 5 | 5 | 3 | 2b | . | . | 2 | . | . | 3 | 2 |
| 10 | Luguru | 7 | . | . | 4 | (4) | 3 | 1(b) | . | . | . | 5e | (2) | (3) | . |
| 11 | Kikuyu | (2) | 2 | . | 4 | 4 | 3 | 1b | 4 | . | [3] | 4e | (3) | 4 | 4 |
| 12 | Ganda | 2 | 3 | 2 | . | . | 3 | 1b | . | . | (1) | 7 | 4 | 4 | 3 |
| 13 | Mbuti | 5 | (1) | 1 | 4 | 3 | 3 | 2b | (4) | . | (3) | 6 | 1 | 3 | (3) |
| 14 | Nkundo Mongo | [6] | (1) | (1) | (4) | (4) | 1 | 2b | [4] | . | (3) | [5] | 3 | 4 | 3 |
| 15 | Banen | 6 | 3 | . | . | . | 1 | 2b | . | . | 3 | 6 | 2 | (3) | 4 |
| 16 | Tiv | 6 | 1 | 1 | 4 | 4 | 1 | 2b | 4 | . | 4 | [6] | (2) | 4 | 4 |
| 17 | Ibo | (2) | . | . | . | . | 1 | 2b | 3 | . | 2 | 7 | 2 | 2 | 3 |
| 18 | Fon | 6 | 1 | 1 | 4 | 3 | 3 | 1b | . | . | [3] | 7 | 4 | 4 | 3 |
| 19 | Ashanti | 6 | (1) | . | . | . | (3) | 1b | (4) | . | 3 | 4 | 2 | 5 | 3 |
| 20 | Mende | 6 | . | . | . | . | 3 | 1b | (3) | . | . | 5 | 3 | 4 | 3 |
| 21 | Wolof | 7 | [1] | [1] | (4) | (4) | 3 | 1b | . | . | 3 | 6e | 2 | 3 | 3 |
| 22 | Bambara | . | . | . | 4 | 4 | 3 | 1b | . | . | 3 | 4 | 3 | 4 | 2 |
| 23 | Tallensi | 6 | 1 | 1 | (4) | (3) | 1 | 2b | 4 | . | 3 | 7 | 3 | 3 | 3 |
| 24 | Songhai | (2) | 3 | 3 | (3) | (3) | 5 | 1a | [4] | [3] | 3 | 4 | 4 | 4 | 3 |
| 25 | Wodaabe Fulani | (6) | (1) | 1 | 4 | 3 | 1 | 1b | (4) | . | (3) | 7e | 2 | (3) | 3 |
| 26 | Hausa | (6) | 4 | 4 | 4 | 4 | 3 | 1b | 4 | (3) | 3 | 6 | 4 | 4 | (3) |
| 27 | Massa | 9 | . | . | . | . | . | . | . | . | 3 | 6 | [1] | (3) | (3) |
| 28 | Azande | 6 | 1 | (1) | . | . | 3 | (2b) | . | . | 2 | 7 | 2 | 4 | 3 |
| 29 | Fur | (2) | . | . | (4) | (4) | 3 | 1b | . | . | 5 | 4 | (2) | 4 | 4 |
| 30 | Otoro Nuba | (5) | . | . | . | . | . | . | . | . | . | . | (3) | [4] | . |
| 31 | Shilluk | 5 | 1 | 1 | 5 | 5 | 2 | 2b | . | . | 4 | 7 | 3 | 4 | 2 |
| 32 | Mao | 5 | . | . | (5) | (5) | 3 | 1b | . | . | . | . | 3 | . | . |
| 33 | Kaffa | (6) | . | . | 5 | (5) | 3 | 1b | . | . | (3) | [3] | 2 | 4 | 2 |
| 34 | Masai | 6 | (1) | (1) | 5 | 4 | 3 | 1b | 5 | . | 3 | 6 | 4 | 3 | 3 |
| 35 | Konso | (6) | . | . | . | . | . | 1(b) | . | . | 3 | 7 | (2) | 3 | 2 |
| 36 | Somali | (6) | 1 | 1 | [4] | [4] | 3 | 1b | . | . | . | 4 | [3] | [3] | (3) |
| 37 | Amhara | [5] | . | . | 5 | 5 | 3 | 1b | . | . | 2 | 4 | 2 | 2 | 2 |
| 38 | Bogo | . | . | . | . | . | . | . | . | . | 2 | . | 2 | 2 | . |
| 39 | Kenuzi Nubians | 6 | . | (1) | 5 | 4 | 2 | 2b | 4 | . | 3 | . | 3 | 4 | 2 |
| 40 | Teda | 9 | [1] | [1] | . | . | . | . | . | . | (2) | (2) | 2 | 4 | 4 |
| 41 | Tuareg | 8 | 3 | (3) | . | . | 2 | 2b | (4) | . | 3 | 4 | 2 | 3 | 2 |
| 42 | Riffians | (5) | . | . | . | . | . | [1] | . | . | (3) | 4 | 4 | 4 | 2 |
| 43 | Egyptians | 7 | . | . | 4 | 4 | 2 | 2b | 4 | . | 4 | 4e | 4 | 4 | 2 |
| 44 | Hebrews | . | 4 | [1] | 4 | 4 | 2 | 3b | . | . | 3 | 4 | 3 | (2) | 3 |
| 45 | Babylonians | . | . | . | . | . | . | . | . | . | . | . | . | (4) | . |
| 46 | Rwala Bedouin | (2) | 4 | (4) | . | . | . | . | [4] | . | 4 | 4 | 3 | 4 | 4 |
| 47 | Turks | (4) | 4 | [4] | [3] | [3] | [4] | 1 | [3] | . | (4) | . | 3 | 4 | 3 |
| 48 | Gheg Albanians | 4 | 5 | (2) | 2 | (2) | 5 | 1(a) | . | . | . | 4 | 3 | 4 | 2 |
| 49 | Romans | . | (4) | (4) | . | . | . | . | . | . | [3] | . | [2] | (4) | . |
| 50 | Basques | 4 | 3 | 3 | 2 | 2 | 2 | 2b | 3 | . | (2) | (2) | (2) | (1) | 5 |
| 51 | Irish | 4 | 3 | 2 | 3 | 3 | 2 | 2a | 4 | (2) | (1) | 4 | 2 | 1 | 4 |
| 52 | Lapps | 4 | 5 | 5 | (3) | (3) | 5 | 1a | 4 | (2) | . | 4e | 2 | 3 | (4) |
| 53 | Yurak Samoyed | 4 | 4 | (2) | . | . | . | . | . | 4 | 3 | [4] | 3 | [3] | . |
| 54 | Russians | 4 | [4] | [1] | (3) | (3) | 2 | . | [4] | [2] | [2] | . | (3) | (3) | (5) |

| Area | 9 W | M | 10 A | E | C | 11 | 12 WMAEC | 13 (a) | (b) | 14 (a) | (b) | 15 (a) | (b) | 16 (a) | (b) |
|---|---|---|---|---|---|---|---|---|---|---|---|---|---|---|---|
| 1 | . | 2 | [4] | (3) | . | 1 | 36–48 | 312.4 | (2) | 4 | [3] | (3) | . | 3 | . | (3L) |
| 2 | . | 1 | . | 1 | 2 | [1] | 36–72 | 31424 | 2 | 2 | 4 | 4 | . | 9 | 5M | 5L |
| 3 | 3 | 2 | . | 4 | . | 1 | 30–36 | 212.4 | 3 | 4 | 2 | 2 | 1 | 9 | 3L | [4L] |
| 4 | . | 2 | . | . | . | 1 | 24–36 | 21..3 | . | . | [2] | [3] | . | . | . | . |
| 5 | 1 | 1 | (4) | (3) | . | . | 36–48 | 312.. | 3 | 3 | 3 | (3) | 1 | 3 | 4M | 3M |
| 6 | 3 | (1) | . | [3] | . | . | 24–36 | 212.. | . | (3) | [3] | (4) | (1) | . | . | . |
| 7 | 1 | 2 | . | 3 | . | 1 | (24–36) | 213.4 | 2 | 4 | [2] | [1] | 1 | 9 | 3H | 4M |
| 8 | . | (1) | . | . | . | 2 | 24–36 | 21..3 | 3 | (3) | (2) | [2] | 4 | 4f | . | . |
| 9 | 1 | 5 | . | (3) | . | 1 | 12 | 123.4 | 2 | 3 | 2 | 3 | 4 | 1s | (4M) | (4M) |
| 10 | 1 | (1) | . | . | . | . | 24–36 | 21... | (2) | . | [3] | . | . | . | . | . |
| 11 | 1 | 1 | 4 | 4 | . | 1 | 24 | 312.4 | 3 | 4 | (2) | (4) | 1 | (3) | 3H | 4M |
| 12 | 2 | 2 | 4 | 4 | (2) | 1 | 36 | 31325 | (3) | 4 | 1 | (2) | 4 | 9 | . | 2H |
| 13 | [2] | (3) | 4 | 3 | . | 1 | 12–36 | 213.5 | 3 | 4 | 4 | 4 | 9 | 3 | 4L | (4L) |
| 14 | [1] | 1 | [4] | . | . | 1 | 24–30 | 21..3 | 2 | 2 | 3 | 3 | (6) | 6 | 4H | (3M) |
| 15 | . | 2 | . | . | . | . | (24) | 21... | 3 | (3) | (3) | (3) | 7 | (9) | . | . |
| 16 | 2 | 2 | 4 | [3] | 3 | 1 | 24–30 | 31425 | 4 | [4] | 3 | 4 | 3 | 6 | (3H) | 4M |
| 17 | . | (1) | . | (4) | . | 1 | 24–36 | 213.5 | 4 | 4 | 3 | 3 | 3 | 7f | 3H | . |
| 18 | 2 | 2 | 5 | 3 | (3) | 1 | 24–36 | 42315 | (1) | (2) | (1) | (2) | . | 3 | 4L | 3L |
| 19 | 1 | 2 | (3) | . | 2 | 1 | 24 | 21.34 | (3) | 4 | (2) | 5 | 4 | . | 4M | 3L |
| 20 | [2] | (1) | . | 1 | . | 5 | 36 | 213.4 | 3 | 4 | [3] | 4 | 4 | 5 | . | . |
| 21 | . | (1) | . | (3) | . | 1 | (24) | 213.4 | (2) | 3 | . | (2) | . | 4f | . | [2H] |
| 22 | . | (1) | . | (1) | . | (1) | 24–36 | 214.3 | 3 | 2 | . | . | 1 | 1s | . | . |
| 23 | 5 | 1 | 3 | 3 | 2 | 1 | 36 | 31425 | 3 | 3 | (3) | 4 | 4 | 3 | 4L | 4H |
| 24 | 1 | (3) | 4 | 1 | (0) | 1 | 18–24 | 21435 | 3 | 3 | (3) | 4 | 6 | 6 | 3M | (3M) |
| 25 | . | 1 | 4 | (3) | 3 | 1 | 24+ | 31425 | 3 | (3) | [3] | 3 | 4 | 4f | 4H | 4H |
| 26 | . | 1 | . | 3 | (5) | (1) | 24 | 32415 | (2) | (2) | (3) | (3) | 6 | 9 | 4L | 4M |
| 27 | . | [3] | (4) | . | . | 0 | 12+ | 12..3 | 3 | . | . | . | 4 | . | . | . |
| 28 | 1 | 1 | . | (1) | . | 1 | 24–48 | 213.3 | 1 | (2) | 2 | 2 | (1) | (3) | (4L) | (3M) |
| 29 | . | . | . | . | . | 1 | 24 | 21..3 | (2) | . | (1) | (1) | 1 | 9 | . | 2L |
| 30 | . | . | . | . | . | . | . | ..... | . | . | [3] | . | . | 3 | . | . |
| 31 | . | (1) | . | . | . | 1 | 24–30 | 21..3 | 2 | . | 3 | 3 | 1 | . | (4H) | (4H) |
| 32 | . | . | . | . | . | 1 | . | ..... | . | . | . | . | . | . | . | . |
| 33 | 1 | . | 4 | . | . | 1 | . | .12.3 | 2 | 4 | (2) | (3) | 7 | 3 | . | . |
| 34 | 1 | 4 | . | 4 | . | (2) | 18–24 | 213.3 | (2) | 4 | 1 | (1) | 7 | 3 | 4H | (4L) |
| 35 | . | (1) | . | . | [2] | 1 | 36 | 31.24 | [1] | . | [2] | [2] | . | 5 | . | . |
| 36 | . | (3) | . | . | . | 1 | (12–24) | 12..3 | (2) | (3) | (2) | . | 1 | . | . | . |
| 37 | 5 | 1 | 3 | 3 | 2 | 1 | 24 | 21335 | 2 | 4 | 2 | 2 | 7 | 3 | 4H | 3H |
| 38 | . | . | . | . | . | . | . | ..... | . | . | . | . | . | . | . | . |
| 39 | . | 2 | (3) | . | . | 5 | 24 | 32..1 | 2 | 2 | 1 | 1 | 1 | 7f | 4H | . |
| 40 | (5) | 1 | . | (3) | . | 1 | (12–48) | 213.4 | (2) | 4 | [3] | 4 | [4] | 7f | [4L] | 3H |
| 41 | . | 1 | . | (3) | . | 1 | 30–36 | 213.4 | 3 | (4) | . | 4 | 7 | 1s | . | . |
| 42 | . | (1) | . | . | . | [5] | (60) | 32..1 | . | . | [3] | . | [4] | . | . | . |
| 43 | 2 | 4 | 5 | 4 | 5 | 5 | 12–18 | 43521 | 2 | 4 | 2 | 2 | 4 | 4(f) | 4H | 2L |
| 44 | . | 1 | . | . | . | . | 36 | 21... | 2 | 2 | 3 | 3 | 7 | 3 | . | . |
| 45 | . | (1) | . | . | . | . | 24–36 | 21... | . | . | . | . | . | . | . | . |
| 46 | . | . | . | [1] | . | 5 | . | .23.1 | 2 | 2 | 2 | 3 | . | . | [4M] | [4L] |
| 47 | . | . | . | . | . | 5 | . | .2..1 | (3) | (3) | 3 | 4 | 4 | 4f | . | (4L) |
| 48 | . | (1) | . | . | . | [5] | 36 | 32..1 | (2) | . | . | (3) | 4 | 7f | . | . |
| 49 | . | . | . | . | . | (5) | . | .2..1 | (6) | (4) | [3] | [4] | 7 | 9 | . | [5M] |
| 50 | 2 | [7] | 4 | 3 | 2 | 5 | [3] | 23451 | 4 | 4 | 3 | 3 | 4 | 4f | 4M | 4L |
| 51 | 2 | (1) | 4 | 3 | 1 | 5 | 24–30 | 32441 | 5 | 4 | 2 | 3 | 4 | 7f | 4H | 4L |
| 52 | . | 3 | 3 | 3 | . | 5 | 12–24 | 324.1 | 2 | 3 | 4 | 4 | [4] | 4f | 4L | 4H |
| 53 | (3) | (1) | . | . | . | . | (60+) | 21... | (2) | . | . | . | . | . | . | . |
| 54 | . | [5] | [5] | [4] | [4] | 5 | [8] | 24531 | (4) | (4) | 4 | 4 | 4 | 6 | 4L | 2H |

| Area Society | 1 | 2 (a) | (b) | 3 (a) | (b) | 4 (a) | (b) | 5 (a) | (b) | 6 | 7 | 8 (a) | (b) | (c) |
|---|---|---|---|---|---|---|---|---|---|---|---|---|---|---|
| 55 Abkhaz | (5) | . | . | . | . | . | [2b] | . | . | . | . | (1) | 3 | 3 |
| 56 Armenians | (5) | . | . | . | . | [2] | [2b] | . | . | . | . | (2) | . | . |
| 57 Kurd | 4 | 5 | (5) | 1 | 1 | 5 | 4 | 2 | (5) | 3 | 4 | 3 | 4 | (3) |
| 58 Basseri | 5 | [3] | . | . | . | . | . | . | . | 4 | . | 2 | 3 | 3 |
| 59 West Punjabi | 5 | . | . | [4] | . | . | (2b) | . | . | 3 | . | 3 | 3 | 4 |
| 60 Gond | (6) | . | . | . | . | 3 | 2b | . | . | . | 3e | 1 | (2) | 2 |
| 61 Toda | (5) | . | . | . | . | [2] | 2b | . | . | (4) | 4e | 3 | (3) | (3) |
| 62 Santal | 9 | . | . | 4 | 4 | 2 | 2b | 4 | . | . | . | 3 | 4 | (2) |
| 63 Uttar Pradesh | 6 | 1 | 1 | (3) | (3) | 2 | 2b | 4 | 1 | 3 | 6 | 3 | 3 | 4 |
| 64 Burusho | 4 | 5 | 5 | 2 | 2 | 3 | 1b | (3) | (3) | 2 | 7 | 3 | 2 | 4 |
| 65 Kazak | 5 | 5 | [5] | . | . | . | . | . | . | 3 | . | (3) | 3 | 2 |
| 66 Khalka Mongols | 5 | . | . | . | . | . | . | [4] | . | 3 | . | 3 | 3 | 1 |
| 67 Lolo | 5 | . | . | . | . | . | . | . | . | . | . | 2 | (2) | (2) |
| 68 Lepcha | 8 | 1 | 1 | 5 | 4 | 3 | 1b | 4 | 1 | 2 | 1 | 2 | 4 | 3 |
| 69 Garo | 8 | 1 | 1 | 5 | 5 | 3 | 1b | 5 | . | 3 | . | 2 | 2 | (2) |
| 70 Lakher | 9 | . | . | . | . | 3 | 3(b) | . | . | 2 | . | 3 | 4 | [2] |
| 71 Burmese | 5 | 4 | 4 | (3) | (3) | (2) | 2b | 4 | 1 | (1) | . | 2 | 4 | 2 |
| 72 Lamet | (8) | . | . | . | . | 3 | 2b | . | . | . | . | [2] | . | . |
| 73 Vietnamese | 5 | [1] | [1] | (4) | (4) | [2] | [2b] | 4 | 1 | . | 4 | [4] | 4 | [3] |
| 74 Rhade | 5 | . | . | . | . | . | . | . | . | . | 4 | (4) | (3) | . |
| 75 Khmer | . | . | . | . | . | . | . | . | . | 2 | 2 | 2 | 3 | (3) |
| 76 Siamese | 4 | 4 | 4 | (3) | (3) | 2 | 2b | 3 | 3 | (2) | 3e | (2) | 4 | 4 |
| 77 Semang | 9 | 1 | 1 | (5) | (4) | 3 | 2b | 4 | (4) | [1] | 6e | (1) | 3 | 4 |
| 78 Nicobarese | 5 | [1] | [1] | [4] | [4] | 1 | 2b | . | . | (2) | . | 3 | 4 | 4 |
| 79 Andamanese | 5 | . | . | . | . | 3 | 2b | . | . | (2) | . | 1 | 2 | 2 |
| 80 Vedda | 5 | [1] | [1] | [3] | [3] | 1 | 2b | [4] | . | . | 3e | 1 | 3 | (2) |
| 81 Tanala | (9) | (1) | (1) | 5 | 5 | 3 | 1b | 4 | . | 3 | 3 | [3] | 3 | 3 |
| 82 Negri Sembilan | 8 | 4 | 1 | 3 | 3 | 3 | 2b | 4 | . | . | 4e | 3 | (4) | 3 |
| 83 Javanese | 9 | 4 | 2 | 5 | 5 | 3 | 3b | 5 | 1 | 2 | 4 | 5 | 5 | 4 |
| 84 Balinese | 8 | 3 | 3 | 5 | 5 | 3 | 2b | 5 | 1 | 2 | 4e | 5 | 4 | 3 |
| 85 Iban | 5 | . | . | . | . | (2) | (3b) | . | . | 3 | . | 4 | 4 | 3 |
| 86 Badjau | 4 | 4 | 2 | . | . | . | . | . | . | 1 | . | 3 | 3 | 3 |
| 87 Toradja | 4 | 5 | 1 | (2) | (3) | 3 | 3b | 4 | (1) | 1 | . | 3 | 4 | 3 |
| 88 Tobelorese | (4) | 4 | (1) | . | . | . | . | 4 | 1 | 2 | . | 5 | 4 | 4 |
| 89 Alorese | 8 | 3 | 1 | 5 | 4 | 3 | 2b | 3 | 3 | 4 | 5 | 2 | 2 | 3 |
| 90 Tiwi | 8 | 1 | 1 | 4 | 3 | 1 | 1b | 4 | (2) | . | [3] | 2 | 3 | 2 |
| 91 Aranda | 5 | . | . | . | . | 4 | 2 | . | . | . | 3e | (3) | 4 | 2 |
| 92 Orokaiva | (8) | 4 | 4 | 3 | 3 | 3 | 1b | 4 | (3) | 3 | . | . | (2) | (2) |
| 93 Kimam | (5) | . | . | . | . | . | . | . | . | . | 4e | 4 | (3) | 3 |
| 94 Kapauku | 2 | 3 | 1 | 4 | 4 | 3 | . | 4 | . | 2 | 3e | 3 | 3 | 2 |
| 95 Kwoma | 8 | . | 1 | 5 | 5 | 1 | 3b | 5 | (1) | 3 | 6 | 1 | 3 | 3 |
| 96 Manus | (8) | 1 | 1 | 3 | (2) | 1 | 1b | 4 | . | 4 | 3 | 2 | 1 | 2 |
| 97 New Ireland | 6 | 1 | 1 | [3] | [3] | 3 | [1b] | 3 | 1 | 3 | 7 | 5 | 3 | . |
| 98 Trobrianders | 9 | 1 | 1 | 4 | (4) | 1 | 2b | (4) | . | [1] | 6 | (2) | [3] | 3 |
| 99 Siuai | (8) | 1 | 1 | 4 | 4 | 1 | 2b | 4 | [4] | 3 | 7 | 4 | 4 | 3 |
| 100 Tikopia | 9 | 1 | 1 | (3) | (3) | 3 | 1b | 4 | (2) | 2 | 2 | 2 | 3 | 3 |
| 101 Pentecost | (6) | . | . | 4 | 4 | 3 | . | . | . | 3 | 6e | 3 | . | . |
| 102 Mbau Fijians | . | (1) | (1) | . | . | 1 | 1b | 4 | . | 3 | . | 2 | (4) | 2 |
| 103 Ajie | (2) | (1) | (1) | (3) | (3) | 4 | 1a | . | . | . | . | (2) | . | . |
| 104 Maori | 5 | (3) | (3) | (4) | 4 | 3 | 1b | [5] | . | (2) | 2e | [3] | 4 | 2 |
| 105 Marquesans | 9 | [1] | [1] | [2] | [2] | (1) | (2b) | [3] | . | (3) | 1 | 4 | 4 | 4 |
| 106 Samoans | 5 | (1) | (1) | . | . | 1 | 2b | . | . | 3 | (6) | 5 | (3) | 3 |
| 107 Gilbertese | . | . | . | . | . | . | 1b | . | . | 3 | 3e | 4 | . | . |
| 108 Marshallese | 5 | . | . | . | . | . | 2b | . | . | 2 | 3 | 3 | 4 | 3 |

| Area | 9 | | 10 | | | 11 | | 12 | 13 | | 14 | | 15 | | 16 | |
|---|---|---|---|---|---|---|---|---|---|---|---|---|---|---|---|---|
| | W | M | A | E | C | | | WMAEC | (a) | (b) | (a) | (b) | (a) | (b) | (a) | (b) |
| 55 | . | . | . | . | . | . | . | ..... | . | . | (1) | . | . | . | . | . |
| 56 | . | . | . | . | 5 | . | . | .2..1 | (3) | . | [3] | [4] | . | [9] | . | . |
| 57 | . | . | . | (4) | 5 | 5 | 6–24 | 34521 | 2 | 4 | . | (3) | 1 | 6 | 2M | 2H |
| 58 | . | . | . | . | . | . | . | ..... | . | . | . | . | . | . | . | . |
| 59 | . | (1) | . | [3] | [0] | . | 24–36 | 2134. | 4 | 3 | (3) | 4 | 3 | 3 | . | [3M] |
| 60 | . | . | . | . | . | . | 24–36 | 21..3 | [2] | . | . | . | . | . | . | . |
| 61 | 2 | 2 | . | . | [5] | 1 | (24) | 32.14 | . | . | (3) | (3) | . | . | . | [2M] |
| 62 | . | (1) | . | 1 | . | . | 60 | 212.. | (2) | (2) | [3] | (3) | . | 7f | [4M] | [4H] |
| 63 | 4 | 1 | 2 | 1 | 4 | 3 | [36] | 43512 | 3 | 3 | 4 | (4) | 4 | 5 | 4H | 4M |
| 64 | . | 1 | 1 | [1] | . | 5 | 36 | 324.1 | 2 | 3 | (3) | . | 3 | 6 | (3M) | 4H |
| 65 | . | 1 | . | . | . | (5) | 48–60 | 32..1 | . | (4) | (4) | (5) | 2 | . | . | . |
| 66 | 1 | 1 | . | (4) | . | 1 | 48–72 | 312.4 | 3 | (4) | (3) | (3) | 7 | 3 | . | (2H) |
| 67 | . | (1) | . | . | . | . | 48–60 | 21... | . | . | (4) | (4) | (7) | 3 | . | . |
| 68 | 1 | 2 | 4 | 2 | 5 | . | 36–48 | 3241. | 3 | 3 | 4 | 4 | 3 | 6 | 4M | 4L |
| 69 | 4 | 2 | 4 | 1 | (5) | 1 | 24 | 32415 | 3 | . | 4 | 4 | 3 | . | 5M | 4L |
| 70 | 1 | [1] | . | . | . | 1 | 24–36 | 21..3 | [2] | . | [3] | [4] | . | . | . | . |
| 71 | . | (1) | . | . | 5 | . | (24–36) | 32.1. | (4) | (3) | (3) | (3) | 6 | 9 | 4H | 4H |
| 72 | . | . | . | . | . | . | . | ..... | 2 | . | . | . | . | 9 | . | . |
| 73 | 2 | (1) | . | [3] | 1 | [1] | (36+) | 21345 | [3] | [4] | [4] | 4 | 6 | 6 | 4H | 3M |
| 74 | . | . | . | . | . | . | . | ..... | (3) | 2 | (3) | (3) | . | 3 | . | . |
| 75 | 1 | 1 | . | . | . | . | 24–48 | 21... | (2) | . | (4) | (4) | 1 | (3) | . | [3L] |
| 76 | 1 | (1) | . | [3] | [1] | (2) | 24–36 | 21344 | 4 | (4) | 3 | 4 | 4 | 6 | (3L) | 3H |
| 77 | . | 1 | (3) | 1 | (2) | 1 | 24–36 | 21435 | [3] | 2 | 4 | 4 | 4 | [3] | 4H | 4H |
| 78 | . | (1) | [3] | (3) | . | 1 | 24 | 213.4 | (2) | [3] | (4) | . | . | 5 | [4M] | . |
| 79 | . | 1 | . | 3 | . | 1 | 36–48 | 213.4 | 3 | 2 | 4 | (3) | 7 | . | 4H | (4M) |
| 80 | . | [1] | . | . | . | 1 | [24] | 21..3 | (2) | [2] | [4] | [4] | . | . | [4M] | . |
| 81 | [2] | [3] | . | . | 5 | 2 | . | 32.14 | 2 | [3] | 3 | [3] | 2 | 3 | 4L | [4L] |
| 82 | 1 | 2 | (4) | 3 | 4 | 1 | 24 | 32415 | 2 | 3 | 3 | 4 | 1 | 3 | 4M | 4L |
| 83 | 1 | (3) | 4 | 1 | 4 | 2 | 14–24 | 32514 | 2 | 3 | 3 | 5 | 4 | 4f | 5L | 4M |
| 84 | 1 | 1 | 5 | 4 | (2) | 1 | 30 | 41235 | 3 | 4 | 4 | 4 | 6 | 4(f) | 5L | 4M |
| 85 | 1 | . | . | . | . | . | . | .1... | (3) | . | . | . | 3 | . | . | . |
| 86 | 1 | . | . | . | . | 1 | . | .1..2 | 2 | 2 | 4 | 4 | 4 | 4f | . | [4H] |
| 87 | (2) | 1 | 4 | (3) | . | . | 24–36 | 213.. | 2 | (3) | [2] | [3] | 1 | 4f | 4H | 4L |
| 88 | 1 | (1) | (4) | . | . | . | (24) | 21..3 | 2 | (3) | (3) | 4 | [7] | 3 | (4H) | . |
| 89 | 1 | (2) | 3 | 3 | 2 | 1 | (24–30) | 41325 | 5 | 4 | 4 | (3) | 3 | 6 | 2H | 4L |
| 90 | 4 | 1 | [3] | 3 | . | 0 | (36–48) | 213.4 | 2 | 3 | 4 | 4 | 4 | 3 | 5L | 5L |
| 91 | . | 1 | 4 | . | . | 0 | 36 | 21..3 | (2) | (2) | (3) | . | (7) | . | [4L] | [4M] |
| 92 | 3 | (1) | . | (4) | . | 1 | 36 | 312.4 | 3 | 3 | 4 | 5 | 2 | 2 | 3M | 2H |
| 93 | . | . | . | . | . | (1) | . | .1..2 | . | [3] | . | [4] | . | . | . | [4H] |
| 94 | 5 | 1 | . | 1 | 3 | 3 | 24 | 41522 | 2 | 2 | 2 | 2 | (4) | 3 | 4M | 3H |
| 95 | 2 | 2 | . | 2 | 2 | 0 | 18–48 | 21425 | 1 | 4 | 3 | 3 | 7 | 6 | 5M | 2M |
| 96 | 1 | 2 | 5 | 3 | 2 | 5 | 30–36 | 31325 | 3 | 5 | 3 | 5 | 4 | 3 | 4L | 3L |
| 97 | 1 | 1 | (3) | (3) | 2 | (5) | 24–36 | 31425 | 4 | 3 | 4 | 5 | 4 | 6 | 4H | 4L |
| 98 | 1 | 1 | . | 1 | . | 1 | 24 | 213.4 | 4 | 3 | 5 | 5 | 4 | 1s | 5L | (4H) |
| 99 | 2 | 1 | 4 | 1 | 2 | 1 | 36 | 31425 | 3 | 2 | 4 | 4 | 4 | 3 | 4H | 4M |
| 100 | (1) | 5 | . | (3) | . | 1 | (9) | 123.4 | 3 | 3 | 4 | 5 | 4 | 1s | 4H | 3H |
| 101 | . | . | . | . | . | 2 | . | .1..2 | (2) | [3] | 3 | (3) | . | 3 | . | . |
| 102 | . | 1 | . | . | . | 1 | 30 | 21..3 | [2] | . | (2) | (2) | 4 | . | . | (3L) |
| 103 | . | . | . | . | . | 1 | . | .1..2 | . | . | . | . | . | . | . | . |
| 104 | . | (6) | 5 | . | . | 1 | (10–24) | 12..3 | 3 | 2 | 5 | 5 | 1 | 4f | 4H | 4M |
| 105 | 2 | 3 | [3] | . | [3] | 0 | 12 | 13.14 | 3 | [4] | 4 | 4 | (6) | (6) | . | 4H |
| 106 | 1 | (2) | . | . | . | 1 | (24) | 21..3 | (3) | . | (3) | (3) | 1 | 4f | [3L] | (2H) |
| 107 | . | 3 | . | . | . | 1 | 18–36 | 21..3 | [2] | 2 | . | . | . | 3 | . | . |
| 108 | 2 | (2) | . | 1 | . | (2) | 24–36 | 214.3 | 3 | 4 | (3) | (3) | 4 | 3 | . | 4H |

| Area | Society | 1 | 2(a) | 2(b) | 3(a) | 3(b) | 4(a) | 4(b) | 5(a) | 5(b) | 6 | 7 | 8(a) | 8(b) | 8(c) |
|---|---|---|---|---|---|---|---|---|---|---|---|---|---|---|---|
| 109 | Trukese | 5 | (4) | 1 | (3) | (2) | 2 | 2b | 2 | 4 | 3 | 5 | 2 | 4 | 4 |
| 110 | Yapese | [9] | 3 | 2 | 4 | 4 | [1] | [2b] | . | . | 3 | 6 | [3] | 3 | 3 |
| 111 | Palauans | . | 1 | 1 | (3) | (4) | 1 | 3b | 4 | . | 2 | (5) | 2 | 3 | 3 |
| 112 | Ifugao | 5 | . | . | . | . | 3 | 1b | . | . | [1] | . | [2] | 3 | (2) |
| 113 | Atayal | 9 | . | . | (4) | (4) | 2 | 2b | . | . | . | . | 2 | . | . |
| 114 | Chinese | 9 | [4] | [4] | (4) | (4) | . | . | 5 | . | [3] | . | 2 | 3 | [3] |
| 115 | Manchu | (4) | 4 | 4 | (2) | (2) | 5 | 1(a) | . | . | [3] | . | 3 | 4 | 2 |
| 116 | Koreans | . | . | . | (3) | (3) | 3 | 1b | 4 | . | 3 | . | 5 | (3) | (2) |
| 117 | Japanese | 9 | . | . | 4 | 4 | 3 | 1b | 4 | . | 4 | 3e | 5 | 3 | 4 |
| 118 | Ainu | 5 | 4 | 4 | (2) | (2) | 3 | 1b | 1 | 4 | 3 | 4 | 3 | 4 | (3) |
| 119 | Gilyak | 4 | 4 | 5 | [3] | [3] | 5 | 1a | . | . | . | . | (1) | 4 | 3 |
| 120 | Yukaghir | 5 | . | . | . | . | 5 | . | . | . | . | 3e | (2) | 4 | 3 |
| 121 | Chukchee | 5 | 4 | 4 | . | . | 3 | 1 | 3 | . | (3) | 3 | (3) | 3 | 4 |
| 122 | Ingalik | 4 | 4 | 2 | . | . | 3 | 1b | 4 | . | 3 | 3 | 1 | 4 | 3 |
| 123 | Aleut | 5 | 4 | (4) | (1) | (1) | 4 | . | (1) | . | (4) | (4) | 2 | 1 | 3 |
| 124 | Copper Eskimo | 9 | (4) | (4) | 4 | 4 | 3 | 1b | 3 | . | 2 | 3e | 2 | 3 | 2 |
| 125 | Montagnais | . | 4 | 4 | [2] | [2] | 3 | 3 | . | . | 2 | 2 | 2 | 3 | 4 |
| 126 | Micmac | 4 | 5 | 5 | . | . | 5 | 1a | (4) | . | [4] | 5e | 4 | 3 | 4 |
| 127 | Saulteaux | 4 | 5 | 5 | (3) | (3) | 5 | 1a | (3) | [3] | 1 | 3 | 2 | 4 | (3) |
| 128 | Slave | 4 | 4 | 1 | (3) | (3) | 3 | 1b | 4 | . | (2) | 4 | 2 | 3 | (3) |
| 129 | Kaska | 4 | 5 | 1 | [3] | . | 3 | 1a | 4 | . | 3 | 4 | 2 | 3 | 4 |
| 130 | Eyak | 5 | 4 | 4 | . | . | 3 | 1a | 4 | . | [2] | . | (2) | 3 | 2 |
| 131 | Haida | 5 | 5 | 5 | . | . | 5 | . | . | . | 4 | 7e | (4) | 2 | 3 |
| 132 | Bellacoola | 5 | 1 | (1) | . | . | 1 | . | 4 | . | 5 | 3e | 2 | 5 | 5 |
| 133 | Twana | 8 | 5 | [3] | (3) | (3) | 5 | 1a | (3) | . | 5 | (4) | [3] | 4 | 4 |
| 134 | Yurok | (2) | 4 | [4] | (3) | (3) | 4 | 1a | . | . | (1) | 5 | (3) | 4 | 3 |
| 135 | Pomo | 5 | 4 | 1 | 2 | (2) | 4 | 1a | . | . | 3 | . | 4 | 4 | 4 |
| 136 | Yokuts | 4 | 5 | 5 | (2) | (2) | 5 | 1a | [3] | (1) | 3 | [4] | (2) | 4 | 4 |
| 137 | Paiute | 8 | 5 | 5 | 2 | 2 | 5 | 1a | 4 | (2) | 3 | [3] | (1) | 3 | (3) |
| 138 | Klamath | 4 | 4 | 5 | 2 | 2 | 5 | 1a | 4 | . | 4 | 4e | 1 | 3 | 4 |
| 139 | Kutenai | 5 | 5 | (5) | (3) | (3) | 5 | 1a | . | . | (2) | 4e | (2) | (3) | 3 |
| 140 | Gros Ventre | 4 | 5 | 4 | [3] | [3] | 5 | 1 | . | . | 4 | 4 | 2 | 4 | 4 |
| 141 | Hidatsa | 5 | 4 | 4 | (1) | (1) | [5] | 1b | . | . | 2 | . | 2 | 3 | 3 |
| 142 | Pawnee | (4) | 5 | (5) | . | . | 5 | 1a | . | . | [4] | 3e | 3 | [3] | (3) |
| 143 | Omaha | 4 | 5 | 3 | (2) | 3 | 5 | 1a | 4 | 2 | . | 3e | 4 | 4 | 4 |
| 144 | Huron | 9 | 5 | 5 | . | . | 5 | 1b | . | . | 2 | 7 | 2 | 3 | (2) |
| 145 | Creek | . | . | . | . | . | . | . | . | . | 4 | 4 | . | (2) | 3 |
| 146 | Natchez | 4 | 5 | 1 | . | . | (5) | (1a) | 3 | (3) | 5 | . | . | (3) | 3 |
| 147 | Comanche | (9) | 5 | 1 | (3) | (3) | 5 | 1a | (2) | . | . | . | 2 | (1) | 3 |
| 148 | Chiricahua | (8) | 5 | 1 | 2 | 3 | 5 | 1a | 4 | (1) | 2 | 7 | 5 | 4 | 4 |
| 149 | Zuni | (4) | 5 | 5 | 3 | 3 | 5 | 1a | 4 | 4 | 3 | 3 | (2) | 5 | (4) |
| 150 | Havasupai | 5 | 5 | 5 | . | . | 5 | 3b | (3) | . | 2 | . | 1 | 3 | 2 |
| 151 | Papago | 9 | 4 | 4 | (3) | (3) | 5 | 1a | 5 | [2] | 1 | 3 | 2 | 3 | 3 |
| 152 | Huichol | 4 | 4 | . | 2 | 4 | 3 | 1b | (4) | . | 3 | . | 5 | 4 | 2 |
| 153 | Aztec | 5 | 4 | . | . | . | 4 | 1 | . | . | 5 | (7) | 5 | 5 | (4) |
| 154 | Popoluca | (5) | 4 | 4 | . | . | [2] | [2b] | . | . | . | . | (2) | 3 | [2] |
| 155 | Quiche | (5) | 4 | (4) | (3) | (3) | 3 | 1b | 4 | . | 1 | 3 | 4 | 4 | 3 |
| 156 | Miskito | 5 | 3 | 3 | (4) | (4) | 3 | 1b | . | 1 | . | 3e | 2 | (3) | (3) |
| 157 | Bribri | 5 | 3 | (3) | 4 | (4) | 3 | 1b | 4 | . | (1) | 4e | 2 | 3 | 3 |
| 158 | Cuna | 5 | 3 | 3 | [3] | [3] | 2 | 2b | . | . | 1 | . | 1 | (2) | 3 |
| 159 | Goajiro | (2) | 3 | 3 | 4 | 3 | 2 | 2b | 3 | . | 5 | 2 | 2 | 3 | 2 |
| 160 | Haitians | 9 | (4) | . | . | . | . | 1 | 4 | . | 4 | 4 | (3) | 5 | 3 |
| 161 | Callinago | 6 | (3) | 1 | 4 | 3 | 3 | 2b | . | . | 4 | 4 | 3 | 2 | 3 |
| 162 | Warrau | 9 | 3 | 3 | 4 | 4 | 3 | 2b | 4 | (1) | 2 | 4e | (1) | (3) | (3) |

| Area | 9 | | 10 | | | 11 | | 12 | 13 | | 14 | | 15 | | 16 | |
|---|---|---|---|---|---|---|---|---|---|---|---|---|---|---|---|---|
| | W | M | A | E | C | | | WMAEC | (a) | (b) | (a) | (b) | (a) | (b) | (a) | (b) |
| 109 | 2 | 4 | 4 | 3 | 3 | 2 | 12–24 | 31425 | 3 | 3 | 4 | 4 | 4 | 3 | 2H | 2M |
| 110 | 1 | 1 | 3 | 3 | [2] | 1 | 24–36 | 31425 | 2 | 3 | 4 | 4 | 6 | 6 | 5L | 3H |
| 111 | . | . | . | 2 | 1 | 1 | . | .1324 | 3 | 2 | 4 | 4 | 6 | 4f | 4H | 4M |
| 112 | . | (1) | . | (3) | . | 1 | 24–36 | 213.4 | (3) | . | (3) | [3] | 3 | 1s | . | . |
| 113 | . | . | . | . | . | . | . | ..... | 2 | . | . | . | . | . | . | . |
| 114 | . | 1 | . | . | . | . | 36 | 21... | 2 | (2) | (3) | (3) | 1 | 6 | 4L | (3L) |
| 115 | 2 | 1 | . | (1) | . | . | 60+ | 312.4 | (2) | (3) | [3] | [4] | (4) | (7s) | [4L] | (4M) |
| 116 | (2) | 1 | . | . | 3 | . | 24–36 | 31.2. | 2 | (3) | 3 | 4 | 1 | 9 | (4L) | (2H) |
| 117 | . | 1 | . | . | (2) | 5 | 48 | 42.31 | 3 | 3 | (3) | (3) | 4 | 1s | 4M | 4M |
| 118 | . | 1 | . | . | . | 5 | 48–60 | 32..1 | (3) | 3 | (3) | (4) | 6 | . | 2L | [2H] |
| 119 | . | [1] | . | . | . | . | 24 | 21... | . | . | (3) | (4) | [4] | . | 4L | . |
| 120 | . | 1 | . | . | . | (5) | 48 | 32..1 | (2) | 2 | . | . | 4 | 4f | [4H] | (5M) |
| 121 | 5 | 1 | . | [4] | . | 5 | 36–72 | 423.1 | (2) | [2] | 3 | 3 | [6] | [9] | (3H) | 4M |
| 122 | 5 | 1 | 4 | . | 4 | 4 | 24–48 | 43.21 | 2 | (2) | 3 | 3 | 1 | 3 | 4M | 2M |
| 123 | . | [3] | . | . | . | . | 12 | 12... | . | . | (2) | . | . | 7s | . | . |
| 124 | 5 | 1 | . | . | . | 5 | 36–60 | 423.1 | 2 | (3) | 4 | . | . | 3 | (4L) | (4H) |
| 125 | . | (3) | (3) | . | . | [5] | 12–60 | 32..1 | 2 | (3) | 3 | (4) | . | [3] | [4M] | (3H) |
| 126 | . | 1 | . | (3) | . | 5 | 24–36 | 323.1 | (2) | . | (3) | 4 | . | 1s | 4H | [4M] |
| 127 | (5) | 1 | 1 | 1 | . | (5) | 48–60 | 324.1 | 3 | 2 | (2) | (2) | 4 | 5 | 4M | 4M |
| 128 | [5] | (2) | (4) | 3 | (2) | 5 | 24–36 | 32331 | 3 | 3 | (4) | 4 | 2 | 5 | 4H | 3M |
| 129 | 5 | 1 | 4 | (3) | 3 | 5 | 24–36 | 435.1 | 2 | 4 | 3 | 3 | . | 6 | 4H | 4L |
| 130 | (1) | (1) | . | . | . | 5 | 24–36 | 32..1 | [2] | . | (4) | (4) | . | 9 | . | . |
| 131 | . | (1) | . | . | . | . | 24 | 21... | . | . | (3) | (4) | . | 9 | . | . |
| 132 | [2] | 2 | . | . | . | . | 24–36 | 21... | 2 | . | 3 | [3] | 4 | . | (4M) | (2L) |
| 133 | . | . | [3] | 3 | . | [1] | . | .12.3 | 3 | (3) | (4) | [4] | 6 | 9 | (3M) | (2M) |
| 134 | 1 | [1] | 4 | . | 2 | 1 | [24–36] | 31.24 | (2) | (2) | (2) | . | (7) | 5 | (4L) | [4M] |
| 135 | 3 | (3) | 3 | . | . | [2] | 15+ | 21..3 | (2) | . | [3] | . | 4 | . | . | . |
| 136 | [2] | [1] | (4) | . | [2] | [1] | [36] | 31.24 | (2) | (2) | [3] | . | [4] | . | [3H] | [3H] |
| 137 | 2 | 1 | (2) | 3 | 2 | 1 | 24 | 21425 | 3 | 3 | 3 | . | 4 | 3 | 4M | 3H |
| 138 | . | 2 | 4 | 4 | 2 | . | 24–36 | 3142. | 2 | 3 | 3 | 4 | 4 | 3 | 3H | 2H |
| 139 | . | (1) | . | (3) | . | 5 | 24+ | 323.1 | 3 | . | 3 | (4) | 1 | 6 | (3H) | (2H) |
| 140 | . | 2 | 4 | 3 | 4 | [5] | 24+ | 43521 | 2 | (3) | . | . | 4 | 6 | [4L] | 3L |
| 141 | . | . | 4 | . | 1 | . | . | .12.3 | 3 | 4 | 2 | 2 | 4 | 4s | . | . |
| 142 | . | (1) | . | (4) | . | 1 | 36 | 213.4 | . | 5 | . | . | (4) | 7f | . | [2H] |
| 143 | . | 1 | . | . | . | 2 | 36 | 21..3 | 3 | (3) | (3) | 4 | 4 | 9 | (4M) | 3M |
| 144 | . | (1) | . | . | . | (1) | 24–36 | 21..3 | . | . | . | . | . | . | . | . |
| 145 | . | . | . | . | . | 1 | . | .1..2 | 2 | 2 | 2 | (2) | 4 | 7s | . | . |
| 146 | . | 1 | 4 | (3) | . | 1 | . | .12.3 | 2 | (4) | . | (2) | 1 | (7s) | 2H | (4L) |
| 147 | . | . | 4 | (4) | . | 1 | . | .12.3 | [3] | 4 | 2 | 2 | 4 | 3 | 2M | [2H] |
| 148 | 5 | 1 | (3) | (1) | 2 | 2 | 30–36 | 31524 | 3 | 3 | 4 | 4 | 4 | 4f | 4H | 4M |
| 149 | . | (1) | 4 | 3 | 2 | 1 | 12–60 | 21333 | 3 | 4 | 4 | 4 | 4 | 9 | 4M | 3M |
| 150 | 5 | 3 | (4) | [4] | . | 1 | 18 | 213.4 | (2) | (3) | 3 | 4 | 1 | . | 4L | 4M |
| 151 | 4 | 1 | 3 | 3 | 2 | 1 | 18–36 | 21435 | 3 | 3 | 3 | (3) | 4 | 3 | 5L | 5L |
| 152 | 3 | 1 | (4) | 3 | 4 | 1 | 36 | 42315 | (2) | (3) | 4 | 4 | 3 | 3 | 4M | 4L |
| 153 | . | (1) | . | [4] | . | (1) | 36 | 213.4 | [2] | . | . | 4 | . | . | . | 1H |
| 154 | . | . | . | . | . | 2 | . | .1..2 | . | . | 3 | . | . | 3 | . | . |
| 155 | . | 1 | . | (1) | (1) | 5 | 36–48 | 32441 | 2 | 2 | (3) | 4 | 1 | 6 | 4H | 5L |
| 156 | . | (1) | . | [3] | . | [2] | (36) | 212.4 | (2) | [2] | 4 | 4 | [4] | [7f] | [4M] | [3L] |
| 157 | . | 3 | (4) | . | 5 | . | 18–24 | 32.1. | . | . | . | (3) | . | . | 4H | [4M] |
| 158 | . | 1 | . | . | . | 1 | 48–60 | 21..3 | 3 | [3] | (3) | (3) | 1 | 6 | [4L] | (3H) |
| 159 | 3 | 2 | 5 | 3 | 5 | 1 | 36 | 42315 | 3 | 4 | 3 | (4) | 3 | 7 | 3H | 1H |
| 160 | 3 | 4 | 5 | . | 5 | . | 18 | 32.1. | 2 | (3) | [2] | (3) | 1 | 3 | (3H) | (2L) |
| 161 | 1 | 2 | . | . | (1) | 1 | 48+ | 31.24 | 1 | (2) | 1 | 2 | (1) | 3 | 4M | 5L |
| 162 | [2] | (1) | . | [1] | . | 1 | 24–36 | 213.4 | 2 | 3 | (4) | 4 | 4 | 9 | 4H | 4M |

| Area | Society | 1 | 2 (a) | (b) | 3 (a) | (b) | 4 (a) | (b) | 5 (a) | (b) | 6 | 7 | 8 (a) | (b) | (c) |
|---|---|---|---|---|---|---|---|---|---|---|---|---|---|---|---|
| 163 | Yanomamo | 8 | 1 | 1 | [4] | [2] | 1 | . | . | (4) | . | 7 | . | 4 | (2) |
| 164 | Carib | (4) | . | . | . | . | 3 | 2b | . | . | 4 | 3 | 2 | 2 | 3 |
| 165 | Saramacca | (6) | . | . | . | . | [3] | [1b] | . | . | . | 6 | (2) | 3 | 3 |
| 166 | Mundurucu | (6) | . | . | . | . | . | [3b] | . | . | . | . | (2) | (2) | . |
| 167 | Cubeo | 8 | 3 | (3) | 3 | 3 | 3 | 2b | 4 | 1 | (1) | 6 | 3 | 2 | 3 |
| 168 | Cayapa | 5 | 4 | (4) | . | . | 2 | 2b | 3 | 3 | 3 | . | 3 | 1 | 3 |
| 169 | Jivaro | 2 | (4) | . | (4) | (4) | 3 | 1b | . | . | (3) | 7 | 3 | 4 | (2) |
| 170 | Amahuaca | 8 | . | . | 5 | 5 | 3 | 2b | [4] | . | 3 | 3 | [3] | 1 | 3 |
| 171 | Inca | 4 | 5 | 5 | 2 | 2 | 5 | 1 | 1 | . | 4 | . | 3 | 3 | (3) |
| 172 | Aymara | 9 | 4 | [1] | (4) | . | 3 | 1(b) | 4 | . | (1) | 3e | 3 | 4 | 3 |
| 173 | Siriono | 8 | 1 | 1 | (4) | (4) | 3 | 2b | 4 | (4) | 4 | 3 | 2 | 3 | 3 |
| 174 | Nambicuara | 8 | [1] | [1] | (4) | . | 3 | 2b | (5) | . | 2 | 6 | 1 | (3) | 3 |
| 175 | Trumai | 8 | . | . | . | . | . | . | . | . | 2 | 6 | (1) | 2 | [3] |
| 176 | Timbira | 9 | (1) | (1) | 4 | (4) | 1 | 2b | (4) | . | (2) | [5] | 3 | 3 | 4 |
| 177 | Tupinamba | 5 | 3 | (3) | (4) | (4) | 3 | 1b | [4] | (2) | 3 | . | (3) | 4 | 4 |
| 178 | Botocudo | 5 | . | . | 5 | 5 | 3 | 1b | . | . | . | . | . | . | . |
| 179 | Shavante | 8 | 4 | 1 | 4 | (3) | 4 | 1 | 4 | (4) | 3 | 7e | (1) | 2 | . |
| 180 | Aweikoma | 7 | . | . | (4) | (4) | 3 | 1b | 4 | . | 4 | 4 | 3 | 3 | (2) |
| 181 | Cayua | 5 | . | . | (4) | (4) | 4 | 1 | . | . | . | (7) | [1] | 2 | 3 |
| 182 | Lengua | (5) | [3] | . | . | . | 3 | 1b | (4) | . | [3] | 7 | . | (3) | 2 |
| 183 | Abipon | (5) | (1) | (1) | . | . | [3] | . | . | . | 4 | 7 | 2 | 2 | 2 |
| 184 | Mapuche | 7 | 5 | . | (3) | (3) | 5 | 1a | 3 | (4) | 3 | 5e | 3 | 3 | 5 |
| 185 | Tehuelche | 5 | 5 | 4 | . | . | 3 | 1 | . | . | . | (5) | 2 | 4 | 3 |
| 186 | Yahgan | 8 | (1) | 1 | 4 | 3 | 1 | 1b | 5 | 1 | 3 | 4 | 1 | 3 | 3 |
| 11a | Chagga | 6 | 2 | 2 | 5 | . | 2 | 2b | 3 | 3 | (5) | 7 | 5 | 5 | 4 |
| 29a | Katab | (2) | . | . | . | . | 3 | 1b | . | . | 2 | 7 | 3 | 1 | (2) |
| 38a | Dorobo | 6 | . | . | . | . | [3] | 1b | . | . | 3 | 4 | 3 | 1 | 2 |
| 46a | Lebanese | 8 | 4 | . | . | . | . | . | 4 | 2 | . | . | . | . | . |
| 60a | Chenchu | 5 | . | . | 5 | (5) | 2 | 2b | 4 | . | (1) | 3 | 1 | 1 | 3 |
| 68a | Sherpa | 5 | . | . | . | . | 4 | 1b | . | . | . | . | 2 | . | . |
| 90a | Murngin | 5 | . | . | (3) | 3 | 1 | 4b | . | . | . | 3 | (1) | 4 | 2 |
| 95a | Wogeo | 7 | 4 | 2 | (3) | (4) | 1 | 1b | 5 | 1 | (3) | 7 | 3 | 5 | 3 |
| 106a | Pukapukans | 8 | . | . | (3) | (3) | 2 | (3b) | 4 | [2] | 3 | [3] | 2 | 1 | 3 |
| 138a | Washo | 5 | 5 | 5 | . | . | 5 | 1a | . | . | . | 5e | 3 | 4 | 4 |
| 141a | Crow | 5 | [5] | 5 | . | . | 5 | (1a) | . | . | 4 | 3e | 2 | 3 | 2 |
| 149a | Navaho | 4 | 5 | 5 | 2 | 3 | 5 | (1a) | 4 | 2 | 2 | 4 | 3 | 4 | 3 |
| 175a | Bororo | (5) | (3) | . | . | . | 1 | 4b | . | . | 2 | . | 2 | (4) | . |
| 179a | Caraja | 7 | 3 | . | 5 | 5 | 1 | 2b | . | . | 3 | (7) | 2 | 4 | 2 |
| 183a | Mataco | 5 | . | . | (4) | (4) | 3 | 2b | (4) | . | . | 5 | 3 | 4 | (2) |

A few variables included in the coding sheet are omitted from Table 1. Role of the Breast for nursing and pacifying the infant or young child was coded on a scale from 1 (No special importance as a pacifier, for feeding only) to 5 (Breast used regularly as a pacifier in transition period). A code could be specified for fewer than 25 per cent of the societies. The age was specified when possible for onset of each of the five aspects of development, but the only age code included in Table 1 is Weaning (Column 11). For each aspect the approximate age of onset is specified by the codes in Column 10, and the relative ages for the five aspects are obtainable from the ranks in Column 12. For Motor Activity, the age at onset was generally assumed to

| Area | 9 W | 10 M | 10 A | 10 E | 10 C | 11 | 12 WMAEC | 13 (a) | 13 (b) | 14 (a) | 14 (b) | 15 (a) | 15 (a) | 16 (a) | 16 (b) |
|---|---|---|---|---|---|---|---|---|---|---|---|---|---|---|---|
| 163 | 5 | (1) | . | 3 | . | 0 | 36 | 213.4 | (2) | 3 | (4) | 4 | 6 | 4f | [4L] | [4L] |
| 164 | . | (3) | 4 | . | . | 1 | 15–24 | 21..3 | . | . | . | . | . | 4f | [2H] | [2H] |
| 165 | 2 | (3) | . | (4) | . | 1 | 3–24 | 213.4 | [2] | 4 | (1) | 2 | . | 5 | . | . |
| 166 | . | . | . | . | . | . | | ..... | 3 | . | (2) | (3) | 1 | . | . | . |
| 167 | . | 4 | 5 | 4 | (2) | . | (18) | 2142. | 2 | 4 | 3 | 3 | 4 | 4f | (5L) | 4L |
| 168 | 2 | 2 | (3) | (1) | 5 | 1 | 36 | 32415 | 3 | (3) | 3 | 3 | 4 | 6 | 2L | 2L |
| 169 | . | (1) | . | (4) | . | . | 36 | 213.. | (3) | . | (3) | 4 | 1 | (3) | . | 4M |
| 170 | 2 | 2 | . | [3] | 5 | 2 | 36 | 32414 | 2 | (2) | . | . | [4] | . | 4M | 3H |
| 171 | . | (1) | . | . | . | [1] | 24 | 21..3 | (2) | . | . | . | . | . | 1M | . |
| 172 | 5 | 1 | 3 | 4 | . | 5 | 24–30 | 324.1 | 2 | 3 | 2 | 3 | [1] | 4f | 3M | 3L |
| 173 | 4 | 1 | (3) | 3 | (3) | 0 | 36–48 | 41325 | 2 | (3) | (3) | (4) | [4] | 3 | (4L) | 4L |
| 174 | 3 | 1 | 4 | [1] | (2) | 0 | 24–36 | 31425 | 3 | 3 | 5 | 4 | (4) | . | 5L | 5L |
| 175 | 3 | 1 | 4 | . | 1 | 0 | 60–72 | 31.24 | [3] | 3 | . | 4 | . | 9 | . | 4H |
| 176 | [4] | (1) | 4 | (3) | . | 1 | 24 | 213.4 | 2 | (3) | (4) | 4 | 4 | (7f) | (4H) | 4H |
| 177 | [2] | 1 | [4] | [1] | . | 0 | 60 | 213.4 | 2 | 2 | 4 | 4 | . | . | 4H | 4M |
| 178 | . | [1] | . | . | . | 0 | . | 21..3 | (2) | . | . | . | . | . | . | . |
| 179 | 1 | 1 | . | 3 | . | 1 | 24–36 | 212.4 | 3 | (4) | 4 | 4 | 4 | 1s | 4L | 5L |
| 180 | . | . | . | . | . | . | . | ..... | 3 | [3] | (4) | 4 | 7 | 9 | 4H | [4M] |
| 181 | . | 1 | . | . | . | 1 | . | 21..3 | (3) | . | 4 | 4 | (6) | [3] | (4H) | [4H] |
| 182 | . | (1) | 3 | (3) | . | [1] | 36–48 | 312.4 | (3) | . | . | (4) | 1 | . | [4H] | [5L] |
| 183 | . | 1 | [4] | [3] | . | . | 36 | 213.4 | . | . | . | 4 | . | [1s] | . | (4M) |
| 184 | . | 3 | 4 | (1) | . | 5 | 12–24 | 224.1 | 3 | 2 | 4 | 4 | 7 | 6 | 3H | 3H |
| 185 | . | 1 | 4 | . | . | 1 | 60+ | 21..2 | . | . | [3] | [3] | . | . | . | . |
| 186 | (3) | 1 | 3 | 3 | [2] | (1) | 24 | 31425 | 3 | 2 | 4 | 4 | 7 | 4f | 4H | 3M |
| 11a | 1 | 2 | 5 | 3 | 4 | . | 36 | 3241. | 4 | (3) | 3 | 2 | 7 | 3 | 3M | 1H |
| 29a | . | (1) | . | (3) | . | . | 36 | 213.. | 3 | . | 1 | (2) | 4 | . | . | . |
| 38a | 3 | 4 | . | . | . | . | 12 | 12... | 3 | 2 | 2 | (2) | 1 | . | . | (2H) |
| 46a | . | 6 | . | . | 4 | 5 | 11 | 34.21 | 2 | 3 | 4 | 4 | 5 | 5 | 4L | 2M |
| 60a | 3 | 1 | . | 4 | . | 1 | . | 312.4 | 2 | 4 | 3 | 3 | 1 | 1s | 5L | 4L |
| 68a | . | . | . | (4) | . | . | . | .12.. | . | (4) | [2] | [2] | 5 | . | . | . |
| 90a | . | 1 | 4 | (2) | . | . | 48 | 212.. | 3 | 2 | [2] | 3 | 4 | (9) | [4M] | . |
| 95a | 2 | 1 | 1 | 3 | 2 | 1 | 36 | 31425 | 1 | 3 | 1 | 3 | 4 | 3 | 5M | 4L |
| 106a | 2 | 3 | 4 | 4 | 3 | 1 | 15 | 21425 | 3 | 4 | (3) | . | 4 | 3 | 4H | 3M |
| 138a | . | 3 | . | [4] | 2 | . | 12–24 | 4122. | . | . | . | . | 4 | . | . | (2H) |
| 141a | . | . | . | . | . | . | . | ..... | . | . | . | [3] | (4) | . | . | [2M] |
| 149a | 2 | 1 | 4 | 3 | 2 | 2 | 31 | 51222 | 2 | 4 | (2) | 3 | 6 | 5 | 4M | 4L |
| 175a | . | 1 | . | . | . | 1 | 60–84 | 21..3 | . | . | (1) | (1) | . | . | . | . |
| 179a | . | 1 | . | . | . | 1 | 60–72 | 21..3 | 3 | . | 3 | (3) | 4 | . | . | . |
| 183a | 4 | 3 | . | . | . | 1 | 12 | 12..3 | (2) | . | . | . | (4) | . | (4M) | [4H] |

be 15 months, the usual age when walking unsupported begins in most human societies. A different age or range of ages was specified for fewer than 20 per cent of the societies.

## CODING PROBLEMS

Although the societies were selected for the sample largely on the basis of adequate ethnographic information, the material on infancy and early childhood was insufficient in many cases. This is evident in the substantial number of cases when the coders found the information insufficient for a confident code or for any code at all. Some ethnographers, who give excellent accounts of other cultural variables, appear uninterested in infancy and childhood or unable to obtain information on these topics. The fact that most ethnographers are men may be an obstacle to observing the intimate mother-infant relationships. Some of the best accounts of child training in our sample have been by female ethnologists. The more recent ethnographies, whether written by men or women, are generally superior to the earlier ones in description of infancy and early childhood.

The coders noted any reported deviations from the cultural norms for male, middle-born children. Sex differences were identified in 82 of the 186 societies. These applied to only a single code in the majority of these societies, with a maximum of four codes showing a sex difference for two societies (110 Yapese, 158 Cuna). The codes with the largest number of sex differences were Covering Genitals (10C) and Role of Father in early childhood (14b), 30 societies each; others with substantial incidence were Nonmaternal Care in early childhood (13b), 21 societies; Ceremonialism (8a), 20; and Pain Infliction (6), 11. In accordance with the statement by Barry, Bacon, and Child (1957), there were very few reports of sex difference during infancy. Some of the codes listed above included both infancy and early childhood, but the only instances of sex differences, specifically for the infancy period, were Role of Father (14a) in two societies (25 Wodaabe Fulani, 163 Yanomamo) and Gerneral Indulgence (16a) in two societies (110 Yapese, 146 Natchez). Girls were given a lower score than boys in each of these four cases.

A less frequent source of differences from the norm was based on birth order, reported for sixteen societies. This was applied to the code for Ceremonialism (8a) in 12 of these societies. Usually the score was higher for the firstborn child or firstborn son; an exceptional case (19 Ashanti) had a higher score for the third, sixth, and ninth child. A higher score in Ceremonialism for twins was noted in two societies (5 Mbundu, 160 Haitians). Another source of differences from the cultural norm was status or wealth groups, but only a few instances of such differences were reported. In general, the norms for middle-born boys appear adequate for coding ethnographic reports on infancy and early childhood. Differences on the basis of sex, birth order, or other categories pertain to less than 5 per cent of the coded data.

A problem concerning the applicability of the source material arose for several societies with adequate information on infants and young children available only for a different time or location from the specifications on the pinpointing sheets. Examples are the Russians (Area 54), Vietnamese (Area 73), and Marquesans (Area 105). These codes are generally enclosed in brackets, indicating a low degree of confidence, unless corroborative evidence indicated that the information applied to the pinpointed time and place.

For some codes it was difficult to decide how much of the available information should be used. For example, some societies are very magically oriented, thus giving indirect evidence for a high degree of Magical Protectiveness (Column 8b). This was coded only if the ethnographic information indicated that it was applied to infants and young children. Nevertheless, the problem remains that the application of magical procedures to children is probably more likely to be reported and emphasized if magic is prevalent in the adult culture.

Most of the codes on treatment of infants and young children were based on many different types of behavior, reported in diverse situations. Therefore, coding required careful inspection and evaluation of the relevant information. For some codes, the definitions or coding categories were particularly difficult to apply to the ethnographic accounts. Changes from the early to the later stages of infancy (Columns 2-3) did not occur at a uniform time or in a clear-cut manner in all the societies. The difference in treatment, when reported, most typically seemed to occur at the age when the infant begins to crawl, approximately 9 months. In some societies there was a gradual, progressive change throughout infancy, as from high to low Bodily Restrictiveness for the Kaska (Area 129). In this and other such cases, the highest extreme was coded for the earlier period and the lowest extreme for the later period. The code for Carrying Technique (Column 4) made no distinction between stages of infancy, and a change was sometimes reported, usually at about 4 months of age. The code was generally based on the technique used during the longer time span. The same problem and coding method applied to changes during early childhood in Non-maternal Relationships (Column 13b). In several societies, where the young children spent progressively more time away from the mother during this time span, it was difficult to code earliness of onset of Autonomy (Column 10A). Some ethnographers emphasize the transition from lap child to yard child, but a yard child was not classified as developing autonomy if the mother maintained close watch and supervision.

Some specific ambiguities in coding categories may be noted. In Column 15 (Principal Relationships), it was uncertain whether the father's co-wives should be defined as female family members (category 4) or other females (category 7). Such cases were usually assigned to category 7, but category 4 was generally used for societies where the co-wives were the mother's sisters living in the same house, especially if the grandmother was also an important caretaker or companion. In Column 15b, the lack of differential codes for Caretakers and Companions during early childhood was a source of difficulty because in most societies different categories of people had these two types of relationships with the child. The generally more important and prevalent type of relationship was selected for the code.

Ambiguities were caused by the lack of a coding category needed for information on some societies. For Sleeping Proximity (Column 1), there was no category for societies in which one parent slept in the same room as the infant, without specification of whether in the same bed. The code for New Foods (Column 9) lacked a category for forced feeding. In the code for Weaning (Column 10W), a report of late onset was often not accompanied by information on whether it was gentle (category 1) or severe (category 2). Such cases were usually given a code of 1, enclosed in parentheses. The code for Elimination Control (Column 10E) lacked a category

for societies where the child learned only by imitation. These were coded
0 or 1.

Identification of the ambiguities was helped by the procedure of a conference between coders to agree on a set of consensus codes. The discussion
often resolved specific problems and also helped in formulating uniform,
explicit criteria for coding all the societies. In a number of instances, the
conference easily resolved disagreements due to an item of information being
overlooked or misinterpreted by one coder. The consensus codes were
thereby more accurate and complete than either person's independent codes.

In spite of the difficulties, a high degree of success was achieved in coding
most of the societies on most of the measures. This is partly due to the
fact that adequacy of ethnographic information, specifically on infancy and
childhood, was a criterion for selecting some of the area representatives.
Extensive pretesting of preliminary versions of the code helped to identify
and devise codes which could be applied to the ethnographic information
generally available. Some of the difficulties in coding on infants and young
children may have contributed to the high degree of success. Most of the
codes were based on diverse information, obtainable from various portions of
the text or from pictures. For many societies, a large number of sources were
used, as is indicated by the more extensive ethnographic bibliography in
the present article than in the report by Murdock and Morrow (1970) on
codes concerning subsistence economy.

### RELATIONSHIPS AMONG CODES

A single dimension of quantitative variation, with a progressive increase
in score from 0 or 1 to the highest number, characterized 30 of the 34
numerical codes in Table 1. The four exceptions were: Sleeping Proximity
(Column 1), Carrying Position (Column 4b), and Principal Relationships
(Columns 15a and 15b). For most of the 30 codes with ordinal, unidimen-
sional scales, the societies were preponderantly rated at an intermediate
score, with relatively few at the lowest and highest extremes. These characteristics made the codes suitable for statistical analysis by parametric tests,
including product-moment correlation for assessing the reliability and validity
of the codes.

Reliability is a measure of the degree to which the same codes are re-
peatable, rather than varying by random error. This can be measured by
the independent ratings by the two people, prior to their consensus codes,
available for the majority of the 186 societies. These showed high correlations
for most of the codes, indicating high reliability. However, a more important
issue is the degree of validity, which is a measure of the degree to which the
codes apply to the variable specified in the definitions. If a code is highly
correlated with another code similarly defined but rated independently, both
reliability and validity are thereby shown to be high. This test of reliability
and validity was made possible for the present set of codes by the existence of
previous codes which included a few similar measures, applied to a substantial portion of the sample of societies (Barry, Bacon, and Child 1967;
Whiting and Child 1953). The present sample of 186 societies contains 46

in one earlier sample (Barry, Bacon, and Child 1967) and 42 in the other (Whiting and Child 1953). Of these, 31 were in both earlier samples. Among the fifteen alternate societies, six were in both earlier samples with one additional in Barry, Bacon, and Child (1967).

General Indulgence during infancy (Column 16a) closely resembled the definition of Over-all Indulgence (Barry, Bacon, and Child 1967). The correlation between these two variables was sufficiently high to indicate a satisfactory degree of reliability and validity for both ($r = .60$, $N = 37$, $p < .01$). Whiting and Child (1953: 50) defined initial satisfaction potential in terms of four criteria: duration, freedom, encouragement, and concurrent anxiety, applied to five separately coded types of behavior: oral, anal, sexual, dependence, and aggression. Although these criteria partially differ from the present code for General Indulgence, its correlation with one of their five codes (Dependence Satisfaction Potential) was fairly high ($r = .51$, $N = 27$, $p < .01$). High correlations with Barry, Bacon, and Child (1967) measures for the infancy period were found for Non-maternal Relationships during infancy (Column 13a) with Diffusion of Nurturance ($r = .65$, $N = 42$, $p < .01$) and for the use of Carrying Devices for infants (Column 4a) with Protection from Environmental Discomforts ($r = .52$, $N = 38$, $p < .01$).

Age of Weaning (Column 11), using the earliest age when a range was given, showed a correlation of .82 ($N = 41$, $p < .01$) with the same measure in Barry, Bacon, and Child (1967) and .66 ($N = 26$, $p < .01$) with the same measure in Whiting and Child (1953). The code for Earliness and Severity of Weaning (Column 10W) showed slightly lower relationships with these earlier measures of Age of Weaning ($r = -.52$, $N = 42$, $p < .01$ and $r = -.51$, $N = 27$, $p < .01$ respectively). The code for Earliness and Severity of Elimination Control was highly related to the Whiting and Child (1953) measure of Anal Satisfaction Potential ($r = -.60$, $N = 15$, $p < .05$). Non-maternal Relationships during Childhood (Column 13b) was negatively related to a Barry, Bacon, and Child (1967) measure of Age at Reduced Contact with Mother ($r = -.43$, $N = 28$, $p < .01$) and to a Whiting and Child (1953) measure of Age at Beginning of Independence Training ($r = -.59$, $N = 19$, $p < .01$).

In general, a satisfactory degree of reliability and validity is demonstrated by high correlations between some of the present codes and equivalent measures in two prior studies with entirely different coders. These results are especially impressive because of differences for some of the societies in the pinpointed time and location and in the sources used, which should tend to decrease the relationships. The more limited coverage of infancy and early childhood by the earlier codes curtails these tests of reliability and validity to a small proportion of the present codes. A few of these codes failed to show high correlations with codes in the earlier studies which appeared to be defined similarly. General Indulgence during early childhood (Column 16b) showed little relationship with the Barry, Bacon, and Child (1967) measures of Transition Anxiety or Childhood Indulgence. A possible reason is that General Indulgence during early childhood (Column 16b) was defined primarily in terms of absence of pressures and punishments.

The highest scale scores would be found in socieities where the young children are mostly disregarded, because a high degree of affectionate attention is generally accompanied by some pressures and punishments. The five codes for Earliness and Severity of Development (Column 10) showed low correlations with age at onset of corresponding aspects coded in the two prior studies. The ethnographic information on ages is often incomplete and conflicting, so that the measures were probably unreliable in some of these studies.

The 30 codes in Table 1 measuring a progressive change in a single dimension of variation showed a preponderance of low intercorrelations, with remarkably few higher than $+.50$ or $-.50$, among the total of 435 correlation coefficients. This indicates a high degree of differentiation among the present codes, with very few of them correlated with each other so closely as to raise any doubt of their value as separate variables. There was usually little difference between the early and later stage of infancy, indicated by high correlations between these stages for Bodily Contact ($r = .89$, $N = 117$) and for Bodily Restrictiveness ($r = .70$, $N = 121$). In the comparisons between infancy and early childhood, the correlation was equivalently high for Role of Father ($r = .76$, $N = 139$). General Indulgence during infancy was highly correlated with Reward for Crying ($r = .78$, $N = 95$). The code for earliness and severity of Weaning (10W) was negatively related to Age of Weaning ($r = -.57$, $N = 153$). Each of the five aspects of development might also be expected to show a negative correlation between the code for earliness and severity (Column 10) and rank order for age of onset (Column 12), but a high correlation was found only for Covering Genitals ($r = -.76$, $N = 146$) and for Elimination Control ($r = -.71$, $N = 64$). The rank order for Motor Activity was positively correlated with the codes for earliness and severity in Covering the Genitals ($r = .64$, $N = 146$) and Elimination Control ($r = .61$, $N = 65$), indicating that the prevalent age of 15 months at onset of Motor Activity tended to have a low rank in societies with lenient training and a high rank in societies with severe training in these other developmental aspects.

Some generally lower but still highly reliable correlations may indicate important features of the codes. In the earlier infancy period, Bodily Restrictiveness was correlated positively with Carrying Device ($r = .67$, $N = 120$) and negatively with Bodily Contact ($r = -.57$, $N = 99$). The coders usually gave a low score for Bodily Restrictiveness in societies where the infants were held continuously while awake. During infancy, Reward for Crying was negatively correlated with Frequency of Crying ($r = -.52$, $N = 44$), as might be expected if the infant's expression of discomfort is effectively minimized by prompt attention on the part of the caretaker. An opposite tendency for any type of rewarded behavior to be strengthened and expressed more frequently (Miller 1969) apparently is not manifested at this early stage, indicating that crying by infants is primarily a reflex response to discomfort rather than a learned, instrumental response. Bodily Contact, in the later infancy period, was closely related to Reward for Crying ($r = .63$, $N = 82$) and to General Indulgence during infancy ($r = .44$,

N = 96). A moderate degree of similarity in treatment between infancy and early childhood is indicated by the correlation between these two stages for General Indulgence (r = .47, N = 112) and Non-maternal Care (r = .35, N = 132). Among the rank-order scores for age of onset (Column 12 of Table 1), Motor Activity correlated positively with Autonomy (r = .54, N = 106) and negatively with Covering Genitals (r = −.55, N = 150). The intercorrelations among the codes for earliness and severity (Column 10) were all less than .40; Autonomy was highly related to Column 13b, Non-maternal Care in early childhood (r = .52, N = 97).

All of the foregoing correlations among the present set of codes were statistically significant beyond the .01 level. Although the other correlations were generally lower, many of them were also highly reliable. With samples of more than 100 societies available for most of the correlations, a coefficient as low as .25 is sufficient for statistical significance at the .01 level.

The present set of codes can be used for testing relationships with independent sets of codes which measure different features of culture. This is expected to be an effective means for assessing the cultural importance of the present measures of infancy and early childhood. The present paper gives a few samples of such relationships with two of the new codes in order to indicate some potential directions for more thorough investigations.

Studies reviewed by Barry (1969b) give evidence of the importance of the father in personality development. Role of Father during infancy (Column 14a) is likely to be influenced by the social and economic activities of adult males. This infancy code shows close relationships with various codes of social organization and cultural customs in the Ethnographic Atlas (Murdock 1967), which includes all but Areas 55, 102, 114 of the 186 societies in this sample. Role of the Father during infancy tends to be important in societies with bilateral or matrilineal rather than patrilineal descent, with monogamy or limited polygyny, without circumcision of males, without a high god, without segregation of adolescent boys, and with games of physical skill but not games which include strategy. More recent codes for subsistence activity and supportive practices (Murdock and Morrow 1970) show further that role of the father during infancy tends to be important in societies where birds or small mammals rather than large game are hunted, where animal husbandry is absent or unimportant, and where land transport is by humans rather than pack animals. In accordance with relationships previously reported between subsistence economy and child-training practices (Barry, Child, and Bacon 1959), correlations with the Barry, Bacon, and Child (1967) codes show that the role of the father during infancy tends to be important in societies with relatively lenient training of children to be responsible and obedient. Sawyer and Le Vine (1966) and Barry (1968) have pointed out differences among six major regions of the world in various features of social organization and economy. Role of the father during infancy tends to be important in East Eurasia and the Insular Pacific, unimportant in Africa and the Circum-Mediterranean, and intermediate in North and South America.

Some students of culture have suggested that physical restraint in swaddling or a cradle board during infancy might have an important effect on personality development (Benedict 1949). The present code of Bodily Restrictiveness during early infancy (Column 2a) shows a negligible correlation (r = —.11, N = 115) with Role of Father during infancy (Column 14a). However, both of these variables show similar relationships with some of the other variables. For example, Role of Father and Bodily Restrictiveness both tend to have high scores in societies without circumcision and without segregation of adolescent boys. In other aspects, these two infancy variables differ. High Bodily Restrictiveness tends to be found in societies with games of both skill and chance but not in those with games of skill alone. Bodily Restrictiveness tends to be high in societies where agriculture is absent or limited to a nonfood crop, and in societies where the agricultural product is in the form of cereal grains rather than roots, tubers, trees, or vines. Other variables associated with high Bodily Restrictiveness are hunting of large rather than small animals, land transport by pack animals or vehicles rather than by humans, and relatively severe training of children in nurturant and self-reliant behavior. Societies high in Bodily Restrictiveness occur preponderantly in North America, whereas those low in Bodily Restrictiveness are preponderantly found in Africa and the Insular Pacific.

These sample findings for two of the 34 present codes indicate interrelationships among diverse features of culture. These might lead to the identification of several culture types, as in a factor analysis by Sawyer and Le Vine (1966). Their sophisticated statistical analysis was limited to measures of social organization and economy, which were the only types of code available for a large sample of societies. The present paper presents various codes on infancy and early childhood, most of them applied to a majority of the societies in a new, improved sample. These greatly broaden the potential scope of interrelated variables in future identification of culture types with the aid of factor analysis. Codes are being prepared on various additional features of the same sample of societies.

The fifteen alternative area representatives, at the end of Table 1, have been excluded from all the data analyses in this paper in order to provide a single case for each distinctive culture area. However, the availability of two societies in some areas enables use of the technique of matched pairs for enhancing sensitivity and specificity in measuring relationships between variables (Barry 1969a). Future codes applied to this sample may include alternate societies in additional culture areas.

## NOTES

This project (Cross-Cultural Cumulative Coding Center) was supported by a National Science Foundation Research Grant (No. GS-2111). The senior author was supported by a Public Health Service Research Scientist Development Award (No. K2-MH-5921) from the National Institute of Mental Health. The data were analyzed with the aid of IBM 360 and IBM 7090 digital computers at the University of Pittsburgh Computer Center. George P. Murdock and Edith Lauer helped in planning and conducting the research and preparing the article. The authors wish to express gratitude to the following individuals who generously provided coded materials on the basis of their own personal field work: Pilar C. Greenwood, Eileen Kane, Mildred Stroop Luschinsky, and Morris E. Opler.

## REFERENCES CITED

Barry, H., III. 1968. Regional and Worldwide Variations in Culture. Ethnology 7: 207-217.

—— 1969a. Cross-Cultural Research with Matched Pairs of Societies. Journal of Social Psychology 79: 25-33.

—— 1969b. Cultural Variations in the Development of Mental Illness. Changing Perspectives in Mental Illness, ed. S. C. Plog and R. B. Edgerton, pp. 155-179. New York.

Barry, H., III, M. K. Bacon and I. L. Child. 1957. A Cross-Cultural Survey of Some Sex Differences in Socialization. Journal of Abnormal and Social Psychology 55: 327-332.

—— 1967. Definitions, Ratings, and Bibliographic Sources for Child-Training Practices of 110 Cultures. Cross-Cultural Approaches, ed. C. S. Ford, pp. 293-331. New Haven.

Barry, H., III, I. L., Child, and M. K. Bacon. 1959. Relation of Child Training to Subsistence Economy. American Anthropologist 61: 51-63.

Benedict, R. 1949. Swaddling in Eastern Europe. American Journal of Ortho-psychiatry 19: 342-350.

Miller, N. E. 1969. Learning of Visceral and Glandular Responses. Science 163: 434-445.

Murdock, G. P. 1967. Ethnographic Atlas. Pittsburgh. (See also installments in Ethnology, v. 1-10.)

Murdock, G. P., and D. O. Morrow. 1970. Subsistence Economy and Supportive Practices: Cross-Cultural Codes 1. Ethnology 9: 302-330.

Murdock, G. P., and D. R. White. 1969. Standard Cross-Cultural Sample. Ethnology 8: 329-369.

Naroll, R. 1970. What Have We Learned from Cross-Cultural Surveys? American Anthropologist 72: 1227-1288.

Sawyer, J., and R. A. LeVine. 1966. Cultural Dimensions: A Factor Analysis of the World Ethnographic Sample. American Anthropologist 68: 708-731.

Textor, R. B. 1967. A Cross-Cultural Summary. New Haven.

Whiting, J. W. M., and I. L. Child. 1953. Child Training and Personality. New Haven.

## BIBLIOGRAPHY OF ETHNOGRAPHIC SOURCES

For each society, after its identifying co-ordinates and dates, are listed the sources used by the coders in the approximate order of the quantity of pertinent information derived from each.

1. Nama Hottentot of the Gei//Khauan tribe (27°30'S, 17°E) in 1860.
Schultze, L. 1907. Aus Namaland und Kalahari. Jena.
Schapera, I. 1930. The Khoisan Peoples. London.
2. Kung Bushmen of the Nyae Nyae region (19°50'S, 20°35'E) in 1950.
Marshall, L. 1959. Marriage Among !Kung Bushmen. Africa 29: 335-364.
—— 1960. !Kung Bushman Bands. Africa 30: 325-355.
—— 1961. Sharing, Talking, and Giving. Africa 31: 231-249.
3. Thonga of the Ronga subtribe (25°50'S, 32°20'E) in 1895.
Junod, H. A. 1927. The Life of a South African Tribe. 2d edit. 2v. London.
4. Lozi (14° to 18°S, 22° to 25°E) in 1900.
Holub, E. 1895. Seven Years in South Africa, v.2. London
Gluckman, M. 1951. The Lozi of Barotseland. Seven Tribes of British Central Africa, ed. E. Colson and M. Gluckman, pp. 1-93. London.
5. Mbundu of the Bailundo subtribe (12°15'S, 16°30'E) in 1890.
Childs, G. M. 1949. Umbundu Kinship and Character. London.
6. Suku of Feshi Territory (6°S, 18°E) in 1920.
Kopytoff, I. 1965. The Suku of Southwestern Congo. Peoples of Africa, ed. J. L. Gibbs, Jr., pp. 441-477. New York.

——— 1964. Family and Lineage Among the Suku. The Family Estate in Africa, ed. R. F. Gray and P. H. Gulliver, pp. 83-116. Boston.

Van de Ginste, F. 1947. Le mariage çhez les Basuku. Bulletin des Jurisdictions Indigènes et du Droit Coutumier Congolais, nos. 1-2.

7. Bemba of Zambia (9° to 12°S, 29° to 32°E) in 1897.

Richards, A. I. 1939. Land, Labour and Diet in Northern Rhodesia. Oxford.

——— 1940. Bemba Marriage and Present Economic Conditions. Rhodes-Livingstone Papers 4.

——— 1948. Hunger and Work in a Savage Tribe. Glencoe.

——— 1956. Chisnugu: A Girl's Initiation Ceremony Among the Bemba. London.

Gouldsbury, C., and A. Sheane. 1911. The Great Plateau of Northern Rhodesia. London.

8. Nyakyusa near Mwaya and Masoko (9°30'S, 34°E) in 1934.

Wilson, M. 1957. Rituals of Kinship Among the Nyakyusa. London.

Wilson, G. 1936. An Introduction to Nyakyusa Society. Bantu Studies 10: 253-292.

——— 1938. The Land Rights of Individuals Among the Nyakyusa. Rhodes-Livingstone Papers 1: 1-52.

Lehmann, F. R. 1951. Notes on the Daily Life of the Nyakyusa. Sociologus 1: 138-148.

9. Hadza (3°20' to 4°10'S, 34°40' to 35°25'E) in 1930.

Kohl-Larsen, L. 1958. Wildbeuter in Ostafrika. Berlin.

Woodburn, J. 1964. The Social Organization of the Hadza of North Tanzania. Ph.D. dissertation, Cambridge University.

Bleek, D. F. 1931. The Hadzapi or Watindiga of Tanganyika Territory. Africa 4: 273-286.

10. Luguru around Morogoro (6°50'S, 37°40'E) in 1925.

Scheerder and Tastevin. 1950. Les Wa lu guru. Anthropos 45: 241-286.

11. Kikuyu of the Fort Hall or Metume district (0°40'S, 37°10'E) in 1920.

Cagnolo, C. 1933. The Akikuyu. Nyeri.

Kenyatta, J. 1939. Facing Mount Kenya. London.

Middleton, J. 1953. The Kikuyu and Kamba of Kenya. London.

12. Ganda of the Kyaddondo district (0°20'N, 32°30'E) in 1875.

Roscoe, J. 1911. The Baganda. London.

Southwold, M. 1965. The Ganda. Peoples of Africa, ed. J. L. Gibbs, Jr., pp. 81-118. New York.

13. Mbuti Pygmies of the Epulu group (1°30' to 2°N, 28°20'E) in 1950.

Turnbull, C. N. 1965a. Wayward Servants. New York.

——— 1961. The Forest People. New York.

——— 1965b. The Mbuti Pygmies. Anthropological Papers of the American Museum of Natural History 50: iii, 1-282.

Putnam, P. 1948. The Pygmies of the Ituri Forest. A Reader in General Anthropology, ed. C. S. Coon, pp. 322-342. New York.

14. Nkundo Mongo of the Ilanga group (0°15' to 1°15'S, 18°35' to 19°45'E) in 1930.

Hulstaert, G. 1938. Le mariage des Nkundó. Mémoires de l'Institut Royal Colonial Belge 8: 1-520. Brussels.

Van der Kerken, G. 1944. L'ethnie Mongo. Mémoires de l'Institut Royal Colonial Belge 3: 1-1143.

15. Banen of the Ndiki subtribe (4°35' to 4°45'N, 10°35' to 11°E) in 1935.

Dugast, I. 1959. Monographie de la tribu des Ndiki. Travaux et Mémoires de l'Institut d'Ethnologie 58: ii, 1-635. Paris.

Tessman, G. 1934. Die Bafia und die Kultur der Mittelkamerun Bantu. Stuttgart.

McCulloch, M., M. Littlewood, and I. Dugast. 1954. Peoples of the Central Cameroons. London.

16. Tiv of Benue Province (6°30' to 8°N, 8° to 10°E) in 1920.

Bohannan, P., and L. Bohannan. 1958. Three Source Notebooks in Tiv Ethnography. New Haven.
—— 1953. The Tiv of Central Nigeria. London.
Abraham, R. C. 1940. The Tiv People. London.
East, R., ed. 1939. Akiga's Story. London.
17. Ibo of the Isu-Ama division (5°20′ to 5°40′N, 7°10′ to 7°30′E) in 1935.
Leith-Ross, S. 1939. African Women: A Study of the Ibo of Nigeria. New York.
Green, M. M. 1947. Ibo Village Affairs. London.
Uchendu, V. C. 1965. The Igbo of Southeast Nigeria. New York.
18. Fon of the city and environs of Abomey (7°12′N, 1°56′E) in 1890.
Herskovits, M. J. 1938. Dahomey. 2v. New York.
19. Ashanti of Kumasi state (6° to 8°N, 0° to 3°W) in 1895.
Fortes, M. 1950. Kinship and Marriage Among the Ashanti. African Systems of Kinship and Marriage, ed. A. R. Radcliffe-Brown and D. Forde, pp. 252-284.
Rattray, R. S. 1927. Religion and Art in Ashanti. Oxford.
—— 1929. Ashanti Law and Constitution. Oxford.
—— 1916. Ashanti Proverbs. Oxford.
20. Mende near the town of Bo (7°50′N, 12°W) in 1945.
Little, K. L. 1951. The Mende of Sierra Leone. London.
21. Wolof of Upper and Lower Salum in the Gambia (13°45′N, 15°20′W) in 1950.
Gamble, D. P. 1957. The Wolof of Senegambia. London.
Ames, D. W. 1953. Plural Marriage Among the Wolof in the Gambia. Ph.D. dissertation, Northwestern University.
Faladé, S. 1963. Women of Dakar and the Surrounding Urban Area. Women of Africa, ed. D. Paulme, pp. 217-229. London.
22. Bambara between Segou and Bamako (12°30′N, 6° 8′W) in 1902.
Monteil, C. 1924. Les Bambara du Ségou et du Kaarta. Paris.
Pacques, V. 1954. Les Bambara. Paris.
Henry, J. 1910. L'âme d'un peule africain: Les Bambara. Bibliotheque Anthropos 1: ii, 1-240.
Dieterlen, G. 1951. Essai sur la religion Bambara. Paris.
23. Tallensi (10°30′ to 10°45′N, 0°30′ to 0°40′W) in 1934.
Fortes, M. 1949. The Web of Kinship Among the Tallensi. London.
—— 1938. Social and Psychological Aspects of Education in Taleland. Supplement to Africa v. 9, no. 4. London.
24. Songhai of the Bamba division (16° to 17°15′N, 0°10′E to 3°10′W) in 1940.
Rouch, J. 1954. Les Songhay. Paris.
Miner, H. 1965. The Primitive City of Timbuctoo. Princeton.
25. Wodaabe Fulani of Niger (13° to 17°N, 5° to 10°E) in 1951.
Dupire, M. 1962. Peuples nomades. Travaux et Mémoires de l'Institut d'Ethnologie 64: 1-327.
—— 1963. The Position of Women in a Pastoral Society (Wodaabe). Women of Tropical Africa, ed. D. Paulme, pp. 47-92. Berkeley and Los Angeles.
26. Hausa of Zaria or Zazzau (9°30′ to 11°30′N, 6° to 9°E) in 1900.
Smith, M. F. 1954. Baba of Karo: A Woman of the Muslim Hausa. London.
Smith, M. G. 1965. The Hausa of Northern Nigeria. Peoples of Africa, ed. J. L. Gibbs, pp. 119-155. New York.
Dry, E. 1956. The Social Development of the Hausa Child. Proceedings of the International West African Conference held at Ibadan, 1949, pp. 164-170.
Greenberg, J. H. 1946. The Influence of Islam on a Sudanese Religion. Monographs of the American Ethnological Society 10: 1-73.
27. Massa of Cameroon (10° to 11°N, 15° to 16°E) in 1910.
Hagen, G. von. 1912. Die Bana. Baessler-Archiv 2: 77-116.
Lembezat, B. 1961. Les populations paiennes du Nord-Cameroun et de l'Adamoua. Paris.

28. Azande of the Yambio chiefdom (4°20' to 5°50'N, 27°40' to 28°50'E) in 1905.
Evans-Pritchard, E. E. 1937. Witchcraft, Oracles and Magic Among the Azande. Oxford.
———— 1932. Heredity and Gestation, as the Azande See Them. Sociologus 8: 400-414.
Lagae, C. R. 1926. Les Azande ou Niam-Niam. Bibliotheque-Congo 18: 1-224.
Larkin, G. M. 1926-27. An Account of the Azande. Sudan Notes and Records 9: 235-247; 10: 85-134.
Baxter, P. T. W., and A. Butt. 1953. The Azande and Related Peoples of the Anglo-Egyptian Sudan and Belgian Congo. London.
Seligman, C. G., and B. Z. Seligman. 1932. Pagan Tribes of the Nilotic Sudan. London.
29. Fur around Jebel Marra (13°30'N, 25°30'E) in 1880.
Felkin, R. W. 1885. Notes on the Fur Tribe. Proceedings of the Royal Society of Edinburgh 13: 205-265.
Beaton, A. C. 1948. The Fur. Sudan Notes and Records 29: 1-39.
Muhammad Ibn 'Umar, al-Tūnusi. 1845. Voyage au Darfour, traduit de l'Arabe par le Dr. Perron. Paris.
30. Otoro of the Nuba Hills (11°20'N, 30°40'E) in 1930.
Nadel, S. F. 1947. The Nuba. London.
31. Shilluk (9° to 10°30'N, 31° to 32°E) in 1910.
Hofmayr, W. 1925. Die Schilluk. Wien.
Seligman, C. G., and B. Z. Seligman. 1932. Pagan Tribes of the Nilotic Sudan. London.
32. Northern Mao (9° to to 9°35'N, 34°30' to 34°50'E) in 1939.
Grottanelli, V. L. 1940. I Mao. Missione Etnografica nel Uollaga Occidentale 1: 1-387. Roma.
Cerulli, E. 1956. Peoples of South-West Ethiopia and Its Borderland. London.
33. Kaffa (6°50' to 7°45'N, 35°30' to 37°E) in 1905.
Bieber, F. J. 1920-23. Kaffa. 2v. Münster.
34. Masai of Tanzania (1°30' to 5°30'S, 35° to 37°30'E) in 1900.
Merker, M. 1904. Die Masai. Berlin.
35. Konso of the vicinity of Busc (5°15'N, 37°30'E) in 1935.
Hallpike, C. R. 1969. The Konso of Ethiopia. Ms.
Jensen, A. E. 1936. Im Lande des Gada. Stuttgart.
36. Somali of the Dolbahanta subtribe (7° to 11°N, 45°30' to 49°E) in 1900.
Lewis, I. M. 1961. A Pastoral Democracy. London.
———— 1965. The Northern Pastoral Somali. Peoples of Africa, ed. J. L. Gibbs, Jr., pp. 319-360. New York.
———— 1955. Peoples of the Horn. London.
Puccioni, N. 1936. Antropologia e etnographia delle genti della Somalia 3: 1-140. Bologna.
Paulitschke, P. 1888. Beiträge zur Ethnographie und Anthropologie der Somal, Gaua und Harari. Leipzig.
37. Amhara of the Gondar district (11° to 14°N, 36° to 38°30'E) in 1953.
Messing, S. D. 1957. The Highland-Plateau Amhara of Ethiopia. Ph.D. dissertation, University of Pennsylvania.
Lipsky, G. A. 1962. Ethiopia. New Haven.
38. Bogo or Belen (15°45'N, 38°45'E) in 1855.
Munzinger, W. 1859. Ueber die Sitten und das Recht der Bogos. Winterthur.
39. Kenuzi Nubians (22° to 24°N, 32° to 33°E) in 1900.
Schäfer, H. 1935. Nubisches Frauenleben. Mitteilungen des Seminars für Orientalische Sprachen zu Berlin 38.
Herzog, R. 1957. Die Nubier. Berlin.
40. Teda nomads of Tibesti (19° to 22°N, 16° to 19°E) in 1950.
Chapelle, J. 1957. Nomades noirs du Sahara. Paris.
Fuchs, P. 1956. Ueber die Tubbu von Tibesti. Archiv für Völkerkunde 11: 43-66.

Cline, W. 1950. The Teda of Tibesti, Borku and Kawar. General Series in Anthropology 12: 1-52.

41. Tuareg of Ahaggar (21° to 25°N, 4° to 9°E) in 1900.
Lhote, H. 1944. Les Touaregs du Hoggar. Paris.
Nicolaisen, J. 1963. Ecology and culture of the Pastoral Tuareg. National-museets Skrifter, Etnografisk Raeke 9: 1-540. Copenhagen.
Benhazera, M. 1908. Six mois chez les Touareg de Ahaggar. Alger.

42. Riffians of northern Morocco (34°20' to 35°30'N, 2°30' to 4°W) in 1926.
Coon, C. S. 1931. Tribes of the Rif. Harvard African Studies 9: 1-417.

43. Egyptians of the town and environs of Silwa (24°45'N, 33°E) in 1950.
Ammar, H. 1954. Growing Up in an Egyptian Village. London.

44. Hebrews of the kingdom of Judah (30°30' to 31°55'N, 34°20' to 35°30'E) in 621 B.C.
Patai, R. 1959. Sex and Family in the Bible and the Middle East. Garden City.
DeVaux, R. 1961. Ancient Israel. New York.

45. Babylonians of the city and environs of Babylon (32°35'N, 44°45'E) in 1750 B. C.
Saggs, H. W. F. 1962. The Greatness that was Babylon. London.
Driver, G. R., and J. C. Miles. 1952-55. The Babylonian Laws. 2v. Oxford.

46. Rwala Bedouin (31° to 35°30'N, 36° to 41°E) in 1913.
Musil, A. 1928. The Manners and Customs of the Rwala Bedouins. New York.

47. Turks of the Anatolian plateau (38°40' to 40°N, 32°40' to 35°50'E) in 1950.
Pierce, J. E. 1964. Life in a Turkish Village. New York.
Makal, M. 1954. A Village in Anatolia. London.
Stirling, P. 1965. Turkish Village. London.
Yasa, I. 1957. Hasanoglan. Ankara.

48. Gheg Albanians (41°20' to 42°40'N, 19°30' to 20°30'E) in 1910.
Durham, M. E. 1928. Some Tribal Origins, Laws and Customs of the Balkans. London.
Hasluck, M. 1954. The Unwritten Law in Albania. Cambridge.
Pisko, J. E. 1896. Gebräuche bei der Geburt und Behandlung der Neugeborenen bei den Albanesen. Mitteilungen der Anthropologischen Gesellschaft zu Wien 26: 141-146.
Coon, C. S. 1950. The Mountain of Giants. Papers of the Peabody Museum of Archaeology and Ethnology, Harvard University 23: iii, 1-105.

49. Romans of the city and environs of Rome (41°50'N, 13°30'E) in A.D. 110.
Carcopino, J. 1940. Daily Life in Ancient Rome, ed. H. T. Howell. New Haven.
Pellisson, M. 1901. Roman Life in Pliny's Time. Philadelphia.
Friedländer, L. 1908. Roman Life and Manners Under the Early Empire. London.

50. Basques of Vera de Bidasoa (43°12' to 43°20'N, 1°35' to 1°45'W) in 1940.
Greenwood, P. C. 1971. Personal Communication.
Douglass, W. A. 1969. Death in Murelaga. Seattle.
Caro Baroja, J. 1944. La vida rural en Vera de Bidasoa. Madrid.

51. Irish of Kinvarra parish (53°5'N, 9°W) in 1955.
Kane, E. 1970. Personal Communication.
Cresswell, R. 1969. Une communauté rurale d'Irlande. Travaux et Mémoires de l'Institut d'Ethnologie 74: 1-571. Paris.

52. Lapps of Könkämä district (68°20' to 69°5'N, 20°5' to 23°E) in 1950.
Haglund, S. 1935. Life Among the Lapps. London.
Bernatzig, H. A. 1938. Overland with the Nomad Lapps. New York.
Collinder, B. 1949. The Lapps. Princeton.
Pehrson, R. N. 1957. The Bilateral Network of Social Relations in Könkämä Lapp District. Indiana University Publications, Slavic and East European Series 5: 1-128.
Turi, J. 1931. Turi's Book of Lapland. New York.

53. Yurak Samoyed (65° to 71°N, 41° to 62°E) in 1894.

Islavin, V. 1847. Samoiedy v domashnem i obshchestvennom bytu. St. Petersburg.

Kopytoff, I. 1955. The Samoyed. New Haven.

Donner, K. 1954. Among the Samoyed in Siberia. New Haven.

54. Russians of the peasant village of Viriatino (52°40′N, 41°20′E) in 1955.

Dunn, S. P., and E. Dunn. 1967. The Peasants of Central Russia. New York.

Dunn, S. P. 1971. Structure and Functions of the Soviet Rural Family. The Soviet Rural Community. ed. J. R. Millar, pp. 325-345. Urbana.

Fitzsimmons, T., ed. 1957. RSFSR. 2v. New Haven.

Black, C. E. 1960. The Transformation of Russian Society. Cambridge.

Mace, D., and V. Mace. 1963. The Soviet Family. Garden City.

55. Abkhaz (42°50′ to 43°25′N, 40° to 41°35′E) in 1880.

Dzhanashvili, M. G. 1894. Abkhaziya i Abkhaztsy. Zapiski Kavkazkago Otdiela Inperalorskago Russkago Geograficheskago Obshchestva 16: 1-59. Tiflis.

Luzbetak, L. J. 1951. Marriage and the Family in Caucasia. Mödling bei Wien.

56. Armenians in the vicinity of Erevan (40°N, 44°30′E) in 1843.

Haxthausen, A. von. 1854. Transcaucasia. London.

Klidschian, A. 1911. Das armenische Eherecht. Zeitschrift für Vergleichende Rechtswissenschaft 25: 257-377.

57. Kurd in and near the town of Rowanduz (36°30′N, 44°30′E) in 1951.

Masters, W. M. 1953. Rowanduz. Ph.D. dissertation, University of Michigan.

Hausen, H. H. 1961. The Kurdish Woman's Life. Copenhagen Ethnographic Museum Record 7: 1-213.

58. Basseri of the nomadic branch (27° to 31°N, 53° to 54°E) in 1958.

Barth, F. K. 1961. Nomads of South Persia. London.

59. West Punjabi of the village of Mohla (32°30′N, 74°E) in 1950.

Eglar, Z. S. 1960. A Punjabi Village in Pakistan. New York.

Honigmann, J. J. 1957. Women in West Pakistan. Pakistan: Society and Culture, ed. S. Maron, pp. 154-176. New Haven.

———— 1958. Third Village: Punjab Province, Chak 41MB. Three Pakistan Villages, pp. 68-95. Chapel Hill.

Wilbur, D. N. 1964. Pakistan. New Haven.

60. Gond of the Hill Maria division (19°15′ to 20°N, 80°30′ to 81°20′E) in 1930.

Grigson, W. V. 1938. The Maria Gonds of Bastar. London.

61. Toda of the Nilgiri Hills (11° to 12°N, 76° to 77°E) in 1900.

Rivers, W. H. R. 1906. The Todas. London.

Peter, Prince. 1855. The Todas. Man 55: 89-93.

Marshall, W. E. 1873. A Phrenologist Amongst the Todas. London.

62. Santal of Bankura and Birbhum districts (23° to 24°N, 86°50′ to 87°30′E) in 1940.

Culshaw, W. J. 1949. Tribal Heritage. London.

Datta-Majumder, N. 1956. The Santal. Memoirs of the Department of Anthropology, Government of India 2: 1-150.

Das, A. K. 1967. Scientific Analysis of "Santal" Social System. Bulletin of the Cultural Research Institute, 6: i-ii, 5-9.

63. Uttar Pradesh in and near Senapur village (25°55′N, 83°E) in 1945.

Luschinsky, M. S. 1971. Personal communication.

Opler, M. E., and R. D. Singh. 1954. The Division of Labor in an Indian Village. A Reader in General Anthropology, ed. C. S. Coon, pp. 464-496. New York.

———— 1952. Economic and Social Change in a Village of North Central India. Human Organization 11: 5-12.

Opler, M. E. 1956. The Extensions of an Indian Village. Journal of Asian Studies 16: 5-10.

64. Burusho of Hunza State. (36°20′ to 36°30′N, 74°30′ to 74°40′E) in 1934.

Lorimer, E. O. 1939. Language Hunting in the Karakoram. London.

———— 1938. The Burusho of Hunza. Antiquity 12: 5-15.
65. Kazak of the Great Horde (37° to 48°N, 68° to 81°E) in 1885.
Grodekov, N. I. 1889. Kirghizy i Karakirgizy sur Dar'inskoi Oblasti. Tashkent.
Sedel'nikov, A. N., *et al.* 1903. Kirgizshii Krai. Polnoe Geographicheskoe Opisanie nashego etechestva 18: 138-222.
Murdock, G. P. 1934. Our Primitive Contemporaries, pp. 135-162. New York.
Hudson, A. E. 1938. Kazak Social Structure. Yale University Publication in Anthropology 20: 1-109.
66. Khalka Mongols of Narobanchin territory (47° to 47°20′N, 95°10′ to 97°E) in 1920.
Vreeland, H. H. 1954. Mongol Community and Kinship Structure. New Haven.
Maiskii, I. 1921. Sovremennaia Mongolia. Ordelenie.
67. Lolo of Taliang Shan mountains (26° to 29°N, 103° to 104°E) in 1910.
Lin, Y. H. 1961. The Lolo of Liang Shan. Shanghai.
D'Ollone, H. M. 1912. In Forbidden China. Boston.
Tseng, C. L. 1945. The Lolo District in Liang-Shan. Chungking.
68. Lepcha of Lingthem and vicinity (27° to 28°N, 89°E) in 1937.
Gorer, G. 1938. Himalayan Village. London.
Morris, J. 1938. Living with the Lepchas. London.
69. Garo of Rengsanggri and neighboring villages (26°N, 91°E) in 1955.
Burling, R. 1963. Rengsanggri. Philadelphia.
70. Lakher (22°20′N, 93°E) in 1930.
Parry, N. E. 1932. The Lakhers. London.
71. Burmese of Nondwin village (22°N, 95°40′E) in 1960.
Nash, M. 1965. The Golden Road to Modernity. New York.
Scott, J. G. (Shway Yoe). 1882. The Burman: His Life and Notions. London.
72. Lamet of northwestern Laos (20°N, 100°40′E) in 1940.
Izikowitz, K. G. 1951. Lamet. Etnologiska Studier 17: 1-375. Göteborg.
73. North Vietnamese of the Red River delta (20° to 21°N, 105°30′ to 107°E) in 1930.
Hickey, G. C. 1964. Village in Vietnam. New Haven.
Donoghue, J. D. n.d. Cam An: A Fishing Village in Central Vietnam. East Lansing.
Coughlin, R. J. 1950. The Position of Women in Vietnam. New Haven.
Gourou, P. 1936. Les paysans du delta tonkinois. Paris.
74. Rhade of the village of Ko-sier (13°N, 108°E) in 1962.
Donoghue, J. D., D. D. Whitney, and I. Ishino. 1962. People in the Middle. East Lansing.
75. Khmer of Angkor (13°30′N and 103°50′E) in 1292.
Steinberg, D. J. 1959. Cambodia. New Haven.
Porée, G., and E. Maspero. 1938. Moeurs et coutumes des Khmers. Paris.
Briggs, L. P. 1951. The Ancient Khmer Empire, Transactions of the American Philosophical Society 41: 237-250.
76. Siamese of the village of Bang Chan (14°N, 100°52′E) in 1955.
Hanks, J. R. 1963. Maternity and Its Rituals in Bang Chan. Ithaca.
Hanks, L. M., Jr., and J. R. Hanks. 1961. Thailand: Equality Between the Sexes. Women in the New Asia, ed. B. J. Ward, pp. 424-451.
Sharp, R. L., H. M. Hauck, K. Janlekha, and R. B. Textor. 1954. Siamese Village. Bangkok.
Sharp, L., and L. M. Hanks. n.d. Bang Chan: The Social History of a Thai Village. Ms.
Phillips, H. P. 1965. Thai Peasant Personality. Berkeley.
Benedict, R. F. 1946. Thai Culture and Behavior. Ithaca.
77. Semang of the Jahai subtribe (4°30′ to 5°30′N, 101° to 101°30′E) in 1925.
Schebesta, P. 1952-57. Die Negrito Asiens. Studia Instituti Anthropos v. 6, i; 12, ii; 13, ii. Mödling bei Wien.
———— 1927. Among the Forest Dwarfs of Malaya. London.

78. Nicobarese of the northern islands (8°15′ to 9°15′N, 92°40′ to 93°E) in 1870.
    Man, E. H.  1932.  The Nicobar Islands and Their People. Guilford.
    Whitehead, G.  1924.  In the Nicobar Islands. London.
    Svoboda, W.  1892-93.  Die Bewohner des Nikobaren-Archipels. Internationales Archiv für Ethnographie 5: 149-168.
79. Andamanese of the Aka Bea tribe (11°45′ to 12°N, 93° to 93°10′E) in 1860.
    Man, E. H.  1932.  On the Aboriginal Inhabitants of the Andaman Islands. London.
    Radcliffe-Brown, A. R.  1922.  The Andaman Islanders. Cambridge.
80. Forest Vedda (7°30′ to 8°N, 81° to 81°30′E) in 1860.
    Seligmann, C. G., and B. Z. Seligmann.  1911.  The Veddas. Cambridge.
    Bailey, J.  1963.  An Account of the Wild Veddahs of Ceylon. Transactions of the Ethnological Society of London 2: 278-320.
81. Tanala of the Menabe subtribe (20°S, 48°E) in 1925.
    Linton, R.  1933.  The Tanala. Field Museum of Natural History Anthropological Series 22: 1-334.
    ———  1939.  The Tanala of Madagascar. The Individual and His Society, ed., A. Kardiner, pp. 251-290. New York.
82. Negri Sembilan of Inas district (2°30′ to 2°40′N, 102°10′ to 102°20′E) in 1958.
    Lewis, D. K.  1962.  The Minangkabau Malay of Negri Sembilan. Ph.D. dissertation, Cornell University.
    Wilkinson, R. J.  1911.  Notes on the Negri Sembilan. Papers on Malay Subjects, ser. 1: History, pt. 5.
83. Javanese in the vicinity of Pare (7°43′S, 112°13′E) in 1955.
    Geertz, H.  1961.  The Javanese Family. New York.
    Geertz, C.  1960.  The Religion of Java. Chicago.
84. Balinese of the village of Tihingan (8°30′S, 115°20′E) in 1958.
    Mead, M., and F. C. MacGregor.  1951.  Growth and Culture: A Photographic Study of Balinese Childhood. New York.
    Belo, J.  1936.  A Study of the Balinese Family. American Anthropologist 38: 12-31.
    Covarrubias, M.  1937.  The Island of Bali. New York.
85. Iban of the Ulu Ai group (2°N, 112°30′ to 113°30′E) in 1950.
    Gomes, E. H.  1911.  Seventeen Years Among the Sea Dyaks of Borneo. London.
    Roth, H. L., ed.  1892.  The Natives of Borneo. Journal of the Royal Anthropological Institute 21: 110-137.
    Howell, W.  1908-10.  The Sea Dyak. Sarawak Gazette, v. 38-50.
86. Badjau of Tawi-Tawi and adjacent islands (5°N, 120°E) in 1863.
    Nimmo, H. A.  1964.  Nomads of the Sulu Sea. Ph.D. dissertation, University of Hawaii.
    ———  1965.  Social Organization of the Tawi-Tawi Badjaw. Ethnology 4: 421-439.
87. Toradja of the Bare'e subgroup (2°S, 121°E) in 1910.
    Adriani, N., and A. C. Kruijt.  1912.  De Bare'e-sprekende Toradja's. 3v. Batavia.
    Downs, R. E.  1956.  The Religion of the Bare'e-speaking Toradja. Gravenhage.
88. Tobelorese of Tobelo district (1°N, 128°30′E) in 1900.
    Hueting, A.  1921.  De Tobeloreezen in hun denken en doen. Bijdragen tot de Taal-, Land-, en Volkenkunde 77: 217-385; 78: 137-342.
    Riedel, J. G. F.  1885.  Galela und Tobeloresen. Zeitschrift für Ethnologie 17: 58-89.
89. Alorese of Atimelang (8°20′S, 124°40′E) in 1938.
    DuBois, C.  1944.  The People of Alor. Minneapolis.
    ———  1945.  The Alorese. The Psychological Frontiers of Society, ed. A. Kardiner, pp. 101-145. New York.
90. Tiwi (11° to 11°45′S, 130° to 132°E) in 1929.

Goodale, J. C. 1959. The Tiwi Women of Melville Island. Ph.D. dissertation, University of Pennsylvania.
91. Aranda of Alice Springs (23°30′ to 25°S, 132°30′ to 134°20′E) in 1896.
Spencer, B., and F. J. Gillen. 1927. The Arunta. 2v. London.
Murdock, G. P. 1934. Our Primitive Contemporaries, pp. 20-47. New York.
Strehlow, C. 1907-11. Die Aranda und Loritja Stämme in Zentral-Australien. Frankfurt.
92. Orokaiva of the Aiga subtribe (8°20′ to 8°40′S, 147°50′ to 148°10′E) in 1925.
Reay, M. 1953. Social Control Amongst the Crokaiva. Oceania 24: 110-118.
Williams, F. E. 1930. Orokaiva Society. London.
93. Kimam of the village of Bamol (7°30′S, 38°30′E) in 1960.
Serpenti, L. M. 1965. Cultivators in the Swamps. Assen.
94. Kapauku of Botukebo village (4°S, 36°E) in 1955.
Pospisil, L. 1958. Kapauku Papuans and Their Law. Yale University Publications in Anthropology 54: 1-296.
95. Kwoma of the Hongwam subtribe (4°10′S, 142°40′E) in 1937.
Whiting, J. W. M. 1941. Becoming a Kwoma. New Haven.
Whiting, J. W. M., and S. W. Reed. 1938. Kwoma Culture. Oceania 9: 170-216.
96. Manus of Peri village (2°10′S, 147°10′E) in 1929.
Mead, M. 1930. Growing Up in New Guinea. New York.
———— 1934. Kinship in the Admiralty Islands. Anthropological Papers of the American Museum of Natural History 34: 180-358.
———— 1932. An Investigation of the Thought of Primitive Children with Special Reference to Animism. Journal of the Royal Anthropological Institute 62: 173-190.
———— 1969. New Lives for Old. New York.
97. New Irelanders of Lesu village (2°30′S, 151°E) in 1930.
Powdermaker, H. 1933. Life in Lesu. New York.
98. Trobrianders of Kiriwina island (8°38′S, 151°4′E) in 1914.
Malinowski, B. 1929. The Sexual Life of Savages in Northwestern Melanesia. 2v. New York.
———— 1935. Coral Gardens and Their Magic. 2v. New York.
———— 1927. Sex and Repression in Savage Society. London.
99. Siuai of the northeastern group (7°S, 155°20′E) in 1939.
Oliver, D. L. 1955. A Solomon Island Society. Cambridge.
100. Tikopia (12°30′S, 168°30′E) in 1930.
Firth, R. 1936. We the Tikopia. London.
———— 1956. Ceremonies for Children and Social Frequency in Tikopia. Oceania 27: 12-55.
101. Pentecost Islanders of Bunlap village (16°S, 168°E) in 1953.
Lane, B. S., and R. B. Lane. Untitled, undated manuscript.
Lane, R. B. 1965. The Melanesians of South Pentecost. Gods, Ghosts and Men in Melanesia, ed. P. Lawrence and M. G. Meggitt, pp. 250-279. London.
102. Fijians of Mbau island (18°S, 178°35′E) in 1840.
Williams, T. 1884. Fiji and the Fijians. Rev. edit. London.
Toganivalu, D. 1911. The Customs of Bau before the Advent of Christianity. Transactions of the Fijian Society.
Waterhouse, J. 1866. The King and People of Fiji. London.
Deane, W. 1921. Fijian Society. London.
103. Ajie of Neje chiefdom (21°20′S, 165°40′E) in 1845.
Leenhardt, M. 1930. Notes d'ethnologie néo-calédonienne. Travaux et Mémoires de l'Institut d'Ethnologie 8: 1-340. Paris.
104. Maori of the Nga Puhi tribe (35°10′ to 35°30′S, 174° to 174°20′E) in 1820.
Reed, A. W. 1963. Illustrated Encyclopedia of Maori Life. New Zealand.
Polack, J. S. 1838. New Zealand. 2v. London.
Cruise, R. A. 1824. Journal of a Ten Month's Residence in New Zealand. 2nd edit. London.

Earle, A. 1832. A Narrative of Nine Month's Residence in New Zealand in 1827. London.

Gudgeon, T. W. 1885. The History and Doings of the Maoris. Auckland.

Best, E. 1924. The Maori. 2v. Wellington.

105. Marquesans of southwest Nuku Hiva (8°55'S, 140°10'W) in 1800.

La Barre, R. W. 1934. Marquesan Culture. Ms.

Tautain. 1896. Notes sur l'ethnographie des Iles Marquises. Anthropologie 7: 542-552.

———— 1898. Étude sur la depopulation de l'Archipel des Marquises. Anthropologie 9: 298-318.

Suggs, R. C. 1963. Marquesan Sexual Behavior. Ms. New Haven.

Handy, E. S. C. 1923. The Native Culture in the Marquesans. Bulletins of the Bernice P. Bishop Museum 9: 1-358.

Linton, R. 1939. Marquesan Culture. The Individual and His Society, ed. A. Kardiner, pp. 138-196. New York.

106. Samoans of western Upolu (13°48' to 14°S, 172°W) in 1829.

Turner, G. 1884. Samoa. London.

Stair, J. B. 1897. Old Samoa. London.

Grattan, F. J. H. 1948. An Introduction to Samoan Custom. Apia.

Murdock, G. P. 1934. The Samoans. Our Primitive Contemporaries, pp. 48-84. New York.

107. Gilbertese of Makin island (3°30'N, 172°20'E) in 1890.

Lambert, B. 1964. Fosterage in the Northern Gilbert Islands. Ethnology 3: 232-258.

Finsch, O. 1893. Ethnologische Erfahrungen und Belegstücke aus der Südsee 3: 19-89. Wien.

Krämer, A. 1906. Hawaii, Ostmikronesien, und Samoa, pp. 253-315. Stuttgart.

Grimble, A. 1921. From Birth to Death in the Gilbert Islands. Journal of the Royal Anthropological Institute 51: 25-54.

108. Marshallese of Jaluit atoll (6°N, 169°15'E) in 1900.

Erdland, P. A. 1914. Die Marshall-Insulaner. Anthropos Bibliothek Ethnological Monographs 2: 1-376 Münster i. Wien.

Wedgewood, C. 1942. Notes on the Marshall Islands. Oceania 13: 1-23.

Spoehr, A. 1949. Majuro: A Village in the Marshall Islands. Fieldiana: Anthropology 39: 1-266.

Krämer, A., and H. Nevermann. 1938. Ralik-Ratak. Ergebnisse der Südsee-Expedition 1908-1910, ed. G. Thilenius 2: xi, 1-438. Hamburg.

109. Trukese of Romonum island (7°24'N, 151°40'E) in 1947.

Gladwin, T., and S. B. Sarason. 1953. Truk: Man in Paradise. Viking Fund Publications in Anthropology 20: 1-655.

Fischer, A. The Role of the Trukese Mother and Its Effect on Child Training. Undated Ms.

110. Yapese (9°30'N, 138°10'E) in 1910.

Hunt, E. E., Jr., D. M. Schneider, N. R. Kidder, and W. D. Stevens. 1949. The Micronesians of Yap and Their Depopulation. Washington.

Müller, W. 1917. Yap. Ergebnisse der Südsee-Expedition 1908-1910, ed. G. Thilenius 2: B, iii, 1-380. Hamburg.

Salesius. 1906. Die Karolineninsel Jap. Berlin.

Schneider, D. M. Miscellaneous unpublished manuscripts.

———— 1953. Yap Kinship Terminology and Kin Groups. American Anthropologist 55: 215-236.

Murdock, G. P., C. S. Ford, and J. W. M. Whiting. 1944. West Caroline Islands. Civil Affairs Handbook OPNAV 50E-7: 1-222.

111. Palauans of Koror island (7°N, 134°30'E) in 1873.

Barnett, H. G. 1949. Palauan Society. Eugene.

———— 1960. Being a Palauan. New York.

112. Ifugao of the Kiangan group (16°50'N, 121°10'E) in 1910.

Barton, R. F. 1930. The Half-Way Sun. New York.
—— 1938. Philippine Pagans. London.
—— 1946. The Religion of the Ifugaos. Memoirs of the American Anthropological Association 65: 1-219.
—— 1919. Ifugao Law. University of California Publications in American Archaeology and Ethnology 15: i, 1-186.
113. Atayal (23°50′ to 24°50′N, 120°20′ to 120°50′E) in 1930.
Ruey Yih-Fu. 1955. Ethnographical Investigation of Some Aspects of the Atayal. Bulletin, Department of Archaeology and Anthropology, National Taiwan University 5: 113-127.
114. Chinese of Kaihsienkung village in north Chekiang (31°N, 120°5′E) in 1936.
Fei, H. 1946. Peasant Life in China. New York.
Fried, M. 1953. Fabric of Chinese Society. New York.
Lang, O. 1946. Chinese Family and Society. New Haven.
115. Manchu of the Aigun district (50°N, 125°30′E) in 1915.
Shirokogoroff, S. M. 1924. Social Organization of the Manchus. Royal Asiatic Society, North China Branch, Extra Volume 3: 1-196. Shanghai.
116. Koreans of Kanghwa island (37°37′N, 126°25′E) in 1950.
Osgood, C. 1951. The Koreans and Their Culture. New York.
Hewes, G. W., and C. H. Kim. 1952. Korean Kinship Behavior and Structure. Research Monographs on Korea, Ser. F, no. 2. P'yongyang.
Rutt, R. 1964. Korean Works and Days. Rutland.
117. Japanese of southern Okayama prefecture (34°30′ to 35°N, 133°40′E) in 1950.
Beardsley, R. K., J. W. Hall, and R. E. Ward. 1959. Village Japan. Chicago.
DeVos, G. 1965. Social Values and Personal Attitudes in Primary Human Relations in Niiike. University of Michigan Center for Japanese Studies Occasional Papers.
118. Ainu of the Tokapchi and Saru basins (42°40′ to 43°N, 142° to 144°E) in 1880.
Munro, N. G. 1962. Ainu Creed and Cult, ed. B. Z. Seligman. New York.
Batchelor, J. 1895. The Ainu of Japan. New York.
—— 1927. Ainu Life and Lore. Tokyo.
Hilger, M. I. 1971. Together with the Ainu. Norman.
Sutherland, I. L. G. 1948. The Ainu People of Northern Japan. Journal of the Polynesian Society 57: 203-226.
119. Gilyak (53° to 54°30′N, 139° to 143°10′E) in 1880.
Shternberg, L. 1933. Semya i rod u narodov severovostochnoi Azii. Leningrad.
Seeland, N. 1882. Die Ghiliaken. Russische Revue 21: 97-130, 222-254.
120. Yukaghir of the upper Kolyma River (63°30′ to 66°N, 150° to 157°E) in 1900.
Jochelson, W. 1926. The Yukaghir and Yukaghirized Tungus. Memoirs of the American Museum of Natural History 13: 1-469.
121. Chukchee of the Reindeer group (63° to 70°N, 171°E to 171°W) in 1900.
Bogoras, W. 1904-09. The Chukchee. Memoirs of the American Museum of Natural History 11: 1-703.
Sverdrup, H. U. 1938. Hos tendrafolket. Oslo.
122. Ingalik of Shageluk village (62°30′N, 159°30′W) in 1885.
Osgood, C. 1958. Ingalik Social Culture. Yale University Publications in Anthropology 55: 1-289.
—— 1940. Ingalik Material Culture. Yale University Publications in Anthropology 22: 1-500.
123. Aleut of the Unalaska branch (53° to 57°30′N, 158° to 170°W) in 1778.
Veniaminov, I. E. P. 1840. Zapiski ob ostrovakh unalashkinskago otdela. St. Petersburg.
Elliott, H. W. 1886. Our Arctic Province. New York.
Coxe, W. 1804. Account of Russian Discoveries Between Asia and America. London.
124. Copper Eskimo of the mainland (66°40′ to 69°20′N, 108° to 117°W) in 1915.

Jenness, D. 1922 The Life of the Copper Eskimos. Report of the Canadian Arctic Expedition, 1913-18, 12: 5-227. Ottawa.

Rasmussen, K. 1932. Intellectual Culture of the Copper Eskimos. Report of the Fifth Thule Expedition 9: 1-350. Copenhagen.

125. Montagnais of the Lake St. John and Mistassini bands (48° to 52°N, 73° to 75°W) in 1910.

Lips, J. E. 1947. Naskapi Law. Transactions of the American Philosophical Society, n.s., 37: 379-492.

Burgesse, J. A. 1944. The Woman and Child Among the Lac-St.-Jean Montagnais. Primitive Man 17: 1-18.

126. Micmac of the mainland (43°30' to 50°N, 60° to 66°W) in 1650.

Denys, N. 1908. The Description and Natural History of the Coasts of North America. Publications of the Champlain Society 2: 1-625.

Le Clercq, C. 1910. New Relation of Gaspesia. Publications of the Champlain Society 5: 1-452.

Wallis, W. D., and R. S. Wallis. 1955. The Micmac Indians of Eastern Canada. Minneapolis.

127. Saulteaux of the Berens River, Little Grand Rapids, and Pekangekum bands (51°30' to 52°30'N, 94° to 97°W) in 1930.

Dunning, R. W. 1959. Social and Economic Change Among the Northern Objibwa. Toronto.

Hallowell, A. I. 1955. Culture and Experience. Philadelphia.

Skinner, A. 1912. Notes on the Eastern Cree and Northern Saulteaux. Anthropological Papers of the American Museum of Natural History 9: i, 1-177.

128. Slave in the vicinity of Fort Simpson (62°N, 122°W) in 1940.

Helm, J. 1961. The Lynx Point People. Bulletin of the National Museum of Canada 176: 1-193.

Honigmann, J. J. 1946. Ethnography and Acculturation of the Fort Nelson Slave. Yale University Publications in Anthropology 33: 1-169.

129. Kaska of the upper Liard River (60°N, 131°W) in 1900.

Honigmann, J. J. 1949. Culture and Ethos of Kaska Society. Yale University Publications in Anthropology 40: 1-368.

———— 1954. The Kaska Indians. Yale University Publications in Anthropology 51: 1-163.

Teit, J. A. 1956. Field Notes on the Tahltan and Kaska Indians, 1912-1915. Anthropologica 3: 39-171.

130. Eyak (60° to 61°N, 144° to 146°W) in 1890.

Birket-Smith, K., and F. de Laguna. 1938. The Eyak Indians. Copenhagen.

131. Haida of the village of Masset (54°N, 132°30'W) in 1875.

Murdock, G. P. 1934. Our Primitive Contemporaries, pp. 221-263. New York.

———— 1934. Kinship and Social Behavior Among the Haida. American Anthropologist 36: 355-385.

Niblack, A. P. 1890. The Coastal Indians of Southern Alaska and Northern British Columbia. Annual Reports of the Board of Regents, Smithsonian Institution, for the year ending June 30, 1888, pp. 225-386.

132. Bellacoola (52°20'N, 126° to 127°W) in 1880.

McIlwraith, T. F. 1948. The Bella Coola Indians. 2v. Toronto.

Smith, H. I. 1925. Sympathetic Magic Among the Bellacoola. American Anthropologist 27: 116-121.

Drucker, P. 1950. Northwest Coast. Anthropological Records 9: 157-294.

133. Twana (47°20' to 47°30'N, 123°10' to 123°20'W) in 1860.

Elmendorf, W. W. 1960. The Structure of Twana Culture. Washington State University Research Studies, Monographic Supplement 2: 1-576.

134. Yurok (41°30'N, 124°W) in 1850.

Loeffelholz, K. von. 1893. Die Zoreisch-Indianer der Trinidad-Bai. Translation in R. F. Heizer and J. E. Mills, The Four Ages of Tsurai. Berkeley, 1952.

Kroeber, A. L. 1925. Handbook of the Indians of California. Bulletins of the Bureau of American Ethnology 78: 1-97.
—— 1960. Comparative Notes on the Structure of Yurok Culture. Washington State University Research Studies, Monographic Supplement 2.
Erikson, E. H. 1943. Observations on the Yurok: Childhood and World Image. University of California Publications in American Archaeology and Ethnology 25: 257-302.
135. Eastern Pomo of Clear Lake (39°N, 123°W) in 1850.
Loeb, E. M. 1926. Pomo Folkways. University of California Publications in American Archaeology and Ethnology 19: 149-404.
Gifford, E. W. 1926. Clear Lake Pomo Society. University of California Publications in American Archaeology and Ethnology 18: 287-390.
Kroeber, A. L. 1953. Handbook of the Indians of California. Berkeley.
136. Yokuts around Tulare Lake (35°10′N, 119°20′W) in 1850.
Gayton, A. H. 1948. Yokuts and Western Mono Ethnography. Anthropological Records 10: 1-301.
Latta, F. F. 1949. Handbook of Yokuts Indians. Oildale.
137. Wadadika Paiute of Harney Valley (43° to 44°N, 118° to 120°W) in 1870.
Whiting, B. B. 1950. Paiute Sorcery. Viking Fund Publications in Anthropology 15: 1-110.
138. Klamath (42° to 43°15′N, 121°20′ to 122°20′W) in 1860.
Pearsall, M. 1950. Klamath Childhood and Education. Anthropological Records 9: 339-353.
Spier, L. 1930. Klamath Ethnography. University of California Publications in American Archaeology and Ethnology 30: 1-328.
Voegelin, E. W. 1942. Northeast California. Anthropological Records 7: 47-251.
Stern, T. 1965. The Klamath Tribe, Seattle.
139. Kutenai of the Lower or eastern branch (48°40′ to 49°10′N, 116°40′W) in 1890.
Turney-High, H. H. 1941. Ethnography of the Kutenai. Memoirs of the American Anthropological Association 56: 1-202.
Chamberlain, A. F. 1892. Report on the Kootenay Indians. Reports of the British Association for the Advancement of Science 62: 539-617.
140. Gros Ventre (47° to 49°N, 106° to 110°W) in 1880.
Flannery, R. 1953. The Gros Ventres of Montana. Catholic University of America Anthropological Series 15: 1-221.
Cooper, J. M. 1956. The Gros Ventres of Montana: Religion and Ritual. Catholic University of America Anthropological Series 16: 1-491.
141. Hidatsa of Hidatsa village (47°N, 101°W) in 1836.
Bowers, A. W. 1965. Hidatsa Social and Ceremonial Organization. Bulletins of the Bureau of American Ethnology 194: 1-528.
Curtis, E. S. 1909. The North American Indian 4: 129-172, 180-196.
Wied-Neuwied, M.zu. 1906. Travels in the Interior of North America. Early Western Travels, ed. R. G. Thwaites 22: 357-366; 23: 252-385.
Matthews, W. 1877. Ethnography and Philology of the Hidatsa Indians. U.S. Geological and Geographical Survey Miscellaneous Publication 7: 1-239.
142. Pawnee of the Skidi band (42°N, 100°W) in 1867.
Dorsey, G. A., and J. R. Murie. 1940. Notes on Skidi Pawnee Society, ed. A. Spoehr. Field Museum of Natural History Anthropological Series 27: 67-119.
Weltfish, G. 1965. The Lost Universe. New York.
143. Omaha (41°10′ to 41°40′N, 96° to 97°W) in 1860.
Fletcher, A. C., and F. LaFlesche. 1911. The Omaha Tribe. Annual Reports of the Bureau of Ethnology 27: 17-672.
Dorsey, J. O. 1884. Omaha Sociology. Annual Reports of the Bureau of American Ethnology 3: 205-320.
144. Huron of the Attignawantan and Attigneenongnahac tribes (44° to 45°N, 78° to 80°W) in 1634.

Trigger, B. G.   1969.   The Huron. New York.
Tooker, E.   1964.   An Ethnography of the Huron Indians. Bulletins of the
    Bureau of American Ethnology 190: 1-183.
145. Creek of the Upper Creek division (32°30' to 34°20'N, 85°30' to 86°30'W) in
    1800.
    Swanton, J. R.   1928.   Social Organization and `Social Usages of the Creek Con-
    federacy. Annual Reports of the Bureau of American Ethnology 42: 23-472,
    859-900.
    ———— 1946.   The Indians of the Southeastern United States. Bulletins of the
    Bureau of American Ethnology 137: 1-943.
146. Natchez (31°30'N, 91°25'W) in 1718.
    Swanton, J. R.   1911.   Indian Tribes of the Lower Mississippi Valley. Bulletins
    of the Bureau of American Ethnology 43: 1-387.
147. Comanche (30° to 38°N, 98° to 103°W) in 1870.
    Wallace, E., and E. A. Hoebel.   1952.   The Comanches. Norman.
    Gladwin, T.   1948.   Comanche Kin Behavior. American Anthropologist 50:
    73-94.
148. Chiricahua Apache of the Central band (32°N, 109°30'W) in 1870.
    Opler, M. E.   1941.   An Apache Life-Way. Chicago.
    ———— 1971.   Personal communication.
149. Zuni (35°50' to 35°30'N, 108°30' to 109°W) in 1880.
    Leighton, D. C., and J. Adair.   1966.   People of the Middle Place: A Study of
    the Zuni Indians. New Haven.
    Gifford, E. W.   1940.   Apache-Pueblo. Anthropological Records 4: 1-207.
    Benedict, R.   1934.   Patterns of Culture, pp. 57-129. Boston.
    Stevenson, M. C.   1904.   The Zuni Indians. Annual Reports of the Bureau of
    American Ethnology 23: 1-634.
    Roberts, J. M.   1956.   Zuni Daily Life. University of Nebraska Laboratory of
    Anthropology Monographs, Note Book 3: i, 1-23.
    Parsons, E. C.   1919.   Mothers and Children at Zuni. Man 19: 168-173.
150. Havasupai (35°20' to 36°20'N, 111°20' to 113°W) in 1918.
    Spier, L.   1928.   Havasupai Ethnography. Anthropological Papers of the Amer-
    ican Museum of Natural History 24: 81-408.
151. Papago of the Archie division (32°N, 112°W) in 1910.
    Underhill, R. M.   1936.   The Autobiography of a Papago Woman. Memoirs of
    the American Anthropological Association 46: 1-64.
    ———— 1939.   Social Organization of the Papago Indians. Columbia University
    Contributions to Anthropology 30: 1-280.
    Joseph, A., R. B. Spicer, and J. Chesky.   1949.   The Desert People. Chicago.
    Lumholtz, C.   1912.   New Trails in Mexico. New York.
152. Huichol (22°N, 105°W) in 1890.
    Zingg, R. M.   1938.   The Huichols. University of Denver Contributions to An-
    thropology 1: 1-826.
    Lumholtz, C.   1902.   Unknown Mexico, v. 2. London.
    Klineberg, O.   1934.   Notes on the Huichol. American Anthropologist 36: 446-
    460.
    Grimes, J. E., and T. B. Hinton.   1969.   The Huichol and Cora. Handbook of
    Middle American Indians, ed. R. Wauchope, 7: i, 792-813. Austin.
153. Aztec of the city and environs of Tenochtitlan (19°N, 99°10'W) in 1520.
    Höltker, G.   1930.   Die Familie bei den Azteken in Altmexiko. Anthropos 25:
    465-526.
    Sahagun, B. de.   1950-57.   Florentine Codex: General History of the Things of
    New Spain. Translated from the original Aztec by A. J. O. Anderson and
    C. F. Dibble. Monographs of the School of American Research 14: pts. 2,
    3, 4, 8, 9, 13, 14. Sante Fe.
    Soustelle, J.   1961.   Daily Life of the Aztecs. New York.
    Vaillant, G. C.   1941.   Aztecs of Mexico. New York.

Murdock, G. P. 1934. Our Primitive Contemporaries, pp. 359-402. New York.
154. Popoluca around the pueblo of Soteapan (18°15′N, 94°50′W) in 1940.
Foster, G. M. 1940. Notes on the Popoluca of Veracruz. Publications del Instituto Panamericano de Geografia e Historia 51: 1-41.
———— 1942. A Primitive Mexican Economy. Monographs of the American Ethnological Society 5: 1-115.
155. Quiche of the town of Chichicastenango (15°N, 91°W) in 1930.
Bunzel, R. 1952. Chichicastenango. Publications of the American Ethnological Society 22: 1-438.
Schultze-Jena, L. 1933. Indiana 1: Leben, Glaube und Sprache der Quiché von Guatemala. Jena.
156. Miskito near Cape Gracias a Dios. (15°N, 83°W) in 1921.
Conzemius, E. 1932. Ethnographic Survey of the Miskito and Sumu Indians. Bulletins of the Bureau of American Ethnology 106: 1-191.
Helms, M. W. 1971. Asang. Gainesville.
157. Bribri tribe of Talamanca (9°N, 83°15′W) in 1917.
Stone, D. 1962. The Talamancan Tribes of Costa Rica. Papers of the Peabody Museum, Harvard University 43: ii, 1-108.
Gabb, W. M. 1876. On the Indian Tribes and Languages of Costa Rica. Proceedings of the American Philosophical Society 14: 483-602.
Skinner, A. 1920. Notes on the Bribri of Costa Rica. Indian Notes and Monographs 6: 37-106.
158. Cuna of San Blas Archipelago (9° to 9°30′N, 78° to 79°W) in 1927.
Stout, D. C. 1947. San Blas Cuna Acculturation. Viking Fund Publications in Anthropology 9: 1-124.
Nordenskiöld, E. 1938. An Historical and Ethnological Survey of the Cuna Indians. Comparative Ethnographical Studies 10: 1-686. Göteborg.
Krieger, H. W. 1926. Material Culture of the People of Southeastern Panama. Bulletins of the United States National Museum 134: 1-133.
159. Goajiro (11°30′ to 12°20′N, 71° to 72°30′W) in 1947.
Gutiérrez de Pineda, V. 1948. Organización social en la Guajira. Revista del Instituto Etnológico Nacional 3: ii, 1-225. Bogotá.
Bolinder, G. 1957. Indians on Horseback. London.
Armstrong, J. M., and A. Métraux. 1948. The Goajiro. Bulletins of the Bureau of American Ethnology 143: iv, 360-383.
160. Haitians of Mirebalais (18°50′N, 72°10′W) in 1935.
Herskovits, M. J. 1937. Life in a Haitian Valley. New York.
Romain, J. B. 1955. Quelques moeurs et coutumes des paysans haitiens. Theses de Doctoral (typescript). Paris.
Simpson, G. E. 1943. Sexual and Familial Institutions in Northern Haiti. American Anthropologist 44: 655-674.
Bastien, R. 1951. La familia rural haitiana. México.
161. Callinago of Dominica (15°30′N, 60°30′W) in 1650.
Breton, R. 1665. Observations of the Island Carib. Auxerre.
Breton, R., and A. de la Paix. 1929. Relation de l'ile de la Guadeloup, ed. J. Rennard. Histoire Coloniale 1: 45-74. Paris.
Du Tertre, J. B. 1667. Histoire generale des Antilles habitées par les Francois, v. 2. 2d edit. Paris.
Taylor, D. 1946. Kinship and Social Structure of the Island Carib. Southwestern Journal of Anthropology 2: 180-212.
Rouse, I. 1948. The Carib. Bulletins of the Bureau of American Ethnology 143: iv, 547-565.
Hodge, W. H., and D. M. Taylor. 1957. The Ethnobotany of the Island Caribs of Dominica. Webbia 12: ii, 513-644.
162. Warrau of the Orinoco delta (8°30′ to 9°50′N, 60°40′ to 62°30′W) in 1935.
Turrado Moreno, A. 1945. Etnographía de los Indios Guaraunos. Caracas.
Hill, G. W., et al. 1956. Los Guarao del delta Amacuro. Caracas.

Suárez, M. M. 1968. Los Warao. Caracas.

Wilbert, J. 1958. Die soziale und politische Organisation der Warrau. Kölner Zeitschrift für Soziologie und Sozialpsychologie, ns, 10: 272-291.

163. Yanomamo of the Shamatari tribe (2° to 2°45′N, 64°30′ to 65°30′W) in 1965.
Chagnon, N. A. 1968. The Fierce People. New York.

164. Carib along the Barama River (7°10′ to 7°40′N, 59°20′ to 60°20′W) in 1932.
Gillin, J. 1936. The Barama River Caribs. Papers of the Peabody Museum, Harvard University 14: ii, 1-274.

——— 1948. Tribes of the Guianas. Bulletins of the Bureau of American Ethnology 143: iii, 799-860.

Roth, W. E. 1924. An Introductory Study of the Arts, Crafts and Customs of the Guiana Indians. Annual Reports of the Bureau of American Ethnology 38: 25-720.

165. Saramacca of the upper Suriname River (3° to 4°N, 55°30′ to 56°W) in 1928.
Kahn, M. C. 1931. Djuka: The Bush Negroes of Dutch Guiana. New York.

Herskovits, M. J., and F. S. Herskovits. 1934. Rebel Destiny. New York.

166. Mundurucu of Cabrua village (7°S, 57°W) in 1850.
Murphy, R. F. 1960. Headhunter's Heritage. Berkeley and Los Angeles.

Tocantins, A. M. G. 1877. Estudos sobre a tribu "Mundurucú." Revista Trimensal do Instituto Histórico, Geographico e Ethnográphico do Brasil 40: ii, 73-161.

Martius, C. F. P. von. 1863-67. Beiträge zur Ethnographie und Sprachenkunde Amerika's, zumal Brasiliens. 2v. Leipzig.

167. Cubeo of the Caduiari River (1° to 1°50′N, 70° to 71°W) in 1939.
Goldman, I. 1963. The Cubeo Indians. Illinois Studies in Anthropology 2: 1-305.

168. Cayapa of the Rio Cayapas drainage (0°40′ to 1°15′N, 78°45′ to 79°10′W) in 1908.
Barrett, S. A. 1925. The Cayapa Indians. Indian Notes and Monographs 40: 1-476.

Altschuler, M. 1965. The Cayapa. Ph.D. dissertation, University of Minnesota.

169. Jivaro (2° to 4°S, 77° to 79°W) in 1920.
Karsten, R. 1935. The Head-Hunters of Western Amazonas. Societas Scientiarum Fennica, Commentationes Humanarum Litterarum 7: 1-588.

Harner, M. J. 1960. Machetes, Shotguns, and Society: An Inquiry into the Social Impact of Technological Change Among the Jivaro Indians. Ph.D. dissertation, University of California at Berkeley.

Stirling, M. W. 1938. Historical and Ethnographical Material on the Jivaro Indians. Bulletins of the Bureau of American Ethnology 117: 1-148.

170. Amahuaca of the upper Inuya River (10°10′ to 10°30′S, 72° to 72°30′W) in 1960.
Huxley, M., and C. Capa. 1964. Farewell to Eden. New York.

Tessman, G. 1930. Die Indianer Nordost-Perus. Hamburg.

171. Inca in the vicinity of Cuzco (13°30′S, 72°W) in 1530.
Cobo, B. 1890-95. Historia del Nuevo Mundo. 4v. Seville.

Rowe, J. H. 1946. Inca Culture at the Time of the Conquest. Bulletins of the Bureau of American Ethnology 143: ii, 183-330.

Baudin, L. 1961. A Socialist Empire: The Incas of Peru. New York.

Murdock, G. P. 1934. Our Primitive Contemporaries, pp. 403-450. New York.

172. Aymara of Chucuito (16°S, 65°45′W) in 1940.
Tschopik, H., Jr. 1946. The Aymara. Bulletins of the Bureau of American Ethnology 143: ii, 501-573.

——— 1948. The Aymara of Chucuito. Anthropological Papers of the American Museum of Natural History 44: 137-308.

LaBarre, W. 1948. The Aymara Indians of the Lake Titicaca Plateau. Memoirs of the American Anthropological Association 68: 1-250.

173. Siriono near the Rio Blanco (14° to 15°S, 63° to 64°W) in 1942.
Holmberg, A. R. 1950. Nomads of the Long Bow. Publications of the Institute

of Social Anthropology, Smithsonian Institution 10: 1-104.
174. Nambicuara of the Cocozu group (12°30′ to 13°30′S, 58°30′ to 59°W) in 1940.
Lévi-Strauss, L. 1948. La vie familiale et sociale des Indiens Nambikwara. Journal de la Société des Américanistes 37: 1-131. Paris.
Oberg, K. 1953. Indian Tribes of Northern Mato Grosso. Publications of the Institute of Social Anthropology, Smithsonian Institution 15: 82-105.
175. Trumai (11°50′S, 53°40′W) in 1938.
Murphy, R. F., and B. Quain. 1955. The Trumai Indians. Monographs of the American Ethnological Society 24: 1-108.
176. Timbira of the Ramcocamecra subtribe (6° to 7°S, 45° to 46°W) in 1915.
Nimuendajú, C. 1946. The Eastern Timbira. University of California Publications in American Archaeology and Ethnology 41: 1-357.
Snethlage, E. H. 1930. Unter nordostbrasilianischen Indianern. Zeitschrift für Ethnologie 62: 111-205.
Arnaud, E. 1964. Noticia sobre los Indios Gavioes de Oeste. Antropológia 20.
177. Tupinamba in the vicinity of Rio de Janeiro (22°35′ to 23°S, 42° to 44°30′W) in 1550.
Yves d'Evreux. 1864. Voyage dans le nord du Brésil fait durant les années 1613 et 1614, ed. F. Denis. Leipzig and Paris.
Thevet, A. 1878. Les singularitez de la France antarctique, ed. P. Gaffarel. Paris.
Soares de Souza, G. 1851. Tratado descriptivo do Brazil em 1587. Revista do Instituto Histórico e Geográphico do Brazil 14: 1-423.
Léry, J. de. 1906. Extracts out of the Historie of John Lerius, ed. S. Purchas. Hakluytus Posthumus or Purchas His Pilgrimes 16: 518-579. Glasgow.
Métraux, A. 1948. The Tupinamba. Bulletins of the Bureau of American Ethnology 143: iii, 95-133.
178. Botocudo of the Naknenuk subtribe (18° to 20°S, 41°30′ to 43°30′W) in 1884.
Ehrenreich, P. 1887. Ueber die Botocudos. Zeitschrift für Ethnologie 19: 49-82.
Métraux, A. 1946. The Botocudo. Bulletins of the Bureau of American Ethnology 143: i, 531-540.
179. Shavante in the vicinity of São Domingo (13°30′S, 51°30′W) in 1958.
Maybury-Lewis, D. 1967. Akwë-Shavante Society. Oxford.
180. Aweikoma (28°S, 50°W) in 1932.
Henry, J. 1941. Jungle People. New York.
Métraux, A. 1946. The Caingang. Bulletins of the Bureau of American Ethnology 143: i, 445-475.
181. Cayua of southern Mato Grosso (23° to 24°S, 54° to 56°W) in 1890.
Koenigswald, G. von. 1908. Die Cayuás. Globus 93: 376-381.
Ambrosetti, J. B. 1895. Los Indios Cainguá del Alto Parana. Boletín del Instituto Geográfico Argentino 15: 661-744.
182. Lengua (23° to 24°S, 58° to 59°W) in 1889.
Baldus, H. 1931. Indianerstudien im nordöstlichen Chaco. Forschungen zur Völkerpsychologie und Soziologie 11: 1-239.
Grubb, W. B. 1911. An Unknown People in an Unknown Land. London.
183. Abipon (27° to 29°S, 59° to 60°W) in 1750.
Dobrizhoffer, M. 1822. An Account of the Abipones. 3v. London.
Métraux, A. 1946. Ethnography of the Chaco. Bulletins of the Bureau of American Ethnology 143: i, 197-370.
184. Mapuche in the vicinity of Temuco (38°30′S, 72°35′W) in 1950.
Hilger, M. I. 1957. Araucanian Child Life and Its Cultural Background. Smithsonian Miscellaneous Collections 133: 1-495.
Titiev, M. 1951. Araucanian Culture in Transition. Occasional Contributions from the Museum of Anthropology, University of Michigan 15: 1-164.
Faron, L. C. 1961. Mapuche Social Structure. Illinois Studies in Anthropology 1: 1-247.
185. Tehuelche (40° to 50°S, 64° to 72°W) in 1870.

Musters, G. C.   1873.   At Home with the Patagonians. London.
—— 1872.   On the Races of Patagonia. Journal of the (Royal) Anthropological Institute 1: 193-207.
Viedma, A. de.   1837.   Descripción de la costa meridional del sur. Coleción de obras y documentos relativos a la historia antigua y moderna de las provincias del Rio de la Plata, ed. P. de Angelis, 6: 63-81. Buenos Aires.
Bourne, B. F.   1874.   The Captive in Patagonia. Boston.

186.   Yahgan (54°30′ to 56°30′S, 67° to 72°W) in 1865.
Gusinde, M.   1937.   Die Feuerland-Indianer 2: Yamana. Mödling bei Wien.

11a.   Chagga of Mt. Kilimanjaro (3° to 4°S, 37° to 38°E) in 1906.
Raum, O. F.   1940.   Chaga Childhood. London.
Gutmann, B.   1926.   Das Recht der Dschagga. Arbeiten zur Entwicklungspsychologie 7: 1-733. München.
Dundas, C.   1924.   Kilimanjaro and Its Peoples. London.

16a.   Katab of the Jos plateau (10°N, 8°E) in 1925.
Meek, C. K.   1931.   Tribal Studies in Northern Nigeria, v.2. London.
Gunn, H. D.   1956.   Pagan Peoples of the Central Area of Northern Nigeria. London.

34a.   Dorobo of the North Tindiret Forest band (0°10′N, 35°30′E) in 1927.
Huntingford, G. W. B.   1951.   The Social Institutions of the Dorobo. Anthropos 46: 1-48.
—— 1929.   Modern Hunters. Journal of the Royal Anthropological Institute 59: 333-378.

46a.   Lebanese of Al-Munsif village (34°25′N, 35°40′E) in 1950.
Prothro, E. T.   1961.   Child Rearing in the Lebanon. Cambridge, Mass.

60a.   Chenchu of the Forest group (16°15′N, 79°E) in 1940.
Fürer-Haimendorf, C. von.   1943.   The Chenchus. London.

68a.   Sherpa of the Khumbu region (86°40′ to 86°50′E, 17°48′ to 27°54′N) about 1950.
Fürer-Haimendorf, C. von.   1964.   The Sherpas of Nepal. London.

90a.   Northeastern Murngin of Capes Arnhem and Wilburforce (136°10′ to 137°E, 11°45′ to 12°35′S) about 1930.
Warner, W. L.   1937.   A Black Civilization. New York.
Thompson, D. F.   1949.   Economic Structure and the Ceremonial Exchange Cycle in Arnhem Land. Melbourne.
Webb, T. T.   1934.   The Aborigines of East Arnhem Land. Victoria.

95a.   Wogeo Islanders of Wonevaro district (3°S, 144°E) in 1930.
Hogbin, H. I.   1943.   A New Guinea Infancy: From Conception to Weaning in Wogeo. Oceania 13: 285-309.
—— 1946.   A New Guinea Childhood: From Weaning till the Eighth Year in Wogeo. Oceania 16: 275-296.

106a.   Pukapukans of Danger Island (10°53′S, 165°50′W) in 1915.
Beaglehole, E., and P. Beaglehole.   1938.   Ethnology of Pukapuka. Bulletins of the Bernice P. Bishop Museum 150: 1-419.
—— 1941.   Personality Development in Pukapukan Children. Language, Culture and Personality, ed. L. Spier, A. I. Hallowell, and S. S. Newman, pp. 282-298. Menasha.

138a.   Washo around Lake Tahoe and Washoe Lake (38°20′ to 40°10′N, 119°30′ to 120°15′W) about 1860.
d'Azevedo, W. L., ed.   1963.   The Washo Indians of California and Nevada. University of Utah, Department of Anthropology, Anthropological Papers 67: 1-201.
Downs, J. F.   1966.   The Two Worlds of the Washo. New York.

141a.   Crow Indians (42°30′ to 47°N, 105° to 111°W) in 1870.
Lowie, R. H.   1935.   The Crow Indians. New York.
—— 1912.   Social Life of the Crow Indians. Anthropological Papers of the American Museum of Natural History 9: 179-248.

———— 1922. The Religion of the Crow Indians. Anthropological Papers of the American Museum of Natural History 25: 309-444.

Denig, E. T. 1961. Five Indian Tribes of the Upper Missouri. Norman.

Murdock, G. P. 1934. Our Primitive Contemporaries, pp. 264-290. New York.

McAllester, D. 1941. Water as a Disciplinary Agent Among the Crow and Blackfoot. American Anthropologist 43: 593-604.

149a. Ramah Navaho, centered around the town of Ramah (35°N and 108°30′W) in 1940.

Kluckhohn, C. 1947. Some Aspects of Navaho Infancy and Early Childhood. Psychoanalysis and the Social Sciences 1: 37-86.

Kluckhohn, C., and D. Leighton. 1946. The Navaho. Cambridge.

Leighton, D. C., and C. Kluckhohn. 1947. Children of the People. Cambridge.

Bailey, F. L. 1950. Some Sex Beliefs and Practices in a Navaho Community. Papers of the Peabody Museum of American Archaeology and Ethnology, Harvard University 40: ii, 1-108.

Roberts, J. M. 1951. Three Navaho Households. Papers of the Peabody Museum of American Archaeology and Ethnology, Harvard University 40: iii, 1-89.

175a. Bororo of the Rio Vermelho (15°30′ to 16°S, 54°30′ to 55°W) in 1936.

Steinen, K. von den. 1894. Unter den Naturvölkern Zentral-Brasiliens. Berlin.

Cook, W. A. 1909. Through the Wildernesses of Brazil by Horse, Canoe and Float. New York.

Lowie, R. H. 1953. The Bororo. Bulletins of the Bureau of American Ethnology 143: i, 419-434.

Lévi-Strauss, C. 1936. Contribution a l'étude de l'organisation sociale des Indiens Bororo. Journal de la Société des Américanistes 28: 269-304.

Frič, V. A., and P. Radin. 1906. Contributions to the Study of the Bororo Indians. Journal of the Royal Anthropological Institute 36: 382-406.

179a. Carajá along the west bank of the Araguaya River (10°12′ to 15°15′S, 50°25′ to 51°50′W) in 1908.

Krause, F. 1911. In den Wildnissen Brasiliens. Leipzig.

Lipkind, W. 1948. The Carajá. Bulletins of the Bureau of American Ethnology 143: iii, 179-191.

Ehrenreich, P. 1891. Beiträge zur Völkerkunde Brasiliens. Veröffentlichungen aus dem Königlichen Museum für Völkerkunde 2: 1-80. Leipzig.

Dietschy, H. 1956. Geburtshütte und "Männerkindbett" bei den Karajă. Verhandlungen der Naturforschenden Gesellschaft zu Basel 68: 114-132.

183a. Mataco of the Guisnay and Vejó divisions in Argentina (22° to 24°S, 62° to 64°W) in 1875.

Pelleschi, J. 1896. Los Indios Mataco y su lengua. Boletin del Instituto Geografico Argentina 17: 559-662; 18: 173-350.

Karsten, R. 1932. Indian Tribes of the Argentine and Bolivian Chaco. Societas Scientiarum Fennica, Commentationes Humanarum Litterarum 4: i, 1-246.

Métraux, A. 1944. Nota etnográfica sobre los indios Mataco. Relaciones de la Sociedad Argentina de Antropologia 4: 7-18.

# 7

# Traits Inculcated in Childhood:
# Cross-Cultural Codes 5[1]

*Herbert Barry III, Lili Josephson,*

*Edith Lauer,* and *Catherine Marshall*

The experiences of children express and in part determine the general values of the culture. A prior cross-cultural study has shown that traits necessary for the adult subsistence economy activities are inculcated during childhood (Barry, Child, and Bacon 1959). Various aspects of adult personality are shaped by experiences in early stages of development (Barry 1969). Important cultural variations may be revealed by different approaches to the universal problems of training children. There is more scope for cultural and sexual differentiation in the treatment of children than of infants, as has been indicated in a study of differentiation between boys and girls (Barry, Bacon, and Child 1957).

The present article provides a new set of codes on child training in a world sample of 186 societies, selected by Murdock and White (1969). A prior article by Barry and Paxson (1971) has given codes on infancy for this sample. Two stages were differentiated, infancy up to the age of one year and the transitional years up to the age of approximately four to five years. The new code begins after this transitional stage and ends prior to the major changes associated with puberty. It differentiates between two stages of childhood, early and late, and also between boys and girls, who were so seldom differentiated during infancy that sex differences were not reported by Barry and Paxson (1971).

Although ethnographic reports vary greatly in the thoroughness and accuracy with which child training is observed, children constitute an important part of the community and family. Therefore, most ethnographies contain some information on this stage of development. Cross-cultural studies of child training prior to the present report have been less thorough and were applied to smaller samples. Codes reported by Whiting and Child (1953) for a sample of 75 societies did not include information on late childhood or sex differences. Barry, Bacon, and Child (1967) measured socialization pressures on boys and girls in a sample of 110 societies. These codes were limited to a small number of traits, without differentiating between the early and late stages of childhood.

The present sample, in addition to being larger, has advantages of greater scope and information. It includes representation of technologically advanced civilizations, whereas the earlier samples were almost entirely preliterate societies. The new sample avoids duplication of closely related societies and was selected partly on the basis of adequacy of information on various cultural characteristics, including child training. Inclusion of a substantial number of the societies in both earlier samples enables comparison of the new codes with earlier equivalent ones.

TABLE 1

Traits Inculcated in Boys (B) and Girls (G) during Early (E) and Late (L) Childhood

| Area | Society | D | Fortit. E (B B) | Fortit. L (B G) | Aggress. E (B G) | Aggress. L (B G) | Compet. E (B G) | Compet. L (B G) | Self-Rel. E (B G) | Self-Rel. L (B G) | Achiev. E (B G) | Achiev. L (B G) |
|---|---|---|---|---|---|---|---|---|---|---|---|---|
| 1 | Nama Hottentot | 3 | . . | 3 3 | 2 2 | 3 3 | 2 2 | 3 3 | 2+2+ | 4 2+ | 3-3- | 3-3- |
| 2 | Kung Bushmen | 2 | 2+2+ | 3+3+ | 2 2 | 3 3 | 1 1 | 2 2 | 2+2+ | 3+3+ | 2+2+ | 3+3+ |
| 3 | Thonga | 3 | 3 . | 3 . | 3+. | 3+. | 2 2 | 2 2 | 3+2+ | 3+2+ | 2+2+ | 2+2+ |
| 4 | Lozi | 3 | 3 3 | 3 3 | 3+3+ | 3+3+ | . . | . . | . . | . . | 3 . | 3 . |
| 5 | Mbundu | 3 | 2+2+ | 3+3+ | . . | . . | 2+2+ | 2+2+ | 2+2+ | 3+3+ | 2 2 | 3+3+ |
| 6 | Suku | 3 | . . | 3+. | . . | 3+. | . . | . . | . . | . . | 2 2 | 3 3 |
| 7 | Bemba | 3 | 2 2 | 3 3 | 3 3 | 3+3+ | 3-3- | 3 3 | 3-3- | 4 3+ | 2 2+ | 2 2+ |
| 8 | Nyakyusa | 3 | 3 3 | 3 3 | 3 3 | 3+3+ | . . | 3+. | 3 2+ | 4-3 | . . | 3+3+ |
| 9 | Hadza | 1 | 3 2+ | 3 2+ | 3 3+ | 3 3+ | 3-3- | 3-3- | 3+2 | 4 3- | 2 2 | 3 3 |
| 10 | Luguru | 3 | . . | . . | . . | . . | . . | . . | 3 2+ | 3 2+ | . . | . . |
| 11 | Kikuyu | 1 | . . | 4-3+ | 3 2 | 3 2 | 2 2 | 4 3 | 2+2+ | 3+3+ | 3 3 | 4 4 |
| 12 | Ganda | 1 | 2 2 | 3+3+ | . . | 3+3+ | . . | 3+. | 3 3 | 4 3 | 2 2 | 3 3+ |
| 13 | Mbuti Pygmies | 3 | 3-3- | 3+3+ | 2 2 | 3+3+ | 2 2 | 2 2 | 3+3+ | 4 4 | 3+3+ | 3+3+ |
| 14 | Nkundo Mongo | 1 | 2+2+ | 3+3+ | 3 . | 3 . | . . | . . | 3-2+ | 3-2+ | 3-3- | 3-3- |
| 15 | Banen | 1 | 2 2 | 3+3+ | 4 4 | 4 4 | 3 3 | 3 3 | 3 3 | 3 3 | . . | . . |
| 16 | Tiv | 3 | 3+3 | 3+3 | 2 2 | 3 3 | 3 3 | 3 3 | 2+2+ | 4 3+ | 3 3 | 3 3 |
| 17 | Ibo | 3 | 3 3 | 3+3+ | 3+3+ | 3+3+ | 3+3+ | 3+3+ | 2 2 | 3+2+ | 3 3 | 3+3+ |
| 18 | Fon | 2 | . . | 3+3+ | . . | . . | 3+3+ | 3+3+ | 2+2+ | 3+3+ | 3 3 | 4-4- |
| 19 | Ashanti | . | . . | . . | . . | . . | . . | . . | . . | . . | . . | . . |
| 20 | Mende | 1 | 2+2+ | . . | . . | . . | . . | . . | 2 2 | 3 2+ | . 2 | 3+3+ |
| 21 | Wolof | 3 | . . | 4 3- | . . | 3 . | 3 3 | 4 4 | 3 3 | 4 4 | 2 2 | 3+4 |
| 22 | Bambara | 2 | 3 2+ | 4 3+ | 2+2+ | 3+3+ | 3 3 | 3 3 | 2+2- | 2+2- | 2 2 | 3 3 |
| 23 | Tallensi | 3 | 2+2+ | 2+2+ | 2+2+ | 2+2+ | 2 2 | 2 2 | 3 2+ | 4 3+ | 2 2 | 3+3+ |
| 24 | Songhai | 1 | 3 3 | 3 3 | 3 . | 3+. | . . | . . | 2 2 | 3+3 | . . | . . |
| 25 | Wodaabe Fulani | 1 | 2+2+ | 3+3 | 2+2 | 3+3 | . . | 3+3 | 3 3 | 4 3 | 2 2 | 3 3 |
| 26 | Zazzagawa Hausa | 1 | 3-3- | 3-3- | 3 3 | 3 3 | 2+2+ | 2+2+ | 2+2+ | 4 4 | 2 2 | 3 3 |
| 27 | Massa | 3 | . 3 | . 3 | 3 3 | 3 3 | 3 3 | 3 3 | 3 . | 3 . | . . | . . |
| 28 | Azande | 1 | . . | . . | 3 3 | 3+3+ | . . | . . | 2-2- | 2-2- | . . | . . |
| 29 | Fur | 2 | 3+3+ | 3+3+ | 3 . | 3+. | . . | 3 3 | 3-2 | 4-3 | 3 2+ | 3+3 |
| 30 | Otoro Nuba | 2 | 3 . | 3+3 | . . | 3+2 | . . | 4 3 | 3 2 | 4+3 | . . | 4+3- |
| 31 | Shilluk | 1 | 3 3 | 4 3+ | . 2+ | 4 3 | . 3 | . 3+ | 3 2 | 4 3 | 2 2+ | 3 3+ |
| 32 | Northern Mao | . | 3+3+ | 3+3+ | . . | . . | . . | . . | . . | . . | . . | . . |
| 33 | Kaffa | 3 | 2 2 | 4 4 | . . | 3+. | . . | 2+3- | 2 2 | 3-. | 2+. | 3+3- |
| 34 | Masai | 3 | 4 3+ | 5-4 | 4 3 | 5 4 | . . | . . | 4 4 | 4 4 | 2 2 | 2 2 |
| 35 | Konso | 3 | . . | 3 3 | 3+2 | 3+2 | 2 . | 2 . | 3+3+ | 3+3+ | 3+3+ | 3+3+ |
| 36 | Somali | 2 | . . | 4-4- | . . | . . | . . | 3 3 | 2+2+ | 3+2+ | . . | 3 3 |
| 37 | Amhara | 1 | . . | 3+. | . . | 4 2- | . . | . . | 2 2 | 3+3 | 1 1 | 3+. |
| 38 | Bogo | . | 4-4- | 4-4- | 4 4 | 4 4 | 3+3+ | 3+3+ | . . | 3 . | 2+2+ | 2+2+ |
| 39 | Kenuzi Nubians | 1 | . . | 3 3+ | . . | 3+3+ | . . | . . | 2 2 | 3 2+ | . . | 3 2+ |
| 40 | Teda | 1 | 4 4 | 4 4 | 4 4 | 4 4 | . . | . . | 3+3 | 4+. | 3 . | 3+3 |

## DEFINITION OF CODES

Table 1 identifies for each of 186 world areas the representative society selected by Murdock and White (1969). Codes are shown for all of them except four, omitted because of insufficient information about childhood (75 Khmer;

Table 1 Continued

| Area | Dutifulness — Indust. E (B G) | Indust. L (B G) | Respon. E (B G) | Respon. L (B G) | Obedien. E (B G) | Obedien. L (B G) | Submission — Self-Rstr. E (B G) | Self-Rstr. L (B G) | Sex Rstr. E (B G) | Sex Rstr. L (B G) | Sociability Ge | Tr | Ho |
|---|---|---|---|---|---|---|---|---|---|---|---|---|---|
| 1 | 2 2 | 3-3+ | 2 2 | 3+3 | 3 3 | 3 3 | . . | . . | 2 2 | 3-3- | . | 3+ | . |
| 2 | 2 2 | 3 3+ | 2-2- | 3-3+ | 2 2 | 3+3+ | 2+2+ | 3+3+ | 3+3+ | 3+3+ | 4 | 4+ | 5 |
| 3 | 2+3 | 3 3+ | 3-3- | 3 3 | 3+3+ | 3+3+ | 2 2 | 2 2 | . . | . . | 4 | 3 | 2 |
| 4 | 2 2+ | 3 3+ | . . | . . | . . | . . | 2+2+ | 2+2+ | 3-3- | 3-3- | 3 | 2 | . |
| 5 | 2 3- | 3+4- | 2+3 | 3+3+ | 3+3+ | 3+3+ | 3 3 | 3+3 | 3+3+ | 3+3+ | . | . | 3- |
| 6 | 2 3 | 2+3+ | 2 2 | 2 3 | 4 4 | 4 4 | . . | . . | . . | 3-3- | . | . | . |
| 7 | 2 2+ | 3 3+ | 2 2+ | 2 3+ | 2 2 | 2 2 | 2 2 | 3-3- | . . | . . | . | 3 | 2+ |
| 8 | 2 2 | 3 3 | 3 3 | 3+3 | 3 3 | 3 3 | 3 3 | 3 3 | 2+2+ | 2 3- | 3 | . | 3- |
| 9 | 2 2 | 2+. | 2 2 | 2+. | 1 3 | 1 3 | . . | . . | 2 2 | 2 2 | 3- | 2+ | . |
| 10 | 3-3- | 3-3- | 2+2+ | 2+2+ | . . | . . | . . | . . | 2 2 | 2 2 | 3+ | 3 | . |
| 11 | 3-3- | 4 4 | 3 3 | 3 3 | 3 3 | 4 4 | 3 3 | 3 3 | 2+3 | 3 4- | 3+ | . | 2 |
| 12 | 2 2+ | 3+4 | 2 2 | 3+3+ | 4 4 | 4 4 | 2 3 | 3 3 | 3-3- | 3-3- | 3+ | . | 2+ |
| 13 | 2+2+ | 3 3 | 2 2 | 2 2 | 3-3- | 3-3- | 2 2 | 2 2 | 2 2 | 2 2 | 5 | 5 | 4 |
| 14 | 2+3 | 3 3+ | 2+3 | 2+3+ | 2 2 | 2+2+ | 2+2 | 2+2 | 2 2 | 2 2 | 3- | 4- | . |
| 15 | 3 3 | 4 4+ | 2 2 | 3+3+ | 4 4 | 4 4 | 3 3 | 3 3 | 2-2- | 2+2+ | . | 2 | 3- |
| 16 | 2 2 | 4 4 | 2 2 | 4 4 | 4 4 | 4 4 | 2+2+ | 3+3+ | . . | . . | 4 | 3 | 4 |
| 17 | 2 2 | 3 2+ | 2 2+ | 2+3 | 2 3 | 2 3 | 2 2 | 2 2 | 2 2 | 2 3 | 4- | 3- | 2+ |
| 18 | 3 3+ | 3+4 | 2+2+ | 3+4- | 3+3+ | 3+3+ | . . | . . | 2 2 | 3-3 | 3+ | . | 2+ |
| 19 | 2 2 | 3 3 | 2+2+ | 3 3 | 3 3 | 4 4 | 3 3 | 3+3+ | 2 2+ | 3 3+ | 3 | 3+ | . |
| 20 | 2 3 | 3 4 | . 2+ | 2+4 | 4 4 | 4 4 | 3 3 | . 3 | 3 3 | 3 3 | . | . | . |
| 21 | 2 3 | 4 4 | 2 3 | 4 4 | 4+4+ | 4+4+ | 3 3 | 4 4 | 3 3 | 3 3+ | 4 | 3- | 3 |
| 22 | 2+2+ | 3 3+ | 3 3 | 3 3 | 3 3 | 3 3 | 3 3 | 3 3 | 2 2 | 3-3+ | . | 3 | 2+ |
| 23 | 2 2 | 3+3+ | 3-3- | 3+3+ | 3 3 | 4 4 | 2+2+ | 3 3 | 2 2 | 2+2+ | 4 | 3+ | 3+ |
| 24 | . 2+ | 3 3 | . . | . . | 3 3 | 3 3 | 3 3 | 3 3 | 2+2+ | 3 3+ | 3 | 3- | 2+ |
| 25 | 3 2 | 4 3+ | 3 2 | 4 3+ | 2+2+ | 3+3 | 2+2+ | 3+3+ | 1 1 | 3-3 | 3+ | . | . |
| 26 | 2 2 | 3 3 | 2 2 | 3 3 | 2 2 | 3 3 | 2 2 | 3-3- | 2 2 | 2+3- | 3+ | 4- | 2+ |
| 27 | 3+3+ | 3+3+ | 3+. | 3+. | . . | . . | . . | . . | 2 2 | 2 3- | . | 3+ | . |
| 28 | 2+2+ | 3+4 | . . | . . | 3 3 | 4 4 | . . | . . | 2 . | 2+3+ | . | . | . |
| 29 | 2+2+ | 3+3+ | 2+2+ | 3+3+ | 3 3+ | 3+4 | 2+3 | 2+3 | 2-2 | 2-2 | 2+ | 2 | 4 |
| 30 | 2 2 | 4+3 | 2 2 | 4+3 | 4 4 | 4 4 | . . | . . | 2+2+ | 3 3 | . | 4 | 3 |
| 31 | 2+2+ | 3+3+ | 3 3 | 4 4 | 2+2+ | 2+2+ | . . | . . | 2 2 | 2 2 | . | . | . |
| 32 | . . |  |  |  |  |  |  |  | 2+3- | 2+3+ | . | . | . |
| 33 | . . | 3+3+ | 2 2 | 3-3 | 3+3+ | 4-4- | . . | 2+3 | 2+3 | 3 5 | . | 2 | 2 |
| 34 | 4 3 | 3-4 | 4 4 | 3-3- | 3 3 | 3 3 | 4 3+ | 4 3+ | 2 2 | 2 2 | 4 | 3 | 2- |
| 35 | 3-3- | 4-4- | 3 3 | 3 3 | 3 3 | 4 . | 2 2 | 2 2 | 2+3 | 3 3+ | . | 3 | . |
| 36 | . . | 3 3 | . . | 3+3+ | 2 2 | 3 3 | . . | . . | 3 3+ | 3 4 | . | 3 | . |
| 37 | 1 1 | 3 3+ | 1 1 | 3 4- | . . | 3+3+ | . . | 3 . | 2 2 | 3+4- | . | . | . |
| 38 | . . | 2+2+ | 2 2 | 3 3 | 3 4 | 3 4 | 3+3+ | 3+3+ | 3 4 | 3 4 | . | 2 | . |
| 39 | 2 2 | 3-3+ | 2 2 | 3 3- | 3 3 | 4+4+ | 2+3 | 3 3+ | 2 4 | 3 5 | 3 | 2 | . |
| 40 | 3+3+ | 3+4 | 3+3+ | 4 4 | 3 3 | 3 3 | 2+2+ | 2+2+ | . . | 3 4 | 2 | 2 | 2+ |

88 Tobelorese; 101 Pentecost; 103 Ajie). The codes are applied to children between the approximate ages of four and twelve years. The starting point is the age when the child is walking and talking proficiently, or when the society considers the child past infancy. The end of this age span is defined by the onset

TABLE 1 Continued

| Area | Society | D | Fortit. E B G | Fortit. L B G | Aggress. E B G | Aggress. L B G | Compet. E B G | Compet. L B G | Self-Rel. E B G | Self-Rel. L B G | Achiev. E B G | Achiev. L B G |
|---|---|---|---|---|---|---|---|---|---|---|---|---|
| | | | | | Toughness | | | | Maturity | | | |
| 41 | Ahaggaren Tuareg | 1 | 3 3 | 3+3+ | 3 3 | 3+3+ | 2+2+ | 2+2+ | 3 3 | 3+3+ | 2+2+ | 2+3 |
| 42 | Riffians | 2 | 3 . | 3 . | 4+4+ | 4+4+ | 3 3 | 4 4 | 3 3 | 4 4 | 3+. | 3+. |
| 43 | Egyptians | 1 | 3+2+ | 3+2+ | 3 3- | 4-3 | 4+3+ | 4+3+ | 2 2 | 3 2+ | 2 2 | 3-3- |
| 44 | Hebrews | 1 | . . | . . | . . | . . | 4+4+ | 4+4+ | 2+3 | 3+3 | . . | . . |
| 45 | Babylonians | 3 | . . | . . | 3 . | 3 . | 3 . | 3 . | 2 2 | 2+2+ | 3-2 | 3+3- |
| 46 | Rwala Bedouin | 1 | 3 3 | 4+3 | 4+3 | 4+3 | 3 . | 3+. | 3+. | 3+. | 3+. | 3+. |
| 47 | Turks | 1 | 3 3 | 3 3 | . . | 3+3- | 2+2+ | 2+2+ | 2 2 | 3 2 | . . | 2+2+ |
| 48 | Gheg Albanians | 2 | 3+3 | 4+4- | 3+2+ | 4 2+ | . . | . . | 2+2+ | 3+3+ | . . | 3 3+ |
| 49 | Romans | 1 | 2+2+ | 3+3+ | 3 3- | 3+3- | 3+3+ | 3+3+ | 2 2 | 2 2 | 3+2+ | 4+3+ |
| 50 | Spanish Basques | 2 | . . | . . | 2 2- | 3 2 | 2+2+ | 2+2+ | 2 2 | 3 3 | 3 3 | 3+3+ |
| 51 | Irish | 3 | 2 2 | 3-3- | . . | 3 3 | . . | 3+3+ | 2 2 | 3 3 | 2 2 | 3+3+ |
| 52 | Kǒnkämä Lapps | 1 | 3 3 | 3+3 | 2+2+ | 3-3- | 3 3 | 3 3 | . . | 3+3+ | 3 3 | 3 3 |
| 53 | Yurak Samoyed | 3 | 3+3+ | 3+3+ | . . | . . | . . | . . | . . | . . | 3 3 | 4 4 |
| 54 | Russians | 1 | 3 3 | 3 3 | 2-2- | 2-2- | 2 2 | 2 2 | -3 3 | 3 3 | 3 3 | 4 4 |
| 55 | Abkhaz | 3 | 3 3 | 4-4- | 3 3 | 4 4 | 2+2+ | 3 3 | . . | . . | 3+3+ | 3+3+ |
| 56 | Armenians | 1 | . . | . . | . . | . . | . . | . . | . . | . . | . . | . . |
| 57 | Kurd | 1 | 3 3 | 3 3 | 3+3+ | 3+3+ | 3 3 | 3 3 | 3 3- | 4 3+ | 2 2+ | . 3+ |
| 58 | Basseri | 1 | . . | 3-. | 3+3+ | 3+3+ | . . | . . | 3+3+ | 4-4- | . . | . . |
| 59 | West Punjabi | 2 | . . | . . | 2+2+ | 2+2+ | 3+3+ | 3+3+ | 2 1 | 2+1 | 2+2+ | 2+2+ |
| 60 | Maria Gond | 3 | 3 3 | 3+3+ | . . | . . | . . | . . | . . | 4+4+ | 2+2+ | 3+3+ |
| 61 | Toda | 3 | . . | 3-. | 2-2- | 2-2- | . . | . . | . . | 3 . | 2+. | . . |
| 62 | Santal | 1 | 3 3 | 3+3+ | 3 3 | 3 3 | 3 3 | 3 3 | . . | 3 . | 2+. | 3 . |
| 63 | Uttar Pradesh | 1 | 3 3 | 3 3 | . . | . . | 3 3 | 3+3 | 2 2 | 3 2+ | 2 2 | 3 2+ |
| 64 | Burusho | 1 | 3 3 | 3 3 | 2 2 | 2+2+ | 2 2 | 2+2+ | 3+3+ | 4 4 | 3 3 | 3+3+ |
| 65 | Kazak | 3 | 3+3+ | 3+3+ | 3+3+ | 3+3+ | 3+3+ | 3+3+ | 3 3 | 3 3 | 3 3 | 3 3+ |
| 66 | Khalkha Mongols | 1 | 3 3 | 3 3 | 3 3 | 3 3 | 2 2 | 2 2 | 3 3 | 4 4 | 3 3 | 4-4- |
| 67 | Lolo | 1 | 3 3 | 3+3+ | 3 3 | 4-3 | 3 3 | 3 3 | . . | . . | . . | 3+3 |
| 68 | Lepcha | 3 | . . | . . | 2-2- | 2 2 | 1 1 | 1 1 | 2+2 | 3-2+ | 2+2+ | 2+2+ |
| 69 | Garo | 1 | 2 2 | 2 2 | . . | 3 3 | . . | 2+2+ | 3 2+ | 4 3 | . . | 2 2 |
| 70 | Lakher | 2 | . . | . . | 3 2 | 3 2 | 3-3- | 3-3- | 3 3 | 3 3 | 2 2 | 2 2 |
| 71 | Burmese | 2 | . . | 3+2+ | 2 2 | 3 3 | . . | 2+2 | 2-2- | 2 2 | . . | 2 2+ |
| 72 | Lamet | 3 | 2+2+ | 2+2+ | 2 2 | 2 2 | . . | . . | 2+2+ | 3+3+ | 3+3+ | 3+3+ |
| 73 | North Vietnamese | 2 | . . | . . | . . | . . | 2 2 | 2 2 | 3+3 | 3+3 | . . | 2+2+ |
| 74 | Rhade | 2 | . . | . . | . . | . . | . . | . . | 3-2 | 3-3- | . . | . . |
| 75 | Khmer | . | . . | . . | . . | . . | . . | . . | . . | . . | . . | . . |
| 76 | Siamese | 2 | . . | . . | 2-2- | 2-2- | . . | . . | 2 2 | 3 3 | 2+2+ | 3+3+ |
| 77 | Semang | 1 | 3-3- | 3-3- | 3+3+ | 3+3+ | 3 3 | 3 3 | 3 3 | 3 3 | 3 3 | 3 3 |
| 78 | Nicobarese | 3 | 3 3 | 3 3 | 2 2 | 2+2+ | 2 2 | 2 2 | 2+2+ | 3 3 | 3 3 | 3 3 |
| 79 | Andamanese | 3 | 3 3 | 4 4 | 3 . | 3 . | 3-3- | 3-3- | . . | . . | . . | . . |
| 80 | Forest Vedda | 1 | 3+3+ | 3+3+ | . . | . . | . . | . . | 2+2+ | 3+3+ | 2 . | 3-. |

of major physiological or status changes, usually associated with puberty at approximately the age of twelve years.

Duration of early childhood (D) specifies three different ages at which an important changes in treatment or status marks the transition from early to late

TABLE 1 Continued

| Area | Dutifulness | | | | Submission | | | | | | Sociability | | |
|---|---|---|---|---|---|---|---|---|---|---|---|---|---|
| | Indust. | | Respon. | | Obedien. | | Self-Rstr. | | Sex Rstr. | | Ge | Tr | Ho |
| | E | L | E | L | E | L | E | L | E | L | | | |
| | B G | B G | B G | B G | B G | B G | B G | B G | B G | B G | | | |
| 41 | 3-3- | 3+3+ | 3+3+ | 4 4 | 3 3 | 3 3 | 3-3- | 3-3- | 2 2 | 2+2+ | 3 | 3 | 3 |
| 42 | 3-. | 3+. | 3-. | 3+. | . . | . . | . . | . . | 3 3 | 3 4 | . | 3- | 2 |
| 43 | 3+3+ | 4 4 | 3 3 | 4 3+ | 3+3+ | 4+4+ | 2+2+ | 4-3+ | 2 2+ | 3+4 | . | 2 | 2 |
| 44 | 2+2+ | 3+3+ | 2 2 | 4 3 | 4+5 | 4+5 | 4 4+ | 4 4+ | 3 3 | . 5 | 4 | 2 | 3+ |
| 45 | 2 2 | 3 3 | . . | 3 3 | 3+3+ | 3+3+ | . . | . . | . . | . . | . | 2 | . |
| 46 | 2+2+ | 3+3+ | 2+2+ | 3+3+ | 4+4+ | 4+4+ | 3 3 | 3 3 | 3 3 | 3 4 | 4 | 3- | . |
| 47 | 2 . | 3 4 | 1 . | 3 3+ | 3+3+ | 3+3+ | . . | 3+3+ | 3 3 | 4 4+ | . | . | . |
| 48 | 3-3+ | 3+4 | 2 2 | 3 3 | 4+4+ | 4+4+ | 4 4 | 4 4 | 3-4- | 3+5 | . | 2 | 2+ |
| 49 | 3-3- | 4 4 | 3-3- | 3-3- | 3 3 | 3 3 | 2 2 | 3+3+ | 3 3 | 3 4 | . | 2 | 3 |
| 50 | 2 2 | 3+3+ | 3 3 | 3+3+ | 4 4 | 4 4 | 3+3+ | 4 4 | 3 3 | 3+3+ | 3 | 3+ | . |
| 51 | . . | 3 3+ | 2+2+ | 2+2+ | 3 3 | 4 4 | 3+3+ | 3+3+ | 3 3 | 3+4- | 4 | 3 | 3 |
| 52 | 2+3 | 3 3+ | 2 2 | 3 3+ | 3+3 | 3+3+ | 3+3+ | 3+3+. | 3 3 | 3 3 | . | 4- | 3 |
| 53 | 2+2+ | 2+3+ | . . | . . | . . | . . | . . | . . | . . | . . | 4 | . | . |
| 54 | 3 3 | 4 4 | 3 3 | 4 4 | 4 4 | 4 4 | 3 3 | 4 4 | 3+3+ | 3+3+ | . | 4 | 3+ |
| 55 | 2+3 | 3 3+ | 2 2 | 3 3 | 4 4+ | 4 4+ | . . | . . | . 3 | . 4+ | 3 | 2 | 2- |
| 56 | . . | . . | . . | . . | 3+3+ | 3+3+ | 3 3 | 3 3 | . . | . 4+ | 3+ | 3+ | . |
| 57 | 2+3- | 3+4- | 3-3- | . . | . . | . . | . . | . . | 3 3 | 3 4 | . | 3 | 2+ |
| 58 | 2+2+ | 3+3+ | 3+3+ | 4-4- | 3+3+ | 3+3+ | 2+2+ | 2+2+ | . . | . . | . | 3 | 2- |
| 59 | 2 2 | 3 3 | 2 2 | 2+3- | 4 4 | 4 4 | 2 2 | 3+2+ | 3-3- | 3+4+ | 4 | . | 3+ |
| 60 | 3-3- | 3+3+ | 2 2 | 3+3+ | 3-3- | 3-3- | 2+2+ | 2+2+ | 2 2 | 2 2 | 4 | 3+ | 3+ |
| 61 | 2+2+ | 2+2+ | 2+2+ | 2+2+ | . . | . . | . . | . . | . . | . . | . | . | . |
| 62 | 2 2+ | 3 3+ | 2 2+ | 3 3+ | 3 3 | 3 3 | . . | . . | 2+2+ | 3-3- | . | 3 | . |
| 63 | 2 2 | 3 3+ | 2 2 | 3-3- | 3+3+ | 3 3+ | 2+3 | 2+3 | 3 3+ | 3+4 | 2+ | 3 | 2+ |
| 64 | 3 3 | 3+3+ | 3+3+ | 4 4 | 3 3 | 3 3 | 3 3 | 3 3 | 2+2+ | 3-3- | 3+ | 4 | 3+ |
| 65 | 3 3 | 3 3 | 3 3 | 3 3 | 4 4 | 4 4 | . . | . . | 3 3 | 3 3 | . | . | 2+ |
| 66 | 3-3- | 4-4- | 3 3 | 4 4 | 3+3+ | 4+4+ | 3 3 | 3 3 | 3-3- | 3-3- | . | 3 | 3- |
| 67 | 2 2 | . . | . . | . . | 2 2 | 2 2 | . . | . . | 2+2+ | 2+2+ | . | 2 | . |
| 68 | 2 2+ | 3 3+ | 2 2+ | 3 3+ | 3 3 | 3 3 | 3 3 | 3 3 | 2-2- | 2 2 | 4 | 4 | 3+ |
| 69 | 2 2 | 3 3 | 2 2 | 3 3 | 4-4- | 3 3 | 3+3+ | 3-3 | 2 2 | 3-3- | 3+ | 4 | 3 |
| 70 | 2+2+ | 2+2+ | 2+2+ | 2+2+ | 2+2+ | 3 3 | 2 2 | 2 2 | 2 2 | 2 2 | 3- | 4- | 3+ |
| 71 | 2 2 | 2+2+ | 1 1 | 3-3- | 2 2 | 3 3 | 2-2- | 3-3- | 2 2 | 3-3- | . | 4- | . |
| 72 | 3-3- | 3+3+ | 2+2+ | 2+2+ | 4 . | 4 . | . . | . . | . . | . . | : | 3+ | . |
| 73 | 2+2+ | 3 3 | 2+2+ | 3 3 | 3 4 | 3 4 | 3 3 | 3 3 | 2+2 | 2+3+ | . | 4 | . |
| 74 | . . | 3+3 | . . | 3+3 | 3 3 | 3 3 | . . | . . | . . | 3 3 | . | . | . |
| 75 | . . | . . | . . | . . | . . | . . | . . | . . | . . | . . | . | . | . |
| 76 | 2+2+ | 3+3+ | 3 3 | 3+3+ | 3 3+ | 3 3+ | 3+3+ | 3+3+ | 2+2+ | 2+3+ | 4+ | 4 | . |
| 77 | 2 2 | . 3 | . . | . 3 | 2+2+ | 2+2+ | 2+2+ | 3+3+ | 2 2 | 3-3- | . | . | . |
| 78 | 2 2 | 3 3 | 2 . | 3 . | 3 3 | 3 3 | 3 3 | 3 3 | 2 2 | 2 2 | 3+ | 4 | 4- |
| 79 | 2 2 | 3 3 | 2 2 | 3 3 | . . | . . | . . | . . | 2 2 | 2 2 | 3+ | 3 | . |
| 80 | 2 2 | 3 3 | . . | . . | 2 2 | 3+3+ | . . | . . | 2-2 | 2-2 | . | . | . |

childhood: 1 = Short (ending at about 7 years of age); 2 = Medium (ending at about 9 years of age); and 3 = Long (ending at about 11 years of age or later).

The remaining codes designate the degree to which specified traits are inculcated, on a scale of 1 to 5. A code of 3 indicates moderately strong

TABLE 1 Continued

| Area | Society | D | Toughness Fortit. E (B G) | Fortit. L (B G) | Aggress. E (B G) | Aggress. L (B G) | Compet. E (B G) | Compet. L (B G) | Maturity Self-Rel. E (B G) | Self-Rel. L (B G) | Achiev. E (B G) | Achiev. L (B G) |
|---|---|---|---|---|---|---|---|---|---|---|---|---|
| 81 | Menabe Tanala | 1 | 3+3- | 3+3- | 3 3 | 3 3 | 3 3 | 3 3 | 2 2 | 3 3 | 2+2 | 3+2+ |
| 82 | Negri Sembilan | 3 | . . | . . | . . | . . | 3 3 | 3 3 | 3 3 | 4 3 | 3+3+ | 3+3+ |
| 83 | Javanese | 1 | 2 2 | 2 2 | 2-2 | 2-2 | 2 2 | 2+2+ | 1 1 | 3+3- | . . | 2 3 |
| 84 | Balinese | 2 | 3 3 | 3 3 | 2+2+ | 2+2+ | 2 2 | 2 2 | 4 4- | 4 4- | 3 3 | 3 3 |
| 85 | Iban | 3 | 3 3 | 3 3 | 3 3 | 3 3 | 3 3 | 3 3 | 3 3 | 3 3 | 3+3+ | 3+3+ |
| 86 | Tawi-Tawi Badjau | 1 | . . | . . | 2 2 | 2 2 | 1 1 | 1 1 | 2-2- | 2-2- | 2+2+ | 2+2+ |
| 87 | Toradja | 2 | 3 . | 4 4- | 3+2+ | 3+2+ | 3 3 | 3 3 | 3+3+ | 3+3+ | 2 2 | 2 3 |
| 88 | Tobelorese | . | . . | . . | | | | | | | | |
| 89 | Alorese | 1 | 2 2 | 3 2+ | 3 3 | 3-3- | 3-3- | 3-3- | 2 2 | 3+3 | 2 2+ | 2+3 |
| 90 | Tiwi | 2 | 3 3 | 3 3 | 3+3+ | 3+3+ | . . | . . | . 3+ | . 4 | 2 3 | 2 4 |
| 91 | Aranda | 3 | 2+. | 3+ | | | | | | | 2+2+ | 2+2+ |
| 92 | Orokaiva | 3 | 3 2 | 3+3 | 3+3 | 3+3 | 1 1 | 1 1 | 2 2 | 3 3 | 2-2- | 2-2- |
| 93 | Kimam | 3 | 2 2 | 4 4 | . . | 4 . | 2 2 | 4 3+ | 2 2 | 3 3 | 2 2 | 3 3 |
| 94 | Kapauku | 1 | 2 2 | 3 2+ | 2 2 | 4 2 | 2 2 | 4 3 | 3 3 | 4 4- | 3+3+ | 4+4+ |
| 95 | Kwoma | 1 | 2+2 | 3+3 | 2 . | 4+. | . . | 3 3 | 3 3 | 4 4 | 2 2 | 3 3 |
| 96 | Manus | 1 | 3 3 | 3 3 | 4-4- | 4-4- | 3 3 | 3 3 | 4+4 | 4+4 | 4 4 | 3 3+ |
| 97 | Lesu | 1 | | 2+. | 3-3- | 3-3- | 2 2 | 2 2 | 2 2 | 3 3 | 2 2 | 2 2 |
| 98 | Trobrianders | 1 | . . | . . | 3 3 | 3 3 | 3 3 | 3+3+ | 3 3 | 4 4 | 3 . | 3+. |
| 99 | Siuai | 1 | 3-3- | 3-3- | 3+3+ | 3+3+ | . . | 3 . | 2+2+ | 3 3 | . . | 3+3+ |
| 100 | Tikopia | 1 | 2 2 | 3+2 | 2 2 | 2 2 | . . | . . | 2+2+ | 3+3+ | . . | 3 3 |
| 101 | Bunlap | . | . . | . . | | | | | . . | . . | . . | . . |
| 102 | Mbau Fijians | 1 | 3 3 | 4-4- | 5 5 | 5 5 | 3+3+ | 4-4- | 3 3 | 4 4 | 3 3 | 4 4 |
| 103 | Ajie | . | . . | . . | | | | | . . | . . | | |
| 104 | Maori | 3 | 3+3 | 4 3 | 3 3 | 4+3+ | 4-3 | 4+3 | . . | . . | 3+3 | 4+4 |
| 105 | Marquesans | 3 | 3-3- | 4-4- | 3+3+ | 3+3+ | 3+3+ | 3+3+ | 3-3- | 5 5 | 3 3 | 4 4 |
| 106 | Samoans | 3 | . . | 3+3+ | 3 3 | 3 3 | 3 3 | 3 3 | 3-3- | 3+3 | . . | 3-3- |
| 107 | Makin Gilbertese | 2 | 3 2 | 4 3+ | 2 2 | 3 3 | 3-3- | 3-3- | 2 2 | 3 2 | 3 2 | 4 3 |
| 108 | Jaluit Marshallese | 1 | 3+3+ | 3+3+ | 3-3- | 3 3 | 3-3- | 3 3 | 3 2+ | 4 3+ | 3 3 | 4 4 |
| 109 | Trukese | 1 | 3 3 | 3 3 | . . | . . | . . | 3 3 | 3+3+ | 4+4+ | 2 2 | 3 3 |
| 110 | Yapese | 3 | 3+3+ | 3+3+ | 3 3 | 3 3 | 3 3 | 3 3 | 3-3- | 4 3+ | 2+2+ | 3 3 |
| 111 | Palauans | 1 | 3 3 | 3 3 | 2 2 | 2 2 | . . | 3 3 | 2+2+ | 3+3+ | 2 2 | 3 3 |
| 112 | Ifugao | 1 | 3+3+ | 3+3+ | 4 4 | 4 4 | 2 2 | 2 2 | 4-4- | 4-4- | 2 2 | 3-3+ |
| 113 | Atayal | 3 | 3 . | 3+3+ | . . | . . | | | . . | . . | 3+3+ | 3+3+ |
| 114 | Chekiang Chinese | 1 | 2+3 | 3 3+ | 3 3 | 3 3 | . . | . . | 2 2 | 2+2+ | 2 2 | 3 3 |
| 115 | Aigun Manchu | 1 | . . | . . | . . | . . | 3 . | 3 . | 2 2 | 2 2 | . . | 2+3 |
| 116 | Koreans | 1 | . . | . . | 2+. | 4 . | . . | 3+. | 2 2 | 3 3 | 2+2+ | 3+3+ |
| 117 | Japanese | 1 | . . | 3 3 | 2 2 | 3-2+ | . . | 2+2 | 2+2+ | 3+3+ | 2+2+ | 4 4 |
| 118 | Saru Ainu | 1 | 3-3- | 3+3+ | 2 2 | 2 2 | 3+3+ | 3+3+ | 3+3+ | 3+3+ | 4-3+ | 4-3+ |
| 119 | Gilyak | 3 | 3 3 | 4 4 | 3-3- | 3 3 | 2+2+ | 2+2+ | 3-3- | 3+3 | 3 3 | 4 4 |
| 120 | Yukaghir | 2 | . . | 3 3 | . . | 3 3 | . . | 3 3 | . . | . . | | |

inculcation, 5 indicates extremely strong inculcation, and 1 indicates no inculcation of the trait or strong inculcation of the opposite trait. More precise values were indicated by codes for levels above or below the middle of the category, for example 3+ for a code slightly above 3, and 3— for a code slightly below 3.

TABLE 1 Continued

| Area | Dutifulness | | | | Submission | | | | | | Sociability | | |
|---|---|---|---|---|---|---|---|---|---|---|---|---|---|
| | Indust. | | Respon. | | Obedien. | | Self-Rstr. | | Sex Rstr. | | Ge | Tr | Ho |
| | E B G | L B G | E B G | L B G | E B G | L B G | E B G | L B G | E B G | L B G | | | |
| 81 | 2 2 | 4 4 | 2 2 | 4 4 | 5 5 | 5 5 | 3 4 | 4 3 | 3 3 | 3 3+ | 3 | 2 | 3 |
| 82 | 2 3 | 2 4- | 1 3- | 2 3+ | 3-4+ | 3-4+ | 2 2 | 2+3 | 2 3 | 2 5 | 3 | 4 | . |
| 83 | . . | 3 3+ | . 2- | 2 3+ | 2 2 | 3+3+ | 2 2- | 4 3 | 2 2 | 3 3+ | . | . | 2 |
| 84 | 2 3 | 3 4 | 3 3 | 3+4 | 2+2+ | 3 3 | 2-2- | 3-3 | 2 2+ | 3 3+ | 4 | . | 3 |
| 85 | 2 2+ | 3 3+ | 3 3 | 3+3+ | 3-3- | 3-3- | 3 3 | 3 3 | 2 2 | 2+2+ | 3 | 4 | 4 |
| 86 | 3 3 | 3 3 | 3 3 | 3 3 | 2 2 | 2 2 | 3+3+ | 3+3+ | 2-2- | 2-2 | 4 | 4 | . |
| 87 | 2 2+ | 3 3+ | 2 2+ | 3 3+ | 2 2+ | 2 3 | 2 2+ | 2 3 | . . | 3-3- | . | 3- | 3 |
| 88 | . . | . . | . . | . . | . . | . . | . . | . . | . . | . . | . | . | . |
| 89 | 2 2+ | 3 3+ | 2-2+ | 3-3+ | 3-3- | 3-3- | 2-2- | 3-3- | 2 2 | 2+2+ | 2+ | . | . |
| 90 | 2 3+ | 2 4 | 1 3 | 1 4 | . 3- | . 3- | 2+2+ | 2+2+ | 3 3 | 3 3 | . | . | . |
| 91 | 2 2 | 2+2+ | . . | . . | 2-2- | 3+3+ | 2 2 | 3+. | . . | . . | . | . | . |
| 92 | 2+3 | 2+3 | 3-3+ | 3-3+ | 3 3 | 3+3+ | 2 2 | 2 2 | 3 3 | 3 3 | . | . | 3 |
| 93 | 2 2 | 3+3+ | . . | 3 3 | 2 2 | 4 4 | 2+2+ | 3+3- | . . | 2+2+ | . | . | 3- |
| 94 | 3-3- | 4 4 | 2+2+ | 4 4 | 2 2 | 2 2 | 2 2 | 3 3 | 2-2- | 3-3- | 2 | 2+ | 2 |
| 95 | 1 1 | 3 3+ | 1 1 | 3 3+ | 3-3- | 3+3+ | 2 2 | 3-3- | 3+3- | 4 3+ | . | 1 | 1 |
| 96 | 1 1 | 2+3 | 1 1 | 1 3- | 2-2- | 3 3 | 2 2 | 3 . | 3 3 | 4-4 | 4 | . | 4+ |
| 97 | 2 2+ | 3-3+ | 2 2+ | 3-3+ | 3+3+ | 3+3+ | . . | . . | 2 2 | 2+2+ | 3+ | 4 | . |
| 98 | 3 3 | 3+3+ | 2+2+ | 3 3 | 3-3 | 3-3- | 2+2+ | 3 3 | 2 2 | 2 2 | 3 | 4 | . |
| 99 | 2 2+ | 3 4- | 2 2+ | 3-3+ | 2+3 | 2+3 | 2 2 | 2 2 | 2 2+ | 2 2+ | 4 | 3+ | . |
| 100 | 2 2 | 3 3+ | 2+2+ | 3+3+ | 3+3+ | 3+3+ | 2 2 | 3 3 | 3-3- | 3-3- | . | 4+ | 3 |
| 101 | . . | . . | . . | . . | . . | . . | . . | . . | . . | . . | . | . | . |
| 102 | 2 2 | 2 2 | 2 2 | 2+2+ | 3-3- | 3-3- | . . | . . | 2+3 | 3 3+ | 3+ | 2- | 2 |
| 103 | . . | . . | . . | . . | . . | . . | . . | . . | . . | . . | . | . | . |
| 104 | 2 2 | 3 3 | 2 2 | 3-3 | 2 2 | 2 2 | . . | . . | 2 2 | 2 . | . | . | 2 |
| 105 | 2 2 | 2 2 | 2 2 | 3 3 | . . | . . | 2+2+ | 2+2+ | 2-2- | 2-2- | 4 | . | . |
| 106 | 3 3 | 3+3+ | 2+2+ | 3+3+ | 4 4 | 4 4 | . . | . . | 2 . | 2+. | 3+ | 3+ | 2+ |
| 107 | 3 2 | 4 3 | 3 2 | 4 3 | 3 2 | 4 3 | 2+2+ | 2+2+ | 2 2 | 3 4- | 4 | 4 | 2+ |
| 108 | 2-2 | 3-3 | 1 2 | 2 3 | 2-2- | 2-2+ | 2 2 | 2 2 | 2 2 | 2 2 | 4 | 4 | 3 |
| 109 | 2 2 | 3 3 | 2-2- | 3 3 | 2 2 | 3 3+ | 2-2- | 3+3 | 3-3- | 3+3+ | . | 2 | . |
| 110 | 2 2 | 2 2+ | 2 2 | 2+3- | 3-3- | 3-3- | 2+2+ | 2+2+ | 2 2 | 2 2 | . | 3 | 2 |
| 111 | 2 2+ | 3 3+ | 2 2+ | 3 3+ | 2 2 | 2 2 | 2 2+ | 2 2+ | 2 2+ | 2+3 | 2+ | 3- | . |
| 112 | 2 2 | 3 3- | 2 2 | 2+2+ | 2+2+ | 2+2+ | 2+2+ | 2+2+ | 2 2 | 2 2 | 2+ | . | 2- |
| 113 | . 3 | 3 3+ | . . | . . | 3+3+ | 3+3+ | . . | . . | 2 3 | 2 3 | 3 | 2+ | 3 |
| 114 | 3 3 | 4 4 | 2 2 | 3+3+ | 4 4 | 4 4 | 2 3 | 3 4+ | 2 3- | 3 4 | 3 | 3 | 3 |
| 115 | . . | 2+3 | 2-2- | 3-3 | 3 3 | 3 3 | 3-3- | 3-3- | 2 2 | 3-3- | . | 3+ | . |
| 116 | 2 2+ | 3 4 | 2 2+ | 3 3+ | . 4 | . 4 | 3-3- | 4 4 | 3+3+ | 3+4 | . | 3+ | 3- |
| 117 | 2-2- | 3 3 | 2 2 | 3+3+ | 3+4 | 3+4 | 2+3 | 3 4- | 2 2 | 3+4- | 3 | . | . |
| 118 | 3 3 | 4 4 | 2 2 | 3 3 | 4 4 | 4 4 | 3+3+ | 3+3+ | 3-3- | 3-3- | . | 3 | 3+ |
| 119 | 2+2+ | 3 3+ | 3 3 | 3+3+ | 3 3+ | 3 4- | . . | . . | 2 2 | 2+2+ | 4 | 4- | 4- |
| 120 | . . | . . | . . | . . | 4 4 | 4 4 | . . | . . | . . | 2 2 | . | 4 | 3+ |

This scale of 1-5 was applied to thirteen traits which have subsequently been arranged and designated on the basis of five categories: (1) Toughness (Fortitude, Aggression, Competitiveness); (2) Maturity (Self-Reliance, Achievement); (3) Dutifulness (Industry, Responsibility); (4) Submission (Obedience, Self-Restraint, Sexual Restraint); (5) Sociability (Generosity,

TABLE 1 Continued

| | | | Fortit. | | Toughness Aggress. | | Compet. | | Maturity Self-Rel. | | Achiev. | |
|---|---|---|---|---|---|---|---|---|---|---|---|---|
| Area | Society | D | E B G | L B G | E B G | L B G | E B G | L B G | E B G | L B G | E B G | L B G |
| 121 | Reindeer Chukchee | 2 | 3 3 | 4 4 | 2-2- | 3 3 | 2+2+ | 3+3+ | 3+3+ | 4+4+ | 3 3 | 3+3+ |
| 122 | Ingalik | 1 | 3 3 | 3 3 | 3+3+ | 3+3 | 3+3+ | 3+3+ | 2-2- | 3 3- | 3 3 | 3+3+ |
| 123 | Aleut | 1 | 4-3+ | 4-3+ | 2 2 | 2 2 | . . | . . | 2 2 | . . | 2 2 | 3+3+ |
| 124 | Copper Eskimo | 3 | 3+3+ | 3+3+ | 2 2 | 3 3 | 3 3 | 3 3 | 4 4- | 4+4- | 3 3 | 3+4- |
| 125 | Montagnais | 2 | . . | . . | 3 . | 3 . | . . | . . | . . | 4 . | 2+2+ | 3+3+ |
| 126 | Micmac | 3 | 4 4 | 4 4 | 3-. | 3-. | . . | . . | 4 3- | 4 3- | 4 . | 4 . |
| 127 | North Saulteaux | 2 | 3 . | 4-. | 3+. | 3+. | . . | 3+3+ | 2 2 | 4 3 | 2 2 | 3+3+ |
| 128 | Slave | 3 | 2 2 | 3 3 | 3+3+ | 4-4- | . . | 3 3 | 3+3+ | 4+4+ | 2 2 | 3 3 |
| 129 | Kaska | 2 | 3 3 | 3+3+ | 2 2- | 2 2- | . . | 2 2 | 4-4- | 4-4- | 2 2 | 2+2+ |
| 130 | Eyak | 3 | 3 3 | 4-4- | . . | 3 3 | . . | 3 3 | 2 2 | 3 3 | 3+3+ | 3+3+ |
| 131 | Masset Haida | 3 | 3+3+ | 4-4- | 3+3+ | 3+3+ | 3+3+ | 3+3+ | . . | . . | 2 2 | 3+3+ |
| 132 | Bellacoola | 3 | 3 3 | 4 4 | 3 3 | 4 4 | 3 3 | 3 3 | . . | . . | 3 3 | 3 3 |
| 133 | Twana | 2 | 4+4+ | 4+4+ | 3+3- | 3+3- | 3 3 | 3 3 | 3 3 | 4 3- | 3 3 | 4 3 |
| 134 | Yurok | 1 | 2 2- | 3 2+ | 2+2+ | 2+2+ | 2+2+ | 2+2+ | 2 2 | 4-3 | 2 2 | 3 3 |
| 135 | Eastern Pomo | 3 | 3 3 | 4 4 | 3+3+ | 3+3+ | 3 3 | 3 3 | 2 2 | 2 2 | 2 . | 2+. |
| 136 | Lake Yokuts | 2 | 3-3- | 4-4- | . . | . . | 3+3+ | 3+3+ | . . | 3 3 | 2 2 | 3+3+ |
| 137 | Wadadika Paiute | 1 | 2+2+ | 2+2+ | . . | . . | 3 3 | 3 3 | 2+2+ | 4 3 | 3+3+ | 3+3+ |
| 138 | Klamath | 1 | 3 3 | 4-4- | 2+2+ | 3 3 | 4-4- | 4 4 | 2 2 | 3 3 | 3 3 | 4 4 |
| 139 | Lower Kutenai | 1 | 3+3 | 4 3+ | 3 . | 3 . | 3+. | 3+. | 4+4 | 4+4 | 4+3+ | 4+3+ |
| 140 | Gros Ventre | 1 | 3+3 | 4+3+ | 4 3+ | 4 3+ | 3+3+ | 3+3+ | 4 3 | 4 2+ | 2+3+ | 3 4 |
| 141 | Hidatsa | 3 | 3+3 | 4+3 | 3 . | 3 . | 3+3+ | 4 4 | 2+2+ | 3+3+ | 2 2 | 3+3+ |
| 142 | Skidi Pawnee | 3 | 3 3 | 3+3 | 3+3 | 4 3 | 3 3 | 3 3 | 2+2+ | 3+2+ | 2 2 | 2 2 |
| 143 | Omaha | 2 | 3 3 | 4+3 | 3 3 | 3 3 | 3 2 | 3 2 | 3 2 | 4+3- | 3 3 | 3 3 |
| 144 | Huron | 1 | 4 . | 4 . | 4 4 | 4 4 | . . | . . | 3 2 | 4 3 | 2 2 | 2+3 |
| 145 | Upper Creek | 1 | 3+3 | 5 3+ | 3 3 | 4 4 | 3 3 | 4 4 | . . | . . | 3 3 | 4 4 |
| 146 | Natchez | 3 | 3+3+ | 3+3+ | 2 2 | 3-2+ | 2+2+ | 3+3+ | 2 2 | 2 2 | 2+2+ | 3 3 |
| 147 | Comanche | 3 | 3+3- | 4 3 | 3 2 | 3+3 | 3 3 | 4 4 | 3 3 | 4 3+ | 2+2 | 4 3 |
| 148 | Chiricahua Apache | 1 | 3 3- | 4+3 | 2+2 | 3+2+ | 3 2+ | 4-2+ | 3 3 | 3+3+ | 3 3- | 3+3 |
| 149 | Zuni | 2 | 3-2+ | 3-2+ | 2+2+ | 2+2+ | 2+2+ | 2+2+ | 2 2 | 3 3 | 2+2+ | 3+3 |
| 150 | Havasupai | 1 | 3 3 | 3 3 | 3 3- | 3 3- | 3 3 | 3 3 | 3 3- | 4 3 | 2 2 | 2+3 |
| 151 | Papago | 2 | 3 3 | 4 3+ | . . | . . | 3 3 | 3+3+ | 3 3 | 4 3+ | 3+3+ | 3+3+ |
| 152 | Huichol | 1 | 3-3- | 3-3- | 2 2 | 2 2 | . . | . . | 3 2 | 4 2 | 2 2 | 3 3 |
| 153 | Aztec | 1 | 4+4+ | 4+4+ | 3+2+ | 4 3+ | 3 3 | 3 3 | 2-2- | 2-2- | 3 3+ | 4 4+ |
| 154 | Sierra Popoluca | 1 | . . | . . | . . | . . | 1 1 | 1 1 | . . | . . | . . | . . |
| 155 | Quiche | 2 | 2+2+ | 3 3 | 2 2 | . . | 1 1 | 1 1 | 2+2+ | 3+4 | . . | 3 3+ |
| 156 | Miskito | 3 | 3 2 | 3 2 | 3+3+ | 3+3+ | . . | . . | 4 3 | 4 3 | 2 2 | 2 2 |
| 157 | Bribri Talamanca | 1 | . . | . . | 2+2+ | 2+2+ | 2+2+ | 2+2+ | 2 2 | 3+3+ | 3 3 | 3 3 |
| 158 | Cuna | 1 | . . | . . | 2 2 | . . | . . | . . | 3 3- | 4 3- | 2+2+ | 4 3+ |
| 159 | Goajiro | 1 | 3+3+ | 3+3+ | . . | . . | 3+3+ | 4 4 | 2 2+ | 3 3+ | 3 3 | 3 3 |
| 160 | Haitians | 1 | 3 3 | 3 3 | . . | 2+2+ | . . | . . | 4 4 | 4 4 | 3 3 | 3 3 |

Trust, Honesty). For the first four categories (ten traits), separate codes differentiate between two stages of childhood, early (E) and late (L). Within both stages, separate codes differentiate between boys (B) and girls (G). The last category (three traits) has a single code for both stages and sexes because these were differentiated for very few of the societies.

TABLE 1 Continued

| Area | Dutifulness Indust. E (B G) | Indust. L (B G) | Respon. E (B G) | Respon. L (B G) | Obedien. E (B G) | Obedien. L (B G) | Submission Self-Rstr. E (B G) | Self-Rstr. L (B G) | Sex Rstr. E (B G) | Sex Rstr. L (B G) | Sociability Ge | Tr | Ho |
|---|---|---|---|---|---|---|---|---|---|---|---|---|---|
| 121 | 3 3 | 4 4 | 3 3 | 4 4 | 3 3 | 3+3+ | 2+2+ | 2+2+ | 2 2 | 2 2 | 4 | 3+ | 3- |
| 122 | 2 2+ | 3-3 | 2 2 | 2+3 | 3-3- | 3-3- | 2 2 | 3 3 | 3 3 | 3 3 | 3+ | 4- | 3+ |
| 123 | 2-2 | 2+3- | 2-2 | 2+3- | 3+3+ | 3+3+ | 3+3+ | 3+3+ | 2+2+ | 2+3 | 3+ | 3+ | 3+ |
| 124 | 2 2 | 3 3 | 2 2 | 3 3+ | 2+2+ | 2+2+ | 2+2+ | 2+2+ | 2-2- | 2-2- | 3+ | 4- | 3- |
| 125 | 2 2+ | 3 3+ | 2+2+ | 3+3+ | 3 3 | 3 3 | . . | . . | 3 3 | 3 3 | . | . | 3- |
| 126 | 3-3+ | 3-3+ | . . | . . | 3 3 | 3 3 | 3 3 | 3 3 | 4 4 | 4 4 | . | . | . |
| 127 | 2 2 | 2+3+ | 2 2 | 3+3 | 3-3 | 2+3 | . . | . . | . . | 2 2+ | 3 | 3- | . |
| 128 | 2 2 | 3 3 | 2+2+ | 3+3+ | 2+2+ | 2+2+ | 2 2 | 3 3 | . . | 2 2+ | . | 4 | 2+ |
| 129 | 2-2- | 3 3+ | 2 2 | 3 3+ | 3-3- | 3-3- | 4 4 | 4 4 | 3+3+ | 3-3- | . | 3- | . |
| 130 | . . | 3-3- | . . | . . | . . | . 4+ | 3+3+ | 3+3+ | . . | . . | . | . | . |
| 131 | 3+3+ | 3+3+ | 2 2 | 3 3 | 3 3 | 3 3 | 3 3 | 3 3 | 2 2 | 2 2 | 3+ | 3+ | 3 |
| 132 | 2 2 | 3 3 | 2 2 | 2+2+ | 3 3 | 3 3 | 2 2 | 3-3- | 2 2 | 2+2+ | 3 | 3 | . |
| 133 | 2 2 | 4 3 | . . | . . | 4 4 | 4 4 | 3+3+ | 4+4+ | 3 3 | 3 4- | 4+ | 3- | . |
| 134 | 2 2 | 2+2+ | 2 2 | 2+2+ | . . | . . | 2+3- | . . | 2+2+ | 2+. | 3 | 3- | 3 |
| 135 | 2 2 | 2 2 | 2 2 | 2 2 | 3+3+ | 3+3+ | 3-3- | 3-3- | 3-3- | 3-3- | 3 | 2- | 3 |
| 136 | 2 2 | 3 3 | 2 2 | 3 3 | 4 4 | 4 4 | . . | . . | 3 3 | 3 3 | 4 | 3- | 4 |
| 137 | 2 2 | 3 3 | 2 2 | 3 3 | 3+3+ | 3+3+ | 4 4 | 4 4 | 3 3+ | 3 3+ | 3 | 2+ | 3 |
| 138 | 2 2 | 3 4 | 2 2 | 3 4 | 3+3+ | 3+3+ | 3 3- | 4-3 | 2+2+ | . 3+ | . | 3 | . |
| 139 | 3 3 | 3+4+ | 3+3 | 4 4 | 3+3+ | 3+3+ | 4 4 | 4 4 | 3 3+ | 3 3+ | . | 4 | 3+ |
| 140 | 2 3 | 3 4 | . 3 | 3-4 | 3 4 | 3 4 | 2+2+ | 3+3+ | 2+3+ | 3 4 | 4+ | 4 | 4- |
| 141 | 2 3- | 3 3+ | 2 2 | 3 3 | 3 3 | 3 3 | 3 3- | 4 3 | 2 2 | 2+3- | 4 | 4 | 3 |
| 142 | 2-2- | 3-3- | . . | 3-3- | 3 3 | 3 3 | 3 3 | 3 3 | 2 2 | 2+3 | 3 | . | 3 |
| 143 | 2 3 | 4-4 | 2 3 | 4-4 | 4 4 | 4 4 | 3-3 | 4 4 | 3-3+ | 3+4 | 3+ | 4 | 4 |
| 144 | 2-2 | 2 3 | 2-2 | 2 3 | 2 2 | 2 2 | 2 2 | 2 2 | 2 2 | 2 2 | . | 3- | 2 |
| 145 | 2 2 | 3 3+ | . . | . . | . . | 4 . | 3+3+ | 3+3+ | . . | 2+3- | 3+ | 3 | 3+ |
| 146 | 2 2+ | 3-3+ | 2 2 | 2+2+ | 4 4 | 4 4 | 3 3 | 3 3 | 2 2 | 2 2 | . | 3 | . |
| 147 | 2-2 | 3-3+ | 2-2 | 2 3+ | 2 2 | 3 3 | 2+2+ | 3+3+ | 2-2 | 3 2+ | 3+ | 3 | 2 |
| 148 | 3 3+ | 3+4 | 3 3 | 3+3+ | 3 3+ | 4 4+ | 2+2+ | 4 3 | 3-3 | 4 4+ | 4- | 4- | 3 |
| 149 | 2 2 | 3 3 | 2 2 | 3+3 | 3 3 | 3 3 | 2+2+ | 2+2+ | 2 2 | 3-3 | 3- | 2 | 3- |
| 150 | 3-3 | 3 3+ | 2 2+ | 3 3+ | 3 3 | 3 3 | 3 3 | 3 3 | 2-2- | 2+3- | 3+ | 4+ | 3- |
| 151 | 2+3 | 3+4 | 2 2+ | 3+3+ | 2+2+ | 3+3+ | 2+2+ | 4 4 | 3-3 | 3-3+ | 3+ | . | 4- |
| 152 | 2 2 | 2+2+ | 2 2 | 3-3- | 3 3+ | 3 3+ | 2+2+ | 2+2+ | 2 2 | 2+2+ | 3+ | 2 | 3 |
| 153 | 3+3+ | 4+4+ | 3+3+ | 4 4 | 5 5 | 5 5 | 4 4 | 4 4 | 3 4 | 3 5 | 3 | . | 4 |
| 154 | 2+2+ | 3+3+ | . . | . . | . . | . . | . . | . . | 2+3 | 2+3. | . | 3 | . |
| 155 | 2 2 | 3-4- | 2 2 | 3 4 | 3+3+ | 4+4+ | 3 3 | 3 3 | 3 3 | 3 3 | 2 | 2- | . |
| 156 | 3 3+ | 3 3+ | 2+3+ | 2+3+ | 3-3 | 3-3 | . . | . . | 3 3+ | 3 3+ | . | 2+ | 3- |
| 157 | 2 2 | 3 3 | 2+2+ | 3+3+ | . . | . . | . . | . . | 2 3 | 2 3 | 3 | 3 | . |
| 158 | 2+. | 3+3 | . . | 3+3+ | 3 3 | 3 3 | . . | . . | 3 3+ | 4-4 | 3+ | 3+ | . |
| 159 | 3 3 | 4 4 | 3 3 | 4 4 | . . | . . | . . | . . | 2+3 | 3-3 | . | . | . |
| 160 | 3 3 | 3+4 | 3 3 | 3+4 | 4 4 | 4 4 | 2+2+ | 2+2+ | 2 2+ | 2 2+ | . | 3 | . |

The inculcated traits were coded, if possible, on the basis of reports of the pressures exerted by the people who train the child. The codes were also based on the behavior of the child and were inferred only with great caution from reports of the customary adult behavior or of adult ideology.

For all the codes in Table 1, a dot designates insufficient information for a

TABLE 1 Continued

| Area | Society | D | Fortit. E B G | Fortit. L B G | Aggress. E B G | Aggress. L B G | Compet. E B G | Compet. L B G | Self-Rel. E B G | Self-Rel. L B G | Achiev. E B G | Achiev. L B G |
|---|---|---|---|---|---|---|---|---|---|---|---|---|
| | | | Toughness | | | | | | Maturity | | | |
| 161 | Callinago | 1 | 3 3 | 4-4- | . . | 3+3+ | . . | 3+3+ | 3 3 | 3+3+ | 3 3 | 3 3 |
| 162 | Warrau | 1 | 2 2 | 2 2 | 3+. | 3+. | 2+. | 2+. | 2+2 | 4 2 | 2 2 | 2 3 |
| 163 | Yanomamo | 3 | . . | . . | 4+. | 4+. | . . | . . | 2 2 | 3+3+ | 2 2 | 3 3 |
| 164 | Barama Carib | 3 | 3 3 | 3 3 | 3-3- | 3-3- | 2 2 | 3-3- | 2 2 | 4 3 | . . | 2+2+ |
| 165 | Saramacca | 1 | 3 3 | 3 3 | . . | . . | . . | . . | 3 3- | 4+3 | 4 4- | 4 4- |
| 166 | Mundurucu | 2 | 3 3 | 3+3+ | . . | . . | 2 2 | 2 2 | 4 3 | 4 3 | 3 3 | 4 4 |
| 167 | Cubeo | 1 | 2 2 | 3+3 | 2 2 | 3 3 | . . | . . | 2+2 | 3+3- | 2-2 | 3-3+ |
| 168 | Cayapa | 1 | 3 3 | 3+3+ | 3-3- | 3-3- | . . | . . | 2-2- | 3 3 | 3 3 | 4 4 |
| 169 | Jivaro | 1 | . . | 4 3+ | . . | 4+. | . . | . . | 3 2 | 4 3 | 3+3+ | 3+3+ |
| 170 | Amahuaca | 2 | 3+3 | 3+3 | 2+2+ | 2+2+ | 3 3 | 3 3 | 3 3 | 4 4 | 3 . | 3 . |
| 171 | Inca | 3 | 4-3+ | 4-3+ | . . | . . | . . | . . | 2-2- | 2-2- | 3-3- | . . |
| 172 | Aymara | 1 | 3-3- | 3-3- | 3 3 | 3+4- | 3+3+ | 3+3+ | 3-3- | 3-3- | 2 2 | 2 2 |
| 173 | Siriono | 2 | 2+2+ | 3+3+ | 3 3 | 4-4- | . . | 2+2+ | 3 3 | 4 4 | 3 3 | 3 3 |
| 174 | Nambicuara | 3 | 3 3 | 3 3 | 3+4- | 3+4- | 3-3- | 3-3- | 2+3 | 2+3 | 2 2+ | 2 2+ |
| 175 | Trumai | 1 | 2 . | 3+. | 2+2+ | 2+2+ | 2+2+ | 2+2+ | 2+2+ | 3+3+ | 2 2 | 3 3 |
| 176 | Ramcocamecra Timbira | 1 | 3 3 | 4 3 | 3 3 | 3 3 | 3 3 | 3 3 | 4 3 | 4 3+ | 3 4 | 4 4 |
| 177 | Tupinamba | 2 | 4 4 | 4 4 | . . | . . | . . | . . | 2 . | 3 . | 2 2 | 3 3 |
| 178 | Botocudo | 1 | . . | . . | . . | . . | . . | . . | 2 2 | 3+3+ | 2-2- | 3 2- |
| 179 | Shavante | 1 | 4 . | 4 . | 4 . | 4 . | 2 2 | 2 2 | 4 3 | 4 3 | . . | . . |
| 180 | Aweikoma | 1 | 3-3- | 3-3- | 3+3+ | 3+3+ | . . | . . | . . | . . | . . | . . |
| 181 | Cayua | 2 | 2+2+ | 3 3 | . . | . . | . . | 3-3- | 3 3 | 2 2 | 2 2 | 3-3- |
| 182 | Lengua | 3 | 3+3 | . 3 | 3+3 | . 3 | 3-3- | 3-3- | 3+3+ | 3+3+ | 3 3 | 3 3 |
| 183 | Abipon | 1 | 3 3 | 4 4 | 3 3 | 4 4 | 2+2+ | 3+2+ | . . | . . | 3 2 | 4 3 |
| 184 | Mapuche Araucanians | 1 | 2 2 | 3 3 | 3+2 | 3+2 | 2 2 | 3+3+ | 2 2 | 3+3+ | 3 3 | 4 4 |
| 185 | Tehuelche | 2 | 2+2+ | 2+2+ | . . | 3 3 | . . | . . | 3 3 | 4 4 | 2+2 | 3+3 |
| 186 | Yahgan | 1 | 3 3 | 3 3 | 3-3- | 3-3- | 3+3+ | 3+3+ | 3+3+ | 4 4 | 3+3+ | 4 4 |

rating. This symbol is used for cases in which the rating was designated as inferential or based on a single instance, or the information was contradictory, such as a discrepancy between "word and deed," and the few cases in which the two stages of childhood or the two sexes were differentiated for the three measures of Sociability (Generosity, Trust, Honesty). Therefore, the numerical codes are limited to ratings which were made with a high degree of confidence and without qualifications.

The coders used the following definitions of the thirteen traits. The sequence in which they were listed on the rating sheet differed only slightly from the present sequence, grouped into the five categories.

## Toughness

This category includes three traits: Fortitude, Aggressiveness, and Competitiveness.

Fortitude (Fortit.) or Fearlessness. This measures suppressions of visible reaction to pain, exertion, frightening situations, discomfort, e.g., the hardening

TABLE 1 Continued

| Area | Dutifulness | | | | Submission | | | | | | Sociability | | |
|---|---|---|---|---|---|---|---|---|---|---|---|---|---|
| | Indust. | | Respon. | | Obedien. | | Self-Rstr. | | Sex Rstr. | | Ge | Tr | Ho |
| | E B G | L B G | E B G | L B G | E B G | L B G | E B G | L B G | E B G | L B G | | | |
| 161 | 2+2+ | 2+2+ | 2 2 | 3 3 | 2 2 | 2 2 | 2 2 | 2 2 | . . | . . | 3+ | 3 | 3 |
| 162 | . . | 2+3 | . . | . 3 | 2 3 | 2 3 | 2 2 | 2 2 | 2 2 | 2 2 | . | 4 | 2 |
| 163 | 2-3 | 2-4 | 1 3 | 1 4 | 2 3+ | 2 3+ | 2 3 | 2 3 | . . | . . | . | 3 | 2 |
| 164 | 2 2 | 3 3+ | . . | 2 3 | 3+3+ | 3+3+ | 2 2 | 2 2 | 2-2- | 2 2 | 3+ | 3- | 3 |
| 165 | 3-3+ | 4 4 | 2 2 | 3 3 | 3 3 | 3 3 | . . | . . | 2 2 | 2 3 | . | 2 | . |
| 166 | 2+3 | . 4 | 2 3 | 3 4 | 3 3 | 3 3 | . . | . . | 3-3- | 3-3- | . | 3 | . |
| 167 | 2 2 | 3-4- | 1 2- | 2 3+ | 2 2 | 3 3+ | 2-2- | 2-2- | 2-2- | 3 2+ | . | 4- | 3 |
| 168 | 3 3 | 4 4 | 2+3 | 3+4 | 3+3+ | 3+3+ | 2 2 | 3 3+ | 2+2+ | 3+3+ | 3+ | 4 | . |
| 169 | 2 2+ | 3 3+ | 2 2 | 3 3 | 3+3+ | 3+3+ | . . | . . | . . | 3 3 | . | 2- | . |
| 170 | 2 3 | 3 4 | 2 3 | 3 4 | 2 2 | 2 2 | 2 2 | 2 2 | 2 2 | 2 2 | . | 3- | . |
| 171 | 3+3+ | 4+4+ | . . | . . | 5 5 | 5 5 | . . | . . | 2 2 | 2 2 | . | 3 | . |
| 172 | 3 3 | 4 4 | 3 3 | 3+4 | 4-4- | 4-4- | 3 3 | 3 3 | 2-2- | 2-2- | 2- | 2- | 2- |
| 173 | 2 2 | 3-3- | 2 2 | 3 3 | 2 2 | 3 3 | 2 2 | 3 3 | 2+2+ | 2+2+ | 2 | 4- | . |
| 174 | 2-2 | 2 2+ | 2 2 | 2 2 | 2+2+ | 2+2+ | 2 . | 2 . | 2 2 | 2 2 | 2+ | 3 | . |
| 175 | 2 2 | 3 3 | 2 2 | 3 3 | 3 3 | 3 3 | 2-2- | 3+3+ | 2 2 | 2 2 | . | 3+ | 2 |
| 176 | 2+3 | 3+4 | 2+3 | 3+4 | 3 3 | 3 3 | 3 3 | 4 3 | 2+2+ | . . | 3+ | 4 | 4- |
| 177 | . . | 3+3+ | . . | 4 . | 3+3+ | 3+3+ | 4 4 | 4 4 | . . | 2 2 | 4+ | . | 4 |
| 178 | . . | . . | 2 2 | 3+3+ | . . | . . | . . | . . | 2 2 | 2 2 | . | . | 3- |
| 179 | 1 3 | 3 3+ | 1 3 | 2+3 | 1 2+ | 2+2+ | 2+2+ | 3+3+ | . . | 4 3+ | 4 | 3 | . |
| 180 | 2 2 | 2 2 | . . | . . | . . | . . | 2 2 | 2 2 | 2-2- | 2-2- | 3 | 2- | 2 |
| 181 | 2 2 | 3 3+ | 2 2 | 2 3 | . . | . . | 2 2 | 3-3- | 2 . | 2+. | 3+ | . | 2 |
| 182 | 2 2 | 3 3 | 2 2+ | 2 2+ | . . | . . | . . | . . | 2 2 | 2 2 | 3+ | 3+ | 3 |
| 183 | 2 2+ | 3 3+ | 2 2+ | 3 3+ | 3-3- | 3-3- | 2 2+ | 2 2+ | 3 4 | 3 4 | . | . | . |
| 184 | 2+2+ | 3+4 | 2 2 | 3+3+ | 4 4 | 4 4 | 2+2+ | 3+3+ | 3-3- | 3-3- | 4 | . | 3+ |
| 185 | 2-2 | 2 3- | 2-2 | 2 3- | 2 2 | 2 2 | 2 2 | 2 2 | 2 2 | . 3+ | . | 3 | 2 |
| 186 | 2+3+ | 3+4 | 2+3 | 3 3+ | 3+3+ | 3+3+ | 3+3+ | 4 4 | 3+3+ | 4 4 | 4 | 4 | 3 |

of boys who are forced to display their stoicism while being plunged into cold water.

5 = Consistent hardening by adults or age-mates and selves with show of courage or stoicism; or punishments (severe) for lack of courage or stoicism.

4 = Child is expected to bear pain without showing any signs.

3 = Child is expected to bear pain but parents or others numb or cushion the pain, are tolerant of expressions of pain. If it is clearly stated that courage is not highly valued of its own accord, rating should not be over 3.

2 = Pain or hardship is present but child is protected from experiencing much of it.

Aggressiveness (Aggress.). This is aggressive behavior toward people (including peers) or animals, which may be implicitly inculcated or condoned by adults, e.g., parental urging to stand up for oneself or retaliate against aggression. Exhortations or frequent retelling of heroic myths may also instill aggressiveness; overt and covert inculcation are both included.

Competitiveness (Compet.). This refers specifically to achievement of superiority over other people, especially peers, e.g., competitive sports or superiority in a craft. The mere existence of competitive games denotes some competitiveness but not a high degree unless there is a very strong value on winning the game.

5 = Competitiveness seems an outstanding feature of the society (constant inculcation, comparison of children by parents).

4 = Strong competition, definitely inculcated.

3 = Moderate, there are competitive games and other signs of inculcation.

2 = Some competitiveness, e.g., competitive games but without special emphasis.

### Maturity

This category includes two traits: Self-Reliance and Achievement.

Self-Reliance (Self-Rel.) or Initiative. This measure is based on encouragement of the child to act without supervision, e.g., children playing by themselves while their parents are away on economic pursuits, or children performing tasks such as food gathering or hunting by themselves.

Achievement (Achiev.). This is the pleasure in or demand for acquisition of skills or a demand for excellence in those skills, e.g., the weaving of baskets or hunting at an early age. Early performance generally indicates a high degree of this trait as does general admiration of work well done or strong emphasis on teaching of skills. Industry does not necessarily denote high achievement.

4 = General admiration of work well done or strong emphasis on teaching of skills.

3 or 4 = Very high emphasis on games of skill.

### Dutifulness

This category includes two traits: Industry and Responsibility.

Industry (Indust.) or Diligence. This is based on the demand that the child keep busy on activities which involve responsibility or obedience. The best indication of high industry is that the child has very little spare time for pleasure or idleness, idle time being disapproved. An ideology in the adult culture opposing laziness or idleness is pertinent although inferential if not specifically applied to children, e.g., demands that boys fish or hunt daily, that a girl weave baskets in her spare time, or that children perform their schoolwork diligently.

5 = A great deal of work is expected of children, with very little or no leisure.

4 = Many duties, but occasional leisure.

3 = Regular duties but children have free time, adults accept the notion of playtime for children.

Responsibility (Respon.). The main emphasis for this trait is on regular performance of duties or economic activities without continual supervision. If these are usually performed on command, they are examples of obedience. Typical examples of responsibility are older siblings' care of younger children, schoolwork, or any other expected activity done independently (spontaneously). Other instances are observance of taboos or ritual performances, but not etiquette or general deferential behavior.

### Submission

This category includes three traits: Obedience, Self-Restraint, and Sexual Restraint.

Obedience (Obedien.). This is primarily a measure of the degree to which children are expected to obey specific requests by the parents and others in authority. In addition to consistency of obeying, promptness of obeying should be taken into account, e.g., unquestioning response to maternal uncle's demand for assistance. Some degree of obedience is necessarily encouraged in all societies, so that a high score should be given only if there is an unusual insistence on this trait.

Self-Restraint (Self-Rstr.). The principal criterion is information on the discouragement of children's open expression of emotions, including crying, anger, or effusiveness. Stoicism is more related to fortitude, while suppression of dependency is more related to self-reliance.

Sexual Restraint (Sex Rstr.). This is a measure of taboo or restrictions on heterosexual play, masturbation, or other erotic behavior in children. A high degree of modesty, such as the requirement to keep the genitals constantly covered in public, indicates moderately high restraint in the absence of encouragment or permission of sexual play. A rating of high restraint requires both prohibition and evidence that the prohibition is generally effective.

## Sociability

This category includes three traits: Generosity, Trust, and Honesty.

Generosity (Ge). This refers to the specific behavior encouraged rather than a general attitude, but a wide range of actions may exemplify generosity. These include giving and sharing of food, possessions, time, or services to others of the community or outsiders, e.g., sharing the product of a hunt among the community members whether or not they were active in its attainment, or sharing and giving of treats or toys. Expressions of kindness and affection are included, especially toward younger children or aged, ill, or infirm people. Reciprocity is not necessarily generosity.

Trust (Tr) or Mutual confidence. This refers to confidence in social relationships, especially toward community members outside the family, e.g., children are welcome in any home in the village, possessions are left unguarded. Sorcery and witchcraft generally indicate a low rating of trust. The code is omitted where in-group and out-group differ widely.

Honesty (Ho). This refers to desire and strong approval for truthfulness under all circumstances. Stealing or other criminal or anti-social behavior by children indicate low honesty. It is possible to have high emphasis on honesty toward one's own social group along with approval for lying, cheating, and stealing against an out-group. It takes into account societies where the concept of honesty differs from ours, e.g., lying is considered "smart," but stealing is dishonest.

## PROCEDURES FOR CODING AND DATA ANALYSIS

The ratings were made from ethnographic sources as listed by Barry and Paxson (1971), with substitutions or additions specified in the Supplementary Bibliography of the present article. A rating sheet was usually filled out for each source containing substantial information in order to enhance the accuracy and completeness of the rating sheet based on the total material.

For each inculcated trait, the early and late stages of childhood were entered for boys, followed by the corresponding ratings for girls. Table 1 shows boys and girls at the early stage, followed by boys and girls at the late stage, because of the subsequent observation (Table 2) that differences between the two stages were generally greater than between the two sexes. These ratings on traits were also preceded by several measures of the social environment (Residence, Agents of Socialization, Type of Education) and followed by measures of socialization techniques (Reward and Punishment), children's tasks, and parental and societal attitudes. These further codes will be reported in a subsequent article and are mentioned here because of their possible influence on the type of information sought by the raters.

The ratings in Table 1 were made by one of the authors (L. J., E. L., or C. M.) on 85 societies and independently by two of these authors on 96 societies. All three made ratings on one society. After the independent codes had been completed on the same society, the raters prepared a new set of "consensus" ratings based on comparison and discussion of their separate ratings.

In order to include the plus and minus qualifications in the analyses and summaries of the data on inculcated traits, the original codes (1, 2−, 2, 2+, 3−, 3, 3+, 4−, 4, 4+, 5) were converted into a corresponding ordinal scale of numbers (0, 1, 2, 3, 4, 5, 6, 7, 8, 9, 10). Thus in the converted scale, 5 is median, 10 is highest, and 0 is lowest. In the original codes, there were no ratings of 1−, 1+, or 5+, and the single instance of 5− (Fortitude in late childhood for boys in society 34) was assigned a score of 10 in the converted scale.

The data shown in Tables 2-10 are based on this converted scale of eleven numerical categories. The large number of categories is especially advantageous

TABLE 2

Ratings of Ten Traits

| | | Number Rated | | | | Mean Rating | | | |
|---|---|---|---|---|---|---|---|---|---|
| | | E | | L | | E | | L | |
| | | B | G | B | G | B | G | B | G |
| (1) | TOUGHNESS | | | | | | | | |
| | Fortit. | 140 | 131 | 155 | 145 | 4.7 | 4.4 | 6.0 | 5.5 |
| | Aggress. | 133 | 118 | 148 | 128 | 4.5 | 4.0 | 5.5 | 4.7 |
| | Compet. | 111 | 106 | 135 | 126 | 4.1 | 4.0 | 4.7 | 4.5 |
| (2) | MATURITY | | | | | | | | |
| | Self-Rel. | 155 | 153 | 160 | 153 | 4.0 | 3.5 | 6.2 | 5.2 |
| | Achiev. | 146 | 136 | 162 | 153 | 3.8 | 3.6 | 5.3 | 5.3 |
| (3) | DUTIFULNESS | | | | | | | | |
| | Indust. | 166 | 165 | 175 | 175 | 2.8 | 3.3 | 5.2 | 6.0 |
| | Respon. | 151 | 150 | 161 | 158 | 2.7 | 3.1 | 4.9 | 5.6 |
| (4) | SUBMISSION | | | | | | | | |
| | Obedien. | 160 | 161 | 162 | 162 | 4.9 | 5.2 | 5.6 | 5.9 |
| | Self-Rstr. | 134 | 133 | 135 | 132 | 3.7 | 3.8 | 4.9 | 4.9 |
| | Sex Rstr. | 156 | 154 | 164 | 165 | 3.0 | 3.4 | 3.8 | 4.8 |

Number of societies rated, among the total of 182, and mean rating on a scale of 0 - 10, for the first 10 inculcated traits listed in Table 1, comparing the early (E) with the late (L) stage of childhood and in both stages comparing boys (B) with girls (G).

because in the original scale the extreme categories (1 and 5) were seldom used. The increased precision introduced by the plus and minus qualifications in many instances is necessary for detecting small differences between boys and girls or between the early and late stages for the same trait in a society. Table 1 shows a large number of codes with the plus or minus qualifications, although the majority of ratings were made without either qualification. There were more than twice as many plus as minus ratings.

## COMPARISONS AMONG TRAITS

Table 2 shows for each of the first ten traits the number of societies on which a numerical rating was made and the mean rating. Both measures are given separately for the two stages of childhood and for the two sexes.

Each of these ten traits was rated on more than half of the sample of societies. A larger number of societies were rated for late than for early childhood; and for all the traits except one (Obedien.), slightly more societies were rated for boys than for girls. For all ten traits, the mean rating of degree of inculcation was higher in the late than in the early stage. This increase with advancing age was much larger for the measures of Dutifulness (Indust., Respon.) and Maturity (Self-Rel., Achiev.) than for the measures of Toughness (Fortit., Aggress., Compet.) and Submission (Obedien., Self-Rstr., Sex Rstr.).

The difference between boys and girls was generally smaller than the difference between the early and late stage. However, consistent sex differences were found for each of the four groups of measures in Table 2. Boys were inculcated more strongly in Toughness (but with a small sex difference in Compet.) and in Maturity (but with a negligible sex difference in Achiev.). Girls were inculcated more strongly in Dutifulness and in Submission (but with a negligible sex difference in Self-Rstr.). Most of the traits listed in Table 2 showed a consistent interaction between the two stages and the two sexes, the difference between boys and girls being larger in late than in early childhood. Therefore, the sex with stronger inculcation of a trait in the early stage generally showed a larger increase in this measure from the early to the late stage.

The last three traits listed in Table 1, measuring Sociability, are omitted from Table 2 because they were not differentiated between the two stages and sexes. The mean rating for Generosity (Ge) was 6.0 (N = 104), for Trust (Tr) was 5.2 (N = 138), and for Honesty (Ho) was 4.4 (N = 110). The differences between the two stages of childhood generally consisted of higher ratings for Generosity and lower ratings for Trust in late childhood. These few cases, in addition to the even rarer differential ratings for boys and girls, were omitted from the quantitative scores and thus are included among the dots in Table 1.

Duration of early childhood, the first measure in Table 1, is an overall judgment for the society with respect to the age at which late childhood began. All but three of the 182 societies were rated on this measure. Early childhood ended at about seven years of age (short duration) in 87 (49%), at about nine years of age (medium duration) in 36 (20%), and at about eleven years of age (long duration) in 56 (31%).

## INTERCORRELATIONS AMONG MEASURES

The product-moment correlations among the traits in the late stage of childhood are summarized for boys in Table 3 and for girls in Table 4. The late stage

TABLE 3

Relationships among Ten Traits in Late Childhood for Boys

| | | Ft | Ag | Cm | Rl | Ac | Nd | Rp | Ob | Rt | Sx |
|---|---|---|---|---|---|---|---|---|---|---|---|
| **(1) TOUGHNESS** | | | | | | | | | | | |
| Fortit. | (Ft) | – | .45 | .38 | -.03 | .29 | .14 | .18 | .13 | .32 | .10 |
| Aggress. | (Ag) | (134) | – | .45 | .14 | .06 | -.06 | -.04 | -.07 | -.05 | .13 |
| Compet. | (Cm) | (119) | (117) | – | .10 | .40 | .21 | .16 | .12 | .27 | .10 |
| **(2) MATURITY** | | | | | | | | | | | |
| Self-Rel. | (Rl) | (136) | (133) | (125) | – | .22 | -.07 | .11 | -.26 | -.06 | .01 |
| Achiev. | (Ac) | (143) | (137) | (127) | (149) | – | .39 | .33 | .15 | .27 | .21 |
| **(3) DUTIFULNESS** | | | | | | | | | | | |
| Indust. | (Nd) | (150) | (145) | (131) | (157) | (158) | – | .72 | .51 | .43 | .18 |
| Respon. | (Rp) | (137) | (135) | (126) | (150) | (151) | (159) | – | .39 | .40 | .10 |
| **(4) SUBMISSION** | | | | | | | | | | | |
| Obedien. | (Ob) | (141) | (135) | (123) | (148) | (151) | (157) | (148) | – | .51 | .35 |
| Self-Rstr. | (Rt) | (120) | (119) | (107) | (124) | (127) | (133) | (124) | (128) | – | .44 |
| Sex Rstr. | (Sx) | (141) | (134) | (125) | (147) | (149) | (158) | (147) | (147) | (122) | – |

The Pearson product-moment correlation coefficients are shown to the upper right of the diagonals and the number of societies rated on both traits are shown in parentheses to the lower left of the diagonals.

is chosen because there is usually better information and greater differentiation between the sexes than in the early stage, as shown in Table 2.

The categories of traits, shown in Table 2, are demonstrated by the correlations in Tables 3 and 4. Fairly high positive correlations are found between traits in the same category, except that the correlation is rather low between Self-Reliance and Achievement. The correlations are not so high, how-

TABLE 4

Relationships among Ten Traits in Late Childhood for Girls

| | | Ft | Ag | Cm | Rl | Ac | Nd | Rp | Ob | Rt | Sx |
|---|---|---|---|---|---|---|---|---|---|---|---|
| **(1) TOUGHNESS** | | | | | | | | | | | |
| Fortit. | (Ft) | – | .36 | .21 | .01 | .19 | .04 | .00 | .12 | .16 | .11 |
| Aggress. | (Ag) | (112) | – | .37 | .12 | .00 | -.11 | -.10 | -.14 | -.20 | .00 |
| Compet. | (Cm) | (109) | (100) | – | .07 | .31 | .08 | -.03 | .10 | .12 | .13 |
| **(2) MATURITY** | | | | | | | | | | | |
| Self-Rel. | (Rl) | (123) | (111) | (112) | – | .29 | .04 | .21 | -.20 | -.05 | -.19 |
| Achiev. | (Ac) | (129) | (113) | (114) | (137) | – | .28 | .27 | .06 | .19 | .11 |
| **(3) DUTIFULNESS** | | | | | | | | | | | |
| Indust. | (Nd) | (141) | (124) | (122) | (150) | (150) | – | .69 | .36 | .36 | .27 |
| Respon. | (Rp) | (126) | (115) | (115) | (142) | (143) | (157) | – | .18 | .21 | .12 |
| **(4) SUBMISSION** | | | | | | | | | | | |
| Obedien. | (Ob) | (131) | (116) | (115) | (142) | (143) | (158) | (147) | – | .48 | .44 |
| Self-Rstr. | (Rt) | (111) | (101) | (96) | (118) | (118) | (131) | (122) | (126) | – | .48 |
| Sex Rstr. | (Sx) | (134) | (117) | (116) | (140) | (139) | (158) | (144) | (150) | (123) | – |

The measures for girls in this table correspond to the measures for boys in Table 3.

ever, as to indicate that the measures are redundant. The highest is between Industry and Responsibility (.72 for boys, .69 for girls). For both sexes the square of the correlation coefficient is approximately .50, which indicates that about half the variance among the scores for either measure is accounted for by its relationship with the other measure.

The last three traits (Sociability) are omitted from Tables 2, 3, and 4 because they are uniform for both sexes. The correlation of Generosity (Ge) with Trust (Tr) is .45 (N = 85) and with Honesty (Ho) is .40 (N = 72). The correlation of Trust with Honesty is .45 (N = 88).

The correlations between traits in different categories are generally very low. The highest are Competitiveness with Achievement (.40 for boys, .31 for girls), Achievement with Industry (.39 for boys, .28 for girls), Achievement with Responsibility (.33 for boys, .27 for girls), Industry with Obedience (.51 for boys, .36 for girls), and Industry with Self-Restraint (.43 for boys, .36 for girls). These correlations are all higher for boys than for girls. The three measures of Sociability are all more highly correlated with each other than with any of the other traits. Among the measures in Tables 3 and 4, Generosity is most highly correlated with Fortitude (.28 for boys, .22 for girls), Trust with Aggressiveness (−.39 for boys, −.30 for girls), and Honesty with Aggressiveness (−.36 for boys, −.29 for girls) and with Self-Restraint (.29 for boys, .32 for girls).

Almost all of the correlations between traits in different categories are lower than the correlations between traits in the same category. Among the 45 separate correlations in Table 3, however, only eight are negative, and likewise only eight are negative in Table 4. These few negative correlations are generally very small, the largest being for Self-Reliance with Obedience (−.26 for boys, −.20 for girls). This preponderance of positive correlations suggests the existence of a general tendency for some societies to have relatively strong inculcation of all the traits whereas other societies have weak inculcation of all the traits. Such a general cultural variation in strength of inculcation seems to apply to boys more than girls. A comparison between the two sexes with respect to each of the 45 correlations between the same pairs of traits shows that the correlation was higher positive or lower negative for boys in 33 instances and for girls in 12 instances.

For most of the traits listed in Table 1, the mean strength of inculcation shows little difference among the societies divided into the three categories of duration of the early stage of childhood, which is the first measure in Table 1. In the late stage of childhood, however, Industry, Responsibility, Self-Restraint, and Sexual Restraint on the average are inculcated least strongly, both in boys and girls, in the societies with the longest duration of early childhood. The increase for these measures from early to late chilhood tends to be smallest for these same societies. Generosity on the average is inculcated least strongly in societies with the shortest duration of early childhood.

## VALIDITY AND RELIABILITY

Four of the thirteen inculcated traits rated in the present study correspond closely to four of the six traits rated for degree of socialization pressure in an earlier study (Barry, Bacon and Child 1967). Some of the societies are the same, although the same ethnographic sources were not always used. Correlations between the corresponding traits constitute measures of validity of the ratings in both studies. The validity also provides a minimal estimate of the reliability which might have been demonstrated if the present ratings had been completed independently by two coders.

Table 5 summarizes the intercorrelations between the four equivalently named measures in the two studies, for the same sex. The present study in addition differentiates between the early and late stages of childhood. All of the correlations shown in Table 5 are reasonably high and each difference from zero is statistically significant. The correlations are higher for late than early childhood, except for an appreciably higher correlation for Responsibility in early childhood for boys. Most of these correlations are decreased when the quantitative scores for inculcated traits are converted by selective grouping (0, 1-3, 4-6, 7-9, 10) to correspond to the original rating scale of 1-5. This further finding indicates that the qualifications of the original ratings (plus and minus) add valid information.

The correlations not shown in Table 5, between boys in one study and girls in the other study for the same traits, differed only slightly from the corresponding correlations for the same sex. In general, the correlations between different sexes tended to be slightly lower, in accordance with the difference to be expected if societies differ from each other in degree of sex difference in child training, as has been reported by Barry, Bacon, and Child (1957).

The four measures in the earlier study generally showed higher correlations with the corresponding measures in the present study (Table 5) than with any of the other measures in Table 1. This indicates a high degree of specificity in the correlation between corresponding traits in the two studies. An exception was that Achievement in the earlier study was correlated more highly with Competitiveness for boys in late childhood ($r = .62$, $N = 31$). Also, Responsibility in the earlier study was correlated more highly with Industry for

TABLE 5

Relation between Inculcation and Pressure for Several Traits

|  |  | Early Childhood | | Late Childhood | |
|---|---|---|---|---|---|
|  |  | Boys | Girls | Boys | Girls |
| Self-Reliance | r | .53 | .54 | .60 | .70 |
|  | N | 42 | 40 | 41 | 39 |
| Achievement | r | .46 | .55 | .47 | .62 |
|  | N | 34 | 27 | 36 | 28 |
| Responsibility | r | .60 | .38 | .35 | .42 |
|  | N | 41 | 40 | 43 | 41 |
| Obedience | r | .62 | .60 | .65 | .67 |
|  | N | 43 | 41 | 43 | 42 |

Correlations, and number of societies on which the correlations are based, between the new ratings of degree of inculcation of traits and the earlier ratings (Barry, Bacon and Child, 1967) of socialization pressure toward the corresponding traits.

girls, both in early childhood (r = .49, N = 42) and in late childhood (r = .63, N = 44).

Further indications of validity of one of the new variables are shown in Tables 6 and 7. In Table 6, average degree of inculation of Sexual Restraint increases progressively with earlier ages at which the child is trained to cover the genitals (Barry and Paxson 1971). The late stage for girls shows the closest relationship of sexual restraint with age at which covering the genitals is trained. In Table 7, the average inculation of Sexual Restraint shows a logical progression of increase with categories which indicate increasing restriction on sex behavior of unmarried females (Murdock 1967), from freely permitted sex behavior to insistence on virginity. The differences in average Sexual Restraint are greater in late childhood, especially for girls. Sexual Restraint is inculcated to a low and almost uniform degree in both stages of childhood, for both sexes, in the societies where the child is never trained to cover the genitals (Table 6) and where sex behavior is freely permitted in unmarried females (Table 7). Sexual Restraint differs greatly between the stages of childhood and between the sexes in the opposite categories of societies, where training to cover the genitals begins in early infancy (Table 6) and where virginity is required in unmarried females (Table 7).

## Traits Related to Other Cultural Variables

The new ratings of inculcated traits in childhood can be related to various other measures which have been obtained independently on the same sample of societies.

Table 8 shows the average degree to which three traits (Fortitude, Aggressiveness, and Achievement) are inculcated in boys and girls in later childhood, separately for each of four categories which distinguish amount of contact with the mother during early infancy (Barry and Paxson 1971). High contact is associated with low Fortitude and low Achievement but high Aggressiveness. This inverse relationship of Fortitude and Aggressiveness is found in spite of the fact that these two traits are positively correlated with each other (Tables 3 and 4). Barry and Roberts (1972) have found that several cultural attributes, in particular absence of games of chance, tend to be found in societies where the infant experiences high contact with the mother.

Table 9 shows the same sample of societies divided into six categories on the basis of importance of animal husbandry (Murdock and Morrow 1970). Increasing importance of animal husbandry is associated with increasing inculation of Competitiveness and Responsibility, but with decreasing inculation of Trust and Honesty. These combinations of traits suggest some resistance to the high degree of training in compliance, which was previously shown to be related to the extremely high degree of accumulation of food resources in societies where animal husbandry is important (Barry, Child, and Bacon 1959).

In Table 10 the societies are divided into five categories on the basis of a measure of cultural complexity (political integration beyond the local community) reported by Murdock and Provost (1973b). Increasing levels of political hierarchy are associated with decreasing degrees of inculation in Self-Reliance but increasing degrees of inculation in Obedience and Sexual Restraint. For Self-Reliance the differences are greater in boys than in girls; for

TABLE 6

Relation between Two Measures of Sex Training

| | | Age at which Child is Trained to Cover Genitals | | | | |
|---|---|---|---|---|---|---|
| | | Never | Childhood | After Walking | Late Infancy | Early Infancy |
| Sexual Restraint in Early Childhood | | | | | | |
| Boys | Mean | 2.9 | 2.6 | 3.3 | 3.7 | 4.1 |
| | (N) | (8) | (75) | (13) | (3) | (29) |
| Girls | Mean | 2.6 | 3.0 | 3.8 | 4.0 | 4.6 |
| | (N) | (8) | (72) | (13) | (3) | (29) |
| Sexual Restraint in Late Childhood | | | | | | |
| Boys | Mean | 3.0 | 3.6 | 4.1 | 5.0 | 4.6 |
| | (N) | (9) | (77) | (13) | (3) | (32) |
| Girls | Mean | 3.0 | 4.6 | 5.1 | 5.7 | 5.8 |
| | (N) | (9) | (74) | (13) | (3) | (33) |

Mean degree to which Sexual Restraint is inculcated and number of societies rated for boys and girls in the early and late stages of childhood, separately for five groups of societies with the specified differences in the age at which the child is trained to cover the genitals (Barry and Paxson 1971). The category for training to cover genitals in late infancy combines categories in the original codes for training after 6 months and after one year.

TABLE 7

Sexual Restraint Related to Premarital Sex in Girls

| | | Freely Permitted | Trial Marriage | Censured if Pregnancy | Weakly Censured | Early Marriage | Insistence on Virginity |
|---|---|---|---|---|---|---|---|
| Sexual Restraint in Early Childhood | | | | | | | |
| Boys | Mean | 2.2 | 2.3 | 2.9 | 3.4 | 3.5 | 3.7 |
| | (N) | (31) | (3) | (14) | (34) | (8) | (32) |
| Girls | Mean | 2.3 | 2.7 | 3.0 | 3.8 | 4.3 | 4.3 |
| | (N) | (31) | (3) | (13) | (33) | (8) | (32) |
| Sexual Restraint in Late Childhood | | | | | | | |
| Boys | Mean | 2.5 | 3.3 | 3.5 | 4.0 | 4.3 | 5.1 |
| | (N) | (32) | (3) | (15) | (34) | (10) | (31) |
| Girls | Mean | 2.7 | 3.7 | 3.9 | 5.1 | 5.1 | 7.1 |
| | (N) | (31) | (3) | (15) | (34) | (10) | (33) |

Mean degree to which Sexual Restraint is inculcated and number of societies rated for boys and girls in the early and late stages of childhood, separately for six groups of societies with the specified differences in norms of heterosexual behavioral for unmarried females (Murdock 1967).

TABLE 8

Traits Inculcated in Childhood Related to Infant's Contact with Mother

| Fortitude in Late Childhood | | Contact with Mother | | | | |
|---|---|---|---|---|---|---|
| | | Very low | Low | Medium | High | Very High |
| Boys | Mean | 7.0 | 6.8 | 5.9 | 5.8 | 5.6 |
| | (N) | (3) | (13) | (28) | (41) | (18) |
| Girls | Mean | 5.3 | 5.9 | 5.1 | 5.1 | 4.9 |
| | (N) | (3) | (3) | (26) | (39) | (17) |
| **Aggressiveness in Late Childhood** | | | | | | |
| Boys | Mean | 4.3 | 4.9 | 4.8 | 5.7 | 5.4 |
| | (N) | (3) | (12) | (25) | (39) | (17) |
| Girls | Mean | 4.0 | 3.6 | 3.9 | 4.9 | 4.5 |
| | (N) | (2) | (11) | (21) | (31) | (15) |
| **Achievement in Late Childhood** | | | | | | |
| Boys | Mean | 6.0 | 5.5 | 5.4 | 5.2 | 4.4 |
| | (N) | (2) | (15) | (31) | (44) | (19) |
| Girls | Mean | 6.0 | 5.9 | 5.3 | 5.4 | 4.1 |
| | (N) | (3) | (14) | (30) | (42) | (17) |

Societies are divided into five groups on the basis of the amount of contact with the mother during early infancy, defined as the first few months after birth (Barry and Paxson 1971). For each group the mean score and number of societies are shown for degree of inculcation of three traits (Fortitude, Aggressiveness, Achievement).

Sexual Restraint the differences are greater in girls, corresponding to the stronger relationships of Sexual Restraint for girls than boys with age at which the child is trained to cover the genitals (Table 6) and with restriction on sexual behavior for unmarried females (Table 7).

The sources used for the measures in Tables 8, 9, and 10 contain many other codes which show relationships with traits inculcated in childhood. Additional sets of codes on the same sample of societies are available in Murdock and Provost (1973a), Murdock and Wilson (1972), and Tuden and Marshall (1972). Differences in degree to which some of the traits are inculcated are also found among the six major regions of the world, as may be expected from large regional differences in various cultural characteristics (Barry 1968; Murdock and Wilson 1972; Tuden and Marshall 1972; Murdock and Provost 1973a; 1973b).

## CONCLUSIONS

The present paper provides a new code intended to fill a need for comparative cultural data on child training. Previous codes have been expanded to define a larger number of inculcated traits and to distinguish between two stages of childhood as well as between boys and girls. These methods are applied to a large world sample which has been coded previously on a number of other cultural variables.

Although sizable sex differences were found for some of the traits, the differences between the two stages of childhood were generally larger. Inculcation was much stronger in the late than early stage for ten of the thirteen traits, and sex differences were generally larger in the late than early stage.

Intercorrelations among the thirteen traits indicate that they can be grouped into five categories, labeled Toughness (Fortitude, Agressiveness, Competitiveness), Maturity (Self-Reliance, Achievement), Dutifulness (Industry, Responsibility), Submission (Obedience, Self-Restraint, Sexual Restraint), and Sociability (Generosity, Trust, Honesty). Factor analyses of the data, using a program with various options (Nie, Bent, and Hull 1970), confirm the existence of these five categories or factors. The second (Maturity) is least distinct, as indicated by the relatively low intercorrelations between the two component traits and relatively high correlations with some of the other traits.

Correlations of some of the traits with equivalent or similar variables, measured independently on the same societies, indicate a high degree of validity of the ratings. Since the other measures were defined somewhat differently and not always rated on the basis of the same ethnographic information, the reliability of the new codes is probably higher than indicated by these correlations.

Some correlations of the new traits with measures of infancy, subsistence economy, and cultural complexity are also reported. These are only a few of the correlations with other cultural measures, available for the same sample of

TABLE 9

Traits Inculcated in Childhood Related to Subsistence Economy

| | | None | No Food | Little Food | Meat | Milk | Most Important |
|---|---|---|---|---|---|---|---|
| | | | | Animal Husbandry | | | |
| **Competitiveness in Late Childhood** | | | | | | | |
| Boys | Mean | 2.8 | 4.9 | 4.7 | 4.7 | 4.9 | 5.3 |
| | (N) | (6) | (33) | (45) | (24) | (16) | (11) |
| Girls | Mean | 2.8 | 4.8 | 4.4 | 4.0 | 5.1 | 5.1 |
| | (N) | (6) | (32) | (43) | (20) | (15) | (10) |
| **Responsibility in Late Childhood** | | | | | | | |
| Boys | Mean | 4.4 | 4.5 | 4.3 | 5.4 | 5.7 | 6.3 |
| | (N) | (8) | (35) | (55) | (30) | (18) | (15) |
| Girls | Mean | 4.8 | 5.8 | 5.5 | 5.6 | 5.6 | 6.2 |
| | (N) | (8) | (34) | (56) | (29) | (16) | (15) |
| Trust | Mean | 6.4 | 5.8 | 5.2 | 4.5 | 4.8 | 4.4 |
| | (N) | (8) | (32) | (48) | (22) | (17) | (11) |
| Honesty | Mean | 5.6 | 4.9 | 4.1 | 4.6 | 4.5 | 3.0 |
| | (N) | (5) | (28) | (35) | (21) | (12) | (9) |

Societies are divided into six groups on the basis of importance of animal husbandry (Murdock and Morrow 1970), showing for each the mean score and number of societies rated on degree of inculcation of four traits (Competitiveness, Responsibility, Trust, Honesty).

TABLE 10

Traits Inculcated in Childhood Related to Political Structure

|  |  | None | Local Communities | One Level | Two Levels | Three or More Levels |
|---|---|---|---|---|---|---|
| **Self-Reliance in Late Childhood** | | | | | | |
| Boys | Mean | 7.8 | 6.4 | 6.3 | 6.1 | 5.2 |
|  | (N) | (9) | (61) | (40) | (26) | (24) |
| Girls | Mean | 6.3 | 5.4 | 5.0 | 5.2 | 4.3 |
|  | (N) | (10) | (58) | (37) | (25) | (23) |
| **Obedience in Late Childhood** | | | | | | |
| Boys | Mean | 4.0 | 5.1 | 5.6 | 6.3 | 6.6 |
|  | (N) | (8) | (62) | (41) | (25) | (26) |
| Girls | Mean | 4.6 | 5.3 | 5.9 | 6.5 | 7.0 |
|  | (N) | (9) | (61) | (41) | (24) | (27) |
| **Sexual Restraint in Late Childhood** | | | | | | |
| Boys | Mean | 2.6 | 3.8 | 3.7 | 4.0 | 4.5 |
|  | (N) | (11) | (62) | (42) | (24) | (25) |
| Girls | Mean | 2.7 | 4.3 | 4.7 | 5.8 | 6.0 |
|  | (N) | (10) | (63) | (42) | (24) | (26) |

Societies are divided into five groups with the specified levels of political integration (Murdock and Provost 1973b), showing for each the mean score and number of societies rated on degree of inculcation of three traits (Self-Reliance, Obedience, Sexual Restraint).

societies, which can be calculated. Further investigations of these relationships may be expected to increase our understanding of child training, both as an expression of cultural characteristics and as an influence on the development of the individuals who maintain cultural traditions.

### NOTE

1. This project (Cross-Cultural Cumulative Coding Center) was supported by a National Science Foundation Research Grant (No. GS-2111). The senior author was supported by a Public Health Service Research Scientist Development Award (No. K2-MH-5921) from the National Institute of Mental Health. The data were analyzed with the aid of the PDP 10 digital computer at the University of Pittsburgh Computer Center. George P. Murdock helped in planning the research. Mrs. Priscilla A. Oyekan and the Social Science Information Center at the University of Pittsburgh helped to prepare the data for analysis. The authors wish to express their gratitude to L. Keith Brown, John P. Gillin, Ian Rawson, John M. Roberts, and Alexander Spoehr, who contributed information on societies 117 (Japanese), 164 (Carib), 160 (Haitians), 149 (Zuni), and 108 (Marshallese), respectively.

### BIBLIOGRAPHY

Barry, H., III. 1968. Regional and Worldwide Variations in Culture. Ethnology 7:207-217.
———— 1969. Cultural Variations in the Development of Mental Illness. Changing Perspectives in Mental Illness, ed. S. C. Plog and R. B. Edgerton, pp. 155-179. New York.
Barry, H., III., M. K. Bacon, and I. L. Child. 1957. A Cross-Cultural Survey of Some Sex Differences in Socialization. Journal of Abnormal and Social Psychology 55:327-332.

———— 1967.   Definitions, Ratings, and Bibliographic Sources for Child Training Practices of 110 Cultures. Cross-Cultural Approaches, ed. C. S. Ford, pp. 293-331. New Haven.

Barry, H., III., I. L. Child, and M. K. Bacon.   1959.   Relation of Child Training to Subsistence Economy. American Anthropologist 61:51-63.

Barry, H., III, and L. M. Paxson.   1971.   Infancy and Early Childhood: Cross-Cultural Codes 2. Ethnology 10:466-508.

Barry, H., III, and J. M. Roberts.   1972.   Infant Socialization and Games of Chance. Ethnology 11:296-308.

Murdock, G. P.   1967.   Ethnographic Atlas. Pittsburgh.

Murdock, G. P., and D. O. Morrow.   1970.   Subsistence Economy and Supportive Practices: Cross-Cultural Codes 1. Ethnology 9:302-330.

Murdock, G. P., and C. Provost.   1973a.   Factors in the Division of Labor by Sex: A Cross-Cultural Analysis. Ethnology 12:203-225.

———— 1973b.   Measurement of Cultural Complexity. Ethnology 12:379-392.

Murdock, G. P., and D. R. White.   1969.   Standard Cross-Cultural Sample. Ethnology 8:329-369.

Murdock, G. P., and S. F. Wilson.   1972.   Settlement Patterns and Community Organization: Cross-Cultural Codes 3. Ethnology 11:254-295.

Nie, N. H., D. H. Bent, and C. H. Hull.   1970.   Statistical Package for the Social Sciences. New York.

Tuden, A., and C. Marshall.   1972.   Political Organization: Cross-Cultural Codes 4. Ethnology 11:436-464.

## SUPPLEMENTARY BIBLIOGRAPHY

This bibliography is supplementary to that published in Barry and Paxson (1971). Where the usefulness of the sources for this code differs from the infancy code, their rank order is indicated by the number preceding the citation; full citations are given only for works which did not appear in the previous article. Omission of the society name signifies the same rank order as in Barry and Paxson (1971) or not coded (societies 75, 88, 101, 103).

1. Nama Hottentot.
    3. Murdock, G. P.   1934.   Our Primitive Contemporaries. New York.
    4. Hoernlé, A. W.   1925.   The Social Organization of the Nama Hottentots. American Anthropologist 27: 1-24.
2. Kung Bushmen.
    4. Thomas, E. M.   1959.   The Harmless People. New York.
    5. Schapera, I.   1930.   The Khosian Peoples of South Africa. London.
4. Lozi.
    3. Turner, V. W.   1952.   The Lozi Peoples of North-Western Rhodesia. London.
6. Suku.
    2. Kopytoff, I.   1971.   The Suku of the Congo. Kinship and Culture, ed. F.L.K. Hsu, pp. 69-86. Chicago.
    3. Van de Ginste, F.   1947.
    4. Kopytoff, I.   1964.
8. Nyakyusa.
    1. Wilson, M.   1951.   Good Company. London.
    2. ———   1936.
    3. ———   1957.
9. Hadza.
    1. Woodburn, J.   1964.
    2. Kohl-Larsen, L.   1958.
10. Luguru.
    2. Christiansen, J. B.   1963.   Utani: Joking, Sexual License and Social Obligations Among the Luguru. American Anthropologist 65:1314-1327.
11. Kikuyu.
    1. Kenyatta, J.   1939.
    2. Cagnolo, C.   1933.
    3. Lambert, H. E.   1956.   Kikuyu Social and Political Institutions. London.
12. Ganda.
    2. Mair, L. P.   1934.   An African People in the Twentieth Century. London.
    3. Southwold, M.   1965.
    4. Murdock, G. P.   1934.   The Ganda of Uganda. Our Primitive Contemporaries, pp. 508-550. New York.
13. Mbuti Pygmies.
    1. Turnbull, C. N.   1961.
    2. ———   1965.   The Mbuti Pygmies of the Congo. Peoples of Africa, ed. J. L. Gibbs, Jr., pp. 279-317. New York.
    3. ———   1965.   Wayward Servants.
16. Tiv.
    3. Bohannan, P.   1965.   The Tiv of Nigeria. Peoples of Africa, ed. J. L. Gibbs, Jr., pp. 515-546. New York.
    4. East, R., ed.   1939.
18. Fon.
    2. Herskovits, M. J.   1937.   A note on 'Woman Marriage' in Dahomey. Africa 10: 335-341.
    3. Bohannan, L.   1949.   Dahomean Marriage. Africa 19:273-278.
19. Ashanti.
    1. Fortes, M.   1949.   Time and Social Structure: An Ashanti Case Study. Social Structure, ed. M. Fortes, pp. 54-84. London.
    2. Lystad, R. A.   1958.   The Ashanti. New Brunswick.
    3. Manoukian, M.   1950.   Akan and Ga-Adangme Peoples of the Gold Coast. London.

20. Mende.
    2. Little, K. L.   1954.   The Mende in Sierra Leone. African Worlds, ed. D. Forde, pp. 111-137. London.
    3. McCulloch, M.   1950.   The Peoples of Sierra Leone Protectorate. London.
    4. Crosby, K. M.   1937.   Polygamy in Mende Country. Africa 10:224-264.
21. Wolof.
    1. Ames, D. W.   1953.
    2. Gamble, D. P.   1957.
    3. Ames, D. W.   1959.   Wolof Co-operative Work Groups. Continuity and Change in African Cultures, eds. W. R. Bascom and M. J. Herskovits, pp. 224-237. Chicago.
    4. Faladé, S.   1963.
25. Wodaabe Fulani.
    2. Stenning, P. J.   1959.   Savannah Nomads. London.
    3. Hopen, C. E.   1959.   The Pastoral Fulbe Family in Gwandu. London.
27. Massa.
    2. Garine, I. de.   1964.   Les Massa du Cameroun. Paris.
    3. Lembezat, B.   1961.
28. Azande.
    1. Lagae, C. R.   1926.
    2. Baxter, P. T. W., and A. Butt.   1953.
    3. Evans-Pritchard, E. E.   1937.
    4. Reining, C. C.   1966.   The Zande Scheme. Evanston.
29. Fur.
    4. Barth, F.   1967.   Economic Spheres in Darfur. Themes in Economic Anthropology, ed. R. Firth, pp. 149-174. Association for Social Anthropology Monographs 6.
31. Shilluk.
    3. Cann, G. P.   1929.   A Day in the Life of an Idle Shilluk. Sudan Notes and Records 12:251-253.
    4. Pumphrey, M. E. C.   1941.   The Shilluk Tribe. Sudan Notes and Records 24:1-45.
34. Masai.
    2. Huntingford, G. W. B.   1953.   The Southern Nilo-Hamites. London.
    3. Baumann, O.   1894.   Durch Massailand zur Nilquelle. Berlin.
    4. Jacobs, A. H.   1958.   Masai Age-groups and Some Functional Tasks. Ms.
35. Konso.
    3. Cerulli, E.   1956.   Peoples of South-west Ethiopia and Its Borderland. London.
36. Somali.
    1. Lewis, I. M.   1965.   The Northern Pastoral Somali. Peoples of Africa, ed. J. L. Gibbs, Jr., pp. 319-360. New York.
    2. Paulitschke, P.   1888.
    3. Lewis, I. M.   1962.   Marriage and the Family in Northern Somaliland. Kampala: East African Institute for Social and Economic Research.
    4. ———   1955.
    5. Puccioni, N. 1936.
39. Kenuzi Nubians.
    1. Herzog, R.   1957.
    2. Callender, C., and F. el Guindi.   1971.   Life-Crisis Rituals Among the Kenuz. Case Western Reserve University Studies in Anthropology. 3.
    3. Schäfer, H.   1935.
40. Teda.
    3. Nachtigal, G.   1879.   Sahara und Sudan I:377-464. Berlin.
    4. Cline, W.   1950.
42. Riffians.
    2. Hart, D. M.   1954.   An Ethnographic Survey of the Riffian Tribe of Aith Waryaghil. Tamuda I:55-86. Tetuan.
44. Hebrews.
    3. Dalman, G.   1932.   Arbeit und Sitte in Palestina. 8v. Gütersloh.
45. Babylonians.
    1. Saggs, H. W. F.   1965.   Everyday Life in Babylonia and Assyria. New York.

2. Saggs, H. W. F.   1962.
3. Driver, G. R., and J. C. Miles.   1952-55.
46. Rwala Bedouin.
   2. Raswan, C. R.   1947.   Black Tents of Arabia. New York.
48. Gheg Albanians.
   1. Coon, C. S.   1950.
   2. Durham, M. E.   1909.   High Albania. London.
   3. Hasluck, M.   1954.
   4. Lane, R. W.   1923.   Peaks of Shala, New York.
49. Romans.
   1. Balsdon, J. P. V. D.   1969.   Life and Leisure in Ancient Rome. New York.
   2. Davis, W. St.   1959.   A Day in Old Rome. New York.
   3. Carcopino, J. 1940.
   4. Balsdon, J. P. V. D.   1963.   Roman Women, New York.
   5. Pliny.   1969.   Letters and Panegyricus, 2v., trans. B. Radice. Cambridge.
   6. Paoli, V. E.   1963.   Rome: Its People, Life and Customs, trans. R. D. Macnaghten. New York.
50. Spanish Basques.
   1. Caro-Baroja, J.   1944.
   2. Douglass, W. A.   1969.
51. Irish.
   1. Arensberg, C. M., and S. T. Kimball.   1940.   Family and Community in Ireland. Cambridge.
   2. O'Donoghue, J.   1958.   In a Quiet Land. New York.
   3. Cresswell, R.   1969.
52. Könkämä Lapps.
   1. Bernatzig, H. A.   1938.
   2. Pehrson, R. N.   1957.
   3. Haglund, S.   1935.
53. Yurak Samoyed.
   3. Englehardt, E. A.   1899.   A Russian Province of the North. Westminster.
   4. Jackson, F. G.   1895.   The Great Frozen Land. London.
54. Russians.
   1. Benet, S., ed.   1970.   The Village of Viriatino. New York.
   2. Alt, H., and E. Alt.   1959.   Russia's Children. New York.
   3. Mace, D., and V. Mace.   1963.   The Soviet Family. Garden City.
   4. Dunn, S. P., and E. Dunn.   1967.
55. Abkhaz.
   3. Byhan, A.   1926.   Die kaukasischen Völker. Illustrierte Völkerkunde, ed. G. Buschan, 2:ii, 749-844. Stuttgart.
56. Armenians.
   1. Klidschian, A.   1911.
   2. Haxthausen, A. von.   1854.
   3. Lynch, H. F. B.   1901.   Armenia, v. 1. London.
   4. Kohler, J.   1887, 1906.   Das Recht der Armenier. Zeitschrift für vergleichende Rechtswissenschaft 7:385-436, 19:103-130.
57. Kurd.
   3. Barth, F.   1953.   Principles of Social Organization in Southern Kurdistan. Universitetets Etnografiske Museum Bulletin 7:1-146.
   4. Leach, E. R.   1938.   Social and Economic Organization of the Rowanduz Kurds. London School of Economics Monographs on Social Anthropology 3:1-74.
58. Basseri.
   2. Barth, F. K.   1964.   Capital, Investment and Social Structure of a Pastoral Nomadic Group. Capital, Saving and Credit in Peasant Societies, eds. R. Firth and B. S. Yamey, pp. 69-81. Chicago.
59. West Punjabi.
   2. Wilbur, D. N.   1964.

3. Eglar, Z. 1957. Panjabi Village Life. Pakistan: Society and Culture, ed. S. Maron, pp. 62-80. New Haven.
4. Honigmann, J. J. 1957.
5. ———— 1958.
6. Kennedy, M. J. 1957. Panjabi Urban Society. Pakistan: Society and Culture, ed. S. Maron, pp. 81-103. New Haven.

63. Uttar Pradesh.
1. Luschinsky, M. S. 1963. The Life of a Woman in a Village of North India. Ph.D. Dissertation, Cornell University.

67. Lolo.
2. Liétard, A. 1913. Au Yun-nan: Les Lo-Lo P'o. Anthropos I:1-272.
3. Pollard, S. 1921. In Unknown China. Philadelphia.
4. Tseng, C. L. 1945.

74. Rhadé.
2. Sabatier, L. 1940. Recueil des coutumes rhadées du Darlac. Hanoi.

76. Siamese.
1. Hanks, L. M., Jr., and J. R. Hanks. 1961.
2. Sharp, R. L. et al. 1954.
3. Sharp, L., and L. M. Hanks, n.d. Bang Chan.
4. Hanks, J. R. 1963.
5. Phillips, H. P. 1965. Thai Peasant Personality. Berkeley.

77. Semang.
1. Schebesta, P. 1927.

79. Andamanese.
1. Radcliffe-Brown, A. R. 1922.
2. Man, E. M. 1932.

80. Forest Vedda.
2. Spittel, R. L. 1945. Wild Ceylon. 3rd edit. Colombo.
3. Bailey, J. 1963.

81. Menabe Tanala.
3. Kardiner, A. 1939. The Analysis of Tanala Culture. The Individual and his Society, pp. 291-351. New York.

83. Javanese.
2. Jay, R. R. 1969. Javanese Villagers, Cambridge.
3. Koentjaraningrat, R. M. 1960. The Javanese of South Central Java. Social Structure in Southeast Asia, ed. G. P. Murdock, pp. 88-115. Chicago.
4. ———— 1961. Some Social-Anthropological Observations on Gotong Rojong Practices in Two Villages of Central Java. Ithaca.

84. Balinese.
1. Belo, J. 1936. A Study of the Balinese Family. American Anthropologist 38:12-31.
2. Covarrubias, M. 1937.
3. Belo, J. 1970. Traditional Balinese Culture. New York.
4. Mead, M., and F. C. MacGregor. 1951.

85. Iban.
2. Freeman, J. D. 1955. Iban Agriculture. Colonial Research Studies 18:1-148.
3. ———— 1957. Iban Pottery. Sarawak Museum Journal 8:53-176.
4. ———— 1958. The Family System of the Iban. Cambridge Papers in Social Anthropology 1:15-52.

87. Toradja.
1. Adriani, N., and A. C. Kruijt. 1950-1951. De Bare'e-sprekende Toradja's. 2nd edit. 3v. Amsterdam.

90. Tiwi.
1. Goodale, J. C. 1971. Tiwi Wives. Seattle.
2. ———— 1960. Sketches of Tiwi Children. Expedition 2, no. 4:4-13.
3. Pilling, A. R. 1957. Law and Feud in an Aboriginal Society of North Australia. Ph.D. Dissertation, University of California at Berkeley.
4. Hart, C. W. M, and A. R. Pilling. 1960. The Tiwi of North Australia. New York.

92. Orokaiva.

1. Williams, F. E. 1930.
2. Reay, M. 1953.
94. Kapauku.
  2. Pospisil, L. 1963. The Kapauku Papuans of West New Guinea. New York.
  3. ———— 1963. Kapauku Papuan Economy. Yale University Publications in Anthropology 67:1-502.
102. Mbau Fijians.
  2. Thomson, B. 1908. The Fijians: A Study of the Decay of Custom. London.
  3. Waterhouse, J. 1866.
  4. Deane, W. 1921.
104. Maori.
  1. Reed, A. W. 1963.
  2. Best, E. 1924.
  3. Polack, J. S. 1838.
  4. Buck, P. 1949. The Coming of the Maori. Wellington.
106. Samoans.
  1. Krämer, A. 1901-1902. Die Samoa-Inseln. 2v. Stuttgart.
  2. Turner, G. 1884.
  3. Grattan, F. J. H. 1948.
  4. Krämer, A. 1906. Hawaii, Ostmikronesien und Samoa, pp. 143-193, 460-522. Stuttgart.
  5. Murdock, G. P. 1934. The Samoans. Our Primitive Contemporaries, pp. 48-84. New York.
107. Makin Gilbertese.
  1. Grimble, A. 1921.
  2. Lambert, B. 1964.
  3. Krämer, A. 1906.
  4. Finsch, O. 1893.
108. Jaluit Marshallese.
  2. Spoehr, A. personal communication.
109. Trukese.
  3. Goodenough, W. H. 1969. Changing Social Organization on Romonum, Truk: 1947-1965. Ms.
110. Yapese.
  1. Müller, W. 1917.
  2. Salesius. 1906.
  3. Tetens, A. 1958. Among the Savages of the South Seas. Trans. F. M. Spoehr. Stanford.
  4. Schneider, D. M. 1953.
111. Palauans.
  2. Kubary, J. S. 1873. Die Palau-Inseln in der Südsee. Journal des Museum Godeffroy 1:181-238. Hamburg.
112. Ifugao.
  1. Barton, R. F. 1938.
  2. ———— 1930.
  3. ———— 1919.
  4. ———— 1946.
113. Atayal.
  1. Okada, Y. 1949. The Social Structure of the Atayal Tribe. (Ms translated from Essays Presented to Teizo Toda, pp. 393-433.) Tokyo.
  2. Ruey Yih-Fu. n.d. The Atayal. Ms.
  3. ———— 1955.
114. Chekiang Chinese.
  1. Lang, O. 1946.
  2. Fei, H. 1946.
  3. Fried, M. 1953.
116. Koreans.
  3. Kang, Y. 1931. The Grass Roof. New York.
  4. Rutt, R. 1964.

117. Japanese.
    3. Smith, R. S., and J. B. Cornell.   1956.   Two Japanese Villages. Ann Arbor.
    4. Brown, L. K. personal communication.
118. Saru Ainu.
    1. Hilger, M. I.   1971.
    2. Batchelor, J.   1895.
    3. Murdock, G. P.   1934.   The Ainus of Northern Japan. Our Primitive Contemporaries, pp. 163-191. New York.
121. Reindeer Chukchee.
    3. Krenova, J.   1936.   The Chukchee Children. Indians at Work 3:35-37.
122. Ingalik.
    3. Osgood, C.   1959.   Ingalik Mental Culture. Yale University Publications in Anthropology 56:1-195.
123. Aleut.
    2. Lantis, M.   1970.   Ethnohistory in Southwestern Alaska and the Southern Yukon. Lexington.
124. Copper Eskimo.
    2. Jenness, D.   1928.   People of the Twilight. New York.
    3. Rasmussen, K.   1932.
125. Montagnais.
    1. Burgess, J. A.   1944.
    2. Lips, J. E.   1947.
126. Micmac.
    1. Wallis, W. D., and R. S. Wallis.   1955.
    2. Le Clerq, C.   1910.
129. Kaska.
    2. Underwood, F. W., and I. Honigmann.   1947.   A Comparison of Socialization and Personality in Two Simple Societies. American Anthropologist 49:557-577.
    3. Honigmann, J. J.   1954.
131. Masset Haida.
    4. Swanton, R., Jr.   1909.   Contributions to the Ethnology of the Haida. Memoirs of the American Museum of Natural History 8:1-300.
133. Twana.
    2. Eells, M.   1877.   Twana Indians of the Skokomish Reservation. Bulletins of the U. S. Geographical and Geological Survey of the Territories 3:57-114.
134. Yurok.
    1. Erikson, E. H.   1943.
    2. Loeffelholz, K. von.   1893.
    3. Kroeber, A. L.   1960.
    4. ———   1925.
135. Eastern Pomo.
    2. Aginsky, B. W., and E. G. Aginsky.   1967.   Deep Valley. New York.
    3. Gifford, E. W.   1926.
136. Lake Yokuts.
    1. Latta, F. F.   1949.
    2. Gayton, A. H.   1948.
137. Wadadika Paiute.
    2. Stewart, O. C.   1941.   Northern Paiute. Anthropological Records 4:361-446.
139. Lower Kutenai.
    3. Ray, V. F.   1943.   Plateau. Anthropological Records 8:99-257.
140. Gros Ventre.
    3. Kroeber, A. L.   1908.   Ethnology of the Gros Ventre. Anthropological Papers of the American Museum of Natural History I:141-281.
142. Skidi Pawnee.
    1. Weltfish, G.   1965.
    2. Dorsey, G. A., and J. R. Murie.   1940.
143. Omaha.
    3. Mead, M.   1932.   The Changing Culture of an Indian Tribe. Columbia University Contributions to Anthropology 15:1-313.

145. Upper Creek.
　　1. Swanton, J. R. 1946.
　　2. ———— 1928.
　　3. Speck, F. G. 1907. The Creek Indians of Taskigi Town. Memoirs of the American Anthropological Association 2:99-164.
148. Chiricahua Apache.
　　2. Opler, M. E. 1955. An Outline of Chiricahua Apache Social Organization. Social Organization of North American Tribes, ed. F. Eggan, pp. 173-242. Chicago.
　　3. ———— 1936. An Interpretation of Ambivalence of Two American Indian Tribes. Journal of Social Psychology 7:82-116.
149. Zuni.
　　2. Roberts, J. M. personal communication.
150. Havasupai.
　　1. Smithson, C. L. 1959. The Havasupai Woman. Department of Anthropology, University of Utah, Anthropological Papers 38:1-170.
　　2. Spier, L. 1928.
　　3. Iliff, F. G. 1954. People of the Blue Water. New York.
　　4. James, G. W. 1903. The Indians of the Painted Desert Region. Boston.
151. Papago.
　　1. Underhill, R. M. 1939.
　　2. Joseph, A., R. B. Spicer, and J. Chesky. 1949.
　　3. Underhill, R. M. 1936.
　　4. Lumholtz, C. 1912.
153. Aztec.
　　2. Seler-Sachs, C. 1919. Frauenleben im Reiche der Azteken. Berlin.
　　3. Soustelle, J. 1961.
　　4. Sahagun, B. de. 1950-1957.
　　5. Murdock, G. P. 1934.
154. Sierra Popoluca.
　　2. Foster, G. M. 1945. Sierra Popoluca Folklore and Beliefs. University of California Publications in American Archaeology and Ethnology 42:177-250.
　　3. ———— 1942.
157. Bribri Talamanca.
　　2. Pittier de Fabrega, H. 1938. Apuntaciones etnológicas sobre los indios Bribri. Museo Nacional, Serie Etnológica 1:pt. 1. San José.
　　3. Skinner, A. 1920.
160. Haitians.
　　2. Underwood, F. W., and I. Honigmann. 1947. A Comparison of Socialization and Personality in Two Simple Societies. American Anthropologist 49:557-577.
　　3. Rawson, I. personal communication.
　　4. Métraux, A. 1960. Haiti Black Peasants and Their Religion. Trans. P. Lengyel. Neuchâtel.
　　5. Leyburn, J. G. 1941. The Haitian People. New Haven.
164. Barama Carib.
　　2. Gillin, J. P. personal communication.
　　3. Roth, W. E. 1924.
165. Saramacca.
　　1. Price, R. 1972. Saramaka Social Structure. Ms.
　　2. Herskovits, M. J., and F. S. Herskovits. 1934.
　　3. Neumann, P. 1967. Wirtschaft und materielle Kultur der Buschneger Surinames. Abhandlungen und Berichte des Staatlichen Museums für Völkerkunde Dresden 25:1-181.
166. Mundurucu.
　　4. Murphy, R. F. 1957. Intergroup Hostility and Social Cohesion. American Anthropologist 59:1018-1035.
167. Cubeo.
　　2. Goldman, I. 1948. Tribes of the Uaupés-Caqueta Region. Bulletins of the Bureau of American Ethnology 143:iii, 763-798.

169. Jivaro.
    4. Harner, M. J. 1962. Jivaro Souls. American Anthropologist 64:258-272.
170. Amahuaca.
    2. Carneiro, R. L. 1968. Hunting and Hunting Magic Among the Amahuaca. Ms.
    3. ———. 1964. The Amahuaca and the Spirit World. Ethnology 3:6-11.
    4. Dole, G. E. 1961. The Influence of Population Density on the Development of Social Organization Among the Amahuaca of East Peru. Paper presented at American Anthropological Association meeting, Philadelphia.
171. Inca.
    1. Rowe, J. H. 1946.
    2. Baudin, L. 1962. Daily Life in Peru. New York.
    3. Cobo, B. 1890-1895.
172. Aymara.
    3. Bouroncle Carreon, A. 1964. Contribucion al estudio de los Aymaras. America Indigena 24:129-169, 233-269.
175. Trumai.
176. Ramcocamecra Timbira.
    2. Arnaud, E. 1964.
    3. Lowie, R. H. 1946. The Northwestern and Central Ge. Bulletins of the Bureau of American Ethnology 143:i, 477-517.
177. Tupinamba.
    4. Staden, H. 1928. The True Story of His Captivity, ed. M. Lotts. London.
178. Botocudo.
    3. Saint-Hilaire, A. 1930-1933. Voyages dans l'intérieur du Brésil. Paris.
181. Cayua.
    1. Ambrosetti, J. B. 1895.
    2. Koenigswald, G. von. 1908.
    3. Müller, F. 1934-1935. Beiträge zur Ethnographie der Guarani-Indianer im östlichen Waldgebiet von Paraguay. Anthropos 29:177-208, 441-460, 695-702; 30:151-164, 433-450, 767-783.
182. Lengua.
    1. Grubb, W. B. 1911.
    2. Baldus, H. 1931.
    3. Métraux, A. 1946. Ethnography of the Chaco. Bulletins of the Bureau of American Ethnology 143:8, 197-370.
185. Tehuelche.
    2. Bourne, B. F. 1874.
    3. Cooper, J. M. 1946. The Patagonian and Pampean Hunters. Bulletins of the Bureau of American Ethnology 143:i, 127-168.
    4. Viedma, A. de. 1837.
    5. Musters, G. C. 1872.

# 8

# Agents and Techniques for Child Training: Cross-Cultural Codes 6

*Herbert Barry III, Lili Josephson,*

*Edith Lauer,* and *Catherine Marshall*

A previous article (Barry *et. al.,* 1976) has provided a set of quantitative codes on the degree to which various traits are inculcated during childhood in a world sample of 186 societies, selected by Murdock and White (1969). Differential ratings for boys and girls, in two stages of childhood, enable comparisons on the basis of sex and age. Independently measured cultural variations in treatment of infants, and in attributes of social organization and subsistence economy, were shown to be related to differences in the degree to which several traits are inculcated.

The present article provides a further set of codes, obtained from the same ethnographic sources at the same time and by the same group of coders. Agents of child training are specified in terms of functions, types, and sexes of the people who interact with the child. Techniques of child training include methods of exhorting, punishing, and rewarding the child, and attitudes expressed by the caretakers and by the society. In common with the ratings of traits inculcated, these measures were rated differentially when possible for boys and girls, during the early and late stages of childhood.

These measures of agents and techniques are expected to provide new information about important attributes of child training. Some relationships are identified between these new measures and the previously published ratings of traits inculcated during childhood (Barry, *et. al.,* 1976). These relationships may be expected to clarify the meanings of both sets of ratings. In addition, the new measures of agents and techniques in child training are closely related to independent measures of equivalent or similar cultural customs, derived by other cross-cultural researchers. These relationships further amplify the meanings of the measures presented here and indicate their validity as measures of general attributes of culture.

## DEFINITIONS OF CODES

Table 1 identifies for each of 186 world areas the representative society selected by Murdock and White (1969). Four of them are not coded on any of the variables because of meager information about childhood (75 Khmer; 88 Tobelorese; 101 Pentecost; 103 Ajie). The codes are applied to the span of ages from approximately four years, when the child is walking and talking proficiently, or when the society regards infancy as having ended, to approximately

TABLE 1

Agents and Techniques of Training in Early and Late Childhood

| SOCIETY | COMPANION | | RESIDENCE | | | | CARETAKER | | | |
| | I-NF | SEX | I-NP | CAT. | S-P | S-NP | I-NP | CAT. | S-P | S-NP |
| | E L | E L | E L | E L | E L | E L | E L | E L | E L | E L |
| | BGBG | BGBG | BGBG | BGBG | BGBG | BGBG | BGBG | BGBG | BGBG | BGBG |
| 1 Nama Hottentot | 3 | 3324 | 1122 | --CC | 3 | --15 | 2 | N | 5 | 3 |
| 2 Kung Bushmen | 3344 | 2424 | 1177 | --IG | 33-- | ---5 | 5557 | SSSG | 444- | 3535 |
| 3 Thonga | 5 | 2424 | 6 | G | 5 | 3 | 55.. | SS.. | 55.. | 55.. |
| 4 Lozi | 5 | 1515 | 4455 | F | 4 | 3 | 1 | - | 5 | - |
| 5 Mbundu | 3344 | 3315 | 3377 | UGUG | 44-- | 1515 | 55.. | SS.. | 44.. | 45.. |
| 6 Suku | 3 | 3 | 2233 | F | 4 | 3 | 4 | S | 5 | 5 |
| 7 Bemba | 3 | 3315 | 1 | - | 3 | - | 3 | G | 5 | 5 |
| 8 Nyakyusa | 3353 | 2424 | 2272 | FFCN | 44-4 | 3311 | 5 | G | 5 | 5 |
| 9 Hadza | 3344 | 2424 | 2 | RRCR | 4433 | 3313 | 3373 | RRIR | 55-5 | 55-5 |
| 10 Luguru | 5 | 3 | 2 | F | 3 | 3 | 1 | - | 5 | - |
| 11 Kikuyu | 4433 | 3324 | 1 | - | 5 | - | 5 | S | 5 | 5 |
| 12 Ganda | 4455 | 2415 | 6677 | RNRN | 35-- | 3131 | 6363 | RNRN | 5 | 5 |
| 13 Mbuti Pygmies | 5 | 3 | 5 | F | 3 | 3 | 6677 | CCII | 33-- | 33-- |
| 14 Nkundo Mongo | 3 | 3 | 2224 | FFFN | 4 | 3 | 5 | G | 5 | 3 |
| 15 Banen | 3 | 3 | 1363 | -GCG | 5515 | -515 | 3331 | SSS- | 5 | 333- |
| 16 Tiv | 3344 | 2424 | 1144 | --RR | 5 | --33 | 7 | SSII | - | 24-- |
| 17 Ibo | 4455 | 3 | 3342 | GGCN | 5 | 3313 | 3 | S | 4 | 3 |
| 18 Fon | 3 | 3 | 4474 | RRCG | 45-5 | 3315 | 5575 | GSIS | 55-5 | 35-5 |
| 19 Ashanti | 3 | 3 | 1 | - | 4433 | - | 2277 | RRUU | 55-- | 3311 |
| 20 Mende | 3344 | 3324 | 2557 | GNRR | 445- | 5533 | 15.5 | -N.N | 45.5 | -5.5 |
| 21 Wolof | 3353 | 2425 | 1171 | --N- | 55-5 | --1- | 4474 | SSCS | 55-5 | 5515 |
| 22 Bambara | 5 | 1524 | 2 | FNFN | 3 | 3 | 3 | N | 5 | 5 |
| 23 Tallensi | 3 | 3315 | 2 | R | 5 | 3 | 55.. | SS.. | 33.. | 33.. |
| 24 Songhai | 3355 | 3315 | 4477 | FFCC | 44-- | 3315 | 5 | N | 5 | 3 |
| 25 Wodaabe Fulani | 3 | 3324 | 4373 | FGIG | 55-5 | 33-3 | 5 | G | 5 | 3 |
| 26 Zazzagawa Hausa | 4 | 3324 | 1444 | -CCC | 3 | -515 | 1212 | -G-G | 5 | -5-5 |
| 27 Massa | 3 | 2424 | 4 | F | 5 | 3 | 2 | N | 5 | 5 |
| 28 Azande | 2232 | 3315 | 3363 | RRCR | 5515 | 1 | 2211 | NN-- | 5515 | 55-- |
| 29 Fur | 3355 | 3324 | 3154 | G-NC | 5345 | 3-33 | 5 | S | 5 | 5 |
| 30 Otoro Nuba | 3233 | 3315 | 1177 | --CC | 55-- | --15 | 22.. | GG.. | 55.. | 33.. |
| 31 Shilluk | 3344 | 2424 | 4477 | C | 33-- | 1515 | .1.1 | .-.- | .5.5 | .-.- |
| 32 Northern Mao | . | . | 2 | F | 4 | 3 | 1 | - | 5 | - |
| 33 Kaffa | 3 | 3315 | 4242 | F | 4 | 3 | 44.. | N | 55.. | 55.. |
| 34 Masai | 3 | 3324 | 1166 | --IN | 5 | ---1 | 4 | N | 5 | 5 |
| 35 Konso | 3344 | 3324 | 2172 | F-NC | 44-4 | 3-15 | 447. | SSI. | 55-. | 44-. |
| 36 Somali | 3343 | 3315 | 2271 | FFR- | 33-5 | 331- | . | . | . | . |
| 37 Amhara | 3355 | 3315 | 4 | F | 3 | 3 | 3 | G | 5 | 3 |
| 38 Bogo | 4 | 2424 | 2121 | N-N- | 3 | 1-1- | 2 | N | 5 | 5 |
| 39 Kenuzi Nubians | 3343 | 3325 | 1144 | --RR | 3 | --33 | 5575 | GGIG | 55-5 | 55-5 |
| 40 Teda | 3 | 2424 | 5 | G | 4 | 5 | 5577 | GGII | 55-- | 55-- |

| SOC | AUTHORITY | | | | DISCIPLINARIAN | | | | EDUCATOR | | | | SCH |
|---|---|---|---|---|---|---|---|---|---|---|---|---|---|
| | I-NP E L BGBG | CAT. E L BGBG | S-P E L BGBG | S-NP E L BGBG | I-NP E L BGBG | CAT. E L BGBG | S-P E L BGBG | S-NP E L BGBG | I-NP E L BGBG | CAT. E L BGBG | S-P E L BGBG | S-NP E L BGBG | E L BGBG |
| 1 | 1171 | --C- | 33-3 | --1- | | | | | 1171 | --C- | 45-5 | --1- | 3 |
| 2 | 1 | - | 2 | - | . | . | . | . | 1 | - | 3315 | - | 3 |
| 3 | 5 | R | 1 | 1 | 5.5. | G.G. | 1.1. | 1.1. | 6262 | CTCT | 1515 | 1313 | 5 |
| 4 | 5 | C | 4 | 1515 | | | | | 1 | - | 5515 | - | 3344 |
| 5 | 5454 | R | 3315 | 3315 | | | | | 6555 | S | 3515 | 1515 | 3344 |
| 6 | 6 | R | 1 | 1 | | | | | 4 | R | 1515 | 1515 | 1 |
| 7 | 2 | G | 2424 | 3 | 1 | - | 1 | - | 2243 | GGCC | 4515 | 3315 | 1133 |
| 8 | 4171 | C-C- | 22-2 | 1-1- | 5.5. | N.N. | 1.1. | 1.1. | 7464 | C | -515 | 1515 | 5354 |
| 9 | 1 | - | 5 | - | 7 | I | - | - | 6 | G | 2525 | 5 | 3 |
| 10 | 6 | U | 3 | 1 | | | | | . | . | . | . | . |
| 11 | 5 | R | 2 | 1 | | | | | 4454 | GGSN | 4525 | 3515 | 4 |
| 12 | 5377 | URRR | 22-- | 1124 | | | | | 2321 | RRR- | 2525 | 252- | 3344 |
| 13 | 4 | N | 2424 | 2424 | 5 | N | 3 | 3 | 5 | N | 2424 | 2424 | 3 |
| 14 | 1 | - | 2 | - | | | | | 5354 | N | 1515 | 3335 | 5 |
| 15 | 1 | - | 1212 | - | 3 | S | 1414 | 3 | 2 | SSTT | 3315 | 3 | 3355 |
| 16 | 5544 | R | 3324 | 3324 | 5511 | CC-- | 3324 | 24-- | 4411 | CC-- | 3315 | 24-- | 4 |
| 17 | 1 | - | 2424 | - | 1 | - | 5 | - | 5 | T | 3 | 5 | 6 |
| 18 | 5353 | UGUG | 3 | 1515 | 2 | R | 4 | 3 | 3355 | UUNN | 1515 | 1115 | 3 |
| 19 | 4474 | RRUR | 22-2 | 3313 | 4 | S | 2 | 3 | 2211 | RR-- | 5115 | 33-- | 3344 |
| 20 | 6575 | UNNN | 14-4 | 1515 | | | | | 5 | N | 15-- | 1533 | 2365 |
| 21 | 4 | GGSG | 2212 | 2212 | 4454 | SSTS | 2212 | 5515 | 6162 | G-CT | 1515 | 1-13 | 2265 |
| 22 | 2177 | C-NN | 22-- | 1-15 | | | | | 2277 | CCNN | 15-- | 1515 | 3344 |
| 23 | 4 | S | 1212 | 3 | | | | | 6 | S | 3515 | 1515 | 1133 |
| 24 | 4477 | RRCC | 15-- | 1515 | 1 | - | 3 | - | 7424 | RRTR | -515 | 1515 | 1151 |
| 25 | 4 | S | 2 | 1 | ..11 | ..-- | ..15 | ..-- | 5 | S | 3515 | 3515 | 3 |
| 26 | 1277 | -GCC | 22-- | -515 | | | | | 2 | NNTT | 1515 | 1533 | 1155 |
| 27 | 1 | - | 3 | - | . | . | . | . | 1 | - | 3 | - | 3 |
| 28 | 1171 | --N- | 22-2 | --1- | | | | | 1122 | --NN | 2515 | --15 | 3344 |
| 29 | 2171 | G-T- | 22-5 | 3-1- | 1171 | --C- | 45-5 | --3- | 5 | GGSS | 3315 | 3315 | 3365 |
| 30 | 4161 | R-C- | 1313 | 1-1- | 1152 | --CN | 1515 | --11 | 7171 | C-N- | -5-5 | 1-1- | 1144 |
| 31 | 5457 | SSSN | 151- | 1115 | .7.7 | .S.S | .-.- | .1.1 | 5 | C | 1515 | 1515 | 1 |
| 32 | . | . | . | . | | | | | . | . | . | . | . |
| 33 | 1 | - | 2 | - | 1 | - | 1 | - | 1121 | --T- | 1515 | --1- | 3354 |
| 34 | 1171 | --N- | 22-2 | --1- | 1 | - | .5 | - | 5151 | N-N- | 1515 | 1-1- | 2323 |
| 35 | 5573 | GGNG | 33-3 | 1 | 4 | U | 5 | 1 | ...7 | ...N | ...- | ...5 | ...4 |
| 36 | 1 | - | 2 | - | | | | | 1161 | --C- | 2515 | --1- | 3344 |
| 37 | 3 | S | 2 | 1515 | | | | | 7761 | CCT- | --15 | 333- | 1164 |
| 38 | 4242 | S | 1 | 1 | 3232 | S | 1 | 1 | 4141 | S-S- | 1515 | 1-1- | 3 |
| 39 | 4 | G | 2 | 5 | | | | | 5 | RRNR | 4515 | 5515 | 1165 |
| 40 | 1 | - | 2 | - | . | . | . | . | 1127 | --TT | 333- | --33 | 1156 |

| | EXAMPLE | OPINION | LECTURE | TEASE | SCOLD | WARN | CORPORAL |
|---|---|---|---|---|---|---|---|
| | E  L | E  L | E  L | E  L | E  L | E  L | E  L |
| | B G B G | B G B G | B G B G | B G B G | B G B G | B G B G | B G B G |
| 1 | 3+ | 3 | 3 | 3 | 3 | . | 3 |
| 2 | 4+ | 4 | 2 | 3 | . . 2+2+ | . | 1 |
| 3 | 4 | . | 3+ | 3 . 3 . | 3 | 3+ | 3+. 3+. |
| 4 | . | . | . | . . 3 3 | . | . | 3 |
| 5 | 4 | . | 4 | 3 | 3 | 4 4 2-2- | 3 |
| 6 | 4 | 3+ | . . 3 . | . . 4 3 | . | . | . |
| 7 | 3+ | 3 | . | 3 | 3 | 3+ | 3 |
| 8 | 3 3 3+3 | 4+ | . . . 3 | . . 3+3+ | 3 | 3+ | 3 |
| 9 | 3+ | . | . | . | . 3 . 3 | . | 2 |
| 10 | . | . | . | . | . | . | 2+ |
| 11 | 3+ | 4 | 4 | 2 2 3 3 | 3 | 4 | 2 2 3 3 |
| 12 | 4+ | . | 3+ | 3 | 2 2 3 3 | 3+ | 2+2+. . |
| 13 | 4+ | 3- | 3 | 4 | 3 | 2 | 3 |
| 14 | 3+ | 3- | 2 2 3 3 | 3 | 2 2 3 3 | 3 | 2 3+3 3+ |
| 15 | 3 3 4 4 | . | 3 3 4 4 | . | 3 3 4 4 | 3 | 3+3 4 3+ |
| 16 | 4 | 4 | 3 | 4 | 4 | 3 | 3 |
| 17 | 4+ | 3+ | 3 | 3+ | 3 | 3+ | 3- |
| 18 | 4 | 3+ | 4- | 3+ | . | 3+ | 4 |
| 19 | 3+ | . | 3 3 3+3+ | . | . | . | . |
| 20 | 4 | . | 3 3 4 4 | . | . | 4 | . |
| 21 | 4 4+4 4+ | 3 | 3 | . . . 4 | 4 | 4 | 4 |
| 22 | 4 | 3 | 3+ | 3 | . | . | 3+. 3+. |
| 23 | 4+ | 3+ | . | 2+2+3 3 | 3-3-3+3+ | . . 2+2+ | 2+2+3 3 |
| 24 | . | . | . . 3 3 | . . 2+2+ | . | . | . |
| 25 | 4 | 3+ | 3+ | 3-3-3+3+ | 3 3 3+3+ | . | 2 2 4-3- |
| 26 | 3+ | . | . | 3+ | 3 | . | 3 |
| 27 | . | . | . | . | . | . | 3+3+4 4 |
| 28 | 3 | 4 | 3 | . | . | . | 3+ |
| 29 | 4 | . | 3+ | 3 | . | 3+ | 3+3+4+3+ |
| 30 | 4 | . . 4 . | . | . . 3 . | . | . | . |
| 31 | 4 | . | 3 . 3 . | . | . | . | 2+ |
| 32 | . | . | . | . | . | . | . |
| 33 | 4 | 4 | 3 | 3+ | . | 4+ | 3 |
| 34 | 4 | 4 | . | 4 | 3+ | 3 | 3+ |
| 35 | 3 | . | 3 | 3 | . | . | . |
| 36 | . | . | . | . | . | . | . |
| 37 | . | . | . | . . 3+3+ | . . 3+3+ | . . 3 3 | . . 4 3 |
| 38 | 4 | . | . | . | . | 3 | 2 |
| 39 | 4+ | . | . | 3+ | 3 | 4 | 2 |
| 40 | 4 | . | . | 2+ | . | . | 3 |

| SOC | CEREMONY E(B G) L(B G) | GIFTS E(B G) L(B G) | PERMISS. E(B G) L(B G) | AFFECTION E(B G) L(B G) | VALUE E(B G) L(B G) | INCORP. E(B G) L(B G) |
|---|---|---|---|---|---|---|
| 1 | 2+ | 3 | 4-3+3+3 | 3 | 3+3-3+3- | 2+2+3 3+ |
| 2 | 3+ | 3 | 5-5-4+4+ | 4+4+4-4- | 4- | 2+2+3+3+ |
| 3 | 2 | . 2+. 2+ | 4 3+4 3+ | 3- | 4- | 2 3 3 3 |
| 4 | . . 2+. | 3 | 3+3 3 3- | 3 | 3 | . |
| 5 | . | . | 3 | 3- | 4- | 2+2+4 4 |
| 6 | . . 3+. | . | 4 3 4 3 | . | 4 | 2+2+3+3+ |
| 7 | 2 | 3 3 3 3+ | 4 4 3+3 | 3+ | 4 | 3-3 4-3+ |
| 8 | 2 2 3 2 | . | 3+3+3 3 | 3 | 4- | 2 2 3-3+ |
| 9 | 3 3+3 3+ | 3 | 4+3 4+3 | 2+3+2+3+ | 3 | 2 2+3-4- |
| 10 | . | . | . | 3 | 3 3+3 3+ | . . 3+3+ |
| 11 | 2 2 3 4 | 3- | 4-4-3 3 | 4- | 4-3+4-3+ | 2 2 3 3+ |
| 12 | 2 2 3 3 | 3 | 3 3-2+2- | 3- | 3 | 2 2 3 3 |
| 13 | 1 1 3 3 | . . 2 2 | 4-4-3 3 | 4+4+3+3+ | 4- | 3 3 4-4- |
| 14 | . 2+2+2+ | 2+ | 4-4-3+3- | 3+3+3 3 | 3+ | 2 3-3+4 |
| 15 | 3 2-3 2- | 3 | . | . | 3 3-3 3- | 2-2-3 3- |
| 16 | 3 . 3 . | . | 3 | 3+ | 4- | 2+2+4 4- |
| 17 | 3+ | 3+ | 4 3+3 3+ | 4 | 4-3+4-3+ | 3 3 4+4+ |
| 18 | 3+ | 3+. . 3+ | 3 | . | 4- | 3-3-3 3 |
| 19 | . | 3 | 3+3+3 3 | 4- | 3+ | . . 3 3 |
| 20 | . 3-. . | 2 . 3 3 | 2+3 . 2+ | 2 | 3 3+3 3+ | 2 2 . . |
| 21 | 2 2 3+2 | 2 3 3+3 | 3 3-3-2+ | 3 4-3 4- | 4+ | 2+3 4-4+ |
| 22 | 3+ | 3+ | 3 | 3+ | 4-3+4-3+ | 3 3 4-4- |
| 23 | 2+ | 3 | 4+4+4 4 | 4 | 5 5-5 5- | 2+2+3+3+ |
| 24 | . . 3+2+ | 3+ | 4- | 4- | 3+ | 2 2 3 3 |
| 25 | . . 3 2+ | 3 3 4 4 | 4 4 3-3 | . | 4+4-4+4- | 2 2 3+3 |
| 26 | 3 | 3+ | 4-4-3 3 | 3+ | 3 | 2+2+3 3 |
| 27 | . | . | . | . | 4 4+4 4+ | . |
| 28 | . . 3 . | 2 3 2 3 | 3 3 2 2 | 3+3+2 2 | 3 3+3 3+ | 2 2 3 3+ |
| 29 | 2 2 3 3 | 3 | 3- | 3- | 3 3+3 3+ | 2+2+3 3 |
| 30 | . 1 3 2 | 2 | 2+ | 3- | 3+ | 2+2+2+3 |
| 31 | 2 2 3 3 | 2+ | 3+ | 3+ | 3+3 3+3 | 3-3-4-4- |
| 32 | 2+ | 2+ | . | . | . | . |
| 33 | 2 2-2 2- | 3 | . | 3 | . | 2-2-2+4 |
| 34 | 2 | 3 2+4 2+ | 3 | 3- | 4 3 4 3 | 3 3 3 4 |
| 35 | 3 | . | 3 | 2 | 3- | 2+2-2+2- |
| 36 | . | . | 4-3+3 3- | 3 | 3+3-3+3- | 2 2 4-4- |
| 37 | . | . . 3 3 | 4 4 3-3- | 3 | 3+3+4 3+ | 2-2-3 3 |
| 38 | 3 . . . | . | 3+ | 3- | 3+3-3+3- | 2 2-3 3 |
| 39 | 3 3+3+3+ | 2 2 3 3 | 4+3 3 3- | 3 | 4-3+4-3+ | 2 2 3 3 |
| 40 | . . 3 . | . . 3 . | 3 | . | 3 | 3 3 4-4- |

| SOCIETY | COMPANION | | RESIDENCE | | | | CARETAKER | | | |
|---|---|---|---|---|---|---|---|---|---|---|
| | I-NF | SEX | I-NP | CAT. | S-P | S-NP | I-NP | CAT. | S-P | S-NP |
| | E L | E L | E L | E L | E L | E L | E L | E L | E L | E L |
| | B G B G | B G B G | B G B G | B G B G | B G B G | B G B G | B G B G | B G B G | B G B G | B G B G |
| 41 Ahaggaren Tuareg | 3 | 2424 | 1 | – | 3 | – | 4646 | N | 4515 | 5515 |
| 42 Riffians | 4455 | 2415 | 4141 | N-N- | 3 | 3-3- | 2 | C | 5 | 5 |
| 43 Egyptians | 3344 | 3324 | 1 | – | 3 | – | 7 | S | – | 4 |
| 44 Hebrews | 5 | 3 | 2 | F | 3 | 3 | 1 | – | 5 | – |
| 45 Babylonians | 4 | 2424 | 2252 | FFNF | 3 | 3 | 4 | N | 5151 | 5151 |
| 46 Rwala Bedouin | 2255 | 3315 | 4111 | F--- | 4515 | 3--- | 4 | N | 5 | 3 |
| 47 Turks | 2242 | 3315 | 2 | RFRF | 3 | 3 | 66.. | US.. | 55.. | 55.. |
| 48 Gheg Albanians | 3 | 3324 | 1 | – | 3 | – | 3 | G | 5 | 5 |
| 49 Romans | 4455 | 3324 | 2122 | F-FN | 3 | 3-33 | 6646 | N | 4515 | 3313 |
| 50 Spanish Basques | 4 | 2415 | 2 | F | 3 | 3 | 2 | G | 5 | 5 |
| 51 Irish | 3 | 3315 | 1122 | --FF | 3 | --33 | 5511 | GG-- | 5 | 55-- |
| 52 Könkämä Lapps | 3 | 3 | 4455 | FFRR | 3 | 3 | 5 | G | 4435 | 3 |
| 53 Yurak Samoyed | 2 | 3 | 1 | – | 3 | – | . | . | . | . |
| 54 Russians | 4455 | 3324 | 1122 | --NN | 3 | --33 | 6 | G | 5 | 3 |
| 55 Abkhaz | 5 | 3 | 6611 | FF-- | 3 | 33-- | 6 | N | 5 | 3 |
| 56 Armenians | 3 | 3324 | 4 | F | 3 | 3 | 1 | – | 5 | – |
| 57 Kurd | 3 | 3324 | 1121 | --R- | 3 | --3- | 5 | S | 5 | 4 |
| 58 Basseri | 3 | 2424 | 2 | F | 3 | 3 | 1 | – | 3 | – |
| 59 West Punjabi | 4433 | 3324 | 1213 | -F-F | 3 | -3-3 | 3 | S | 4 | 4 |
| 60 Maria Gond | 4 | 3 | 1141 | --C- | 3313 | --1- | 1 | – | 3 | – |
| 61 Toda | . | . | 1212 | -N-N | 3 | -3-3 | 1 | – | 5 | – |
| 62 Santal | 4452 | 2425 | 1 | – | 3 | – | 6 | G | 5 | 3 |
| 63 Uttar Pradesh | 5 | 2425 | 1 | – | 5515 | – | 5 | G | 5 | 3 |
| 64 Burusho | 5 | 3 | 2 | G | 3 | 3 | 3 | S | 4 | 3 |
| 65 Kazak | 3 | 3 | 4242 | F | 3 | 3 | 4 | S | 5 | 3 |
| 66 Khalkha Mongols | 3355 | 3324 | 4252 | F | 3 | 3 | 1 | – | 4 | – |
| 67 Lolo | 4 | 3324 | 2121 | F-F- | 3 | 3-3- | 4 | N | 5 | 5 |
| 68 Lepcha | 4 | 2424 | 2121 | F-F- | 3 | 3-3- | 4 | S | 4 | 3 |
| 69 Garo | 4 | 2424 | 2273 | GGCG | 33-3 | 3313 | 5353 | S | 4 | 3 |
| 70 Lakher | 4 | 2424 | 2177 | F-CC | 33-- | 3-55 | 1 | – | 5 | – |
| 71 Burmese | 3 | 3 | 1 | – | 3 | – | 5 | R | 3 | 3 |
| 72 Lamet | 3355 | 3324 | 2212 | FF-F | 3 | 33-3 | 5 | R | 5 | 5 |
| 73 North Vietnamese | 3 | 2424 | 4242 | F | 3 | 3 | 55.. | GG.. | 33.. | 33.. |
| 74 Rhade | 3 | 3315 | 2 | F | 3 | 3 | 4 | S | 5 | 3 |
| 75 Khmer | . | . | . | . | . | . | . | . | . | . |
| 76 Siamese | 3 | 3 | 5 | F | 3 | 3 | 5 | S | 3 | 3 |
| 77 Semang | 3 | 3324 | 2 | F | 3 | 3 | 11.. | --.. | 33.. | --.. |
| 78 Nicobarese | 3 | 2424 | 2 | F | 3 | 3 | 4242 | C | 5 | 3 |
| 79 Andamanese | 3 | 1515 | 4474 | FFCN | 33-3 | 3313 | 1 | – | 2424 | – |
| 80 Forest Vedda | 5 | 2424 | 1 | – | 3 | – | 2 | S | 5 | 5 |

| SOC | AUTHORITY I-NP E L BGBG | CAT. E L BGBG | S-P E L BGBG | S-NP E L BGBG | DISCIPLINARIAN I-NP E L BGBG | CAT. E L BGBG | S-P E L BGBG | S-NP E L BGBG | EDUCATOR I-NP E L BGBG | CAT. E L BGBG | S-P E L BGBG | S-NP E L BGBG | SCH E L BGBG |
|---|---|---|---|---|---|---|---|---|---|---|---|---|---|
| 41 | 4 | U | 2424 | 1 | | | | | 5525 | CCTN | 1525 | 3315 | 3356 |
| 42 | 1 | - | 3 | - | 114. | --C. | 333. | --1. | 4171 | T-C- | 45-5 | 1-1- | 6161 |
| 43 | 3355 | SSTT | 3 | 1115 | 1164 | --TT | 4424 | --15 | 6 | CCSS | 3315 | 1515 | 6 |
| 44 | 4545 | G | 2 | 1 | | | | | 5131 | T-N- | 4515 | 1-1- | 6364 |
| 45 | 1 | - | 2 | - | 1.4. | -.T. | 1.1. | -.1. | 2253 | NNTN | 1515 | 1535 | 4465 |
| 46 | 1414 | -S-S | 2313 | -1-1 | 4 | N | 3 | 3 | 1 | - | 3315 | - | 1 |
| 47 | 3 | S | 1 | 1 | 6 | S | 3 | 3 | 1152 | --NT | 1515 | --11 | 1165 |
| 48 | 4 | R | 2 | 1 | 1 | - | 2 | - | 525. | RGT. | 151. | 151. | 236. |
| 49 | 1 | - | 2 | - | 4 | T | 1313 | 1313 | 6 | N | 4545 | 3 | 6 |
| 50 | 4 | N | 3 | 3 | | | | | 5377 | TGTT | 14-- | 3533 | 6 |
| 51 | 5 | R | 2424 | 3315 | | | | | 6655 | S | 5115 | 3315 | 6 |
| 52 | 4 | G | 3 | 3 | | | | | 5 | G | 2424 | 3 | 3636 |
| 53 | 4 | G | 1 | 1 | | | | | 2121 | T-T- | 1515 | 3-3- | 5454 |
| 54 | 5577 | T | 33-- | 3 | . | . | . | . | 7 | GGTT | - | 3 | 5566 |
| 55 | 6111 | R--- | 2515 | 1--- | | | | | 6 | N | 2415 | 1515 | 3366 |
| 56 | 5 | S | 2 | 1 | | | | | 1141 | --T- | 1 | --3- | 3366 |
| 57 | 5 | S | 2 | 2 | 1 | - | 1212 | - | 7642 | SSTT | -515 | 3315 | 2355 |
| 58 | 1 | - | 2 | - | 1 | - | 1 | - | 6644 | CCTT | 2415 | 3 | 3366 |
| 59 | 3 | S | 3 | 1 | 1141 | --T- | 2 | --1- | 5523 | GGTN | 3515 | 5515 | 3355 |
| 60 | 1177 | --CC | 33-- | --15 | | | | | 4177 | N-CN | 15-- | 3-33 | 1133 |
| 61 | 4 | R | 1 | 1 | . | . | . | . | . | | | | 1 |
| 62 | 1144 | --NN | 1 | --11 | 1.1. | -.-. | 1.1. | -.-. | 2 | TSTS | 1515 | 3535 | 5353 |
| 63 | 4 | G | 2424 | 4242 | 5544 | RRTT | 4415 | 3313 | 5525 | CCTR | 1515 | 1515 | 5 |
| 64 | 1 | - | 3 | - | | | | | 5 | NNTN | 3 | 3 | 3363 |
| 65 | 4 | N | 2 | 5 | 1 | - | 1155 | - | 2121 | T-T- | 4545 | 3-3- | 5454 |
| 66 | 4421 | SST- | 4415 | 153- | 5 | R | 3 | 3 | 4454 | S | 3324 | 3315 | 1153 |
| 67 | 1 | - | 3 | - | | | | | ..44 | ...NN | ..15 | ..15 | ..44 |
| 68 | 1 | - | 3 | - | 1 | - | 4 | - | 1131 | --S- | 2515 | --1- | 2252 |
| 69 | 5 | U | 3315 | 1 | | | | | 6461 | CCC- | 2424 | 333- | 1155 |
| 70 | 4 | U | 3 | 1 | | | | | 1 | - | 1515 | - | 3 |
| 71 | 3 | R | 3 | 1 | | | | | 3355 | NNTT | 3325 | 3313 | 1166 |
| 72 | 5454 | R | 1 | 1 | | | | | 4141 | N-N- | 1515 | 1-1- | 3131 |
| 73 | 4 | S | 1 | 1 | 1 | - | 1 | - | 4455 | G | 3315 | 3315 | 4465 |
| 74 | 1 | - | 1 | - | | | | | 5 | G | 3 | 3 | 5 |
| 75 | . | . | . | . | | | | | . | . | . | . | . |
| 76 | 4455 | S | 3 | 3 | | | | | 1177 | --TT | 33-- | --33 | 1166 |
| 77 | 1 | - | 3 | - | | | | | 1414 | -S-S | 1515 | -5-5 | 1 |
| 78 | 1 | . | . | . | | | | | 6 | C | 1515 | 1515 | 1155 |
| 79 | 6 | S | 3 | 1515 | | | | | 1 | - | 1515 | - | 3 |
| 80 | 1 | - | 2525 | - | | | | | 5 | U | 1515 | 1 | 3 |

| | EXAMPLE E L B G B G | OPINION E L B G B G | LECTURE E L B G B G | TEASE E L B G B G | SCOLD E L B G B G | WARN E L B G B G | CORPORAL E L B G B G |
|---|---|---|---|---|---|---|---|
| 41 | 3+ | . | 3+ | 2+ | 2+ | . | 2 |
| 42 | 4 | 3+ | 3+ | 4 | . | 4 | . |
| 43 | 3+ | 4 | 3+ | 4 | 3 3 4 4 | 4 4 3 3 | 3+3+4 4 |
| 44 | 4+ | 4 | 4+ | . | 4 | . | 4+ |
| 45 | 3 | 3+ | 4 | . | 3+ | . | . . 4 4 |
| 46 | 4 | . | 3 | . | . | 3 | 3+3+4 4- |
| 47 | 4 | . | . | 3 | 3- | . | 2 |
| 48 | 4+ | 4- | 4+ | . | . 3+. 3+ | . | . |
| 49 | 4 | . | 4 | 3+ | . . 4 4 | 3+ | 3 3 4 4 |
| 50 | . | . | . | . | . | . | . |
| 51 | 4 | 3+ | 3 3 4 4 | 3 | . | 4 | . . 4 4 |
| 52 | 4 | 3 | 3- | 3- | 2 | 3 | 1 |
| 53 | . | . | 3 | . | . | . | 2 |
| 54 | 4 | 3 3 4 4 | 3 | 4 | 2 | 2 | 2 |
| 55 | . | . | 3 | . | . | . | . |
| 56 | . | . | 2+ | . | . | . | . |
| 57 | 3+ | . . 3 3+ | 3 | 3 | 3 | 3 | 3 |
| 58 | . | . | 3 | 3+ | . | . | 3 |
| 59 | 3+ | 4+ | 3 | . | 3 2 3 2 | . | 3+2 3+2 |
| 60 | 4 | 4 | . . 3 3 | 3 | . | . | . |
| 61 | . | . | . | . | . | . | . |
| 62 | 3 | . | 3 | . | 3 | 3 | 2 |
| 63 | 4 | 4 4+4 4+ | 3 | 4-4-3+3+ | 3 3 4 4 | 3 | 3-3-4 4 |
| 64 | 4 | 3 | 3 | 2 | 2+ | . | 2+ |
| 65 | 4 | . | 3 | 3 | . | 3 | 3 |
| 66 | 4+ | 3+ | . | . | . | . | 3 3 4 4 |
| 67 | 3 | . | . | 3 | 3- | 3+ | . |
| 68 | 4 | 4+ | 3 | 3 | 3- | 3+3+ . . | 3 |
| 69 | 4 | 3 | 3 | 4 | 3 | 3 | 3 |
| 70 | 4- | 3 | 2+ | . | 3 | 3+ | 2+2 3 3 |
| 71 | . | . | 3 3 3+3+ | 3- | . . 3 3 | . | 2 2 3 3 |
| 72 | 4 | 3 | . | . | . | 4 | . |
| 73 | . | . | 3 | . | 3- | 3+ | 3- |
| 74 | . | . | . | . | . | . | . |
| 75 | . | . | . | . | . | . | . |
| 76 | 4+ | . | . | . | . | 2+ | 3- |
| 77 | 4+ | . | . | 2+ | 3 | 3+ | 2 |
| 78 | 3 | . | 3 | . | . | 3+ | 2- |
| 79 | . | . | 2 | . | 3 | . | 1 |
| 80 | 4 | . | . | . | 3 | . | . |

| SOC | CEREMONY<br>E L<br>B G B G | GIFTS<br>E L<br>B G B G | PERMISS.<br>E L<br>B G B G | AFFECTION<br>E L<br>B G B G | VALUE<br>E L<br>B G B G | INCORP.<br>E L<br>B G B G |
|---|---|---|---|---|---|---|
| 41 | 2+ | 3 | 3- | 3+ | 4- | 3 3 4 4 |
| 42 | 3 . 3 . | 3 . 3 . | 2+ | . | 4-3+4-3+ | 2+2+3-3- |
| 43 | 3+2+3+2+ | 3 | 3-3-2 2 | 3-3-2 2 | 3 2+3+3 | 2+2+3 3 |
| 44 | 4 | 3 | . | . | 4+4-4+4- | 2 2 3 3 |
| 45 | . | 3 | 2+ | 3- | . | 2 2 2+2+ |
| 46 | 3 2 3 2 | 3+ | 3- | 2 | 3+2+3+2+ | 2 2 3+3+ |
| 47 | 3 . 3 . | 3-2+3-2+ | 4 3+3+3+ | 3+ | 4+2 4+2 | 2 2 3 3+ |
| 48 | . | . | 3-2 3-2 | 3-2 3-2 | 3+2+3+2+ | 2 2 3-3- |
| 49 | 3+3 3+3 | 4 | 3+ | 3 | 3 3-3 3- | 2 2 3+4- |
| 50 | 2 2 3 3 | 3+ | 2+2+2-2- | 3 3 2+2+ | 3 | 3-3-4-4- |
| 51 | 2 2 3 3 | 3 | 4-4-2+3 | 4 | 4 | 2-2-2+2+ |
| 52 | 2 | 3+ | 4- | 4 4 3+3+ | 4+4-4+4- | 3-3-3 3+ |
| 53 | . | 2+ | 4 | 3- | 3+ | . . . 3+ |
| 54 | 2+ | 3 | 2 2 3-3- | 4- | 4+ | 3-3-4-4- |
| 55 | 2 2 3 3 | . | 3-2+3-2+ | 2+ | 3-2+3-2+ | 3-3-4 4 |
| 56 | . | . | 2+ | . | 3+3 3+3 | 2 |
| 57 | 3+2 . . | 3 | 3+3 3+3- | 3 3-3 3- | 4 3 4 3 | 3 |
| 58 | . | 3 | 2+ | 3 | 4-3+4-3+ | 3 3 4 4 |
| 59 | 2+2 3 2 | 3+4 3+4 | 3+3+3 3 | 3+ | 4 3+4 3+ | 3-3-3+3+ |
| 60 | . . 3+3- | 3 | 3+ | . | 3+ | 2+2+4+4+ |
| 61 | 2+. 3 2+ | 3- | . | . | . 2 . 2 | 2 2 3 3 |
| 62 | 2 2 3 2 | 3 . 3 . | 3+3 3+3 | 3 3-3 3- | 3+2+3+2+ | 2+2+3+3+ |
| 63 | 3 3+3 3+ | 2+ | 3 3-3 3- | 3+3 3+3 | 4 3 4 3 | 2+2+3 3 |
| 64 | . | . | 3+3+3 3 | 3+ | 4-3+4 4- | 3+3+4+4+ |
| 65 | 3 . 3 . | . | 3+ | 3+ | 4-3-4-3- | 2+2+4-4- |
| 66 | . | 3 | 3 3 2+2+ | 3+ | 4- | 2+2+3+3+ |
| 67 | 2 | 2+ | . | 3 | 3 | 2 2 3 3 |
| 68 | 2+ | 3+ | 3 3-3-2+ | 3- | 3 | 2+3-3+4- |
| 69 | 3 | 3- | 4- | 4- | 3 3+3 3+ | 2 2 3 3 |
| 70 | 3 2+3 2+ | 3 | 3+3+3 3 | 3 | 3 | 3-3-3 3 |
| 71 | . . 2+2+ | 3 | 4 | 4- | 4 | 2+2+3+3+ |
| 72 | 3- | 3 | 3 3 3-3- | 3 | 3+3 3+3 | 3-3-4-4- |
| 73 | 3 | 3 | 4- | 4-4-3 3 | 4 3 4 3 | 2+2+3+3+ |
| 74 | . | . 3 . 3 | 4 4 3 3 | 4 | 4-4 4-4 | 2+2+3 3 |
| 75 | . | . | . | . | . | . |
| 76 | 3+3 3+3 | 4 | 4 | 3+ | 3 | 3- |
| 77 | . | 2+ | 4 | 4 | 3 | 3 |
| 78 | 2 2 3 . | 2+ | 3+ | 3+ | 3+ | 3 3 4-4- |
| 79 | . | 3 | 4-4-3 3 | 3+ | 3+ | 2+2+3+3+ |
| 80 | . | 3+ | . | 4- | 3 | 3-3-4-4- |

| SOCIETY | COMPANION | | RESIDENCE | | | | CARETAKER | | | |
| | I-NF<br>E L<br>BGBG | SEX<br>E L<br>BGBG | I-NP<br>E L<br>BGBG | CAT.<br>E L<br>BGBG | S-P<br>E L<br>BGBG | S-NP<br>E L<br>BGBG | I-NP<br>E L<br>BGBG | CAT.<br>E L<br>BGBG | S-P<br>E L<br>BGBG | S-NP<br>E L<br>BGBG |
|---|---|---|---|---|---|---|---|---|---|---|
| 81 Menabe Tanala | 4443 | 3324 | 2 | F | 4 | 3 | 5577 | SSII | 44-- | 33-- |
| 82 Negri Sembilan | 4455 | 3315 | 2 | F | 3 | 3 | 2 | S | 3 | 5 |
| 83 Javanese | 2253 | 2315 | 2255 | R | 3 | 3 | 5544 | GGSS | 4455 | 5 |
| 84 Balinese | 4443 | 3315 | 4 | F | 3 | 3 | 5571 | RRI- | 33-5 | 55-- |
| 85 Iban | 4455 | 3324 | 4 | F | 3 | 3 | 5 | G | 4 | 3 |
| 86 Tawi-Tawi Badjau | 3 | 3 | 2 | F | 3 | 3 | 3 | S | 3 | 3 |
| 87 Toradja | 3 | 3324 | 2 | F | 3 | 3 | 55.. | SS.. | 55.. | 44.. |
| 88 Tobelorese | . | . | . | . | . | . | . | . | . | . |
| 89 Alorese | 3355 | 2424 | 2 | FFRR | 3 | 3 | 6 | S | 4 | 3 |
| 90 Tiwi | 3 | 3324 | 2224 | FFFN | 5 | 3331 | 55.. | NN.. | 55.. | 55.. |
| 91 Aranda | 5 | 3315 | 1171 | --C- | 55-5 | --1- | 1 | - | 5 | - |
| 92 Orokaiva | 3 | 3 | 2 | UNUN | 4 | 1313 | 6 | S | 2 | 3 |
| 93 Kimam | 444. | 332. | 4477 | FFCN | 33--. | 3313 | 5 | U | 3 | 1 |
| 94 Kapauku | 3344 | 3315 | 1 | - | 5515 | - | 5571 | SSI- | 55-5 | 33-- |
| 95 Kwoma | 2244 | 3324 | 4242 | F | 3 | 3 | 2 | N | 5 | 5 |
| 96 Manus | 1144 | 2424 | 4 | F | 3 | 3 | 1177 | --II | 22-- | - |
| 97 Lesu | 445. | 331. | 1141 | --N- | 3 | --1- | 5 | G | 3 | 5 |
| 98 Trobrianders | 4 | 2424 | 2 | F | 3 | 3 | 22.2 | RR.R | 33.3 | 55.5 |
| 99 Siuai | 3 | 3324 | 1112 | ---N | 4 | ---3 | 4 | S | 5 | 5 |
| 100 Tikopia | 3 | 3324 | 5 | R | 3 | 3 | 5 | S | 3 | 3 |
| 101 Bunlap | . | . | . | . | . | . | . | . | . | . |
| 102 Mbau Fijians | 3 | 2424 | 5272 | FGNG | 44-4 | 3515 | 4 | N | 5 | 5 |
| 103 Ajie | . | . | . | . | . | . | . | . | . | . |
| 104 Maori | 4 | 3315 | 4545 | F | 3 | 3 | 5575 | GGIG | 33-3 | 33-3 |
| 105 Marquesans | 4 | 3 | 4477 | FFII | 33-- | 33-- | 6677 | NNII | 11-- | 22-- |
| 106 Samoans | 5353 | 1515 | 3 | F | 3 | 3 | 4 | S | 5 | 3 |
| 107 Makin Gilbertese | 4 | 3315 | 4165 | F-GF | 2414 | 3-13 | 5577 | NNRG | 45-- | 5515 |
| 108 Jaluit Marshallese | 4 | 2424 | 4 | F | 3 | 3 | 5 | R | 4 | 3 |
| 109 Trukese | 4433 | 2424 | 4 | FFRR | 3 | 3 | 6677 | RRII | 33-- | 33-- |
| 110 Yapese | 4 | 2424 | 4 | F | 3 | 3 | 4 | G | 5 | 3 |
| 111 Palauans | 3 | 3 | 4 | F | 3 | 3 | 5 | S | 3535 | 3535 |
| 112 Ifugao | 5 | 2424 | 5 | C | 3 | 1515 | 5 | G | 3 | 3 |
| 113 Atayal | 2 | 3 | 2 | F | 3 | 3 | 1 | - | 4 | - |
| 114 Chekiang Chinese | 3334 | 2315 | 4447 | FFNN | 333- | 3332 | 5544 | RRSS | 5515 | 5515 |
| 115 Aigun Manchu | 3 | 2424 | 2 | FNFN | 3 | 3 | 6 | R | 5 | 2 |
| 116 Koreans | 3332 | 2425 | 4242 | F | 3 | 3 | 5575 | SSIS | 55-5 | 35-5 |
| 117 Japanese | 4 | 3315 | 4 | F | 3 | 3 | 5 | G | 5 | 5 |
| 118 Saru Ainu | 3 | 3 | 5 | F | 3 | 3 | 2 | S | 5 | 5 |
| 119 Gilyak | 3 | 2424 | 1212 | -N-N | 3 | -3-3 | 1 | - | 5 | - |
| 120 Yukaghir | 5 | 3315 | 2 | F | 3 | 3 | 4 | R | 5 | 5 |

| SOC | AUTHORITY I-NP E L BGBG | CAT. E L BGBG | S-P E L BGBG | S-NP E L BGBG | DISCIPLINARIAN I-NP E L BGBG | CAT. E L BGBG | S-P E L BGBG | S-NP E L BGBG | EDUCATOR I-NP E L BGBG | CAT. E L BGBG | S-P E L BGBG | S-NP E L BGBG | SCH E L BGBG |
|---|---|---|---|---|---|---|---|---|---|---|---|---|---|
| 81 | 4111 | G--- | 2212 | 1--- | 1141 | --N- | 4515 | --1- | 4161 | N-N- | 3515 | 1-1- | 2343 |
| 82 | 4 | U | 4 | 1 | | | | | 7662 | CCCT | -515 | 3315 | 5565 |
| 83 | 1 | - | 3434 | - | 4 | G | 5 | 5 | 1475 | -STT | 55-5 | -533 | 3366 |
| 84 | 2 | S | 3 | 3 | | | | | 2167 | C-TT | 252- | 3-34 | 3364 |
| 85 | 5 | G | 3 | 3 | | | | | 5552 | GGTT | 3315 | 3315 | 3365 |
| 86 | 2 | R | 2 | 3 | | | | | 1 | - | 1515 | - | 1 |
| 87 | 11.1 | --.- | 35.5 | --.- | | | | | 1125 | --TN | 3515 | --35 | 1155 |
| 88 | . | . | . | . | | | | | . | . | . | . | . |
| 89 | 4 | R | 3 | 3 | 5 | S | 3 | 3 | 6441 | SCC- | 3415 | 351- | 1314 |
| 90 | 12.7 | -U.N | 33.- | -1.1 | | | | | 2227 | TTTN | 333- | 3331 | 5 |
| 91 | 1 | - | 2 | - | | | | | 1141 | --N- | 3515 | --1- | 1141 |
| 92 | 1 | - | 2 | - | 1 | - | 5 | - | 1141 | --N- | 2424 | --1- | 1 |
| 93 | 5 | USUS | 2 | 1 | | | | | 1177 | --RR | 24-- | --15 | 2266 |
| 94 | 1144 | --SS | 4414 | --11 | 1144 | --CS | 5514 | --11 | 5141 | C-C- | 5515 | 1-1- | 3344 |
| 95 | 1155 | --SS | 3 | --33 | 5 | S | 3 | 3 | 5554 | S | 3335 | 3335 | 3 |
| 96 | 7 | I | - | - | 4 | C | 5 | 3 | 5557 | CCCG | 121- | 3335 | 2223 |
| 97 | 1 | - | 3 | - | 3 | R | 3 | 3 | 3272 | CNTN | 15-5 | 1333 | 3353 |
| 98 | 1171 | --U- | 33-3 | --1- | . | . | . | . | 5 | NNUN | 2313 | 1515 | 3 |
| 99 | 6161 | U-U- | 1313 | 1-1- | | | | | 1454 | -NUN | 4515 | -515 | 1152 |
| 100 | 4 | G | 1 | 1 | 4 | G | 3 | 3 | 4441 | SSU- | 3315 | 331- | 3 |
| 101 | . | . | . | . | | | | | | | | | |
| 102 | 4 | N | 3 | 1 | 2 | R | 3 | 3 | 5511 | NN-- | 3324 | 33-- | 3344 |
| 103 | . | . | . | . | | | | | . | . | . | . | . |
| 104 | 4 | R | 2 | 1515 | . | . | . | . | 5454 | R | 2525 | 1515 | 4253 |
| 105 | 5577 | UUII | 11-- | 11-- | 7 | I | - | - | 6655 | C | 3323 | 3 | 1165 |
| 106 | 4 | N | 3 | 3 | 5 | S | 3 | 3 | 4 | SSCC | 5115 | 3315 | 3344 |
| 107 | 5552 | RGRN | 2413 | 3515 | 5552 | UGGN | 2413 | 1515 | 2233 | R | 3351 | 3315 | 1133 |
| 108 | 46.6 | SS.S | 12.2 | 33.3 | . | . | . | . | 5 | R | 2415 | 2415 | 2255 |
| 109 | 5 | G | 2 | 3 | 5577 | GGTT | 33-- | 3 | 5574 | RRTT | 33-5 | 3 | 1155 |
| 110 | 5 | G | 1515 | 1515 | | | | | 5511 | SS-- | 3315 | 33-- | 1133 |
| 111 | 6 | G | 1 | 1 | | | | | 5577 | S | 35-- | 3315 | 6 |
| 112 | 1 | - | 3 | - | 1 | - | 5 | - | 6655 | CCNN | 3315 | 1515 | 3344 |
| 113 | 4 | S | 2 | 1 | | | | | 1 | - | 1515 | - | 3 |
| 114 | 3222 | SSSN | 2215 | 1115 | 1142 | --TN | 2215 | --15 | 2255 | CCNR | 1515 | 1515 | 3366 |
| 115 | 5 | R | 1 | 1 | . | . | . | . | 1145 | --TS | 5525 | --35 | 3363 |
| 116 | 5454 | S | 1212 | 1 | 1 | - | 2 | - | 6155 | G-GR | 2515 | 1-15 | 2365 |
| 117 | 1177 | --TT | 22-- | --33 | 5 | G | 5 | 5 | 5 | G | 4242 | 5151 | 6 |
| 118 | 5 | S | 2424 | 1 | | | | | 4555 | G | 4515 | 1515 | 3344 |
| 119 | 1 | - | 5 | - | | | | | 3 | R | 1515 | 1515 | 3 |
| 120 | 2 | S | 3 | 3 | | | | | 4447 | N | 333- | 3331 | 2223 |

| | EXAMPLE E L B G B G | OPINION E L B G B G | LECTURE E L B G B G | TEASE E L B G B G | SCOLD E L B G B G | WARN E L B G B G | CORPORAL E L B G B G |
|---|---|---|---|---|---|---|---|
| 81 | 3+ | . | 3 | . | 3 | 4 | . |
| 82 | . . . 4 | . | 3+ | . | . | . | 2-2-3 3 |
| 83 | 3 3 4 4 | 2 2 3 3 | 3 | 2 2 3+3+ | 2-2-3 3 | 4 4 2 2 | 1 1 3-3- |
| 84 | 4 | . | 3+ | 4 4 3 3 | 3- | 3+ | 2- |
| 85 | 4 | 4 | 3- | . | . | . | . |
| 86 | 4 | . | . | 2+ | 2 | . | 1 |
| 87 | 4+ | 4 | 3- | 4 | 2+3 2+3 | 3 | 2 |
| 88 | . | . | . | . | . | . | . |
| 89 | 4+ | 4 | 3- | 4 | 2+2+3+3+ | 3+ | 2+2+3+3+ |
| 90 | . 4 . 4 | . | 3 3-3 3- | . | 3 | . | 3 2+3 2+ |
| 91 | . | . | 3 2+3+2+ | . | . | 3+ | . |
| 92 | 5 | . | . . 2+2+ | 3 2+3 2+ | 3+ | . | 3 |
| 93 | 4 | . | 2 2 3+3+ | 3 3 3+3+ | 3 | . | 2-2-4 4 |
| 94 | 4 | . | 3 3 4 4 | 2 2 3 3 | 3-3-3+3+ | . | 3-3-3+3+ |
| 95 | 3 3 4 4 | . . 3+3+ | 3 3 4 4 | 3 3 4 4 | 3+3+4+4+ | 3+3+4+4+ | 3 3 4 4 |
| 96 | 4+ | 4 | 4 4 2 2 | 3+ | 4 | 3- | 3+ |
| 97 | 4 3+4 3+ | . | 3 | 3+ | 3 | 2 | 3 |
| 98 | 4 | . | 2+ | 2+ | 3+ | . | 2+ |
| 99 | 4 | . | 3 | 3+ | 3 | 3+ | 2 |
| 100 | 3 | 4 | 4- | 3- | 3 | . | 2+ |
| 101 | . | . | . | . | . | . | . |
| 102 | 5 | 4 | 4 | 4 | 3+ | 4 | 4+ |
| 103 | . | . | . | . | . | . | . |
| 104 | 4 | 4 | 4+3 4+3 | . | 2 | 4+ | 3 2 3 2 |
| 105 | . . 3 3 | . | . | . | 1 | 4+ | 1 |
| 106 | . | . | . | 3 | 3+ | 3+ | 3 |
| 107 | 3+ | 4 | 4 | . . 4-4- | 3 | . | 3 3 3+3+ |
| 108 | 4+ | . | 4 | 4 | . | . | 2 |
| 109 | 4 | 3 | 4 | 4+ | 3 | 4+4+3 3 | 4 |
| 110 | 3 | . | 2 | 3 | . | 3+ | 2 |
| 111 | 3+ | . | 3 | 3+ | 4-4-5-5- | . | 3 |
| 112 | 3 | 2+ | 3+ | 4- | 3 | 3 | 3- |
| 113 | . | . | 3 | . | . | . | 2+ |
| 114 | 3+ | 3 | 4 | 3 3 4 4 | 3 3 4 4 | 2 | 3+3+4 4 |
| 115 | 4 | 3+ | 2+ | 3 | . | . | 2+ |
| 116 | 4 | . | 3+ | 3 | 3 | 2+ | 3+ |
| 117 | 4+ | 3 | 3 | . . 3 3 | 2 | . | 2 |
| 118 | 4 | 4 | 4 | . | 3 | 3 | 3- |
| 119 | 4 | 4 | 4- | . | . | 3- | . |
| 120 | . | . | . | 3 | . | 3 | . . |

| SOC | CEREMONY E L B G B G | GIFTS E L B G B G | PERMISS. E L B G B G | AFFECTION E L B G B G | VALUE E L B G B G | INCORP. E L B G B G |
|---|---|---|---|---|---|---|
| 81 | 3 . 3 2 | 3 | 2+3 2+3 | 3 3 2+2+ | 3+ | 2-2-3 3 |
| 82 | 3-3 3+3 | 3+ | 4 3+4-2- | 4+4+3+3+ | 4-4+4-4+ | 2-3 2 4 |
| 83 | . . 3-2 | 2 2 3 3 | 4+4+3 3 | 4+4+. . | 4+ | 1 1 3 3+ |
| 84 | 4 | . | 3+3+4 4 | 3+ | 4+ | 4 4 4+4+ |
| 85 | 2 2 3 3 | 2 | 4 4-3+3 | . | 4 4-4 4- | 3-3 3 3+ |
| 86 | . | . | 4 | 4 | 4+ | 3 3 4 4 |
| 87 | 2+3+2+3+ | 2 | 4 4 4 3+ | 3+3+. . | 3 3+3 3+ | 2+2+2+3+ |
| 88 | . | . |  |  | . | . |
| 89 | 2 2 3+2 | 2 2 2+2+ | 4 4-3+3 | 3+3+3 3 | 3+ | 2 2+3+4- |
| 90 | 2+ | 2 . 2 . | 3+3+3+3 | 3 3 3 3- | 2+3+2+3+ | 2-3 2-4+ |
| 91 | 2 2 3+2 | . | 3+3+2 . | 3+ | 3- | . |
| 92 | 2 2 3+3+ | 2+ | 4- | . | 3 | 2+2+. . |
| 93 | 2 2 3+2 | . | 4-4-2 3 | 3+ | 4 | 2 2 3 4- |
| 94 | . . 2 2 | 3 | 3+3+3-3- | 3+ | 3-3-3+3 | 2 2 4 4 |
| 95 | 2+. 3 . | . . 3 3 | 2 | 2 | 3 | 2-2-3-3- |
| 96 | 2 | 3 | 3+3+3+3 | . | 4+4+3+3+ | 2-2-2 3- |
| 97 | 2 2 3+3- | 3 | 4 3 4 3 | 3 | 3+ | 2 3-4-4- |
| 98 | 2+ | 3+ | 4 | 4 4 3+3+ | 4 | 3 |
| 99 | 3 | 3+ | 4+4+4-3 | 4 4 3 3 | 4 | 2+2+2+3+ |
| 100 | 3-2+3+2+ | 3 | 4 | 4 4 3+3+ | 4 | 3-3-3 3 |
| 101 | . | . | . | . | . | . |
| 102 | 2 2-3+3- | . | . | 2 | 3-2-3-2- | 2-2-3 3+ |
| 103 | . | . | . | . | . | . |
| 104 | 3 | . | 4+4+3+3+ | 3 | . | 3 3 4-4- |
| 105 | . | 4 | 4+ | . | . | 1 1 2+2+ |
| 106 | 2 2 3+3+ | . | 3- | 3- | 3+ | 3 3 4-4- |
| 107 | 3 | 3 | 4 4 2+3 | 4- | 4-3+4-3+ | 2 2 3+4- |
| 108 | . . . 3 | . . . 2 | 4+4 4+4 | 3+ | 3+ | 2-2-3-3+ |
| 109 | . | . | 3 . 4-3 | . | 3+ | 2-2-3+3+ |
| 110 | 2+ | 3- | 4- | 3 | 3 | 2-2-3+3- |
| 111 | 2 | . | 4-3+3+3- | 2+2+2 2 | 3 3+3 3+ | 2 2+3-3 |
| 112 | 2 | 2 | 4 4 3+3+ | 3 | 4- | 2 2 3-3- |
| 113 | . | . | 3 | 3 | . | . . 4 4+ |
| 114 | . | 3 2 3 2 | 3-2 2-2- | 3 2 3 2 | 3 2 4-2+ | 2 2 3 3 |
| 115 | 3- | 3 | 4-4-3+3+ | 4- | 3+3+3+3 | 2+3-2+3 |
| 116 | 3+2+3+2+ | 3 | 3 3-3 2+ | . | 3+3 3+3 | 2 2 3 3- |
| 117 | 3 | 3+ | 4-3 3 3- | 4 4-4 4- | 4 3+4 3+ | 2 2 3 3 |
| 118 | 3- | 3+ | 3- | 3+ | 3+3-3+3- | 2-2-3 3 |
| 119 | 2 2 3 3 | 3 | 3+ | 3+ | 3+ | 3 3 4+4 |
| 120 | 2+ | 2+ | 4-4-3+3+ | 4 | 4-3+4-3+ | 2 2 3 3 |

| SOCIETY | COMPANION | | RESIDENCE | | | | CARETAKER | | | |
|---|---|---|---|---|---|---|---|---|---|---|
| | I-NF<br>EL<br>BGBG | SEX<br>EL<br>BGBG | I-NP<br>EL<br>BGBG | CAT.<br>EL<br>BGBG | S-P<br>EL<br>BGBG | S-NP<br>EL<br>BGBG | I-NP<br>EL<br>BGBG | CAT.<br>EL<br>BGBG | S-P<br>EL<br>BGBG | S-NP<br>EL<br>BGBG |
| 121 Reindeer Chukchee | 3 | 3324 | 4343 | F | 4 | 3 | 3 | G | 4 | 3 |
| 122 Ingalik | 4455 | 3315 | 2212 | FF-N | 3 | 33-3 | 2211 | SS-- | 5 | 55-- |
| 123 Aleut | 3 | 3 | 3 | U | 3 | 1 | 1 | - | 5 | - |
| 124 Copper Eskimo | 3 | 3 | 5 | F | 3 | 3 | 1 | - | 5 | - |
| 125 Montagnais | 3 | 3315 | 2 | F | 3 | 3 | 44.. | SS.. | 55.. | 55.. |
| 126 Micmac | 5 | 1515 | 2 | F | 3 | 3 | 11.. | --.. | 55.. | --.. |
| 127 North Saulteaux | 2233 | 3324 | 1 | - | 3 | - | 5577 | GGII | 55-- | 33-- |
| 128 Slave | 3 | 2424 | 3 | F | 3 | 3 | 4 | S | 5 | 4 |
| 129 Kaska | 2 | 3 | 4 | F | 3 | 3 | 6677 | SSII | 44-- | 33-- |
| 130 Eyak | 3 | 3315 | 2 | F | 3 | 3 | 1 | - | 4 | - |
| 131 Masset Haida | 3 | 3 | 2141 | F-U- | 3 | 3-1- | 4424 | G | 4424 | 2415 |
| 132 Bellacoola | 3 | 3315 | 2 | F | 3 | 3 | 5111 | U--- | 4515 | 1--- |
| 133 Twana | 4455 | 3315 | 2 | F | 3 | 3 | 6 | G | 3 | 3 |
| 134 Yurok | 3 | 2424 | 2 | F | 3 | 3 | 1 | - | 5 | - |
| 135 Eastern Pomo | 4455 | 3324 | 5 | U | 5 | 1 | 5 | G | 5 | 4545 |
| 136 Lake Yokuts | 3 | 2424 | 1 | - | 3 | - | 4545 | SSRR | 5 | 5 |
| 137 Wadadika Paiute | 3 | 3342 | 5 | R | 3 | 3 | 5 | G | 5 | 3 |
| 138 Klamath | 3444 | 3424 | 4 | F | 3 | 3 | 3 | G | 5 | 3 |
| 139 Lower Kutenai | 3 | 2415 | 4 | F | 3 | 3 | 7477 | SSII | -5-- | 45-- |
| 140 Gros Ventre | 4343 | 2414 | 5556 | FFFG | 3 | 3335 | 5 | N | 5 | 5 |
| 141 Hidatsa | 4 | 3315 | 2 | F | 3 | 3 | 3 | S | 5 | 3535 |
| 142 Skidi Pawnee | 3355 | 2424 | 2211 | FF-- | 3 | 33-- | 6 | G | 4 | 5 |
| 143 Omaha | 4343 | 2415 | 1 | - | 3 | - | 5 | N | 5 | 5 |
| 144 Huron | 3354 | 2415 | 2 | F | 3 | 3 | 1 | - | 4 | - |
| 145 Upper Creek | 3 | 2415 | 4442 | F | 3 | 3331 | 2117 | S--R | 451- | 1--5 |
| 146 Natchez | 4 | 3324 | 1 | - | 3 | - | 2 | S | 5 | 5 |
| 147 Comanche | 3345 | 3324 | 5353 | F | 3 | 3 | 7 | GGII | - | 35-- |
| 148 Chiricahua Apache | 4443 | 3315 | 2 | F | 3 | 3 | 3535 | RGRG | 3 | 5353 |
| 149 Zuni | 3 | 3324 | 2 | F | 3 | 3 | 5 | G | 5 | 4 |
| 150 Havasupai | 4455 | 3324 | 2 | F | 3 | 3 | 3 | R | 3 | 5 |
| 151 Papago | 3 | 3324 | 2 | F | 3 | 3 | 5 | S | 3 | 3 |
| 152 Huichol | 5 | 2424 | 2 | F | 3 | 3 | 2 | S | 5 | 4 |
| 153 Aztec | 3355 | 2415 | 2277 | N | 33-- | 3 | 5544 | TNTT | 2515 | 1515 |
| 154 Sierra Popoluca | 5 | 3315 | 1 | - | 3 | - | 1 | - | 5 | - |
| 155 Quiche | 2232 | 3323 | 1 | - | 3 | - | 5 | S | 4 | 5 |
| 156 Miskito | 3 | 2424 | 2 | F | 3 | 3 | 5 | G | 5 | 3 |
| 157 Bribri Talamanca | 5 | 3315 | 1 | - | 2 | - | 1 | - | 5 | - |
| 158 Cuna | 3343 | 2414 | 2 | F | 3 | 3 | 66.1 | SS.- | 55.5 | 44.. |
| 159 Goajiro | 3353 | 2424 | 1 | - | 3 | - | 3 | RRSR | 3315 | 5515 |
| 160 Haitians | 3 | 3324 | 2 | F | 3 | 3 | 4 | S | 5 | 3 |

| SOC | AUTHORITY | | | | DISCIPLINARIAN | | | | EDUCATOR | | | | SCH |
|---|---|---|---|---|---|---|---|---|---|---|---|---|---|
| | I-NP | CAT. | S-P | S-NP | I-NP | CAT. | S-P | S-NP | I-NP | CAT. | S-P | S-NP | |
| | E L | E L | E L | E L | E L | E L | E L | E L | E L | E L | E L | E L | E L |
| | B G B G | B G B G | B G B G | B G B G | B G B G | B G B G | B G B G | B G B G | B G B G | B G B G | B G B G | B G B G | B G B G |
| 121 | 2 | S | 3 | 1 | | | | | 6 | S | 1515 | 1515 | 2255 |
| 122 | 5 | G | 3 | 3 | | | | | 2232 | CCGS | 3315 | 3315 | 3344 |
| 123 | 6 | U | 4 | 1 | 1 | - | 5 | - | 6465 | UGUG | 1515 | 1515 | 3344 |
| 124 | 5 | N | 3 | 3 | | | | | 6 | C | 2424 | 3 | 3 |
| 125 | 4 | S | 2 | 2 | . | . | . | . | 1141 | --N- | 4515 | --1- | 3 |
| 126 | 1 | - | 1 | - | | | | | 1144 | --NN | 1515 | --33 | 3 |
| 127 | 5151 | S-S- | 1212 | 1-1- | 1 | - | 1 | - | 5575 | SSGG | 15-5 | 1515 | 1155 |
| 128 | 4 | S | 3 | 5 | 4 | S | 3535 | 5 | 5111 | S--- | 1515 | 1--- | 1323 |
| 129 | 4 | S | 4424 | 3315 | | | | | 5454 | S | 4414 | 3315 | 1 |
| 130 | 4555 | S | 3313 | 1 | | | | | 4454 | URUR | 1515 | 1515 | 2343 |
| 131 | 1141 | --U- | 2424 | --1- | | | | | 3341 | GGU- | 2515 | 331- | 3344 |
| 132 | 1 | - | 1 | - | | | | | 6611 | SS-- | 3315 | 33-- | 3 |
| 133 | 5 | G | 3 | 3 | 7 | N | - | 3 | 7 | G | - | 2415 | 4 |
| 134 | 4 | R | 3 | 3 | | | | | 6565 | R | 1515 | 3 | 3 |
| 135 | 7 | G | - | 3 | 7 | NGNG | - | 1515 | 7565 | USRS | -515 | 1515 | 3343 |
| 136 | 1 | - | 2 | - | | | | | 6451 | CCU- | 3314 | 111- | 2244 |
| 137 | 1 | - | 2 | - | | | | | 6 | G | 3 | 3 | 3 |
| 138 | 3 | G | 3 | 3 | | | | | 3372 | CGGG | 15-5 | 1515 | 3344 |
| 139 | 5 | S | 3 | 3 | | | | | 4151 | R-R- | 1414 | 1-1- | 3 |
| 140 | 6667 | UUUG | 232- | 1115 | | | | | 4556 | RRUR | 1515 | 1515 | 1133 |
| 141 | 3373 | USNS | 55-5 | 1424 | | | | | 6555 | S | 3515 | 1515 | 3 |
| 142 | 5 | G | 3 | 3 | 4 | G | 3 | 3 | 5565 | UGGG | 3515 | 1515 | 3444 |
| 143 | 4 | U | 2 | 1 | 4545 | U | 2525 | 1 | 6 | N | 1515 | 1 | 4 |
| 144 | . | . | . | . | 7 | I | - | - | 4 | C | 3 | 1515 | 3 |
| 145 | 2177 | S-NR | 45-- | 1-15 | 7 | N | - | 1515 | 4472 | SSNN | 44-5 | 1515 | 3344 |
| 146 | 5454 | G | 1313 | 1 | | | | | 6161 | N-N- | 5 | 1-1- | 4 |
| 147 | 7 | S | - | 3515 | 7 | S | - | 5 | 7755 | UGSG | --15 | 1515 | 3344 |
| 148 | 2 | G | 2424 | 3 | 5 | N | 3 | 1515 | 5575 | RRNR | 15-5 | 1515 | 3343 |
| 149 | 2 | S | 3 | 3 | | | | | 5552 | GGST | 3315 | 3313 | 6 |
| 150 | 1 | - | 3 | - | | | | | 2533 | CGNN | 2515 | 3311 | 2255 |
| 151 | 6 | G | 1313 | 1313 | | | | | 5 | S | 3315 | 3315 | 5 |
| 152 | 1 | - | 2 | - | | | | | 2211 | CC-- | 1515 | 15-- | 3344 |
| 153 | 5 | RRTT | 3324 | 3315 | 4 | T | 2424 | 1515 | 2244 | T | 1515 | 1515 | 5566 |
| 154 | . | . | . | . | | | | | . | . | . | . | . |
| 155 | 1 | - | 2 | - | 1 | - | 5515 | - | 1177 | --RN | 33-- | --15 | 2155 |
| 156 | 1 | - | 3 | - | | | | | 5 | N | 1515 | 1515 | 6 |
| 157 | 1 | - | 5 | - | | | | | 1122 | --TT | 2415 | --33 | 3344 |
| 158 | 1 | - | 3 | - | | | | | 3545 | SRTR | 1515 | 1535 | 5565 |
| 159 | 5353 | GRGR | 5 | 5 | | | | | 5366 | SRUG | 5515 | 5515 | 1134 |
| 160 | 5 | NGNG | 2 | 3 | 5577 | SSRR | 33-- | 3 | 5566 | C | 2415 | 1515 | 1166 |

| | EXAMPLE E L B G B G | OPINION E L B G B G | LECTURE E L B G B G | TEASE E L B G B G | SCOLD E L B G B G | WARN E L B G B G | CORPORAL E L B G B G |
|---|---|---|---|---|---|---|---|
| 121 | 3+ | 3 | . | 2 2 3 3 | . . 3-3- | . | 2 |
| 122 | 4 | 3 | 3+ | . | 3 | 3+ | 3-3-3 3 |
| 123 | 4 | . | 2+ | . | . | . | 2 |
| 124 | 4 | 4- | 3+ | 3+ | 3 | 3- | 3- |
| 125 | 4 | 3+ | 3 | 3+ | 3 | 2+ | 2 |
| 126 | . | . | 2+2+3+3+ | . | . | . | 3 |
| 127 | 4 | 3+ | 2+ | 3 | 2 | 3 | 2- |
| 128 | 3 | 4 | . | 4 | 3 | 3 | 2 |
| 129 | 3+ | . | 3- | 2 | 3 | 3+ | 3 3 2 3 |
| 130 | 4 | 4 | 4 | . | 3 | 3+ | 2+ |
| 131 | 4 | 4+ | 4 | . | . | . | . |
| 132 | 3 | 3+ | 3+ | . | . | 3 . | 3+ |
| 133 | 4 | 3+ | 5 5 4-5 | . | . | 3 | 2 |
| 134 | 3 | . | 3+3+3+4- | . | 2+ | 3+ | 2 |
| 135 | 3+ | 3+ | 3+3+4+4+ | . | 3 | 4+ | 3 . 3 . |
| 136 | 4 | 3+ | 3+ | . | . | . | 2 |
| 137 | 4 | . | 3+ | . | 3 | 4 | 3 |
| 138 | 4 | 3+ | 3 3 3+3+ | 3+ | 3+ | 3+ | 3 3 4 3 |
| 139 | 3 4+3 4+ | 3 | 4+ | 4 | . | 3+ | 3 |
| 140 | 4 | 4 | 5 | 4 | 4 | 3+ | 2+2+2+4 |
| 141 | 4 | 4 | 4 | 4 | 4 | . | 2+ |
| 142 | 3 | 2 | 2+2+3+3+ | 3+ | 3+ | 3 | 3+ |
| 143 | 4 | 3 | 4+ | 3 | 3 4 3 4 | 3 | 3 3+3 3+ |
| 144 | 4+ | 4 | 3 | . | 2 | . | 1 |
| 145 | 4 | 3+ | 3 3 4+4+ | 3 3 3+3+ | . | . | 3+3 4+4 |
| 146 | 3+ | 3+ | 4 | . 2+3-3- | 3- | . | 2 |
| 147 | 3+ | 3+ | 3+ | 3 3 4 4 | 2+ | 3+ | 3 |
| 148 | 4 | 3+ | 4- | 3+ | 3 | 3+ | 3 |
| 149 | 4 | 3 | 3-3-. 3- | 2+ | 3 | 3+ | 2+ |
| 150 | 4 | 3+ | 2 2 3 3 | 3+ | 2+ | 3 | 3 |
| 151 | 3 3 4 4 | 4 | 5 | 3+ | 2 2 3-3- | 3 | 2 2 2+2+ |
| 152 | 3+ | 3 | 4 | . . 3 3 | . | . | 2+ |
| 153 | 4 | 4 | 4 | 4 | 3+ | 4 | 5 |
| 154 | . | . | 2 | . | . | . | . |
| 155 | 4 | . | 2 2 4 4 | . | 3 | . | 1 |
| 156 | 3 | 4 | 4 | . | 3+ | . | 3 |
| 157 | 3+ | . | 3 | . | . | 3 | . |
| 158 | 4- | . | 4 | 3+ | 3 | 3+ | 2 |
| 159 | 4+ | . | 4+ | 4 | 3 3 5 5 | 3+ | 5-5-4 4 |
| 160 | 4 | 3+ | 4 | 2+ | 3+ | 3+ | 3+ |

| SOC | CEREMONY | GIFTS | PERMISS. | AFFECTION | VALUE | INCORP. |
|---|---|---|---|---|---|---|
| | E L | E L | E L | E L | E L | E L |
| | B G B G | B G B G | B G B G | B G B G | B G B G | B G B G |
| 121 | 3 | 3 | 3+3+3-3 | 4 4 3 3 | 4 4 3 3 | 2+2+4-4- |
| 122 | . . 3 2+ | 3 | 3+3+3 3 | 3 | 3+ | 2+2+3 3+ |
| 123 | 2+ | 3 | . | 4 | 3+ | . |
| 124 | 2+2+3+3 | 3 | 4+4-4+4- | 3 3-3 3- | 3+3 3+3 | 2 2 3-3+ |
| 125 | . | 2 | 3+3+3 3 | 3+ | 3+3 3+3 | 3-3-4 4 |
| 126 | 3+. 3+. | 2 . 2 . | 3 3 3-3- | 4-4-3-3- | 4 | 2+2+3+3+ |
| 127 | 2 | 3+ | 4-3+4-3+ | 3 . 3 . | 4-3-4-3- | 2-2-3 3+ |
| 128 | 2 2 2+2+ | 3 | 4 4-4-3+ | 4 4 3-3- | 3+ | 3-3-4-4- |
| 129 | 2 | 2 | 4- | . | 3 | 2 2+3-3+ |
| 130 | . . 3 . | 3 3 3+3+ | 3 3-3 3- | 3- | 3- | 2 2 3 3 |
| 131 | 3+ | 3+ | 3 | 4- | 3 3+3 3+ | 3 3 3+3+ |
| 132 | 2 2 3 3 | 3 | 3+ | 3+ | 3+ | 2+2+3+3+ |
| 133 | 4 | 3 2 3 2 | 2 2 3 2 | . | 4- | 2+2+4-4- |
| 134 | 2 | 2+ | 3+3 3 3- | 3 | 3 3-3 3- | 2 2 3 3 |
| 135 | 2+2+3 3 | 2+ | 3 | . | 3- | 2-2-2+2+ |
| 136 | . . 3 . | . | 3+3+3-3- | 3+ | 3+ | 2+2+3 3+ |
| 137 | 3 3 3+3 | . | 3+ | 3 | 3 | 2-2-2+3- |
| 138 | 1 1 3 2 | 2+ | 3+3+3-3- | 3+ | 4-3+4-3+ | 2+2+3+4- |
| 139 | 3 | 2 | 3- | 4-4-3 3 | 4 | 3+3+4 4 |
| 140 | 3 3 3+3+ | 4 | 3 3-3 3- | 3+ | 3 3-3 3- | 2+3-3 4- |
| 141 | 3 | 3+ | 3+3+3 3 | 4 | 4 | 2+2+4-4- |
| 142 | 2 | 3- | 4-4-3+3 | . | 3+ | 2-2-2+3 |
| 143 | 3 2 4 2 | 3+3-3+3- | 3-2 3-2 | 4- | 4- | 2+3-3+3+ |
| 144 | 2+ | . | 4 | 4- | 4-4 4-4 | 3-3 3+4- |
| 145 | . . 4-. | 3 | . | 3 3-3 3- | 3-3-3 3 | 3-2+3+4 |
| 146 | 2 2-3 2 | . . 2+2+ | 3 3-3-2 | . | 3- | 2-2-3 3+ |
| 147 | . . 2 . | 3 2 3 2 | 3+3 3 3- | 3-2 3-2 | 3 3-3 3- | 2 2 3+3+ |
| 148 | 3 | 3 | 3-3 2-3- | 3+ | 4- | 2+2+4-4- |
| 149 | 3 2+3+2+ | 2+2+3 3 | 3+3+3 3 | 3 | 3+. 3+. | 2 2 3+4- |
| 150 | 2 2 3 3 | 3 | 4-3+3+3 | 4 | 4 4-4 4- | 2+3-3 3+ |
| 151 | 2 2 3 3 | 3 | 4 4 3 2+ | 4 4 3+3+ | 4- | 3-3-4-4- |
| 152 | 3 | 3 | 3+3+3 3 | 4 | 4+4 4+4 | 2+2+3 3 |
| 153 | 3+3+4 4 | 3+ | 1 | 3 | 4 | 1 1 3 3 |
| 154 | . | . | . | . | . | . |
| 155 | 3 3 4 4 | 3 | 4-4-3 3 | . . 3-3- | 2+ | 2+2+3 3 |
| 156 | . | 3 | 3+ | 3+3 3+3 | 3-2+3-2+ | 2 2+2 2+ |
| 157 | . | 3 | 3 | 3+ | . | 3 3 4-4- |
| 158 | 1 1 1 3 | 3+3+3+4 | 3+3+3 3- | 3+4-3+4- | 3 4-3 4- | 2 2 3+4- |
| 159 | 3 3 3+4 | 3 | 2+. 2 2- | . 2-. 2- | 3+3 3+3 | 3 3 4 4 |
| 160 | 2 2 3 3 | 2 | 3 3 3-3- | 3 | 4-3-4-3- | 3-3 3+4 |

| SOCIETY | COMPANION I-NF E L BGBG | COMPANION SEX E L BGBG | RESIDENCE I-NP E L BGBG | RESIDENCE CAT. E L BGBG | RESIDENCE S-P E L BGBG | RESIDENCE S-NP E L BGBG | CARETAKER I-NP E L BGBG | CARETAKER CAT. E L BGBG | CARETAKER S-P E L BGBG | CARETAKER S-NP E L BGBG |
|---|---|---|---|---|---|---|---|---|---|---|
| 161 Callinago | 4 | 3324 | 1 | - | 5515 | - | 3313 | SS-S | 5515 | 55-5 |
| 162 Warrau | 3 | 3324 | 1 | - | 3 | - | 44.. | SS.. | 55.. | 55.. |
| 163 Yanomamo | 3 | 2415 | 1114 | ---N | 3 | ---1 | 4 | S | 5 | 5 |
| 164 Barama Carib | 3 | 3 | 5151 | R-R- | 5 | 3-3- | 3313 | SS-S | 4515 | 55-5 |
| 165 Saramacca | 1 | 2424 | 5477 | FFFR | 55-- | 2425 | 5571 | URI- | 45-1 | 15-- |
| 166 Mundurucu | 3343 | 2424 | 4171 | F-N- | 55-5 | 3-1- | 5 | R | 5 | 5 |
| 167 Cubeo | 3355 | 4415 | 1 | - | 3 | - | 6671 | SSC- | 45-5 | 551- |
| 168 Cayapa | 3 | 3315 | 1 | - | 3 | - | 5 | S | 5 | 5 |
| 169 Jivaro | 3 | 3315 | 1112 | ---N | 5515 | ---5 | 4 | S | 5 | 5 |
| 170 Amahuaca | 3 | 2424 | 4447 | FFFN | 333- | 3 | 5 | R | 5 | 5 |
| 171 Inca | 2255 | 3315 | 2144 | F-CC | 3 | 3-15 | 2121 | N-N- | 5 | 5-5- |
| 172 Aymara | 3 | 3 | 2 | F | 3 | 3 | 3 | S | 3 | 3 |
| 173 Siriono | 3 | 2415 | 2 | F | 3 | 3 | 1 | - | 5 | - |
| 174 Nambicuara | 4453 | 2425 | 2 | F | 3 | 3 | 2277 | GGII | 44-- | 55-- |
| 175 Trumai | 3 | 2415 | 1 | - | 3 | - | 3535 | S | 4 | 3 |
| 176 Ramcocamecra Timbira | 3344 | 2424 | 1171 | --C- | 33-3 | --1- | 1171 | --I- | 55-5 | - |
| 177 Tupinamba | 3 | 2424 | 1212 | -N-N | 4 | -3-3 | 11.. | --.. | 55.. | --.. |
| 178 Botocudo | 4 | 3324 | 1212 | -F-F | 3 | -3-3 | 11.. | --.. | 55.. | --.. |
| 179 Shavante | 3355 | 2415 | 1171 | --C- | 33-3 | --1- | 7 | CCII | - | 33-- |
| 180 Aweikoma | 4 | 3 | 1212 | -F-F | 3 | -3-3 | 3311 | GG-- | 3315 | 55-- |
| 181 Cayua | 3 | 3315 | 1 | - | 3 | - | 1 | - | 4 | - |
| 182 Lengua | 4 | 3 | 1 | - | 3 | - | 5 | R | 4 | 3 |
| 183 Abipon | 3 | 1515 | 1 | - | 3 | - | 1 | - | 4545 | - |
| 184 Mapuche Araucanians | 3 | 3324 | 4 | F | 3 | 3 | 5 | G | 4 | 5 |
| 185 Tehuelche | 3 | 3324 | 1 | - | 4 | - | 1 | - | 4 | - |
| 186 Yahgan | 3 | 2415 | 1 | - | 3 | - | 77.. | II.. | --.. | --.. |

twelve years, at the onset of puberty or other major changes in physical attributes or social status.

Six functions of social agents are distinguished: companion, residence, caretaker, authority figure, disciplinarian, and educator. Two or more sets of codes are defined for each function, and each set is coded separately for different stages of childhood (E-early; L-late) and the two sexes (B-boy; G-girl). Each group of four columns in Table 1, therefore, shows successively the codes for early boyhood, early girlhood, late boyhood, and late girlhood. The transition from the early to the late stage occurs between seven and eleven years of age. Variations among the societies in this respect are coded by Barry *et. al.* (1976).

## Companions

Companions are defined as those persons involved in the same activities as the child, on a more or less equal status. Type of companion is coded on a scale of

| SOC | AUTHORITY | | | | DISCIPLINARIAN | | | | EDUCATOR | | | | SCH |
|-----|------|------|------|------|------|------|------|------|------|------|------|------|------|
| | I-NP E L B G B G | CAT. E L B G B G | S-P E L B G B G | S-NP E L B G B G | I-NP E L B G B G | CAT. E L B G B G | S-P E L B G B G | S-NP E L B G B G | I-NP E L B G B G | CAT. E L B G B G | S-P E L B G B G | S-NP E L B G B G | E L B G B G |
| 161 | 1 | - | 2 | - | | | | | 6611 | CC-- | 3315 | 33-- | 3344 |
| 162 | 1 | - | 5 | - | | | | | 6 | C | 3 | 3 | 1155 |
| 163 | .1.1 | .-.- | .5.5 | .-.- | | | | | 5151 | C-C- | 3535 | 1-1- | 1 |
| 164 | 1 | - | 2 | - | 1 | - | 1515 | - | 1 | - | 2415 | - | 3344 |
| 165 | 6661 | UUU- | 1511 | 111- | 6 | U | 5 | 1 | 1333 | -RUR | 2515 | -515 | 3444 |
| 166 | . | . | . | . | | | | | 6565 | CRCR | 4515 | 1515 | 2323 |
| 167 | 4171 | R-C- | 15-5 | 1-1- | .171 | .-C- | .5-5 | .-1- | 5641 | RSC- | 1515 | 151- | 3344 |
| 168 | 2 | G | 3 | 3 | | | | | 4411 | RR-- | 1515 | 15-- | 3344 |
| 169 | 4 | G | 1212 | 1 | | | | | 4445 | R | 1515 | 1515 | 2244 |
| 170 | 1 | - | 3 | - | 6 | S | 3 | 3 | 4141 | R-R- | 1515 | 1-1- | 3 |
| 171 | 1177 | --TT | 22-- | --15 | | | | | 1154 | --TT | 1515 | --15 | 3366 |
| 172 | 2 | S | 2 | 1515 | 1 | - | 1 | - | 6 | C | 5 | 3 | 1 |
| 173 | 1 | - | 2 | - | | | | | 4 | S | 3315 | 3315 | 3 |
| 174 | 1 | - | 1212 | - | | | | | 1414 | -N-N | 4515 | -5-5 | 1133 |
| 175 | 4 | R | 2 | 1 | | | | | 5 | S | 3 | 3 | 1 |
| 176 | 4575 | UUCU | 55-5 | 1 | 1777 | -NCN | 1--- | -121 | 7477 | CNNC | -5-- | 1215 | 2343 |
| 177 | 1515 | -R-R | 1 | -1-1 | 7 | N | - | 1 | 1144 | --NN | 1515 | --15 | 3 |
| 178 | 1 | - | 3 | - | 11.. | --.. | 55.. | --.. | 4 | C | 1515 | 1515 | 1 |
| 179 | 2 | N | 1515 | 1515 | 1 | - | 5 | - | 5171 | N-N- | 15-5 | 1-1- | 1133 |
| 180 | 1211 | -G-- | 4424 | -1-- | | | | | 7711 | CC-- | --11 | 33-- | 1144 |
| 181 | 1 | - | 2424 | - | | | | | 7741 | SSN- | --15 | 351- | 1144 |
| 182 | 4 | R | 3 | 3 | | | | | 4 | N | 3 | 3 | 3 |
| 183 | 1 | - | 1515 | - | | | | | 1 | - | 2424 | - | 3 |
| 184 | 4 | S | 2215 | 3315 | 1 | - | 3 | - | 5 | S | 4415 | 3315 | 3366 |
| 185 | . | . | . | . | | | | | 1 | - | 2515 | - | 1122 |
| 186 | 4 | N | 2 | 4242 | 1 | - | 3 | - | 4 | N | 2424 | 2424 | 3 |

importance of non-family (I-NF) ranging from 1 to 5; that is, the scale goes from least importance of non-family to most importance of non-family.

1 Parents predominantly.
2 Siblings; not other children.
3 Primarily siblings, secondarily other children.
4 Primarily other children, secondarily siblings.
5 Other children; not siblings.

Sex of companions (SEX) is coded on the following scale of 1 to 5, which is also used for the subsequently listed functions of agents.

1 Male exclusively.
2 Male predominantly.
3 Both sexes equally.
4 Female predominantly.
5 Female exclusively.

| | EXAMPLE<br>E   L<br>B G B G | OPINION<br>E   L<br>B G B G | LECTURE<br>E   L<br>B G B G | TEASE<br>E   L<br>B G B G | SCOLD<br>E   L<br>B G B G | WARN<br>E   L<br>B G B G | CORPORAL<br>E   L<br>B G B G |
|---|---|---|---|---|---|---|---|
| 161 | . | . | 3+ | . . 3 3 | . | 3+ | 2 2 3 3 |
| 162 | 4 | . | . | . | 2+ | . | 2 |
| 163 | 4+ | 3+ | . | 3+. 3+. | . | 4- | 2 . 2 . |
| 164 | 4 | 2 | 4 | . . 2 2 | 3 | 3+ | 3- |
| 165 | 4 | 4 | 4 | . | 4 | 4+ | . |
| 166 | 4 | . | 3 | . | . | . | . |
| 167 | 3 3 4+4+ | 3+ | . | 3 | 2-2 3-3+ | . | 2 |
| 168 | 4+ | . | 3+ | 4 | 3 | 3 | 3 |
| 169 | 4 | . | 5 | 2 | . | . | 3+ |
| 170 | 4 | . | 2 | 3 | 3 | 3 | 3 3 2 2 |
| 171 | 3 | . | 3+ | . | . | . | . |
| 172 | 4 | 3+ | . | 3+ | 3+ | 3+ | 3+ |
| 173 | 4 | . | 2+ | 3+ | . | 3 | 2+ |
| 174 | 3 | 2+ | 2+ | 3+ | 3- | . | 1 |
| 175 | 4 | 3 | . | 3 | 3 | . | 2+ |
| 176 | 4+4 4+4 | . 4 4 4 | . . 3 3 | 2 4 4 4 | 3 | . | 2 2 3 2 |
| 177 | 4 | . | 3+. 3+. | . | 1 | . | 1 |
| 178 | . | . | 3+ | . | . | 3+ | 2 |
| 179 | . | . | 1 . 3 . | . | 3+ | . | 3 |
| 180 | . | . | . | . | 3- | . | . |
| 181 | 3 | . | . | . | . | 3 | . |
| 182 | 4 | . | 3 | 3 | 2- | . | 2- |
| 183 | 4 | 3+ | 3- | . 3 . 3 | 2 | . | 2 |
| 184 | 4 | 3+ | 3 3 4 4 | 3+ | 3 3 4 4 | 3- | 3-3-3+3 |
| 185 | 3 | . | . | . | . | . | . |
| 186 | 5 | 4 | 2 2 4 4 | 2 | 3+ | . | 3+. 3+. |

## Residence

Residence refers to the principal home, where the child sleeps and eats.

Importance of non-parent (I-NP) designates by the following scale of 1-7 the degree to which categories of people other than the parents are the proprietors of the child's residence. The same scale is also used for the subsequently listed functions of agents.

1 Exclusively parental.

2 Single atypical or occasional category of non-parent.

3 Two or more atypical or occasional categories of non-parent.

4 Single category that is typical and frequent but less important than the parents.

5 Two or more categories, at least one of which is typical and frequent, but less important than the parents.

| SOC | CEREMONY E L B G B G | GIFTS E L B G B G | PERMISS. E L B G B G | AFFECTION E L B G B G | VALUE E L B G B G | INCORP. E L B G B G |
|---|---|---|---|---|---|---|
| 161 | 3 | 2 2 3 3 | 4–4–3 3 | 3+3+3 3 | 3+ | 2 2 3+3+ |
| 162 | . | 2 | 5 | 3 3 2 2 | 3 4 3 4 | 2 2 3 3 |
| 163 | . | . | 5 3–5 3– | 3+ | 4 2 4 2 | 2–3 2–3+ |
| 164 | 3 | 3 | 3+ | 3 | 3+3–3+3– | 2+2+3+3+ |
| 165 | 2 2 3 3 | 2 3 2 3 | 3 | 4– | 3+4–3+4– | 2 2+4–4– |
| 166 | 2 | . | 4 3 3+3– | . | 4– | 2+3–3+4 |
| 167 | 2+2+3+3– | 3 | 3+3 5–2+ | 4–3–4–3– | 3 3–3 3– | 2–2–2 3 |
| 168 | 2 2 3 3 | 3 | 3 | 4– | 3+ | 2+2+3+4– |
| 169 | 3 | 2 | 4–3+3 3– | 3+ | 4 | 3–3 3+4– |
| 170 | 2 . 2 . | 2 | 3 3–3–2 | 3 | 3–2+3–2+ | 3–3 3+4+ |
| 171 | 3– | 2+ | 2– | 3– | 3+ | 3 3 . . |
| 172 | 2+2+2 2 | . | 2 2 2–2– | 2 | 2 | 2–2–2 2 |
| 173 | 2 2 . 3– | 3– | 4 4–3+3 | 4 | 4 4–4 4– | 2+2+4–4+ |
| 174 | 2–2–2+. | 2 | 5–4 5–4 | 3 3 3–3– | 2 | 2 2 2+2+ |
| 175 | 2 2 3+2 | 3 | 4–4–3 3 | 3+ | 3 3–3 3– | 2 2 3+3+ |
| 176 | 3 4 4 4 | 2 4 3 4 | 4–3+3 3 | 4– | 3+ | 2+3 4–4– |
| 177 | 3+ | 2 | 3+3 3+3 | 4 2+4 2+ | 3 | 2+3–3 3+ |
| 178 | 3 | . | 3 | 3 3 3–3– | . | 2+2+3 3 |
| 179 | 2 . 4 2+ | 3 . 3 . | 5–4–4 3 | 3+ | 3+ | 2 3 2 4+ |
| 180 | . | 3 | 4– | 3+ | 3+ | 3– |
| 181 | 3 | 3 2+3 2+ | 4–4–3 3 | 4 | 3 2+3 2+ | . . 3 5 |
| 182 | 2 | 3– | 4+ | 3 | 2+2 2+2 | 2 2 2+2+ |
| 183 | . | . | 3+3 3+3 | 3+ | 3 | . |
| 184 | 3 | 2 2 3 3 | 4–4–3 3 | 4 4 3 3 | 4 4–4 4– | 2+2+4–3+ |
| 185 | 2 | 2+ | 4 4 4–3+ | 4 | 4– | 2 2+3–3 |
| 186 | . | 2+ | 3 | 3+ | 4+ | 3+3+4+4+ |

6 More typical and frequent than the parents.
7 Exclusively non-parental.
The principal category of non-parental agent is designated by the following alphabetical codes. The first code, foster parent (F), applies only to the proprietor of the child's residence. Two of the codes, sibling (S) and teacher (T), apply only to the subsequently listed functions of agents.
F Foster parent.
S Sibling.
G Grandparent.
U Uncle (mother's brother only).
R Relative (including father's brother).
C Child.
N Nonrelative.
T Teacher.

I Independence of child; no agent.

Sex of parents (S-P) with whom the child resides is rated on the same scale of 1-5 as for companion.

Sex of non-parents (S-NP) refers to the principal type of non-parental proprietors of the child's residence, rated on the same scale of 1-5 as for companions.

## Caretakers

Caretakers are defined as those persons contributing to the physical and emotional needs of the child.

Non-parental involvement is designated by the same scale of 1-7 as for residence.

The principal category of non-parental caretaker is designated by the alphabetical codes listed for proprietors of the child's residence.

Sex of parental caretakers and of principal category of non-parental caretakers are rated on the same scale of 1-5 as for companions.

## Authority figures

Authority figures are defined as the socializing agents, who inculcate traits and other cultural values.

Non-parental involvement in authority, principal category of non-parental authority figures, sex of parental authority figures, and sex of principal category of non-parental authority figures, are coded as described for caretakers.

## Disciplinarians

Disciplinarians are defined as those socializing agents who administer punishments.

Non-parental involvement in discipline, principal category of non-parental disciplinarians, sex of parental disciplinarians, and sex of principal category of non-parental disciplinarians, are coded as described for caretakers. The codes for disciplinarians are left blank when they are all the same as for authority figures.

## Educators

Educators are defined as those persons who train the child for adult knowledge and skills.

Non-parental involvement in education, principal category of non-parental educators, sex of parental educators, and sex of principal category of non-parental educators, are coded as described for caretakers.

## Schooling

Guidance or formal schooling (SCH) as a method of education is coded on the following scale of 1-6.

1 Informal training only, with minimal guidance.
2 Apprenticeship (guidance) is atypical or occasional.
3 Apprenticeship is typical and frequent but informal training is more prevalent.
4 Apprenticeship is predominant.
5 Formal schooling is atypical or occasional.

6 Formal schooling is typical and frequent.

The third and fourth pages of Table 1 list the quantitative ratings for nine techniques of child training, classified under exhorting, punishing, rewarding, and four attitudes toward children. The ratings, on a scale of 1 to 5, are sometimes followed by a minus ($-$), designating a value below the median of the scale score, or by a plus ($+$), designating a value above the median of the scale score.

Exhorting describes the use of three techniques: example, public opinion, and lecturing.

## Example

Example refers to imitation of elders and a low level of verbal instructions. Scale categories 2-5 are defined as follows.

2 Children have different activities from adults and are not expected to behave like them, but are occasionally shown how to perform tasks or behave on special occasions.

3 Children are expected to do things more or less by example.

4 Children are frequently shown things and example is considered very important in socializing children.

5 Example is given by the ethnographer as the most important method of education, or adults are constantly showing children how to do things.

## Public Opinion

The degree to which approval by people in general controls the behavior of children is the basis for the rating of public opinion.

## Lecturing

Lecturing includes moralizing, explaining reasons for commands, verbal exhortations, or stories, myths, and songs as educative or socializing devices. Scale categories 3-5 are defined as follows.

3 Often, but not constant lectures or myths.

4 Almost daily.

5 Constant and one of the most important methods used in socializing the child.

Punishing describes the use of four techniques: teasing, scolding, warning, and corporal punishment.

## Teasing

Teasing refers to shaming and exposure to ridicule for misconduct.

## Scolding

Scolding includes verbal reprimands, nagging, scolding for misbehavior.

## Warning

Warning is defined as threats of punishment by supernatural beings or strangers.

*Corporal punishment*

Corporal punishment includes whipping and any other pain-inflicting treatment.

Rewarding describes the use of two techniques: ceremonies and gifts.

*Ceremonies*

Included here are such ceremonies as those for the first animal killed or the first basket woven by the young child, or ceremonies like birthday parties or children's days. Inclusion of children in cultural ceremonies justifies only moderate scores.

*Gifts*

This coding is based on material rewards for approved behavior, e.g., gifts or conferring of privileges.

Attitudes toward children include two attitudes of relevant social agents (permissiveness, affection) and two societal attitudes (evaluation, incorporation in adult life).

*Permissiveness*

Permissiveness refers primarily to absence or mildness of punishment. Scale categories 1-5 are defined as follows.
1 Harsh socialization by parents or other authority figures. Severe punishment for deviant behavior or persistent lesser punishments with little flexibility or overlooking of mistakes.
2 Generally harsh treatment, but no extreme severity.
3 Generally moderate or balanced degree of both harshness and permissiveness.
4 Prevalently indulgent, but no extreme permissiveness.
5 Prevalently lenient and indulgent permissiveness, with minimal punishment or expression of disapproval.

*Affection*

Affection refers primarily to attention and positive interest expressed toward the child. Scale categories 1-4 are defined as follows.
1 Minimal expression of affection, attention, or positive interest in the child, who is generally ignored by parents or other authority figures and caretakers.
2 Generally low expression of affection and attention.
3 Moderate or sporadic expression of affection and attention.
4 Consistent, or occasionally strong, expression of affection, attention, and positive interest.

*Evaluation by Society*

This refers to the degree to which children are desired and valued. Scale categories 1-5 are defined as follows.
1. Children are viewed indifferently or as a liability by the society and local community.

2 Only slight, sporadic expression of valuation of children.
3 Moderate or occasionally strong expression of the value of children.
4 Strong, but no extreme valuation of children.
5 Intense, repeated expression of cultural valuation for children.

## *Incorporation into Society*

This refers to the inclusion of children in adult activities. Scale categories 1-5 are defined as follows.

1 Children are almost completely excluded from membership in the adult working, ceremonial, and social activities.
2 Children are usually excluded from membership in adult activities.
3 Inconsistent but substantial participation by children in adult activities.
4 Children are closely integrated in adult family activities with substantial participation in adult community life.
5 Almost complete, continual inclusion of children in adult activities.

The following two symbols designate inability to enter a code for the specified reason.

Dash (-): code not applicable. This is entered for sex of parent when the code for non-parental involvement is 7 (exclusively non-parental) and for category and sex of non-parent when the code for non-parental involvement is 1 (exclusively parental).

Dot (.): ethnographic information is insufficient.

When the code is the same for early boyhood, early girlhood, late boyhood, and late girlhood, it is entered for early boyhood and left blank for the other three categories.

### PROCEDURES FOR CODING AND DATA ANALYSIS

The bibliography of ethnographic sources was listed by Barry and Paxson (1971), with modifications listed in a subsequent, supplementary bibliography (Barry *et. al.*, 1976). The procedures for using these sources and for preparing the coding sheets were the same as described in the later article.

On the original coding sheets, the ratings of agents of child training were entered at the top of the first page, followed by the ratings of inculcated traits, reported by Barry *et. al.* (1976). These were followed by the ratings of techniques for exhorting, punishing, and rewarding, in the same sequence as in Table 1 except that the techniques for rewarding (Ceremonies, Gifts) were the first two instead of the last two measures. Eight additional techniques, interspersed in the list, are not included in the present article because less than half the societies had sufficient information for a rating. These techniques were Praise, Promises of reward, Pacification, Atonement, Threats of punishment, Rejection, Isolation, and Other.

The coding sheet also contained a list of sixteen types of tasks performed by children. The ratings of importance of these have not yet been published; less than half the societies were rated on most of them. The four measures of attitudes, in Table 1, were the last measures coded.

The codes in the first two pages of Table 1 summarize more extensive listings by the coders for categories of agents. An alphabetical letter designated each category of agent reported in the ethnographic accounts, including parent (P) and non-parental categories, separately for residence proprietor, caretaker, authority figure, disciplinarian, and educator. Categories were designated as typical or frequent by capital letters and as atypical or occasional by lower-case letters. The letter was followed by a number to designate the sex of the agent: 1 for same as child, 2 for opposite sex, and 3 for both sexes. Combinations of numbers (1-3, 1-2, 2-1, or 3-1) designated preponderantly but not exclusively one sex.

Some of the alphabetical letters for categories of non-parent, in the present article, combine additional categories that were used in a few instances by the coders. The code of C (Child) for residence includes codes of B (Boy's house) and G (Girl's house), and for the other functions of agents includes O (Older child). The code of N (Non-relative) includes S (School), M (Men's house), and husband's household for a girl married during childhood.

In the third and fourth pages of Table 1, showing the thirteen techniques of child training, the code is omitted and thereby designated by a dot whenever the rating was based on an inference. The letter V preceding a code on the coding sheet, denoting variation, was treated in the same manner as an inferential rating. In the first and second pages of Table 1, an inferential rating for a particular agent was treated as equivalent to an atypical or occasional designation.

The codes in Table 1 constitute ordinal, numerical scales except for the categories of non-parental agents, identified by alphabetical letters in the first two pages of the table. These alphabetical symbols were converted into numbers (1-8) for greater economy and versatility of data processing. The ratings of techniques and attitudes, on pages three and four of Table 1, were transformed in the same way as the ratings of inculcated traits (Barry *et. al.*, 1976). The ordinal code values 1, 2−, 2, 2+, 3−, 3, 3+, 4−, 4, 4+, 5) were converted into a scale of 0-10. In order to obtain the convenient range from 0 to 10, with 5 as the midpoint, it was necessary to group together codes of 1− and 1+ with 1 in the lowest transformed score (0), and similarly 5− and 5+ with 5 in the highest transformed score (10). The codes of 1−, 1+, and 5+ were never used, and the 5− code was used very seldom (for societies 2, 23, 111, 159, 167, 174, and 179, shown in Table 1).

Data tabulations and summaries were done with the aid of a package of statistical programs for use on large digital computers (Nie *et. al.*, 1975). The new measures were related to various other codes on the same world sample of societies (see below). These other codes included infancy and early childhood (Barry and Paxson, 1971), attributes of the family and community (Murdock and Wilson, 1972), measures of cultural complexity (Murdock and Provost, 1973), and traits inculcated in childhood (Barry, *et. al.*, 1976). Other codes, on a portion of this sample, were reported by Whiting and Child (1953), Barry, Bacon, and Child (1967), and Rohner (1975).

## SUMMARY OF NEW DATA

Tables 2 to 5 summarize the large amount of information shown in Table 1. Boys are compared with girls in all of these, and early childhood is compared with late childhood for both sexes in Tables 2, 4, and 5.

The scores in Table 2 show the average importance of non-family companion

TABLE 2
Summary for Agents and Schooling

| | Number of Societies | | | | Mean Score | | | |
| | Early | | Late | | Early | | Late | |
| | B | G | B | G | B | G | B | G |
|---|---|---|---|---|---|---|---|---|
| Companion (I-NF) | 180 | 180 | 180 | 178 | 3.4 | 3.3 | 3.8 | 3.6 |
| Non-Parental Role (I-NP) | | | | | | | | |
|     Residence | 182 | 182 | 182 | 182 | 2.5 | 2.3 | 3.2 | 2.8 |
|     Caretaker | 179 | 180 | 160 | 163 | 3.7 | 3.7 | 4.0 | 3.7 |
|     Authority | 175 | 176 | 172 | 176 | 3.1 | 3.0 | 3.7 | 3.3 |
|     Disciplinarian | 162 | 161 | 161 | 160 | 3.1 | 3.1 | 3.7 | 3.3 |
|     Educator | 176 | 176 | 177 | 177 | 4.0 | 3.5 | 4.4 | 3.6 |
| Formal Schooling (SCH) | 180 | 180 | 180 | 178 | 3.4 | 3.3 | 3.8 | 3.6 |

Number of societies coded and mean score for importance of non-family companion (I-NF) on a scale of 1-5, importance of non-parent (I-NP) on a scale of 1-7 for five types of social agents, and formal schooling (SCH) on a scale of 1-6. These are shown separately for boys (B) and girls (G) in early and late childhood.

(I-NF) on a scale of 1-5, importance of non-parent (I-NP) on a scale of 1-7 for residence, caretaker, authority, disciplinarian, and educator, and degree of formal schooling (SCH) on a scale of 1-6. The average for companion is between 3 (primarily siblings) and 4 (primarily other children). A code of 1 (parents predominantly) occurs in only two societies (numbers 96 and 165, shown in Table 1). The average for non-parental role of five agents generally ranges from 3 (two or more atypical or occasional categories of non-parent) to 4 (single non-parental category that is typical and frequent but less important than the parents). The average for schooling is between 3 (predominantly informal training) and 4 (predominantly apprenticeship).

For each measure shown in Table 2, the average scores are generally higher for boys than girls, but in early childhood the only measure with a substantial sex difference is non-parental role for educator. The average scores increase in late childhood, and this change is greater for boys than for girls, so that the sex difference is larger in the late than in the early stage. Non-parental role for residence is the only measure with a large increase in both sexes from early to late childhood. In general, the average differences between sexes and ages, shown in Table 2, are smaller than the differences among the individual societies, shown in Table 1.

Table 3 identifies the percentages of societies with several categories of principal non-parent in late childhood, for the five categories of social agent coded for importance of non-parent (I-NP) in Table 1 and summarized in Table 2. For residence, an additional category not included in Table 3 is foster parent (56 per cent for boys and 55 per cent for girls). With this exception, all the coded categories are shown in Table 3. The occasional small differences from 100 per cent for the total family plus total non-family for a specified agent and

TABLE 3
Summary for Types of Agents

| | Grand-parent (G) | | Mother's brother (U) | | Sibling (S) | | Relative (R) | | Total family | |
|---|---|---|---|---|---|---|---|---|---|---|
| | B | G | B | G | B | G | B | G | B | G |
| Residence | 3 | 8 | 4 | 2 | 0 | 0 | 11 | 10 | 18 | 20 |
| Caretaker | 20 | 26 | 2 | 2 | 31 | 34 | 10 | 11 | 63 | 73 |
| Authority | 18 | 23 | 12 | 7 | 26 | 28 | 15 | 19 | 71 | 77 |
| Disciplinarian | 18 | 19 | 11 | 8 | 22 | 29 | 14 | 17 | 65 | 73 |
| Educator | 8 | 12 | 7 | 1 | 14 | 17 | 8 | 15 | 37 | 45 |

| | Teacher (T) | | Independent (I) | | Child (C) | | Non-relative (N) | | Total non-family | |
|---|---|---|---|---|---|---|---|---|---|---|
| | B | G | B | G | B | G | B | G | B | G |
| Residence | 0 | 0 | 3 | 1 | 15 | 7 | 9 | 18 | 27 | 26 |
| Caretaker | 1 | 1 | 18 | 10 | 3 | 2 | 14 | 15 | 36 | 28 |
| Authority | 6 | 4 | 2 | 2 | 7 | 4 | 14 | 13 | 29 | 23 |
| Disciplinarian | 9 | 6 | 3 | 3 | 10 | 4 | 14 | 15 | 36 | 28 |
| Educator | 23 | 18 | 0 | 0 | 17 | 10 | 23 | 27 | 63 | 55 |

Percentage of societies in which the designated category is the principal non-parental social agent, separately for boys (B) and girls (G) in late childhood. Four categories of family agents (Grandparent, Mother's brother, Sibling, Relative) and four categories of non-family agents (Teacher, Independent, Child, Non-relative) are shown for each of five functions (Residence, Caretaker, Authority, Disciplinarian, Educator).

sex are due to rounding the percentage for each category to the last digit shown in Table 3.

For residence, foster parent is by far the most common category. For caretaker, sibling is most common and grandparent is second.. For authority and disciplinarian, sibling is most common. The principal educator is divided fairly evenly among several categories. The sex differences in Table 3 are generally small. For each of the five social agents, the percentage is higher for girls for the total of the four categories of family members, although the percentage is generally higher for boys for one of these categories (mother's brother). Conversely, the percentage is higher for boys for the total of the four non-family categories, although the percentage is generally higher for girls for the category of non-relative. Boys show a higher percentage for unusual and specialized categories, including mother's brother, whereas girls show a higher percentage for typical and generalized categories, including non-relative.

Table 4 summarizes the average score for sex of social agent on a scale from 1

TABLE 4
Summary for Sexes of Agents

| | Number of Societies | | | | Mean Score | | | |
|---|---|---|---|---|---|---|---|---|
| | Early | | Late | | Early | | Late | |
| | B | G | B | G | B | G | B | G |
| Companion | 180 | 180 | 180 | 178 | 2.6 | 3.4 | 1.9 | 4.2 |
| Residence | | | | | | | | |
|    Parent | 182 | 182 | 158 | 168 | 3.4 | 3.4 | 3.1 | 3.4 |
|    Non-Parent | 126 | 120 | 134 | 133 | 2.9 | 3.1 | 2.5 | 3.1 |
| Caretaker | | | | | | | | |
|    Parent | 173 | 175 | 132 | 145 | 4.4 | 4.5 | 4.2 | 4.5 |
|    Non-Parent | 145 | 144 | 103 | 111 | 3.9 | 4.1 | 3.6 | 4.0 |
| Authority | | | | | | | | |
|    Parent | 172 | 173 | 147 | 160 | 2.3 | 2.8 | 2.2 | 2.9 |
|    Non-Parent | 113 | 108 | 121 | 112 | 1.9 | 2.4 | 1.7 | 2.8 |
| Disciplinarian | | | | | | | | |
|    Parent | 154 | 151 | 139 | 141 | 2.6 | 3.1 | 2.4 | 3.2 |
|    Non-Parent | 93 | 93 | 108 | 98 | 2.2 | 2.7 | 1.9 | 2.9 |
| Educator | | | | | | | | |
|    Parent | 163 | 170 | 155 | 160 | 2.4 | 4.3 | 1.4 | 4.7 |
|    Non-Parent | 140 | 125 | 154 | 124 | 2.1 | 3.9 | 1.6 | 4.3 |

Number of societies coded and mean score for sex on a scale from 1 (male only) to 5 (female only) for companion and for parent or non-parent among the other social agents who interact with boys (B) and girls (G) in the early and late stages of childhood.

(male only) to 5 (female only). The five agents listed in Table 3 are divided into sex of parent (SP) and sex of non-parent (S-NP) shown in Table 1.

Most of the averages in Table 4 are below 3.0 for boys, signifying predominantly male agents, and above 3.0 for girls, signifying predominantly female agents. Thus the agents tend to be the same sex as the child. For boys, the only exceptions are parental residence, showing a slight tendency to be female, and parental and non-parental caretaker, showing a strong tendency to be female. For girls the only exceptions are parental authority and non-parental disciplinarian, showing a slight tendency to be male, and non-parental authority, showing a larger tendency to be male. Educator is the agent with the strongest tendency to be the same sex as the child, and all five agents show a stronger tendency to be of the same sex as the child in late than in early childhood.

Regardless of sex and age of the child, the caretaker tends strongly to be female and the parental residence tends slightly to be female. Authority and disciplinarian are predominantly male; this tendency is stronger for authority than for disciplinarian and for non-parent than for parent.

Table 5 summarizes the mean score on a 0-10 scale for three measures of exhorting, four measures of punishing, two measures of rewarding, and four measures of attitudes. Differences between boys and girls and between early and late childhood are generally small, indicated in Table 1 by the high proportion of societies with the same rating for both sexes and ages.

The most frequent technique for exhorting the child is by example, indicated in Table 5 by the high average scores and by the large number of societies rated. Among the four techniques for punishing the child, corporal punishment is rated for the largest number of societies and shows the largest increase from early to late childhood. The rewarding technique of ceremonies increases greatly in late childhood and is higher for boys than girls. Two attitudes of the parents or other caretakers toward the child (permissiveness and affection) both decrease in late childhood and are expressed more strongly toward boys than

TABLE 5
Summary for Techniques of Training

| | Number of Societies | | | | Mean Score | | | |
|---|---|---|---|---|---|---|---|---|
| | Early | | Late | | Early | | Late | |
| | B | G | B | G | B | G | B | G |
| **EXHORTING** | | | | | | | | |
| Example | 152 | 153 | 153 | 155 | 7.4 | 7.4 | 7.5 | 7.5 |
| Public Opinion | 91 | 92 | 95 | 94 | 6.4 | 6.4 | 6.4 | 6.4 |
| Lecturing | 137 | 134 | 141 | 139 | 5.6 | 5.6 | 5.9 | 5.9 |
| **PUNISHING** | | | | | | | | |
| Teasing | 101 | 101 | 113 | 112 | 5.4 | 5.4 | 5.6 | 5.6 |
| Scolding | 110 | 112 | 115 | 117 | 4.6 | 4.7 | 5.1 | 5.1 |
| Warning | 99 | 99 | 100 | 100 | 5.8 | 5.8 | 5.6 | 5.6 |
| Corporal punishment | 145 | 140 | 147 | 142 | 3.8 | 3.7 | 4.4 | 4.2 |
| **REWARDING** | | | | | | | | |
| Ceremonies | 132 | 124 | 146 | 131 | 3.6 | 3.3 | 4.7 | 4.0 |
| Gifts | 141 | 136 | 145 | 143 | 4.4 | 4.4 | 4.6 | 4.6 |
| **ATTITUDES** | | | | | | | | |
| Permissiveness | 169 | 167 | 168 | 168 | 6.2 | 5.8 | 5.4 | 4.9 |
| Affection | 155 | 155 | 154 | 154 | 5.9 | 5.7 | 5.5 | 5.3 |
| Evaluation | 172 | 172 | 172 | 172 | 6.3 | 5.8 | 6.3 | 5.8 |
| Incorporation in adult life | 170 | 170 | 171 | 172 | 2.8 | 3.1 | 5.4 | 6.1 |

Number of societies coded and mean score on a scale of 0-10 for the specified attributes of behavior toward boys (B) and girls (G) in the early and late stages of childhood.

toward girls. The societal attitude of evaluation is higher toward boys; the societal attitude of incorporation in adult life increases greatly in late childhood and is higher toward girls than boys.

## Relationships Among Quantitative Ratings

With the exception of the categories of social agents, designated by alphabetical letters, the variables in Table 1 are ordinally scaled categories, indicated by the numerical values. Therefore, correlation coefficients can be used to measure quantitatively the relationships among the variables. These correlations can be computed not only for the variables shown in Table 1 but also for each of these variables with the degree of inculcation of diverse traits, rated by the same set of coders and reported by Barry *et al.* (1976).

The product-moment correlations among the functions of social agents (summarized in Table 2) indicate that these measures are prevalently independent of each other. Correlations between different functions (residence proprietor, caretaker, authority figure, educator) are generally low, even for corresponding measures (importance of non-parent, sex of parent, or sex of principal non-parent) for the same sex and age. An exception is a fairly high positive correlation for sex of principal non-parent, for boys but not girls, between authority figure and educator. For both sexes the corresponding measures show high correlations between authority figure and disciplinarian, due to the fact that for most societies these were coded as the same.

Intercorrelations among the measures for the same function revealed high positive correlations between sex of parent and sex of principal non-parent for caretaker, authority figure, disciplinarian, and educator, but not for residence proprietor. Neither of these measures shows consistent relationships with importance of non-parent.

The categories of social agents can be grouped into two types, family and non-family, shown in Table 3. Among four functions (caretaker, authority figure, disciplinarian, educator), a society with one type of agent (family or non-family) in one function tends to have the same type of agent in the other functions. For disciplinarian, societies with a non-family type of agent tend to have a high degree of non-parental involvement. Authority figure and caretaker showed the same relationship between non-family agent and non-parental involvement, but only in late childhood and more strongly for boys than girls.

Some of the thirteen attributes of behavior toward children (Table 5) show close relationships with each other. Frequency of corporal punishment is positively correlated with frequency of scolding (r = .59, N = 105 in early boyhood; r = .58, N = 103 in early girlhood; r = .67, N = 110 in late boyhood; r = .70, N = 108 in late girlhood). To a lesser degree, frequency of corporal punishment is negatively correlated with degree of permissiveness (r = −.51, N = 139 for early boyhood; r = −.49, N = 132 for early girlhood; r = −.57, N = 141 for late boyhood; r = −.50, N = 136 for late girlhood). Frequency of lecturing and of teasing are positively correlated with each other and with corporal punishment, and negatively correlated with permissiveness.

Affection is highly correlated with degree of societal evaluation of the child (r = .49, N = 149 in early boyhood; r = .57, N = 148 in early girlhood; r = .41, N = 148 in late boyhood; r = .43, N = 147 in late girlhood). Affection is also correlated with permissiveness, but to a lesser degree, especially in late boyhood (r = .43, N = 148 in early boyhood; r = .52, N = 147 in early girlhood; r = .25, N = 146 in late boyhood; r = .39, N = 146 in late girlhood).

Most of the other correlations among the thirteen attributes of behavior are small and inconsistent. These measures show only a few high correlations with the measures of social agents. High permissiveness in both sexes is correlated with opposite sex companion in late childhood (r = .24, N = 168 for boys; r = −.31, N = 166 for girls).

The meanings of some of the thirteen attributes of behavior may be amplified by correlations with traits inculcated in childhood, included in the same set of codes but reported earlier (Barry *et. al.,* 1976). Permissiveness is negatively correlated with obedience (r = −.63, N = 153 in early boyhood; r = −.59, N = 153 in early girlhood; r = −.61, N = 153 in late boyhood; r = −.48, N = 154 in late girlhood). Warning is negatively correlated with trust (r = −.56 in early boyhood and girlhood, and −.55 in late boyhood and girlhood; N = 74). Incorporation in adult culture is positively correlated with responsibility (r = .46, N = 145 in early boyhood; r = .51, N = 145 in early girlhood; r = .44, N = 156 in late boyhood; r = .35, N = 154 in late girlhood).

Other correlations with traits are lower for attributes of behavior and also for social agents. In general, most of the new measures reported in the present paper show no close relationships with the traits inculcated during childhood.

## THE RELATIONSHIP OF THE NEW MEASURES TO INDEPENDENTLY CODED MEASURES

The relationships of the new measures with each other and with traits could be attributable to the attitudes or expectations on the part of the particular group of coders, or to the ethnographic sources or portions of these sources that were read by the coders. Therefore, the validity of the new measures should be assessed by correlating them with equivalent or similar measures obtained independently. High correlations will help to specify the definitions of the new measures and will demonstrate that the ratings do not depend on the perceptions or procedures of a single group of coders. These tests of validity for some of the new measures are summarized in terms of four general attributes: family structure, sex differentiation, cultural complexity, and indulgence toward children. Each of these attributes is an important measure of variation with respect to child training and also with respect to other cultural customs. Therefore, specification of these attributes of the new measures may facilitate the future task of relating the measures of child training to other important attributes of culture.

### Family Structure

The measures of social agents presented in the first two pages of Table 1 provide diverse information on important attributes of the child's family environment. The present paper analyzes only a small sample of this information.

The new measures of caretakers during early childhood show close relationships with similar variables reported by Barry and Paxson (1971). Non-maternal caretakers and companions were classified as having minor roles during infancy

(Barry and Paxson, 1971) in 58 societies (65 per cent) among 89 in early boyhood, and in 65 societies (64 per cent) among 101 in early girlhood, in which the codes for sex of parent classify the mother as the exclusive caretaker, but in only 21 societies (34 per cent) among 61 in early boyhood, and in only fifteen societies (29 per cent) among 51 in early girlhood, in which the father participates as caretaker. This measure of non-maternal caretakers and companions during infancy shows weaker relationships with the new measure of importance of non-parent, but a close relationship is found when importance of non-parent is combined with sex of parent. Non-maternal caretakers and companions have minor roles in all of the twelve societies in early boyhood, and in fifteen among sixteen societies in early girlhood, in which the mother is the exclusive parental caretaker and there is no non-parental caretaker according to the new codes.

A five-category scale of degree of proximity or companionship of the father with the infant (Barry and Paxson, 1971) was correlated with the new five-category measure of degree to which the parental caretaker is the mother rather than the father. The results are a product-moment correlation of $-.39$ (N = 143) in early boyhood and $-.40$ (N = 145) in early girlhood.

These relationships of the Barry and Paxson (1971) measures in infancy with the new measures in early childhood are closer than with the new measures in late childhood, as is to be expected. A surprising finding is that the same Barry and Paxson measures, applied to early childhood instead of infancy, show slightly less relationship with the new measures for early childhood. The beginning of early childhood at twelve to eighteen months of age, as defined by Barry and Paxson, is earlier than in the new codes. Therefore, it is probably necessary to distinguish between two stages of early childhood.

A measure of household form, reported by Murdock and Wilson (1972), included three categories that indicate a single-parent dwelling: husband resides with his wives in rotation, or in a separate dwelling such as a men's house, or the married couple occupy separate dwellings. According to the new codes for sex of parent, residence in late boyhood is with the mother exclusively in 47 per cent of seventeen societies with single-parent dwellings but in only 2 per cent of 141 societies where both parents reside together. Residence in late girlhood is with the mother exclusively in 81 per cent of 21 societies with single-parent dwellings but in only 5 per cent of 147 societies where both parents reside together.

Murdock and Wilson (1972) classify most of the societies in the sample into three rules of descent: patrilineal, matrilineal, and bilateral. This variation in the characteristics of the kinship group may be expected to have important effects on the child's family environment. Table 6 summarizes some differences among the three rules of descent with respect to frequencies of several categories in the new codes for authority figure during late childhood. The principal non-parent is most often an older sibling or child in patrilineal societies, the mother's brother in matrilineal societies, and a grandparent in bilateral societies. The principal non-parent is predominantly one sex in patrilineal and matrilineal societies; Table 4 shows that it is usually a male, especially for boys. In the majority of bilateral societies, however, the principal non-parent is shared equally by both sexes. The corresponding relationship of rules of descent with sex of parent is influenced by the separate measure of importance of non-parent. In societies where the authority figures are exclusively parental, one sex pre-

TABLE 6
Rule of Descent Related to Authority Figure

| Authority Figure | Late Boyhood | | | Late Girlhood | | |
|---|---|---|---|---|---|---|
| | Pat. | Mat. | Bil. | Pat. | Mat. | Bil. |
| **Principal Non-Parent** | | | | | | |
| Total Sample | 52 | 20 | 39 | 45 | 16 | 40 |
| Sibling or Child | 24 | 4 | 9 | 18 | 5 | 10 |
| Mother's Brother | 4 | 8 | 2 | 3 | 5 | 0 |
| Grandparent | 5 | 4 | 12 | 7 | 3 | 14 |
| **Sex of Principal Non-Parent** | | | | | | |
| Both Sexes Equally | 5 | 3 | 21 | 4 | 4 | 22 |
| One Sex Predominant | 47 | 17 | 17 | 41 | 12 | 17 |
| **Sex of Parent** | | | | | | |
| Parents Exclusively | | | | | | |
| Both Sexes Equally | 5 | 1 | 8 | 7 | 3 | 7 |
| One Sex Predominant | 14 | 3 | 16 | 20 | 6 | 17 |
| Parents Not Exclusively | | | | | | |
| Both Sexes Equally | 8 | 3 | 19 | 10 | 4 | 21 |
| One Sex Predominant | 32 | 12 | 14 | 29 | 11 | 12 |

Number of patrilineal (pat.), matrilineal (mat.), and bilateral (bil.) societies divided into categories on the basis of the specified attributes of authority figures, separately in late boyhood and late girlhood.

dominates regardless of rule of descent. In societies where the authority figures include a non-parent, one sex of parental authority figure predominates in patrilineal and matrilineal but not bilateral societies. Thus a tendency for the parents to share equally in the role of authority figure, in bilateral societies, is effective only if that role is shared with a non-parent.

*Sex Differentiation*

Tables 2 to 5 demonstrate some differences between boys and girls, especially in late childhood. These sex differences are not uniform, however, and for most of the new measures, boys and girls are differentiated in a minority of the societies. Functions of the sex differences, in the societies where they occur, can be investigated by relating the presence or absence of a difference between boys and girls with other features of culture.

The average importance of non-parental role for educator is substantially higher in late boyhood than in late girlhood, as shown in Table 2. This

TABLE 7
Relationships with Sex Difference in Valuation

|  | Number of Societies | | |
|---|---|---|---|
|  | Girls Higher | No Difference | Boys Higher |
| Total Sample | 16 | 93 | 62 |
| Rule of Descent | | | |
|    Patrilineal | 3 | 32 | 37 |
|    Matrilineal | 9 | 14 | 1 |
|    Bilateral | 3 | 38 | 22 |
| Attitude Toward Premarital Sex (Female) | | | |
| 1   Expected, approved | 3 | 19 | 6 |
| 2-5  Restrictions | 4 | 38 | 20 |
| 6   Strongly disapproved | 1 | 14 | 19 |

Number of societies with the designated sex differences in the degree to which the society values boys and girls in late childhood, for different categories of rules of descent (Murdock and Wilson, 1972) and of attitude toward premarital sex in females (Broude and Greene, 1976).

difference is consistent with previous findings of stronger training in self-reliance for boys than girls (Barry, Bacon, and Child, 1957; Barry *et al.*, 1976). The rule of descent (Murdock and Wilson, 1972) influences the frequency of this sex difference. The non-parental role is higher for boys than girls in 34 societies (47 per cent) among 71 with patrilineal descent, in eleven societies (44 per cent) among 25 with matrilineal descent, and in only sixteen societies (24 per cent) among 66 with bilateral descent. Since patrilineal descent is related to polygyny in a world sample of societies (Barry, 1968), these differences are consistent with a report by Barry, Bacon, and Child (1957) that sex differences in child training were larger in polygynous societies.

Table 5 shows a higher average societal value of boys than girls, and Table 7 demonstrates influences of other cultural attributes on this measure of variation among societies. Boys are valued more highly than girls in the majority of patrilineal societies, whereas a higher evaluation is found more often for girls than for boys in matrilineal societies. Bilateral societies are intermediate, with a much higher frequency of higher evaluation for boys than girls, but with no difference in the majority of societies. Table 7 also shows that boys are valued more highly than girls in the majority of societies in which premarital sex behavior of females is strongly disapproved but only in a small proportion of societies in which this behavior is expected and approved. Insistence on virginity

TABLE 8
Cultural Complexity Related to Schooling

| SEX | STAGE | | SCHOOLING | | | | | |
| | | | 1 | 2 | 3 | 4 | 5 | 6 |
|-----|-------|------|------|------|------|------|------|------|
| Boys | Early | Mean | 16.1 | 17.1 | 15.5 | 22.1 | 22.5 | 31.2 |
| | | (N) | (46) | (20) | (78) | (8) | (14) | (11) |
| Girls | Early | Mean | 16.6 | 14.2 | 16.4 | 20.2 | 24.8 | 28.3 |
| | | (N) | (47) | (11) | (88) | (11) | (10) | (10) |
| Boys | Late | Mean | 11.4 | 9.5 | 10.9 | 14.7 | 19.0 | 30.0 |
| | | (N) | (13) | (6) | (42) | (43) | (33) | (41) |
| Girls | Late | Mean | 12.4 | 15.0 | 12.0 | 17.2 | 22.9 | 28.4 |
| | | (N) | (16) | (3) | (55) | (47) | (32) | (25) |

Schooling, on a scale from 1 (Informal) to 6 (Formal), related to a scale of cultural complexity, with a range from 0 to 40, which is the sum of ten measures reported by Murdock and Provost (1973). The mean cultural complexity and number of societies in each category of schooling are shown for boys and girls in early and late childhood.

by the culture apparently does not express a protective attitude toward a cherished, highly valued category of person, but instead is associated with inferior status of females.

*Cultural Complexity*

Societies are often characterized by their degree of technological development. Several measures of subsistence economy and of social and political organization have been used as criteria for specifying variations in a general scale of cultural complexity. Murdock and Provost (1973) rated all 186 societies in the present sample with a score ranging from 0 to 4 on each of ten measures of cultural complexity. A total scale of cultural complexity, with a possible range of scores from 0 to 40, was obtained by summing the scores on the ten measures. The cultural complexity scores for the sample of 186 societies include both of the opposite possible extremes (0 and 40).

Among the new variables, schooling (SCH) is most closely related to cultural complexity. Table 8 shows the average cultural complexity and number of societies for each of six categories of schooling, separately for the different sexes and ages. The average cultural complexity is always higher in societies where apprenticeship is predominant (schooling category 4) than for the same sex and age where informal training is prevalent (schooling categories 1-3). Increasing degrees of formal schooling (categories 5 and 6) are associated with progressive increases in average cultural complexity. The product-moment correlation between cultural complexity and schooling is .30 ($N = 177$) in early boyhood, .25 ($N = 177$) in early girlhood, .62 ($N = 178$) in late boyhood, and .50 ($N = 178$) in late girlhood. The differences from zero are all statistically significant (p < .01), but the correlations also differ substantially among each other. In accordance with the differences between sexes and ages, Table 7 shows that the increase in average cultural complexity from the first three schooling categories (informal training prevalent) to the sixth category (formal schooling) is larger in late childhood, especially for boys.

For both sexes and ages, schooling is correlated more highly with total cultural complexity than with any of the ten component measures of cultural complexity. The correlation between schooling in late boyhood and the sum of any nine of the measures of cultural complexity ranges from .60 to .63, compared with correlations ranging from .49 to .74 between any one of the component measures of cultural complexity and the sum of the other nine. Therefore, schooling in late boyhood would be a suitable additional measure of cultural complexity. A desirable increase in scope might be obtained for total cultural complexity by inclusion of this new measure of child training.

Roberts and Barry (1976) have reported that a three-category scale of complexity of competitive games, which is closely related to most of the measures of cultural complexity, shows high correlations with some of the new measures and with traits inculcated in childhood (Barry *et. al.* 1976). Societies high in game complexity, defined as presence of games of physical skill, chance, and strategy, tend to have a high frequency of corporal punishment and a low degree of permissiveness toward children.

*Indulgence Toward Children*

The two new codes of degree of permissiveness and affection, included in Table 1 and summarized in Table 5, are intended to differentiate between two attributes of indulgence toward children. Product-moment correlations between these measures for corresponding sexes and ages are .43 (N = 148) in early boyhood, .52 (N = 147) in early girlhood, .25 (N = 146) in late boyhood, and .39 (N = 146) in late girlhood. These positive correlations indicate a strong tendency for societies to be low or high in both measures rather than low in one and high in the other. The correlations are low enough, however, so that they measure differential attributes. These can be distinguished by comparing the correlations of both measures with other variables.

Table 9 shows that the two measures of permissiveness and affection have differential relationships with several prior, independent measures of indulgence or severity toward young children. Permissiveness is more highly correlated with sexual and aggression socialization anxiety (Whiting and Child, 1953) and with the measure of childhood indulgence reported by Barry and Paxson (1971). Affection is more highly correlated with parental acceptance (Rohner, 1975). Permissiveness and affection do not differ consistently in their correlations with the remaining measures in Table 9, oral socialization anxiety (Whiting and Child, 1953) and childhood indulgence (Barry, Bacon, and Child, 1967).

Parental acceptance was defined by Rohner (1975: 195) as warmth and affection. Discipline, such as physical punishment or scolding, affected the rating only when it expressed rejection of the child. These specifications account for the higher correlations with affection than warmth. Two other measures reported by Rohner (1975), rated for slightly fewer societies, are parental hostility and parental neglect. These two variables are highly correlated with parental acceptance and show closely similar correlations with permissiveness and affection.

TABLE 9
Correlations Among Measures of Indulgence

| | | Permissiveness | | | | Affection | | | |
| | | Early | | Late | | Early | | Late | |
| | | B | G | B | G | B | G | B | G |
|---|---|---|---|---|---|---|---|---|---|
| **Whiting and Child (1953)** | | | | | | | | | |
| Socialization Anxiety | | | | | | | | | |
| Oral | r | -.27 | -.38 | -.12 | -.18 | -.36 | -.31 | -.20 | -.16 |
| | (N) | (35) | (35) | (35) | (35) | (32) | (32) | (32) | (32) |
| Sexual | r | -.56 | -.50 | -.57 | -.52 | -.18 | -.12 | -.31 | -.24 |
| | (N) | (33) | (33) | (33) | (33) | (29) | (29) | (29) | (29) |
| Aggression | r | -.30 | -.21 | -.48 | -.39 | -.02 | -.06 | -.12 | -.03 |
| | (N) | (36) | (36) | (36) | (36) | (33) | (33) | (33) | (33) |
| **Barry et al. (1967)** | | | | | | | | | |
| Indulgence | r | .41 | .41 | .31 | .28 | .53 | .34 | .49 | .30 |
| | (N) | (46) | (45) | (46) | (45) | (42) | (42) | (42) | (42) |
| **Barry and Paxson (1971)** | | | | | | | | | |
| Indulgence | r | .61 | .56 | .41 | .47 | .34 | .36 | .49 | .30 |
| | (N) | (129) | (127) | (129) | (128) | (116) | (116) | (115) | (115) |
| **Rohner (1975)** | | | | | | | | | |
| Parental Acceptance | r | .25 | .36 | .12 | .25 | .58 | .61 | .38 | .42 |
| | (N) | (29) | (28) | (29) | (29) | (25) | (25) | (24) | (24) |

Product-moment correlations (r) and number of societies (N) for the relationships between two of the new measures (Permissiveness, Affection), separately for boys and girls in early and late childhood, and previous, independent ratings of various aspects of indulgence or severity toward young children.

The measures of socialization anxiety and indulgence, in Table 9, were defined to include both permissiveness and affection. The correlations shown in Table 9 indicate that permissiveness was an important and for some measures a preponderant criterion for the ratings. In addition to the three measures of socialization anxiety in Table 9, Whiting and Child (1953) reported on anal and dependence socialization anxiety. Both were rated for slightly fewer societies than the measures in Table 9. The correlations with permissiveness and affection were very small for anal socialization anxiety and were closely similar for dependence and oral socialization anxiety.

The correlations shown in Table 9 give evidence for a substantial degree of validity of the new measures. Different sets of raters, independently reading the ethnographic information, generated the data for the present study and each of the previous four studies cited in Table 9. The correlations are preponderantly in the same direction and some of them are high enough to indicate satisfactory reliability, especially in view of differences among the studies in definitions of the variables and in the ethnographic sources used. The highest correlation in Table 9 (.61 in early boyhood with Permissiveness) is based on the largest number of cases, in a study on the same sample of 186 societies (Barry and

Paxson, 1971). The other studies were applied to smaller numbers of societies, only a portion of which were also in the present sample.

The correlations shown in Table 9 also give evidence for the validity of the distinction between early and late childhood in the new measures. Barry and Paxson (1971) rated indulgence for the ages from infancy to five years; Rohner (1975) rated parental acceptance for the ages from two to six years. Accordingly, the correlations are substantially higher with early childhood (before seven to eleven years of age) than with late childhood. Barry, Bacon, and Child (1967) rated indulgence for five to twelve years of age, and the correlations are only slightly higher with early than late childhood. Whiting and Child (1953) rated socialization anxiety for the entire span of childhood. The correlations are consistently higher with early than late childhood only for oral socialization, the onset of which is usually earlier than sexual and aggression socialization.

Validity of the difference between boys and girls in the new measures is indicated by some of the correlations in Table 9. Indulgence was reported for boys by Barry, Bacon, and Child (1967) and by Barry and Paxson (1971) in the few instances when a sex difference was noted. The correlation is higher for boys than for girls with the new measures and ages most closely related to the prior measures. This sex difference can be seen for affection in early childhood correlated with indulgence reported by Barry, Bacon, and Child (1967) and for permissiveness in early childhood correlated with indulgence reported by Barry and Paxson (1971).

The measure of total cultural complexity (Table 8) shows appreciable negative correlations with permissiveness ($r = -.23$, $N = 169$ in early boyhood; $r = -.24$, $N = 167$ in early girlhood; $r = -.25$, $N = 168$ in late boyhood; $r = -.25$, $N = 168$ in late girlhood). These correlations are consistent with the conclusion by Rohner (1975) that the degree of parental acceptance is generally lower in the more highly developed societies. His measure of parental acceptance, however, is more closely related to affection (Table 9), which shows little relationship with cultural complexity ($r = -.12$, $N = 155$ in early boyhood; $r = -.13$, $N = 155$ in early girlhood; $r = -.12$, $N = 154$ in late boyhood; $r = -.13$, $N = 154$ in late girlhood). In general, the relationship between cultural complexity and childhood indulgence appears to be weak and inconsistent in the present sample.

## Summary

This paper reports new measures of social agents and attributes of behavior toward children, separately for the two sexes and for two stages (approximately five to eight and eight to twelve years of age). Quantitative scales of nonparental involvement, sex of parent, and sex of principal non-parent were applied to five functions of social agents (residence, caretaker, authority figure, disciplinarian, educator). The quantitative codes also include type and sex of companion, and degree of formal schooling. Quantitative codes for techniques of child training include three measures of exhorting (example, public opinion, lecturing), four measures of punishing (teasing, scolding, warning, corporal punishment), two measures of rewarding (ceremonies, gifts), and four attitudes (permissiveness and affection by the relevant social agents, evaluation by the society, and incorporation in adult life).

These measures are applied to a world sample of 186 societies (Murdock and White, 1969). Summaries of the scores are shown, including differences between boys and girls and between early and late childhood. High correlations are reported for several of these measures with each other and with the degree to which various traits are inculcated in childhood, rated at the same time by the same group of coders but reported previously (Barry *et al.* 1976). Most of the correlations are low, however, indicating that the measures of social agents and behavior toward children are prevalently independent of each other and of the traits inculcated in childhood.

Relationships with variables coded in other studies, applied independently to the same or some of the same sample of societies, demonstrate the validity of certain of the new variables as measures of family structure, sex differences, cultural complexity, and indulgence toward children. The independently coded variables, related to some of the new measures, include importance of the father and other non-maternal agents during infancy (Barry and Paxson, 1971), rules of descent (Murdock and Wilson, 1972), attitudes toward premarital sex behavior of females (Broude and Greene, 1976), cultural complexity (Murdock and Provost, 1973), and childhood indulgence (Whiting and Child, 1953; Barry, Bacon, and Child, 1967; Barry and Paxson, 1971; Rohner, 1975).

## NOTE

1. This article reports a portion of a project (Cross-Cultural Cumulative Coding Center) supported by a National Science Foundation Research Grant (No. GS-2111) directed by George P. Murdock. The senior author was supported by a Public Health Service Research Scientist Development Award (No. K2-MH-5921) from the National Institute of Mental Health. The data were analyzed with the aid of the PDP 10 digital computer at the University of Pittsburgh Computer Center. Preparation of the data was also partly supported by the Social Science Information Center at the University of Pittsburgh.

## BIBLIOGRAPHY

Barry, H., III.   1968.   Regional and Worldwide Variations in Culture. Ethnology 7: 207-217.
Barry, H., III, M. K. Bacon, and I. L. Child.   1957.   A Cross-Cultural Survey of Some Sex Differences in Socialization. Journal of Abnormal and Social Psychology 55: 327-332.
———   1967.   Definitions, Ratings, and Bibliographic Sources for Child Training Practices of 110 Cultures. Cross-Cultural Approaches, ed. C. S. Ford, pp. 293-331. New Haven.
Barry, H., III, and L. M. Paxson.   1971.   Infancy and Early Childhood: Cross-Cultural Codes 2. Ethnology 10: 466-508.
Barry, H., III, L. Josephson, E. Lauer, and C. Marshall.   1976.   Traits Inculcated in Childhood: Cross-Cultural Codes 5. Ethnology 15: 83-114.
Broude, G. J., and S. J. Greene.   1976.   Cross-Cultural Codes on Twenty Sexual Attitudes and Practices. Ethnology 15: 409-429.
Murdock, G. P., and C. Provost.   1973.   Measurement of Cultural Complexity. Ethnology 12: 379-392.
Murdock, G. P., and D. R. White.   1969.   Standard Cross-Cultural Sample. Ethnology 8: 329-369.
Murdock, G. P., and S. F. Wilson.   1972.   Settlement Patterns and Community Organization: Cross-Cultural Codes 3. Ethnology 11: 254-295.
Nie, N. H., C. H. Hull, J. G. Jenkins, K. Steinbrenner, and D. H. Bent.   1975.   Statistical Package for the Social Sciences, 2nd ed. New York.
Roberts, J. M., and H. Barry, III.   1976.   Inculcated Traits and Game-Type Combinations: A Cross-Cultural View. The Humanistic and Mental Health Aspects of Sports, Exercise and Recreation, ed. T. T. Craig, pp. 5-11. Chicago.
Rohner, R. P.   1975.   They Love Me, They Love Me Not. New Haven.
Whiting, J. W. M., and I. L. Child.   1953.   Child Training and Personality. New Haven.

# 9

# Adolescent Initiation Ceremonies:
# A Cross-Cultural Code[1]

*Alice Schlegel* and *Herbert Barry III*

Commonly held assumptions about adolescent initiation ceremonies are that ceremonies for boys are more common than those for girls, that most ceremonies are rather large and dramatic spectacles, that the theme of death and rebirth is common if not ubiquitous, and that genital operations or some other form of pain are almost universal. None of these assumptions receives support from this study.

The discussion and tables below present the data from a cross-cultural study of adolescent initiation ceremonies. We define an adolescent initiation ceremony as some social recognition, in ceremonial form, of the transition from childhood into the next stage (in most societies, this will be an adolescent stage).[2] The ceremony can take place within a rather large period of the early life cycle; during pre-pubescence, at or shortly after puberty, or during late biological adolescence—any time between the ages of about eight and eighteen. Its distinguishing characteristic is that it marks a social transition from one age status to another, excluding those ceremonies that are pertinent to only one aspect of social life; thus, the Bar Mitzvah as currently practiced by American Jews does not constitute an initiation ceremony as we have defined it, for its significance is limited to participation in religious life and does not induce broader social recognition of changed social status. A ceremony as we define it must include at least two participants: at least one initiate, and at least one initiator. This excludes solitary rituals, such as a Plains Indian vision quest, unless at some point a private or public ceremony is conducted.

## THE METHOD

The sample selected was Murdock's and White's (1969) Standard Cross-Cultural Sample of 186 societies representative of the world regions. This sample was selected to facilitate testing with data already coded for that sample. It is representative of all but modern industrial societies.

Information was available on at least presence or absence of adolescent initiation ceremonies for most societies. Exceptions are the Babylonians (45), the Natchez (146), and the Botocudo (178), for which there was no information on either sex. In addition, there was no information for boys' ceremonies among the Amahuaca (170). Thus, the final sample for girls contains 183 societies, while that for boys contains 182.

TABLE 1
Societies where adolescent initiation ceremonies are not reported in either sex.

**AFRICA**

14 Nkundo Mongo
15 Banen
16 Tiv
23 Tallensi
32 Northern Mao

**CIRCUM-MEDITERRANEAN**

26 Zazzagawa Hausa
33 Kaffa
35 Konso
37 Amhara
39 Kenuzi Nubians

42 Riffians
43 Egyptians
44 Hebrews
45 Babylonians *
46 Rwala Bedouin

47 Turks
48 Gheg Albanians
49 Romans
50 Spanish Basques
51 Irish

52 Konkama Lapps
54 Russians
55 Abkhaz
56 Armenians
57 Kurd

**EAST EURASIA**

53 Yurak Samoyed
58 Basseri
59 West Punjabi
60 Maria Gond
63 Uttar Pradesh

64 Burusho
65 Kazak
66 Khalkha Mongols
67 Lolo
68 Lepcha

69 Garo
70 Lakher
71 Burmese
72 Lamet
73 North Vietnamese

74 Rhade
76 Siamese
77 Semang
80 Forest Vedda
81 Menabe Tanala

114 Chekiang Chinese
115 Aigun Manchu
118 Saru Ainu
119 Gilyak
120 Yukaghir

121 Reindeer Chukchee

**INSULAR PACIFIC**

84 Balinese
85 Iban
89 Alorese
98 Trobrianders
99 Siuai

101 Pentecost
104 Maori
109 Trukese
111 Palauans
112 Ifugao

113 Atayal

**NORTH AMERICA**

124 Copper Eskimo
125 Montagnais
128 Slave
140 Gros Ventre
141 Hidatsa

142 Skidi Pawnee
144 Huron
146 Natchez *
147 Comanche
152 Huichol

153 Aztec
154 Sierra Popoluca

**SOUTH AMERICA**

155 Quiche
160 Haitians
166 Mundurucu
168 Cayapa
170 Amahuaca **

172 Aymara
178 Botocudo *
180 Aweikoma
181 Cayua
184 Araucanians

* No information about ceremonies for either sex.

** No information about ceremonies for boys.

The study employed three coders who were trained by coding a pilot sample of twelve societies. (The use of this pilot sample also permitted us to refine or alter operational definitions, thus improving the final coding schedule.) Each trait was coded present, absent, or no information; in case of ambiguity or coder uncertainty, another coder assisted in making the final coding decision. Data were analyzed with the aid of the SPSS Cross-Tabulations program (Nie et al. 1975) at the University of Pittsburgh Computer Center.

TABLE 2

Number (N) and percentage (%) of societies coded with the designated attributes of initiation ceremonies for boys and girls.

| | | Boys | | Girls | |
|---|---|---|---|---|---|
| | | N | % | N | % |
| 1. | Occurrence | 182 | 100% | 183 | 100% |
| | 1.  Absent | 119 | 64% | 98 | 54% |
| | 2.  Present | 63 | 36% | 85 | 46% |
| 2. | Time | 62 | 100% | 83 | 100% |
| | 2.  before genital maturation | 13 | 21% | 9 | 11% |
| | 3.  at first signs of genital maturation | 18 | 29% | 11 | 13% |
| | 4.  at genital maturation | 6 | 10% | 57 | 69% |
| | 5.  within one year after genital maturation | 17 | 27% | 5 | 6% |
| | 6.  later (up to 18 years) | 8 | 13% | 1 | 1% |
| 3. | Number of Concurrent Initiates | 63 | 100% | 84 | 100% |
| | 2.  Single | 29 | 47% | 73 | 87% |
| | 3.  Small group | 7 | 11% | 6 | 7% |
| | 4.  Large group | 27 | 43% | 5 | 6% |
| 4. | Duration of Ceremony | 63 | 100% | 84 | 100% |
| | 2.  Short | 28 | 44% | 36 | 43% |
| | 3.  Medium | 7 | 11% | 21 | 25% |
| | 4.  Long | 28 | 44% | 27 | 32% |
| 5. | Number of Participants | 61 | 100% | 84 | 100% |
| | 2.  Immediate family | 7 | 12% | 40 | 48% |
| | 3.  Local group | 25 | 41% | 29 | 35% |
| | 4.  Large group | 29 | 48% | 15 | 18% |
| 6. | Sexes of Participants | 63 | 100% | 84 | 100% |
| | 2.  Both sexes | 12 | 19% | 10 | 12% |
| | 3.  Partially limited to same sex as initiates | 17 | 27% | 28 | 33% |
| | 4.  Exclusively same sex as initiates | 34 | 54% | 46 | 55% |

Table 1 identifies the societies, grouped according to the six world regions, in which an adolescent initiation ceremony was not reported for either sex.

## THE VARIABLES

We selected those variables that would give the best measures of the behavior and treatment of initiates, the social importance of the ceremony, and the symbolic significance to the society. The discussion that follows defines each of these variables and presents the findings (see Table 2). The findings were discussed further by Schlegel and Barry (1975) and by Barry and Schlegel (1976).

*Occurrence.* The ceremonies are absent in the majority of societies; for those societies holding ceremonies, the number with ceremonies for girls is greater than those for boys (39 societies—girls only, 17 societies—boys only, 46 societies—both sexes [cf. Table 4]). As we discovered upon further analysis,

TABLE 2 (continued)

| | | Boys | | Girls | |
|---|---|---|---|---|---|
| | | N | % | N | % |
| 7. | Primary Physical Components | 63 | 100% | 84 | 100% |
| 2. | None | 6 | 10% | 11 | 13% |
| 3. | Manipulations or activities | 17 | 27% | 45 | 54% |
| 4. | Pain other than genital operation | 20 | 32% | 21 | 25% |
| 5. | Genital operation | 13 | 21% | 7 | 8% |
| 6. | Genital operation and other pain | 7 | 11% | 0 | 0% |
| 8. | Secondary Physical Components | 63 | 100% | 84 | 100% |
| 2. | Neither manipulations nor activities | 15 | 24% | 20 | 24% |
| 3. | Activities | 14 | 22% | 10 | 12% |
| 4. | Manipulations | 9 | 14% | 26 | 31% |
| 5. | Both manipulations and activities | 25 | 40% | 28 | 33% |
| 9. | Primary Cognitive or Performance Components | 63 | 100% | 84 | 100% |
| 2. | Symbolic only | 20 | 32% | 15 | 18% |
| 3. | Learning skills, sharing secrets, or other | 3 | 5% | 3 | 4% |
| 4. | Observing taboos | 8 | 13% | 1 | 1% |
| 5. | Seclusion | 7 | 11% | 9 | 11% |
| 6. | Both seclusion and observing taboos | 18 | 29% | 54 | 64% |
| 7. | Fear | 7 | 11% | 2 | 2% |
| 10. | Secondary Cognitive or Performance Components | 63 | 100% | 84 | 100% |
| 2. | Neither learning skills nor sharing secrets | 42 | 67% | 61 | 73% |
| 3. | Sharing secrets | 8 | 13% | 2 | 2% |
| 4. | Learning skills | 4 | 6% | 11 | 13% |
| 5. | Both learning skills and sharing secrets | 9 | 14% | 10 | 12% |
| 11. | Primary Emic Interpretations | 63 | 100% | 84 | 100% |
| 2. | None | 4 | 6% | 5 | 6% |
| 3. | Status marker, physical change, or behavior change | 41 | 65% | 75 | 89% |
| 4. | Spiritual change | 11 | 18% | 2 | 2% |
| 5. | Death-rebirth | 7 | 11% | 2 | 2% |
| 12. | Secondary Emic Interpretations | 63 | 100% | 84 | 100% |
| 2. | No status marker | 8 | 13% | 8 | 10% |
| 3. | General status marker | 17 | 27% | 25 | 30% |
| 4. | Status marker for adolescence or youth | 14 | 22% | 12 | 14% |
| 5. | Status marker for full adulthood | 24 | 38% | 39 | 46% |
| 13. | Tertiary Emic Interpretations | 63 | 100% | 84 | 100% |
| 2. | Neither physical nor behavior change | 30 | 48% | 48 | 57% |
| 3. | Behavior change | 11 | 18% | 12 | 14% |
| 4. | Physical change | 11 | 18% | 17 | 20% |
| 5. | Both physical and behavior change | 11 | 18% | 7 | 8% |
| 14. | Primary Social Consequences | 63 | 100% | 84 | 100% |
| 2. | None | 19 | 30% | 32 | 38% |
| 3. | Familial integration, familial independence, or other | 14 | 22% | 19 | 23% |
| 4. | Heterosexual intercourse | 7 | 11% | 27 | 32% |
| 5. | Same-sex bonding | 17 | 27% | 3 | 4% |

TABLE 2 (continued)

| | | | Boys | | Girls | |
|---|---|---|---|---|---|---|
| | | | N | % | N | % |
| 6. | | Both same-sex bonding and heterosexual intercourse | 6 | 10% | 3 | 4% |
| 15. | | Secondary Social Consequences | 63 | 100% | 84 | 100% |
| | 2. | None | 35 | 56% | 58 | 69% |
| | 3. | Other | 6 | 10% | 8 | 10% |
| | 4. | Familial independence | 13 | 21% | 9 | 11% |
| | 5. | Familial integration | 9 | 14% | 9 | 11% |
| 16. | | Principal Focus | 62 | 100% | 84 | 100% |
| | 2. | Fertility | 10 | 16% | 34 | 41% |
| | 3. | Sexuality | 10 | 11% | 18 | 21% |
| | 4. | Valor | 7 | 11% | 1 | 1% |
| | 5. | Wisdom | 7 | 11% | 1 | 1% |
| | 6. | Responsibility | 26 | 42% | 23 | 27% |
| | 7. | Other | 2 | 3% | 7 | 8% |

this imbalance is particularly true for food collecting rather than food producing societies (cf. Schlegel and Barry 1975).

*Time.* For both sexes, the time of the ceremony is usually at or close to puberty, that is, first menstruation for girls and first ejaculation for boys. More societies conduct ceremonies at the first signs of genital maturation; i.e., at the first appearance of pubic hair or breasts or when the body begins to conform to adult shape, than within one year afterward. When a group of children are initiated together, coders were instructed to use their judgement about a typical age, generally either the median or highest age.

*Number of Concurrent Initiates.* "Small group" includes up to five or six children, while "large group" is larger than that. If all the children of a community, tribe, large clan, or age-set are initiated concurrently, coders were instructed to code "large group." Girls are preponderantly initiated singly. Interestingly, almost as many societies initiate boys singly as in groups.

*Duration of the Ceremony.* "Short" is up to about three days; "medium" is up to about two weeks; "long" refers to an initiation period lasting from several weeks to a year, in which case there might be a series of ceremonies.

*Number of Participants.* "Immediate family" refers to the household; "local group" includes kin from other households, the neighborhood, or the camp. Where the participation is larger than any of the above groups, community participation is coded "large group." "Large group" also includes the entire society or a large segment of it. For girls, participation tends to include the immediate family or the local group; for boys, it tends to include the local or large group.

*Sexes of Participants.* In every case, initiates belong to single-sex groups, so this variable refers to initiating adults. Where both sexes have important roles in the ceremony, "both sexes" is coded. "Partially limited to same sex as initiates" characterizes some participation of women in boys' ceremonies or men in girls' ceremonies other than as spectators or suppliers of provisions. Expression of emotion on the part of spectators is not considered participation.

While sexual exclusiveness characterizes the majority of ceremonies for both sexes, it is by no means universal. We predict that the degree of exclusiveness in the ceremony reflects the degree to which males and females are distinguished as social categories and socially separated in their activities.

*Primary and Secondary Physical Components.* "Genital operation" means such treatment as circumcision or clitorectomy, with "pain" referring to such treatment as beating, tatooing, tooth extraction, or eating of obnoxious substances. "Manipulation" involves such directly physical, but not painful, treatment as massage, sweat baths, bathing, or body painting. "Activities" refers to activities the initiate must perform, rather than things done to the initiate. It is clear from the percentages in Table 2 that pain (including genital operations) is more characteristic of ceremonies for boys (64 per cent) than for girls (33 per cent); nevertheless, a substantial proportion of girls' ceremonies are painful.

*Primary and Secondary Cognitive or Performance Components.* "Skills" refers to information given that aids in performance, such as sexual skills taught in some girls' ceremonies. "Secrets" refers to knowledge permitted only to those who have been initiated. When initiates are kept in a special location away from persons not involved in the ceremony for more than one day and one night, they are considered to be in seclusion. "Symbolic only" refers to cases in which nothing is specifically taught to the initiate nor does he or she observe taboos or seclusion. For neither sex is learning skills or sharing secrets a prevalent characteristic of the ceremonies, and thus we can question whether the ceremonies are generally instructive in function. Seclusion is a more frequent characteristic, as a means of marking the liminal period the initiate enters. Its preponderance for girls seems to be related to menstrual seclusion.

*Primary, Secondary, and Tertiary Emic Interpretations.* "Death-rebirth" means that the initiate has undergone a total transformation. If there has been some physical change due to the ceremony such as tatooing or symbolic remolding of the body through massage, or the ceremony magically causes physical change, "physical change" is coded present. If the initiate is expected to, or in fact does, behave differently after the ceremony, "behavior change" is coded present. It is true by definition that all initiation ceremonies are status markers, so "status marker" here refers to an important change in the initiate's social standing or function.

It is remarkable, in light of the emphasis in the literature on the theme of death and rebirth (cf. Eliade 1958), that a world-wide sample such as this contains so few cases of this symbolic interpretation; indeed, it may be that this theme is more localized by region or societal type than it is characteristic of symbolic interpretation generally. We are somewhat doubtful about the greater frequency of status markers for movement into full adulthood than into adolescence or youth; our current cross-cultural study on adolescent socialization suggests that adolescence as a post-childhood social stage is more common than the coding here indicates.

*Primary and Secondary Social Consequences.* "Same-sex bonding" refers to the ceremony as intended for or clearly resulting in the formation or intensification of same-sex bonds outside the family. "Heterosexual intercouse" means that the ceremony is intended for or clearly results in the initiation of sexual relations. Familial independence and integration were coded present if (a) the initiate

## TABLE 3

Percentage of societies in which the designated attribute of initiation ceremonies is present in boys and in girls, comparing societies in which there is no initiation ceremony for the opposite sex with societies in which there is an initiation ceremony for both sexes. * p < .05 ** p < .01 for the sex difference.

| Attribute | | Codes | % of Societies | | | |
|---|---|---|---|---|---|---|
| | | | No Ceremony for Opposite Sex | | Ceremony for Both Sexes | |
| | | | Boys | Girls | Boys | Girls |
| | | | (N=17) | (N=39) | (N=45) | |
| 2. | Before genital maturation | 2-3 | 38% | 10% * | 55% | 36% |
| 3. | Group of initiates | 3-4 | 59% | 3% ** | 51% | 22% ** |
| 4. | Medium or long duration | 3-4 | 53% | 69% | 56% | 47% |
| 5. | Local or large group | 3-4 | 94% | 44% ** | 86% | 61% ** |
| 5. | Large group | 4 | 50% | 5% ** | 45% | 30% * |
| 6. | Exclusively same sex | 4 | 65% | 54% | 51% | 56% |
| 7. | Painful procedures | 4-6 | 47% | 26% | 69% | 40% ** |
| 7. | Genital operation | 5-6 | 29% | 0% ** | 31% | 16% |
| 8. | Manipulations | 4-5 | 47% | 72% | 56% | 58% |
| 9. | Seclusion | 5-6 | 35% | 87% ** | 42% | 64% * |
| 9. | Observing taboos | 4,6 | 24% | 82% ** | 47% | 51% |
| 10. | Learning skills | 4-5 | 12% | 31% | 24% | 20% |
| 10. | Sharing secrets | 3,5 | 24% | 10% | 29% | 18% |
| 11. | Spiritual change or death-rebirth | 4-5 | 35% | 3% ** | 27% | 7% ** |
| 12. | Marker for youth | 4 | 6% | 8% | 27% | 20% |
| 12. | Marker for adulthood | 5 | 41% | 51% | 38% | 42% |
| 13. | Physical change | 4-5 | 29% | 23% | 36% | 33% |
| 14. | Same-sex bonding | 5-6 | 35% | 3% ** | 36% | 11% |
| 14. | Heterosexual intercourse | 4,6 | 18% | 39% | 20% | 33% |
| 15. | Familial independence | 4 | 6% | 13% | 24% | 9% * |
| 15. | Familial integration | 5 | 24% | 10% | 11% | 11% |
| 16. | Responsibility | 6 | 56% | 33% | 38% | 22% * |
| 16. | Fertility, Sexuality | 2-3 | 31% | 51% | 33% | 71% ** |

clearly breaks away from the family of origin as a consequence of the ceremony (for girls, this might mean that she marries and moves away immediately after the ceremony), or (b) if the initiate becomes more tightly integrated into the family of origin in such ways as taking on significantly greater familial responsibilities.

The major point of interest here is the difference between the sexes. Same-sex bonding is characteristic of 37 per cent of boys' ceremonies and only eight per cent of girls', whereas heterosexual intercourse characterizes 21 per cent of boys' ceremonies and 36 per cent of girls'. Initiation ceremonies for both sexes tend to lead to cross-sex relationships, but only for boys is there an emphasis on same-sex relationships. This supports the widely-held assumption that men form same-sex bonds outside the kin circle much more than do women. However, support is not proof; this finding applies only to societies that hold initiation ceremonies and tells us nothing about the majority of societies in the sample, which do not. As we have discussed previously (Schlegel and Barry 1975), adolescent initiation ceremonies may be more likely to be held in societies in which gender identity has great social significance.

*Principal Focus.* This variable refers to the central theme of the ceremony. We have identified the following as common foci: "fertility" refers to reproductive capacity; "sexuality" refers to sexual capacity or attractiveness; "valor" refers to courage, usually in warfare or childbirth; "wisdom" refers to knowledge or enlightenment, particularly in spiritual matters; and "responsibility" refers to the importance of adult duties, particularly productive ones. "Other" is a residual category.

For both sexes, the major themes are fertility-sexuality and responsibility, but the emphasis differs by sex. For boys, responsibility has a slight edge over fertility-sexuality; but for girls, fertility-sexuality clearly predominates. The meaning of this was discussed by Schlegel and Barry (1975).

## BOYS' AND GIRLS' CEREMONIES COMPARED

Tables 3 and 4 contain selected variables and allow for comparisons between boys' ceremonies and girls' ceremonies. The tendencies discussed above in the commentary on Table 2 are summarized in these two tables.

TABLE 4

Number of societies in which the designated attribute of initiation ceremonies is absent, present in boys only, present in girls only, and present in both sexes. The phi coefficient measures the degree to which presence of the attribute in one sex predicts its presence in the other sex. $*p < .05$ $**p < .01$ $***p < .001$

| | Attribute | Codes | Absent in Both | Present in Boys | Present in Girls | Present in Both | Phi Coefficient |
|---|---|---|---|---|---|---|---|
| 1. | Occurrence of Ceremony | 2 | 80 | 17 | 39 | 46 | .39 *** |
| 2. | Before genital maturation | 2-3 | 15 | 13 | 5 | 11 | .22 |
| 3. | Group of initiates | 3-4 | 22 | 13 | 0 | 10 | .52 ** |
| 4. | Medium or long duration | 3-4 | 16 | 8 | 4 | 17 | .48 ** |
| 5. | Local or large group | 3-4 | 6 | 11 | 0 | 27 | .50 *** |
| 5. | Large Group | 4 | 23 | 8 | 1 | 12 | .94 *** |
| 6. | Exclusively same sex | 4 | 13 | 7 | 9 | 16 | .29 |
| 7. | Painful procedures | 4-6 | 10 | 17 | 4 | 14 | .16 |
| 7. | Genital operation | 5-6 | 29 | 9 | 2 | 5 | .37 * |
| 8. | Manipulations | 4-5 | 14 | 5 | 6 | 20 | .50 ** |
| 9. | Seclusion | 5-6 | 13 | 3 | 13 | 16 | .35 * |
| 9. | Observing taboos | 4,6 | 18 | 4 | 6 | 17 | .56 *** |
| 10. | Learning skills | 4-5 | 32 | 4 | 2 | 7 | .62 *** |
| 10. | Sharing secrets | 3,5 | 32 | 5 | 0 | 8 | .73 *** |
| 11. | Spiritual change or death-rebirth | 4-5 | 33 | 9 | 0 | 3 | .44 ** |
| 12. | Marker for youth | 4 | 32 | 4 | 1 | 8 | .70 *** |
| 12. | Marker for adulthood | 5 | 23 | 3 | 5 | 14 | .63 *** |
| 13. | Physical change | 4-5 | 25 | 5 | 4 | 11 | .56 *** |
| 14. | Same-sex bonding | 5-6 | 29 | 11 | 0 | 5 | .48 ** |
| 14. | Heterosexual intercourse | 4,6 | 28 | 2 | 8 | 7 | .47 ** |
| 15. | Familial independence | 4 | 34 | 7 | 0 | 4 | .55 ** |
| 15. | Familial integration | 5 | 39 | 1 | 1 | 4 | .78 *** |
| 16. | Responsibility | 6 | 28 | 7 | 0 | 10 | .69 *** |
| 16. | Fertility or Sexuality | 2-3 | 13 | 0 | 17 | 15 | .45 ** |

## TABLE 5

Codes on measures 1-16, separately for boys (B) and girls (G), for each society in which an adolescent initiation ceremony is present for either sex. For measures 2-16, when a ceremony is coded present, a dash indicates no information for that variable; when a ceremony is coded absent, subsequent measures are marked with a dash.

| SOCIETY | 1 BG | 2 BG | 3 BG | 4 BG | 5 BG | 6 BG | 7 BG | 8 BG | 9 BG | 10 BG | 11 BG | 12 BG | 13 BG | 14 BG | 15 BG | 16 BG |
|---|---|---|---|---|---|---|---|---|---|---|---|---|---|---|---|---|
| **AFRICA** | | | | | | | | | | | | | | | | |
| 1 Nama Hottentot | 22 | 64 | 22 | 44 | 33 | 33 | 43 | 55 | 66 | 32 | 33 | 55 | 32 | 44 | 22 | 33 |
| 2 Kung Bushmen | 22 | 54 | 22 | 23 | 33 | 43 | 43 | 54 | 46 | 42 | 33 | 55 | 33 | 22 | 22 | 63 |
| 3 Thonga | 22 | 53 | 43 | 44 | 33 | 44 | 64 | 55 | 23 | 33 | 33 | 52 | 44 | 54 | 42 | 63 |
| 4 Lozi | 12 | -4 | -2 | -3 | -3 | -3 | -4 | -4 | -6 | -4 | -3 | -5 | -3 | -4 | -4 | -3 |
| 5 Mbundu | 22 | 55 | 43 | 44 | 44 | 43 | 65 | 52 | 55 | 55 | 33 | 55 | 44 | 53 | 55 | 66 |
| 6 Suku | 21 | 5- | 4- | 4- | 4- | 4- | 6- | 3- | 7- | 2- | 3- | 5- | 4- | 6- | 3- | 3- |
| 7 Bemba | 12 | -3 | -2 | -4 | -3 | -3 | -3 | -4 | -6 | -5 | -3 | -5 | -2 | -3 | -5 | -6 |
| 8 Nyakyusa | 12 | -4 | -2 | -4 | -3 | -3 | -3 | -5 | -6 | -4 | -3 | -5 | -3 | -4 | -4 | -2 |
| 9 Hadza | 22 | 44 | 22 | 22 | 22 | 44 | 22 | 22 | 22 | 22 | 22 | 22 | 22 | 22 | 22 | 22 |
| 10 Luguru | 22 | 34 | 42 | 44 | 44 | 43 | 53 | 44 | 66 | 55 | 33 | 55 | 55 | 64 | 22 | 33 |
| 11 Kikuyu | 22 | 33 | 44 | 44 | 44 | 33 | 55 | 55 | 46 | 55 | 33 | 55 | 55 | 33 | 33 | 66 |
| 12 Ganda | 12 | -4 | -2 | -3 | -2 | -3 | -3 | -5 | -6 | -2 | -3 | -4 | -2 | -3 | -3 | -2 |
| 13 Mbuti Pygmies | 12 | -4 | -2 | -4 | -4 | -2 | -3 | -3 | -6 | -5 | -3 | -5 | -2 | -5 | -4 | -2 |
| 17 Ibo | 22 | 3- | 42 | 24 | 22 | 44 | 25 | 22 | 75 | 32 | 43 | 44 | 22 | 55 | 22 | 53 |
| 18 Fon | 12 | -4 | -2 | -2 | -2 | -4 | -3 | -5 | -5 | -2 | -3 | -4 | -4 | -3 | -3 | -7 |
| 19 Ashanti | 12 | -4 | -2 | -3 | -3 | -4 | -3 | -5 | -2 | -2 | -3 | -3 | -2 | -4 | -2 | -2 |
| 20 Mende | 22 | 52 | 44 | 44 | 44 | 44 | 43 | 55 | 66 | 55 | 54 | 25 | 23 | 66 | 22 | 66 |
| 22 Bambara | 22 | 22 | 44 | 44 | 44 | 33 | 55 | 24 | 66 | 22 | 55 | 22 | 22 | 66 | 42 | 33 |
| 27 Massa | 21 | 4- | 4- | 3- | 3- | 4- | 4- | 3- | 7- | 3- | 5- | 2- | 4- | 2- | 2- | -- |
| 28 Azande | 21 | -- | 4- | 4- | 3- | 4- | 5- | 2- | 6- | 2- | 3- | 5- | 5- | 6- | 2- | 3- |
| 30 Otoro Nuba | 22 | 33 | 43 | 22 | 42 | 44 | 44 | 22 | 25 | 22 | 33 | 44 | 22 | 44 | 22 | 33 |
| 31 Shilluk | 21 | 5- | 3- | 2- | 3- | 2- | 3- | 5- | 2- | 2- | 3- | 5- | 2- | 5- | 5- | 6- |
| 34 Masai | 22 | 6- | 3- | 4- | 4- | 3- | 5- | 5- | 4- | 2- | 3- | 4- | 5- | 6- | 4- | 4- |
| **CIRCUM-MEDITERRANEAN** | | | | | | | | | | | | | | | | |
| 21 Wolof | 21 | 3- | 4- | 4- | 4- | 4- | 6- | 5- | 5- | 3- | 5- | 3- | 4- | 5- | 2- | 6- |
| 24 Songhai | 22 | 24 | 43 | 32 | 42 | 34 | 22 | 22 | 52 | 42 | 33 | 55 | 22 | 52 | 22 | 22 |
| 25 Wodaabe Fulani | 21 | 5- | 3- | 2- | 4- | 4- | 2- | 2- | 2- | 2- | 3- | 3- | 3- | 2- | 2- | 6- |
| 29 Fur | 22 | 33 | 22 | 22 | 33 | 44 | 55 | 22 | 33 | 22 | 33 | 44 | 22 | 22 | 22 | 22 |
| 36 Somali | 22 | 22 | 22 | 22 | 32 | 44 | 55 | 24 | 66 | 22 | 43 | 33 | 44 | 22 | 22 | 22 |
| 38 Bogo | 21 | 6- | 2- | 3- | 4- | 4- | 3- | 4- | 2- | 2- | 3- | 3- | 2- | 2- | 2- | 2- |
| 40 Teda | 21 | 3- | 4- | 2- | 4- | 3- | 5- | 5- | 5- | 2- | 3- | 5- | 2- | 3- | 4- | 6- |
| 41 Ahaggaren Tuareg | 22 | 54 | 22 | 22 | 33 | 22 | 33 | 44 | 22 | 22 | 33 | 55 | 33 | 33 | 33 | 22 |
| **EAST EURASIA** | | | | | | | | | | | | | | | | |
| 61 Toda | 12 | -2 | -2 | -3 | -3 | -2 | -4 | -5 | -2 | -2 | -3 | -5 | -2 | -4 | -2 | -3 |
| 62 Santal | 21 | 2- | 2- | 2- | 3- | 2- | 3- | 2- | 2- | 2- | 3- | 5- | 2- | 4- | 5- | 6- |
| 75 Khmer | 22 | 24 | 22 | 34 | 44 | 22 | 33 | 55 | 26 | 22 | 33 | 55 | 22 | 33 | 55 | 63 |
| 78 Nicobarese | 12 | -4 | -2 | -3 | -3 | -3 | -3 | -4 | -6 | -2 | -3 | -5 | -5 | -4 | -2 | -3 |
| 79 Andamanese | 22 | 34 | 22 | 22 | 33 | 43 | 43 | 35 | 46 | 22 | 33 | 44 | 53 | 53 | 44 | 66 |

TABLE 5 (continued)

| SOCIETY | 1 BG | 2 BG | 3 BG | 4 BG | 5 BG | 6 BG | 7 BG | 8 BG | 9 BG | 10 BG | 11 BG | 12 BG | 13 BG | 14 BG | 15 BG | 16 BG |
|---|---|---|---|---|---|---|---|---|---|---|---|---|---|---|---|---|
| 82 Negri Sembilan | 22 | 54 | 22 | 22 | 33 | 44 | 34 | 54 | 22 | 22 | 23 | 23 | 22 | 33 | 55 | 66 |
| 116 Koreans | 22 | 25 | 22 | 22 | 33 | 24 | 33 | 55 | 22 | 22 | 33 | 55 | 22 | 33 | 55 | 66 |
| 117 Japanese | 21 | 5- | 2- | 2- | 3- | 2- | 3- | 4- | 2- | 2- | 4- | 5- | 2- | 3- | 5- | 6- |
| INSULAR PACIFIC | | | | | | | | | | | | | | | | |
| 83 Javanese | 22 | 53 | 22 | 22 | 32 | 44 | 52 | 32 | 22 | 22 | 33 | 44 | 52 | 52 | 42 | 32 |
| 86 Tawi-Tawi Badjau | 21 | 5- | 2- | 2- | 3- | 2- | 5- | 4- | 2- | 2- | 3- | 4- | 4- | 3- | 5- | 6- |
| 87 Toradja | 22 | 62 | 22 | 22 | 22 | 22 | 44 | 22 | 22 | 22 | 33 | 33 | 55 | 44 | 22 | 33 |
| 88 Tobelorese | 21 | 3- | 4- | 3- | 4- | 3- | 4- | 5- | 6- | 2- | 2- | 2- | 2- | 2- | 2- | 2- |
| 90 Tiwi | 12 | -4 | -2 | -3 | -3 | -3 | -4 | -4 | -6 | -2 | -3 | -3 | -2 | -3 | -3 | -7 |
| 91 Aranda | 22 | 34 | 22 | 44 | 42 | 34 | 63 | 45 | 76 | 32 | 43 | 55 | 24 | 54 | 22 | 52 |
| 92 Orokaiva | 22 | 44 | 42 | 44 | 43 | 33 | 33 | 55 | 77 | 55 | 33 | 33 | 44 | 33 | 33 | 55 |
| 93 Kimam | 22 | 44 | 42 | 42 | 44 | 34 | 43 | 53 | 76 | 53 | 53 | 25 | 22 | 56 | 42 | 62 |
| 94 Kapauku | 12 | -4 | -2 | -2 | -2 | -4 | -4 | -2 | -7 | -4 | -3 | -5 | -3 | -2 | -2 | -2 |
| 95 Kwoma | 22 | 44 | 42 | 42 | 44 | 34 | 62 | 32 | 55 | 22 | 53 | 33 | 55 | 55 | 44 | 66 |
| 96 Manus | 12 | -4 | -2 | -4 | -3 | -3 | -3 | -4 | -6 | -2 | -3 | -3 | -3 | -3 | -5 | -6 |
| 97 Lesu | 22 | 23 | 32 | 42 | 44 | 34 | 53 | 54 | 53 | 22 | 33 | 55 | 44 | 33 | 44 | 66 |
| 100 Tikopia | 22 | 22 | 32 | 22 | 32 | 24 | 52 | 52 | 22 | 22 | 32 | 52 | 52 | 42 | 52 | 62 |
| 102 Mbau Fijians | 22 | 32 | 42 | 22 | 32 | 44 | 25 | 22 | 42 | 22 | 43 | 33 | 44 | 33 | 33 | 77 |
| 103 Ajie | 22 | 34 | 42 | 22 | 42 | 34 | 63 | 34 | 62 | 22 | 32 | 42 | 22 | 52 | 22 | 32 |
| 105 Marquesans | 22 | 22 | 33 | 22 | 33 | 44 | 54 | 33 | 66 | 22 | 33 | 33 | 44 | 42 | 22 | 22 |
| 106 Samoans | 22 | 65 | 42 | 42 | 44 | 24 | 42 | 52 | 42 | 22 | 43 | 33 | 22 | 52 | 22 | 42 |
| 107 Makin Gilbertese | 22 | 64 | 22 | 42 | -2 | 43 | 43 | 44 | 66 | 44 | 33 | 55 | 24 | 23 | 22 | 42 |
| 108 Jaluit Marshallese | 22 | 53 | 22 | 43 | 33 | 43 | 34 | 55 | 46 | 22 | 33 | 45 | 22 | 44 | 42 | 33 |
| 110 Yapese | 12 | -3 | -2 | -4 | -3 | -3 | -3 | -5 | -6 | -2 | -3 | -5 | -2 | -4 | -2 | -3 |
| NORTH AMERICA | | | | | | | | | | | | | | | | |
| 122 Ingalik | 12 | -4 | -2 | -4 | -2 | -4 | -3 | -5 | -6 | -2 | -3 | -3 | -3 | -3 | -5 | -6 |
| 123 Aleut | 12 | -4 | -2 | -4 | -2 | -4 | -3 | -5 | -6 | -2 | -3 | -5 | -2 | -2 | -2 | -6 |
| 126 Micmac | 12 | -4 | -2 | -2 | -2 | -4 | -3 | -4 | -6 | -2 | -3 | -3 | -2 | -2 | -2 | -6 |
| 127 North Saulteaux | 22 | 23 | 22 | 42 | 22 | 44 | 33 | 33 | 56 | 24 | 53 | 55 | 52 | 34 | 42 | 63 |
| 129 Kaska | 12 | -4 | -2 | -3 | -2 | -4 | -3 | -3 | -6 | -2 | -3 | -5 | -3 | -4 | -2 | -6 |
| 130 Eyak | 12 | -4 | -2 | -3 | -2 | -4 | -3 | -3 | -6 | -4 | -3 | -5 | -4 | -4 | -2 | -6 |
| 131 Masset Haida | 12 | -4 | -2 | -4 | -2 | -4 | -2 | -2 | -6 | -2 | -3 | -3 | -2 | -2 | -2 | -7 |
| 132 Bellacoola | 12 | -4 | -2 | -4 | -2 | -3 | -3 | -3 | -6 | -4 | -3 | -5 | -4 | -4 | -2 | -7 |
| 133 Twana | 12 | -4 | -2 | -2 | -2 | -4 | -2 | -2 | -6 | -2 | -3 | -5 | -2 | -4 | -2 | -6 |
| 134 Yurok | 12 | -4 | -2 | -3 | -2 | -2 | -4 | -3 | -6 | -2 | -3 | -3 | -4 | -2 | -2 | -3 |

Table 3 shows where one sex differs significantly from the other for a particular variable[3] While there are some clear tendencies in the direction of one sex or the other, there are many features for which there is no significant difference between the sexes. In societies having ceremonies for one sex only, girls are significantly less likely than boys to be initiated before genital maturation, to undergo genital operations, and to experience same-sex bonding, and they are significantly more likely to observe taboos. In societies having ceremo-

TABLE 5 (continued)

| SOCIETY | 1 BG | 2 BG | 3 BG | 4 BG | 5 BG | 6 BG | 7 BG | 8 BG | 9 BG | 10 BG | 11 BG | 12 BG | 13 BG | 14 BG | 15 BG | 16 BG |
|---|---|---|---|---|---|---|---|---|---|---|---|---|---|---|---|---|
| 135 Eastern Pomo | 12 | -6 | -2 | -4 | -2 | -4 | -4 | -5 | -6 | -5 | -3 | -5 | -2 | -3 | -5 | -6 |
| 136 Lake Yokuts | 12 | -4 | -2 | -2 | -2 | -4 | -3 | -5 | -4 | -2 | -3 | -3 | -2 | -2 | -2 | -2 |
| 137 Wadadika Paiute | 22 | 34 | 22 | 23 | 22 | 23 | 33 | 45 | 46 | 24 | 33 | 33 | 22 | 24 | 22 | 66 |
| 138 Klamath | 12 | -4 | -2 | -2 | -3 | -2 | -3 | -5 | -6 | -2 | -3 | -3 | -2 | -2 | -2 | -2 |
| 139 Lower Kutenai | 12 | -4 | -2 | -2 | -2 | -4 | -3 | -4 | -6 | -4 | -3 | -5 | -2 | -2 | -2 | -2 |
| 143 Omaha | 21 | 2- | 2- | 3- | -- | 4- | 4- | 3- | 6- | 2- | 4- | 3- | 2- | 2- | 2- | 5- |
| 145 Upper Creek | 21 | 5- | 3- | 2- | 4- | 4- | 2- | 2- | 2- | 2- | 3- | 3- | 3- | 2- | 2- | 6- |
| 148 Chiricahua Apache | 12 | -4 | -2 | -2 | -4 | -3 | -3 | -5 | -6 | 2- | -3 | 5- | 4- | 4- | 2- | -7 |
| 149 Zuni | 12 | -4 | -2 | -2 | -2 | -2 | -3 | -5 | -2 | -2 | -3 | -3 | -2 | -2 | -2 | -2 |
| 150 Havasupai | 12 | -4 | -2 | -3 | -2 | -4 | -4 | -4 | -6 | -2 | -3 | -3 | -2 | -2 | -2 | -6 |
| 151 Papago | 12 | -4 | -2 | -3 | -3 | -3 | -4 | -5 | -6 | -2 | -3 | -5 | -2 | -2 | -2 | -6 |

SOUTH AMERICA

| SOCIETY | 1 BG | 2 BG | 3 BG | 4 BG | 5 BG | 6 BG | 7 BG | 8 BG | 9 BG | 10 BG | 11 BG | 12 BG | 13 BG | 14 BG | 15 BG | 16 BG |
|---|---|---|---|---|---|---|---|---|---|---|---|---|---|---|---|---|
| 156 Miskito | 21 | 2- | 2- | 2- | 2- | 4- | 3- | 3- | 2- | 2- | 2- | 2- | 2- | 2- | 2- | 2- |
| 157 Bribri Talamanca | 12 | -4 | -2 | -3 | -2 | -4 | -3 | -4 | -6 | -2 | -3 | -3 | -2 | -2 | -2 | -2 |
| 158 Cuna | 12 | -4 | -2 | -4 | -3 | -3 | -3 | -4 | -6 | -2 | -3 | -3 | -2 | -2 | -2 | -2 |
| 159 Goajiro | 12 | -4 | -2 | -4 | -3 | -4 | -3 | -5 | -6 | -5 | -5 | -2 | -2 | -4 | -3 | -3 |
| 161 Callinago | 22 | 33 | 22 | 44 | 32 | 44 | 44 | 54 | 66 | 22 | 33 | 33 | 32 | 23 | 25 | 42 |
| 162 Warrau | 22 | 34 | 22 | 22 | 22 | 44 | 44 | 22 | 26 | 22 | 33 | 33 | 22 | 22 | 22 | 22 |
| 163 Yanomamo | 12 | -4 | -2 | -2 | -2 | -4 | -3 | -4 | -6 | -2 | -3 | -5 | -4 | -4 | -4 | -2 |
| 164 Barama Carib | 12 | -4 | -2 | -3 | -2 | -4 | -2 | -2 | -5 | -4 | -3 | -4 | -3 | -2 | -2 | -6 |
| 165 Saramacca | 21 | 5- | 2- | 4- | 3- | 4- | 3- | 3- | 3- | 5- | 4- | 3- | 2- | 5- | 2- | 5- |
| 167 Cubeo | 22 | 34 | 42 | 42 | 43 | 43 | 44 | 35 | 36 | 32 | 33 | 45 | 25 | 24 | 22 | 73 |
| 169 Jivaro | 22 | 64 | 22 | 43 | 33 | 33 | 33 | 54 | 66 | 32 | 43 | 54 | 32 | 22 | 22 | 52 |
| 171 Inca | 22 | 54 | 42 | 43 | 42 | 33 | 44 | 54 | 66 | 22 | 33 | 44 | 22 | 22 | 22 | 62 |
| 173 Siriono | 12 | -2 | -3 | -2 | -3 | -3 | -3 | -5 | -6 | -4 | -3 | -5 | -2 | -4 | -2 | -6 |
| 174 Nambicuara | 22 | 44 | 22 | 22 | 34 | 44 | 43 | 24 | 75 | 22 | 32 | 42 | 22 | 32 | 32 | 52 |
| 175 Trumai | 22 | 34 | 22 | 24 | 42 | 44 | 42 | 52 | 66 | 22 | 33 | 35 | 52 | 54 | 22 | 42 |
| 176 Ramcocamecra Timbira | 21 | 6- | 4- | 4- | 4- | 4- | 3- | 5- | 6- | 5- | 4- | 5- | 3- | 5- | 2- | 6- |
| 177 Tupinamba | 12 | -4 | -2 | -4 | -2 | -4 | -4 | -4 | -6 | -2 | -3 | -3 | -2 | -2 | -2 | -2 |
| 179 Shavante | 22 | 25 | 44 | 43 | 44 | 33 | 43 | 33 | 65 | 42 | 33 | 44 | 34 | 52 | 42 | 47 |
| 182 Lengua | 22 | 34 | 42 | 44 | 33 | 32 | 33 | 44 | 22 | 22 | 33 | 44 | 22 | 22 | 22 | 22 |
| 183 Abipon | 12 | -4 | -2 | -3 | -2 | -4 | -4 | -2 | -6 | -2 | -3 | -5 | -4 | -4 | -4 | -4 |
| 185 Tehuelche | 12 | -4 | -2 | -2 | -3 | -2 | -2 | -2 | -5 | -2 | -2 | -2 | -2 | -2 | -2 | -2 |
| 186 Yahgan | 22 | 55 | 44 | 33 | 44 | 22 | 44 | 33 | 66 | 55 | 44 | 55 | 33 | 33 | 44 | 66 |

nies for both sexes, boys are significantly more likely than girls to undergo painful procedures other than genital operations and to have ceremonies that result in familial independence and focus on responsibility, while girls are significantly more likely to have ceremonies that focus on fertility and sexuality. For both classes of societies, boys are significantly more likely to be initiated in groups, to have local or large group participation in their ceremonies, and to experience spiritual change, while girls are significantly more likely to go into seclusion.

Table 4 measures concordance of one sex with the other against discordance.[4] For most measures there is a statistically significant level of concordance indicated; that is, traits are more likely to be present and absent for both sexes than they are to be present for one but absent for the other. In spite of a high level of concordance, however, there are clear tendencies in the direction of one sex or the other, as discussed above.

## THE CODE

The coded information is found in Table 5. The serial identification numbers for the societies are those specified by Murdock and White (1969). Each column stands for one variable, coded separately for boys and girls. The numbers within each column refer to the codes for that variable. If the ceremony is coded absent (1), all subsequent variables are marked with a dash. If it is coded present (2), dashes indicate absence of information.

## NOTES

1. This study was made possible through the generosity of the University of Pittsburgh Provost Development Fund. We are grateful to the University and to Joseph Shoben, then Associate Provost, for his interest and support. Also we thank the coders (Caterina Provost, Marlee Myers, and Ben Perrino) for their skillful and diligent work.

2. We are currently conducting a cross-cultural study of adolescent socialization with the same sample used for this study.

3. Ceremonies for both sexes are held in 46 societies while Table 3 shows an N of 45; this is because information on all the measures was missing for girls in one society (34: Masai). For societies with no ceremony for the opposite sex, the sex differences were tested for statistical significance by the chi square test. For societies with a ceremony for both sexes, the sex difference was tested for statistical significance by the binomial sign test, comparing the number in the column labeled "Present for Boys" with the number in the column "Present for Girls" in Table 4.

4. Phi coefficient, and the statistical significance of the association between the two sexes for the attribute (tested by the chi square) were obtained from the SPSS Cross-tabulation program (Nie et al. 1975).

## BIBLIOGRAPHY

Barry, H. III, and A. Schlegel.   1976.   Cultural Variations in Adolescent Initiation Ceremonies Related to Traits Inculcated in Earlier Childhood. Paper presented at the annual meeting of the Society for Cross-Cultural Research, New York.

Elaide, M.   1958.   Birth and Rebirth: The Religious Meaning of Initiation in Human Culture, trans. W. R. Trask. New York.

Murdock, G. P., and D. R. White.   1969.   Standard Cross-Cultural Sample. Ethnology 8: 329-369.

Nie, N. H., C. H. Hull, J. G. Jenkins, K. Steinbrenner, and D. H. Bent.   1975.   SPSS: Statistical Package for the Social Sciences. New York.

Schlegel, A., and H. Barry III.   1975.   Cultural Correlates of Adolescent Initiation Ceremonies. Paper presented at the annual meeting of the Society for Cross-Cultural Research, Chicago.

# 10

# Factors in the Division of Labor
# by Sex: A Cross-Cultural Analysis

*George P. Murdock* and *Caterina Provost*

A division of labor between the sexes has long been recognized by economists, sociologists, and other behavioral scientists as (1) the original and most basic form of economic specialization and exchange, and as (2) the most fundamental basis of marriage and the family and hence the ultimate source of all forms of kinship organization. On the whole, however, scholars have focused their major attention on the consequences rather than the causes of the division of labor by sex, seeking, for example, to ascertain its bearing on such matters as the status of women and the forms of social organization. In the present paper the emphasis shifts to an inquiry into the factors governing the assignment of particular tasks to men or to women in the cultures of the world.

## CODING OPERATIONS

The data are derived from an assessment of the ethnographic sources on a representative sample of the world's societies—those selected by Murdock and White (1969) and used in a series of previously published cross-cultural codes (Barry and Paxson 1971; Murdock and Morrow 1970; Murdock and Wilson 1972; Tuden and Marshall 1972). One of the sample societies, the Pentecost islanders of Bunlap village in the New Hebrides (#101), was eliminated because of insufficient data, but the remaining 185 were coded for the presence or absence and the sex assignment of 50 technological activities or tasks, yielding a total of 9,250 items of information. Each activity in each of the sample societies was classified under one of the following symbols:

A  Activity absent in the society.
O  No relevant data available for the society.
P  Activity present in the society but sex participation not specified in the sources.
M  Activity performed exclusively by males at the pinpointed date (or at a somewhat earlier date in the case of activities which had recently lapsed

in consequence of culture contact—a qualification likewise applying to the following symbols).

N   Activity performed by both sexes but predominantly by males.

E   Activity performed by both sexes with approximately equal participation or with a roughly equivalent division of subtasks.

G   Activity performed by both sexes but predominantly by females.

F   Activity performed exclusively by females, male participation being negligible.

Information was also coded on related matters, such as the relative importance of the particular activity in the total cultural context, the degree of occupational specialization involved, and the extent to which the coding depended upon inference. These data are omitted in the present paper.

The basic coding was done by Caterina Provost for 99 of the 185 societies and by Diana Morrow for 56. Lili Josephson coded the remaining 30 societies and the German sources on a number of others. The present authors reviewed all the coded information and together rendered a final decision in all cases of doubt or discrepancy. They refrained from making inferences regarding sex participation except where the supporting evidence impressed them as reasonably strong.

The 50 technological activities assessed are listed and defined below, classified by categories. After each are listed the totals of societies coded as A, O, and P. Those on which data on sex participation were available are separately listed in Table 1.

### Food Collection

Gathering of wild vegetal foods (#44 in Table 1). A-10, O-6, P-34.

Gathering of eggs, insects, and/or small land fauna (#27). A-18, O-52, P-48.

Gathering of shellfish and/or other small aquatic fauna (#39). A-85, O-23, P-22.

Collection of wild honey (#16). A-38, O-79, P-20.

Fowling, i.e., hunting of birds (#7). A-16, O-28, P-2.

Fishing, excluding shellfishing and aquatic hunting (#18). A-29, O-3, P-10.

Trapping or otherwise catching small land fauna (#9). A-20, O-15, P-1.

Hunting of large land fauna (#5). A-36, O-5, P-0.

Hunting of large aquatic fauna (#1). A-127, O-8, P-2.

### Food Production

Land clearance for agriculture (#17). A-44, O-1, P-1.

Soil preparation, e.g., with hoe or plow (#21). A-49, O-1, P-1.

Crop planting and/or transplanting (#28). A-44, O-0, P-0.

Crop tending, e.g., weeding, irrigation (#31). A-48, O-3, P-3.

Harvesting, including preparation for storage (#30). A-44, O-0, P-0.

Care of small domestic animals, e.g., poultry, dogs, pigs (#36). A-13, O-5, P-70.

Tending large domestic animals, e.g., sheep, cattle, horses (#19). A-76, O-1, P-10.

Milking (#32). A-127, O-0, P-10.

### Food Preparation

Preparation of vegetal foods prior to cooking, e.g., grain grinding (#50). A-2, O-7, P-2.

Butchering, including dressing of game (#15). A-8, O-18, P-16.

Preservation of meat and/or fish, e.g., drying, smoking (#37). A-31, O-24, P-64.

Preparation of drinks, e.g., tea, kava, beer (#42). A-37, O-15, P-42.

Dairy production, e.g., making butter or cheese (#45). A-130, O-15, P-20.

Cooking (#49). A-0, O-0, P-1.

### Extractive Industries

Mining and/or quarrying (#13). A-106, O-38, P-6.

Fuel gathering (#40). A-1, O-6, P-12.

Lumbering, i.e., obtaining wood other than for fuel (#4). A-14, O-16, P-16.

Water fetching (#48). A-0, O-0, P-25.

### Intermediate Processing of Raw Materials

Preparation of skins, e.g., scraping, tanning (#26). A-48, O-12, P-44.

Spinning, i.e., manufacture of thread (#46). A-56, O-29, P-9.

Loom weaving, excluding other techniques for making fabrics (#38). A-81, O-15, P-1.

Smelting of metal ores (#2). A-125, O-23, P-0.

### Manufacture of Finished Artifacts

Matmaking (#35). A-29, O-22, P-31.

Netmaking (#22). A-45, O-31, P-38.

Basketmaking (#33). A-21, O-15, P-19.

Making of rope and/or cordage (#23). A-3, O-15, P-56.

Manufacture of leather products, exclusive of clothing (#29). A-57, O-22, P-32.

Making of clothing, exclusive of footwear and head gear (#41). A-36, O-22, P-5.

Potterymaking, including other ceramic arts (#43). A-61, O-13, P-6.

Work in wood, i.e., manufacture of wooden artifacts (#6). A-1, O-3, P-17.

Work in bone, horn, and/or shell (#12). A-14, O-45, P-44.

Stoneworking, i.e., manufacture of stone artifacts (#11). A-39, O-42, P-31.

Metalworking, e.g., forging or casting of metal artifacts (#3). A-93, O-6, P-0.

Manufacture of musical instruments (#8). A-8, O-15, P-74.

*Miscellaneous Technological Activities*

Generation of fire (#24). A-3, O-0, P-96.

Laundering (#47). A-52, O-58, P-9.

Bodily mutilation, e.g., tattooing, circumcision (#25). A-13, O-21, P-45.

Bonesetting and/or other surgery (#14). A-37, O-87, P-17.

Burden carrying, including porterage (#34). A-3, O-30, P-6.

Boatbuilding (#10). A-79, O-10, P-5.

Housebuilding, including erection of portable shelters (#20). A-1, O-0, P-6.

The relative adequacy or inadequacy of the ethnographic coverage for a particular activity can be estimated from the number of societies coded as O or P in the above list. Thus the evidence is revealed to be scantiest, i.e., lacking for more than half of the sample societies, on bonesetting, the gathering of small land fauna, the collection of wild honey, and the generation of fire, and the fullest data are available on cooking, housebuilding, hunting, and the several agricultural operations.

## CLASSIFICATION OF CODED DATA

The assignment of tasks by sex is indicated in Table 1, where the 50 activities are rearranged in descending rank order of male participation. The first five columns give the number of societies for which the particular activity is coded, respectively, as M (exclusive male participation), N (predominant male participation), E (equal or equivalent participation by both sexes), G (predominant female participation), and F (exclusive female participation). The last column presents an index of the average percentage of male participation, giving a weight of 1 to each case of M, of .8 to each N, of .5 to each E, of .2 to each G, and of 0 to each F.

The data in Table 1 confirm, on the whole, the results of an earlier study (Murdock 1937). Indeed, for eight activities (numbers 1, 3, 8, 10, 11, 20, 48, and 49 in Table 1) the indices of male participation differ by less than 1 per cent in the two studies. The larger discrepancies are mainly a product of improvements in the selection of the sample.

Table 1, in presenting indices of sex participation for the world as a whole, ignores important regional differences in the sexual allocation of particular tasks. When indices are calculated separately for the six major ethnographic regions—A Africa, C Circum-Mediterranean, E East Eurasia, I Insular Pacific, N North America, and S South and Central America—the 50 activities break down into four clusters with clearly distinguishable statistical characteristics.

The first cluster, consisting of what we shall designate as strictly masculine activities, has the following statistical characteristics:

1. It includes the fourteen activities with the highest worldwide indices of masculinity in Table 1, these indices being in all cases above 92.5.

2. The regional indices are likewise high, falling below 87.0 in only a single exceptional instance.

3. These indices show minimal differentiation from region to region.

## TABLE 1
### Sex Allocation of 50 Technological Activities in 185 Societies

| Task | M | N | E | G | F | Index |
|------|---|---|---|---|---|-------|
| 1. Hunting large aquatic fauna | 48 | 0 | 0 | 0 | 0 | 100.0 |
| 2. Smelting of ores | 37 | 0 | 0 | 0 | 0 | 100.0 |
| 3. Metalworking | 85 | 1 | 0 | 0 | 0 | 99.8 |
| 4. Lumbering | 135 | 4 | 0 | 0 | 0 | 99.4 |
| 5. Hunting large land fauna | 139 | 5 | 0 | 0 | 0 | 99.3 |
| 6. Work in wood | 159 | 3 | 1 | 1 | 0 | 98.8 |
| 7. Fowling | 132 | 4 | 3 | 0 | 0 | 98.3 |
| 8. Manufacture of musical instruments | 83 | 3 | 1 | 0 | 1 | 97.6 |
| 9. Trapping of small land fauna | 136 | 12 | 1 | 1 | 0 | 97.5 |
| 10. Boatbuilding | 84 | 3 | 3 | 0 | 1 | 96.6 |
| 11. Stoneworking | 67 | 0 | 6 | 0 | 0 | 95.9 |
| 12. Work in bone, horn, and shell | 71 | 7 | 2 | 0 | 2 | 94.6 |
| 13. Mining and quarrying | 31 | 1 | 2 | 0 | 1 | 93.7 |
| 14. Bonesetting and other surgery | 34 | 6 | 4 | 0 | 0 | 92.7 |
| 15. Butchering | 122 | 9 | 4 | 4 | 4 | 92.3 |
| 16. Collection of wild honey | 39 | 5 | 2 | 0 | 2 | 91.7 |
| 17. Land clearance | 95 | 34 | 6 | 3 | 1 | 90.5 |
| 18. Fishing | 83 | 45 | 8 | 5 | 2 | 86.7 |
| 19. Tending large animals | 54 | 24 | 14 | 3 | 3 | 82.4 |
| 20. Housebuilding | 105 | 30 | 14 | 9 | 20 | 77.4 |
| 21. Soil preparation | 66 | 27 | 14 | 17 | 10 | 73.1 |
| 22. Netmaking | 42 | 2 | 5 | 1 | 15 | 71.2 |
| 23. Making of rope or cordage | 62 | 7 | 18 | 5 | 19 | 69.9 |
| 24. Generation of fire | 40 | 6 | 16 | 4 | 20 | 62.3 |
| 25. Bodily mutilation | 36 | 4 | 48 | 6 | 12 | 60.8 |
| 26. Preparation of skins | 39 | 4 | 2 | 5 | 31 | 54.6 |
| 27. Gathering of small land fauna | 27 | 3 | 9 | 13 | 15 | 54.5 |
| 28. Crop planting | 27 | 35 | 33 | 26 | 20 | 54.4 |
| 29. Manufacture of leather products | 35 | 3 | 2 | 5 | 29 | 53.2 |
| 30. Harvesting | 10 | 37 | 34 | 34 | 26 | 45.0 |
| 31. Crop tending | 22 | 23 | 24 | 30 | 32 | 44.6 |
| 32. Milking | 15 | 2 | 8 | 2 | 21 | 43.8 |
| 33. Basketmaking | 37 | 9 | 15 | 18 | 51 | 42.5 |
| 34. Burden carrying | 18 | 12 | 46 | 34 | 36 | 39.3 |
| 35. Matmaking | 30 | 4 | 9 | 5 | 55 | 37.6 |
| 36. Care of small animals | 19 | 8 | 14 | 12 | 44 | 35.9 |
| 37. Preservation of meat and fish | 18 | 2 | 3 | 3 | 40 | 32.9 |
| 38. Loom weaving | 24 | 0 | 6 | 8 | 50 | 32.5 |
| 39. Gathering small aquatic fauna | 11 | 4 | 1 | 12 | 27 | 31.1 |
| 40. Fuel gathering | 25 | 12 | 12 | 23 | 94 | 27.2 |
| 41. Manufacture of clothing | 16 | 4 | 11 | 13 | 78 | 22.4 |
| 42. Preparation of drinks | 15 | 3 | 4 | 4 | 65 | 22.2 |
| 43. Potterymaking | 14 | 5 | 6 | 6 | 74 | 21.1 |
| 44. Gathering wild vegetal foods | 6 | 4 | 18 | 42 | 65 | 19.7 |
| 45. Dairy production | 4 | 0 | 0 | 0 | 24 | 14.3 |
| 46. Spinning | 7 | 3 | 4 | 5 | 72 | 13.6 |
| 47. Laundering | 5 | 0 | 4 | 8 | 49 | 13.0 |
| 48. Water fetching | 4 | 4 | 8 | 13 | 131 | 8.6 |
| 49. Cooking | 0 | 2 | 2 | 63 | 117 | 8.3 |
| 50. Preparation of vegetal foods | 3 | 1 | 4 | 21 | 145 | 5.7 |

TABLE 2

Strictly Masculine Activities, with Regional Indices of Sex Participation

| | Activity | A | C | E | I | N | S |
|---|---|---|---|---|---|---|---|
| 1. | Hunting large aquatic fauna | 100.0 | 100.0 | 100.0 | 100.0 | 100.0 | 100.0 |
| 2. | Smelting of ores | 100.0 | 100.0 | 100.0 | 100.0 | 100.0 | 100.0 |
| 3. | Metalworking | 100.0 | 100.0 | 100.0 | 100.0 | 100.0 | 97.7 |
| 4. | Lumbering | 100.0 | 98.5 | 99.2 | 100.0 | 98.5 | 100.0 |
| 5. | Hunting large land fauna | 99.3 | 100.0 | 100.0 | 97.6 | 98.7 | 100.0 |
| 6. | Work in wood | 100.0 | 99.1 | 100.0 | 100.0 | 96.7 | 97.5 |
| 7. | Fowling | 100.0 | 97.2 | 99.0 | 100.0 | 95.4 | 99.3 |
| 8. | Making musical instruments | 96.9 | 97.7 | 95.5 | 100.0 | 98.5 | 97.5 |
| 9. | Trapping | 100.0 | 98.8 | 98.3 | 98.0 | 95.5 | 98.7 |
| 10. | Boatbuilding | 100.0 | 100.0 | 100.0 | 100.0 | 87.1 | 100.0 |
| 11. | Stoneworking | 100.0 | 93.8 | 100.0 | 96.9 | 92.9 | 100.0 |
| 12. | Work in bone, horn, shell | 100.0 | 97.5 | 90.0 | 97.9 | 93.3 | 90.7 |
| 13. | Mining and quarrying | 100.0 | 90.9 | 93.3 | 100.0 | 100.0 | 100.0 |
| 14. | Bonesetting | 90.9 | 92.9 | 91.3 | 87.1 | 92.5 | 100.0 |

4. In only seven scattered cases out of the 1,215 for which data were available was any of these activities reported as assigned either exclusively or predominantly to females.

The few exceptional cases deserve special mention:

Work in wood among the Pawnee. The ethnographer (Weltfish 1965) specifically notes that the assignment of this task to women is unique among North American Indians.

Manufacture of musical instruments among the Tuareg. Based on an inference from a picture in Nicolaisen (1963) showing two drums reportedly made by women.

Trapping among the Mbuti Pygmies. Although men do the important hunting, women are reported to catch small, slow animals by hand or net.

Boatbuilding among the Hidatsa. Women constructed the skin coracles or "bull boats" used for crossing the Missouri River.

Work in bone, horn, and shell. Santal women are reported to fashion ornaments of shell and Pawnee women utensils of horn, but in neither case is there conclusive evidence that female participation in the activity is exclusive or even preponderant.

Mining among the Fur. The collection of iron ore in the form of dust by women for sale to smiths has been coded as mining.

The second cluster includes a series of activities which we term quasi-masculine because, though most commonly assigned to males, their assignment predominantly or exclusively to females is by no means uncommon. They are listed in Table 3 and exhibit the following common statistical characteristics:

1. They reveal worldwide indices of masculine participation of between approximately 70 and 92 without any overlap with the activities of either the first or the third cluster.

TABLE 3
Quasi-masculine Activities, with Regional Indices of Sex Participation

| Activity | A | C | E | I | N | S |
|---|---|---|---|---|---|---|
| 15. Butchering | 100.0 | 95.2 | 96.2 | 100.0 | 79.0 | 87.5 |
| 16. Collection of wild honey | 96.9 | 100.0 | 97.8 | 87.5 | 50.0 | 96.9 |
| 17. Land clearance | 89.1 | 97.5 | 92.4 | 86.7 | 74.6 | 95.2 |
| 18. Fishing | 82.6 | 92.0 | 88.8 | 81.0 | 85.8 | 87.1 |
| 19. Tending large animals | 90.6 | 77.6 | 82.0 | 83.3 | 91.5 | 70.0 |
| 20. Housebuilding | 73.5 | 75.4 | 80.0 | 91.0 | 67.9 | 77.3 |
| 21. Soil preparation | 53.4 | 94.6 | 82.1 | 73.9 | 53.1 | 72.0 |
| 22. Netmaking | 100.0 | 50.0 | 57.8 | 68.4 | 72.1 | 57.1 |
| 23. Making rope and cordage | 80.0 | 76.7 | 66.7 | 71.2 | 53.5 | 72.7 |

2. Their regional indices in no instance fall below 50.0.

3. These indices show substantially greater variation from region to region than do those of the first cluster.

4. All are assigned either exclusively or predominantly to females in a not inconsiderable fraction of the sample societies.

The third cluster embraces what we designate as swing activities because they are assigned predominantly to males in some regions but predominantly to females in others. They exhibit the following common statistical characteristics:

1. They reveal intermediate worldwide indices of masculine participation, which range between approximately 31 and 62.

2. Their regional indices range from 100.0 to 0.0, thus covering the entire gamut from exclusively masculine to exclusively feminine, and for particular activities the average difference between the region with the

TABLE 4
Swing Activities, with Regional Indices of Sex Participation

| Activity | A | C | E | I | N | S |
|---|---|---|---|---|---|---|
| 24. Generation of fire | 40.7 | 14.3 | 70.6 | 70.6 | 68.6 | 83.6 |
| 25. Bodily mutilation | 63.2 | 68.3 | 46.2 | 74.4 | 34.0 | 68.2 |
| 26. Preparation of skins | 87.5 | 66.7 | 58.9 | — | 30.7 | 44.4 |
| 27. Gathering small land fauna | 39.2 | 55.0 | 85.0 | 40.0 | 47.5 | 68.0 |
| 28. Crop planting | 29.6 | 75.0 | 61.9 | 54.4 | 46.9 | 53.3 |
| 29. Manufacture of leather products | 90.8 | 67.6 | 61.1 | — | 24.6 | 46.7 |
| 30. Harvesting | 24.3 | 67.1 | 63.3 | 39.6 | 35.4 | 34.4 |
| 31. Crop tending | 23.2 | 69.1 | 57.8 | 24.2 | 44.6 | 50.0 |
| 32. Milking | 62.5 | 30.0 | 61.1 | — | 0.0 | 40.0 |
| 33. Basketmaking | 63.8 | 50.0 | 61.1 | 22.6 | 13.1 | 55.0 |
| 34. Burden carrying | 20.4 | 48.5 | 67.2 | 40.7 | 32.2 | 32.3 |
| 35. Matmaking | 54.2 | 45.6 | 50.0 | 17.8 | 6.3 | 63.6 |
| 36. Care of small animals | 69.3 | 36.0 | 33.3 | 19.5 | 38.0 | 21.8 |
| 37. Preservation of meat or fish | 50.0 | 40.0 | 47.5 | 71.7 | 6.4 | 41.7 |
| 38. Loom weaving | 100.0 | 40.0 | 16.8 | 2.9 | 12.5 | 17.0 |
| 39. Gathering small aquatic fauna | 30.0 | — | 33.3 | 9.2 | 47.0 | 75.0 |
| 41. Manufacture of clothing | 62.5 | 28.3 | 13.3 | 6.5 | 14.3 | 26.7 |
| 43. Potterymaking | 5.0 | 28.9 | 61.7 | 29.2 | 13.8 | 10.9 |

greatest and that with the lowest masculine participation is 57 percentage points.

The fourth cluster consists of activities which we designate as quasi-feminine because they are usually, though not universally, assigned to fe-

TABLE 5

Quasi-feminine Activities, with Regional Indices of Sex Participation

| Activities | A | C | E | I | N | S |
|---|---|---|---|---|---|---|
| 40. Fuel gathering | 20.0 | 24.6 | 36.4 | 18.1 | 36.7 | 26.1 |
| 42. Preparation of drinks | 20.6 | 35.8 | 22.1 | 42.9 | 13.0 | 14.8 |
| 44. Gathering of wild vegetal foods | 11.0 | 13.3 | 15.0 | 46.7 | 12.3 | 21.1 |
| 45. Dairy production | 11.7 | 7.7 | 28.6 | — | 0.0 | 0.0 |
| 46. Spinning | 47.6 | 11.8 | 1.2 | 25.0 | 11.1 | 9.2 |
| 47. Laundering | 25.0 | 18.9 | 10.0 | 11.7 | 0.0 | 8.3 |
| 48. Water fetching | 0.0 | 8.1 | 18.5 | 6.1 | 14.3 | 4.3 |
| 49. Cooking | 7.9 | 3.4 | 9.7 | 17.1 | 4.2 | 7.1 |
| 50. Preparation of vegetal food | 0.7 | 4.1 | 4.1 | 21.0 | 0.6 | 4.0 |

males. They show the following common statistical characteristics:

1. They reveal relatively low worldwide indices of masculine participation, in no instance as high as 28.

2. Their regional indices are invariably under 50, but in no case does the highest such index fall below 17.

3. Male participation in the activity is equal or subordinate in many of the sample societies, and exclusive or preponderant in at least a minority of them.

The nine quasi-feminine activities counterbalance, or are comparable to, the nine quasi-masculine activities. Interestingly enough, the statistics reveal no technological activities which are strictly feminine. One can, of course, name activities that are strictly feminine, e.g., nursing and infant care, but they fall outside the range of technological pursuits.

## FACTORS INFLUENCING THE SEXUAL ALLOCATION OF TECHNOLOGICAL TASKS
### A: AS DETERMINED BY CONVENTIONAL MODES OF ANALYSIS

Having presented a fourfold classification of technological activities based on a statistical analysis of their assignment to males or females for the world as a whole and by major ethnographic regions, we may now examine the activities themselves for features which may help to account for their assignment to one sex or the other. Using conventional modes of analysis, we have isolated a series of tentative explanatory factors which are named and discussed below. In the next section the more rigorous techniques of factor analysis will be employed to test these factors and identify additional ones.

### Factor A: Masculine Advantage

The probability that any activity will be assigned to males is increased to the extent that it has features which give males a definite advantage, and/

or females a definite disadvantage, in its performance, regardless of whether the distinction is innate or socio-cultural. Thus males tend in general to be endowed with greater physical strength than females and probably also a superior capacity for mobilizing it in brief bursts of excessive energy, whereas females tend to be more closely attached to the home by the burdens of pregnancy and infant care and to this extent suffer a disadvantage in undertaking tasks which must be performed at a distance from the household. These relative masculine advantages clearly characterize most of the activities classed above as strictly masculine or quasi-masculine and are therefore presumably a factor favoring the widespread assignment of these tasks to males, especially since they are absent or less apparent in the remaining 27 activities.

### Factor B: Feminine Advantage

Except for the 23 activities which we have classed as strictly masculine or quasi-masculine, including several (notably netmaking and the manufacture of rope and cordage) for which the evidence is purely statistical rather than functional, none of the activities in our list seems inherently better suited to the capacities of either sex. In the case of the eighteen swing activities, indeed, their assignment to one sex rather than the other appears almost random and can be accounted for only on the basis of other factors. In the case of the nine activities classed as quasi-feminine, however, a definite feminine advantage, relative rather than absolute, is strongly to be suspected. Judith Brown (1970: 1074), despite a noticeable feminist bias, identifies this advantage fairly adequately when she suggests that

the degree to which women participate in subsistence activities depends upon the compatibility of the latter with simultaneous child-care responsibilities. Women are most likely to make a substantial contribution when subsistence activities have the following characteristics: the participant is not obliged to be far from home; the tasks are relatively monotonous and do not require rapt concentration; and the work is not dangerous, can be performed in spite of interruptions, and is easily resumed once interrupted.

These specifications fit the nine quasi-feminine activities particularly well and go far toward accounting for their widespread assignment to females, provided that one adds, from the masculine point of view which Brown ignores, that these activities require practically daily attention and are thus relatively incompatible with such masculine tasks as warfare, hunting, fishing, and herding which commonly require periods of absence from the household.

### Factor C: Qualities of Raw Materials

It is clear from an examination of Table 1 that manufacturing activities tend strongly to be assigned to males when the materials processed are hard or tough, as in the cases of metalworking (#3), work in wood (#6), manufacture of musical instruments (#8), stoneworking (#11), and work in bone, horn, or shell (#13), but to females when the raw materials are soft or pliable, as in the manufacture of leather products (#29), basketmaking (#33), matmaking (#35), loom weaving (#38), potterymaking (#43), and spinning (#46). The partial exceptions, such as netmaking (#22) and the manufacture of rope and cordage (#23), are accounted for by Factor D. The reasons why the qualities of raw materials should make a difference in sex assignment are obscure; the masculine advantage in physical strength, though a possible explanation, seems scarcely an adequate one.

### Factor D: Sequential Series

Our data indicate a general tendency for the sex which uses a product to be the same as the sex that produces it. This is most obvious in the cases where activities fall into sequential production series, e.g.:

Mining (#14), Smelting (#2), Metalworking (#3);
Land clearance (#17), Soil preparation (#21), Crop planting (#28), Crop tending (#31), Harvesting (#30);
Tending large animals (#19), Milking (#32), Dairy production (#45);
Spinning (#46), Loom weaving (#38), Manufacture of clothing (#41);
Gathering of vegetal foods (#44), Preparation of vegetal foods (#50), Cooking (#49).

Cases where the users of a product differ in sex from its producers interrupt such sequences. Thus textile materials, which our unanalyzed findings reveal to be usually procured by women, are normally processed by women when the products are used principally by women, e.g., baskets, mats, and cloth, but by men when the products have a predominantly masculine use, e.g., nets and rope.

### Factor E: Replacement of Simpler by More Complex Artifacts or Processes

When the invention of a new artifact or process supplants an older and simpler one, both the activity of which it is a part and closely related activities tend more strongly to be assigned to males. The introduction of the plow, for example, seems to have increased masculine participation in all agricultural operations and not alone in soil preparation. Table 6, for ex-

TABLE 6
Sex Participation in Planting and Use of the Plow

| Sex Assignment of Planting | In Societies Having the Plow | In Societies Lacking the Plow | Total |
|---|---|---|---|
| M or N | 23 | 39 | 62 |
| E, G, or F | 13 | 66 | 79 |
| Total | 36 | 105 | 141 |

$\chi^2 = 5.27$, corrected for continuity; $P < .03$.
The sample societies possessing the plow are those numbered 33, 37–38, 42–45, 47–51, 54–57, 59, 62–64, 66–68, 71, 73, 75–76, 82–84, 114–117, 172, and 184.

ample, reveals its influence on the sex assignment of crop planting. Correlations with other indices of agricultural complexity, e.g., irrigation, yield comparable results.

## Factor F: Degree of Occupational Specialization

With the development of a complex division of labor by occupation, our data reveal a tendency to assign fully specialized tasks to male craftsmen, even in regions where the same activity is ordinarily performed by women in neighboring societies with a less complex economic organization. Examples in our sample include male potters among the Aztecs, Babylonians, Ganda, Hebrews, and Romans; male weavers among the Burusho, Punjabi, and Uttar Pradesh; and male matmakers among the Aztecs, Babylonians, and Javanese. Even the most feminine tasks in the entire list, namely, cooking and the preparation of vegetal foods, tend to be assumed by specialized male bakers, chefs, and millers in the more complex civilizations of Europe and Asia.

## Factor G: Fixity of Residence

In coding the information on housebuilding (#50), it became apparent that this normally quasi-masculine activity tends strongly to be assigned to females where the mode of life is strictly nomadic, as among most pastoral nomads and among hunters and gatherers who wander throughout the year rather than at certain seasons only. Under such conditions dwellings tend to be portable or else made of flimsy materials, and to be erected anew at each campsite by the women while the men hunt, herd, or guard the camp. The construction of a substantial structure of wood or masonry is scarcely worth the effort if it is to be occupied for no more than a few days. Table 7, which combines our information on the sex to which housebuilding is assigned and that from Murdock and Wilson (1972) on fixity of settlement, reveals a remarkably high correlation.

TABLE 7
Fixity of Residence and the Sexual Assignment of Housebuilding

| Assignment by Sex | Strict Nomadism | Sedentary or Semi-Sedentary Mode of Life | Total |
|---|---|---|---|
| M or N | 3 | 132 | 135 |
| F or G | 21 | 8 | 29 |
| Total | 24 | 140 | 164 |

$\chi^2 = 87.95$, corrected for continuity; $P < .000001$

### FACTORS INFLUENCING THE SEXUAL ALLOCATION OF TECHNOLOGICAL TASKS
### B: AS DETERMINED BY FACTOR ANALYSIS OF CO-VARIATION

The foregoing attempt to shed light by conventional means on the factors underlying the division of labor by sex has yielded some positive results, though these tend to be disappointingly meager with respect to the allocation of what we have called "swing activities." On the advice of Douglas R. White and Joel Gunn, therefore, we decided to supplement the conventional techniques with the more complex one of factor analysis. Since the authors had had no previous experience with factor analysis, they owe a heavy debt of gratitude to their consultants for the assistance they have so generously given, and in particular to Gunn for assuming the laborious task of all computer calculations.

The first step was to ascertain the incidence of co-variation, i.e., the extent to which particular activities tend to be assigned primarily to males under one set of conditions and to females under other conditions. To this end a principal components factor analysis was performed on all 50 variables, and the resulting factor structure was rotated by the varimax technique to isolate the most distinctive such factors. Two factors proved to be especially significant. Factor loadings of tasks on these two factors will be given below. The square of these loadings indicates the proportion of variance in each task that is accounted for by the factor.

## Factor H: Processing of Animal Products

The first of these factors is revealed in the following set of activities which are correlated through the sex which performs them:

| | | |
|---|---|---|
| 29 | Manufacture of leather products | .86 |
| 26 | Preparation of skins | .84 |
| 41 | Making of clothing | .50 |
| 15 | Butchering | .37 |
| 50 | Housebuilding | .33 |
| 10 | Boatbuilding | .29 |
| 38 | Loom weaving | .29 |
| 22 | Netmaking | .29 |
| 37 | Preservation of meat and fish | .28 |
| 8 | Manufacture of musical instruments | .28 |

Factor H clearly centers on the processing of meat and skins and on the manufacture of artifacts commonly made of leather, such as clothing, drums, and tents. These activities tend to be performed by women in societies which subsist by hunting or pastoral nomadism, where the men are often away from home, but by men in societies which depend more strongly upon sedentary agriculture and animal husbandry. Factor H obviously bears a close relationship to Factor G (Fixity of Residence). It goes far toward accounting for the sharp differentiation in the sexual allocation of tasks between regions with a heavy incidence of hunters and gatherers, like North America, and those, like Africa, with well developed agriculture and animal husbandry. It reveals an association, which would not have been suspected from techniques other than factor analysis, between the processing of animal products and such seemingly unrelated activities as loom weaving, netmaking, and boatbuilding.

*Factor I: Intensity of Agriculture*..

Another factor brought to light by factor analysis is revealed in the association of a second set of activities in terms of their sexual allocation:

| | | |
|---|---|---|
| 30 | Harvesting | .78 |
| 28 | Crop planting | .77 |
| 31 | Crop tending | .76 |
| 21 | Soil preparation | .71 |
| 17 | Land clearance | .47 |
| 34 | Burden carrying | .39 |
| 43 | Potterymaking | .30 |
| 48 | Water fetching | .28 |
| 40 | Fuel gathering | .25 |

Factor I centers on the complex of agricultural operations and bears a close relationship to Factor E. Where agriculture is simple or extensive, these operations and the associated tasks, such as potterymaking, tend to be performed by females, but with their increase in complexity or intensity they tend to be assigned increasingly to males.

In general, factor analysis has confirmed and clarified the results of the more conventional modes of analysis. It has also brought to light a series of additional relationships which account for much of the otherwise unexplained variance, especially with regard to certain of the more puzzling swing activities.

### FACTORS INFLUENCING THE SEXUAL ALLOCATION OF TECHNOLOGICAL TASKS C: AS DETERMINED BY FACTOR ANALYSIS OF TASK SIMILARITIES

The validity of the rank order of tasks by assignment to males (Table 1) and of the fourfold classification of tasks (Tables 2-5) was subsequently tested by a factor analysis of similarities in order to assess the functional coherence of factors A (masculine advantage) and B (feminine advantage) relative to other factors. Ordinary factor analysis of co-variance (correlation coefficients) is not sufficient for this purpose, since there is very little variance for some of the tasks, particularly those ranking highest and lowest in Table 1. To check the functional association between tasks, coefficients of similarity were computed between pairs of tasks, and this matrix of coefficients was then factor analyzed. Each pair of task variables was compared for the 185 societies in order to compute a standard coefficient of similarity.

Four factors were found statistically significant in the factor analysis of similarities after rotation. These are identical with factors A (masculine advantage), B (feminine advantage), G-H (nomadic/sedentary differences in allocation of housebuilding and processing of animal products), and E-F-I (increased specialization and intensification of agriculture). Factors C and D, which relate to smaller subsets of tasks, do not appear in this factor analysis. Of the variance accounted for by the four factors, masculine advantage (A) accounts for 75 per cent, feminine advantage (B) for 18 per cent, and the two other factors (G-H and E-F-I) together for the remaining 7 per cent.

This independent confirmation of the factor structure in the division of labor by sex underscores the importance of universal functional similarites in the sex assignment of tasks. When tasks were plotted by their scores on Factors A and B (masculine and feminine advantage) a linear order of tasks emerged which was practically identical with the rank order by frequency of masculine assignment in Table 1. The clusters of tasks in this linear order, ranging from the most masculine to the most feminine tasks, fall into categories in the similarities analysis whi ʰ correspond closely to the classification into strictly masculine, quasi-masculine, swing, and quasi-feminine activities. That 93 per cent of the variance in the similarities analysis is accounted for by the masculine and feminine factors is strong support for the importance of universal functional similarities in the sex allocation of tasks. This does not, however, account for the variance in the swing activities, which is accounted for in large part by the two remaining factors. Factor G-H corresponds to the technological shift from nomadic hunting or pastoralism to sedentary exploitation of domestic plants and animals, with housebuilding and processing of animal products (as well as loom weaving and other tasks) tending to be assigned to males under the latter circumstances. The E-F-I factor corresponds to the technological shift in intensification of agriculture and in associated development of greater occupational specialization. In both cases the general principle applies that greater technological complexity is associated with a shift in sexual allocation of the more complex tasks from females to males.

## CODED MATERIAL

Of the very large body of data coded for the present study it seems sufficient to present detailed information here only on those activities that have proved especially pertinent in the analysis and on a few others, such as metalworking, potterymaking, loom weaving, and milking, which seem most likely to yield significant results in intercorrelations with other bodies of coded data. Table 8 therefore presents only a selection of the coded material for the individual societies of the sample. Column R presents the symbol (e.g., A for Africa) for the region in which the society is classed, and the numbered columns list the symbols for presence or absence of information and the sex allocation of tasks for the activities bearing these numbers in Table 1.

### TABLE 8
#### Coded Data on Selected Societies

| | R | 3 | 15 | 17 | 20 | 21 | 23 | 26 | 28 | 30 | 32 | 33 | 34 | 38 | 43 | 49 |
|---|---|---|----|----|----|----|----|----|----|----|----|----|----|----|----|----|
| 001 Nama | A | M | M | A | E | A | G | G | A | A | F | P | G | A | F | F |
| 002 Kung | A | A | M | A | F | A | E | M | A | A | A | A | G | A | A | G |
| 003 Thonga | A | M | M | G | M | G | M | A | G | F | M | M | G | O | F | F |
| 004 Lozi | A | A | M | M | E | G | P | M | G | G | M | G | G | M | F | F |
| 005 Mbundu | A | M | M | N | M | G | M | P | G | G | A | G | E | O | F | F |
| 006 Suku | A | M | M | M | M | F | P | P | F | F | A | M | O | M | F | F |
| 007 Bemba | A | M | M | N | N | E | M | M | G | F | A | M | G | M | F | F |
| 008 Nyakyusa | A | M | M | M | N | M | P | A | G | F | M | M | F | A | A | G |

| | R | 3 | 15 | 17 | 20 | 21 | 23 | 26 | 28 | 30 | 32 | 33 | 34 | 38 | 43 | 49 |
|---|---|---|---|---|---|---|---|---|---|---|---|---|---|---|---|---|
| 009 Hadza | A | A | M | A | F | A | M | N | A | A | A | A | E | A | A | G |
| 010 Luguru | A | M | M | M | N | N | P | M | F | A | E | A | F | N | A | F |
| 011 Kikuyu | A | M | M | M | E | E | E | M | E | F | F | M | F | A | A | G |
| 012 Ganda | A | M | O | M | M | F | M | M | F | F | M | F | F | A | M | F |
| 013 Mbuti | A | A | M | A | F | A | F | P | A | A | F | F | G | A | A | M |
| 014 Nkundo | A | M | M | N | M | F | M | P | F | A | F | A | G | G | M | F |
| 015 Banen | A | M | O | M | N | F | E | M | F | F | A | M | G | M | F | F |
| 016 Tiv | A | M | M | E | M | M | M | P | G | G | A | M | F | M | F | G |
| 017 Ibo | A | M | M | N | M | N | M | A | G | E | A | P | F | M | F | G |
| 018 Fon | A | M | M | M | M | M | P | P | E | F | A | M | N | M | F | G |
| 019 Ashanti | A | M | M | M | P | F | P | O | F | F | A | O | F | M | F | G |
| 020 Mende | A | M | M | M | P | M | M | M | N | G | A | M | E | M | F | G |
| 021 Wolof | C | M | M | M | M | N | M | M | N | N | F | M | O | M | F | F |
| 022 Bambara | A | M | M | M | N | M | P | M | N | E | F | N | F | M | F | F |
| 023 Tallensi | A | M | M | M | N | M | N | M | N | N | M | P | O | A | F | F |
| 024 Songhai | C | M | M | M | N | M | M | F | N | N | F | G | O | M | F | F |
| 025 Fulani | C | A | M | A | F | A | E | P | A | A | F | E | F | A | A | F |
| 026 Hausa | C | M | M | M | M | M | M | M | M | N | F | M | O | E | F | F |
| 027 Massa | A | M | M | N | M | N | M | M | E | E | N | O | O | F | F | F |
| 028 Azande | A | M | M | M | N | F | E | M | F | G | A | M | P | A | F | F |
| 029 Fur | C | M | M | M | E | M | P | P | E | E | A | M | P | E | F | F |
| 030 Otoro | A | M | M | N | M | E | P | M | E | E | M | E | F | M | F | G |
| 031 Shilluk | A | M | M | M | M | M | M | P | N | N | M | E | F | O | F | G |
| 032 Mao | A | M | M | M | M | N | M | A | E | E | P | G | G | A | G | G |
| 033 Kaffa | C | M | M | M | M | M | M | M | M | N | E | F | E | M | F | F |
| 034 Masai | A | M | M | A | F | A | M | F | A | A | F | A | F | A | F | G |
| 035 Konso | C | M | M | N | M | N | P | F | N | E | A | E | M | F | F | G |
| 036 Somali | C | M | M | A* | F | A* | F | M | A* | A* | E | F | F | A | A | G |
| 037 Amhara | C | M | M | M | M | M | E | M | M | M | E | E | P | M | F | G |
| 038 Bogo | C | O | P | M | P | M | O | P | M | N | M | F | O | O | F | F |
| 039 Kenuzi | C | A | M | M | M | M | M | P | E | E | F | P | M | F | F | F |
| 040 Teda | C | M | M | N | E | N | M | M | E | G | E | F | E | A | F | F |
| 041 Tuareg | C | M | N | F | M | M | M | F | F | E | E | E | O | A | F* | F |
| 042 Riffians | C | M | M | M | M | M | E | M | M | N | E | E | E | E | E | F |
| 043 Egyptians | C | M | O | M | M | M | P | P | M | N | F | N | F | P | P | F |
| 044 Hebrews | C | M | M | M | M | M | P | M | M | N | M | P | O | G | M | F |
| 045 Babylonians | C | M | M | M | M | M | P | M | M | M | M | M | M | G | M | G |
| 046 Rwala | C | M* | M | A | F | A | P | F | A | A | M | A | O | A | O | F |
| 047 Turks | C | M | M | M | M | M | O | P | N | G | F | P | O | F | O | F |
| 048 Gheg | C | M | M | M | M | M | O | P | G | E | F | F | F | F | G | F |
| 049 Romans | C | M | M | M | M | M | M | M | M | M | P | O | M | E | M | G |
| 050 Basques | C | M | M | M | E | M | M | P | M | E | F | M | N | M | O | F |
| 051 Irish | C | M | M | M | M | M | M | P | N | N | G | M | O | A | O | F |
| 052 Lapps | C | A | M | A | M | A | O | P | A | A | F | O | O | F | O | G |
| 053 Yurak | C | A | F | A | F | A | P | F | A | A | A | P | O | A | A | F |
| 054 Russians | C | M | P | N | N | N | P | P | G | G | F | O | O | F | M | F |
| 055 Abkhaz | C | M | M | M | E | M | O | F | E | E | P | P | O | F | A | F |
| 056 Armenians | C | M | O | M | M | M | O | M | N | N | F | O | O | F | F | F |
| 057 Kurd | C | M | M | M | M | M | F | P | N | N | P | E | G | F | F | F |
| 058 Basseri | E | M | P | M | M | M | M | P | M | M | G | O | O | F | A | G |
| 059 Punjabi | E | M | M | M | M | M | P | A | M | N | M | O | N | M | M | G |
| 060 Gond | E | M | P | N | E | N | M | P | N | N | A | E | G | A | A | F |
| 061 Toda | E | A | A | A | M | A | A | A | A | A | N | A | M | A | A | E |
| 062 Santal | E | A | M | M | E | M | M | O | N | N | A | P | N | O | A | F |
| 063 U. Pradesh | E | M | M | M | M | M | P | P | M | N | F | E | M | M | N | F |
| 064 Burusho | E | M | M | M | M | M | P | P | M | E | M | E | N | M | A | F |
| 065 Kazak | E | M | M | M | F | M | F | M | M | M | E | A | A | F | A | F |

## TABLE 8   (continued)

| | R | 3 | 15 | 17 | 20 | 21 | 23 | 26 | 28 | 30 | 32 | 33 | 34 | 38 | 43 | 49 |
|---|---|---|----|----|----|----|----|----|----|----|----|----|----|----|----|----|
| 066 Khalka | E | M | M | M | N | M | N | N | M | M | F | P | A | A | A | F |
| 067 Lolo | E | M | M | P | M | E | P | P | E | E | A | P | O | F | A | G |
| 068 Lepcha | E | A | M | E | N | E | G | O | E | E | P | N | M | F | A | G |
| 069 Garo | E | M | M | M | M | N | P | P | E | E | A | M | M | F | F | G |
| 070 Lakher | E | M | M | M | M | E | M | P | G | E | A | M | E | F | F | F |
| 071 Burmese | E | M | P | M | M | M | M | O | E | N | A | E | E | F | N | G |
| 072 Lamet | E | A | M | N | M | A | E | M | E | N | A | M | E | A | A | F |
| 073 Vietnamese | E | M | O | M | M | M | P | O | E | N | A | F | O | F | A | G |
| 074 Rhade | E | A | M | M | M | M | P | M | E | N | A | M | O | F | F | G |
| 075 Khmer | E | M | O | M | M | M | P | P | G | G | A | M | O | F | P | G |
| 076 Siamese | E | A | M | O | N | N | P | A | N | E | A | N | O | O | | G |
| 077 Semang | E | A | O | M | G | A | E | O | F | F | A | N | G | A | A | F |
| 078 Nicobarese | E | M | O | M | M | N | P | A | E | E | A | F | P | A | E | F |
| 079 Andamanese | E | A | M | A | E | A | M | A | A | A | A | F | G | A | E | G |
| 080 Vedda | E | A | M | M | M | E | F | P | E | A | G | A | P | M | A | E | G |
| 081 Tanala | E | M | M | M | M | A | P | A | N | E | M | G | N | F | O | G |
| 082 N. Sembilan | I | A | M | N | M | G | P | A | F | G | A | F | G | A | O | F |
| 083 Javanese | I | M | M | M | N | M | O | A | G | E | A | M | E | F | F | G |
| 084 Balinese | I | M | M | M | M | M | P | A | M | N | A | F | F | N | F | G |
| 085 Iban | I | M | P | N | M | M | P | P | E | G | A | G | N | F | F | F |
| 086 Badjau | I | A | A | A | A | A | P | A | A | A | A | O | A | A | A | F |
| 087 Toradja | I | M | M | N | M | P | P | P | E | F | A | G | E | A | F | G |
| 088 Tobelorese | I | O | P | N | M | M | P | P | F | E | A | F | E | A | O | F |
| 089 Alorese | I | A | M | E | M | G | O | A | G | G | A | F | O | A | A | F |
| 090 Tiwi | I | A | M | A | P | A | A | A | A | A | A | A | F | A | A | G |
| 091 Aranda | I | A | M | A | F | A | P | P | A | A | A | A | F | A | A | G |
| 092 Orokaiva | I | A | M | E | N | A | E | A | M | F | A | F | G | A | A | F |
| 093 Kimam | I | A | M | N | M | M | F | A | M | N | A | F | G | A | A | G |
| 094 Kapauku | I | A | M | N | M | G | E | A | G | G | A | A | G | A | A | G |
| 095 Kwoma | I | A | M | N | M | E | F | A | N | E | A | O | G | A | M | F |
| 096 Manus | I | A | O | A | N | A | P | A | A | A | A | E | M | A | F | F |
| 097 New Ireland | I | A | M | M | M | M | M | A | G | F | A | E | G | A | A | G |
| 098 Trobrianders | I | A | M | N | N | N | P | A | M | E | A | M | E | A | P | G |
| 099 Siuai | I | A | M | N | M | F | M | A | F | F | A | E | F | A | M | G |
| 100 Tikopia | I | A | A | M | M | M | M | A | N | E | A | G | E | A | A | G |
| 102 Fijians | I | A | O | M | M | M | E | A | N | N | A | P | F | A | F | G |
| 103 Ajie | I | A | M | M | M | M | M | A | N | G | A | F | O | A | F | F |
| 104 Maori | I | A | O | N | M | N | E | A | N | G | A | F | G | A | A | G |
| 105 Marquesans | I | A | A | M | N | M | N | A | M | N | A | P | M | A | A | E |
| 106 Samoans | I | A | A | M | M | M | N | A | M | N | A | G | E | A | A | N |
| 107 Gilbertese | I | A | P | M | M | M | P | A | G | F | A | F | M | A | A | G |
| 108 Marshallese | I | A | M | M | N | N | M | A | N | N | A | F | E | A | A | G |
| 109 Trukese | I | A | M | M | M | M | M | A | M | N | A | G | N | F | A | N |
| 110 Yapese | I | A | M | M | N | M | N | A | E | E | A | G | E | G | F | F |
| 111 Palauans | I | A | M | N | M | G | M | P | G | G | A | F | F | O | F | G |
| 112 Ifugao | I | M | M | N | M | E | P | P | F | E | A | E | M | F | E | G |
| 113 Atayal | I | M | P | N | N | G | P | P | G | G | A | O | O | F | A | F |
| 114 Chinese | E | M | O | M | M | M | O | O | N | M | A | O | M | F | O | F |
| 115 Manchu | E | M | M | M | M | M | P | P | N | N | A | O | M | F | M | G |
| 116 Koreans | E | M | M | M | M | E | M | O | E | N | A | M | M | F | M | F |
| 117 Japanese | E | M | P | N | M | N | G | O | E | E | M | M | E | G | M | F |
| 118 Ainu | E | A | M | G | E | G | F | E | G | G | A | F | G | F | O | F |
| 119 Gilyak | E | M | O | A | N | A | N | F | A | A | A | P | E | A | A | F |
| 120 Yukaghir | E | M | M | A | G | A | P | F | A | A | A | A | G | A | A | F |
| 121 Chukchee | E | M | G | A | F | A | M | F | A | A | A | P | E | A | P | F |

| | R | 3 | 15 | 17 | 20 | 21 | 23 | 26 | 28 | 30 | 32 | 33 | 34 | 38 | 43 | 49 |
|---|---|---|---|---|---|---|---|---|---|---|---|---|---|---|---|---|
| 122 Ingalik | N | A | M | A | N | A | E | G | A | A | A | F | E | A | F | G |
| 123 Aleut | N | A | F | A | M | A | O | E | A | A | A | F | P | A | A | F |
| 124 C. Eskimo | N | M | E | A | N | A | P | G | A | A | A | A | O | A | A | G |
| 125 Montagnais | N | A | M | A | N | A | F | F | A | A | A | G | E | A | A | F |
| 126 Micmac | N | A | F | A | F | A | M | F | A | A | A | F | F | A | O | F |
| 127 Saulteaux | N | A | N | A | F | A | P | F | A | A | A | A | A | A | A | F |
| 128 Slave | N | A | M | M | M | M | O | F | M | G | A | A | O | A | A | G |
| 129 Kaska | N | A | N | A | N | A | F | F | A | A | A | F | G | A | A | F |
| 130 Eyak | N | O | P | A | M | A | O | F | A | A | A | F | P | A | P | G |
| 131 Haida | N | M | M | A | M | A | F | F | A | A | A | F | E | F | A | F |
| 132 Bellacoola | N | O | M | A | M | A | O | P | A | A | A | F | E | A | A | F |
| 133 Twana | N | A | M | A | M | A | F | G | A | A | A | F | E | F | A | F |
| 134 Yurok | N | A | N | A | M | A | M | N | A | A | A | F | G | A | A | F |
| 135 Pomo | N | A | M | A | M | A | P | M | A | A | A | G | G | A | A | F |
| 136 Yokuts | N | A | O | A | G | A | M | N | A | A | A | F | E | A | A | F |
| 137 Paiute | N | A | M | A | G | A | M | M | A | A | A | G | E | A | A | F |
| 138 Klamath | N | A | M | A | E | A | E | F | A | A | A | F | E | A | A | G |
| 139 Kutenai | N | A | M | A | E | A | E | F | A | A | A | F | E | A | M | F |
| 140 Gros Ventre | N | A | N | A | F | A | A | F | A | A | A | F | A | F | F | F |
| 141 Hidatsa | N | A | N | F | G | F | F | F | F | F | A | F | O | A | F | F |
| 142 Pawnee | N | A | G | E | E | F | F | F | F | G | A | A | G | A | F | G |
| 143 Omaha | N | A | M | N | E | G | M | F | G | G | A | A | F | A | F | F |
| 144 Huron | N | A | O | G | M | F | F | F | F | F | A | F | F | A | F | F |
| 145 Creek | N | O | N | N | M | G | O | G | G | G | A | F | F | F | F | F |
| 146 Natchez | N | A | M | N | M | N | P | M | E | E | A | F | F | F | F | F |
| 147 Comanche | N | A | G | A | F | A | O | F | A | A | A | A | F | A | A | F |
| 148 Chiricahua | N | A | M | A | F | A | G | F | A | A | A | F | G | A | G | F |
| 149 Zuni | N | M | M | M | N | N | M | P | N | N | P | F | E | M | F | F |
| 150 Havasupai | N | A | G | M | N | N | M | M | N | G | A | F | G | A | F | F |
| 151 Papago | N | A | M | M | M | M | M | M | E | G | A | F | G | O | F | F |
| 152 Huichol | N | A | M | M | M | E | M | P | E | E | F | M | G | F | F | F |
| 153 Aztec | N | M | O | M | M | N | P | M | N | N | A | M | M | F | M | F |
| 154 Popoluca | N | A | M | N | M | N | P | O | N | N | A | N | N | F | F | G |
| 155 Quiche | S | A | M | M | M | M | M | P | M | M | P | O | M | G | P | G |
| 156 Miskito | S | A | M | M | P | G | M | P | G | G | A | F | G | F | F | F |
| 157 Bribri | S | O | O | M | P | M* | M | P | M* | N* | A | M | E | G | F | F |
| 158 Cuna | S | M | P | M | M | N | E | O | N | N | A | E | M | E | G | F |
| 159 Goajiro | S | A | N | N | M | N | F | M | G | G | N | A | E | F | F | F |
| 160 Haitians | S | M | E | M | M | N | M | M | N | N | P | M | E | O | M | G |
| 161 Callinago | S | A | M | M | M | G | M | A | F | F | A | M | F | F | F | F |
| 162 Warrau | S | A | O | M | M | G | F | A | M | F | A | F | E | F | A | F |
| 163 Yanomamo | S | A | A | M | M | M | P | A | N | G | A | F | E | O | A | G |
| 164 Carib | S | A | M | M | M | M | M | A | N | G | A | M | E | O | F | G |
| 165 Saramacca | S | A | M | M | M | E | M | A | G | F | A | P | G | A | F | G |
| 166 Mundurucu | S | A | F | M | M | M | M | A | E | G | A | M | E | F | F | F |
| 167 Cubeo | S | A | M | M | M | G | M | A | G | G | A | N | E | O | F | F |
| 168 Cayapa | S | A | P | M | M | G | P | A | F | G | A | F | F | F | F | F |
| 169 Jivaro | S | A | M | M | M | G | P | P | E | F | A | M | F | M | G | F |
| 170 Amahuaca | S | A | E | M | M | G | P | A | E | F | A | M | F | F | F | F |
| 171 Inca | S | M | M | N | M | N | P | P | E | E | A | F | E | F | F | F |
| 172 Aymara | S | M | N | M | M | M | M | M | F | G | P | G | E | E | N | F |
| 173 Siriono | S | A | E | E | M | E | F | A | E | E | A | G | E | A | F | G |
| 174 Nambicuara | S | A | P | N | N | N | N | A | N | N | A | M | G | M | A | G |
| 175 Trumai | S | A | A | M | M | M | M | A | N | F | A | N | E | F | A | G |
| 176 Timbira | S | A | M | M | N | O | P | A | E | F | A | E | G | O | O | F |
| 177 Tupinamba | S | A | M | M | M | M | P | O | F | F | A | P | O | F | F | F |
| 178 Botocudo | S | A | M | A | F | A | M | P | A | A | A | A | F | A | A | F |

## TABLE 8 (continued)

| | R | 3 | 15 | 17 | 20 | 21 | 23 | 26 | 28 | 30 | 32 | 33 | 34 | 38 | 43 | 49 |
|---|---|---|----|----|----|----|----|----|----|----|----|----|----|----|----|----|
| 179 Shavante | S | A | M | M | G | A | P | P | N | G | A | M | G | A | A | F |
| 180 Aweikoma | S | A | M | A | G | A | G | A | A | A | A | M | G | O | F | G |
| 181 Cayua | S | A | M | N | M | N | M | M | G | E | A | F | F | F | G | G |
| 182 Lengua | S | A | M | M | G | M | E | F | M | M | A | O | F | F | F | F |
| 183 Abipon | S | A | P | A | F | A | P | F | A | A | A | O | F | F | F | P |
| 184 Mapuche | S | M | P | M | N | M | P | F | N | N | F | G | O | F | F | F |
| 185 Tehuelche | S | N | M | A | F | A | M | F | A | A | A | A | F | A | O | G |
| 186 Yahgan | S | A | M | A | G | A | F | F | A | A | A | F | E | A | A | F |

### Notes on Table 1

36, columns 17, 21, 28, 30: Agriculture is practiced to a limited extent by non-Somali slaves.

41, column 43: Pottery is made by Negro serfs only.

46, column 3: Smiths are Arabs, not Bedouins.

157, columns 21, 28, 30: Coding follows Gabb; Stone has G.

#### REFERENCES CITED

Barry, H., III, and L. M. Paxson. 1971. Infancy and Early Childhood: Cross-Cultural Codes 2. Ethnology 10:466-508.

Brown, J. K. 1970. A Note on the Division of Labor by Sex. American Anthropologist 72: 1073-1078.

Murdock, G. P. 1937. Comparative Data on the Division of Labor by Sex. Social Forces 15: 551-553. (Reprinted in Murdock, Culture and Society, Pittsburgh, 1965, pp. 308-310.)

Murdock, G. P., and D. O. Morrow. 1970. Subsistence Economy and Supportive Practices: Cross-Cultural Codes 1. Ethnology 9: 302-330.

Murdock, G. P., and D. R. White. 1969. Standard Cross-Cultural Sample. Ethnology 8: 329-369.

Murdock, G. P., and S. F. Wilson. 1972. Settlement Patterns and Community Organization: Cross-Cultural Codes 3. Ethnology 11: 254-295.

Tuden, A., and K. Marshall. 1972. Political Organization: Cross-Cultural Codes 4. Ethnology 11: 436-464.

#### SUPPLEMENTARY ETHNOGRAPHIC BIBLIOGRAPHY

Since the ethnographic sources covered for the present study are in the main the same as those used and cited in Murdock and Morrow (1970) and in Murdock and Wilson (1972), only the sources which have not previously been cited are listed below. All the sample societies are precisely identified in Murdock and Wilson (1972).

*4: Lozi*
Turner, V. W. 1952. The Lozi Peoples of Northwestern Rhodesia. London.

*6: Suku*
Torday, E., and T. A. Joyce. 1906. Notes on the Ethnography of the Bayaka. Journal of the Royal Anthropological Institute 36: 39-58.

*13: Mbuti Pygmies*
Turnbull, C. N. 1965. The Mbuti Pygmies. Anthropological Papers of the American Museum of Natural History 50: iii, 1-282.

*15: Banen*
Dugast, I. 1944. L'agriculture chez les Ndiki de population Banen. Bulletin d'Etudes Cameroun 8: 7-130.

*16: Tiv*
Bohannan, P. 1953. Concepts of Time Among the Tiv of Nigeria. Southwestern Journal of Anthropology 9: 251-262.

Bohannan, P., and L. Bohannan. 1954. Tiv Farm and Settlement. London.

——— 1968. Tiv Economy. Northwestern University African Studies. Evanston

East, R., ed. 1939. Akiga's Story. London.

*18: Fon*
Skertchley, J. A. 1874. Dahomey as It really is. London.
Tardits, C., and C. Tardits. 1962. Traditional Market Economy in South Dahomey. Markets in Africa, ed. P. Bohannan and G. Dalton, pp. 89-102. New York.

*19: Ashanti*
Rattray, R. S. 1916. Ashanti Proverbs. Oxford.
——— 1927. Religion and Art in Ashanti. Oxford.
Service, E. E. 1963. The Ashanti of West Africa. Profiles in Ethnology, pp. 366-386. New York.

*22: Bambara*
Henry, J. 1910. L'âme d'un peuple africain: Les Bambara. Bibliothèque Anthropos 1: ii, 1-240.

*23: Tallensi*
Fortes, M. 1937. Communal Fishing and Fishing Magic in the Hinterland of the Gold Coast. Journal of the Royal Anthropological Institute 67: 131-142.

*24: Songhai*
Jacquemond, M. S. 1959. Les pêcheurs du boucle du Niger. Paris.
Miner, H. 1965. The Primitive City of Timbuctoo. Princeton.

*25: Wodaabe Fulani*
Hopen, C. E. 1958. The Pastoral Fulani Family in Gwandu. London.

*26: Hausa of Zaria*
Smith, M. F. 1954. Baba of Karo: A Woman of the Muslim Hausa. London.
Smith, M. G. 1955. The Economy of Hausa Communities of Zaria. Colonial Office Research Studies 16: 1-264.

*28: Azande*
Evans-Pritchard, E. E. 1956. A History of the Kingdom of Gbudwe. Zaire 10: 451-491, 675-710, 815-860.
Lagae, C. R. 1926. Les Azande ou Niam-Niam. Bibliothèque-Congo 18: 1-224.

*31: Shilluk*
Cann, G. P. 1929. A Day in the Life of an Idle Shilluk. Sudan Notes and Records 12: 251-253.

*32: Northern Mao*
Grottanelli, V. L. 1972. Personal communication.

*33: Kaffa*
Cerulli, E. 1932. Etiopia occidentale, v. 1. Roma.

*34: Masai*
Hollis, A. C. 1905. The Masai: Their Language and Folklore. Oxford.

*39: Kenuzi Nubians*
Schäfer, H. 1935. Nubisches Frauenleben. Mitteilungen des Seminars für Orientalische Sprachen zu Berlin 38.

*43: Egyptians*
Blackman, W. S. 1927. The Fellahin of Upper Egypt. London.

*44: Hebrews*
Forbes, R. J. 1964. Studies in Ancient Technology. 2d rev. edit. 9v. Leiden.

*45: Babylonians*
Contenau, G. 1954. Everyday Life in Babylon and Assyria. New York.

*47: Turks*
Hanson, A. H., *et al.* 1955. Studies in Turkish Local Government. Ankara.

*49: Romans*
Maxey, M. 1938. Occupations of the Lower Classes in Roman Society as seen in Justinian's Digest. Chicago.

*51: Irish*
Arensberg, C. M., and S. T. Kimball. 1968. Family and Community in Ireland. Cambridge.
Evans, E. E. 1957. Irish Folk-Ways. London.
Kane, E. 1972. Personal communication.

*54: Russians*
Benet, S., ed. 1970. The Village of Viriatino. New York.

*55: Abkhaz*
Luzbetak, L. J.   1951.   Marriage and the Family in Caucasia. Mödling bei Wien.
*57: Kurd*
Hansen, H. H.   1961.   The Kurdish Woman's Life. Copenhagen Ethnographic Museum Record 7: 1-213.
Leach, E. R.   1938.   Social and Economic Organization of the Rowanduz Kurds. London School of Economics Monographs on Social Anthropolgy 3: 1-74.
*59: West Punjabi*
Honigmann, J. J.   1958.   Three Pakistan Villages, pp. 68-95. Chapel Hill.
*62: Santal*
Mukherjea, C. L.   1943.   The Santals. Calcutta.
*63: Uttar Pradesh*
Pandey, T. N.   1972.   Personal communication.
*65: Kazak*
Hudson, A. E.   1938.   Kazak Social Structure. Yale University Publications in Anthropology 20: 1-109.
Murdock, G. P.   1934.   Our Primitive Contemporaries, pp. 135-162. New York.
*66: Khalka Mongols*
Maiskii, I.   1921.   Sovremennaia Mongolia. Ordelenie.
*67: Lolo*
Pollard, S.   1921.   In Unknown China. Philadelphia.
*71: Burmese*
Scott, J. G. (Shway Yoe).   1882.   The Burman: His Life and Notions. London.
*73: North Vietnamese*
Nguyen-Van-Khoan.   1930.   Essai sur le dinh et le culte du génie tutélaire des villages au Tonkin. Bulletin de l'Ecole Françoise d'Extrême Orient 30: 107-139.
*74: Rhade*
Donoghue, J. D.   1972.   Personal communication.
LeBar, F. G., G. C. Hickey, and J. K. Musgrave.   1964. Ethnic Groups of Mainland Southeast Asia, pp. 251-255. New Haven.
*75: Khmer*
Briggs, L. P.   1951.   The Ancient Khmer Empire. Transactions of the American Philosophical Society 41: 237-250.
Porée, G., and E. Maspero.   1938.   Moeurs et coutumes des Khmers. Paris.
Steinberg, D. J.   1959.   Cambodia. New Haven.
*76: Siamese*
Hanks, L. M., Jr., and J. R. Hanks.   1961.   Thailand: Equality Between the Sexes. Women in the New Asia, ed. B. J. Ward, pp. 424-451.
Janlekha, K. O.   1955.   A Study of the Economy of a Rice Growing Village in Central Thailand. Ph.D. dissertation, Cornell University.
*80: Forest Vedda*
Ryan, B., C. Arulpragasam, and C. Bible.   1949-50. The Agricultural System of a Ceylon Jungle Village. Eastern Anthropologist 3: 151-160.
*82: Negri Sembilan*
Swift, M. G.   1965.   Malay Peasant Society in Jelebu. London School of Economics Monographs on Social Anthropology 29: 1-181.
*83: Javanese*
Geertz, H.   1961.   The Javanese Family. New York.
*84: Balinese*
Franken, H. J., R. Goris, C. J. Grader, V. E. Korn, and J. L. Swellengrebel.   1960. Bali: Studies in Life, Thought, and Ritual. The Hague.
*85: Iban*
Freeman, J.   1957.   Iban Pottery. Sarawak Museum Journal 8: 53-176.
Gomes, E. H.   1911.   Seventeen Years Among the Sea Dyaks of Borneo. London.
Sandin, B.   1968.   The Sea Dayaks of Borneo. East Lansing.
*90: Tiwi*
Goodale, J. C.   1971.   Tiwi Wives. Seattle.
Mountford, C. P.   1958.   The Tiwi, Their Arts and Ceremony. London.

*96: Manus*
Mead, M. 1969. New Lives for Old. New York.
*98: Trobrianders*
Silas, E. 1926. A Primitive Arcadia. London.
*102: Fijians*
Toganivalu, D. 1917. Fijian Property and Gear. Transactions of the Fijian Society, 1917: 1-18.
*104: Maori*
Earle, A. 1832. A Narrative of Nine Months' Residence in New Zealand in 1827. London.
Wright, H. M. 1959. New Zealand, 1769-1840. Cambridge.
*106: Samoans*
Krämer, A. 1906. Hawaii, Ostmikronesien und Samoa, pp. 253-315. Stuttgart.
*109: Trukese*
Gladwin, T., and S. B. Sarason. 1953. Truk: Man in Paradise. Viking Fund Publications in Anthropology 20: 1-655.
Murdock, G. P., C. S. Ford, and J. W. M. Whiting. 1944. East Caroline Islands. Civil Affairs Handbook OPNAV 50-E-5: 1-213. Washington.
*110: Yapese*
Hunt, E. E., Jr., D. M. Schneider, N. R. Kidder, and W. D. Stevens. 1949. The Micronesians of Yap and Their Depopulation. Washington.
Senfft, A. 1903. Ethnographische Beiträge über die Carolineninsel Yap. Petermanns Mitteilungen 49: 46-60, 83-87.
*111: Palauans of Koror Island in 1783*
Kubary, J. S. 1873. Die Palau-Inseln in der Südsee. Journal des Museum Godeffroy 1: 181-238. Hamburg.
*113: Atayal*
Ferrell, R. 1969. Taiwan Aboriginal Groups: Problems in Cultural and Linguistic Classification. Academia Sinica, Institute of Ethnology Monographs 17.
*114: Chinese*
Smith, A. H. 1970. Village Life in China. Boston.
*116: Koreans*
Dallet, C. 1874. Histoire de l'église de Corée, v. 1. Paris.
Heydrich, M. 1931. Koreanische Landwirtschaft. Abhandlungen und Berichte, Museum für Tierkunde and Völkerkunde zu Dresden 19: 1-44.
*117: Japanese*
DeVos, G., and H. Wagatsuma. 1967. Japan's Invisible Race. Berkeley and Los Angeles.
Smith, R. J., and J. B. Cornell. 1956. Two Japanese Villages. Ann Arbor.
*118: Ainu*
Hilger, M. I. 1971. Together with the Ainu. Norman.
*123: Aleut*
Golder, F. A. 1922-25. Bering's Voyages. 2v. New York.
Langsdorff, G. H. von. 1817. Voyages and Travels. London.
Jochelson, A. 1925. Archeological Investigations in the Aleutian Islands. Washington.
*125: Montagnais*
Burgesse, J. A. 1944. The Woman and Child Among the Lac-St.-Jean Montagnais. Primitive Man 17: 1-18.
Lane, K. S. 1952. The Montagnais Indians, 1600-1640. Kroeber Anthropological Society Papers 7: 1-62.
Lips, J. E. 1947. Naskapi Law. Transactions of the American Philosophical Society, n.s., 37: 379-492.
*129: Kaska*
Teit, J. A. Field Notes on the Tahltan and Kaska Indians, 1912-1915. Anthropologica 3: 39-171.
*135: Eastern Pomo*
Gifford, E. W., and A. L. Kroeber. 1937. Culture Element Distributions IV: Pomo.

University of California Publications in American Archaeology and Ethnology 37: 117-254.

*138: Klamath*
Stern, T. 1965. The Klamath Tribe. Seattle.
Voegelin, E. W. 1942. Northeast California. Anthropological Records 7: 47-251.
*139: Kutenai*
Ray, V. F. 1942. Plateau. Anthropological Records 8: 99-257.
*143: Omaha*
Dorsey, J. O. 1884. Omaha Sociology. Annual Reports of the Bureau of American Ethnology 3: 205-320.
*145: Creek*
Bartram, W. 1953. Observations on the Creek and Cherokee Indians. Transactions of the American Ethnological Society 3: 1-81.
Swanton, J. R. 1928. Religious Beliefs and Medical Practices of the Creek Indians. Annual Reports of the Bureau of American Ethnology 42: 473-672.
*147: Comanche*
Lee, N. 1957. Three Years Among the Comanches. Norman.
Rister, C. C. 1955. Comanche Bondage. Glendale.
*149: Zuni*
Leighton, D. C., and J. Adair. 1966. People of the Middle Place: A Study of the Zuni Indians. New Haven.
Roberts, J. M. 1956. Zuni Daily Life. University of Nebraska Laboratory of Anthropology Monographs, Note Book 3: i, 1-23.
Stevenson, M. C. 1909. Ethnobotany of the Zuni Indians. Annual Reports of the Bureau of American Ethnology 30: 31-102.
*150: Havasupai*
Works Projects Administration, Writers Program. 1940. The Havasupai and the Hualapai. Arizona State Teachers College Bulletin 21: v, 1-18.
*152: Huichol*
Klineberg, O. 1934. Notes on the Huichol. American Anthropologist 36: 446-460.
*155: Quiche*
Schultze-Jena, L. 1933. Indiana 1: Leben, Glaube und Sprache der Quiché von Guatemala. Jena.
*156: Miskito*
Helms, M. W. 1971. Asang. Gainesville.
*158: Cuna*
De Puydt, L. 1868. Account of Scientific Explorations in the Isthmus of Darien in the Years 1861 and 1865. Journal of the Royal Geographic Society 38: 69-110.
Krieger, H. W. 1926. Material Culture of the People of Southeastern Panama. Bulletins of the United States National Museum 134: 1-133.
Wafer, L. 1934. A New Voyage and Description of the Isthmus of America, ed. L. E. E. Joyce. Hakluyt Society, ser. 2, 73: 1-220. Oxford.
*160: Haitians*
Bastien, R. 1951. La familia haitiana. México.
Courlander, H. 1960. The Drum and the Hoe: Life and Lore of the Haitian People. Berkeley and Los Angeles.
Métraux, A. 1959. Voodoo in Haiti. New York.
*161: Callinago*
Du Tertre, J. B. 1667. Histoire générale des Antilles habitées par les François, v. 2. 2d edit. Paris.
Hodge, W. H., and D. M. Taylor. 1957. The Ethnobotany of the Island Caribs of Dominica. Webbia 12: ii, 513-644. Firenze.
Taylor, D. 1946. Kinship and Social Structure of the Island Carib. Southwestern Journal of Anthropology 2: 180-212.
*164: Carib*
Roth, W. E. 1924. An Introductory Study of the Arts, Crafts and Customs of the Guiana Indians. Annual Reports of the Bureau of American Ethnology 38: 25-720.

*165: Saramacca*
Hurault, J. 1959. Etude démographique comparée des Indiens Oayana et des noirs refugiés Boni de Haut-Maroni. Population 14: 509-534.
*166: Mundurucu*
Frikel, P. 1959. Agricultura dos Indios Mundurukù. Boletim do Museu Paraense Emilio Goeldi n.s., Antropologia 4: 1-35.
Kruse, A. 1937. Mundurucu Moieties. Primitive Man 7: 51-57.
*167: Cubeo*
Goldman, I. 1948. Tribes of the Uaupés-Caqueta Region. Bulletins of the Bureau of American Ethnology 143: iii, 763-798.
*168: Cayapa*
Murra, J. 1948. The Cayapa and Colorado. Bulletins of the Bureau of American Ethnology 143: iv, 277-291.
*169: Jivaro*
Up de Graff, F. W. 1923. Head Hunters of the Amazon. New York.
*171: Inca*
Métraux, A. History of the Incas. New York.
Molima, C. de. Relación de las fábulas y ritos de los Inca, ed. T. Thayer Ojeda. Revista Chilena de Historia y Geografía 5: 117-190.
*174: Nambicuara*
Oberg, K. 1953. Indian Tribes of Northern Mato Grosso. Publications of the Institute of Social Anthropology, Smithsonian Institution 15: 82-105.
Roquette-Pinto, E. 1935. Rondonia. 3d edit. Brasiliana 39: 1-401.
*175: Trumai*
Lévi-Strauss, C. 1948. Tribes of the Upper Xingu River. Bulletins of the Bureau of American Ethnology 143: iii, 321-348.
*176: Timbira*
Arnaud, E. 1964. Noticia sobre los Indios Gavioes de Oeste. Antropología 20.
Kissenberth, W. 1912. Bei den Canella-Indianern in Zentral Maranhas. Baessler-Archiv 2: 45-54.
*177: Tupinamba*
Abbeville, C. d'. 1614. Histoire de la mission des Pères Capucins en l'isle de Maraguan et terres circonvoisines. Paris.
Cardim, F. 1906. A Treatise on Brasil. Haklyutus Posthumus or Purchas His Pilgrimes 16: 417-517. Glasgow.
Soares de Souza, G. 1851. Tratado descriptivo do Brazil em 1587. Revista do Instituto Histórico e Geográphico do Brazil 14: 1-423.
Yves d'Evreux. 1864. Voyage dans le nord Brésil, ed. F. Denis. Leipzig and Paris.
*178: Botocudo*
Keane, A. H. 1883. On the Botocudos. Journal of the (Royal) Anthropological Institute 13: 199-213.
*179: Shavante*
Nimuendajú, C. 1942. The Šerente. Publications of the Frederick Webb Hodge Anniversary Publications Fund 4: 1-106.
*181: Cayua*
Ambrosetti, J. B. 1895. Los Indios Cainguá del alto Parana. Boletín del Instituto Geográfico Argentino 15: 661-744.
Müller, F. 1934-35. Beiträge zur Ethnographie der Guarani-Indianer im östlichen Waldgebiet von Paraguay. Anthropos 29: 177-208, 441-460, 695-702; 30: 151-164, 433-450, 767-783.
*182: Lengua*
Baldus, H. 1931. Indianerstudien in nordöstlichen Chaco. Forschungen zur Völkerpsychologie und Soziologie 11: 1-239.
*184: Mapuche*
Nutini, H. G. 1972. Personal communication.
Titiev, M. 1951. Araucanian Culture in Transition. Occasional Contributions from the Museum of Anthropology, University of Michigan 15: 1-164.

# 11

# Cross-Cultural Codes on
# Twenty Sexual Attitudes and Practices[1]

*Gwen J. Broude* and *Sarah J. Greene*

The purpose of this article is to present a set of twenty codes measuring a variety of sexual attitudes and practices, along with ratings for each code on 200 societies. The codes were developed for a long-range study on styles of male-female attachment. The goals of the study have been to examine the patterning of opposite-sex relationships in cross-cultural perspective and to isolate any social structural or psychological antecedents that might help to explain variations in heterosexual relationships from one culture to the next. We have been testing hypotheses relating to these two goals and wished to make the full set of codes and ratings on sexual attitudes and practices, constructed in the course of our own work, available to other researchers who are interested in the cultural management of human sexuality. Our intent here, then, is to extend the body of cross-cultural data on sexual beliefs and behaviors rather than to propose any theories or test any hypotheses concerning the cultural handling of sexuality.

## SAMPLE

The codes appearing in this article were rated on Murdock's and White's (1969) Standard Cross-Cultural Sample. Among the reasons for using this sample are the following:

The Standard Sample consists of 186 societies, each of which represents a different and independent culture cluster within the major world areas. The sample was constructed with the specific aim of minimizing the problems of diffusion and historical contamination that have characterized other cross-cultural samples. For this reason, care was taken that the societies in the sample be geographically and linguistically unrelated.

The societies in the Standard Sample have also been defined in terms of both specific locality and ethnographic present. An exhaustive bibliography has been provided for the entire set of societies. All of this means that the researcher is relatively confident that different sets of codes using the Standard Sample will have been rated on the same population at more or less the same point in time.

Finally, a number of anthropologists have recently confined themselves to the Standard Sample in the rating of new sets of codes. Therefore, we wished to continue this trend of having a variety of codes rated on a single sample of societies.

## SELECTION OF VARIABLES FOR CODING

The choice of specific sexual attitudes and practices to be coded was dictated by two considerations; the first being the goals of the research in which we were engaged, and the second being the state of the ethnographic data on sex.

In terms of the research aims, it was one of our intentions to explore the degree to which the patterning of sexual attitudes and practices is consistent within a society. That is, we wanted to determine whether or not societies tend to be generally permissive or restrictive, or generally secure or anxious in their management of sexuality in its many manifestations. The degree to which cultures exhibit regularity in the patterning of sexual beliefs and behaviors has been examined by other researchers, notably Brown (1952); Heise (1967); Minturn, Grosse, and Haider (1969); and Stephens (1972). These studies, however, confined themselves to a consideration of the relationships among a limited set of variables, and we hoped to be able to re-examine the issue of cultural consistency with an expanded and more representative set of sexual attitudes and practices. For this reason, it was our goal to construct as exhaustive a set of codes as possible within the limitations of what was available in the ethnographic literature.

It should be noted that a number of attitudes and practices for which we have constructed codes have also been rated in other cross-cultural work on sexuality. Minturn, Grosse, and Haider (1969) have published scales dealing with divorce, rape, and homosexuality; we have also focused on these variables. Attitudes toward premarital sex, which are also rated in the present article, have been coded by John T. Westbrook (Murdock 1963) and by George W. Goethals and John W. M. Whiting (Palfrey House n.d.). We decided to construct new codes for these variables for two reasons. First, the scales found in other studies were not rated on the Standard Sample, so that the ratings for those codes would have had to be augmented at a minimum. This would have introduced the problem of reliability, as we had some difficulty at times in understanding the underlying rationale for rating particular societies on some of these codes. In any event, we wished to make some modifications in the available scales to better suit our own interests and also to better reflect the data at hand. We, therefore, started from scratch in our construction of scales although we were in some ways duplicating the efforts of other researchers.

## PROBLEMS WITH ETHNOGRAPHIC DATA

It was mentioned that the choice of variables to be coded and utilized in our research project was to some degree dictated by the state of the ethnographic literature. The process of code construction and rating is always difficult in cross-cultural research; however, studies dealing with sexual attitudes and practices face a special set of challenges. In the first place, information of any sort on sexual habits and beliefs is hard to come by, and is a result of a number of factors. The area, to begin with, is not conducive to participant-observation: interviews or questionnaires can clearly be awkward to conduct under certain circumstances; and the ethnographic reporting of sexual matters has not always been considered an appropriate undertaking. When data do exist concerning sexual attitudes and practices, they are often sketchy and vague; what is more, such information is usually suspect in terms of its reliability, either because of distortions on the part of the subjects or because of biases introduced by the ethnographer. Informants may exaggerate or understate regarding their sexual views and activities, depending upon dominant cultural values and also upon personal motives. The propensities of the anthropologist himself are sometimes more insidious. Some field workers are plainly uncomfortable about sexual matters. At the other extreme are the anthropologists whose frank admiration of sexual freedom overshadows their capacity to discern the jealousies and anxieties of the people themselves. And, to a greater extent than is true of other areas of social structure, personality, or behavior, many anthropologists simply neglect any mention of sexual customs because the reporting of such matters is not customary in the traditional ethnography.

The pecularities of the ethnographic data on sex, then, influenced the range and kinds of attitudes and practices which were coded, the form of the scales themselves, and also the procedure that was followed in the isolation of variables and code construction and rating.

## CODE CONSTRUCTION AND RATING

Because of the special problems presented by cross-cultural data on sex, choice of specific attitudes and practices to be coded was preceded by a preliminary review of the ethnographic literature to determine what kinds of sexual beliefs and behaviors were described often enough and in enough detail to be useful for cross-cultural codes. We relied here, as in all subsequent data collection, on the bibliographies provided by researchers using the Standard Sample (Barry and Paxson 1971; Murdock and Morrow 1970; Murdock and Provost 1973; Murdock and White 1969). Supplementary data were also taken from the Human Relations Area Files. This initial survey of the ethnographic data generated a list of some 35 sexual attitudes and practices for which we felt that codes could be written and ratings obtained for a reasonable number of societies in our sample.

We then took verbatim notes on 50 Standard Sample societies for each of the 35 attitudes and practices which we had isolated. From these notes, we constructed a rough set of codes and independently rated the 50 societies on these scales. The codes were then revised on the basis of discussions concerning problems and disagreements encountered in the initial coding attempt. Codes were sometimes expanded to include more detailed discriminations and were sometimes collapsed because of the sketchiness of the data. Wording also had to be modified to reflect the realities represented in the ethnographic material. Verbatim notes were then taken for the remaining Standard Sample societies and these were rated on the revised set of codes. When codes still presented problems, they were further modified; in these cases, the whole sample was recoded on the final scale.

All societies were rated independently by the two authors on all codes. All ratings were checked for agreement between the two judges. Disagreements were discussed, each coder citing evidence in the verbatim notes that led to her rating. The final rating for each code on each society was a product either of initial agreement or of consensus between the two coders after discussion; if no consensus could be reached, the rating was omitted.

## PROBLEMS WITH SPECIFIC CODES

While difficulties with specific codes were largely ironed out by revision of the scales themselves, a number of problems could not be resolved by modification of the scales because their origins rested in the data. The two most serious difficulties were identified with the "present-absent" scales and the frequency scales.

"Present-absent" codes always present the problem that, while the existence of a particular trait or behavior is relatively easy to determine, its absence is not. When a trait is not specifically designated by the ethnographer as absent, the coder either has to infer its absence or to omit any rating for the culture, and this leads to highly skewed distributions where most societies are coded as present or "not ascertainable."

Concerning the present set of codes, we tried to avoid the "present-absent" code, but this was not always possible because the data did not permit any other kinds of distinctions. Therefore, when we did have to resort to the use of this type of code, we generally rated a practice as absent only if this was explicitly stated in the ethnography. Where this convention was ignored, this is stated in the code itself.

The second problem which was encountered in the ethnographic data was the pervasiveness of imprecise and often misleading wording regarding the frequencies of various sexual attitudes and practices. The problem particularly affected the coding of frequencies of premarital sex, extramarital sex, and homosexuality. The most troublesome example of imprecision or ambiguity in reports on frequencies of a behavior is the statement that a practice is "not uncommon." "Not uncommon" could mean almost universal, very common, or typical. Our solution to this difficulty was twofold. First, we attempted to so construct the scales on frequencies that one item would, in fact, include very common to typical. Further, we incorporated the actual wording "not uncommon" into the scales themselves.

Inspection of the twenty codes on sexual attitudes and practices reveals a number of other problems with the rating of cross-cultural management of sexuality. Some of the codes are general, for example those on importance or frequency of homosexuality, while others are highly detailed, the clearest instance of this being the wife-sharing scale. In some cases, the items on a scale are not strictly ordered; in some cases, the "distance" between items is not comparable on a specific code.

In point of fact, the codes, as a set, tend to reflect neither ideal distributions nor ideal codes, but rather, ethnographic reality. They were constructed on the basis of what was available in the literature and, while this clearly has its drawbacks, we feel that this particular set of codes represents our best effort given what there is to work with in the ethnographic material.

## CODES

The final set of twenty codes measuring a variety of sexual attitudes and practices appears below. The coded data appear in Table I following the code descriptions. The list of variables included in this article was reduced from the original 35 attitudes and practices to the present twenty scales for two reasons.

Thirteen of the original codes were dropped because they could not be rated on a large enough sample of societies. These codes dealt with one or another aspect of masturbation, heterosexual play in childhood, modesty in bathing and toilet habits in adulthood, and machismo. Our display of affection code could be rated on a reasonable number of societies, but the code itself was inadequate. It attempted to discriminate between societies that allowed displays of affection in public and those that did not. The discrimination could not be made with any degree of reliability based upon the data at hand. The remaining twenty codes, then, represent the specific sexual attitudes and practices that we felt could be codified with confidence out of the total range of beliefs and behaviors described in the ethnographic literature.

| *Scale* | *Frequency Dist.* | *Percent* | *Cumulative Percent* |
|---|---|---|---|
| *Column 1: Talk about Sex* | | | |
| 1 = Adolescents and adults talk explicitly and without inhibition about sexual matters in front of anyone, including children | 19 | 28.4 | 28.4 |
| 2 = Talk about sex except in front of children | 3 | 4.5 | 32.8 |
| 3 = Talk about sex except in front of specific categories of people (e.g., kin, elders, opposite sex) | 17 | 25.4 | 58.2 |
| 4 = Talk about sex only with small group of intimates (e.g., age-mates, friends) | 10 | 14.9 | 73.1 |
| 5 = Talk about sex always shameful, offensive, improper; euphemisms always used | 18 | 26.9 | 100.0 |
| | 67 | | |
| *Column 2: Attitude Toward Desirability of Frequent Sex in Marriage* | | | |
| 1 = Abstinence undesirable; frequent sex desirable; no concept of abstinence | 12 | 17.1 | 17.1 |
| 2 = Abstinence desirable under some circumstances (e.g., occasional sex taboos); otherwise frequent sex desirable | 42 | 60.0 | 77.1 |
| 3 = Sexual intercourse desirable in moderation; excesses unhealthy, bad, debilitating, but abstinence also undesirable in extremes | 6 | 8.6 | 85.7 |
| 4 = Too much sexual intercourse is undesirable, bad, debilitating; abstinence admired | 10 | 14.3 | 100.0 |
| | 70 | | |
| *Column 3: Belief that Sex is Dangerous* | | | |
| 1 = Sexual intercourse never considered dangerous; sex always normal and natural | 14 | 37.8 | 37.8 |
| 2 = Sexual intercourse dangerous to specified categories of people (e.g., shamans, unmarried, prepubescent) | 4 | 10.8 | 48.6 |
| 3 = Unusual or unsanctioned sexual intercourse dan- | | | |

|  | Frequency Dist. | Percent | Cumulative Percent |
|---|---|---|---|

*Scale*
*Column 1: Talk about Sex*

|  | | | |
|---|---|---|---|
| gerous (e.g., sex at the wrong time, in the wrong place, using the wrong technique) | 10 | 27.0 | 75.7 |
| 4 = Sexual secretions are dangerous; cleansing important after sexual intercourse | 2 | 5.4 | 81.1 |
| 5 = Sexual intercourse is always dangerous; ritual purification always accompanies sexual activity | <u>7</u> | 18.9 | 100.0 |
|  | 37 | | |

*Column 4: Foreplay*

|  | | | |
|---|---|---|---|
| 1 = Present: prolonged non-coital activity before sexual intercourse (e.g., kissing, caressing, fondling) | 21 | 53.8 | 53.8 |
| 2 = Minimal: Some, but not elaborate or extensive non-coital activity | 4 | 10.3 | 64.1 |
| 3 = Absent: no non-coital activity; intercourse is perfunctory | <u>14</u> | 35.9 | 100.0 |
|  | 39 | | |

*Column 5: Age at which Clothing Begins to be Worn (Male)*

|  | | | |
|---|---|---|---|
| 1 = Never: adults wear no clothing | 6 | 14.3 | 14.3 |
| 2 = Adulthood | 1 | 2.4 | 16.7 |
| 3 = At puberty | 9 | 21.4 | 38.1 |
| 4 = Before puberty but after toddler stage | 21 | 50.0 | 88.1 |
| 5 = At toddler stage | 1 | 2.4 | 90.5 |
| 6 = At birth or soon after | <u>4</u> | 9.5 | 100.0 |
|  | 42 | | |

*Column 6: Age at which Clothing Begins to be Worn (Female)*

|  | | | |
|---|---|---|---|
| 1 = Never: adults wear no clothing | 4 | 7.5 | 7.5 |
| 2 = Adulthood | 2 | 3.8 | 11.3 |
| 3 = At puberty | 7 | 13.2 | 24.5 |
| 4 = Before puberty but after toddler stage | 29 | 54.7 | 79.2 |
| 5 = At toddler stage | 7 | 13.2 | 92.5 |
| 6 = At birth or soon after | <u>4</u> | 7.5 | 100.0 |
|  | 53 | | |

*Column 7: Attitude Toward Premartial Sex (Female)*

|  | | | |
|---|---|---|---|
| 1 = Premarital sex expected, approved; virginity has no value | 34 | 24.1 | 24.1 |
| 2 = Premarital sex tolerated; accepted if discreet | 29 | 20.6 | 44.7 |
| 3 = Premarital sex mildly disapproved; pressure towards chastity but transgressions are not punished and non-virginity ignored | 24 | 17.0 | 61.7 |
| 4 = Premarital sex moderately disapproved: virginity valued and token or slight punishment for non-virginity | 12 | 8.5 | 70.2 |
| 5 = Premarital sex disallowed except with bridegroom | 6 | 4.3 | 74.5 |

| Scale | Frequency Dist. | Percent | Cumulative Percent |
|---|---|---|---|

*Column 1: Talk about Sex*

6 = Premarital sex strongly disapproved: virginity required or stated as required (virginity tests, severe reprisals for non-virginity, e.g., divorce, loss of brideprice)

|  | 36 | 25.5 | 100.0 |
|  | 141 | | |

*Column 8: Frequency of Premarital Sex (Male)*

| | Frequency Dist. | Percent | Cumulative Percent |
|---|---|---|---|
| 1 = Universal or almost universal: almost all males engage in premarital sex | 64 | 59.8 | 59.8 |
| 2 = Moderate: not uncommon for males to engage in premarital sex | 19 | 17.8 | 77.6 |
| 3 = Occasional: some males engage in premarital sex but this is not common or typical | 11 | 10.3 | 87.9 |
| 4 = Uncommon: males rarely or never engage in premarital sex | 13 | 12.1 | 100.0 |
| | 107 | | |

*Column 9: Frequency of Premarital Sex (Female)*

| | | | |
|---|---|---|---|
| 1 = Universal or almost universal: almost all females engage in premarital sex | 56 | 49.1 | 49.1 |
| 2 = Moderate: not uncommon for females to engage in premarital sex | 19 | 16.7 | 65.8 |
| 3 = Occasional: some females engage in premarital sex but this is not common or typical | 16 | 14.0 | 79.8 |
| 4 = Uncommon: females rarely or never engage in premarital sex | 23 | 20.2 | 100.0 |
| | 114 | | |

*Column 10: Who Initiates Sexual Activity (Premarital)*

| | | | |
|---|---|---|---|
| 1 = Women always take the initiative in making sexual advances | 6 | 17.6 | 17.6 |
| 2 = Women usually take the initiative but men sometimes do | 0 | 0 | 17.6 |
| 3 = Both sexes take the initiative with more or less equal frequency | 11 | 32.4 | 50.0 |
| 4 = Men usually take the initiative but women sometimes do | 5 | 14.7 | 64.7 |
| 5 = Men always take the initiative; women never do | 12 | 35.3 | 100.0 |
| | 34 | | |

*Column 11: Double Standard in Extramarital Sex*

| | | | |
|---|---|---|---|
| 1 = Single standard prevails: extramarital sex allowed for both husband and wife | 13 | 11.2 | 11.2 |
| 2 = Double standard: extramarital sex is allowed for husband but condemned for wife | 50 | 43.1 | 54.3 |
| 3 = Double standard: extramarital sex is condemned for both sexes but wife's activities are more severely punished (e.g., husband is scolded but wife is divorced) | 26 | 22.4 | 76.7 |

| Scale | Frequency Dist. | Percent | Cumulative Percent |
|---|---|---|---|
| **Column 1: Talk about Sex** | | | |
| 4 = Single standard: extramarital sex condemned for both sexes and punished equally severely | 27 | 23.3 | 100.0 |
| | 116 | | |
| **Column 12: Frequency of Extramarital Sex (Male)** | | | |
| 1 = Universal or almost universal: almost all men engage in extramarital sex | 7 | 12.7 | 12.7 |
| 2 = Moderate: not uncommon for men to engage in extramarital sex | 31 | 56.4 | 69.1 |
| 3 = Occasional: men sometimes engage in extramarital sex but this is not common | 6 | 10.9 | 80.0 |
| 4 = Uncommon: men rarely or never engage in extramarital sex | 11 | 20.0 | 100.0 |
| | 55 | | |
| **Column 13: Frequency of Extramarital Sex (Female)** | | | |
| 1 = Universal or almost universal: almost all women engage in extramarital sex | 7 | 12.5 | 12.5 |
| 2 = Moderate: not uncommon for women to engage in extramarital sex | 25 | 44.6 | 57.1 |
| 3 = Occasional: women sometimes engage in extramarital sex but this is not common | 9 | 16.1 | 73.2 |
| 4 = Uncommon: women rarely or never engage in extramarital sex | 15 | 26.8 | 100.0 |
| | 56 | | |
| **Column 14: Wife Sharing** | | | |
| 1 = Extramarital sex of any kind allowed for wives | 4 | 3.6 | 3.6 |
| 2 = Wife lending and/or exchange institutionalized vis a vis a woman and a group of men (e.g., any man in husband's age grade, husband's clansmen) | 11 | 10.0 | 13.6 |
| 3 = Wife lending and/or exchange institutionalized vis a vis some specific man other than husband (e.g., brother-in-law) | 5 | 4.5 | 18.2 |
| 4 = Wife lending and/or exchange only on occasion and specifically for sexual satisfaction | 7 | 6.4 | 24.5 |
| 5 = Wife lending and/or exchange occurs for reason that benefits husband (e.g., wife exchanged in return for labor, money) | 3 | 2.7 | 27.3 |
| 6 = Wife lending and/or exchange occurs on a one-time basis for a specific purpose over and above sexual satisfaction (e.g., hospitality, alliance, ceremonial) | 13 | 11.8 | 39.1 |
| 7 = No wife lending or exchange allowed | 67 | 60.9 | 100.0 |
| | 110 | | |
| **Column 15: Attitude Toward Rape** | | | |
| 1 = Accepted, ignored | 10 | 25.0 | 25.0 |
| 2 = Ridiculed | 4 | 10.0 | 35.0 |
| 3 = Mildly disapproved: token fine or punishment | 8 | 20.0 | 55.0 |

| Scale | Frequency Dist. | Percent | Cumulative Percent |
|---|---|---|---|
| **Column 1: Talk about Sex** | | | |
| 4 = Strongly disapproved: severe punishment (e.g., severe whipping, exile, death) | 18 | 45.0 | 100.0 |
| | 40 | | |
| **Column 16: Frequency of Rape** | | | |
| 1 = Absent | 8 | 23.5 | 23.5 |
| 2 = Rare; isolated cases | 12 | 35.3 | 58.8 |
| 3 = Common; not atypical | 14 | 41.2 | 100.0 |
| | 34 | | |
| **Column 17: Male Sexual Aggressiveness** | | | |
| 1 = Men are diffident, shy about making sexual overtures | 6 | 9.2 | 9.2 |
| 2 = Males do not make sexual overtures, but this is not due to diffidence | 9 | 13.8 | 23.1 |
| 3 = Men typically forward in sexual overtures, but these are verbal as opposed to physical | 26 | 40.0 | 63.1 |
| 4 = Men are physically aggressive in sexual overtures, but this is solicited and/or desired by women | 7 | 10.8 | 73.8 |
| 5 = Men's sexual advances are occasionally hostile (e.g., rape, unsolicited sleep-crawling, forced intercourse with wives) | 7 | 10.8 | 84.6 |
| 6 = Men are typically hostile in their sexual advances; overtures are rough or aggressive and not solicited or desired by women (e.g., grabbing at sexual organs) | 10 | 15.4 | 100.0 |
| | 65 | | |
| **Column 18: Attitude Toward Homosexuality** | | | |
| 1 = Accepted, ignored | 9 | 21.4 | 21.4 |
| 2 = No concept of homosexuality | 5 | 11.9 | 33.3 |
| 3 = Ridiculed, scorned, but not punished | 6 | 14.3 | 47.6 |
| 4 = Mildly disapproved, considered undesirable, but not punished | 5 | 11.9 | 59.5 |
| 5 = Strongly disapproved and punished | 17 | 40.9 | 100.0 |
| | 42 | | |
| **Column 19: Frequency of Homosexuality** | | | |
| 1 = Absent, rare | 41 | 58.6 | 58.6 |
| 2 = Present, not uncommon | 29 | 41.4 | 100.0 |
| | 70 | | |
| **Column 20: Impotence** | | | |
| 1 = Absent: incidence of and/or concern about impotence absent or atypical | 8 | 20.0 | 20.0 |
| 2 = Present: incidence of and/or concern about impotence present (women complain about partner's impotence; charms, magic, etc. to cure impotence or promote virility; fear of impotence a pervasive preoccupation) | 32 | 80 | 100.0 |
| | 40 | | |

## TABLE 1

### Coded Data on Sex Attitudes and Practices

| Area | Society | 1 | 2 | 3 | 4 | 5 | 6 | 7 | 8 | 9 | 10 |
|------|---------|---|---|---|---|---|---|---|---|---|----|
| 001 | Hottentots | – | 2 | – | 1 | – | – | – | 2 | 2 | – |
| 002 | Kung | 3 | 4 | – | 1 | – | – | – | – | – | – |
| 003 | Thonga | – | 2 | – | – | – | – | 1 | 1 | 1 | – |
| 004 | Lozi | – | – | – | – | – | – | 4 | – | – | – |
| 005 | Mbundu | 2 | – | – | – | – | – | 6 | – | – | – |
| 006 | Suku | – | – | – | – | – | – | – | – | – | – |
| 007 | Bemba | – | 1 | 5 | – | – | – | 1 | – | – | – |
| 008 | Nyakyusa | 4 | – | 4 | – | – | – | 5 | – | – | – |
| 009 | Hadza | – | – | – | – | – | – | 1 | 1 | 1 | – |
| 010 | Luguru | – | – | – | – | – | – | – | – | – | – |
| 011 | Kikuyu | – | – | 1 | – | – | 4 | 6 | 3 | 3 | – |
| 012 | Ganda | 1 | 2 | – | – | 4 | 3 | 3 | 2 | 2 | – |
| 013 | Mbuti | 1 | – | – | – | – | – | 1 | 1 | 1 | – |
| 014 | Nkundo | 4 | 2 | 3 | 1 | – | – | 2 | – | – | – |
| 015 | Banen | – | – | – | – | – | – | – | – | – | – |
| 016 | Tiv | – | 1 | – | – | – | – | 3 | – | – | – |
| 017 | Ibo | 3 | – | 3 | – | 3 | 3 | 6 | – | 3 | – |
| 018 | Fon | 3 | – | – | 1 | – | – | 4 | 2 | 3 | – |
| 019 | Ashanti | – | – | – | – | – | – | 2 | – | – | – |
| 020 | Mende | – | – | – | – | – | – | – | – | – | – |
| 021 | Wolof | – | – | – | – | – | – | 6 | – | – | – |
| 022 | Bambara | – | 2 | 3 | – | – | – | – | 1 | 1 | – |
| 023 | Tallensi | 1 | 4 | 1 | – | 2 | 2 | 1 | 3 | 3 | – |
| 024 | Songhai | 4 | – | – | – | – | – | 2 | 1 | – | – |
| 025 | Fulani | – | – | – | 1 | – | – | 3 | 1 | – | – |
| 026 | Hausa | – | – | – | – | – | 4 | 3 | – | – | – |
| 027 | Massa | – | – | – | – | – | – | – | – | – | – |
| 028 | Azande | – | 2 | 3 | – | – | – | 1 | 1 | 1 | 5 |
| 029 | Fur | – | – | – | – | – | – | 4 | 2 | 2 | – |
| 030 | Nuba | 5 | – | – | – | – | – | 1 | 1 | 1 | – |
| 031 | Shilluk | – | 2 | 5 | – | – | – | 1 | 1 | 1 | – |
| 032 | Mao | – | – | – | – | – | – | 4 | – | – | – |
| 033 | Kaffa | – | – | – | – | – | – | – | – | – | – |
| 034 | Masai | – | – | – | 3 | – | – | 1 | 1 | 1 | – |
| 035 | Konso | 4 | 4 | – | – | 4 | 5 | 3 | 2 | 2 | – |
| 036 | Somali | – | 4 | – | – | – | – | 6 | 4 | 4 | – |
| 037 | Amhara | – | – | – | – | 4 | 4 | 6 | – | 4 | – |
| 038 | Bogo | – | – | – | – | – | – | – | – | – | – |
| 039 | Nubians | – | – | – | – | – | – | – | – | – | – |
| 040 | Teda | – | – | – | – | – | 5 | 6 | – | – | – |

| Area | Society | 11 | 12 | 13 | 14 | 15 | 16 | 17 | 18 | 19 | 20 |
|------|---------|----|----|----|----|----|----|----|----|----|----|
| 001 | Hottentots | 1 | – | – | 4 | 4 | – | – | 1 | 2 | – |
| 002 | Kung | 3 | 3 | 3 | 4 | – | – | – | – | – | – |
| 003 | Thonga | 2 | – | – | 7 | – | – | 3 | – | 1 | 2 |
| 004 | Lozi | 4 | – | – | 7 | – | – | – | – | – | – |
| 005 | Mbundu | 4 | – | – | – | – | – | 2 | 5 | 2 | – |
| 006 | Suku | – | – | – | 7 | – | – | – | – | – | – |
| 007 | Bemba | – | – | – | – | – | – | – | – | – | 1 |
| 008 | Nyakyusa | 2 | 2 | 2 | – | – | – | – | – | 1 | 2 |
| 009 | Hadza | 1 | – | – | 7 | 1 | 3 | 6 | – | – | – |
| 010 | Luguru | – | – | – | – | – | – | – | – | – | – |
| 011 | Kikuyu | 3 | – | 4 | – | 4 | – | 2 | 5 | 1 | 2 |
| 012 | Ganda | 2 | – | – | 7 | – | – | – | – | – | – |
| 013 | Mbuti | 2 | 2 | – | 7 | – | 1 | 4 | 5 | 1 | – |
| 014 | Nkundo | 3 | 2 | 2 | 2 | 4 | 1 | – | – | 2 | – |
| 015 | Banen | – | – | – | 2 | – | – | – | – | – | – |
| 016 | Tiv | 2 | – | – | 6 | – | – | – | – | – | 2 |
| 017 | Ibo | – | – | – | 5 | – | – | – | – | – | – |
| 018 | Fon | – | – | – | – | – | – | – | 4 | 2 | 2 |
| 019 | Ashanti | – | – | – | – | – | – | – | – | – | – |
| 020 | Mende | 1 | – | – | 3 | – | – | – | – | – | 2 |
| 021 | Wolof | 2 | – | – | – | – | – | – | – | 2 | 2 |
| 022 | Bambara | 2 | – | – | 7 | – | – | – | – | – | 2 |
| 023 | Tallensi | 3 | – | – | – | 3 | – | 3 | – | – | – |
| 024 | Songhai | – | 2 | – | – | 4 | – | – | – | – | – |
| 025 | Fulani | 2 | – | – | 7 | – | – | – | – | – | 2 |
| 026 | Hausa | 4 | – | – | – | – | – | – | – | – | 2 |
| 027 | Massa | – | – | – | – | – | – | – | – | – | – |
| 028 | Azande | 2 | – | – | 7 | 4 | 2 | 3 | 1 | 2 | 2 |
| 029 | Fur | 3 | – | – | – | 4 | – | 3 | – | – | – |
| 030 | Nuba | 2 | – | – | 7 | – | – | 5 | – | – | 2 |
| 031 | Shilluk | 2 | – | – | 2 | 4 | – | 3 | – | – | 1 |
| 032 | Mao | – | – | – | – | – | – | – | – | – | – |
| 033 | Kaffa | – | – | – | – | – | – | – | – | – | – |
| 034 | Masai | 1 | – | – | 2 | – | – | – | – | – | – |
| 035 | Konso | 2 | – | – | – | – | – | – | 3 | 2 | – |
| 036 | Somali | 2 | – | – | 7 | – | – | 5 | – | – | – |
| 037 | Amhara | – | – | – | – | – | – | 5 | 1 | 2 | 2 |
| 038 | Bogo | – | – | – | – | – | – | – | – | – | – |
| 039 | Nubians | – | – | – | – | – | – | – | – | – | – |
| 040 | Teda | – | – | – | – | 3 | 3 | – | – | – | – |

TABLE 1 (continued)

| Area | Society | 1 | 2 | 3 | 4 | 5 | 6 | 7 | 8 | 9 | 10 |
|------|---------|---|---|---|---|---|---|---|---|---|----|
| 041 | Tuareg | - | - | - | 1 | - | - | 1 | 1 | 1 | - |
| 042 | Riffians | - | - | - | - | - | - | 6 | - | - | - |
| 043 | Egyptians | 5 | 1 | 1 | - | - | - | 6 | 4 | 4 | - |
| 044 | Hebrews | - | 2 | 5 | - | - | - | 6 | - | - | - |
| 045 | Babylonians | - | 2 | - | - | - | - | 6 | - | - | - |
| 046 | Rwala | - | - | - | - | - | - | 6 | - | - | - |
| 047 | Turks | 5 | - | - | - | - | - | 6 | - | - | - |
| 048 | Gheg | - | - | - | - | - | - | 6 | - | - | - |
| 049 | Romans | - | - | - | - | - | - | - | - | - | - |
| 050 | Basques | - | - | - | - | - | - | - | - | - | - |
| 051 | Irish | - | 2 | - | 3 | 6 | 6 | 6 | 4 | 4 | - |
| 052 | Lapps | - | 2 | - | - | 6 | 6 | 1 | 1 | 1 | - |
| 053 | Yurak | - | - | - | - | - | - | - | - | - | - |
| 055 | Abkhaz | - | - | - | - | - | - | 6 | - | 4 | - |
| 056 | Armenians | - | - | - | - | - | - | - | - | - | - |
| 057 | Kurd | 3 | - | 5 | - | 6 | 6 | 6 | - | - | - |
| 058 | Basseri | - | - | - | - | - | - | 6 | 4 | 4 | - |
| 059 | Punjabi | - | 1 | - | - | - | - | 6 | 4 | 4 | 5 |
| 060 | Maria Gond | - | 2 | 5 | - | - | 4 | 2 | - | 1 | - |
| 061 | Toda | 1 | 1 | - | 2 | - | - | 2 | 1 | 1 | - |
| 062 | Santal | - | - | - | - | - | - | 2 | 2 | 2 | - |
| 063 | U. Pradesh | - | - | - | - | - | - | - | - | - | - |
| 064 | Burusho | - | - | - | - | - | - | - | 4 | 4 | - |
| 065 | Kazak | - | - | - | - | - | - | 5 | 1 | 2 | - |
| 066 | Mongols | - | - | - | - | - | - | - | - | 4 | - |
| 067 | Lolo | - | - | - | - | - | - | 2 | 1 | 1 | - |
| 068 | Lepcha | 1 | 1 | 1 | 2 | 4 | 4 | 1 | 2 | 2 | 4 |
| 069 | Garo | - | - | - | - | 4 | 4 | 2 | 1 | 1 | 5 |
| 070 | Lakher | - | 2 | 3 | - | - | - | 1 | 1 | 1 | 3 |
| 071 | Burmese | - | - | 1 | - | - | - | 3 | 1 | 1 | - |
| 072 | Lamet | - | 2 | - | - | - | - | 1 | 1 | 1 | - |
| 073 | Vietnamese | - | - | - | - | - | - | 3 | - | - | - |
| 074 | Rhade | - | - | - | - | - | - | - | - | - | - |
| 075 | Khmer | 5 | - | - | - | - | - | 5 | 3 | 4 | - |
| 076 | Siamese | 3 | - | - | - | 4 | 4 | 6 | 4 | 4 | - |
| 077 | Semang | - | - | 3 | - | - | - | - | 2 | 2 | - |
| 078 | Nicobarese | - | - | - | - | - | - | 1 | 1 | 1 | - |
| 079 | Andamanese | - | - | - | - | - | - | 2 | 1 | 1 | - |
| 080 | Vedda | - | - | - | - | 4 | 4 | 5 | 3 | 3 | - |
| 081 | Tanala | - | - | - | - | 4 | 4 | 3 | 1 | 4 | - |

| Area | Society | 11 | 12 | 13 | 14 | 15 | 16 | 17 | 18 | 19 | 20 |
|------|---------|----|----|----|----|----|----|----|----|----|----|
| 041 | Tuareg | 3 | 3 | – | – | – | – | 3 | – | 1 | 2 |
| 042 | Riffians | 3 | – | – | 7 | – | – | – | – | 2 | – |
| 043 | Egyptians | – | 4 | 4 | 7 | – | – | 1 | – | 2 | 2 |
| 044 | Hebrews | 2 | – | – | 7 | 4 | – | – | 5 | 2 | – |
| 045 | Babylonians | 2 | – | – | – | 4 | – | – | 5 | 2 | 2 |
| 046 | Rwala | 2 | – | – | 7 | 4 | – | 3 | 5 | 1 | 2 |
| 047 | Turks | 2 | 4 | 4 | 7 | – | – | – | – | – | 2 |
| 048 | Gheg | 2 | – | – | – | – | – | – | – | – | – |
| 049 | Romans | – | 2 | 2 | – | – | – | – | – | – | – |
| 050 | Basques | – | – | – | – | – | – | – | – | – | – |
| 051 | Irish | – | 4 | 4 | 7 | – | – | – | – | 1 | – |
| 052 | Lapps | – | 4 | 4 | 7 | – | – | – | – | – | – |
| 053 | Yurak | – | – | – | – | – | – | – | – | – | – |
| 055 | Abkhaz | 2 | – | – | 7 | 4 | – | – | 5 | 1 | – |
| 056 | Armenians | – | – | – | – | – | – | – | – | – | – |
| 057 | Kurd | – | – | – | – | – | – | – | – | 1 | – |
| 058 | Basseri | – | – | – | 7 | – | – | – | – | – | – |
| 059 | Punjabi | 2 | – | – | 7 | – | – | – | 5 | 2 | – |
| 060 | Maria Gond | – | – | – | – | – | – | – | – | – | 2 |
| 061 | Toda | 1 | – | – | 2 | – | – | – | – | – | – |
| 062 | Santal | 4 | – | – | 7 | – | – | – | – | – | – |
| 063 | U. Pradesh | – | – | – | – | – | – | – | – | – | – |
| 064 | Burusho | – | 4 | 4 | 7 | – | – | – | – | – | – |
| 065 | Kazak | 1 | 2 | 2 | 7 | 4 | 3 | – | – | – | 2 |
| 066 | Mongols | 4 | – | – | 6 | – | – | – | – | – | – |
| 067 | Lolo | – | – | – | – | – | – | – | – | – | – |
| 068 | Lepcha | 1 | 3 | 3 | 1 | 1 | 3 | 3 | 2 | 1 | 1 |
| 069 | Garo | 4 | – | – | 7 | – | – | 3 | – | – | – |
| 070 | Lakher | 2 | – | 4 | – | 4 | 2 | 6 | – | – | 2 |
| 071 | Burmese | 3 | – | – | – | – | – | – | 3 | 2 | – |
| 072 | Lamet | – | – | – | – | – | – | 3 | – | – | – |
| 073 | Vietnamese | – | 2 | 2 | – | – | – | – | – | – | – |
| 074 | Rhade | – | – | – | – | – | – | – | – | – | – |
| 075 | Khmer | 4 | – | – | 7 | – | 2 | – | – | – | – |
| 076 | Siamese | – | – | – | – | – | – | 2 | – | – | 1 |
| 077 | Semang | 4 | – | – | 7 | – | – | – | – | – | – |
| 078 | Nicobarese | – | – | – | – | – | – | – | – | – | – |
| 079 | Andamanese | 1 | 2 | 2 | – | – | – | – | – | 1 | – |
| 080 | Vedda | – | 4 | 4 | 7 | – | – | – | – | – | – |
| 081 | Tanala | 4 | – | – | 7 | – | 3 | – | 1 | 2 | 2 |

TABLE 1 (continued)

| Area | Society | 1 | 2 | 3 | 4 | 5 | 6 | 7 | 8 | 9 | 10 |
|------|---------|---|---|---|---|---|---|---|---|---|----|
| 082 | N. Sembilan | - | - | - | - | - | - | - | - | - | - |
| 083 | Javanese | 5 | - | 1 | - | 4 | 4 | 3 | 1 | 3 | - |
| 084 | Balinese | 1 | - | 3 | 1 | - | - | 2 | 1 | 1 | 4 |
| 085 | Iban | - | 2 | - | - | - | - | 2 | 2 | 2 | - |
| 086 | Badjau | 1 | - | - | 1 | 3 | 4 | 3 | 3 | 3 | - |
| 087 | Toradja | - | - | - | - | - | - | - | - | - | - |
| 088 | Tobelorese | - | - | - | - | - | - | - | - | - | - |
| 089 | Alorese | 1 | 2 | - | 1 | - | - | 3 | 3 | 3 | 3 |
| 090 | Tiwi | - | - | - | - | - | - | - | - | - | - |
| 091 | Aranda | - | - | - | - | - | - | - | - | 4 | - |
| 092 | Orokaiva | - | 2 | - | - | - | - | 3 | - | - | - |
| 093 | Kimam | - | - | 5 | - | - | - | 2 | 1 | 1 | 1 |
| 094 | Kapauku | 5 | 2 | - | - | 4 | 4 | 4 | 1 | 1 | 3 |
| 095 | Kwoma | - | 2 | - | 3 | 1 | 1 | 4 | 1 | 1 | 1 |
| 096 | Manus | 4 | - | - | 3 | - | 4 | 6 | 4 | 4 | - |
| 097 | Lesu | 3 | - | - | 3 | - | - | - | 1 | 1 | - |
| 098 | Trobrianders | - | 2 | - | 1 | - | 4 | 2 | 1 | 1 | 3 |
| 099 | Siuai | - | 4 | - | 3 | 1 | 2 | 4 | 1 | 1 | 4 |
| 100 | Tikopia | 4 | - | - | - | - | - | 3 | 1 | 1 | - |
| 101 | Pentecost | 5 | 2 | - | - | - | - | - | - | - | - |
| 102 | Fijians | - | - | - | - | 3 | 4 | - | - | - | - |
| 103 | Ajie | - | - | - | - | - | - | - | - | - | - |
| 104 | Maori | 1 | - | - | - | 3 | 3 | 1 | 1 | 1 | - |
| 105 | Marquesans | - | - | - | 3 | - | - | 1 | - | - | - |
| 106 | Samoans | 1 | - | - | - | 3 | 3 | 2 | 1 | 1 | - |
| 107 | Gilbertese | - | - | 2 | - | - | - | 6 | - | - | - |
| 108 | Marshallese | 1 | 2 | - | - | 4 | 4 | 1 | 1 | 1 | 5 |
| 109 | Trukese | 3 | 2 | - | 3 | 4 | 4 | 1 | 1 | 1 | 5 |
| 110 | Yapese | - | 4 | - | 1 | - | - | 2 | 1 | 1 | - |
| 111 | Palauans | - | - | - | - | 4 | 4 | 1 | 1 | 1 | - |
| 112 | Ifugao | 3 | 1 | - | 1 | - | - | 1 | 1 | 1 | 5 |
| 113 | Atayal | - | - | - | - | - | - | - | - | - | - |
| 114 | Chinese | - | - | - | - | - | - | 6 | 2 | 4 | - |
| 115 | Manchu | - | - | - | - | - | 4 | 4 | - | 2 | - |
| 116 | Koreans | 3 | - | - | - | - | - | 3 | - | - | - |
| 117 | Japanese | 5 | - | - | 3 | - | - | 4 | - | 3 | - |
| 118 | Ainu | - | - | - | 2 | - | - | 2 | 1 | 1 | - |
| 119 | Gilyak | - | - | - | 1 | - | - | 1 | - | - | - |
| 120 | Yukaghir | 5 | - | - | - | - | - | 1 | 1 | 1 | - |
| 121 | Chukchee | 1 | - | 1 | 1 | - | - | 2 | 1 | 1 | - |

| Area | Society | 11 | 12 | 13 | 14 | 15 | 16 | 17 | 18 | 19 | 20 |
|------|---------|----|----|----|----|----|----|----|----|----|----|
| 082 | N. Sembilan | – | – | – | – | – | – | – | – | – | – |
| 083 | Javanese | 4 | 2 | 4 | 7 | – | – | – | – | – | – |
| 084 | Balinese | – | – | – | – | – | – | – | – | – | – |
| 085 | Iban | – | – | 3 | – | – | – | 4 | 1 | 2 | – |
| 086 | Badjau | – | – | – | – | – | – | – | 3 | 1 | – |
| 087 | Toradja | – | – | – | – | – | – | – | – | – | – |
| 088 | Tobelorese | – | – | – | – | – | – | – | – | – | – |
| 089 | Alorese | 3 | 2 | – | 7 | – | 2 | 3 | 2 | 1 | – |
| 090 | Tiwi | 2 | 1 | 1 | – | – | – | – | – | – | – |
| 091 | Aranda | 2 | – | – | 6 | – | – | – | – | – | – |
| 092 | Orokaiva | 3 | – | – | 6 | – | – | 3 | – | – | – |
| 093 | Kimam | 4 | – | – | 4 | – | – | 2 | – | – | – |
| 094 | Kapauku | 2 | – | 2 | 7 | – | – | 6 | – | – | – |
| 095 | Kwoma | – | 1 | 1 | 7 | 4 | – | 2 | 5 | 1 | – |
| 096 | Manus | – | – | – | 7 | – | – | 6 | 4 | 1 | – |
| 097 | Lesu | 1 | 1 | 1 | 1 | – | 1 | 3 | 2 | 1 | – |
| 098 | Trobrianders | 3 | 2 | 2 | 7 | 1 | – | 3 | 3 | 1 | – |
| 099 | Siuai | 2 | – | 3 | 7 | – | 1 | 4 | – | 1 | – |
| 100 | Tikopia | 3 | – | 4 | 7 | – | – | 5 | – | 2 | – |
| 101 | Pentecost | – | – | – | – | – | 2 | – | – | – | – |
| 102 | Fijians | 2 | 2 | 2 | 6 | – | – | – | – | – | – |
| 103 | Ajie | – | – | – | – | – | – | – | – | – | – |
| 104 | Maori | 4 | – | – | – | – | – | – | – | – | – |
| 105 | Marquesans | – | – | – | – | – | – | – | – | 2 | – |
| 106 | Samoans | 4 | 2 | 2 | 7 | 2 | – | 3 | – | 2 | – |
| 107 | Gilbertese | 2 | – | – | 2 | – | – | – | – | – | – |
| 108 | Marshallese | – | – | – | 3 | – | 3 | 3 | 5 | 1 | – |
| 109 | Trukese | 2 | 2 | 2 | 2 | 2 | – | 3 | 2 | 1 | 1 |
| 110 | Yapese | – | – | – | – | – | – | – | – | – | – |
| 111 | Palauans | 4 | – | – | 5 | – | – | – | – | – | – |
| 112 | Ifugao | 4 | – | – | 7 | 3 | 2 | 6 | – | 1 | – |
| 113 | Atayal | – | – | – | – | – | – | – | – | – | – |
| 114 | Chinese | 2 | 3 | – | 7 | – | – | – | – | – | – |
| 115 | Manchu | 1 | – | – | 2 | – | – | – | – | – | – |
| 116 | Koreans | 2 | – | – | 7 | – | – | – | – | – | 2 |
| 117 | Japanese | – | – | – | – | – | – | – | – | 1 | – |
| 118 | Ainu | – | – | – | – | – | – | – | – | – | – |
| 119 | Gilyak | – | – | 1 | 2 | – | 2 | – | 4 | 1 | – |
| 120 | Yukaghir | – | – | – | – | – | – | 3 | – | – | – |
| 121 | Chukchee | 1 | – | – | 4 | 3 | – | – | 1 | 2 | – |

TABLE 1 (continued)

| Area | Society | 1 | 2 | 3 | 4 | 5 | 6 | 7 | 8 | 9 | 10 |
|------|---------|---|---|---|---|---|---|---|---|---|----|
| 122 | Ingalik | 3 | – | – | 2 | – | – | 2 | 1 | 1 | 4 |
| 123 | Aleut | – | – | 3 | – | – | – | – | – | – | – |
| 124 | C. Eskimo | – | – | – | – | – | – | – | – | – | – |
| 125 | Montagnais | 5 | – | – | – | – | – | 4 | 2 | 2 | – |
| 126 | Micmac | 5 | 1 | – | – | – | – | 6 | – | – | – |
| 127 | Saulteaux | – | 1 | 2 | 3 | – | – | 2 | 2 | 2 | 3 |
| 128 | Slave | 5 | – | – | – | – | – | 3 | 1 | 2 | – |
| 129 | Kaska | 4 | 3 | – | 1 | 4 | 4 | 3 | 2 | 2 | 3 |
| 130 | Eyak | – | 2 | 1 | – | – | – | 6 | – | 4 | – |
| 131 | Haida | – | – | – | – | – | – | 4 | 1 | 2 | – |
| 132 | Bellacoola | 1 | 3 | 1 | – | – | – | – | – | – | – |
| 133 | Twana | – | 2 | – | – | – | – | 6 | 3 | 4 | 5 |
| 134 | Yurok | 5 | 2 | 3 | – | – | – | 2 | – | – | – |
| 135 | Pomo | – | – | – | 1 | – | – | – | – | – | – |
| 136 | Yokuts | – | – | – | – | – | – | – | – | – | – |
| 137 | Paiute | – | 2 | – | – | – | – | 1 | – | – | 4 |
| 138 | Klamath | – | – | – | – | – | – | 6 | – | 3 | – |
| 139 | Kutenai | – | 4 | – | – | – | – | 3 | 3 | 3 | – |
| 140 | Gros Ventre | 3 | – | – | – | – | – | 6 | – | – | – |
| 141 | Hidatsa | – | – | – | – | – | – | – | 1 | – | – |
| 142 | Pawnee | 1 | 2 | – | – | 3 | 3 | 6 | 1 | 3 | – |
| 143 | Omaha | – | 1 | – | – | 4 | 5 | 3 | 4 | 4 | – |
| 144 | Huron | – | – | – | – | – | – | 1 | 1 | 1 | 3 |
| 145 | Creek | – | 4 | – | – | – | – | 2 | – | – | – |
| 146 | Natchez | – | 2 | – | – | – | – | 1 | 1 | 1 | – |
| 147 | Comanche | – | – | – | – | – | – | 2 | 1 | 1 | 1 |
| 148 | Chiricahua | 5 | 3 | – | – | – | – | 6 | 2 | 4 | – |
| 149 | Zuni | – | – | – | – | – | 4 | – | – | – | 5 |
| 150 | Havasupai | – | 2 | 2 | – | 4 | 4 | 3 | 2 | 2 | 5 |
| 151 | Papago | 1 | – | – | – | 4 | 4 | 3 | 3 | 3 | – |
| 152 | Huichol | – | 2 | – | – | – | 4 | 3 | 2 | 2 | – |
| 153 | Aztec | – | – | – | – | – | – | 6 | – | – | – |
| 154 | Popoluca | – | – | – | – | – | – | – | 1 | 1 | – |
| 155 | Quiche | 5 | – | – | – | – | – | 6 | – | – | – |
| 156 | Miskito | – | – | – | – | – | – | – | – | – | – |
| 157 | Bribri | – | 2 | – | – | – | 4 | – | – | – | – |
| 158 | Cuna | 5 | 4 | – | 3 | – | – | 6 | 4 | 4 | – |
| 159 | Goajiro | – | 3 | – | 1 | – | – | 6 | 2 | 3 | – |
| 160 | Haitians | 4 | 2 | 1 | – | 4 | 4 | 3 | 1 | 1 | – |
| 161 | Callinago | – | – | – | – | – | – | – | – | – | 5 |

| Area | Society | 11 | 12 | 13 | 14 | 15 | 16 | 17 | 18 | 19 | 20 |
|------|---------|----|----|----|----|----|----|----|----|----|----|
| 122 | Ingalik | – | 1 | 3 | 7 | 4 | 3 | 6 | – | 1 | – |
| 123 | Aleut | – | – | – | – | – | – | – | – | – | – |
| 124 | C. Eskimo | – | – | – | 4 | 1 | – | – | – | – | – |
| 125 | Montagnais | 3 | – | – | – | 1 | – | – | – | – | – |
| 126 | Micmac | – | 4 | 4 | 7 | – | – | – | – | – | – |
| 127 | Saulteaux | 2 | – | – | – | – | – | 4 | – | – | 1 |
| 128 | Slave | 3 | 2 | – | 7 | 2 | – | – | – | 1 | – |
| 129 | Kaska | 4 | 2 | 3 | 4 | 1 | – | 4 | 4 | 2 | – |
| 130 | Eyak | 4 | – | – | 4 | – | – | – | – | – | – |
| 131 | Haida | 4 | – | – | 2 | – | – | – | – | – | – |
| 132 | Bellacoola | – | – | – | – | – | – | – | – | – | – |
| 133 | Twana | 2 | – | – | 7 | – | – | 3 | – | – | – |
| 134 | Yurok | – | – | – | 6 | – | – | – | 1 | 2 | – |
| 135 | Pomo | – | – | – | – | – | – | – | – | – | – |
| 136 | Yokuts | 3 | – | – | – | – | – | – | – | – | – |
| 137 | Paiute | 4 | 2 | 2 | – | – | – | 3 | – | – | – |
| 138 | Klamath | 3 | 4 | 4 | – | – | – | – | – | 2 | 2 |
| 139 | Kutenai | 2 | 4 | 4 | 7 | 1 | – | 5 | 5 | 1 | – |
| 140 | Gros Ventre | 2 | – | – | 6 | – | – | 1 | – | – | – |
| 141 | Hidatsa | – | – | – | 6 | 4 | 3 | 5 | – | – | – |
| 142 | Pawnee | – | – | – | 5 | – | – | – | – | 1 | – |
| 143 | Omaha | 4 | – | – | – | – | 1 | – | – | 2 | – |
| 144 | Huron | 1 | – | 2 | 6 | – | – | 3 | – | – | – |
| 145 | Creek | – | – | – | – | – | – | – | – | 1 | – |
| 146 | Natchez | 2 | – | 4 | 6 | – | – | – | – | – | – |
| 147 | Comanche | 2 | – | – | – | 2 | 3 | 1 | 5 | 1 | – |
| 148 | Chiricahua | 3 | 2 | 2 | 7 | 4 | 2 | – | 5 | – | 2 |
| 149 | Zuni | – | – | – | – | – | – | – | – | 2 | – |
| 150 | Havasupai | 3 | – | – | – | 3 | – | 1 | 5 | 2 | – |
| 151 | Papago | 3 | 2 | 2 | 7 | 3 | – | 3 | 1 | 2 | – |
| 152 | Huichol | 4 | 2 | 2 | 7 | – | 1 | – | – | 1 | – |
| 153 | Aztec | 2 | – | – | – | – | – | – | – | – | – |
| 154 | Popoluca | – | – | – | – | – | – | – | – | – | – |
| 155 | Quiche | 4 | – | – | 7 | – | – | – | – | – | 2 |
| 156 | Miskito | – | – | – | – | – | – | – | – | – | 2 |
| 157 | Bribri | – | – | – | – | – | – | – | – | – | – |
| 158 | Cuna | – | 2 | 2 | 7 | 4 | 2 | 2 | 5 | 1 | – |
| 159 | Goajiro | 2 | – | – | 7 | – | – | 3 | 5 | 2 | – |
| 160 | Haitians | 3 | – | – | 7 | – | – | – | 3 | 2 | 2 |
| 161 | Callinago | 2 | 2 | 3 | – | 3 | 3 | 6 | – | – | – |

TABLE 1 (continued)

| Area | Society | 1 | 2 | 3 | 4 | 5 | 6 | 7 | 8 | 9 | 10 |
|------|---------|---|---|---|---|---|---|---|---|---|-----|
| 162 | Warrau | - | - | - | - | - | - | - | - | - | - |
| 163 | Yanomamo | - | 2 | - | - | - | - | - | - | - | - |
| 164 | Carib | - | - | - | 3 | 4 | 4 | 1 | 1 | 1 | - |
| 165 | Saramacca | 3 | - | 1 | - | 3 | 3 | 2 | 2 | 2 | - |
| 166 | Mundurucu | - | - | - | - | - | - | - | - | - | - |
| 167 | Cubeo | 5 | - | - | - | 3 | 5 | - | 3 | 3 | 1 |
| 168 | Cayapa | - | - | - | - | 3 | 3 | 2 | 3 | 2 | 1 |
| 169 | Jivaro | 5 | 2 | 2 | - | - | - | 2 | 1 | 1 | - |
| 170 | Amahuaca | - | - | - | - | - | - | - | - | - | - |
| 171 | Inca | - | 2 | - | - | - | - | - | - | - | - |
| 172 | Aymara | - | - | - | - | 5 | 5 | 1 | 1 | 1 | 3 |
| 173 | Siriono | - | - | 1 | - | 1 | 1 | 2 | 1 | 1 | - |
| 174 | Nambicuara | 1 | 2 | - | - | - | - | - | - | - | - |
| 175 | Trumai | 1 | 3 | - | - | 1 | 1 | 2 | 1 | 1 | 5 |
| 176 | Timbira | - | 2 | - | - | 1 | 1 | - | 1 | 3 | - |
| 177 | Tupinamba | - | - | - | - | - | - | 1 | 1 | 1 | - |
| 178 | Botocudo | - | - | - | - | - | - | - | - | - | - |
| 179 | Shavante | 4 | 1 | 1 | - | 1 | - | - | 4 | 4 | - |
| 180 | Aweikoma | 1 | 2 | 1 | 1 | - | - | 1 | 1 | 1 | 3 |
| 181 | Cayua | - | - | - | - | - | - | - | - | - | - |
| 182 | Lengua | - | - | - | - | - | - | - | - | - | - |
| 183 | Abipon | - | - | - | - | - | - | - | 4 | 4 | - |
| 184 | Mapuche | 3 | 3 | - | 3 | - | - | 2 | 1 | 1 | - |
| 185 | Tehuelche | - | - | - | - | - | - | - | - | - | - |
| 186 | Yahgan | 2 | 2 | - | - | - | - | 6 | 4 | 4 | - |

Alternates

| | | | | | | | | | | | |
|------|---------|---|---|---|---|---|---|---|---|---|-----|
| 011A | Chagga | - | - | - | - | - | - | 3 | - | - | - |
| 029A | Katab | - | - | - | - | - | 4 | 5 | - | - | - |
| 038A | Dorobo | 3 | - | - | - | - | - | 1 | - | - | - |
| 046A | Lebanese | 4 | - | - | - | 6 | 6 | 6 | 2 | - | - |
| 060A | Chenchu | - | - | - | - | - | - | - | - | - | - |
| 068A | Sherpa | - | - | - | - | - | - | 1 | - | 1 | - |
| 090A | Murngin | 3 | - | - | 1 | - | - | 5 | 1 | 1 | 3 |
| 095A | Wogeo | 2 | 2 | 5 | 1 | - | - | 2 | 1 | 1 | - |
| 106A | Pukapuka | 1 | 1 | 4 | 1 | - | - | 1 | 1 | 1 | 5 |
| 138A | Washo | - | - | - | - | - | - | - | - | - | - |
| 141A | Crow | 3 | 2 | - | - | - | - | 3 | - | - | - |
| 149A | Navaho | 3 | 4 | 3 | 3 | 4 | 5 | 4 | - | - | 3 |
| 175A | Bororo | - | - | - | - | - | - | - | - | - | - |
| 179A | Caraja | - | - | - | - | - | 5 | - | - | - | - |
| 183A | Mataco | - | - | - | - | 4 | 4 | 1 | 1 | 1 | 1 |

| Area | Society | 11 | 12 | 13 | 14 | 15 | 16 | 17 | 18 | 19 | 20 |
|------|---------|----|----|----|----|----|----|----|----|----|----|
| 162 | Warrau | – | – | – | – | – | – | – | – | – | – |
| 163 | Yanomamo | 2 | 2 | 2 | 3 | – | 3 | – | – | – | – |
| 164 | Carib | 2 | – | – | – | – | – | 3 | – | – | – |
| 165 | Saramacca | – | 1 | 1 | 1 | – | – | – | – | – | 2 |
| 166 | Mundurucu | 3 | 2 | 2 | 7 | 1 | 3 | 6 | – | – | – |
| 167 | Cubeo | 2 | 2 | 2 | 7 | – | – | 2 | – | 1 | 2 |
| 168 | Cayapa | – | 3 | – | 7 | – | – | 1 | – | 1 | – |
| 169 | Jivaro | 2 | – | – | 7 | – | – | – | – | 1 | – |
| 170 | Amahuaca | – | – | – | – | – | – | – | – | – | – |
| 171 | Inca | 4 | – | – | 7 | – | – | – | – | – | – |
| 172 | Aymara | 3 | 2 | 2 | – | – | 1 | 4 | – | – | – |
| 173 | Siriono | 3 | 2 | 2 | 2 | 3 | 2 | – | 1 | 1 | – |
| 174 | Nambicuara | 2 | 2 | 2 | 3 | – | – | – | 3 | 1 | – |
| 175 | Trumai | 3 | 2 | 3 | – | 1 | 3 | 6 | – | 1 | – |
| 176 | Timbira | – | – | – | 6 | – | 1 | 3 | – | 1 | – |
| 177 | Tupinamba | 2 | – | – | 7 | – | – | – | – | – | – |
| 178 | Botocudo | – | – | – | – | – | – | – | – | – | – |
| 179 | Shavante | 2 | 4 | 4 | 3 | – | – | – | – | 1 | 1 |
| 180 | Aweikoma | 1 | 1 | 1 | 1 | – | – | 4 | – | 1 | – |
| 181 | Cayua | – | – | – | – | – | – | – | – | – | – |
| 182 | Lengua | – | – | – | – | – | – | – | – | – | – |
| 183 | Abipon | 2 | – | – | 7 | – | – | – | – | – | – |
| 184 | Mapuche | 2 | – | – | 7 | – | – | 3 | – | – | – |
| 185 | Tehuelche | – | – | – | – | – | – | – | – | – | – |
| 186 | Yahgan | 4 | 3 | 3 | 7 | – | – | – | 5 | – | – |

### Alternates

| Area | Society | 11 | 12 | 13 | 14 | 15 | 16 | 17 | 18 | 19 | 20 |
|------|---------|----|----|----|----|----|----|----|----|----|----|
| 011A | Chagga | – | – | – | – | – | – | – | – | – | 2 |
| 029A | Katab | – | – | – | – | – | – | – | – | – | – |
| 038A | Dorobo | – | – | – | – | – | – | – | – | – | – |
| 046A | Lebanese | – | 4 | – | 7 | – | – | – | 4 | – | – |
| 060A | Chenchu | – | – | – | – | – | – | – | – | – | – |
| 068A | Sherpa | 4 | – | – | 7 | – | – | – | – | – | – |
| 090A | Murngin | 4 | 2 | 2 | 6 | – | 2 | 1 | – | – | – |
| 095A | Wogeo | 3 | 1 | 1 | 7 | – | – | 2 | – | – | – |
| 106A | Pukapuka | 4 | – | – | 7 | – | – | – | 2 | 1 | 2 |
| 138A | Washo | – | – | – | – | – | – | – | – | – | – |
| 141A | Crow | 2 | 2 | 2 | 6 | – | – | 5 | – | – | – |
| 149A | Navaho | 2 | – | – | – | 1 | 3 | 6 | – | – | 1 |
| 175A | Bororo | – | – | – | – | – | – | – | – | – | – |
| 179A | Caraja | – | – | – | – | – | 2 | – | – | – | – |
| 183A | Mataco | 3 | – | – | 7 | – | – | 2 | – | – | – |

## NOTE

1. This research was made possible by a grant from the National Institutes of Health, Grant #HD 07806-01.

## BIBLIOGRAPHY

Barry, H., III, and L. Paxson.   1971.   Infancy and Childhood: Cross Cultural Codes 2. Ethnology 10: 446-508.
Brown, J, S.   1952.   A Comparative Study on Deviations from Sex Mores. American Sociological Review 17: 135-46.
Heise, D. R.   1967.   Cultural Patterning of Sexual Socialization. American Sociological Review 32: 726-39.
Minturn, L., M. Grosse, and S. Haider.   1969.   Cultural Patterning of Sexual Beliefs and Behavior. Ethnology 8: 301-18.
Murdock, G. P.   1967.   Ethnographic Atlas. Pittsburgh.
Murdock, G. P., and D. O. Morrow.   1970.   Subsistence Economy and Supportive Practices. Ethnology 9: 302-330.
Murdock, G. P., and C. Provost.   1973.   Factors in the Division of Labor by Sex: A Cross-Cultural Analysis. Ethnology 12: 203-25.
Murdock, G. P., and D. R. White.   1969.   Standard Cross-Cultural Sample. Ethnology 13: 329-69.
Palfrey House.   n.d.   Cross-Cultural Codes. Harvard University.
Stephens, W. N.   1972.   A Cross-Cultural Study of Modesty. Behavior Science Notes 7: 1.28.

## SUPPLEMENTARY BIBLIOGRAPHY

The following ethnographic sources were used as supplementary texts in the coding procedure.

1: *Nama Hottentots*
    Murdock, G. P.   1936.   Our Primitive Contemporaries. New York.
8: *Nyakyusa*
    Wilson, M.   1959.   Communal Rites of the Nyakyusa. London.
12: *Ganda*
    Mair, L.   1965.   An African People in the Twentieth Century. New York.
    Murdock, G. P.   1936.   Our Primitive Contemporaries. New York.
21: *Wolof*
    Ames, D.   1959.   Selection of Mates. Continuity and Change in African Cultures, ed. W. R. Bascom and M. J. Herskovits, pp. 156-68. Chicago.
36: *Somali*
    Lewis, I. M.   1962.   Marriage and the Family in Northern Somaliland. East African Institute of Social Research. East African Studies 15. Kampala, Uganda.
46: *Rwala*
    Raswan, C. R.   1947.   Black Tents of Arabia. New York.
61: *Toda*
    Murdock, G. P.   1936.   Our Primitive Contemporaries. New York.
73: *Vietnam*
    Coughlin, R. J.   1965.   Pregnancy and Childbirth in Vietnam. Southeast Asian Birth Customs: Three Studies in Human Reproduction, eds. D. V. Hart *et al.* New Haven.
77: *Semang*
    Murdock, G. P.   1936.   Our Primitive Contemporaries. New York.
105: *Marquesans*
    Suggs, R. C.   1971.   Sex and Personality in the Marquesas. Human Sexual Behavior, ed., D. S. Marshall and R. C. Suggs, pp. 163-86. Princeton.
119: *Gilyak*
    Chard, C. S.   1961.   Sternberg's Materials on the Sexual Life of the Gilyak. Anthropological Papers of the University of Alaska 10: 13-23.

159: *Goajiro*
  Watson, L.   1973.   Marriage and Sexual Adjustment in Goajiro Society. Ethnology 12: 153-62.
168: *Cayapa*
  Altschuler, M.   1971.   Cayapa Personality and Sexual Motivation. Human Sexual Behavior, ed., D. S. Marshall and R. C. Suggs, pp. 38-58. Princeton.
46a: *Lebanese*
  Melikian, L. H., and E. T. Prothro.   1954.   Sexual Behavior of University Students in the Arab Near East. Journal of Abnormal and Social Psychology 49: 59-64.
149a: *Navaho*
  Reichard, G.   1928.   Social Life of the Navaho Indians. New York.
183a: *Mataco*
  Fock, N.   1963.   Mataco Marriage. Folk 5: 91-101.

# 12

# Cross-Cultural Codes Dealing with the Relative Status of Women

*Martin King Whyte*

The purpose of this article is to present a set of codes dealing with the status of women relative to men, along with ratings for each code on 93 cultures. The codes were developed in order to investigate how women's status varies in preindustrial societies, and why women do better in some societies than in others. In the larger study for which these codes were developed (Whyte 1978), they were used to test a wide variety of hypotheses dealing with variation in aspects of the status of women, and for this purpose associations with another set of codes for the subsistence base, political structure, and other organizational characteristics of each society were examined. Here we restrict our attention to the women's status codes themselves and their interrelations.

## SAMPLE

The codes appearing here were rated on an alternate-case subsample of Murdock and White's (1969) Standard Cross-Cultural Sample. The Murdock and White Standard Sample was used for two reasons: the lack of expertise of the author in cross-cultural sampling, and the potential for cumulation and comparison afforded by different scholars working with the same sample. The primary reason for using a subsample was economic; limited research funds were available, and the large number of codes employed made it imperative to use fewer than the full 186 cultures of the Standard Sample.[1] The decision to use an alternate-case subsample was based on concern to minimize diffusion effects, or Galton's Problem (see Naroll 1970), even more than the full sample does. (The Standard Sample cultures are arranged in a sequence indicating relative proximity and cultural similarity. Thus, omitting every other culture reduces the likelihood of historical connections and diffusion among adjacent cultures.) A coin flip was used to select which half of the Standard Sample to use, and the odd-number cultures won. The absence of codes for the 93 even-numbered cultures obviously poses a problem for those desiring comprehensive, ready-made codes for the entire Standard Sample, but creates the potential for other scholars to replicate our research, using the omitted cultures. We will not review the distinctive features of the Murdock and White sample here, assuming that the frequent publication of codes based on this sample in *Ethnology* (e.g., Barry and Paxson 1971; Broude and Greene 1976; Murdock and Morrow 1970) serves to make it familiar to readers of this journal. We based our coding on the time and place specifications for each society indicated by Murdock and White, except in the case of the Khmer (#75) and the Marquesans (#105), for both of which we used a somewhat later time period and additional sources besides those specified (see the supplementary bibliography at the end of this article).

## SELECTION OF VARIABLES FOR CODING

The orientation of the research was frankly eclectic. To begin with, we did not define the relative status of women in specific or narrow terms, since there is substantial debate and confusion in the existing cross-cultural literature on women about just what this concept "really" means and how it should be measured. We wanted to include as many different aspects of the relative position of women as we could find mentioned in this amorphous literature, even if the status implications of some measures seemed rather tenuous. Thus the codes we developed were the product of an extensive literature search, and did not emerge from a particular conception or theory of the nature of women's status. Where possible we used or adapted codes developed by others in cross-cultural research on related topics (e.g., Stephens 1963 and Young 1965). However, for the sake of consistency we did all of the rating on such codes anew, rather than relying on existing ratings compiled using different procedures. Where a previous cross-cultural code was not available, we simply tried to devise new measures, ones that would be codable over a cross-cultural sample while tapping aspects of the relative position of women that particular writers had claimed were important.

The range of concerns represented in these codes is thus intentionally broad, and they do not fit into any obvious or simple typology. However, the reader will note that at least the following somewhat distinct aspects of the relative position of women are included: feminine roles in the cosmos (columns 1 and 2); female access to positions of authority (3,7,8,28,38,39); female participation rights (5,9,12,13,14,47,48); female roles in kinship and marriage (30,31,32, 33,34,37); female roles in productive tasks (10,11,20); relations of females to property (15,16,17,18,19); measures of the relative importance given to women (6,41,42,49,51); restrictions on women (21,22,23,24,29,35,36); female procreative roles (25,26); measures of women as dangerous (4,27); socialization of girls as against boys (43,44); and measures of male dominance (40,45,46,50,52).

## CODE CONSTRUCTION AND RATING

A pretest was conducted using a preliminary coding form to rate selected cultures from the other half of the Standard Sample, and as a result some codes were eliminated and others refined. The final coding form contained detailed general instructions and definitions of particular terms that are not published with the codes here, but are available to interested scholars upon request from the author. All codes initially used symmetrical categories (e.g., from "exclusively male" to "exclusively female") even when we had reason to expect that the ratings would be highly skewed in one direction. Two coders rated each culture in our sample independently, using the specified sources. For sources available in the Human Relations Areas Files, coders were instructed to use the full text versions for coding, rather than to rely on the HRAF categorized filing system. The coders were, with the exception of the author, graduate students in sociology or anthropology at the University of Michigan. The coding form contained ample spaces for page references and quotations to support particular rating decisions. Coders were instructed not to "squeeze" information into existing categories in the case of ambiguity, but to use a "no information" or comparable category provided with each code. For "present-absent" items they were instructed to code "absent" if there was discussion of the relevant topic but no mention of the specific custom, but "no information" if details on both the custom and the general topic were lacking. Coders also recorded information on the characteristics of the authorities and sources used, to be employed in later "quality control" checks on our research results (see Naroll 1962). These codes are not published here.

After the independent ratings had been completed, the two coders met to compare their results. Ratings on which there was agreement were recorded on a master sheet, together with an indication of initial agreement. In cases of conflict the coders checked their marginal notes and sources in an effort to reach an agreement. If able to do so they entered their consensus rating on the master sheet; if not they entered a final code of "no information, ambiguous." In either case they also made a separate notation on the master sheet indicating their initial disagreement. The master sheets were then used to prepare ratings for computer analysis.

Several additional steps were required before we could examine our results. First, we eliminated all codes on which specific ratings could be made on fewer than 62 of our 93 cultures, or on which there had been 30 or more cases of initial coder disagreement. We also combined several codes into special types of scales suggested by earlier studies—e.g., Guttman scales to measure menstrual taboos, deference to husbands, and female initiation ceremony elaborateness, and a scale based on twelve separate codes to measure women's relative contribution to overall subsistence. Finally, in many cases we collapsed the original rating categories into a smaller number for manageable analysis. For this reason the codes listed at the end of this article are in many instances no longer symmetrical in wording, and some final categories reveal through their convoluted wording the fact that several original categories were collapsed into them. As a result of this winnowing, combining, and collapsing, we ended up with 52 final codes dealing with the position of women. These are listed at the end of the text, and their ratings are reproduced in columns 1-52 of Table 2.

## CODES AND THEIR INTERRELATIONSHIPS

Several comments are in order about the frequency distributions listed along with the codes for these 52 measures at the end of this article. First, many distributions are skewed in favor of males, as one would expect from the frequent discussions in the cross-cultural literature of the subordinate status of women. However, on a good many codes, such as those dealing with funerals (column 6), subsistence contributions (column 10), and perceived sexual drives (column 26), a pattern of substantial equality is most common. Even for those codes most strongly skewed toward males, e.g., local political leadership (column 7) or control over the fruits of male labor (column 17), there are a few cultures in which women are coded as having equal status or even the upper hand. There are also cases in which a distribution skewed toward male predominance does not have a clearly favorable implication for men, for example, in regard to the gender of witches (column 4). Viewed in overall terms, the distributions on these 52 codes show widely varying patterns ranging from male superiority to rough equality. These results give no support to previous claims of the inevitability of patriarchy and male dominance (see Goldberg 1973), a theme discussed at greater length in the larger study from which this article is drawn.

The content of our 52 codes is very diverse, and we noted at the outset that some have rather tenuous connections to status concerns. One of the primary goals of this research was to establish how these codes were interrelated. Is there a coherent status-of-women syndrome cross-culturally, such that if women have favorable property rights, religious roles, or high subsistence contributions, for instance, they are also likely to have high domestic authority or equality in sexual restrictions? Or is each area of social life essentially independent, so that knowing how well women do in one area does not allow us to predict how well they do in others?

We investigated this question empirically by examining the correlation matrix for these 52 variables. We do not reproduce the matrix in its entirety here, but only a small portion in Table 1. The reader will see that the correlations in Table 1 are generally weak, and as often negative in sign as positive. This pattern was characteristic of the larger matrix as well. In other words, most aspects of the position of women relative to men are not closely related to one another.

This finding calls into question much existing thought about women's roles. Cross-culturally, there appears to be no such thing as the status of women. It is perfectly possible for women in one society to have important property rights while being excluded from key religious posts and ceremonies; they may also do most of the productive work or have an important role in political life while suffering under a severe sexual double standard. There is no basis here for

TABLE 1
Intercorrelations Among Selected Dependent Variables*

|        |                              | DV 7  | DV 10 | DV 15 | DV 35 | DV 50 |
|--------|------------------------------|-------|-------|-------|-------|-------|
| DV 1   | Sex of gods and spirits      | -.026 | -.018 | -.101 | .259  | .085  |
| DV 7   | Sex of local political leaders |       | .101  | .161  | -.145 | .025  |
| DV 10  | Contributions to subsistence |       |       | -.004 | -.109 | .233  |
| DV 15  | Inheritance rights           |       |       |       | -.060 | .165  |
| DV 35  | Ease of divorce              |       |       |       |       | .261  |
| DV 50  | Machismo                     |       |       |       |       |       |

*Ns vary from 50 to the full 93 cultures.

concluding, as Engels (1902) and some later scholars have, that there is some key aspect of the role of women (e.g., their property rights or the role they play in productive labor) which affects their general lot. Aspects of what have often been assumed to be a unitary phenomenon—the status of women—turn out upon closer examination to be largely discrete and unrelated.

Empirically we did not find that any large number of our 52 separate measures were associated together cross-culturally. However, we were able to identify small groups of codes that were correlated with one another. We did this using a statistical searching procedure called Cluster Analysis (see Wallace 1968), which searches a matrix for clusters of items which are consistently related to each other more strongly than some minimum criterion (in our case, this was r = .2 or greater). As a result of this search we identified nine separate clusters, each composed of three to five interrelated codes. In each case we constructed a composite scale by taking the equally weighted average of the ratings on each separate code and dividing the final scores into three to five categories. These scales are described at the end of the text, and the ratings for them are given in columns 53-61 in Table 2. They reflect quite diverse concerns, including the relative property rights of women (column 53), their domestic authority (column 57), separate solidarity of men and women (column 58) and the relative controls on women's marital and sexual lives (column 59). These scales are again largely unrelated to one another empirically in our sample.

Since our results lead to the view that "the status of women" is not a meaningful concept cross-culturally, we cannot hope to test why women have higher status in some societies than in others. However, these nine scales, in combination with some or all of the 52 specific codes, do provide the means to investigate how and why many particular aspects of women's position and roles *vis-à-vis* men vary cross-culturally. We carry out such an investigation in the larger study stemming from this research, and we offer these codes and ratings here in the hope that other scholars will use and adapt them in an effort to throw further light on this fascinating and complex topic area.

## The Codes

| Scale | Frequency | Percent |
|---|---|---|
| *Column 1:* Sex of gods and spirits and other supernatural beings | | |
| 1 = All male | 9 | 13.4 |
| 2 = Both, but male are more numerous or more powerful or both | 24 | 35.8 |
| 3 = Both, with male more numerous while power equal or male more powerful while numbers equal | 13 | 19.4 |
| 4 = Both, and equal in numbers or power or both, or women more numerous while power equal, or women more powerful while numbers equal | 21 | 31.4 |
| Sex of gods and spirits unascertainable | 26 | — |
| | 93 | |

| Scale | Frequency | Percent |
|---|---|---|

*Column 2:* Mythical founders of the culture

| | | |
|---|---|---|
| 1 = All male | 22 | 33.8 |
| 2 = Both sexes, but the role of men more important | 17 | 26.2 |
| 3 = Both sexes, and the role of both sexes fairly equal | 20 | 30.8 |
| 4 = Both sexes, but female role more important, or solely female | 6 | 9.2 |
| No such myth, or no information | 28 | — |
| | 93 | |

*Column 3:* Sex of shamans

| | | |
|---|---|---|
| 1 = All male | 14 | 19.2 |
| 2 = Both, but male more numerous, more powerful, or both | 26 | 35.6 |
| 3 = Both, but male more numerous while power equal, or male more powerful while numbers equal, or about equal in both | 26 | 35.6 |
| 4 = Both, but female more powerful or more numerous or both, or solely female shamans | 7 | 9.6 |
| No shamans, no information | 20 | — |
| | 93 | |

*Column 4:* Sex of reputed witches

| | | |
|---|---|---|
| 1 = All male | 16 | 23.6 |
| 2 = Both, but male predominance in numbers or power or both | 21 | 30.9 |
| 3 = Both, and equal in numbers or power or both | 23 | 33.8 |
| 4 = Both, but female predominance in numbers or power or both, or only female witches | 8 | 11.7 |
| No information or no belief in witches | 25 | — |
| | 93 | |

*Column 5:* Who can participate in collective religious ceremonies and rituals (excluding life-cycle ceremonies)

| | | |
|---|---|---|
| 1 = Only males | 4 | 5.5 |
| 2 = Both, but males more commonly or more prominently, or some joint ceremonies, some male ones, and no solely female ones | 36 | 49.3 |
| 3 = Both, and fairly equal participation (although possibly with the sexes separated) | 28 | 38.4 |
| 4 = Both, but women more prominent, or some only for women, some joint, and none solely for men | 5 | 6.8 |
| No information, or no identifiable ceremonies | 20 | — |
| | 93 | |

| Scale | Frequency | Percent |
|---|---|---|

*Column 6:* Funeral or burial ceremonies held

| | | |
|---|---|---|
| 1 = Only for males, or for both, but male more elaborate | 11 | 13.1 |
| 2 = For both, and roughly equal | 73 | 86.9 |
| No information | 9 | — |
| | 93 | |

*Column 7:* Intermediate or local political leaders (non-kin group)

| | | |
|---|---|---|
| 1 = Only males | 65 | 87.8 |
| 2 = Both sexes, but males more numerous or more powerful or both | 7 | 9.5 |
| 3 = Both sexes, and males more numerous while females equally powerful or males more powerful while females equally numerous | 2 | 2.7 |
| No such posts, or no information | 19 | — |
| | 93 | |

*Column 8:* Clearly defined leadership posts in kinship and/or extended family units

| | | |
|---|---|---|
| 1 = Include men only | 52 | 83.9 |
| 2 = Both, but men have more say and influence | 6 | 9.7 |
| 3 = Both, with roughly equal influence | 4 | 6.4 |
| No such posts, or no information | 31 | — |
| | 93 | |

*Column 9:* In collective fighting and warfare, who participates?

| | | |
|---|---|---|
| 1 = Only men | 62 | 88.5 |
| 2 = Both, but men do most fighting, women only aid | 8 | 11.5 |
| No warfare, or no information | 23 | — |
| | 93 | |

*Column 10:* Proportional contribution of women to overall subsistence (A composite scale constructed from six subsistence importance items and six sexual division of labor items, following procedures adapted from Heath [1957] and Brown [1963])

| *Scale* | *Frequency* | *Percent* |
|---|---|---|
| 1 = Low | 2 | 2.2 |
| 2 | 2 | 2.2 |
| 3 | 14 | 15.2 |
| 4 | 23 | 25.0 |
| 5 | 27 | 29.4 |
| 6 | 18 | 19.5 |
| 7 | 2 | 2.2 |
| 8 = High | 4 | 4.3 |
| Not ascertainable | 1 | — |
| | 93 | |

*Column 11:* Relative time and effort expended on subsistence activities

| | | |
|---|---|---|
| 1 = Men clearly expend more time and effort on subsistence | 14 | 15.9 |
| 2 = Men and women expend roughly equal time and effort | 54 | 61.4 |
| 3 = Women clearly expend more time and effort | 20 | 22.7 |
| Not ascertainable | 5 | — |
| | 93 | |

*Column 12:* Community-wide exclusively male work groups

| | | |
|---|---|---|
| 1 = None | 20 | 25.6 |
| 2 = For one activity | 44 | 56.4 |
| 3 = For two or more activities | 14 | 18.0 |
| No information | 15 | — |
| | 93 | |

*Column 13:* Community-wide exclusively female work groups

| | | |
|---|---|---|
| 1 = None | 45 | 62.5 |
| 2 = For one or more activity | 27 | 37.5 |
| No information | 21 | — |
| | 93 | |

*Column 14:* Degree of segregation in subsistence activities in which both men and women participate

| | | |
|---|---|---|
| 1 = Men and women are sharply segregated | 15 | 19.5 |
| 2 = Some segregation, or segregation in some activities | 41 | 53.2 |
| 3 = Little or no segregation in these activities | 21 | 27.3 |
| No information | 16 | — |
| | 93 | |

| Scale | Frequency | Percent |
|---|---|---|

*Column 15:* Who can inherit property of some economic value?

| | | |
|---|---|---|
| 1 = Only males, or males except in unusual circumstances | 18 | 25.4 |
| 2 = Both, but males have definite preference in inheritance | 27 | 38.0 |
| 3 = Roughly equal inheritance rights by sex | 22 | 31.0 |
| 4 = Female preference, or exclusive female rights | 4 | 5.6 |
| No such property, or no information | 22 | — |
| | 93 | |

*Column 16:* Who owns or controls the use of dwellings?

| | | |
|---|---|---|
| 1 = Owned or controlled solely by men | 22 | 30.6 |
| 2 = Most owned by men, some by women | 12 | 16.7 |
| 3 = Equal ownership, or no preferential rights | 25 | 34.7 |
| 4 = Most or all owned or controlled by women | 13 | 18.1 |
| No information | 21 | — |
| | 93 | |

*Column 17:* Who controls the disposal and use of the fruits of the labor done solely by men?

| | | |
|---|---|---|
| 1 = Men have virtually total say | 30 | 32.6 |
| 2 = Men have predominant say, or no indication of preference | 41 | 44.6 |
| 3 = Men and women have equal say | 12 | 13.0 |
| 4 = Women have the predominant or total say | 9 | 9.8 |
| No such fruits | 1 | — |
| | 93 | |

*Column 18:* Who controls the disposal and use of the fruits of the joint labor of men and women?

| | | |
|---|---|---|
| 1 = Men have virtually total say | 7 | 8.6 |
| 2 = Men have the predominant say | 6 | 7.4 |
| 3 = Men and women have equal say, or no indication of preference | 60 | 74.1 |
| 4 = Women have the predominant or total say | 8 | 9.9 |
| No such fruits | 12 | — |
| | 93 | |

*Column 19:* Who controls the disposal and use of the fruits of the labor done solely by women?

| *Scale* | *Frequency* | *Percent* |
|---|---|---|
| 1 = Men have virtually total say or predominant say | 7 | 7.6 |
| 2 = Men and women have equal say | 9 | 9.8 |
| 3 = Women have the predominant say, or no indication of preference | 62 | 67.4 |
| 4 = Women have virtually total say | 14 | 15.2 |
| No such fruits | 1 | — |
| | 93 | |

*Column 20:* Who does the domestic work?

| | | |
|---|---|---|
| 1 = Males do virtually none | 47 | 51.1 |
| 2 = Males do some, but mostly done by females | 45 | 48.9 |
| No information | 1 | — |
| | 93 | |

*Column 21:* Is there a double standard in regard to premarital sex?

| | | |
|---|---|---|
| 1 = Yes | 32 | 43.8 |
| 2 = No, equal restrictions on male and female | 41 | 56.2 |
| Does not apply or no information | 20 | — |
| | 93 | |

*Column 22:* Is there an extramarital double standard?

| | | |
|---|---|---|
| 1 = Yes | 32 | 42.7 |
| 2 = No, equal restrictions | 41 | 54.7 |
| 3 = Male punished more severely for transgression | 2 | 2.7 |
| No information | 18 | — |
| | 93 | |

*Column 23:* Are married women allowed to, and do they in fact, have extramarital affairs?

| | | |
|---|---|---|
| 1 = Not allowed, and apparently rare | 40 | 46.5 |
| 2 = Not allowed, but apparently not uncommon | 29 | 33.7 |
| 3 = Allowed, or very common | 17 | 19.8 |
| No information | 7 | — |
| | 93 | |

*Column 24:* Guttman scale of menstrual taboos[2]

| | | |
|---|---|---|
| 1 = No menstrual taboos | 10 | 16.1 |
| 2 = Rule vs. intercourse with menstruating woman | 15 | 24.2 |
| 3 = +Personal restrictions on menstruants, e.g., dietary | 9 | 14.5 |
| 4 = +Stated belief that menstrual blood is dangerous to men | 3 | 4.8 |
| 5 = +A rule that menstruating women may not cook for men | 3 | 4.8 |

| Scale | Frequency | Percent |
|---|---|---|

6 = +Menstruating women are segregated from men, perhaps in a menstrual hut   6   9.7

7 = +A rule that menstruating women may not have contact with some male things, e.g., fishing gear, bows   16   25.8

No information   $\underline{31}$   —

93

*Column 25:* How is the role of men and women in procreation understood?

1 = Men are thought to play the more important role   7   7.5

2 = Belief in roughly equal contributions, or no evidence of greater contribution by either sex   81   87.1

3 = Women are thought to play the more important role   $\underline{5}$   5.4

93

*Column 26:* How are sexual drives and urges understood?

1 = Men are thought to have stronger urges   17   18.3

2 = Belief that urges are roughly equal, or no evidence of belief in greater urges by either sex   72   77.4

3 = Women are thought to have stronger urges   $\underline{4}$   4.3

93

*Column 27:* Is there an explicit view that sexual activity is dangerous or contaminating in some way?

1 = Yes   15   22.1

2 = No   53   77.9

No information   $\underline{25}$   —

93

*Column 28:* Role of the older generation in arranging marriages (1st marriages only)

1 = Males monopolize arrangements   13   15.7

2 = Both males and females participate, males have more say   32   38.6

3 = Both participate, and with roughly equal say   29   34.9

4 = Both males and females participate, females have more say   9   10.8

No information, does not apply   $\underline{10}$   —

93

| Scale | Frequency | Percent |
|---|---|---|

*Column 29:* Voice of the potential bride and groom in marriage decisions (1st marriages only)

| | | |
|---|---|---|
| 1 = Only the groom can initiate or refuse a match | 4 | 5.0 |
| 2 = Groom has more ability than bride to initiate or refuse | 27 | 33.8 |
| 3 = Equal ability to initiate or refuse a match | 46 | 57.5 |
| 4 = Bride has more ability than groom to initiate or refuse | 3 | 3.8 |
| No information | 13 | — |
| | 93 | |

*Column 30:* What kind of marriage payments are made? (1st marriages only)

| | | |
|---|---|---|
| 1 = Woman exchange | 5 | 6.5 |
| 2 = Substantial bride price | 36 | 46.8 |
| 3 = Bride service | 10 | 13.0 |
| 4 = Token bride price | 10 | 13.0 |
| 5 = Gift exchange | 10 | 13.0 |
| 6 = Dowry | 6 | 7.8 |
| No information | 16 | — |
| | 93 | |

*Column 31:* Preferred marriage forms

| | | |
|---|---|---|
| 1 = General polygyny (polygynous unions over 20%) | 22 | 23.7 |
| 2 = Limited polygyny (polygynous unions under 20%) | 35 | 37.6 |
| 3 = Monogamy—plural unions either forbidden or non-preferential and infrequent | 34 | 36.6 |
| 4 = Polyandry | 2 | 2.2 |
| | 93 | |

*Column 32:* Are multiple spouses allowed?

| | | |
|---|---|---|
| 1 = Only for males | 71 | 77.2 |
| 2 = For both, but more commonly for males | 4 | 4.3 |
| 3 = For neither | 15 | 16.3 |
| 4 = For both, but more commonly for females | 2 | 2.2 |
| No information | 1 | — |
| | 93 | |

*Column 33:* Levirate

| | | |
|---|---|---|
| 1 = Present | 54 | 71.1 |
| 2 = Absent | 22 | 28.9 |
| No information | 17 | — |
| | 93 | |

| Scale | Frequency | Percent |
|---|---|---|

*Column 34:* What are the relative distances moved by the bride and groom away from their families of orientation at first marriage?

| | Frequency | Percent |
|---|---|---|
| 1 = The female generally moves farther away | 58 | 69.0 |
| 2 = Generally about equal distance | 7 | 8.3 |
| 3 = The male generally moves farther away | 19 | 22.6 |
| No information | 9 | — |
| | 93 | |

*Column 35:* What is the relative ease of initiating divorce?

| | Frequency | Percent |
|---|---|---|
| 1 = Divorce is in theory only available to male | 5 | 5.4 |
| 2 = Divorce is possible for both, but more difficult for female | 12 | 12.9 |
| 3 = Divorce equally possible, no indication of bias | 72 | 77.4 |
| 4 = Divorce is possible for both, but more difficult for male, or in theory only available to female | 4 | 4.3 |
| | 93 | |

*Column 36:* What is the relative ease of remarriage?

| | Frequency | Percent |
|---|---|---|
| 1 = Possible for both, but fewer obstacles for men | 21 | 24.7 |
| 2 = Equally possible for both men and women | 64 | 75.3 |
| No information | 8 | — |
| | 93 | |

*Column 37:* What is the average relative age at first marriage of men and of women?

| | Frequency | Percent |
|---|---|---|
| 1 = Women generally older | 2 | 2.9 |
| 2 = Ages about equal | 7 | 10.0 |
| 3 = Men 1-2 years older | 12 | 17.1 |
| 4 = Men 3-4 years older | 18 | 25.7 |
| 5 = Men more than 4 years older | 31 | 44.3 |
| No information | 23 | — |
| | 93 | |

*Column 38:* Who has final authority over the care, handling and discipline of infant children (under 4 years)?

| | Frequency | Percent |
|---|---|---|
| 1 = Final authority is monopolized by males, or males have more say | 12 | 17.9 |
| 2 = Final authority is divided roughly equally | 11 | 16.4 |
| 3 = Final authority is divided, but females have more say | 21 | 31.3 |
| 4 = Final authority is monopolized by females | 23 | 34.3 |
| No information | 26 | — |
| | 93 | |

| *Scale* | *Frequency* | *Percent* |
|---|---|---|

*Column 39:* Who has final authority over the up-
bringing and discipline of post-infant
unmarried children living in the home

| | | |
|---|---|---|
| 1 = Final authority is virtually monopolized by males | 11 | 16.2 |
| 2 = Final authority is divided, but males have more say | 14 | 20.6 |
| 3 = Final authority is divided roughly equally | 34 | 50.0 |
| 4 = Authority is divided but females have more say, or final say is virtually monopolized by females | 9 | 13.2 |
| No information | 25 | — |
| | 93 | |

*Column 40:* Wife to husband institutionalized deference (Guttman scale)

| | | |
|---|---|---|
| 1 = None of the following coded | 29 | 34.5 |
| 2 = Husband dominates domestic decision making | 15 | 17.9 |
| 3 = +Wife excluded from many social gatherings | 21 | 25.0 |
| 4 = +Wife rarely disputes husband | 9 | 10.7 |
| 5 = +Husband has seating priority | 7 | 8.3 |
| 6 = +Wife kneels and bows when greeting husband | 3 | 3.6 |
| No information | 9 | — |
| | 93 | |

*Column 41:* Is there a stated preference for children
of one sex?

| | | |
|---|---|---|
| 1 = For males | 28 | 30.1 |
| 2 = Equal, no preference | 54 | 58.1 |
| 3 = For females | 11 | 11.8 |
| | 93 | |

*Column 42:* Is there any evidence of infanticide?

| | | |
|---|---|---|
| 1 = Mostly for females | 6 | 8.5 |
| 2 = For both, or for neither | 64 | 90.1 |
| 3 = Mostly for males | 1 | 1.4 |
| No information | 22 | — |
| | 93 | |

*Column 43:* Are boys or girls trained earlier for adult
duties?

| | | |
|---|---|---|
| 1 = Boys are trained earlier generally | 1 | 1.1 |
| 2 = Training begins at roughly equal ages, no stated bias | 70 | 75.3 |
| 3 = Girls are trained earlier generally | 22 | 23.7 |
| | 93 | |

| Scale | Frequency | Percent |
|---|---|---|

*Column 44:* Are boys or girls punished more severely for equal misbehavior?

| | Frequency | Percent |
|---|---|---|
| 1 = Boys are punished more severely | 3 | 3.2 |
| 2 = Punishment about equal, no stated bias | 82 | 88.2 |
| 3 = Girls are punished more severely | 8 | 8.6 |
| | 93 | |

*Column 45:* Is physical punishment of the spouse condoned?

| | Frequency | Percent |
|---|---|---|
| 1 = Only husband hitting wife generally | 39 | 61.9 |
| 2 = Physical punishment by neither | 16 | 25.4 |
| 3 = Either may hit the other, or only wife may hit husband | 8 | 12.7 |
| No information | 30 | — |
| | 93 | |

*Column 46:* Is there an explicit view that men should and do dominate their wives?

| | Frequency | Percent |
|---|---|---|
| 1 = Yes | 42 | 66.7 |
| 2 = No, evidence of rough equality | 19 | 30.2 |
| 3 = No, evidence of wife dominance | 2 | 3.2 |
| No information | 30 | — |
| | 93 | |

*Column 47:* In general community gatherings, activities, and organizations, who can attend and participate (exclude religious and political gatherings already dealt with)?

| | Frequency | Percent |
|---|---|---|
| 1 = Only men, or both, but men more often or more prominently | 27 | 43.5 |
| 2 = Both equally, although perhaps segregated | 35 | 56.5 |
| No information | 31 | — |
| | 93 | |

*Column 48:* Existence of general female initiation ceremonies (Guttman scale)

| | Frequency | Percent |
|---|---|---|
| 1 = No initiations for females | 36 | 47.4 |
| 2 = Customary minimal social recognition | 8 | 10.5 |
| 3 = +Personal dramatization of the initiate | 10 | 13.2 |
| 4 = +Organized social response | 12 | 15.8 |
| 5 = +Affective social response (e.g., punishment or operations) | 10 | 13.2 |
| No information | 17 | — |
| | 93 | |

| Scale | Frequency | Percent |
|---|---|---|

*Column 49:* Is there in folklore or history any belief that the status of women has changed?

| | Frequency | Percent |
|---|---|---|
| 1 = A belief it has declined | 6 | 6.5 |
| 2 = No such belief, or no change | 83 | 89.2 |
| 3 = A belief it has improved | 4 | 4.3 |
| | 93 | |

*Column 50:* Is there a generally high value placed on males being aggressive, strong, and sexually potent (machismo)?

| | Frequency | Percent |
|---|---|---|
| 1 = Marked emphasis | 26 | 32.1 |
| 2 = Moderate emphasis | 33 | 40.7 |
| 3 = Little or no emphasis | 22 | 27.2 |
| Ambiguous | 12 | — |
| | 93 | |

*Column 51:* Is there a clearly stated belief that women are generally inferior to men?

| | Frequency | Percent |
|---|---|---|
| 1 = Yes | 27 | 29.0 |
| 2 = No such belief | 66 | 71.0 |
| | 93 | |

*Column 52:* Does the ethnographer(s) say that women have more informal influence than the formal norms of the society would make it appear?

| | Frequency | Percent |
|---|---|---|
| 1 = No such statement or implication | 49 | 52.7 |
| 2 = A statement or implication that they have somewhat more informal influence | 25 | 26.9 |
| 3 = A statement or implication that they have much more informal influence | 19 | 20.4 |
| | 93 | |

*Column 53:* Property Control Scale (a scale composed of the equally weighted average of the variables in columns 15,16,17,18, and 19; average r = .28)

| | Frequency | Percent |
|---|---|---|
| 1 = Women have low control over property | 4 | 4.3 |
| 2 | 19 | 20.4 |
| 3 | 60 | 64.5 |
| 4 = Women have high control over property | 10 | 10.8 |
| | 93 | |

| Scale | Frequency | Percent |
|---|---|---|
| *Column 54:* Kin Power Scale (a scale composed of the equally weighted average of the variables in columns 8,31,32, and 33; average r =.41) | | |
| 1 = Low power of women in kinship contexts | 19 | 20.4 |
| 2 | 52 | 55.9 |
| 3 = High power of women in kinship contexts | 22 | 23.7 |
| | 93 | |
| | | |
| *Column 55:* Value of Life Scale (a scale composed of the equally weighted average of the variables in columns 41,42, and 45; average r = .27) | | |
| 1 = Low value placed on women's lives | 8 | 8.6 |
| 2 | 37 | 39.8 |
| 3 = High value placed on women's lives | 48 | 51.6 |
| | 93 | |
| | | |
| *Column 56:* Value of labor (a scale composed of the equally weighted average of the variables in columns 10 and 11 and the inverse of that in column 30) | | |
| 1 = Low value of women's labor | 1 | 1.1 |
| 2 | 9 | 9.7 |
| 3 | 40 | 43.0 |
| 4 | 34 | 36.6 |
| 5 = High value of women's labor | 9 | 9.7 |
| | 93 | |
| | | |
| *Column 57:* Domestic Authority Scale (a scale composed of the equally weighted average of the variables in columns 38,39 and 46; average r = 38) | | |
| 1 = Low women's domestic authority | 8 | 9.0 |
| 2 | 21 | 23.6 |
| 3 | 32 | 36.0 |
| 4 = High women's domestic authority | 28 | 31.5 |
| No information | 4 | — |
| | 95 | |

| Scale | Frequency | Percent |
|---|---|---|

*Column 58:* Ritualized Female Solidarity Scale (a scale composed of the equally weighted average of the variables in columns 12,13,24,48, and 51; average r = .25)

| | | |
|---|---|---|
| 1 = Low female solidarity | 26 | 28.0 |
| 2 | 38 | 40.9 |
| 3 = High female solidarity | 29 | 31.2 |
| | 93 | |

*Column 59:* Control of Sex Scale (a scale composed of the equally weighted average of the variables in columns 21,22,36, and 37; average r = .24

| | | |
|---|---|---|
| 1 = Stricter controls over women's marital and sexual lives | 3 | 3.3 |
| 2 | 56 | 60.9 |
| 3 = More equal controls over women's marital and sexual lives | 33 | 35.9 |
| No information | 1 | — |
| | 93 | |

*Column 60:* Ritualized Fear Scale (a scale composed of the equally weighted average of the variables in columns 6,27, and 50; average r = .25)

| | | |
|---|---|---|
| 1 = High ritualized fear of women | 6 | 6.5 |
| 2 | 18 | 19.4 |
| 3 = Low ritualized fear of women | 69 | 74.2 |
| | 93 | |

*Column 61:* Joint Participation Scale (a scale composed of the equally weighted average of the variables in columns 9,14, and 47; average r = .23)

| | | |
|---|---|---|
| 1 = Low joint participation of men and women | 10 | 11.0 |
| 2 | 50 | 54.9 |
| 3 = High joint participation of men and women | 31 | 34.1 |
| No information | 2 | — |
| | 93 | |

TABLE 2

Coded Data and Scales on the Relative Status of Women

| Area | Society | 1 | 2 | 3 | 4 | 5 | 6 | 7 | 8 | 9 | 10 | 11 | 12 | 13 | 14 | 15 | 16 | 17 | 18 | 19 | 20 |
|------|---------|---|---|---|---|---|---|---|---|---|----|----|----|----|----|----|----|----|----|----|----|
| 001 | Nama Hottentot | 1 | 1 | 1 | 2 | 2 | 2 | 2 | 1 | 1 | 5 | 2 | 3 | - | 2 | 3 | 4 | 4 | 3 | 4 | 2 |
| 003 | Thonga | - | 3 | 2 | 3 | 3 | 2 | 1 | 1 | 1 | 4 | 3 | 2 | 2 | 2 | 2 | 3 | 2 | 3 | 3 | 2 |
| 005 | Mbundu | 3 | 2 | 3 | 4 | - | 2 | 2 | 1 | 1 | 5 | 2 | 2 | 2 | 2 | 1 | - | 1 | 3 | 3 | 1 |
| 007 | Bemba | 2 | 3 | - | 2 | 2 | 2 | 3 | 1 | - | 7 | 2 | 3 | 2 | 3 | - | - | 1 | 3 | 3 | 2 |
| 009 | Hadza | - | - | 2 | - | 2 | 2 | - | - | - | 5 | 2 | 2 | 2 | 2 | 2 | - | 2 | 3 | 3 | 2 |
| 011 | Kikuyu | 3 | 4 | 1 | 3 | 2 | - | 1 | 1 | 1 | 5 | 2 | 2 | 2 | 2 | 1 | 3 | 1 | 4 | 3 | 1 |
| 013 | Mbuti | 2 | - | 3 | - | - | - | - | - | - | 6 | 2 | 2 | 1 | 3 | - | 4 | 3 | 3 | 2 | 2 |
| 015 | Banen | - | 1 | 1 | 2 | - | 2 | 1 | 1 | 1 | 8 | 3 | 2 | 2 | 2 | 1 | 3 | 1 | 3 | 4 | 1 |
| 017 | Ibo | 4 | 1 | 1 | - | - | 2 | - | 2 | 1 | 8 | 3 | 2 | 1 | 2 | 1 | 3 | 4 | 4 | 4 | 2 |
| 019 | Ashanti | 2 | - | 1 | 4 | 3 | 2 | 2 | 2 | 2 | 6 | - | - | - | 2 | 2 | 2 | 1 | 2 | 4 | 1 |
| 021 | Wolof | 4 | 2 | 2 | 3 | 3 | - | 1 | 1 | - | 8 | 3 | 2 | 2 | 2 | 2 | 4 | 2 | 2 | 4 | 1 |
| 023 | Tallensi | - | 1 | 1 | 4 | 2 | 1 | 1 | 1 | 2 | 5 | 2 | - | 1 | 2 | 2 | 3 | 2 | 3 | 3 | 1 |
| 025 | Fulani | - | 2 | 1 | 3 | 3 | - | 1 | 1 | 1 | 5 | 2 | 2 | 1 | 2 | 2 | 4 | 2 | - | 4 | 2 |
| 027 | Massa | 4 | 1 | - | - | 2 | 2 | 1 | 1 | 1 | 2 | 1 | 3 | 2 | - | 2 | 1 | 1 | 2 | 2 | 1 |
| 029 | Fur | - | - | 3 | 3 | 3 | 1 | 1 | - | 1 | 5 | 2 | 2 | 1 | 3 | 2 | 3 | 3 | 3 | 4 | 2 |
| 031 | Shilluk | 2 | 2 | - | 3 | 2 | 1 | 1 | 1 | 1 | 4 | 2 | - | - | 3 | 1 | 1 | 1 | 3 | 4 | 2 |
| 033 | Kaffa | 2 | 2 | 2 | 3 | 2 | 1 | 1 | 1 | 1 | 5 | 1 | 1 | - | 3 | 2 | 1 | 2 | 3 | 3 | 2 |
| 035 | Konso | - | 1 | 3 | 2 | 2 | 1 | 1 | 1 | 1 | 5 | 2 | - | 1 | 3 | 1 | 2 | 4 | 4 | 3 | 2 |
| 037 | Amhara | 1 | - | 3 | 1 | 3 | 2 | 1 | 1 | 1 | 2 | 2 | 2 | - | 2 | 2 | - | 2 | - | 3 | 1 |
| 039 | Nubians | 1 | - | - | - | - | 1 | 1 | 3 | 1 | 4 | 1 | - | 2 | - | 2 | 4 | 2 | 3 | 3 | 1 |
| 041 | Tuareg | - | - | 4 | 3 | 3 | - | 1 | 1 | 1 | 3 | 2 | 1 | 1 | 2 | 2 | - | 2 | - | 4 | 1 |
| 043 | Egyptians | 1 | - | 4 | - | 2 | 2 | 1 | - | - | 4 | 1 | 1 | 1 | 1 | 2 | 2 | 4 | 3 | 3 | 1 |
| 045 | Babylonians | 3 | 2 | 1 | 3 | - | - | 1 | - | 1 | - | - | - | - | - | 2 | - | 2 | 3 | 3 | 1 |
| 047 | Turks | 1 | - | 2 | - | 1 | - | 1 | 1 | 1 | 5 | 3 | 2 | 1 | 2 | 2 | 1 | 1 | 1 | 2 | 1 |
| 049 | Romans | 4 | 1 | - | 3 | - | 2 | 2 | - | 1 | 3 | - | - | 1 | - | 3 | 3 | 2 | 3 | 3 | 1 |
| 051 | Irish | 3 | 3 | - | 4 | 3 | 2 | - | 1 | 1 | 5 | 2 | 2 | 2 | 2 | 2 | 1 | - | 1 | - | 4 |
| 053 | Yurak | 2 | 2 | 3 | - | 2 | 2 | - | - | - | 6 | 2 | 1 | 1 | 3 | - | - | 2 | 3 | 3 | 1 |
| 055 | Abkhaz | 4 | - | 4 | 4 | 2 | 2 | 1 | 1 | 2 | 3 | 2 | 1 | 1 | - | 1 | 1 | 1 | 1 | 1 | 1 |
| 057 | Kurd | 2 | - | - | - | 2 | 1 | 1 | 1 | 1 | 4 | 1 | 1 | 1 | 2 | 2 | 2 | 2 | 2 | 1 | 1 |
| 059 | Punjabi | - | - | - | - | 3 | 2 | 1 | - | 1 | 3 | 1 | 2 | - | 2 | 1 | 1 | 3 | 3 | 3 | 2 |
| 061 | Toda | 4 | 4 | 2 | 1 | 1 | 1 | 1 | - | 1 | 1 | 1 | 1 | 1 | - | 1 | 1 | 1 | - | - | 2 |
| 063 | Uttar Pradesh | 4 | - | 1 | - | 4 | 2 | 1 | 1 | 1 | 3 | 1 | 1 | 2 | 1 | - | 1 | - | 3 | 3 | 2 |
| 065 | Kazak | - | 1 | - | - | - | 1 | - | - | - | 6 | - | - | - | 2 | 1 | 2 | 1 | 3 | 3 | 1 |
| 067 | Lolo | - | 1 | 2 | 2 | - | 2 | - | 1 | 2 | 5 | 2 | 1 | 1 | 3 | 3 | 2 | 3 | 3 | 3 | 1 |
| 069 | Garo | - | 4 | 1 | - | 3 | 2 | 1 | 1 | - | 5 | 2 | 2 | - | 3 | 4 | 4 | 3 | 3 | 2 | 2 |
| 071 | Burmese | 4 | 3 | 3 | 4 | 3 | 2 | 1 | 1 | 1 | 6 | 2 | 2 | 2 | 3 | 3 | - | 3 | 3 | 2 | 2 |
| 073 | N. Vietnamese | - | - | - | - | 2 | 2 | 1 | - | - | 6 | 2 | - | - | 2 | 2 | - | 4 | 4 | 3 | 2 |
| 075 | Khmer Cambodians | - | 1 | 3 | 1 | 2 | 2 | 1 | - | 1 | 5 | 2 | - | - | 3 | 3 | - | 2 | 3 | 2 | 1 |
| 077 | Semang | 4 | 3 | - | 1 | 4 | 2 | - | 3 | - | 3 | 2 | 3 | 2 | 2 | 3 | 4 | 2 | 3 | 3 | 1 |
| 079 | Andamanese | 4 | 3 | 2 | 2 | - | 2 | - | - | 1 | 4 | 2 | - | - | 1 | - | 3 | 2 | - | 3 | 2 |
| 081 | Tanala | 3 | - | 2 | 2 | 3 | 2 | 1 | 1 | 1 | 4 | 1 | 1 | 1 | 3 | - | 4 | 1 | 3 | 4 | 2 |
| 083 | Javanese | 4 | 1 | 2 | 1 | 1 | 2 | 1 | - | - | 6 | 2 | 2 | 1 | 2 | 3 | 3 | 4 | 4 | 3 | 1 |
| 085 | Iban | 2 | - | 2 | - | 3 | 2 | 1 | 3 | 1 | 6 | 2 | 1 | 1 | 2 | 3 | 3 | 2 | 3 | 3 | 2 |
| 087 | Toradja | 4 | 3 | 4 | 3 | 4 | 2 | 1 | 1 | 1 | 5 | 2 | 2 | 2 | 3 | 3 | 3 | 3 | 3 | 2 | 2 |
| 089 | Alorese | 4 | 3 | - | 3 | 2 | 2 | - | - | 1 | 3 | 3 | 2 | 1 | - | 2 | - | 1 | - | 4 | 2 |
| 091 | Aranda | 3 | 2 | 2 | 2 | 2 | 2 | - | 1 | 1 | 8 | 3 | 1 | 1 | 1 | - | 3 | 2 | 3 | 3 | 2 |
| 093 | Kimam | 1 | 2 | - | 1 | 3 | 2 | - | 1 | 1 | 5 | 2 | 3 | 2 | 2 | 1 | 1 | 1 | 1 | 1 | 2 |
| 095 | Kwoma | - | 1 | 3 | 3 | 2 | - | - | - | 1 | 5 | 2 | 3 | 2 | 2 | 2 | 1 | 2 | 4 | 4 | 1 |

## TABLE 2 (continued)

| Area | Society | 21 | 22 | 23 | 24 | 25 | 26 | 27 | 28 | 29 | 30 | 31 | 32 | 33 | 34 | 35 | 36 | 37 |
|---|---|---|---|---|---|---|---|---|---|---|---|---|---|---|---|---|---|---|
| 001 | Nama Hottentot | 2 | 2 | 2 | 7 | 2 | 2 | - | 4 | 2 | 3 | 3 | 1 | 1 | 1 | 2 | 2 | - |
| 003 | Thonga | 2 | - | 2 | 7 | 2 | 2 | 1 | 2 | 3 | 2 | 1 | 1 | 1 | 1 | 3 | 2 | - |
| 005 | Mbundu | 2 | - | 2 | 7 | 2 | 2 | - | - | 2 | 2 | 1 | 1 | 1 | 1 | 3 | 2 | 3 |
| 007 | Bemba | 2 | 1 | 1 | 7 | 3 | 2 | 1 | 3 | 3 | 3 | 3 | 1 | - | 3 | 2 | 2 | 5 |
| 009 | Hadza | - | - | - | - | 2 | 1 | - | - | - | 4 | 3 | 1 | 1 | 3 | 3 | 2 | 4 |
| 011 | Kikuyu | 2 | 2 | 3 | - | 2 | 2 | 2 | - | 3 | 2 | 1 | 1 | - | 1 | 3 | 2 | 5 |
| 013 | Mbuti | 2 | 1 | 1 | 1 | 2 | 2 | 2 | 3 | 3 | - | 2 | 1 | - | 1 | 3 | 2 | 3 |
| 015 | Banen | - | - | - | - | 2 | 2 | 2 | 2 | - | 2 | 1 | 1 | 1 | 1 | 3 | 2 | - |
| 017 | Ibo | 1 | 2 | 3 | 7 | 2 | 2 | 2 | 1 | 2 | 2 | 1 | 1 | 1 | 1 | 3 | 2 | 4 |
| 019 | Ashanti | - | 2 | 2 | 7 | 2 | 2 | 2 | 2 | 2 | 4 | 2 | 1 | 1 | 1 | 2 | 2 | 5 |
| 021 | Wolof | 1 | 1 | 2 | - | 1 | 1 | 2 | 2 | 3 | 2 | 2 | 1 | 1 | 1 | 3 | 1 | 5 |
| 023 | Tallensi | 2 | 2 | 1 | 1 | 2 | 2 | 2 | 1 | 2 | 2 | 2 | 1 | 1 | 1 | 3 | 2 | 5 |
| 025 | Fulani | 2 | - | 2 | 2 | 2 | 2 | 2 | 3 | 4 | 2 | 1 | 1 | 1 | 1 | 3 | 2 | 4 |
| 027 | Massa | 2 | 1 | 2 | 1 | 2 | 2 | 2 | 1 | 2 | 2 | 1 | 1 | 1 | 1 | 3 | 1 | 3 |
| 029 | Fur | 2 | 2 | 2 | - | 2 | 2 | 2 | 2 | 2 | 2 | 2 | 1 | 1 | 1 | 3 | 2 | 3 |
| 031 | Shilluk | 2 | 2 | 2 | - | 2 | 2 | 1 | 2 | 3 | 2 | 1 | 1 | 1 | 1 | 3 | 2 | 5 |
| 033 | Kaffa | 1 | 2 | 1 | - | 2 | 2 | - | 2 | 2 | 2 | 1 | 1 | - | 1 | 3 | 1 | 5 |
| 035 | Konso | 1 | 2 | 1 | - | 2 | 2 | 1 | 2 | 2 | 4 | 2 | 1 | 1 | 1 | 3 | 2 | 5 |
| 037 | Amhara | - | 1 | 1 | 2 | 2 | 1 | 2 | 2 | 1 | 5 | 3 | 3 | 2 | 1 | 3 | 2 | 5 |
| 039 | Nubians | 1 | 1 | 1 | - | 2 | 2 | - | 4 | 2 | 2 | 2 | 1 | 2 | 1 | 1 | 1 | 3 |
| 041 | Tuareg | 2 | 2 | 2 | 3 | 2 | 2 | 2 | 2 | 3 | 2 | 3 | 1 | 2 | 1 | 4 | 2 | 5 |
| 043 | Egyptians | 2 | 2 | 1 | - | 2 | 1 | 1 | 2 | 3 | 2 | 3 | 1 | 2 | 1 | 2 | 2 | 5 |
| 045 | Babylonians | - | 1 | 1 | - | 2 | 2 | 2 | 1 | - | 2 | 3 | 1 | 1 | - | 3 | 2 | - |
| 047 | Turks | 1 | - | 1 | - | 2 | 1 | 2 | 2 | 2 | 3 | 1 | 1 | 1 | 1 | 3 | 2 | 4 |
| 049 | Romans | 1 | 2 | 2 | - | 2 | 2 | 2 | 2 | - | 6 | 3 | 3 | 2 | - | 3 | 2 | 4 |
| 051 | Irish | 1 | - | 1 | 1 | 2 | 2 | - | 2 | 3 | 6 | 3 | 3 | 1 | 1 | 3 | - | 5 |
| 053 | Yurak | - | 1 | 2 | - | 2 | 2 | - | 1 | 2 | 3 | 1 | 1 | - | 1 | 3 | 2 | - |
| 055 | Abkhaz | 1 | 1 | 1 | 2 | 2 | 2 | - | 3 | 2 | 6 | 2 | 1 | 1 | 1 | 3 | 1 | 4 |
| 057 | Kurd | 1 | 1 | 1 | 2 | 2 | 2 | 1 | 2 | 3 | 6 | 2 | 1 | 2 | 1 | 2 | 2 | 3 |
| 059 | Punjabi | - | - | - | - | 2 | 2 | - | 3 | 3 | - | 2 | 1 | 1 | 1 | 3 | 1 | 2 |
| 061 | Toda | 2 | 2 | 3 | 2 | 2 | 2 | 1 | 2 | 3 | 6 | 4 | 4 | 1 | - | 3 | 2 | - |
| 063 | Uttar Pradesh | - | - | 1 | - | 2 | 2 | 2 | 2 | 3 | 6 | 2 | 1 | 1 | 1 | 3 | 1 | 5 |
| 065 | Kazak | 1 | 1 | 2 | 2 | 2 | 2 | 2 | 2 | 3 | 2 | 2 | 1 | 1 | 1 | 2 | 1 | 4 |
| 067 | Lolo | 2 | 2 | 1 | - | 2 | 2 | 2 | 3 | - | 2 | 3 | 1 | 1 | 1 | 3 | 1 | 3 |
| 069 | Garo | 2 | 2 | 1 | 2 | 3 | 1 | - | 2 | 4 | 5 | 3 | 1 | 1 | 3 | 3 | 1 | 4 |
| 071 | Burmese | 2 | 2 | 1 | 2 | 2 | 2 | 2 | 3 | 3 | - | 3 | 1 | - | 3 | 3 | 2 | 5 |
| 073 | N. Vietnamese | 1 | 1 | 1 | - | 2 | 3 | - | 4 | - | 4 | 2 | 1 | - | 1 | 2 | 1 | - |
| 075 | Khmer Cambodians | 1 | 1 | 1 | 1 | 2 | 1 | 2 | 4 | 3 | 4 | 3 | 1 | 2 | 3 | 3 | 2 | 4 |
| 077 | Semang | 2 | 2 | 1 | 1 | 3 | 2 | - | 1 | 3 | 2 | 3 | 3 | 2 | 1 | 3 | 2 | 4 |
| 079 | Andamanese | 2 | 2 | 2 | 3 | 2 | 2 | 2 | 3 | 3 | 5 | 3 | 3 | 2 | - | 3 | 2 | - |
| 081 | Tanala | 1 | 2 | 2 | 1 | 2 | 1 | 2 | - | 3 | 4 | 2 | 1 | 1 | 1 | 2 | 1 | 3 |
| 083 | Javanese | 1 | 1 | 1 | - | 2 | 3 | 2 | 2 | 2 | - | 2 | 1 | 2 | 2 | 3 | 2 | 5 |
| 085 | Iban | 2 | 2 | 1 | - | 2 | 2 | 2 | 3 | 3 | - | 3 | 3 | 2 | 2 | 3 | 2 | 5 |
| 087 | Toradja | 2 | 1 | 2 | 3 | 2 | 2 | 2 | 4 | 2 | 2 | 2 | 1 | 2 | 3 | 3 | 2 | - |
| 089 | Alorese | 1 | 1 | 1 | 2 | 2 | 2 | 2 | 2 | 3 | 2 | 2 | 1 | 1 | 1 | 2 | 2 | 4 |
| 091 | Aranda | - | - | 2 | 3 | 3 | 2 | - | 2 | 3 | 1 | 2 | 1 | 1 | - | 3 | 2 | - |
| 093 | Kimam | 2 | 2 | 2 | 7 | 1 | 2 | 1 | 1 | 2 | 2 | 2 | 1 | 1 | 1 | 3 | 2 | - |
| 095 | Kwoma | 1 | 1 | 2 | 6 | 2 | 2 | 2 | 2 | 4 | 2 | 1 | 1 | 1 | 1 | 4 | 2 | - |

TABLE 2 (continued)

| Area | Society | 38 | 39 | 40 | 41 | 42 | 43 | 44 | 45 | 46 | 47 | 48 | 49 | 50 | 51 | 52 | 53 | 54 |
|---|---|---|---|---|---|---|---|---|---|---|---|---|---|---|---|---|---|---|
| 001 | Nama Hottentot | 4 | 4 | 1 | 1 | 1 | 2 | 2 | 1 | 2 | 2 | 4 | 2 | - | 2 | 2 | 4 | 2 |
| 003 | Thonga | - | 1 | 3 | 2 | 2 | 2 | 2 | - | - | 1 | 2 | 2 | 2 | 2 | 2 | 3 | 1 |
| 005 | Mbundu | 4 | 3 | - | 2 | 2 | 2 | 2 | 2 | 1 | 1 | 2 | 2 | 2 | 2 | 2 | 2 | 1 |
| 007 | Bemba | - | - | 6 | 3 | 2 | 2 | 2 | 1 | 1 | 2 | 5 | 2 | 2 | 2 | 3 | 3 | 2 |
| 009 | Hadza | 3 | 3 | 3 | 2 | - | 2 | 2 | 1 | 2 | 1 | 5 | 2 | 2 | 2 | 1 | 3 | 2 |
| 011 | Kikuyu | 4 | 3 | 2 | 2 | 2 | 2 | 2 | 2 | 2 | 1 | 5 | 1 | 2 | 1 | 2 | 3 | 1 |
| 013 | Mbuti | 2 | 3 | 1 | 2 | 2 | 2 | 2 | 3 | 2 | 2 | 3 | 1 | 3 | 2 | 1 | 3 | 2 |
| 015 | Banen | - | - | 1 | 2 | 2 | 2 | 2 | - | 2 | - | 1 | 2 | 3 | 2 | 2 | 3 | 1 |
| 017 | Ibo | - | 3 | 1 | 1 | 2 | 2 | 2 | - | - | 2 | 2 | 2 | - | 2 | 3 | 4 | 2 |
| 019 | Ashanti | 2 | 3 | 1 | 2 | 2 | 2 | 2 | - | - | - | 4 | 2 | - | 2 | 3 | 3 | 2 |
| 021 | Wolof | 3 | 1 | 3 | 1 | 2 | 3 | 2 | 1 | 1 | 2 | 1 | 2 | 2 | 1 | 3 | 3 | 2 |
| 023 | Tallensi | 3 | 2 | 2 | 1 | 2 | 2 | 2 | 1 | 1 | - | 1 | 2 | 3 | 2 | 1 | 3 | 2 |
| 025 | Fulani | - | 2 | 3 | 2 | 2 | 2 | 2 | 2 | - | - | 1 | 2 | 2 | 2 | 2 | 3 | 1 |
| 027 | Massa | - | 2 | 4 | 3 | 2 | 3 | 2 | - | 1 | 1 | 1 | 2 | 1 | 1 | 1 | 2 | 1 |
| 029 | Fur | 2 | 3 | - | 3 | 2 | 2 | 2 | 2 | 1 | 2 | 5 | 2 | 2 | 1 | 2 | 3 | 2 |
| 031 | Shilluk | - | - | 1 | 2 | 2 | 2 | 2 | 1 | 2 | 2 | 1 | 2 | 2 | 2 | 1 | 2 | 1 |
| 033 | Kaffa | 1 | 1 | 3 | 2 | - | 2 | 2 | 1 | 1 | 2 | - | 2 | 1 | 1 | 1 | 3 | 1 |
| 035 | Konso | 3 | 4 | 3 | 1 | - | 2 | 2 | 1 | 1 | 1 | 3 | 2 | 1 | 1 | 1 | 3 | 2 |
| 037 | Amhara | 4 | 3 | 1 | 1 | 2 | 3 | 2 | 1 | 1 | 1 | 1 | 2 | 1 | 2 | 3 | 3 | 3 |
| 039 | Nubians | 4 | 2 | 4 | 1 | 2 | 3 | 2 | 1 | 1 | - | 1 | 2 | - | 2 | 3 | 3 | 3 |
| 041 | Tuareg | - | 3 | 1 | 1 | 2 | 1 | 2 | - | - | 2 | 2 | 2 | 2 | 2 | 1 | 3 | 2 |
| 043 | Egyptians | - | 2 | 5 | 1 | 2 | 2 | 2 | 1 | 1 | 2 | - | 2 | 1 | 1 | 2 | 3 | 3 |
| 045 | Babylonians | 1 | 1 | 2 | 1 | - | 2 | 2 | 1 | - | 1 | - | 2 | - | 2 | 1 | 3 | 2 |
| 047 | Turks | 3 | 3 | 3 | 1 | 2 | 2 | 2 | 1 | 1 | 2 | 1 | 2 | 1 | 1 | 1 | 2 | 2 |
| 049 | Romans | 1 | 2 | 1 | 1 | 2 | 2 | 2 | - | 2 | 2 | - | 3 | 3 | 2 | 2 | 3 | 3 |
| 051 | Irish | - | - | 5 | 2 | 2 | 2 | 2 | - | - | 1 | 1 | 2 | 2 | 2 | 3 | 2 | 2 |
| 053 | Yurak | - | - | 3 | 2 | 2 | 2 | 2 | 1 | 1 | 2 | - | 2 | - | 1 | 1 | 3 | 2 |
| 055 | Abkhaz | 1 | 1 | 3 | 1 | - | 3 | 2 | 2 | 1 | 1 | - | 1 | 1 | 1 | 3 | 1 | 2 |
| 057 | Kurd | - | 2 | 3 | 1 | 2 | 3 | 3 | 1 | 1 | - | 1 | 2 | 1 | 1 | 3 | 2 | 2 |
| 059 | Punjabi | - | - | - | 1 | 2 | 2 | 2 | 1 | - | 1 | 2 | 3 | 2 | 3 | 3 | 3 | 2 |
| 061 | Toda | - | - | 3 | 1 | 1 | 2 | 2 | - | - | 1 | 2 | - | 1 | 1 | 1 | 1 | 3 |
| 063 | Uttar Pradesh | 1 | 2 | 6 | 2 | 1 | 2 | 2 | 1 | 1 | 1 | 1 | 3 | 3 | 1 | 2 | 2 | 2 |
| 065 | Kazak | 2 | 1 | 5 | 3 | 2 | 2 | 2 | 1 | 1 | 1 | - | 2 | 1 | 1 | 2 | 2 | 2 |
| 067 | Lolo | - | - | 1 | 2 | - | 2 | 2 | 2 | 2 | 2 | 3 | 2 | 2 | 2 | 3 | 3 | 2 |
| 069 | Garo | 1 | 1 | 1 | 3 | - | 3 | 2 | 1 | 1 | 2 | 1 | 2 | 3 | 2 | 1 | 4 | 2 |
| 071 | Burmese | 2 | 3 | 1 | 2 | 2 | 2 | 2 | 2 | 2 | 2 | 5 | 2 | 3 | 2 | 3 | 3 | 2 |
| 073 | N. Vietnamese | 1 | - | 4 | 1 | - | 2 | 2 | 1 | 1 | 1 | - | 2 | - | 1 | 3 | 4 | 2 |
| 075 | Khmer Cambodians | 3 | 3 | 4 | 2 | 2 | 2 | 2 | - | 1 | 2 | 1 | 2 | 3 | 2 | 3 | 3 | 3 |
| 077 | Semang | 2 | - | 1 | 1 | 2 | 2 | 2 | - | - | - | - | 2 | 1 | 2 | 1 | 3 | 3 |
| 079 | Andamanese | 3 | 3 | - | 2 | - | 2 | 2 | - | - | 1 | 5 | 2 | 2 | 2 | 1 | 3 | 3 |
| 081 | Tanala | 1 | 1 | 5 | 2 | 2 | 2 | 2 | 1 | - | - | 1 | 2 | 1 | 2 | 1 | 3 | 2 |
| 083 | Javanese | 4 | 4 | 3 | 2 | 2 | 3 | 2 | 2 | 3 | - | 1 | 2 | 3 | 1 | 3 | 4 | 2 |
| 085 | Iban | 2 | 3 | 1 | 2 | 2 | 2 | 2 | - | 2 | 2 | - | 2 | 2 | 2 | 1 | 3 | 3 |
| 087 | Toradja | 2 | 3 | 1 | 3 | 2 | 3 | 2 | 3 | 2 | 1 | 4 | 2 | 2 | 2 | 2 | 3 | 2 |
| 089 | Alorese | 4 | 4 | 1 | 2 | - | 3 | 2 | 1 | - | 1 | 3 | 2 | 2 | 2 | 2 | 3 | 2 |
| 091 | Aranda | 4 | 3 | 3 | 2 | 2 | 3 | 2 | 1 | 1 | - | - | 1 | - | 1 | 1 | 3 | 2 |
| 093 | Kimam | 3 | 1 | 2 | 2 | 2 | 2 | 2 | 1 | - | - | 3 | 2 | 2 | 2 | 2 | 1 | 2 |
| 095 | Kwoma | 4 | 3 | 3 | 2 | 2 | 2 | 2 | 1 | - | - | 5 | 2 | 2 | 2 | 1 | 3 | 1 |

TABLE 2 (continued)

| Area | Society | 55 | 56 | 57 | 58 | 59 | 60 | 61 |
|------|---------|----|----|----|----|----|----|----|
| 001 | Nama Hottentot | 1 | 3 | 4 | 3 | 3 | 3 | 2 |
| 003 | Thonga | 3 | 3 | 1 | 3 | 3 | 2 | 2 |
| 005 | Mbundu | 3 | 3 | 4 | 3 | 3 | 3 | 2 |
| 007 | Bemba | 3 | 3 | 2 | 3 | 2 | 2 | 3 |
| 009 | Hadza | 2 | 4 | 4 | 3 | 3 | 3 | 2 |
| 011 | Kikuyu | 3 | 3 | 4 | 3 | 3 | 3 | 2 |
| 013 | Mbuti | 3 | 4 | 3 | 2 | 2 | 3 | 3 |
| 015 | Banen | 3 | 4 | 3 | 2 | 3 | 3 | 2 |
| 017 | Ibo | 2 | 4 | 4 | 2 | 2 | 3 | 2 |
| 019 | Ashanti | 3 | 2 | 3 | 3 | 3 | 3 | 3 |
| 021 | Wolof | 2 | 4 | 2 | 2 | 2 | 3 | 3 |
| 023 | Tallensi | 2 | 3 | 3 | 1 | 3 | 3 | 3 |
| 025 | Fulani | 3 | 4 | 2 | 2 | 3 | 3 | 2 |
| 027 | Massa | 3 | 2 | 2 | 2 | 2 | 3 | 2 |
| 029 | Fur | 3 | 3 | 3 | 2 | 2 | 2 | 3 |
| 031 | Shilluk | 2 | 3 | 3 | 1 | 3 | 2 | 3 |
| 033 | Kaffa | 2 | 2 | 1 | 1 | 2 | 1 | 3 |
| 035 | Konso | 1 | 4 | 3 | 2 | 2 | 1 | 2 |
| 037 | Amhara | 2 | 5 | 3 | 1 | 2 | 3 | 2 |
| 039 | Nubians | 2 | 2 | 3 | 2 | 2 | 2 | 2 |
| 041 | Tuareg | 2 | 3 | 4 | 2 | 3 | 3 | 2 |
| 043 | Egyptians | 2 | 2 | 2 | 1 | 3 | 2 | 2 |
| 045 | Babylonians | 1 | 3 | 1 | 2 | 2 | 3 | 2 |
| 047 | Turks | 2 | 4 | 3 | 1 | 2 | 2 | 2 |
| 049 | Romans | 2 | 4 | 2 | 2 | 2 | 3 | 3 |
| 051 | Irish | 3 | 4 | - | 2 | 2 | 3 | 2 |
| 053 | Yurak | 2 | 3 | 2 | 1 | 2 | 3 | 3 |
| 055 | Abkhaz | 2 | 4 | 1 | 1 | 2 | 2 | 3 |
| 057 | Kurd | 2 | 3 | 2 | 1 | 2 | 1 | 2 |
| 059 | Punjabi | 2 | 1 | - | 2 | 2 | 3 | 2 |
| 061 | Toda | 1 | 4 | - | 1 | 3 | 2 | - |
| 063 | Uttar Pradesh | 2 | 3 | 2 | 1 | 2 | 3 | 2 |
| 065 | Kazak | 3 | 5 | 2 | 1 | 2 | 2 | 2 |
| 067 | Lolo | 3 | 3 | 3 | 2 | 2 | 3 | 3 |
| 069 | Garo | 3 | 4 | 1 | 2 | 2 | 3 | 3 |
| 071 | Burmese | 3 | 5 | 3 | 3 | 3 | 3 | 3 |
| 073 | N. Vietnamese | 1 | 4 | 2 | 1 | 1 | 3 | 2 |
| 075 | Khmer Cambodians | 3 | 4 | 3 | 1 | 2 | 3 | 3 |
| 077 | Semang | 2 | 2 | 2 | 3 | 3 | 2 | 2 |
| 079 | Andamanese | 3 | 4 | 4 | 3 | 3 | 3 | 1 |
| 081 | Tanala | 2 | 3 | 1 | 1 | 2 | 3 | 3 |
| 083 | Javanese | 3 | 5 | 4 | 1 | 2 | 3 | 2 |
| 085 | Iban | 3 | 4 | 3 | 2 | 3 | 3 | 2 |
| 087 | Toradja | 3 | 4 | 3 | 3 | 2 | 3 | 2 |
| 089 | Alorese | 2 | 4 | 4 | 2 | 2 | 3 | 2 |
| 091 | Aranda | 2 | 5 | 3 | 1 | 3 | 3 | 1 |
| 093 | Kimam | 2 | 3 | 2 | 3 | 3 | 2 | 2 |
| 095 | Kwoma | 2 | 3 | 4 | 3 | 2 | 3 | 2 |

TABLE 2 (continued)

| Area | Society | 1 | 2 | 3 | 4 | 5 | 6 | 7 | 8 | 9 | 10 | 11 | 12 | 13 | 14 | 15 | 16 | 17 | 18 | 19 | 20 |
|---|---|---|---|---|---|---|---|---|---|---|---|---|---|---|---|---|---|---|---|---|---|
| 097 | Lesu | - | 4 | 2 | 1 | - | 2 | 1 | 1 | - | 7 | 2 | 3 | 2 | 2 | - | - | 2 | 3 | 3 | 2 |
| 099 | Siuai | 3 | 3 | 3 | 3 | - | 2 | 1 | - | - | 6 | 3 | - | - | 2 | - | 3 | 2 | 2 | 1 | 2 |
| 101 | Pentecost | 4 | 4 | 2 | 2 | - | 1 | 1 | - | 1 | 5 | - | 1 | 1 | - | - | - | 2 | 3 | 3 | 2 |
| 103 | Ajie | 2 | 1 | 3 | 3 | 2 | 2 | 1 | - | 1 | 3 | 1 | 2 | - | - | 1 | 1 | 1 | 1 | 3 | 1 |
| 105 | Marquesans | 4 | 2 | 4 | 3 | 3 | 2 | 2 | 3 | 1 | 1 | 1 | 3 | 1 | 1 | 2 | 2 | 1 | 3 | 3 | 2 |
| 107 | Gilbertese | - | - | - | - | - | 2 | 1 | 1 | 1 | 6 | 2 | 2 | - | 3 | - | 2 | 3 | 3 | 2 | 2 |
| 109 | Truk | - | 4 | 3 | - | 3 | 2 | 1 | 2 | - | 5 | 2 | - | - | 1 | 3 | 4 | 3 | 3 | 3 | 2 |
| 111 | Palauans | 4 | - | 3 | - | - | 2 | - | 1 | 1 | 4 | 3 | 3 | 2 | 1 | - | 1 | 1 | 1 | 1 | 1 |
| 113 | Atayal | 4 | 2 | 4 | - | 2 | 2 | 1 | 1 | 1 | 6 | 3 | 2 | 1 | 1 | - | - | 3 | - | 2 | 1 |
| 115 | Manchu | - | 3 | 3 | - | - | 2 | 1 | 2 | 1 | 6 | 2 | 1 | 1 | - | - | 1 | 2 | 3 | 3 | 2 |
| 117 | Japanese | 3 | - | - | - | 2 | 2 | 1 | - | 1 | 4 | 2 | 2 | 1 | - | 1 | 1 | 2 | 3 | 3 | 2 |
| 119 | Gilyak | 2 | - | 3 | 2 | 2 | 2 | - | 1 | 1 | 3 | 1 | 1 | 1 | 1 | 2 | 3 | 1 | - | 3 | 1 |
| 121 | Chukchee | 2 | - | 3 | 3 | 2 | 2 | 1 | - | - | 4 | 3 | 3 | 1 | 2 | 2 | 3 | 1 | 1 | 1 | 1 |
| 123 | Aleut | - | 3 | - | 2 | - | 2 | 1 | 1 | 1 | 5 | 2 | 2 | - | - | - | 1 | 1 | 3 | 3 | 1 |
| 125 | Montagnais | 2 | 1 | 2 | 1 | 2 | 2 | 2 | - | - | 4 | 2 | 1 | 1 | 3 | 2 | 3 | 2 | 3 | 4 | 2 |
| 127 | Salteaux | 2 | 2 | 2 | 2 | 3 | 2 | 1 | 1 | - | 3 | 2 | 1 | 1 | 2 | 3 | - | 2 | 3 | 3 | 1 |
| 129 | Kaska | - | - | 2 | 2 | 2 | 2 | 1 | 1 | 1 | 6 | 2 | 1 | - | 2 | 3 | 4 | 3 | 3 | 3 | 1 |
| 131 | Haida | 2 | 3 | 2 | 2 | 3 | 2 | 1 | 2 | 1 | 4 | 2 | 2 | 1 | 3 | 3 | 2 | 2 | 3 | 3 | 2 |
| 133 | Twana | - | 4 | 2 | 3 | - | 2 | 1 | 1 | 1 | 4 | 2 | 2 | 2 | - | 3 | 1 | 2 | 3 | 3 | 1 |
| 135 | Pomo | 2 | 1 | 2 | 2 | 2 | 2 | 1 | - | 2 | 4 | 2 | 2 | 1 | 3 | 3 | 3 | 2 | 3 | 3 | 2 |
| 137 | Paiute | - | - | 3 | 3 | 4 | 2 | - | - | - | 6 | 3 | 3 | - | 2 | - | 3 | 3 | 3 | 3 | 1 |
| 139 | Kutenai | 4 | 1 | 3 | 2 | 3 | 2 | 1 | - | 1 | 4 | 3 | 3 | 2 | 1 | 3 | 3 | 1 | - | 3 | 1 |
| 141 | Hidatsa | 2 | - | - | - | 2 | 2 | 1 | - | 1 | 5 | 2 | 2 | 1 | 1 | 4 | 4 | 2 | 3 | 3 | 1 |
| 143 | Omaha | 2 | 3 | 3 | 3 | 2 | 2 | 1 | - | 1 | 6 | 2 | 2 | 1 | 3 | 2 | - | 2 | 3 | 3 | 2 |
| 145 | Creek | 2 | - | 3 | 3 | 2 | 2 | 2 | 1 | 1 | 6 | 3 | 2 | 1 | 2 | - | 4 | 1 | 3 | 3 | 1 |
| 147 | Comanche | 3 | 3 | 2 | 2 | 3 | 2 | 1 | 1 | 2 | 3 | 3 | 2 | 2 | - | 3 | 2 | 1 | 3 | 3 | 1 |
| 149 | Zuni | 2 | 3 | 3 | 2 | - | 2 | 1 | - | 1 | 4 | 2 | 1 | 1 | 2 | 4 | 4 | 4 | 4 | 4 | 1 |
| 151 | Papago | 2 | 1 | 2 | 2 | 2 | 2 | 1 | - | 1 | 3 | 2 | 2 | 2 | 1 | 2 | 1 | 1 | 1 | 3 | 1 |
| 153 | Aztec | 3 | 3 | 3 | 3 | 3 | 2 | 1 | 1 | 1 | 4 | 1 | 2 | 1 | - | 1 | 1 | 1 | 3 | 3 | 2 |
| 155 | Quiche | 2 | - | 3 | 2 | 2 | 2 | 1 | - | - | 4 | 2 | 2 | 1 | 2 | 2 | 1 | 1 | 3 | 3 | 2 |
| 157 | Bribri | 2 | 1 | - | 1 | - | 2 | - | 1 | - | 4 | 2 | - | 1 | - | 2 | 2 | 3 | 3 | 3 | 1 |
| 159 | Goajiro | 2 | 3 | 3 | - | 3 | 2 | 1 | 1 | 1 | 3 | 2 | 2 | 2 | 3 | 2 | 2 | 2 | 3 | 3 | 2 |
| 161 | Callinago | 4 | 2 | 3 | 4 | 3 | 2 | - | 1 | 1 | 5 | 3 | 2 | - | 1 | 3 | 3 | 2 | 3 | 3 | 1 |
| 163 | Yanomamo | - | 1 | 1 | 1 | 2 | 2 | 1 | 1 | 1 | 4 | 1 | 1 | 1 | 2 | - | 3 | 2 | 3 | 3 | 2 |
| 165 | Saramacca | 3 | 2 | 1 | - | 3 | 2 | 3 | 1 | 1 | 5 | 2 | 2 | 2 | 2 | 4 | 3 | 4 | 3 | 3 | 2 |
| 167 | Cubeo | 1 | 2 | 1 | 1 | 3 | 2 | 1 | 2 | 1 | 4 | 3 | 2 | 1 | 2 | 3 | - | 3 | 3 | 3 | 2 |
| 169 | Jivaro | 4 | 3 | 1 | 1 | 3 | - | 1 | 1 | 2 | 5 | 2 | 3 | - | 2 | 3 | 1 | 4 | 4 | 3 | 2 |
| 171 | Inca | 3 | 3 | 2 | 2 | 2 | 2 | 1 | 1 | 1 | 5 | 2 | 2 | 1 | 3 | 1 | 1 | 2 | 3 | 3 | 1 |
| 173 | Siriono | 1 | 1 | - | - | 3 | 2 | 1 | 1 | - | 5 | 2 | 3 | 1 | 3 | 3 | 3 | 2 | 3 | 3 | 2 |
| 175 | Trumai | 3 | 2 | 2 | 1 | 2 | 2 | 1 | - | 1 | 4 | 2 | - | 1 | 3 | 1 | 1 | 1 | 2 | 2 | 1 |
| 177 | Tupinamba | - | 2 | 2 | 1 | 2 | 2 | 1 | 1 | 2 | 4 | 3 | 2 | 1 | 1 | - | 3 | - | - | 3 | 1 |
| 179 | Shavante | 1 | 2 | - | 1 | 2 | 2 | 1 | 1 | 1 | 6 | 3 | 2 | 2 | 2 | - | 1 | 1 | 3 | 3 | 1 |
| 181 | Cayua | - | - | 3 | 2 | - | 2 | - | 1 | - | 6 | 2 | 2 | 2 | - | 3 | 2 | 3 | 3 | 3 | - |
| 183 | Abipon | 2 | - | 4 | 4 | 3 | 1 | 1 | - | 1 | 5 | 3 | 2 | 2 | 1 | - | - | 2 | 3 | 3 | 2 |
| 185 | Tehuelche | 1 | 1 | 2 | 3 | 4 | 2 | 1 | 1 | 1 | 3 | 2 | 2 | 2 | ꞌ | 3 | - | 2 | - | 3 | 1 |

TABLE 2 (continued)

| Area | Society | 21 | 22 | 23 | 24 | 25 | 26 | 27 | 28 | 29 | 30 | 31 | 32 | 33 | 34 | 35 | 36 | 37 |
|------|---------|----|----|----|----|----|----|----|----|----|----|----|----|----|----|----|----|----|
| 097 | Lesu | 2 | 2 | 3 | 2 | 2 | 2 | 2 | 3 | 3 | 2 | 2 | 2 | - | 3 | 3 | 2 | 5 |
| 099 | Siuai | 2 | 2 | 2 | 1 | 2 | 2 | 2 | 2 | 3 | 4 | 2 | 1 | - | - | 3 | 2 | 5 |
| 101 | Pentecost | - | 2 | 1 | - | 2 | 1 | 1 | - | - | 2 | 3 | - | - | 1 | 3 | - | 4 |
| 103 | Ajie | 2 | - | 1 | 3 | 2 | 2 | - | 3 | 3 | 1 | 3 | 1 | 2 | - | 3 | 2 | 3 |
| 105 | Marquesans | 2 | 2 | 3 | - | 2 | 2 | 1 | 3 | 3 | - | 2 | 4 | - | 2 | 3 | - | - |
| 107 | Gilbertese | 1 | 3 | 3 | - | 2 | 2 | - | 1 | - | - | 1 | 1 | 1 | 1 | 3 | 2 | 5 |
| 109 | Truk | 2 | 2 | 3 | 1 | 1 | 2 | 2 | 3 | 3 | - | 3 | 3 | - | 3 | 3 | 2 | 5 |
| 111 | Palauans | 2 | 2 | 1 | - | 2 | 2 | 2 | 1 | 3 | 2 | 3 | 1 | 2 | 1 | 3 | 2 | - |
| 113 | Atayal | - | 1 | 1 | - | 2 | 2 | - | 1 | 2 | 5 | 3 | 3 | 2 | 1 | 3 | 2 | 1 |
| 115 | Manchu | 1 | 2 | 3 | 4 | 2 | 2 | 2 | 1 | 3 | 2 | 3 | 1 | 2 | 1 | 1 | 1 | 2 |
| 117 | Japanese | 1 | 1 | 1 | 3 | 2 | 2 | 2 | 3 | 3 | 2 | 3 | 3 | - | 1 | 3 | 1 | 3 |
| 119 | Gilyak | 2 | 3 | 3 | 2 | 2 | 2 | 2 | 3 | 2 | 1 | 2 | 1 | 1 | 1 | 4 | 2 | - |
| 121 | Chukchee | 2 | 2 | 3 | 4 | 2 | 2 | 2 | 2 | 2 | 3 | 2 | 2 | 1 | 1 | 3 | 2 | 3 |
| 123 | Aleut | - | - | - | 6 | 2 | 2 | 2 | 2 | - | 2 | 3 | 3 | - | 2 | 3 | 2 | - |
| 125 | Montagnais | 2 | 1 | 2 | 1 | 2 | 2 | - | 3 | 3 | - | 3 | 3 | 1 | 1 | 2 | 2 | 4 |
| 127 | Salteaux | 1 | 1 | 3 | 2 | 2 | 1 | 2 | 1 | - | 4 | 3 | 3 | - | 1 | 3 | 1 | 2 |
| 129 | Kaska | 1 | 2 | 2 | 7 | 2 | 1 | 2 | 1 | 3 | 3 | 2 | 1 | 1 | 3 | 3 | - | 3 |
| 131 | Haida | 2 | 2 | 3 | 2 | 2 | 2 | 1 | 4 | 3 | - | 2 | 1 | 1 | 3 | 3 | 2 | - |
| 133 | Twana | 1 | 1 | 2 | 7 | 2 | 1 | 1 | - | 3 | 5 | 2 | 1 | 1 | 1 | 3 | 2 | - |
| 135 | Pomo | 1 | 2 | 1 | 5 | 2 | 1 | 1 | 3 | 3 | 5 | 3 | 3 | 2 | 2 | 3 | 2 | 5 |
| 137 | Paiute | 1 | 2 | 3 | 7 | 2 | 2 | 2 | 4 | 2 | - | 1 | 2 | 1 | 3 | 3 | 2 | 4 |
| 139 | Kutenai | 2 | 2 | 1 | - | 2 | 2 | 1 | 3 | 2 | - | 3 | 3 | 1 | 3 | 3 | 2 | 5 |
| 141 | Hidatsa | 1 | - | 1 | 6 | 3 | 1 | - | 4 | 3 | 2 | 1 | 1 | 1 | 3 | 3 | 1 | - |
| 143 | Omaha | 2 | 2 | 1 | 6 | 2 | 2 | - | 2 | 3 | 3 | 1 | 1 | 1 | - | 3 | 1 | 5 |
| 145 | Creek | 2 | 2 | 1 | 7 | 3 | 3 | 1 | 3 | 3 | 4 | 2 | 1 | 1 | 3 | 3 | 1 | - |
| 147 | Comanche | 2 | 1 | 2 | 7 | 2 | 2 | 2 | 2 | 2 | 2 | 1 | 2 | 1 | 1 | 3 | 2 | 5 |
| 149 | Zuni | 1 | 1 | 3 | 1 | 2 | 2 | 2 | 3 | 3 | - | 3 | 3 | 2 | 3 | 3 | 2 | 5 |
| 151 | Papago | - | 1 | 2 | 7 | 2 | 2 | 2 | 2 | 3 | - | 1 | 1 | 1 | 1 | 2 | 2 | 4 |
| 153 | Aztec | 1 | 2 | 1 | - | 2 | 2 | 2 | 3 | 3 | 5 | 2 | 1 | 1 | 3 | 2 | 2 | 4 |
| 155 | Quiche | 2 | 2 | 1 | - | 2 | 2 | 2 | 3 | 2 | 4 | 3 | 1 | 2 | 1 | 4 | 1 | - |
| 157 | Bribri | - | - | - | 6 | 2 | 2 | - | - | 2 | 3 | 1 | 1 | - | 1 | 3 | - | 5 |
| 159 | Goajiro | - | 1 | 3 | 3 | 2 | 1 | 2 | 2 | 2 | 2 | 2 | 1 | 1 | 3 | 3 | 2 | 4 |
| 161 | Callinago | - | 1 | 1 | 7 | 2 | 2 | 2 | 3 | - | 1 | 2 | 1 | 1 | 3 | 1 | 2 | 2 |
| 163 | Yanomamo | - | 2 | 2 | 3 | 2 | 2 | 2 | 1 | 2 | 3 | 1 | 1 | 1 | 1 | 3 | 2 | 5 |
| 165 | Saramacca | 1 | - | 3 | 7 | 2 | 2 | - | 3 | 3 | 2 | 1 | 1 | 1 | 2 | 3 | 2 | 2 |
| 167 | Cubeo | - | 1 | 2 | 6 | 1 | 3 | 2 | 3 | 3 | 1 | 3 | 1 | 2 | 1 | 3 | 2 | 2 |
| 169 | Jivaro | 2 | 1 | 2 | 3 | 1 | 1 | - | 2 | 1 | 3 | 1 | 1 | 1 | 1 | 3 | 2 | 5 |
| 171 | Inca | 1 | 2 | 1 | - | 2 | 2 | 2 | 3 | 3 | 5 | 2 | 1 | 1 | 2 | 3 | 1 | - |
| 173 | Siriono | 2 | 1 | 3 | 4 | 2 | 3 | 2 | 3 | 3 | - | 1 | 1 | 1 | 3 | 1 | 2 | 2 |
| 175 | Trumai | 1 | 1 | 2 | 5 | 2 | 2 | - | 4 | 2 | 5 | 2 | 1 | 1 | 1 | 3 | - | 1 |
| 177 | Tupinamba | 2 | 1 | 1 | 5 | 1 | 2 | 2 | - | - | 3 | 2 | 1 | 1 | 1 | 3 | 1 | 5 |
| 179 | Shavante | - | τ | 1 | 2 | 1 | 1 | 2 | 2 | 1 | - | 1 | 1 | 1 | 3 | 2 | 2 | 5 |
| 181 | Cayua | - | - | - | - | 2 | 2 | - | - | - | 3 | 3 | 1 | - | 1 | 3 | - | - |
| 183 | Abipon | 2 | 2 | 1 | - | 2 | 2 | - | 2 | 2 | 2 | 2 | 1 | 2 | - | 1 | 2 | 5 |
| 185 | Tehuelche | 1 | - | - | - | 2 | 2 | 2 | 3 | 3 | 5 | 2 | 1 | 2 | 1 | 3 | - | 4 |

TABLE 2 (continued)

| Area | Society | 38 | 39 | 40 | 41 | 42 | 43 | 44 | 45 | 46 | 47 | 48 | 49 | 50 | 51 | 52 | 53 | 54 |
|------|---------|----|----|----|----|----|----|----|----|----|----|----|----|----|----|----|----|----|
| 097 | Lesu | - | - | 3 | 2 | 2 | 3 | 2 | 1 | 2 | 2 | 4 | 2 | 3 | 2 | 1 | 3 | 2 |
| 099 | Siuai | 3 | 2 | 3 | 2 | - | 3 | 2 | 1 | 1 | 1 | 1 | 2 | 3 | 2 | 2 | 2 | 2 |
| 101 | Pentecost | 3 | - | - | 2 | - | 2 | 2 | - | - | - | 1 | 2 | 1 | 2 | 1 | 3 | 3 |
| 103 | Ajie | 2 | 4 | - | 2 | - | 2 | 2 | - | - | - | 1 | 2 | 1 | 2 | 1 | 2 | 3 |
| 105 | Marquesans | 1 | 2 | 2 | 1 | 2 | 2 | 2 | 1 | 1 | 2 | 1 | 2 | 2 | 1 | 1 | 3 | 3 |
| 107 | Gilbertese | 4 | 3 | 2 | 2 | - | 2 | 2 | 1 | 1 | 2 | - | 2 | 3 | 2 | 1 | 3 | 1 |
| 109 | Truk | 1 | 1 | - | 2 | 2 | 2 | 2 | 1 | 1 | - | 1 | 2 | 3 | 2 | 1 | 4 | 3 |
| 111 | Palauans | 3 | - | 2 | 2 | - | 3 | 2 | 1 | 1 | 1 | 1 | 2 | 2 | 2 | 3 | 1 | 2 |
| 113 | Atayal | - | - | 3 | 2 | 2 | 2 | 2 | - | 2 | 1 | 1 | 2 | - | 2 | 2 | 3 | 3 |
| 115 | Manchu | - | - | 2 | 1 | 2 | 3 | 2 | 2 | 1 | - | - | 1 | 3 | 1 | 1 | 3 | 3 |
| 117 | Japanese | 3 | 4 | 5 | 1 | 2 | 3 | 3 | - | 1 | 1 | 1 | 3 | 3 | 1 | 2 | 2 | 3 |
| 119 | Gilyak | 1 | 1 | 3 | 2 | 2 | 2 | 2 | 1 | 1 | 1 | 2 | 2 | 2 | 2 | 2 | 3 | 2 |
| 121 | Chukchee | - | - | 4 | 1 | 2 | 2 | 1 | 3 | 1 | 2 | 3 | 2 | 1 | 1 | 1 | 2 | 2 |
| 123 | Aleut | 3 | 2 | 2 | 2 | 2 | 2 | 2 | - | - | 1 | - | 2 | 2 | 2 | 1 | 2 | 2 |
| 125 | Montagnais | 4 | 3 | 1 | 1 | 2 | 2 | 2 | 2 | 2 | - | 3 | 2 | 2 | 2 | 1 | 3 | 3 |
| 127 | Salteaux | 4 | 4 | 4 | 2 | - | 2 | 2 | - | 1 | - | 1 | 2 | 2 | 1 | 1 | 3 | 2 |
| 129 | Kaska | 4 | 3 | 4 | 2 | 2 | 3 | 2 | - | 1 | - | 2 | 2 | 2 | 2 | 3 | 4 | 2 |
| 131 | Haida | 4 | 3 | 1 | 3 | 2 | 2 | 2 | 2 | 2 | 2 | 4 | 2 | 3 | 2 | 1 | 3 | 2 |
| 133 | Twana | 2 | 3 | 1 | 2 | - | 2 | 2 | - | - | 2 | 3 | 2 | - | 2 | 1 | 3 | 2 |
| 135 | Pomo | - | 3 | 3 | 2 | 2 | 2 | 1 | 3 | 2 | 2 | 3 | 2 | 3 | 2 | 1 | 3 | 3 |
| 137 | Paiute | 3 | - | 1 | 2 | 2 | 2 | 2 | 3 | 2 | 2 | 4 | 2 | 3 | 2 | 1 | 3 | 2 |
| 139 | Kutenai | 3 | 3 | 1 | 2 | 2 | 2 | 2 | - | - | 1 | 2 | 2 | 2 | 2 | 1 | 3 | 3 |
| 141 | Hidatsa | 4 | 3 | 1 | 2 | 2 | 2 | 2 | - | - | - | 1 | 2 | 1 | 2 | 1 | 4 | 1 |
| 143 | Omaha | 3 | 3 | - | 2 | 2 | 3 | 3 | 3 | - | 1 | 1 | 2 | 2 | 2 | 2 | 3 | 1 |
| 145 | Creek | 4 | 4 | 5 | 2 | 2 | 2 | 2 | - | 1 | 2 | 1 | 2 | 1 | 1 | 1 | 3 | 2 |
| 147 | Comanche | 4 | - | 2 | 1 | 2 | 2 | 3 | 1 | 1 | 2 | 1 | 2 | 1 | 2 | 1 | 3 | 2 |
| 149 | Zuni | 4 | 3 | 1 | 3 | 2 | 3 | 2 | 1 | - | 2 | 1 | 2 | 3 | 2 | 1 | 4 | 3 |
| 151 | Papago | - | 2 | 4 | 2 | 2 | 2 | 3 | 2 | 1 | 2 | 4 | 2 | 2 | 2 | 1 | 2 | 1 |
| 153 | Aztec | 2 | 3 | 2 | 2 | - | 2 | 2 | 2 | - | - | - | 1 | 2 | 2 | 2 | 2 | 2 |
| 155 | Quiche | 4 | 2 | 2 | 2 | 2 | 2 | 2 | 2 | 1 | - | 2 | 2 | 3 | 2 | 2 | 2 | 3 |
| 157 | Bribri | 3 | 4 | 1 | 2 | - | 2 | 2 | 3 | 3 | - | 1 | 2 | - | 2 | 3 | 3 | 1 |
| 159 | Goajiro | 3 | 3 | 6 | 2 | 2 | 2 | 2 | 1 | 1 | 2 | 4 | 3 | 2 | 2 | 2 | 3 | 2 |
| 161 | Callinago | - | - | 2 | 2 | 2 | 2 | 2 | 3 | 1 | 2 | 3 | 2 | 1 | 1 | 1 | 3 | 2 |
| 163 | Yanomamo | 4 | 3 | 2 | 1 | 1 | 3 | 3 | 1 | 1 | 1 | 5 | 2 | 1 | 1 | 1 | 3 | 1 |
| 165 | Saramacca | 4 | 2 | 1 | 2 | - | 2 | 2 | - | - | - | 1 | 2 | 2 | 2 | 3 | 4 | 1 |
| 167 | Cubeo | 3 | - | 1 | 1 | 1 | 3 | 3 | 1 | - | - | 2 | 2 | 2 | 2 | 1 | 3 | 3 |
| 169 | Jivaro | 4 | 3 | 1 | 2 | 2 | 2 | 2 | 1 | - | 2 | 4 | 2 | 1 | 2 | 3 | 3 | 1 |
| 171 | Inca | - | - | 4 | 2 | 2 | 2 | 2 | - | 1 | - | 4 | 2 | 1 | 1 | 1 | 2 | 2 |
| 173 | Siriono | 3 | 3 | 5 | 1 | 2 | 2 | 3 | 2 | 1 | 2 | 4 | 2 | 1 | 2 | 1 | 3 | 1 |
| 175 | Trumai | - | - | 1 | 1 | 1 | 2 | 2 | 1 | 1 | - | - | 2 | 1 | 2 | 1 | 2 | 2 |
| 177 | Tupinamba | 4 | - | 1 | 3 | 2 | 2 | 2 | - | - | 2 | 5 | 2 | 1 | 2 | 1 | 3 | 2 |
| 179 | Shavante | 3 | - | 3 | 2 | 2 | 3 | 1 | - | 1 | - | 1 | 2 | 1 | 2 | 2 | 2 | 1 |
| 181 | Cayua | - | - | - | 3 | - | 2 | 2 | - | - | - | - | 2 | 3 | 2 | 1 | 3 | 2 |
| 183 | Abipon | 1 | 3 | 3 | 3 | 3 | 2 | 2 | - | - | 1 | 5 | 2 | 1 | 2 | 1 | 3 | 2 |
| 185 | Tehuelche | - | 3 | 2 | 2 | - | 2 | 2 | 2 | 2 | 1 | 4 | 2 | 2 | 2 | 2 | 3 | 2 |

TABLE 2 (continued)

| Area | Society | 55 | 56 | 57 | 58 | 59 | 60 | 61 |
|------|---------|----|----|----|----|----|----|----|
| 097 | Lesu | 2 | 5 | 3 | 3 | 3 | 3 | 3 |
| 099 | Siuai | 2 | 5 | 3 | 1 | 3 | 3 | 2 |
| 101 | Pentecost | 3 | 2 | 4 | 1 | 2 | 1 | 2 |
| 103 | Ajie | 3 | 4 | 4 | 2 | 3 | 2 | 2 |
| 105 | Marquesans | 2 | 3 | 2 | 2 | 2 | 2 | 2 |
| 107 | Gilbertese | 2 | 4 | 3 | 2 | 3 | 3 | 3 |
| 109 | Truk | 2 | 3 | 1 | 1 | 3 | 3 | 1 |
| 111 | Palauans | 2 | 3 | 3 | 3 | 3 | 3 | 1 |
| 113 | Atayal | 3 | 5 | 3 | 2 | 2 | 3 | 1 |
| 115 | Manchu | 2 | 3 | 2 | 1 | 2 | 3 | 2 |
| 117 | Japanese | 2 | 4 | 3 | 1 | 2 | 3 | 2 |
| 119 | Gilyak | 2 | 3 | 1 | 1 | 3 | 3 | 1 |
| 121 | Chukchee | 3 | 4 | 2 | 2 | 2 | 3 | 3 |
| 123 | Aleut | 3 | 3 | 3 | 3 | 3 | 3 | 2 |
| 125 | Montagnais | 2 | 3 | 4 | 1 | 2 | 3 | 3 |
| 127 | Salteaux | 3 | 4 | 4 | 1 | 1 | 3 | 2 |
| 129 | Kaska | 3 | 3 | 3 | 2 | 2 | 3 | 2 |
| 131 | Haida | 3 | 4 | 4 | 2 | 3 | 3 | 3 |
| 133 | Twana | 3 | 2 | 3 | 3 | 2 | 3 | 3 |
| 135 | Pomo | 3 | 3 | 4 | 2 | 2 | 3 | 3 |
| 137 | Paiute | 3 | 4 | 4 | 3 | 2 | 3 | 3 |
| 139 | Kutenai | 3 | 4 | 4 | 3 | 3 | 2 | 1 |
| 141 | Hidatsa | 3 | 3 | 4 | 2 | 2 | 2 | 1 |
| 143 | Omaha | 3 | 3 | 4 | 2 | 2 | 3 | 2 |
| 145 | Creek | 3 | 4 | 4 | 2 | 2 | 2 | 2 |
| 147 | Comanche | 2 | 3 | 3 | 3 | 2 | 3 | 3 |
| 149 | Zuni | 3 | 3 | 4 | 1 | 2 | 3 | 2 |
| 151 | Papago | 3 | 2 | 2 | 3 | 2 | ⌐ | ⌐ |
| 153 | Aztec | 3 | 3 | 3 | 2 | 2 | 3 | 2 |
| 155 | Quiche | 3 | 3 | 3 | 2 | 2 | 3 | 2 |
| 157 | Bribri | 3 | 3 | 4 | 2 | 3 | 3 | − |
| 159 | Goajiro | 2 | 3 | 3 | 3 | 2 | 3 | 3 |
| 161 | Callinago | 3 | 3 | 2 | 2 | 2 | 3 | 2 |
| 163 | Yanomamo | 1 | 3 | 3 | 2 | 3 | 3 | 2 |
| 165 | Saramacca | 3 | 3 | 4 | 3 | 2 | 3 | 2 |
| 167 | Cubeo | 1 | 3 | 4 | 2 | 2 | 3 | 2 |
| 169 | Jivaro | 2 | 4 | 4 | 3 | 2 | 1 | 3 |
| 171 | Inca | 3 | 4 | 2 | 2 | 2 | 3 | 3 |
| 173 | Siriono | 2 | 4 | 3 | 3 | 2 | 3 | 3 |
| 175 | Trumai | 1 | 3 | 2 | 2 | 1 | 2 | 3 |
| 177 | Tupinamba | 3 | 4 | 4 | 3 | 2 | 3 | 3 |
| 179 | Shavante | 3 | 5 | 3 | 2 | 3 | 3 | 2 |
| 181 | Cayua | 3 | 4 | − | 3 | − | 3 | 2 |
| 183 | Abipon | 3 | 4 | 2 | 3 | 3 | 1 | 1 |
| 185 | Tehuelche | 3 | 3 | 4 | 3 | 2 | 3 | 1 |

NOTES

1. This research was supported by a small grant from the National Institute of Mental Health, later supplemented by a faculty fellowship of the Rackham Graduate School of the University of Michigan. The author was assisted during the design stage by Kristin Moore and later in the analysis stage by Patricia Paul, both graduate students in sociology at the University of Michigan.
2. The order of steps in this scale departs from that found by most previous researchers. However, reversing steps 6 and 7 (to get the usual order) results in only a slight increase in scaling errors; in other words in our results these two customs tend in most instances to occur together, so that listing them as two separate steps in the scale is somewhat misleading.

## BIBLIOGRAPHY

Barry, H., III, and L. Paxson. 1971. Infancy and Childhood: Cross Cultural Codes 2. Ethnology 10: 446-508.

Broude, G. J., and S. J. Greene. 1976. Cross-Cultural Codes on Twenty Sexual Attitudes and Practices. Ethnology 15: 409-429.

Brown, J. K. 1963. A Cross-Cultural Study of Female Initiation Rites. American Anthropologist 65: 837-853.

Engels, F. 1902. The Origins of the Family, Private Property and the State. Chicago.

Goldberg, S. 1973. The Inevitability of Patriarchy. New York.

Heath, D. B. 1957. Sexual Division of Labor and Cross-Cultural Research. Social Forces 37: 77-79.

Murdock, G. P., and D. O. Morrow. 1970. Subsistence Economy and Supportive Practices. Ethnology 9: 302-330.

Murdock, G. P., and D. R. White. 1969. Standard Cross-Cultural Sample. Ethnology 8: 329-369.

Naroll, R. 1962. Data Quality Control. New York.

——— 1970. Galton's Problem. A Handbook of Method in Cultural Anthropology, ed. R. Naroll and R. Cohen, pp. 974-989. Garden City.

Stephens, W. 1963. The Family in Cross-Cultural Perspective. New York.

Wallace, D. L. 1968. Clustering. International Encyclopedia of the Social Sciences, pp. 519-524. New York.

Whyte, M. K. 1978. The Status of Women in Preindustrial Societies. Princeton.

Young, F. W. 1965. Initiation Ceremonies. Indianapolis.

## SUPPLEMENTARY BIBLIOGRAPHY

The following sources were used as supplementary texts in the coding procedure.

75: *Khmer Cambodians ca. 1860*

Aymonier, E. 1900. The Modern Kingdom of Cambodia. Paris (translated in HRAF).

Porée-Maspéro, E. (ed) 1958. Cérémonies privées des Cambodgiens. Institut bouddhique. Phnom-Penh.

Delvert, J. 1961. Le Paysan Cambodgien. Paris.

Ebihara, M. 1964. Khmer. Ethnic Groups of Mainland Southeast Asia, ed. F. LeBar, G. Hickey, and J. Musgrave, pp. 94-104. New Haven.

Porée, G., and E. Maspéro. 1938. Traditions and Customs of the Khmer. Paris (translated in the HRAF).

Steinberg, D. J. 1959. Cambodia. New Haven.

105: *Marquesans ca. 1860*

Handy, E. S. C. 1923. The Native Culture in the Marquesas. Bulletins of the Bernice P. Bishop Museum No. 9. Honolulu.

Handy, W. C. 1922. Tattooing in the Marquesas. Bulletins of the Bernice P. Bishop Museum No. 1. Honolulu.

Linton, R. 1923. The Material Culture of the Marquesas Islands. Memoirs of the Bernice P. Bishop Museum, Vol. 8, No. 5. Honolulu.

——— 1939. Marquesan Culture. The Individual and His Society, ed. A. Kardiner, pp. 137-196. New York.

Suggs, R. C. 1963. Marquesan Sexual Behavior (ms. in HRAF).

Sullivan, L. R. 1923. Marquesan Somatology with Comparative Notes on Samoa and Tonga. Memoirs of the Bernice P. Bishop Museum, Vol. 9, No. 2. Honolulu.

II. Studies on Kinship from the Ethnographic Atlas

# 13

# Patterns of Sibling Terminology

*George Peter Murdock*

This paper began as a modest attempt to establish a viable classification of the kinship terms used for siblings, along the lines of the widely accepted patterns worked out by Lowie (1928) and Kirchhoff (1932) for avuncular and nepotic terms and by Spier (1925) and Murdock (1949) for cousin terminology. To this end, the terms most commonly employed for siblings were analyzed for 800 societies from all parts of the world, distributed as follows:

|  |  |
|---|---|
| Africa (sub-Saharan) | 200 |
| Circum-Mediterranean | 90 |
| East Eurasia | 95 |
| Insular Pacific | 135 |
| North America | 200 |
| South and Central America | 80 |

For Africa, aboriginal North America, and South America the coverage of the source materials was exhaustive. For the Circum-Mediterranean region, additional coverage, though possible, would merely have multiplied cases of the one predominant pattern found throughout the European and Arab worlds. For East Eurasia and the Insular Pacific the coverage was somewhat less than exhaustive and is possibly insufficient for four areas—India, the China-Indochina borderland, eastern Indonesia, and Melanesia.

As the study progressed, it generated unexpected insights into problems of linguistic classification, of the conditions of cultural diffusion, and of the functional analysis of social systems, with the result that what had appeared like a routine task became converted into an intellectually exciting adventure. It therefore seems advisable to orient the study briefly to previous kinship research.

## KINSHIP STUDY IN HISTORICAL PERSPECTIVE

*Period 1: The Founder.* The importance of kinship terminology was first recognized in the late nineteenth century by Lewis Henry Morgan (1870), whose achievement gains increasing luster with each passing year.

*Period 2: The Early Giants.* In the first quarter of the twentieth century the scientific contribution of Morgan was adopted, substantially revised, and enormously expanded by the anthropological leaders of the period, most notably by Rivers, Boas, Kroeber, Lowie, and Radcliffe-Brown. It was inconceivable to these men, or to the scholars they trained, that any ethnographic report could dispense with a full account and analysis of kinship terms and usages.

*Period 3: The Later Masters.* In the second quarter of the twentieth century, continuing kinship research reached new peaks in the hands of such figures as Firth and Fortes in Great Britain, Spier and Eggan in the United States, and Lévi-Strauss in France. This period witnessed an amazing efflorescence of wholly satisfying descriptive accounts and interpretations of social systems.

*Period 4: The Modern Innovators.* The third quarter of the twentieth century has seen the injection of new vigor and creativeness into the study of kinship terminology through the influence, particularly, of descriptive linguistics and cognitive psychology. The major contributions are (or are contained in) the following: Goodenough (1956, 1964), Lounsbury (1956, 1964), Wallace and Atkins (1960), Burling (1963), Romney and D'Andrade (1964), Buchler (1964, 1967), Hammel (1965), and Fritsch and Schutz (1967). Despite the striking fertility of research on kinship terminology in the hands of these scholars, certain self-styled "social anthropologists" today no longer report kinship terms in their monographs, or do so half-heartedly and incompletely[1]—a tendency that would profoundly have shocked the Early Giants and the Later Masters. Fortunately, this apathy and slackness have infected only a minority of the contemporary generation; satisfactory accounts of kinship terminology and behavior remain the rule rather than the exception.

While this paper continues the central tradition of the four periods outlined above, and is addressed with special appreciation to the Modern Innovators, it also derives inspiration from other sources. One is the reconstruction of patterns of kinship classification in proto-languages, notably by Hoijer (1956) for Athapaskan, by Callender (1962) and Hockett (1964) for Algonkian, and by Elmendorf (1961) for Salishan. A second is a tentative classification of sibling terminology by Nerlove and Romney (1967) with a demonstration of its theoretical significance. And very recently Pans (1967) has made an interesting attempt to establish interrelationships among subsets of kinship terms for a large number of societies in New Guinea.

### THE SYSTEM OF CLASSIFICATION

It has been recognized, ever since the classic study by Kroeber (1909), that cultural patterns for classifying siblings depend on the application or nonapplication, in varying combinations, of particular distinguishing criteria, of which the most important are relative age (older or younger than Ego), sex (male or female), and relative sex (the sex of Ego relative to that of the sibling, i.e., same or opposite). Theoretical preconceptions quickly proved fallible and were abandoned in favor of empiricism. Every pattern of classification in the 800 societies was noted, the frequency of occurrence of each was computed, all patterns of low frequency were given subordinate status, and certain patterns were combined when they were discovered to be functional alternatives.

Although Nerlove and Romney (1967) have shown that 4,140 distinct patterns of classifying siblings are logically possible, using only the criteria of relative age, sex, and relative sex, I have found that seven basic types, even when defined with extreme rigor, are sufficient to encompass all but 70 of the 800 societies surveyed. Moreover, I encountered no difficulty in assigning all 70 of the apparent exceptions to one of the seven basic types as "minor variants" differing from the basic pattern only in some relatively insignificant respect. These minor variants are indicated by an asterisk (*) in the complete listing of the societies by type and linguistic affiliation in an appendix. The seven basic patterns of classification are named and defined below.

*Type A: The Kordofanian or Undifferentiated Sibling Type.* Defined by the absence of any distinctions among siblings, whether of relative age, of sex, or of relative sex. The prevailing pattern is a single term, which may be glossed as "sibling." This pattern was discovered to characterize 69 of the 800 societies.

*Type B: The Yoruba or Relative Age Type.* Defined by a single distinction, that of relative age. The prevailing pattern is a pair of terms, which may be glossed as "elder sibling" and "younger sibling." This pattern was found in 86 of the 800 societies.

*Type C: The Algonkian or Skewed Age Type.* Defined by the distinction of relative age with a supplementary distinction of sex for elder siblings alone. The prevailing pattern consists of three terms, which may be glossed as "elder brother," "elder sister," and "younger sibling." Logically, this type is intermediate between Types B and D, and might have been considered a mere subtype of either. However, the frequency of its occurrence—in 74 of the 800 societies—warrants giving it independent status.

*Type D: The Dravidian or Age-Sex Type.* Defined by distinctions both of relative age and of sex. The prevailing pattern has four terms, which may be glossed as "elder brother," "elder sister," "younger brother," and "younger sister." This pattern was found in 177 of the 800 societies.

*Type E: The European or Brother-Sister Type.* Defined by a single distinction, that of sex. The prevailing pattern has two terms, which may be glossed as "brother" and "sister." The sample includes 156 societies characterized by this pattern. Most of the "minor variants" add partial age distinctions; full recognition of relative age would automatically throw a society into Type D.

*Type F: The Melanesian or Relative Sex Type.* Defined by primary distinctions of relative sex, which may assume one of four essentially alternative forms. Disregarding partial age distinctions, these result in four related patterns:

1. Two terms, which may be glossed as "sibling of the same sex as Ego" and "sibling of opposite sex." This pattern was found in 80 societies.

2. Three terms, glossed as "sibling of the same sex," "brother (woman speaking)," and "sister (man speaking)." This pattern was found in 63 societies.

3. Three terms, glossed as "sibling of opposite sex," "brother (man speaking)," and "sister (woman speaking)." This pattern was found in 32 societies.

4. Four terms, glossed as "brother (man speaking)," "brother (woman speaking)," "sister (man speaking)," and "sister (woman speaking)." This pattern was found in 26 societies.

These four patterns are classed as subtypes in the appendix but are treated as equivalent in the discussion. Together they account for 201 of the 800 societies, and thus constitute the most numerous of the seven types.

*Type G: The Siouan or Complexly Differentiated Type.* Defined by the application of all three distinctions—relative age, sex, and relative sex—to such an extent as to prevent recognition of any possibly more basic pattern. All of the 37 societies placed in this category recognize at least six distinct terms for siblings, and some make the maximum possible number of distinctions, thus arriving at eight different terms—glossed as "elder brother (man speaking)," "elder brother (woman speaking)," "younger brother (man speaking)," "younger brother (woman speaking)," "elder sister (man speaking)," "elder sister (woman speaking)," "younger sister (man speaking)," and "younger sister (woman speaking)."

To Europeans, terms meaning "brother" and "sister" seem somehow "natural." The foregoing classification, however, reveals that only societies with Type E, comprising fewer than 20 per cent of all the world's peoples, actually have terms that can be glossed as "brother" and "sister"—one more example of anthropology's destruction of ethnocentric illusions!

## DISTRIBUTION OF TYPES

The seven basic patterns of sibling classification are distributed very unevenly over the earth. This is shown in Table 1, which for the sake of clarity uses percentages rather than actual figures. Type A is strongest in Africa, Types B and F in the Insular Pacific, Type C in North America, Type D in East Eurasia, and Type G in South America, while Type E preponderates overwhelmingly in the Circum-Mediterranean region.

There are only two regions in the world where the distribution of types of sibling terminology assumes primarily a territorial character, overriding linguistic boundaries. The first covers most of northern and northeastern Africa, all of Europe, and a large section of southwestern Asia; here Type E encompasses nearly all the societies which speak languages of the large Afroasiatic (or Hamito-Semitic), Chari-Nile (or Sudanic), Indo-European, and Uralic linguistic families and the smaller Abasgo-Kerketian, Basque, Georgian, and Koman families. The second such region, characterized by sibling terms of Type D, extends throughout most of the area of ancient higher civilization in Asia and embraces the majority of societies which

TABLE 1

Distribution of Patterns of Sibling Classification by Major Regions
(in percentages)

| Type | Africa | Circum-Medit. | East Eurasia | Insular Pacific | North America | South America | World Total |
|---|---|---|---|---|---|---|---|
| A (Kor.) | 23½ | 1 | 1 | 10 | 1½ | 4 | 9 |
| B (Yor.) | 7½ | 7 | 12½ | 16 | 11½ | 11 | 11 |
| C (Alg.) | 3 | 1 | 13½ | 9 | 17 | 10 | 9 |
| D (Dra.) | 8 | 14½ | 42 | 7 | 39 | 26½ | 22 |
| E (Eur.) | 27½ | 73 | 17 | 3 | 2½ | 12½ | 19½ |
| F (Mel.) | 30½ | 3½ | 8 | 54 | 20 | 20 | 25 |
| G (Siou.) | 0 | 0 | 6 | 1 | 8½ | 16 | 4½ |
| Total | 100 | 100 | 100 | 100 | 100 | 100 | 100 |

speak languages of the Dravidian, Japano-Ryukyuan, and Sinitic linguistic families and of the Indic subfamily of Indo-European, the Munda subfamily of Mon-Khmer, the northern speakers of Tibeto-Burman, and the Tungusic and Turkic subfamilies of Altaic.

Everywhere else in the world the distribution of types of sibling terminology follows very closely the boundaries of known linguistic divisions, especially language families and subfamilies. In only three instances have I found terminological types to coincide with proposed larger linguistic groupings or phyla. The speakers of Mixtecan and of Zapotecan, which together form the proposed Mixteco-Zapotecan phylum, are characterized by sibling terms of Type F, and the Ge phylum, embracing the Caingang and Ge families, employs terms of Type B. Similarly the speakers of Chemakuan, Salishan, and Wakashan languages, which are grouped in the proposed Mosan linguistic phylum, predominantly use sibling terms of Type B. The proposed Papuan or Indo-Pacific phylum is interesting because its 27 representatives in the sample exemplify all seven of the types. Although this phylum has not yet been analyzed definitively into families, a cursory comparison of my typological findings with the language groupings proposed thus far by Cowan, Greenberg, and Wurm strongly suggests that a close correlation will ultimately be established.

By chance alone, since there are seven possible alternatives of classification, it would happen only rarely that the majority of societies of any sizable language family or subfamily would exhibit sibling terms primarily of one particular type. Yet this is what actually happens in most cases. Listed below for each type are all the linguistic groupings of which a clear majority of the component societies surveyed conform to the type in question.[2]

## Type A

Linguistic families of large or moderate size: Kordofanian.
Small families: Ainu, Chocoan, Guatoan, Tarascan, Tequistlatecan.
Subfamilies: Kwa (of Niger-Congo), Wishoskan (of Ritwan).

## Type B

Large or moderate families: Ge, Piman, Salishan, Yukian.
Small families: Andamanese, Caingang, Chemakuan, Thai-Kadai, Trumaian, Wakashan.
Subfamilies: Semang-Sakai (of Mon-Khmer).

## Type C

Large or moderate families: Algonkian, Tanoan.
Small families: Annam-Muong, Chinantecan, Gilyak, Jicaquean, Mizocuavean
Subfamilies: Mongolic (of Altaic), Southern Mayan.

## Type D

Large or moderate families: Arawakan, Athapaskan, Australian, Dravidian, Hokan, Japano-Ryukyuan, Penutian, Shoshonean, Sinitic, Taracahitian.
Small families: Betoyan, Bororan, Chitimachan, Guahiban, Kanuric (Central Saharan), Kitunahan (Kutenai), Mataco-Mateguayo, Nahuatlan, Nambicuaran, Salivan, Songhaic, Tehuelchean, Uru-Chipayan, Washoan, Yakonan, Zunian.
Subfamilies: Aymaran (of Kechumaran), Khasi-Nicobarese (of Mon-Khmer), Lutuamian (of Sahaptin), Mande (of Niger-Congo), Munda (of Mon-Khmer), Northern Iroquoian, Tibetan (of Tibeto-Burman), Tungusic (of Altaic).

## Type E

Large or moderate families: Afroasiatic (Hamito-Semitic), Chari-Nile (Sudanic), Indo-European, Uralic.
Small families: Abasgo-Kerketian, Basque, Georgian, Koman, Tucunan, Uchean (Yuchi), Yahgan, Yeniseian (Ket).
Subfamilies: Southern Khoisan (Bushman-Hottentot).

## Type F

Large or moderate families: Caddoan, Chibchan, Eskimauan, Keresan, Malayo-Polynesian [see special discussion below], Natchez-Muskogean. Also Coastal Nadene (including Eyak, Haida, and Tlingit), herewith suggested as a subphylum of Nadene co-ordinate with Athapaskan on the basis of the similarity of the three societies in the classification of siblings.
Small families: Araucanian, Burushaski (Burusho), Carajan, Chimmesyan (Tsimshian), Furian, Jivaran, Kiowan, Korean, Misumalpan, Mixtecan, Witotan, Zapotecan.
Subfamilies: Bantoid (Central Niger-Congo), Northern Khoisan (Sandawe), Northern Mayan, Quechuan (of Kechumaran), Southern Iroquoian, Weitspekan (of Ritwan).

## Type G

Large or moderate families: Cariban, Siouan, Tupi-Guarani.
Small families: Coahuiltecan, Serian, Warrauan.
Subfamilies: Shahaptian (of Sahaptin).

The above tabulation reveals 108 linguistic groupings in each of which a single type of sibling terminology is numerically preponderant. Contrasting with this showing there are only twelve linguistic groupings within which no single sibling type achieves a majority. Four are small families with two representatives of divergent types—Guaycuran, Luorawetlan, Oto-Manguean, and Miao-Yao. The several types found in Tibeto-Burman are probably correlated with subfamilies, and in six other groups—the Turkic subfamily of Altaic, the Southern subfamily of Athapaskan, the Cambodian subfamily of Mon-Khmer, and the Atlantic, Eastern, and Gur subfamilies of Niger-Congo—the types may well sort out according to linguistic divisions smaller than a subfamily. This leaves only the Chadic subfamily of Afroasiatic as a clearly aberrant case. The Dera, Margi, Masa, and Matakam of the sample stand alone in retaining the Type E classification which predominates in all the other subfamilies of Afroasiatic—Berber, Cushitic, (Ancient) Egyptian, and Semitic. The remaining fourteen Chadic societies are distributed among Types A, B, C, and D in a manner which shows little correlation with the latest linguistic classification of the subfamily (Newman and Ma 1966).

Incidentally, the time depth of Type E in Afroasiatic is phenomenal. It is attested for the Babylonians of the time of Hammurabi, for the Hebrews of the Old Testament, and for the Ancient Egyptians of the New Empire, as well as for the most remote representatives of the Berber and Cushitic subfamilies, respectively the extinct Guanche of the Canary Islands and the Iraqw of Tanzania.

### THE SPECIAL CASE OF MALAYO-POLYNESIAN

The peoples who speak Malayo-Polynesian languages extend from Madagascar in the west to Easter Island in the east; this is a spread of more than 200 degrees of longitude, greater than that of any other linguistic family of the world except Indo-European since the Discoveries Period. The sample of 800 societies includes 104 representatives of the family, a number exceeded only by Niger-Congo. Since World War II the Malayo-Polynesian languages have received an exceptional amount of attention from linguists. Yet, strangely enough, we still lack an authoritative classification into subfamilies such as we possess for practically every other well studied group of languages in the world. We are, however, provided with the basis for such a classification in the monumental lexicostatistical comparison of 245 Malayo-Polynesian languages by Dyen (1963; cf. also Murdock 1964). The present analysis of sibling terminology permits a very modest test of Dyen's results.

Dyen clearly recognizes a western or Hesperonesian subfamily of Malayo-Polynesian and specifies its eastern boundary. This falls between Sumbawa and Sumba (and Flores) in the south, between Celebes and Bura a bit farther north, between the Sangir Islands and Halmahera north of the Equator, between Palau and Yap in western Micronesia, and between the Marianas in the north and the Caroline Islands to the south thereof. Dyen specifically states that the Palauans and the Chamorro (of the Marianas) are most closely akin linguistically to the inhabitants of Celebes, whereas Yap has its affiliations, remote to be sure, with the east. Sibling terminology completely supports this grouping. Of the Malayo-Polynesian societies west of "Dyen's line" the majority (23) have sibling terms of Types A or B, whereas only five have terms of Type F. East of the line, however, 56 have terms of Type F, and only nine have Types A or B. This is strong supporting evidence that Dyen's Hesperonesian is a valid subfamily. And there seems no reason to disagree with him regarding the inclusion of most, if not all, of the Malayo-Polynesian languages of Formosa, the Philippines, western Indonesia, Madagascar, and the Asiatic mainland.

Dyen likewise appears to recognize a Moluccan subfamily extending from Sumba and Flores in the west to the Vogelkop region of western New Guinea in the east, as well as a Carolinian subfamily extending through Micronesia from Yap in the west to the Gilbert Islands in the east. Since the data on sibling terminology do not contradict these groupings, they have been accepted.

The Polynesian languages are distinctive, like the Polynesian cultures, though they are recognized as being closely cognate with the languages of Fiji, Rotuma, and perhaps the central New Hebrides. Until the exact limits of such a larger grouping are firmly established, however, it seems the part of wisdom to treat Polynesian as a fourth subfamily of Malayo-Polynesian, and this is done in the classification of sibling terminology in the appendix.

By a process of elimination this leaves us with Melanesia. Dyen postulates a division of the languages of this region into an old "Austronesian" stratum of scattered divergent groups and a "Heonesian" subfamily of Malayo-Polynesian proper. Since sibling terminology exhibits marked uniformity throughout Melanesia, Dyen's dichotomy receives no confirmation from this study and should probably be at least tentatively rejected. Consequently, Melanesian is herewith assumed to constitute an as yet indivisible subfamily.

The foregoing classification of Malayo-Polynesian subfamilies bears a remarkable resemblance to the traditional division of Oceania into Polynesia, Melanesia, Micronesia, and Indonesia. Perhaps this is what has inhibited its acceptance heretofore. Linguists are never more unhappy than when their meticulous researches merely confirm a previous unscientific classification.

## DIFFUSION AND ITS CIRCUMSTANCES

The evidence thus far presented indicates the stability of patterns of sibling terminology and their tendency to persist, often for thousands of years, among groups of societies which speak related languages. This is scarcely surprising in view of the fact that the terms themselves necessarily belong to the most basic portion of a people's basic vocabulary, which the glottochronologists have demonstrated to be especially resistant to replacement. Nevertheless, sibling terms can change by processes other than the genetic one of normal linguistic evolution. One of these processes is diffusion or cultural borrowing.

There is reason to suspect borrowing in the case of small societies speaking isolated languages when they are surrounded by much larger groups with an identical pattern of sibling terminology but different linguistic affiliations. Thus it is highly probable that the Basques borrowed the Type E pattern from the neighboring Indo-European peoples of France and Spain, rather than that the similarity is the result of pure chance or of diffusion in the opposite direction. The same interpretation is appropriate for the miniscule Uru tribe of Bolivia, which is completely encircled by Aymara with the same Type D pattern. The chances of accidental parallelism become even smaller when the shared pattern is a rare one, as in the case of the Warrau of the Orinoco delta, who must certainly have borrowed Type G from the surrounding Cariban peoples, who normally adhere to this exceptional pattern. Less certain but still reasonable is a similar assumption when the smaller society is merely adjacent to, rather than encircled by, a larger group with the same terminological pattern but a different linguistic affiliation, as in the case of the Tsimshian and the adjacent Coastal Nadene tribes with Type F. Reference to the appendix will reveal numerous other probable examples.

It should be remembered, however, that borrowing is far from inevitable, even for extremely small, isolated, and linguistically independent peoples. Thus the Ainu with Type A and the Gilyak with Type C have successfully resisted adopting the Type D pattern of their far stronger Japanese and Tungusic neighbors; the Burusho of the Hindu Kush with Type F have similarly withstood the surrounding Indo-European, Tibetan, and Turkic peoples with Types E or D; the Fur of Darfur retain Type F, although completely encircled by peoples with Type E; and the Tequistlatec with Type A have succumbed to the patterns of none of the neighboring peoples, neither the Nahua with Type D, the Zapotec with Type F, nor the Mizocuaven and Mayan peoples with Type C.

Diffusion can often be established with a high degree of probability for societies belonging to larger linguistic families by comparison of the prevailing patterns of sibling terminology among neighboring groups of differing languages. If a society belonging to a family normally characterized by one pattern reveals another pattern which is prevalent among neighboring societies of different linguistic affiliations, it is likely that the former has borrowed the pattern from the latter. For example, though Type C (with three terms—for elder brother, elder sister, and younger sibling) is the normal pattern among most Algonkian peoples, the Algonkian Blood of the northwestern Plains follow Type G in its most extreme form—with eight different sibling terms. Since this rare type is characteristic of the neighboring Siouan peoples, it is difficult to escape the conclusion that the Blood borrowed the pattern from the latter.

Numerous comparable examples could be cited, but one must suffice.

Type E is overwhelmingly predominant in the Chari-Nile or Sudanic family, including the Barabra or Nile Nubians of the Nubian subfamily. Yet two Nubian tribes—the Dilling and the Nyima—exhibit terms of Type A. These two tribes happen to live in the Nuba Hills, where most of the inhabitants speak languages of the Kordofanian family. Since most Kordofanians adhere to Type A, it is next to certain that the two Nubian tribes borrowed their pattern of sibling terminology from them.

Mere establishment of the fact, or at least the strong probability, of diffusion has far less theoretical interest than the determination of the circumstances under which diffusion occurs. Since patterns of sibling terminology are borrowed with relative infrequency, instances where this has happened often shed strong light on the predisposing circumstances. Three cases unearthed in the research seem particularly illuminating.

Certain of the Nguni tribes of southeast Africa, notably the Ndebele, Pondo, Swazi, and Zulu, employ sibling terms of Type E, which is exceptional among Bantu peoples and is not found elsewhere among them within a distance of less than 1,500 miles from the Nguni. Type E (the brother-sister type) is, however, the prevalent one among the neighboring Bushmen, from whom some of the Nguni peoples in question are known to have borrowed their "clicks" or implosive consonants. It is in the highest degree probable that sibling classification was borrowed from the Bushmen through the same process as that by which the clicks were transmitted, namely by the marriage of Bantu men to Bushmen women and the resulting acquisition by their children of certain linguistic patterns of their mothers.

In the Sahara Desert and the adjacent Central Sudan, the locus of the very ancient and important caravan trade with the Mediterranean coast, live four groups of peoples with differing linguistic affiliations but the same Type D pattern of classifying siblings. These are the Hausa and Songhai, who controlled the trade at its southern terminus in the east and west respectively, and the Teda and Tuareg, who actually escorted the camel caravans across the Sahara along the principal eastern and western routes respectively. The Tuareg belong to the Berber and the Hausa to the Chadic subfamily of the Afroasiatic family, within which, as we have seen, Type E is overwhelmingly the predominant pattern of sibling classification. Indeed, the three Tuareg tribes in the sample are the only Berbers, and the several Hausa groups almost the only Chadites, who follow Type D. On the other hand, the Songhaic and Kanuric families (the Teda belong to the latter) are normally characterized by Type D. Hence the pattern must have originated with one or the other of the latter groups rather than with either the Hausa or the Tuareg. The Songhai are the more likely source since they dominated the Sahara and Sudan politically from about 1000 to nearly 1600 A.D. What matters more than the determination of priorities, however, is the fact that all four groups were closely related economically through the caravan trade and were thoroughly habituated to intergroup co-operation, so that conditions in the region were supremely propitious for cultural and linguistic diffusion.

Although sibling terms of Type E are otherwise practically universal among peoples of Indo-European speech, the Bengali and Pahari of central India, the Chakma and Mogh of East Pakistan, and the Sinhalese and Vedda of Ceylon use terms of Type D, which is characteristic of most Dravidians. There can be little doubt that the occurrence of this pattern among these members of the Indic subfamily is the product of borrowing associated with the Aryan conquest of India and the prolonged interaction of the conquering group with the indigenous Dravidians.

## FUNCTIONAL DETERMINANTS

It has now been shown that (1) the process which governs the development of patterns of sibling terminology is most typically the genetic one which also governs the evolution of language itself, so that the patterns tend strongly toward correlation with linguistic groupings, but that (2) under particular sets of circumstances a second process intervenes, namely, that of cultural or linguistic borrowing or diffusion. There remains to be considered a third process, one involving functional determinants. This is an integrative process in which certain aspects of culture or social organization exert pressure on other aspects (through individual behavior, of course), thus tending to bring the latter into adaptive conformity with the former.

Functional determinants have been found operative in various aspects of culture, but particularly in social structure. They are known, for example, to affect kinship terminology (cf. Murdock 1949). Thus unilineal forms of social organization tend to result in the development of bifurcate merging terminology for avuncular and nepotic relatives, and the Crow and Omaha patterns of cousin terminology come into being, with insignificant exceptions, only under the influence, respectively, of matrilineally and patrilineally organized kin groups. The question may now be asked whether patterns of sibling terminology similarly reflect functional determinants to any significant extent.

As an exploratory test, the types of sibling terminology in the 800 societies were compared with the prevailing rules of descent in the same societies. These rules revealed the following distribution:

| | | |
|---|---|---|
| Ambilineal descent | 38 societies or | 4.75 per cent of the total |
| Bilateral descent | 262 societies or | 32.75 per cent of the total |
| Double descent | 29 societies or | 3.62 per cent of the total |
| Matrilineal descent | 109 societies or | 13.63 per cent of the total |
| Patrilineal descent | 362 societies or | 45.25 per cent of the total |
| Total | 800 societies or | 100.00 per cent of the total |

The above figures doubtless approximate within a few percentage points the actual distribution among all known societies.

The distribution of patterns of sibling terminology among the several rules of descent is shown in Table 2, where percentages rather than actual figures are employed to facilitate comparisons.

TABLE 2

Distribution of Types of Sibling Terminology by Rules of Descent
(in percentages)

| Sibling Terms | Ambilineal | Bilateral | Double | Matrilineal | Patrilineal |
|---|---|---|---|---|---|
| Type A | 8 | 5 | 17 | 10 | 10 |
| Type B | 10½ | 16 | 3 | 7 | 9 |
| Type C | 3 | 12 | 14 | 6 | 9 |
| Type D | 10½ | 26 | 14 | 21 | 21 |
| Type E | 5 | 16 | 7 | 6 | 29 |
| Type F | 63 | 15 | 45 | 48 | 20 |
| Type G | 0 | 10 | 0 | 2 | 2 |
| Total | 100 | 100 | 100 | 100 | 100 |

Table 2 suggests the following possibilities for the intervention of functional determinants:

1. Ambilineal descent appears especially conducive to the emergence of sibling terms of Type F.[3]
2. Bilateral descent appears relatively conducive to Types B, D, and G, and reveals a negative association with Types A and F.
3. Matrilineal and double descent appear especially conducive to Type F.
4. Patrilineal descent appears particularly conducive to Type E, despite the countervailing influence of a large number of bilateral European societies.
5. Except for differences in Types E and F, matrilineal and patrilineal societies show an almost identical profile, contrasting at almost every point with the profile of bilateral societies. This suggests that, except with respect to Types E and F, the influences exerted by unilineal descent (including double as well as matrilineal and patrilineal descent) are strikingly uniform and contrast as a unit with the impact of bilateral descent.

For reasons of space, and also because my ideas on the subject have not yet crystallized, I intend to content myself here with a presentation of the evidence and to defer until later, or leave to others, an analysis of the precise nature and mode of operation of the indicated functional determinants. Nevertheless, I would like to highlight somewhat more clearly the association between matrilineal descent and the Type F pattern of sibling terminology.

Only 25 per cent of all the societies of the sample exhibit sibling terminology of Type F, whereas 48 per cent of the matrilineal societies are characterized by this pattern. In other words, the incidence of Type F among matrilineal societies is approximately double that which might be expected by chance. Matrilineal societies with Type F sibling terminology number 52 and appear in ten widely scattered areas of the world, and in fourteen different linguistic families, as follows:

*Southern Africa*—Bemba, Chewa, Kunda, Lala, Lamba, Lele, Luwa, Nyanja, Pende, Sakata, Shila, Yao. All are Central Bantu tribes and hence belong to the Bantoid subfamily of the Niger-Congo linguistic family.

*Central Africa*—Fur, Longuda. The Fur belong to the independent Furian family, and the Longuda to the Eastern subfamily of Niger-Congo.

*Southeastern Asia*—Mnong Gar. This tribe belongs to the Cambodian subfamily of Mon-Khmer.

*Melanesia*—Dobuans, Kurtatchi, Lesu, Manus, Mota, Rossel, Rotumans, Santa Cruz, Siuai. The Rossel Islanders, the inhabitants of Santa Cruz, and the Siuai are "Papuan" in language, whereas the rest belong to the Melanesian subfamily of Malayo-Polynesian.

*Micronesia*—Bikinians, Ifaluk, Lamotrek, Majuro, Nomoians, Trukese, Ulithians. All belong to the Carolinian subfamily of Malayo-Polynesian.

*Northwestern North America*—Eyak, Haida, Tlingit, Tsimshian. The Tsimshian belong to the Chimmesyan linguistic family, the others to the Coastal Nadene subphylum.

*Central North America*—Mandan, Pawnee. The former tribe is Siouan in language, the latter Caddoan.

*Southeastern North America*—Cherokee, Chickasaw, Choctaw, Creek, Seminole, Timucua. The Cherokee are Iroquoian in language, whereas the others are Natchez-Muskogean.

*Southwestern North America*—Acoma, Cochiti, Laguna, Santa Ana, Santo Domingo, Sia, Western Apache. The Western Apache belong to the Southern subfamily of Athapaskan, and the remaining groups are Keresan.

*Central America*—Bribri, Guaymi. Both societies belong to the Chibchan family.

The correlation between sibling terminology of Type F and matrilineal descent is subjected to a chi square test in Table 3, and is found reliable. The interpretation of this finding might present a challenge to Schneider (cf. Schneider and Gough 1961) with his demonstrated interest and sophistication in the theoretical analysis of matrilineal institutions.

TABLE 3

Correlation of Type F Sibling Terminology with Matrilineal Descent

| | Type F | Other Types |
|---|---|---|
| Matrilineal descent | 52 | 57 |
| Other rules of descent | 149 | 542 |
| $r_\phi = 0.21$    $\chi^2 = 32.8$, $df = 1$, $p < .001$ | | |

Pans (1967) has argued for another type of functional determinant, namely, one having its source within the terminological system itself rather than in its social structural environment. He believes that the separate subsets within any kinship system, such as sibling terms, cousin terms, terms for parents and children, grandparental and grandchild terms, terms for avuncular and nepotic relatives, and terms for affinal kinsmen, should reveal a statistically demonstrable congruence with each other. Data in sufficient quantity for a test are available to me on only one subset other than siblings, namely, the classification of cousins as reported in Column 27 of the "Ethnographic Atlas." According to the hypothesis of Pans, sibling terminology should exert a strong influence on the pattern of cousin terminology, producing marked correlations between particular types of the two subsets. The actual relationships between these subsets are shown in Table 4.

TABLE 4

Correlations of Patterns of Sibling and Cousin Terminology

| Type of Sibling Terminology | Eskimo Cousin Terms | Hawaiian Cousin Terms | Iroquois Cousin Terms | Omaha Cousin Terms | Crow Cousin Terms | Anomalous Cousin Terms[4] | Total |
|---|---|---|---|---|---|---|---|
| Type A | 5 | 24 | 11 | 7 | 4 | 1 | 52 |
| Type B | 14 | 40 | 14 | 8 | 4 | 1 | 81 |
| Type C | 10 | 21 | 16 | 16 | 3 | 4 | 70 |
| Type D | 13 | 60 | 59 | 11 | 8 | 2 | 153 |
| Type E | 30 | 21 | 14 | 10 | 6 | 2 | 83 |
| Type F | 9 | 69 | 71 | 10 | 25 | 6 | 190 |
| Type G | 4 | 11 | 12 | 6 | 2 | 1 | 36 |
| Total | 85 | 246 | 197 | 68 | 52 | 17 | 665 |

Examination of Table 4 shows the expected correlations to be conspicuously absent; the types of the two subsets vary almost completely independently. The apparently disproportionate association of Eskimo cousin terminology with sibling terminology of Type E is probably an accidental by-product of their concurrence in a large number of European societies. The only other departure from a chance distribution is the greater frequency of Iroquois and Crow terminology in association with sibling terminology of Type F (the relative sex pattern). But this shows nothing that was not more clearly demonstrated in Table 3. Since matrilineal societies, which usually have either Iroquois or Crow cousin terminology, are especially strongly characterized by Type F, Iroquois and Crow terms inevitably preponderate there as well. The hypothesis advanced by Pans thus appears strikingly disconfirmed.

However, I have intentionally withheld from Table 4 one complete category of cousin terms—the descriptive type, in which the exact relationship of each cousin to Ego is spelled out, yielding terms that may be literally glossed as "father's brother's son," etc. There are 59 societies in the sample with descriptive terms for cousins, and these show correlations with patterns of sibling terminology that are by no means random. Not a single society among these 59 has sibling terms of Types B, C, F, or G; six have terms of Type D, and ten of Type A, whereas no fewer than 43, an enormous majority, have terms of Type E (the brother-sister type). This reveals a correlation between Type E sibling terms and descriptive cousin terminology that is highly reliable statistically—an association of precisely the kind that Pans predicted. Rather than supporting the general theory of Pans, however, this unique correlation has a very specific explanation.

The obvious function of descriptive terms is to distinguish different kinds of cousins. They do so by describing the genealogical routes connecting them with Ego through the latter's parents and parents' siblings, utilizing the prevailing sibling terminology for the connecting relatives in the parental generation. Now the various patterns of sibling terminology differ widely in their efficiency for this purpose. Type E distinguishes the kinds of cousins with maximal precision—and with no irrelevant information or "noise"—as "my father's brother's son," "my father's sister's daughter," "my mother's brother's child," etc. Type D does likewise but with unnecessary "noise" about relative age in the parental generation—"my father's elder brother's son," "my father's younger brother's son," etc.—so that the incidence of descriptive terms for cousins is substantially reduced. Type G introduces such excessive "noise"—"my father's elder-brother-man-speaking's son," "my father's younger-brother-man-speaking's son," etc.— that no society resorts to such description. Type A conveys minimal information; "my parent's sibling's child" distinguishes cousins from siblings but conveys nothing else of significance. It accomplishes the same purpose as Eskimo terminology—"my cousin"—in a relatively clumsy fashion, and consequently has a low incidence. Types B and C do likewise but with added "noise" about relative age, and hence do not occur at all. Type F conveys little except "noise"—"my parent's sibling-of-the-same-sex-man-speaking's son," "my parent's sibling-of-the-opposite-sex-woman-speaking's son," etc.—and its patent absurdity accounts for its nonoccurrence. The reason for the skewed distribution of descriptive cousin terminology thus resides in the logic of particular circumstances, not in the applicability of any general principle.

Errors have doubtless occurred in the classification of certain of the included societies. Some presumably result from faulty observation and others from defective analysis. Moreover, I have occasionally been compelled to make arbitrary decisions, as when the sources are in conflict (thus the Koreans are classed as having Type F rather than a variant of Type D) or when two patterns are reported for a society without an indication of which is the prevailing one (e.g., Types A and B in some Philippine groups). In general, however, the consistency in the results argues for high quality in the ethnographic reporting.

## APPENDIX: TYPES OF SIBLING TERMINOLOGY CLASSED BY LINGUISTIC AFFILIATIONS

All the information on sibling typology and language affiliations used in the paper is tabulated below. The name of each of the 800 societies is followed in parentheses by its regional and numerical identification to facilitate reference to the Ethnographic Atlas for bibliographical sources and data on rules of descent and types of cousin terminology. An asterisk (*) before the name of a society indicates that its sibling terminology deviates in some minor way from the prevailing pattern for the type.

Abasgo-Kerketian family—1 society. Type E: Cherkess (Ci4).
Afroasiatic or Hamito-Semitic family—55 societies. Type E predominant.
   Berber subfamily—7 societies.
       Type D: Ahaggaren (Cc9), Antessar (Cc5), Asben (Cc10).
       Type E: Guanche (Cd11), Shluh (Cd5), Siwans (Cc3) Zekara (Cd10).
   Chadic subfamily—18 societies.
       Type A: Hona (Ah37), Tera (Cb6).

Type B: Bata (Ah36), Buduma (Cb5), Karekare (Cb10), Ngizim (Cb29).
Type C: Kapsiki (Ah38).
Type D: Bachama (Cb27), Bolewa (Cb7), Gude (Ah37), Kanawa (Cb9), Kotoko (Ai18), Maguzawa (Cb1), Zazzagawa (Cb25).
Type E: Dera (Cb28), Margi (Ah5), Masa (Ai9), Matakam (Ah7).
Cushitic subfamily—9 societies.
Type D: Konso (Ca1).
Type E: Afar (Ca6), Arusi (Ca11), Baditu (Ca40), Esa (Ca10), Hadendowa (Ca43), Iraqw (Ca4), Kafa (Ca30), Somali (Ca2).
Egyptian subfamily—1 society. Type E: Ancient Egyptians (Cd6).
Semitic subfamily—20 societies.
Type D: *Amhara (Ca7).
Type E: Algerians (Cd12), Ancient Babylonians (Cj4), Ancient Hebrews (Cj3), Berabish (Cc7), Delim (Cc17), Druze (Cj8), Egyptians (Cd2), Falasha (Ca31), Gurage (Ca8), Humr (Cb15), Jordanians (Cj6), Kababish (Cc6), Lebanese (Cj7), Madan (Cj10), Mutair (Cj5), Regeibat (Cc1), Rwala (Cj2), Syrians (Cj1), Tigrinya (Ca3).
Ainu family—1 society. Type A: Ainu (Ec7).
Algonkian family—24 societies. Type C predominant.
Type C: Abnaki (Ng13), Arapaho (Ne9), Attawapiskat Cree (Na7), Cheyenne (Ne5), Delaware (Ng6), Fox (Nf7), Gros Ventre (Ne1), Kickapoo (Nf15), Menomini (Nf9), Montagnais (Na32), Naskapi (Na5), Ottawa (Na40), Penobscot (Ng4), Plains Cree (Ne19), Potawatomi (Na42), Shawnee (Nf13).
Type D: *Blackfoot (Ne12), Bungi (Nf14), Miami (Nf4), Micmac (Na41), *Piegan (Ne18).
Type F, subtype 1: Chippewa (Na36), *Pekangekum (Na34).
Type G: Blood (Ne13)
Altaic family—12 societies. Type C the most common.
Mongolic subfamily—6 societies.
Type C: Buryat (Eb6), Chahar (Eb7), Dagur (Eb4), Kalmyk (Ci1), Khalka (Eb3).
Type D: *Monguor (Eb2).
Tungusic subfamily—2 societies.
Type D: Goldi (Ec9), Manchu (Ed3).
Turkic subfamily—4 societies.
Type D: *Kazak (Eb1), *Uzbeg (Eb8).
Type E: Turks of Anatolia (Ci5).
Type G: Yakut (Ec2).
Andamanese family—1 society. Type B: Andamanese (Eh1).
Annam-Muong family—1 society. Type C: Annamese or Vietnamese (Ej4).
Araucanian family—1 society. Type F, subtype 3: Mapuche (Sg2).
Arawakan family—9 societies. Type D predominant.
Type B: Piapoco (Sc17).
Type D: Curipaco (Sc9), Goajiro (Sb6), Palikur (Sd3), Paressi (Si7), Piro (Sf8).
Type E: *Wapishana (Sc5).
Type F, subtype 1: Terena (Sh2). Subtype 2: Paraujano (Sb5).
Athapaskan family—21 societies. Type D predominant.
Northern subfamily—13 societies.
Type D: Alkatcho (Nb10), Beaver (Na29), Carrier (Na19), Chipewyan (Na30), Dogrib (Ne7), Ingalik (Na8), Kaska (Na4), Kutchin (Na20), Nabesna (Na1), Sarsi (Ne7), Sekani (Na28), Slave (Na17), Tanaina (Na26).
Pacific subfamily—2 societies.
Type D: Hupa (Nb35), Tolowa (Nb6).
Southern subfamily—6 societies.
Type D: Kiowa Apache (Ne2), Navaho (Nh3).
Type E: Chiricahua (Nh1), Mescalero (Nh15).

Type F, subtype 1: Western Apache (Nh17). Subtype 3: Jicarilla (Nh16).
Australian family—10 societies. Evenly divided between Types C and D.
    Type C: Aranda (Id1), Dieri (Id4), Gidjingali (Id11), Murngin (Id2), Yiryoront (Id12).
    Type D: Kariera (Id5), Tiwi (Id3), Walbiri (Id10), Wikmunkan (Id6), Wongaibon (Id9).
Basque family—1 society. Type E: Basques of Labourd (Ce4).
Betoyan or Tucanoan family—2 societies. Type D: Cubeo (Se5), Tukano (Se12).
Bororan family—2 societies of different types.
    Type C: Bororo (Si11).
    Type D: Umotina (Si8).
Burushaski family—1 society. Type F, subtype 2: Burusho (Ee2).
Caddoan family—5 societies. Type F predominant.
    Type D: *Arikara (Ne10).
    Type F, subtype 2: Pawnee (Nf6). Subtype 4: *Caddo (Nf14), Hasinai (Nf8), Wichita (Nf5).
Carajan family—1 society. Type F, subtype 4: Caraja (Sj1).
Cariban family—12 societies. Type G predominant.
    Type D: *Black Carib (Sa7), *Makiritare (Sc16).
    Type E: *Panare (Sc13).
    Type F, subtype 4: Bacairi (Sj3).
    Type G: Barama River Carib (Sc3), Callinago (Sb1), Camaracoto (Sc11), Carinya (Sb4), Iroka (Sb3), Macusi (Sc12), Yabarana (Sc7), Yupa (Sb7).
Chari-Nile or Sudanic family—31 societies. Types E predominant.
  Central Sudanic subfamily—8 societies.
    Type A: Lendu (Ai29), Mangbetu (Ai11), Popoi (Ai28).
    Type D: Bagirmi (Ai21).
    Type E: Logo (Ai31), Lugbara (Ai32), Madi (Ai33), Moru (Ai34).
  Eastern Sudanic or Nilotic subfamily—20 societies.
    Type A: Bari (Aj8), Dorobo (Aa2), Kipsigis (Aj9), Nandi (Aj7).
    Type E: Acholi (Aj10), Dinka (Aj11), Hill Suk (Aj26), Ingassana (Ai4), Karamojong (Aj30), Kuku (Aj15), Labwor (Aj22), Lango (Aj4), Lotuko (Aj12), Masai (Aj2), Nuer (Aj3), Pari (Aj31), Samburu (Aj29), Shilluk (Ai6), Teso (Aj1), Turkana (Aj5).
  Nubian subfamily—3 societies.
    Type A: Dilling (Ai8), Nyima (Ai43).
    Type E: Barabra (Cd1).
Chibchan family—8 societies. Type F predominant.
    Type B: *Cagaba (Sb2).
    Type D: Chibcha (Sf6).
    Type E: *Cayapa (Sf3).
    Type F, subtype 1: Guaymi (Sa14). Subtype 2: Cuna (Sa1). Subtype 4: Bribri (Sa5), Paez (Sf5), *Tunebo (Sf4).
Chimmesyan family—1 society. Type F, subtype 3: Tsimshian (Nb7).
Chinantecan family—1 society. Type C: Chinantec (Nj1).
Chitimachan family—1 society. Type D: Chitimacha (Ng15).
Chocoan family—1 society. Type A: Choco (Sa4).
Coahuiltecan family—1 society. Type G: Coahuilteco (Ne21).
Coastal Nadene subphylum—3 societies. Type F predominant.
  Eyak family—1 society. Type F, subtype 3: Eyak (Nb5).
  Koluschan family—1 society. Type F, subtype 4: *Tlingit (Nb22).
  Skittagetan family—1 society. Type F, subtype 2: Haida (Nb1).
Dravidian family—10 societies. Type D predominant.
    Type C: Toda (Eg4).
    Type D: Chenchu (Eg1), Coorg (Eg5), Kerala (Eg6), Khond (Eg12), Maria Gond (Eg3), Oraon (Ef6), *Reddi (Eg14), Tamil (Eg2), Telugu (Eg10).
Eskimauan or Eskimo-Aleut family—10 societies. Type F predominant.

Type C: Nunamiut (Na12), Nunivak (Na6).
Type D: Tareumiut (Na2).
Type F, subtype 2: Aleut (Na9), *Caribou Eskimo (Na21), *Copper Eskimo (Na3), Greenlanders (Na25), Iglulik (Na22), *Polar Eskimo (Na14), Taqaqmiut (Na44).
Furian family—1 society. Type F, subtype 3: Fur (Cb17).
Ge phylum—6 societies. Type B predominant.
Caingang family—1 society. Type B: Aweikoma (Sj3).
Ge family—5 societies.
Type B: Ramcocamecra (Sj4), Shavante (Sj11), Sherente (Sj2).
Type E: *Apinaye (Sj7), Coroa (Sj9).
Georgian, Grusian, or Kartvelian family—1 society. Type E: Georgians (Ci8).
Gilyak family—1 society. Type C: Gilyak (Ec1).
Guahiban family—1 society. Type D: Guahibo (Sc4).
Guatoan family—1 society. Type A: Guato (Si6).
Guaycuran family—2 societies of different types.
Type D: Toba (Sh8).
Type F, subtype 4: *Caduveo (Sh4).
Hokan family—18 societies. Type D predominates. Cf. also the allegedly Macro-Hokan Coahuiltecan, Jicaquean, Serian, Tequistlatecan, and Washoan families.
Karok or Quoratean subfamily—1 society. Type D: Karok (Nb34).
Pomo or Kulanapan subfamily—3 societies.
Type C: Eastern Pomo (Nc18), Northern Pomo (Nc17), Southern Pomo (Nc19).
Shastan or Shasta-Achomawi subfamily—2 societies. Type D: *Atsugewi (Nc4), *Shasta (Nb32).
Yuman subfamily—11 societies.
Type B: Maricopa (Nh5), Tolkepaya (Nd67), Walapai (Nd65), Yuma (Nh22).
Type C: Diegueno (Nc6), Kiliwa (Nc34).
Type D: Cocopa (Nh19), Havasupai (Nd3), Kamia (Nh20), *Keweyipaya (Nh23).
Type E: Yavapai (Nd66).
Yanan subfamily—1 society. Type G: Yana (Nc11).
Indo-European family—44 societies. Type E predominates.
Albanian subfamily—1 society. Type E: Gheg (Ce1).
Armenian subfamily—1 society. Type E: Armenians (Ci10).
Baltic or Balto-Slavic subfamily—1 society. Type E: Lithuanians (Ch9).
Celtic subfamily—1 society. Type E: Irish (Cg3).
Germanic subfamily—5 societies. Type E: Boers (Cf2), Dutch (Cg1), Icelanders (Cg2), New Englanders (Cf1), Tristan da Cunha (Cf3).
Greek or Hellenic subfamily—1 society. Type E: Greeks (Ce9).
Indic subfamily—11 societies.
Type D: Bengali (Ef2), Chakma (Ei8), Mogh (Ei9), Pahari (Ef7), Sinhalese (Eh6), Vedda (Eh4).
Type E: Ancient Aryans (Ef3), Bihari (Ef10), Kashmiri (Ef8), Kohistani (Ea4), Sindhi (Ea1).
Iranian or Persian subfamily—7 societies. Type E: Bakhtiari (Ea8), Hazara (Ea3), Iranians (Ea9), Kurd (Ci11), Marri Baluch (Ea10), Osset (Ci6), Pathan (Ea2).
Romance or Italic subfamily—10 societies.
Type C: Saramacca Bush Negroes (Sc6).
Type E: Brazilians (Cf4), French Canadians (Cf5), Haitians (Sb9), Imperial Romans (Ce3), Neapolitans (Ce5), Portuguese (Ce2), Romanians (Ch10), Spaniards (Ce6), Walloons (Cg5).
Slavic subfamily—6 societies. Type E: Bulgarians (Ch5), Byelorussians (Ch6), Czechs (Ch3), Hutsul (Ch2), Serbs (Ch1), Ukrainians (Ch7).
Iroquoian family—2 societies.
Northern Iroquoian subfamily. Type D: Seneca Iroquois (Ng10).
Southern Iroquoian subfamily. Type F, subtype 3: Cherokee (Ng5).

Japano-Ryukyuan family—4 societies. Type D predominant.
    Type C: Miyakans (Ed15).
    Type D: *Ishigakians (Ed13), Japanese (Ed5), Okinawans (Ed7).
Jicaquean family—1 society. Type C: Jicaque (Sa11).
Jivaran family—1 society. Type F, subtype 3: Jivaro (Se3).
Kanuric or Central Saharan family—3 societies. Type D predominant.
    Type D: Daza (Cc17), Teda (Cc2).
    Type F, subtype 1: Kanuri (Cb19).
Kechumaran or Quechua-Aymara family—2 societies. Types differ with subfamily.
    Aymaran subfamily. Type D: Aymara (Sf2).
    Quechuan subfamily. Type F, subtype 4: Inca (Sf1).
Keresan family—6 societies. Type F predominant.
    Type F, subtype 3: Cochiti (Nh7), Santo Domingo (Nh27), Sia (Nh25). Sub-
        type 4: Acoma (Nh13), Laguna (Nh14), Santa Ana (Nh12).
Khoisan family—6 societies. Types differ with subfamily.
    Northern subfamily—1 society. Type F, subtype 2: Sandawe (Aa6).
    Southern or Bushman-Hottentot subfamily—5 societies.
    Type C: Kung Bushmen (Aa1), Naron Bushmen (Aa7).
    Type E: Bergdama (Aa4), Nama Hottentot (Aa3), Xam Bushmen (Aa8).
Kiowan family—1 society. Type F, subtype 3: Kiowa (Ne17).
Kitunahan family—1 society. Type D: Kutenai (Nd7).
Koman family—1 society. Type E: Koma (Ai46).
Kordofanian family—7 societies. Type A predominant.
    Type A: Koalib (Ai37), Korongo (Ai38), Mesakin (Ai39), Moro (Ai40), Otoro
        (Ai10), Tira (Ai41).
    Type E: Tullishi (Ai42).
Korean family—1 society. Type F, subtype 2: Koreans (Ed1).
Luorawetlan or Paleo-Siberian family—2 societies of different types.
    Type F, subtype 4: Chukchee (Ec3).
    Type G: Koryak (Ec5).
Malayo-Polynesian or Austronesian family—104 societies. Type F predominant.
    Carolinian subfamily—12 societies.
    Type A: Carolinians of Saipan (If15), Nauruans (If13), Yapese (If6).
    Type E: Ponapeans (If5).
    Type F, subtype 1: Ifaluk (If4), Lamotrek (If16), Nomoians (If10), Onotoa
        (If7), Ulithians (If9). Subtype 2: Bikinians (If12), Majuro (If3), Trukese (If2).
    Hesperonesian or Western subfamily—35 societies.
    Type A: Bunun (Ia10), Chamorro (If8), Ifugao (Ia3), Kalinga (Ia16), Macas-
        sarese (Ic1), Paiwan (Ia6), Punan (Ib9, Subanun (Ia4), Tawi-Tawi (Ia13).
    Type B: Ami (Ia9), Bilaan (Ia17), Bontok (Ia8), Hanunoo (Ia5), Iban (Ib1),
        Malays (Ej8), Manobo (Ia15), Minangkabau (Ib6), Puyuma (Ia11), Sagada
        (Ia2), Sugbuhanon (Ia12), Tagbanua (Ia7), Toradja (Ic5), Yami (Ia14).
    Type C: Balinese (Ib3), Javanese (Ib2).
    Type D: Antaisaka (Eh9), Betsileo (Eh10), Bisayan (Ia18), *Palauans (If1),
        Rhade (Ej10).
    Type F, subtype 1: Atayal (Ia1), Batak (Ib4), Mentaweians (Ib7). Subtype 3:
        Merina (Eh2). Subtype 4: Tanala (Eh3).
    Melanesian subfamily—29 societies.
    Type B: Bgu (Ig14), Dahuni (Ig14), Kwaio (Ig18).
    Type F, subtype 1: Ajie (Ih5), Bakovi (Ig15), Bwaidoga (Ig16), Choiseulese
        (Ig12), Dobuans (Ig5), Koobe (Ig17), Kurtatchi (Ig3), Lau Fijians (Ih4),
        Molima (Ig19), Motu (Ie10), Rotumans (Ih6), Trobrianders (Ig2), Ulawans
        (Ig6), Vanua Levu (Ih8). Subtype 2: Bunlap (Ih3), Manam (Ie29), Mota
        (Ih1), Ranon (Ih13), Seniang (Ih2), Tannese (Ih10), Waropen (Ie6), Wogeo
        (Ie4). Subtype 3: Epi (Ih11), Eromangans (Ih12), Lesu (Ig4), Manus (Ig9).
    Moluccan subfamily—6 societies.
    Type B: Ili-Mandiri (Ic7).

Type C: Belu (Ic3).
Type F, subtype 1: Alorese (Ic2), Tanimbarese (Ic6). Subtype 2: Rotinese (Ic4). Subtype 4: Kodi (Ic13).
Polynesian subfamily—22 societies.
   Type A: Kapingamarangi (Ii7).
   Type B: Easter Islanders (Ij9).
   Type F, subtype 1: Ellice (Ii4), Futunans (Ii8), Ontong-Javanese (Ii5), Puka-pukans (Ii3), Tikopia (Ii2), Tongans (Ii12), Uveans (Ii13). Subtype 2: Hawaiians (Ij6), Mangaians (Ij1), Mangarevans (Ij7), Manihikians (Ij4), Maori (Ij2), Marquesans (Ij3), Niueans (Ii9), Raroians (Ij5), Rennell (Ii10), Samoans (Ii1), Tahitians (Ij8), Tokelau (Ii6), Tongarevans (Ij10).
Mayan family—10 societies. Type C the most common.
   Northern subfamily—1 society. Type F, subtype 4: Huastec (Nj11).
   Southern subfamily—9 societies.
   Type B: Chorti (Sa3), Pokomam (Sa17).
   Type C: Lacandon (Sa10), Quiche (Sa13), Tzeltal (Sa2), Yucatec Maya (Sa6)
   Type D: Cakchiquel (Sa11), Jacaltec (Sa15).
   Type E: *Mam (Sa8).
Mataco-Mateguayo family—2 societies of different types.
   Type C: Choroti (Sh5).
   Type D: Mataco (Sh1).
Miao-Yao family—2 societies of different types.
   Type E: Man (Ed14).
   Type G: Miao (Ed4).
Misumalpan family—1 society. Type F, subtype 1: Miskito (Sa9).
Mixteco-Zapotecan phylum—2 societies. Type F predominant.
   Mixtecan family. Type F, subtype 3: Mixtec (Nj12).
   Zapotecan family. Type F, subtype 3: Zapotec (Nj10).
Mizocuavean family—3 societies. Type C predominant.
   Type B: Huave (Nj6)
   Type C: Mixe (Nj7), Popoluca (Nj3).
Mon-Khmer family—9 societies. Type D the most common.
   Cambodian subfamily—2 societies.
   Type B: Cambodians (Ej5).
   Type F, subfamily 2: Mnong Gar (Ej2).
   Khasi-Nicobarese subfamily—3 societies.
   Type C: Lamet (Ej1).
   Type D: Khasi (Ei8).
   Type F, subtype 2: Nicobarese (Eh5).
   Munda or Kolarian subfamily—3 societies. Type D: Baiga (Eg9), Hill Bhuiya (Eg7), Santal (Ef1).
   Semang-Sakai subfamily—1 society. Type B: Semang (Ej3).
Mosan phylum—18 societies. Type B predominant.
   Chemakuan family—1 society. Type B: Quileute (Nb18).
   Salishan family—14 societies.
   Type B: Bellacoola (Nb9), Comox (Nb14), Cowichan (Nb26), Klallam (Nb16), Lummi (Nb14), Squamish (Nb13), Stalo (Nb27).
   Type C: Lillooet (Nd9), Shuswap (Nd11).
   Type D: Quinault (Nb25), Sinkaietk (Nd15), *Twana (Nb2).
   Type F, subtype 1: Puyallup (Nb17).
   Type G: Flathead (Nd12).
   Wakashan family—3 societies.
   Type B: Haisla (Nb8), Nootka (Nb11).
   Type F, subtype 1: Kwakiutl (Nb3).
Nahuatlan or Mexicano family—2 societies with different types.
   Type C: Huichol (Ni3).

Type D: Aztec (Nj2).
Nambicuaran family—1 society. Type D: Nambicuara (Si4).
Natchez-Muskogean family—6 societies. Type F predominant.
  Type F, subtype 2: Chickasaw (Ng14), Choctaw (Ng12), Creek (Ng3), Seminole
    (Ng2). Subtype 3: Natchez (Ng7), Timucua (Ng8).
Niger-Congo or Nigritic family—152 societies. Type differs with subfamilities.
  Atlantic subfamily—12 societies. Type B the most common.
    Type A: Baga (Ag14).
    Type B: Biafada (Ag17), Bororo Fulani (Cb8), Djafun (Cb21), Serer (Ag22),
      Wodaabe (Cb24).
    Type C: Kissi (Af2).
    Type D: Futajalonke (Ag6), Pepel (Ag20).
    Type E: Sherbro (Af14).
    Type F, subtype 1: Wolof (Cb2). Subtype 2: Diola (Ag19).
  Bantoid or Central subfamily—94 societies. Type F predominant.
    Type A: Amba (Ae1), Ambo (Ab19), Bena (Ad11), Chawai (Ah10), Efik
      (Af19), Giriama (Ad32), Haya (Ad42), Katab (Ah1), Kentu (Ah24), Kwere
      (Ad27), Luchazi (Ac27), Luimbe (Ac28), Mbugwe (Ad5), Ngoni (Ac9),
      Teita (Ad37), Tiv (Ah3), Turu (Ad26), Yako (Af4).
    Type B: Chokwe (Ac12), Jukun (Ah2), Kurama (Ah21), Ndoro (Ah26),
      Thonga (Ab4).
    Type C: Dzing (Ac22), Lenge (Ab16).
    Type E: Babwa (Ae7), Bajun (Ad1), Birom (Ah17), Ekoi (Af17), Fang
      (Ae3), Gure (Ah6), Kadara (Ah19), Kikuyu (Ad4), Kota (Ae41), Ndebele
      (Ab9), Plains Bira (Ae34), Pondo (Ab10), Reshe (Ah15), Swazi (Ab2),
      Vugusu (Ad41), Wute (Ah8), Zulu (Ab12).
    Type F, subtype 1: Chewa (Ac10), Chiga (Ad13), Chopi (Ab22), Fipa (Ad19),
      Ganda (Ad7), Gisu (Ad9), Hehe (Ad8), Herero (Ab1), Kpe (Ae2), Kunda
      (Ac27), Lele (Ac23), Lovedu (Ab14), Lozi (Ab3), Mongo (Ae24), Ngala
      (Ae28), Ngonde (Ad16), Nkundo (Ae4), Nyakyusa (As6), Nyamwezi
      (Ad20), Nyanja (Ac38), Nyankole (Ad45), Pedi (Ab15), Pende (Ac2), Poto
      (Ae29), Rega (Ae6), Sangu (Ad23), Shila (Ac35), Shona (Ab18), Soga
      (Ad46), Sotho (Ab8), Toro (Ad48), Tswana (Ab13), Tumbuka (Ac36),
      Venda (Ab6).
    Type F, subtype 2: Bemba (Ac3), Duala (Ae12), Hunde (Ae15), Kagoro
      (Ah20), Lala (Ac33), Lamba (Ac5), Ruanda (Ae10), Rundi (Ae11), Yao
      (Ac7).
    Type F, subtype 3: Luwa (Ac29), Nyoro (Ad2), Sakata (Ac24), *Shambala
      (Ad10), *Yeke (Ae19).
    Type F, subtype 4: *Bomvana (Ab21), Ila (Ac1), Mbundu (Ab5), *Xhosa
      (Ab11).
  Eastern or Adamawa-Eastern subfamily—10 societies.
    Type A: Mandja (Ai24), Mumuye (Ah31).
    Type D: Azande (Ai3).
    Type E: Baya (Ai7), Daka (Ah29), Fali (Ai12).
    Type F, subtype 1: Banda (Ai1). Subtype 2: Longuda (Ah30), Yungur (Ah33).
  Gur or Voltaic subfamily—11 societies. Type F the most common.
    Type B: Birifor (Ag5), Dagomba (Ag44), Dian (Ag33).
    Type D: Dorosie (Ag34).
    Type E: *Dogon (Ag3), Konkomba (Ag10), Lobi (Ag11).
    Type F, subtype 1: Nankanse (Ag12), Tallensi (Ag4). Subtype 2: Awuna
      (Ag37), Kasena (Ag13).
  Kwa subfamily—18 societies. Type A predominant.
    Type A: Akyem (Af12), Ashanti (Af3), Baule (Af9), Bete (Af7), Edo (Af24),
      Fanti (Af42), Ibo (Af10), Isoko (Af25), Kukuruku (Af26).
    Type B: Egba (Af32), Ife (Af34), Nupe (Af8), Oyo Yoruba (Af6).

Type D: Adangme (Af35), Ewe (Af36).
Type E: *Buem (Af37), Fon (Af1), Ga (Af43).
Mande or Mandingo subfamily—8 societies. Type D predominant.
Type A: Mende (Af5).
Type D: Bambara (Ag1), Dan (Af50), Diula (Ag27), Gbande (Af54), Kpelle (Af15), Malinke (Ag9), Yalunka (Ag54).
Oto-Manguean family—2 societies of different types.
Type E: Mazatec (Nj5).
Type G: Otomi (Nj13).
Papuan phylum—27 societies. Families are not yet established.
Type A: Tobelorese (Ic10).
Type B: Keraki (Ie5), Kimam (Ie18), Koita (Ie20).
Type C: Mailu (Ie21), Muju (Ie23), Samarokena (Ie36), Star Mountain (Ie37).
Type D: Banaro (Ie27), Kiwai (Ie13), Mimika (Ie30).
Type E: Marindanim (Ie19), Orokaiva (Ie9), Wantoat (Ie2).
Type F, subtype 1: *Iatmul (Ie35), Miriam (Ie14), Rossel (Ig11), Siane (Ie17).
Subtype 2: Abelam (Ie15), Kwoma (Ie12), Mekeo (Ie22). Subtype 3: Enga (Ie7), *Kapauku (Ie1), Kutubu (Ie16), Santa Cruz (Ih9), Siuai (Ig1).
Type G: Arapesh (Ie3).
Penutian family—12 societies. Type D predominant.
Chinookan subfamily—1 society. Type D: Wishram (Nd18).
Copehan or Wintun subfamily—3 societies. Type D: Nomlaki (Nc1), Patwin (Nc22), Wintu (Nc14).
Mariposan subfamily—1 society. Type D: Yokuts (Nc3).
Moquelumnan or Miwok subfamily—2 societies of different types.
Type C: Lake Miwok (Nc21).
Type D: Miwok (Nc5).
Pujunan or Maidu subfamily—2 societies. Type D: Maidu (Nc12), Nisenan (Nc13).
Takilman subfamily—1 society. Type D: Takelma (Nb30).
Yakonan subfamily—2 societies. Type D: Alsea (Nb28), Siuslaw (Nb29).
Piman family—3 societies. Type B predominant.
Type B: Papago (Ni2), Pima (Ni6), Tepehuan (Ni9).
Ritwan family—2 societies. Type varies with subfamilies.
Weitspekan subfamily—1 society. Type F, subtype 4: Yurok (Nb4).
Wishoskan subfamily—1 society. Type A: Wiyot (Nb36).
Sahaptin family—4 societies. Type G predominant.
Lutuamian subfamily—1 society. Type D: Klamath (Nc8).
Shahaptian family—3 societies. Type G: Klikitat (Nd17), Nez Perce (Nd20), Tenino (Nd1).
Salivan family—1 society. Type D: Piaroa (Sc8).
Serian family—1 society. Type G: Seri (Ni4).
Shoshonean family—20 societies. Type D predominant.
Type C: Tubatulabal (Nc2).
Type D: Bannock (Nd63), Bohogue (Nd45), Cahuilla (Nc31), Chemehuevi (Nd54), Comanche (Ne3), Cupeno (Nc32), Eastern Mono (Nd30), Gosiute (Nd48), Hopi (Nh18), Hukundika (Nd5), Kaibab (Nd53), Kawaiisu (Nc27), Kidutokado (Nd24), Luiseno (Nc33), Serrano (Nc30), Shivwits (Nd52), Southern Ute (Nd2), Uintah (Nd58), Wind River (Nd64).
Sinitic family—2 societies. Type D: Cantonese (Ed16), Shantung Chinese (Ed10).
Siouan family—10 societies. Type G predominant.
Type D: *Omaha (Nf3).
Type F, subtype 4: *Mandan (Ne6).
Type G: Assiniboin (Ne11), Crow (Ne4), Hidatsa (Ne15), Oto (Nf11), Ponca (Nf12), Santee (Ne20), Teton (Ne8), Winnebago (Nf1).
Songhaic family—1 society. Type D: Songhai (Cb3).
Tanoan family—7 societies. Type varies with subfamilies.

Tewa subfamily—3 societies.
    Type B: San Ildefonso (Nh11), Santa Clara (Nh26).
    Type C: Hano (Nh2).
Tiwa subfamily—3 societies.
    Type C: Picuris (Nh9), Taos (Nh6).
    Type D: Isleta (Nh10).
Towa subfamily—1 society. Type D: Jemez (Nh8).
Taracahitian family—3 societies. Type D predominant.
    Type D: Opata (Ni8), Tarahumara (Ni1), Yaqui (Ni7).
Tarascan family—1 society. Type A: Tarasco (Nj8).
Tehuelchean family—1 society. Type D: Ona (Sg3).
Tequistlatecan family—1 society. Type A: Tequistlatec (Nj14).
Thai-Kadai family—1 society. Type B: Siamese (Ej9).
Tibeto-Burman family—23 societies. Types apparently tend to sort by subfamilies.
    Type B: Aimol (Ei11), Karen (Ei7), *Kuki (Ei20), Lakher (Ei4), *Lhota
      (Ei2), *Rengma (Ei15), Thado (Ei12).
    Type C: Ao Naga (Ei14), Kachin (Ei5), Lepcha (Ee3), Tibetans (Ee4).
    Type D: Akha (Ej7), Garo (Ei1), Lolo (Ed2), *Mikir (Ei17), Minchia (Ed8),
      Purum (Ei6), Sherpa (Ee6).
    Type E: Kachari (Ee7).
    Type F, subtype 2: Chin (Ei19).
    Type G: Angami (Ei13), Burmese (Ei3), Sema (Ei16).
Trumaian family—1 society. Type B: *Trumai (Si2).
Tucunan family—1 society. Type E: Tucuna (Se2).
Tupi-Guarani family—7 societies. Type G predominant.
    Type A: Siriono (Se1).
    Type E: Maue (Sd5).
    Type F, subtype 4: *Cayua (Sj10).
    Subtype G: Aueto (Si9), Camayura (Si5), Tenetehara (Sj6), Tupinamba (Sj8).
Uchean family—1 society. Type E: Yuchi (Ng11).
Uralic family—5 societies. Type E predominant.
    Finnic subfamily—2 societies. Type E: Hungarians (Ch8), Lapps (Cg4).
    Samoyedic subfamily—2 societies. Type E: Selkup (Ec11), Yurak (Ec4).
    Ugric subfamily—1 society. Type E: Ob Ostyak (Ec10).
Uru-Chipayan family—1 society. Type D: Uru (Sf9).
Warrauan family—1 society. Type G: Warrau (Sc1).
Washoan family—1 society. Type D: Washo (Nd6).
Witotan family—1 society. Type F, subtype 4: Witoto (Se6).
Yahgan family—1 society. Type E: Yahgan (Sg1).
Yeniseian family—1 society. Type E: Ket (Ec8).
Yukian family—4 societies. Type B predominant.
    Type B: *Coast Yuki (Nc15), *Huchnom (Nc16), *Yuki (Nc7).
    Type D: Wappo (Nc20).
Zunian family—1 society. Type D: *Zuni (Nh4).

## NOTES

1. A cursory survey of my personal working library reveals such examples as Gulliver on the Jie and Turkana, Skinner on the Mossi, Spencer on the Samburu, Velsen on the Lakeside Tonga, and Winans on the Shambala.
2. Since Type C, as previously noted, is essentially a subtype of Type D, instances of C are grouped with those of D when necessary to achieve a majority.
3. However, this impression is due in considerable measure to an artifact of ethnographic distribution, since fourteen of the ambilineal societies with Type F, accounting by themselves for 37 per cent of the total, are concentrated in Polynesia.
4. The "anomalous" category includes ten societies with genuinely anomalous cousin terminology and nine with the rare "Sudanese" pattern.

## BIBLIOGRAPHY

Buchler, I. R. 1964. Measuring the Development of Kinship Terminologies: Scalogram and Transformational Accounts of Crow-type Systems. American Anthropologist 66: 765-788.

—— 1967. Analyse formelle des terminologies de parenté iroquoises. L'Homme 7: 5-31. (Contains bibliographical references to other kinship publications by the author.)

Burling, R. 1963. Garo Kinship Terms and the Analysis of Meaning. Ethnology 2: 70-85.

Callender, C. 1962. Social Organization of the Central Algonkian Indians. Milwaukee Public Museum Publications in Anthropology 7: 1-140.

Dyen, I. 1963. The Lexicostatistical Classification of the Austronesian Languages. New Haven.

Elmendorf, W. W. 1961. System Change in Salish Kinship Terminologies. Southwestern Journal of Anthropology 17: 365-382.

Frisch, J. A., and N. W. Schutz, Jr. 1967. Componential Analysis and Semantic Reconstruction: The Proto Central Yuman Kinship System. Ethnology 6: 272-293.

Goodenough, W. H. 1956. Componential Analysis and the Study of Meaning. Language 32: 195-216.

Goodenough, W. H., ed. 1964. Explorations in Cultural Anthropology. New York.

Hammel, E. A., ed. 1965. Formal Semantic Analysis. American Anthropologist 67: v, pt. 2 (Special Publication).

Hockett, C. F. 1964. The Proto Central Algonquian Kinship System. Explorations in Cultural Anthropology, ed. W. H. Goodenough, pp. 239-257. New York.

Hoijer, H. 1956. Athapaskan Kinship Systems. American Anthropologist 58: 309-333.

Kirchhoff, P. 1932. Verwandtschaftsbezeichnungen und Verwandtenheirat. Zeitschrift für Ethnologie 64: 41-72.

Lounsbury, F. G. 1956. A Semantic Analysis of Pawnee Kinship Usage. Language 32: 158-194.

—— 1964. A Formal Account of the Crow- and Omaha-type Kinship Terminologies. Explorations in Cultural Anthropology, ed. W. H. Goodenough, pp. 351-393. New York.

Lowie, R. H. 1928. A Note on Relationship Terminologies. American Anthropologist 30: 265-266.

Morgan, L. H. 1870. Systems of Consanguinity and Affinity of the Human Family. Smithsonian Contributions to Knowledge 17: 1-590.

Murdock, G. P. 1949. Social Structure. New York.

—— 1964. Genetic Classification of the Austronesian Languages. Ethnology 3: 117-126.

Nerlove, S., and A. K. Romney. 1967. Sibling Terminology and Cross-Sex Behavior. American Anthropologist 69: 179-187.

Newman, P., and R. Ma. 1966. Comparative Chadic. Journal of African Languages 5: 218-251.

Pans, A. E. M. J. 1967. Verwandtschapsklassificeringen van Nieuw Guinea. Unpublished thesis, University of Amsterdam.

Romney, A. K., and R. G. D'Andrade, eds. 1964. Transcultural Studies in Cognition. American Anthropologist 66: iii, pt. 2 (Special Publication).

Schneider, D. M., and K. Gough. 1961. Matrilineal Kinship. Berkeley and Los Angeles.

Spier, L. 1925. The Distribution of Kinship Systems in North America. University of Washington Publications in Anthropology 1: 69-88.

Wallace, A. F. C., and J. Atkins. 1960. The Meaning of Kinship Terms. American Anthropologist 62: 58-80.

# 14

# Kin Term Patterns
# and Their Distribution

*George Peter Murdock*

The author has been collecting kinship terminologies for the past twenty years and now has in his files over a thousand complete systems. These include virtually all of those which have been published on Africa and aboriginal North and South America and are only slightly less exhaustive for Eurasia and Oceania. This collection makes it possible—perhaps for the first time in the history of anthropology—to analyze an important segment of culture on the basis of an examination of the total universe of described cultures, not merely of a sample or partial survey of such. Selected for presentation herewith are the various patterns prevailing in the world's cultures for the terminological classification of eight sets of kinsmen: grandparents, grandchildren, uncles, aunts, nephews and nieces (male speaking), siblings, cross-cousins, and siblings-in-law.

The objectives are twofold—first, to assure the inclusion of every major variant reported in the literature for each of the eight sets of kinsmen and, second, to avoid duplication of essentially similar patterns in groups of contiguous and closely related cultures. To this end, the data were assessed separately for each of the 200 sampling provinces into which the cultures of the world have been divided (Murdock 1968b). For each of these there was first selected the society for which the kinship data were adjudged most complete. Additional societies were then chosen if they differed from the first, and from each other, in the patterns reported for two or more of the eight sets of kinsmen. In some provinces, e.g., Han Chinese (83), none of the kinship terminologies analyzed differed to this extent, and hence only a single representative could be included. In other provinces as many as four or five societies were found to differ from one another sufficiently to be included. In the very few instances where more than five societies in a province showed such differences, only the five most divergent systems were selected. In general, no society was chosen unless its kinship terminology was relatively completely reported, i.e., unless information was available on the patterns for at least six of the eight sets of kinsmen considered. (The sole exception to this rule is the inclusion of the Nicobarese of Province 93, for which no alternative system was available.)

The application of the above criteria resulted in the selection of 566 societies from 194 of the 200 cultural provinces. The only provinces for which no adequate terminological systems were available are the following: Pygmies (15), Ancient Egypt (50), Ancient Mesopotamia (53), Moluccas (106), Tasmania (110), and East Brazilian Highlands (192). The systems analyzed are distributed geographically as follows:

   108 from Sub-Saharan Africa (A)
    51 from the Circum-Mediterranean region (C)
    80 from East Eurasia (E)
   107 from the Insular Pacific (I)
   143 from aboriginal North America (N)
    77 from South America (S).

This distribution rather accurately reflects the quantity and quality of the descriptive literature on kinship in the several world regions.

## PATTERNS FOR GRANDPARENTS

The kin terms reported for grandparents have been analyzed into fourteen distinct patterns, which are defined below. To each of these is assigned a capital letter and a name. Here, and also subsequently, the earliest letters in the alphabet are assigned to the patterns that occur in 10 per cent or more of the total of 566 societies; the letters from K to Q, to those occurring in from 1 to 10 per cent of the societies; R and subsequent letters, to those found in fewer than 1 per cent. Subcategories with lower-case letters are used for minor variants of the major patterns.

A  *Bisexual Pattern.* Two terms, distinguished by sex, which can be glossed as "grandfather" and "grandmother." With the following variant:
    Aa—with separate terms for GrFa (ms), GrFa (ws), and GrMo.
B  *Merging Pattern.* A single undifferentiated term, which can be glossed as "grandparent." With the following variants:
    Ba—with a separate term for MoMo only.
    Bb—with a separate term for MoMo (ws) only.
    Bc—with separate terms for FaFa (ms) and FaFa (ws).
C  *Bifurcate Bisexual Pattern.* Four terms, distinguished by both sex and the sex of the connecting relative, which can be glossed as "paternal grandfather," "maternal grandfather," "paternal grandmother," and "maternal grandmother." With the following variants:
    Ca—with a single term embracing MoFa and FaMo.
    Cb—with separate terms for FaFa (ms) and FaFa (ws).
K  *Matri-Skewed Pattern.* Three terms, distinguished by sex and for females also by the sex of the connecting relative, which can be glossed as "grandfather," "paternal grandmother," and "maternal grandmother."
L  *Null Pattern.* Special terms are lacking for grandparents, who are called by the same terms as parents. With the following variants:
    La—with a special term for GrFa, GrMo being called "mother."
    Lb—with a special term for GrMo, GrFa being called "father."
M  *Bifurcate Pattern.* Two terms, distinguished by the sex of the connecting relative, which can be glossed as "paternal grandparent" and "maternal grandparent."

N *Patri-Skewed Pattern.* Three terms, distinguished by sex and for males also by the sex of the connecting relative, which can be glossed as "paternal grandfather," "maternal grandfather," and "grandmother."

R A rare pattern distinguishing GrPa (ms) and GrPa (ws).

S A rare pattern distinguishing GrPa of Ego's sex and GrPa of opposite sex.

T A rare pattern distinguishing GrPa of Ego's sex, GrFa (ws), and GrMo (ms).

U A rare pattern, intermediate between C and M, distinguishing FaPa, MoFa, and MoMo.

V A rare pattern, intermediate between C and M, distinguishing FaFa, FaMo, and MoPa.

W A rare pattern distinguishing GrFa (ms), GrFa (ws), GrMo (ms), and GrMo (ws).

X A rare pattern distinguishing FaFa (ms), FaFa (ws), MoFa, FaMo, MoMo (ms), and MoMo (ws). This pattern, the most complex one on record, is reported for the Yucatec Maya at the time of the Spanish Conquest.

TABLE 1

Geographical Distribution of Patterns for Grandparents

| Pattern | Africa | C-Med. | E. Eur. | In. Pac. | N. Amer. | S. Amer. | Total |
|---------|--------|--------|---------|----------|----------|----------|-------|
| A | 64 | 39 | 49 | 30 | 84 | 61 | 327 |
| B | 28 | 8 | 1 | 54 | 9 | 3 | 103 |
| C | 8 | 3 | 20 | 12 | 38 | 5 | 86 |
| K | 0 | 0 | 3 | 0 | 6 | 2 | 11 |
| L | 0 | 0 | 1 | 5 | 1 | 3 | 10 |
| M | 3 | 0 | 1 | 2 | 1 | 0 | 7 |
| N | 1 | 1 | 3 | 1 | 0 | 1 | 7 |
| R–X | 3 | 0 | 0 | 3 | 4 | 2 | 12 |
| No data | 1 | 0 | 2 | 0 | 0 | 0 | 3 |
| Total | 108 | 51 | 80 | 107 | 143 | 77 | 566 |

PATTERNS FOR GRANDCHILDREN

The kin terms reported for grandchildren have been analyzed into the patterns named and defined below.

A *Merging Pattern.* A single undifferentiated term, which can be glossed as "grandchild." With the following variant:

Aa—with separate terms for SoCh (ms) and DaCh (ms) only.

B *Bisexual Pattern.* Two terms, distinguished by sex, which can be glossed as "grandson" and "granddaughter."

C *Self-Reciprocal Pattern.* Grandparental terms, either with or without diminutive affixes, are applied to grandchildren, a grandchild being invariably called by the same term which he applies to the speaker. With the following variant:

Ca—grandparental terms are applied to grandchildren but not always self-reciprocally, i.e., in some instances the grandchild is called by a grandparental term other than that which he applies to the speaker.

D  *Bifurcate Bisexual Pattern.* Four terms, distinguished by both sex and the sex of the connecting relative, which can be glossed as "son's son," "son's daughter," "daughter's son," and "daughter's daughter."

K  *Null Pattern.* Special terms are lacking for grandchildren, who are called by the same term or terms that the speaker applies to his own children.

L  *Speaker's Sex Pattern.* Two terms, differentiated by the sex of the speaker, which can be glossed as "grandchild (ms)" and "grandchild (ws)."

M  *Bifurcate Pattern.* Two terms, distinguished by the sex of the connecting relative, which can be glossed as "son's child" and "daughter's child."

N  *Bifurcate Speaker's Sex Pattern.* Four terms, differentiated by the sex both of the speaker and of the connecting relative, which can be glossed as "son's child (ms)," "son's child (ws)," "daughter's child (ms)," and "daughter's child (ws)." With the following variants:

    Na—with a man's SoCh further distinguished as SoSo (ms) and SoDa (ms).

    Nb—with SoCh (ws) equated with DaCh (ms).

R  A rare pattern, intermediate between D and M, distinguishing SoCh, DaSo, and DaDa.

S  A rare pattern, intermediate between M and N, distinguishing SoCh, DaCh (ms), and DaCh (ws).

T  A rare pattern distinguishing GrSo (ms), GrDa (ms), and GrCh (ws).

U  A rare pattern distinguishing GrCh (ms), GrSo (ws), and GrDa (ws).

V  A rare pattern distinguishing GrSo (ms), GrSo (ws), GrDa (ms), and GrDa (ws).

W  A rare pattern distinguishing SoCh, DaCh (ms), DaSo (ws), and DaDa (ws).

X  A rare pattern distinguishing SoSo (ms), SoDa (ms), SoCh (ws) = DaCh (ms), DaSo (ws) and DaDa (ws).

Y  A rare pattern with maximal differentiation into SoSo (ms), SoSo (ws), SoDa (ms), SoDa (ws), DaSo (ms), DaSo (ws), DaDa (ms), and DaDa (ws).

## PATTERNS FOR UNCLES

The kin terms reported for uncles have been analyzed into the patterns defined below. Like those for aunts and for nephews and nieces below, the names assigned to them are modifications of those proposed by Lowie (1928).

A  *Simple Bifurcate Merging Pattern.* A single special term which can be glossed as "mother's brother," paternal uncles being terminologically equated with father.

B  *Simple Bifurcate Collateral Pattern.* Two special terms, distinguished by

## TABLE 2
### Geographical Distribution of Patterns for Grandchildren

| Pattern | Africa | C-Med. | E. Eur. | In. Pac. | N. Amer. | S. Amer. | Total |
|---|---|---|---|---|---|---|---|
| A | 78 | 18 | 30 | 51 | 68 | 42 | 287 |
| B | 7 | 18 | 28 | 6 | 14 | 17 | 90 |
| C | 7 | 0 | 2 | 30 | 37 | 2 | 78 |
| D | 4 | 9 | 11 | 0 | 5 | 1 | 30 |
| K | 3 | 1 | 0 | 10 | 1 | 5 | 20 |
| L | 3 | 1 | 0 | 1 | 5 | 6 | 16 |
| M | 1 | 1 | 1 | 2 | 4 | 1 | 10 |
| N | 0 | 0 | 1 | 3 | 2 | 1 | 7 |
| R–Y | 2 | 0 | 2 | 2 | 5 | 1 | 12 |
| No data | 3 | 3 | 5 | 2 | 2 | 1 | 16 |
| Total | 108 | 51 | 80 | 107 | 143 | 77 | 566 |

the sex of the connecting relative, which can be glossed as "paternal uncle" and "maternal uncle."

C *Skewed Bifurcate Collateral Pattern.* Three special terms, distinguished by the sex of the connecting relative and in the case of paternal uncles also by relative age, which can be glossed as "father's elder brother," "father's younger brother," and "mother's brother."

D *Lineal Pattern.* A single special term, which can be glossed as "uncle," applying to both the father's and the mother's brothers and distinguishing them from father. With the following variant:
Da—with separate terms for a male and a female speaker.

E *Generation Pattern.* Special terms are lacking for both paternal and maternal uncles, who are terminologically equated with father.

K *Age-Differentiated Bifurcate Collateral Pattern.* Four terms, distinguished by both relative age and the sex of the connecting relative, which can be glossed as "father's elder brother," "father's younger brother," "mother's elder brother," and "mother's younger brother." With the following variant:
Ka—with FaYoBr terminologically equated with father.

L *Relative Age Pattern.* Two special terms, distinguished by age relative to that of the connecting relative, which can be glossed as "parent's elder brother" and "parent's younger brother."

M *Speaker-Differentiated Bifurcate Merging Pattern.* Paternal uncles are terminologically equated with father, while maternal uncles are called by two special terms, differentiated by the sex of the speaker, which can be glossed as "mother's brother (ms)" and "mother's brother (ws)."

N *Speaker-Differentiated Bifurcate Collateral Pattern.* Three special terms, differentiated by the sex of the connecting relative and for maternal uncles also by the sex of the speaker, which can be glossed as "father's brother (ms)," "mother's brother (ms)," and "mother's brother (ws)." With the following variant:
Na—with paternal uncles further distinguished as FaElBr and FaYoBr.

R A rare pattern, intermediate between K and L, distinguishing PaElBr, FaYoBr, and MoYoBr.

TABLE 3

Geographical Distribution of Patterns for Uncles

| Pattern | Africa | C-Med. | E. Eur. | In. Pac. | N. Amer. | S. Amer. | Total |
|---|---|---|---|---|---|---|---|
| A | 50 | 6 | 10 | 53 | 26 | 25 | 170 |
| B | 25 | 27 | 13 | 6 | 55 | 25 | 151 |
| C | 21 | 5 | 33 | 12 | 14 | 4 | 89 |
| D | 4 | 10 | 7 | 13 | 34 | 14 | 82 |
| E | 3 | 1 | 2 | 18 | 1 | 3 | 28 |
| K | 1 | 0 | 5 | 1 | 8 | 1 | 16 |
| L | 0 | 1 | 8 | 4 | 1 | 0 | 14 |
| M | 1 | 0 | 1 | 0 | 3 | 1 | 6 |
| N | 2 | 0 | 0 | 0 | 0 | 4 | 6 |
| R | 1 | 0 | 0 | 0 | 1 | 0 | 2 |
| No data | 0 | 1 | 1 | 0 | 0 | 0 | 2 |
| Total | 108 | 51 | 80 | 107 | 143 | 77 | 566 |

PATTERNS FOR AUNTS

The kin terms reported for aunts have been analyzed into the patterns defined below. It should be noted that the order of frequency, indicated by the order of listing, differs appreciably from that of the analogous patterns for uncles.

A *Simple Bifurcate Collateral Pattern.* Two special terms, distinguished by the sex of the connecting relative, which can be glossed as "paternal aunt" and "maternal aunt." Analogous to Pattern B for uncles.

B *Bifurcate Merging Pattern.* A single special term which can be glossed as "father's sister," maternal aunts being terminologically equated with mother. Analogous to Pattern A for uncles. With the following variant:

Ba—with paternal aunts differentiated by sex of speaker as FaSi (ms) and FaSi (ws).

C *Lineal Pattern.* A single special term, which can be glossed as "aunt," applying to both the father's and the mother's sisters and distinguishing them from mother. Analogous to Pattern D for uncles.

D *Generation Pattern.* Special terms are lacking for both maternal and paternal aunts, who are terminologically equated with mother. Analogous to Pattern E for uncles.

E *Skewed Bifurcate Collateral Pattern.* Three special terms, distinguished by the sex of the connecting relative and in the case of maternal aunts also by relative age, which can be glossed as "father's sister," "mother's elder sister," and "mother's younger sister." Analogous to Pattern C for uncles. With the following variant:

Ea—with MoYoSi terminologically equated with mother.

K *Relative Age Pattern.* Two special terms, distinguished by age relative to the connecting relative, which can be glossed as "parent's elder sister" and "parent's younger sister." Analogous to Pattern L for uncles.

L *Age-Differentiated Bifurcate Collateral Pattern.* Four terms, distinguished by both relative age and the sex of the connecting relative, which can be glossed as "father's elder sister," "father's younger sister," "mother's elder sister," and "mother's younger sister." Analogous to Pattern K for uncles.

M *Speaker-Differentiated Bifurcate Collateral Pattern.* Three special terms, differentiated by the sex of the connecting relative and for paternal aunts also by the sex of the speaker, which can be glossed as "father's sister (ms)," "father's sister (ws)," and "mother's sister." Analogous to Pattern N for uncles.

R A rare pattern distinguishing PaSi (ms) and PaSi (ws) by the sex of the speaker.

S A rare pattern, intermediate between A and L, distinguishing FaElSi, FaYoSi, and MoSi.

T A rare pattern, intermediate between K and R, distinguishing PaElSi, FaYoSi, and MoYoSi.

U A rare pattern, intermediate between L and R, distinguishing FaElSi, MoElSi, and PaYoSi.

TABLE 4

Geographical Distribution of Patterns for Aunts

| Pattern | Africa | C-Med. | E. Eur. | In. Pac. | N. Amer. | S. Amer. | Total |
|---------|--------|--------|---------|----------|----------|----------|-------|
| A       | 27     | 23     | 22      | 7        | 46       | 26       | 151   |
| B       | 38     | 5      | 11      | 42       | 29       | 24       | 149   |
| C       | 6      | 16     | 7       | 11       | 33       | 16       | 89    |
| D       | 18     | 2      | 2       | 35       | 4        | 5        | 66    |
| E       | 12     | 3      | 22      | 7        | 17       | 3        | 64    |
| K       | 2      | 0      | 10      | 2        | 1        | 0        | 15    |
| L       | 0      | 1      | 4       | 3        | 5        | 1        | 14    |
| M       | 2      | 0      | 0       | 0        | 3        | 2        | 7     |
| R–U     | 2      | 0      | 1       | 0        | 5        | 0        | 8     |
| No data | 1      | 1      | 1       | 0        | 0        | 0        | 3     |
| Total   | 108    | 51     | 80      | 107      | 143      | 77       | 566   |

PATTERNS FOR NEPHEWS AND NIECES (MALE SPEAKING)

The kin terms reported for nieces and nephews (male speaking) have been analyzed into the patterns defined below.

A *Simple Bifurcate Merging Pattern.* A single special term which can be glossed as "sister's child," a brother's children (ms) being terminologically equated with the speaker's own children. With three variants as follows:

Aa—with SiSo alone distinguished terminologically from own child.
Ab—with SiDa alone distinguished terminologically from own child.
Ac—with ElSiCh alone distinguished terminologically from own child.

B　*Sex-Differentiated Bifurcate Merging Pattern.* Two special terms, differentiated by sex, which can be glossed as "sister's son" and "sister's daughter," fraternal nephews and nieces (ms) being terminologically equated with the speaker's own children.

C　*Simple Bifurcate Collateral Pattern.* Two special terms, differentiated by the sex of the connecting relative, which can be glossed as "brother's child (ms)" and "sister's child (ms)."

D　*Simple Lineal Pattern.* A single special term which can be glossed as "sibling's child (ms)." With the following variant:

　　Da—with nieces only distinguished from own child, nephews being terminologically equated with sons.

E　*Generation Pattern.* Special terms are lacking for siblings' children (ms), who are terminologically equated with the speaker's own children.

F　*Sex-Differentiated Lineal Pattern.* Two special terms, differentiated by sex, which can be glossed as "nephew" and "niece."

G　*Sex-Differentiated Bifurcate Collateral Pattern.* Four special terms, differentiated by both sex and the sex of the connecting relative, which can be glossed as "brother's son (ms)," "brother's daughter (ms)," "sister's son (ms)," and "sister's daughter (ms)."

K　*Age-Skewed Bifurcate Collateral Pattern.* Three special terms, differentiated by the sex of the connecting relative and for brothers' children also by relative age, which can be glossed as "elder brother's child (ms)," "younger brother's child (ms)," and "sister's child (ms)." With the following variant:

　　Ka—with SiCh further differentiated as SiSo and SiDa.

L　*Age-Differentiated Bifurcate Collateral Pattern.* Four special terms, differentiated by sex and relative age, which can be glossed as "elder brother's child (ms)," "younger brother's child (ms)," "elder sister's child (ms)," and "younger sister's child (ms)." With two variants as follows:

　　La—with ElBrCh further distinguished as ElBrSo and ElBrDa.

　　Lb—with ElBrCh equated with the speaker's own child rather than distinguished.

M　*Sister-Skewed Bifurcate Collateral Pattern.* Three special terms, differentiated by the sex of the connecting relative and for sisters' children also by sex, which can be glossed as "brother's child (ms)," "sister's son (ms)," and "sister's daughter (ms)."

N　*Brother-Skewed Bifurcate Collateral Pattern.* Three special terms, differentiated by the sex of the connecting relative and for brothers' children also by sex, which can be glossed as "brother's son (ms)," "brother's daughter (ms)," and "sister's child (ms)."

R　A rare pattern distinguishing ElSbCh and YoSbCh by relative age only.

S　A rare pattern, intermediate between E and G, distinguishing BrSo, SiSo, and SbDa.

T　A rare pattern distinguishing ElBrSo=SiSo, YoBrCh, and SbDa.

U　A rare pattern distinguishing ElSbSo, ElSbDa, YoSbSo, and YoSbDa.

V A rare pattern distinguishing ElBrSo, YoBrSo, ElBrDa, YoBrDa, and SiCh.

W A rare pattern distinguishing ElBrCh, YoBrCh, YoBrDa, ElSiSo=SiDa, and YoSiDa.

X A rare pattern distinguishing ElBrSo, YoBrSo, ElBrDa, YoBrDa, SiSo, and SiDa.

Y A rare pattern, maximally differentiated, distinguishing ElBrSo, ElBrDa, YoBrSo, YoBrDa, ElSiSo, ElSiDa, YoSiSo, and YoSiDa.

## PATTERNS FOR SIBLINGS

The kin terms reported for siblings have been analyzed into the patterns defined below. The classification is essentially the same as that previously set forth by the author (Murdock 1968a) except that the patterns here labeled F, G, H, K, M, N, and O represent a sharpened reclassification of the group of patterns previously called "Melanesian."

Table 5

Geographical Distribution of Patterns for Nephews and Nieces

| Pattern | Africa | C-Med. | E. Eur. | In. Pac. | N. Amer. | S. Amer. | Total |
|---------|--------|--------|---------|----------|----------|----------|-------|
| A | 56 | 2 | 3 | 44 | 25 | 11 | 141 |
| B | 2 | 2 | 13 | 12 | 17 | 18 | 64 |
| C | 9 | 10 | 10 | 5 | 20 | 5 | 59 |
| D | 1 | 4 | 10 | 16 | 22 | 5 | 58 |
| E | 14 | 3 | 5 | 20 | 4 | 6 | 52 |
| F | 1 | 9 | 6 | 3 | 15 | 17 | 51 |
| G | 6 | 12 | 14 | 0 | 7 | 9 | 48 |
| K | 4 | 1 | 2 | 2 | 6 | 0 | 15 |
| L | 4 | 0 | 2 | 1 | 6 | 0 | 13 |
| M | 0 | 1 | 1 | 0 | 6 | 4 | 12 |
| N | 0 | 1 | 1 | 2 | 3 | 1 | 8 |
| R–Y | 1 | 0 | 4 | 0 | 8 | 1 | 14 |
| No data | 10 | 6 | 9 | 2 | 4 | 0 | 31 |
| Total | 108 | 51 | 80 | 107 | 143 | 77 | 566 |

A *Dravidian Pattern.* Four terms, distinguished by both sex and relative age, which can be glossed as "elder brother," "younger brother," "elder sister," and "younger sister." With seven variants as follows:
Aa—with ElBr further distinguished as ElBr (ms) and ElBr (ws).
Ab—with YoBr further distinguished as YoBr (ms) and YoBr (ws).
Ac—with YoSi further distinguished as YoSi (ms) and YoSi (ws).
Ad—with Si (ms) further distinguished from ElSi and YoSi.
Ae—with YoSi (ws) equated with YoBr rather than with YoSi (ms).
Af—with YoBr (ms) equated with YoSi rather than with YoBr (ws).
Ag—with YoBr (ws) equated with YoSi rather than with YoBr (ms).

B *European Pattern.* Two terms, distinguished by sex, which can be glossed as "brother" and "sister." With the following variant:
Ba—with separate terms for Br (ms) and Br (ws).

C  *Yoruban Pattern.* Two terms, distinguished by relative age, which can be glossed as "elder sibling" and "younger sibling." With two variants as follows:
   Ca—with a separate term for Si (ms).
   Cb—with YoSb further distinguished as YoBr (ms), YoSi (ms), and YoSb (ws).

D  *Algonkian Pattern.* Three terms, distinguished by relative age and for elder siblings also by sex, which can be glossed as "elder brother," "elder sister," and "younger sibling." With the following variant:
   Da—with ElBr further distinguished as ElBr (ms) and ElBr (ws).

E  *Kordofanian Pattern.* A single undifferentiated term, which can be glossed as "sibling."

F  *Southern Bantu Pattern.* Three terms, distinguished by relative sex and for siblings of the speaker's sex also by relative age, which can be glossed as "elder sibling of the speaker's sex," "younger sibling of the speaker's sex," and "sibling of the opposite sex." With two variants as follows:
   Fa—with YoSb of speaker's sex further distinguished as YoBr (ms) and YoSi (ws).
   Fb—with ElSb of speaker's sex further distinguished as ElBr (ms) and ElSi (ws).

G  *East Polynesian Pattern.* Four terms, distinguished by relative sex and for siblings of the speaker's sex also by relative age, which can be glossed as "elder sibling of the speaker's sex," "younger sibling of the speaker's sex," "brother (ws)," and "sister (ms)."

H  *Quechuan Pattern.* Four terms, distinguished by both sex and the sex of the speaker, which can be glossed as "brother (ms)," "brother (ws)," "sister (ms)," and "sister (ws)." With the following variant:
   Ha—with Br (ms) further distinguished as ElBr (ms) and YoBr (ms).

K  *Carolinian Pattern.* Two terms, distinguished by relative sex, which can be glossed as "sibling of the speaker's sex" and "sibling of the opposite sex."

L  *Siouan Pattern.* Any pattern with extensive differentiation by sex, sex of speaker, and relative age which results in a total of seven or eight distinct terms for siblings. With the following variant:
   La—any similar pattern with six distinct terms for siblings which include specific terms for either YoBr (ms) and YoBr (ws) or ElSi (ms) and ElSi (ws).

M  *Caddoan Pattern.* Six terms, distinguished by sex, by sex of speaker, and for siblings of the speaker's sex also by relative age, which can be glossed as "elder brother (ms)," "younger brother (ms)," "brother (ws)," "sister (ms)," "elder sister (ws)," and "younger sister (ws)." With two variants as follows:
   Ma—with YoBr (ms) equated with YoSi (ws).
   Mb—with YoBr (ms) equated with Br (ws).

N  *Malagasy Pattern.* Three terms, distinguished by relative sex and for siblings of the speaker's sex also by sex, which can be glossed as "sibling of the speaker's sex," "brother (ws)," and "sister (ms)." With the following variant:

Na—with Br (ws) further distinguished as ElBr (ws) and YoBr (ws).

O *Jivaran Pattern.* Three terms, distinguished by relative sex and for siblings of the opposite sex also by sex, which can be glossed as "brother (ms)," "sister (ws)," and "sibling of the opposite sex." With the following variant:

Oa—with Br (ms) further distinguished as ElBr (ms) and YoBr (ms).

P *Voltaic Pattern.* Three terms, distinguished by sex and for brothers also by relative age, which can be glossed as "elder brother," "younger brother," and "sister." With two variants as follows:

Pa—with Si further distinguished as Si (ms) and Si (ws).

Pb—with ElBr further distinguished as ElBr (ms) and ElBr (ws).

Q *Yukian Pattern.* Three terms, distinguished by relative age and for younger siblings also by sex, which can be glossed as "elder sibling," "younger brother," and "younger sister."

R   A rare pattern distinguishing Br (ms), Br (ws), ElSi, and YoSi.

S   A rare pattern distinguishing ElBr=YoBr (ws), ElSi (ws), Si (ms), and YoSb of the speaker's sex.

T   A rare pattern distinguishing ElBr (ms), YoBr (ms), ElSi (ws), YoSi (ws), and sibling of the opposite sex.

U   A rare pattern distinguishing ElBr (ms), ElBr (ws), YoBr, Si (ms), and Si (ws).

V   A rare pattern distinguishing ElBr (ms), ElBr (ws), YoBr (ms), ElSi, and YoSi=YoBr (ws).

W   A rare pattern distinguishing ElBr (ms), ElBr (ws), YoBr=YoSi (ws), ElSi (ws), and Si (ms).

X   A rare pattern distinguishing ElSb of the speaker's sex, YoSb of the speaker's sex, ElBr (ws), YoBr (ws), ElSi (ms), and YoSi (ms).

## PATTERNS FOR CROSS-COUSINS

The kin term patterns for cross-cousins have been analyzed according to the categories that have long been traditional, as defined below. Unfortunately, the data in the author's files do not enable him to make some of the finer distinctions that have recently been suggested, such as that between Iroquois proper and Kariera.

A *Hawaiian Pattern.* Special cousin terms are lacking, both cross and parallel cousins being called by the terms for siblings.

B *Iroquois Pattern.* One or more special terms for first cross-cousins, which differ from those for siblings, parallel cousins, and avuncular and nepotic relatives. With one variant as follows:

Ba—with a combination of Iroquois and Hawaiian features.

C *Eskimo Pattern.* One or more special terms for first cousins, differing

TABLE 6

| | | | | | | | |
|---|---|---|---|---|---|---|---|
| | Geographical Distribution of Patterns for Siblings | | | | | | |
| Pattern | Africa | C-Med. | E. Eur. | In. Pac. | N. Amer. | S. Amer. | Total |
| A | 9 | 6 | 33 | 8 | 50 | 24 | 130 |
| B | 21 | 35 | 12 | 9 | 6 | 8 | 91 |
| C | 8 | 4 | 7 | 14 | 10 | 8 | 51 |
| D | 3 | 1 | 10 | 9 | 23 | 1 | 47 |
| E | 30 | 0 | 1 | 7 | 2 | 2 | 42 |
| F | 13 | 0 | 1 | 10 | 2 | 3 | 29 |
| G | 6 | 0 | 2 | 9 | 6 | 4 | 27 |
| H | 4 | 2 | 3 | 6 | 7 | 4 | 26 |
| K | 4 | 0 | 0 | 16 | 0 | 3 | 23 |
| L | 0 | 0 | 2 | 0 | 11 | 7 | 20 |
| M | 0 | 1 | 3 | 1 | 7 | 5 | 17 |
| N | 1 | 0 | 3 | 7 | 2 | 1 | 14 |
| O | 2 | 0 | 0 | 4 | 3 | 3 | 12 |
| P | 3 | 1 | 1 | 2 | 5 | 1 | 13 |
| Q | 1 | 1 | 0 | 2 | 4 | 1 | 9 |
| R–X | 1 | 0 | 1 | 2 | 5 | 1 | 10 |
| No data | 2 | 0 | 1 | 1 | 0 | 1 | 5 |
| Total | 108 | 51 | 80 | 107 | 143 | 77 | 566 |

from those for siblings but not distinguishing cross from parallel cousins. With two variants as follows:

Ca—with a combination of Eskimo and Hawaiian features.

Cb—with a combination of Eskimo and Iroquois features.

D   *Omaha Pattern.* The children of a mother's brother and of a father's sister are terminologically distinguished from siblings, parallel cousins, and each other but are not designated by special terms. Instead, a mother's brother's children are terminologically equated with relatives of an ascending generation, normally with mother's brother and mother, and a father's sister's children are equated with relatives of a descending generation, normally with a man's sisters' children and a woman's own children. With three variants as follows:

Da—with a combination of Omaha and Hawaiian features.

Db—with a combination of Omaha and Iroquois features.

Dc—with a combination of Omaha and Sudanese features.

E   *Crow Pattern.* The mirror image of the Omaha pattern, with a mother's brother's children terminologically equated with relatives of a descending generation, normally with a man's own children and a woman's brother's children, while a father's sister's children are equated with relatives of an ascending generation, normally with father and father's sister. With three variants as follows:

Ea—with a combination of Crow and Hawaiian features.

Eb—with a combination of Crow and Iroquois features.

Ec—with a combination of Crow and Sudanese features.

F   *Descriptive Pattern.* Special terms of a descriptive character for all first cousins, automatically distinguishing mother's brothers children and father's sister's children from each other and also from siblings, parallel cousins, and avuncular and nepotic relatives.

K *Sudanese Pattern.* Special terms, not descriptive in character or at least not wholly or obviously so, which distinguish a mother's brother's children from a father's sister's child and also from siblings and parallel cousins. With two variants as follows:

Ka—with a combination of Sudanese and Hawaiian features.
Kb—with a combination of Sudanese and Iroquois features.

## PATTERNS FOR SIBLINGS-IN-LAW

The terminology for siblings-in-law presents substantially greater problems of classification than do the terms for the seven sets of relatives previously analyzed. Not only are data lacking or seriously incomplete for a larger proportion of the kinship systems surveyed (nearly one-fourth of the total number) but the sources consulted probably contain more errors, if one may take as an indication the larger proportion of "disjunctive" patterns (see Nerlove and Romney 1967) reported. The number of possible distinctions is greater; differentiation by sex, relative age, sex of speaker, and sex of connecting relative, which permit a maximum of eight distinct terms for siblings, grandchildren, or nepotic relatives, allow for as many as sixteen for siblings-in-law: WiElBr, WiYoBr, WiElSi, WiYoSi, HuElBr, HuYoBr, HuElSi, HuYoSi, ElBrWi (ms), ElBrWi (ws), YoBrWi (ms), YoBrWi (ws), ElSiHu (ms), ElSiHu (ws), YoSiHu (ms), and YoSiHu (ws). Moreover, siblings-in-law of opposite sex may be equated terminologically as potential levirate or sororate spouses as well as distinguished on the basis of sex or other criteria. The problem of classification is thus exceptionally complicated, and the patterns distinguished below should be considered appreciably less definitive than those presented for the other seven sets of relatives.

A *Merging Pattern.* A single undifferentiated term, which can be glossed as "sibling-in-law." With three variants as follows:

Aa—with an additional special term or pair of terms for Bril (ms).
Ab—with an additional special term or pair of terms for Siil (ws).
Ac—with a comparable exception for another pair of Sbil.

### TABLE 7
Geographical Distribution of Patterns for Cross-Cousins

| Pattern | Africa | C-Med. | E. Eur. | In. Pac. | N. Amer. | S. Amer. | Total |
|---------|--------|--------|---------|----------|----------|----------|-------|
| A | 28 | 5 | 12 | 39 | 63 | 24 | 171 |
| B | 40 | 8 | 18 | 38 | 34 | 29 | 167 |
| C | 3 | 16 | 14 | 11 | 20 | 10 | 74 |
| D | 15 | 2 | 13 | 5 | 8 | 5 | 48 |
| E | 9 | 0 | 1 | 9 | 17 | 4 | 40 |
| F | 5 | 14 | 12 | 0 | 0 | 1 | 32 |
| K | 7 | 4 | 7 | 4 | 0 | 2 | 24 |
| No data | 1 | 2 | 3 | 1 | 1 | 2 | 10 |
| Total | 108 | 51 | 80 | 107 | 143 | 77 | 566 |

B *Simple Bisexual Pattern.* Two terms, differentiated by sex, which can be glossed as "brother-in-law" and "sister-in-law." With the following variant:

Ba—with additional distinctions based on relative age.

C *Speaker's Sex Bisexual Pattern.* Four terms, distinguished by sex and the sex of the speaker, which can be glossed as "brother-in-law (ms)," "brother-in-law (ws)," "sister-in-law (ms)," and "sister-in-law (ws)." With two variants as follows:

Ca—with one or two of the four categories further distinguished as follows:

Bril (ms) as WiBr and SiHu (ms), Bril (ws) as HuSi and BrWi (ws), Siil (ms) as WiSi and BrWi (ms), Siil (ws) as HuSi and BrWi (ws).

Cb—with siblings-in-law of opposite sex distinguished as SpSb and SbSp rather than by sex and sex of speaker.

D *Opposite Sex Pattern.* Three terms, distinguished by relative sex and for siblings-in-law of the speaker's sex also by sex, which can be glossed as "sibling-in-law of opposite sex," "brother-in-law (ms)," and "sister-in-law (ws)." With the following variant:

Da—with siblings-in-law of the speaker's sex otherwise differentiated.

E *Null Pattern.* Special affinal terms are absent or rare, siblings-in-law being called by terms for consanguineal relatives, mainly those applying primarily to cousins rather than siblings. With the following variant:

Ea—siblings-in-law are called by consanguineal terms which are primarily those applied to siblings.

J *Differentiated Pattern.* Any pattern having seven or eight distinct terms for siblings-in-law exclusive of those differentiated by relative age. Analogous to the Siouan pattern for siblings.

K *Strongly Differentiated Pattern.* Any pattern having more than eight distinct terms for siblings-in-law and thus necessarily involving a proliferation of terms based on distinctions of relative age.

L *Relative Sex Pattern.* Two terms, distinguished by relative sex, which can be glossed as "sibling-in-law of the speaker's sex" and "sibling-in-law of the opposite sex."

M *Sex-of-link Bisexual Pattern.* Six terms, distinguished by both sex and the sex of the connective relative, which can be glossed as "wife's brother," "husband's brother," "wife's sister," "husband's sister," "sister's husband," and "brother's wife." With three variants as follows:

Ma—with WiBr equated with SiHu and/or BrWi (ms) distinguished from BrWi (ws).

Mb—with WiBr equated with WiSi.

Mc—with WiBr equated with SiHu and HuSi with BrWi.

N *Spouse's Sibling vs. Sibling's Spouse Pattern.* Two terms, distinguished by the affinal or consanguineal character of the connecting relative, which can be glossed as "spouse's sibling" and "sibling's spouse." With three variants as follows:

Na—with SbSp further distinguished as BrWi and SiHu.

Nb—with SpSb further distinguished as WiSb and HuSb.

Nc—with the further distinctions of both Na and Nb.

O *Skewed Bisexual Pattern.* Three terms, distinguished by sex and for females also by the sex of the speaker, which can be glossed as "brother-in-law," "sister-in-law (ms)," and "sister-in-law (ws)."

P *Paired Bisexual Pattern.* Four terms, distinguished by sex and by additional but different criteria for spouse's siblings and sibling's spouses, which can be glossed as "spouse's brother," "spouse's sister," "sister's husband," and "brother's wife." With two variants as follows:

Pa—with WiBr equated with SiHu rather than with WiBr.

Pb—with a further differentiation of either SpBr or SpSi.

Q *Potential Spouse Pattern.* Any of several variant patterns which have in common the terminological equating of HuBr with BrWi (ms) and of WiSi with SiHu (ws), who are potential spouses under the levirate and sororate respectively.

R *Same Sex Pattern.* Three terms, distinguished by relative sex and for siblings-in-law of the opposite sex also by sex and sex of speaker, which can be glossed as "sibling-in-law of the speaker's sex," "brother-in-law (ws)," and "sister-in-law (ms)." With the following variant:

Ra—with siblings-in-law of opposite sex otherwise differentiated.

S *Relative Age Pattern.* Two terms, distinguished by relative age, which can be glossed as "sibling-in-law older than the connecting sibling or spouse" and "sibling-in-law younger than the connecting relative."

T A rare pattern with one term for sisters-in-law and two for brothers-in-law.

U A rare pattern distinguishing siblings-in-law by sex, by relative age, and for sisters-in-law younger than the connecting relative also by sex of speaker.

V A rare pattern distinguishing WiBr=SiHu (ms), SiHu (ws), HuBr, SpSi, BrWi (ms), and BrWi (ws).

W A series of patterns, otherwise difficult to classify, which have in common the terminological equating of potential levirate spouses, namely, HuBr and BrWi (ms). They are listed below with the societies for which they are reported:

Aimol: HuBr=BrWi, WiBr, SiHu, and SpSi.

Kewa: HuBr=BrWi(ms)=WiSi, WiBr=SiHu, Siil (ws).

Kipsigis: HuBr = BrWi(ms) = WiSi, WiBr = SiHu = BrWi(ws), HuSi.

Kutubu: HuBr=BrWi(ms)=SiHu(ws), WiSb, SiHu (ms), HuSi=BrWi (ws).

Lango: HuBr=BrWi=WiSi, WiBr, SiHu, HuSi.

Swazi: HuSb=BrWi, WiSb=SiHu(ms), SiHu (ws).

Waura: HuBr=BrWi(ms)=SiHu(ws), WiBr=SiHu(ms), SpSi=BrWi(ws).

X A series of patterns, otherwise difficult to classify, which have in common the terminological equating of potential sororate spouses, namely,

WiSi and SiHu (ws). They are listed below with the societies for which they are reported:

Bari, Diegueno, and Kiwai: WiSb=SiHu, HuBr, HuSi=BrWi.

Cocopa and Yuma: WiSi=SiHu(ws), WiBr=SiHu(ms), HuSi, BrWi.

Jivaro: WiSi=SiHu(ms), SpBr, HuSi=BrWi.

Keweyipaya and Kurama: WiSb=SiHu, HuSb, BrWi.

Maori: WiSi=SiHu(ws), WiBr=Siil(ws), HuBr, BrWi (ms).

Teso: WiSi=SiHu, WiBr, HuBr, HuSi, BrWi.

Y   A series of disjunctive and otherwise unclassifiable patterns, some of which doubtless reflect errors in reporting or transcribing. They are listed below with the societies for which they are reported:

Atayal: Bril (ms), HuBr, SpSi, BrWi(ms)=SiHu(ws), BrWi(ws).

Chipewyan: WiBr=HuSi, HuBr=SiHu, WiSi=BrWi.

Eromangans: SpSb=SiHu(ms)=HuSi, WiSi, BrWi, SiHu(ws).

Ingassana and Molima: WiSb=BrWi, HuSb=SiHu.

Malinke: SpElBr=YoSiHu(ms), WiYoBr=ElSiHu(ms), HuYoBr= ElSiHu(ws), SpElSb=YoBrWi(ws), WiYoSi=ElBrWi(ms), YoBrWi(ms)=HuYoSi=YoSiHu(ws).

Washo: Bril(ms)=HuSi, HuBr, SiHu(ws), HuSi, BrWi(ms), BrWi(ws).

Yokuts: WiBr, SiHu, HuBr=WiSi, BrWi.

TABLE 8

Geographical Distribution of Patterns for Siblings-in-Law

| Pattern | Africa | C-Med. | E. Eur. | In. Pac. | N. Amer. | S. Amer. | Total |
|---|---|---|---|---|---|---|---|
| A | 38 | 4 | 4 | 21 | 21 | 5 | 93 |
| B | 6 | 17 | 4 | 2 | 12 | 9 | 50 |
| C | 5 | 0 | 1 | 3 | 18 | 20 | 47 |
| D | 2 | 1 | 0 | 7 | 28 | 8 | 46 |
| E | 4 | 2 | 6 | 15 | 2 | 4 | 33 |
| J | 4 | 2 | 10 | 2 | 4 | 1 | 23 |
| K | 2 | 0 | 16 | 2 | 1 | 2 | 23 |
| L | 2 | 0 | 2 | 12 | 3 | 0 | 19 |
| M | 2 | 1 | 4 | 3 | 7 | 2 | 19 |
| N | 1 | 2 | 0 | 2 | 8 | 1 | 14 |
| O | 2 | 1 | 3 | 0 | 4 | 0 | 10 |
| P | 0 | 3 | 4 | 0 | 1 | 2 | 10 |
| Q | 2 | 0 | 0 | 2 | 4 | 2 | 10 |
| R | 0 | 0 | 2 | 1 | 2 | 1 | 6 |
| S | 3 | 2 | 0 | 1 | 1 | 0 | 7 |
| T–Y | 8 | 1 | 2 | 7 | 8 | 4 | 30 |
| No data | 27 | 15 | 22 | 27 | 19 | 16 | 126 |
| Total | 108 | 51 | 80 | 107 | 143 | 77 | 566 |

## Conclusions

This paper has been concerned only with an analysis of the patterns of classification of the kin terms for eight sets of relatives and with the distribution of these patterns by geographical regions. The more interesting problem of ascertaining the extent to which the several patterns correlate with particular features of social organization or other elements of culture must be postponed for further consideration. To aid readers who may wish to test hypotheses of such correlations on their own, the data for all the systems surveyed are assembled in Table 9, ordered by cultural provinces. The second column in the Appendix gives the identifying numbers of the societies that have been covered to date in the Ethnographic Atlas of this journal, thereby providing such readers with access to masses of coded data for potential correlations. Only 49 of the 566 societies have not as yet been included in the Atlas.

## BIBLIOGRAPHY

Lowie, R. H. 1928. A Note on Relationship Terminologies. American Anthropologist 30: 265-266.

Murdock, G. P. 1968a. Patterns of Sibling Terminology. Ethnology 7: 1-24.

———— 1968b. World Sampling Provinces. Ethnology 7: 305-326.

Nerlove, S., and A. K. Romney. 1967. Sibling Terminology and Cross-Sex Behavior. American Anthropologist 69: 179-187.

# APPENDIX

## Kin Term Patterns for 566 Societies by Cultural Provinces

| Province & Society | Atlas Number | GrPa | GrCh | PaBr | PaSi | SbCh | Sibl | CrCo | Sb-il |
|---|---|---|---|---|---|---|---|---|---|
| **Hottentots (1)** | | | | | | | | | |
| Bergdama | Aa4:201 | A | B | B | A | G | B | Ka | . |
| Nama | Aa3:102 | A | B | A | B | B | A | B | C |
| **Bushmen (2)** | | | | | | | | | |
| Kung | Aa1:1 | Aa | Ca | D | C | E | D | C | E |
| Xam | Aa8:635 | A | B | B | A | C | B | A | J |
| **Southeast Bantu (3)** | | | | | | | | | |
| Mpezeni Ngoni | Ac9:351 | B | A | A | B | F | E | B | Ea |
| Pondo | Ab10:402 | B | A | B | A | A | A | B | Ma |
| Swazi | Ab2:3 | A | A | A | B | A | B | B | W |
| Thonga | Ab4:104 | B | A | C | E | A | C | D | B |
| Zezuru Shona | Ab18:410 | C | A | C | E | A | F | D | Da |
| **Sotho (4)** | | | | | | | | | |
| Kgatla Tswana | Ab13:405 | A | A | C | E | K | F | B | Cb |
| Lozi | Ab3:103 | B | A | C | E | F | F | A | A |
| Venda | Ab6:204 | B | A | C | E | A | F | B | J |
| **Southwest Bantu (5)** | | | | | | | | | |
| Ambo | Ab19:411 | A | A | A | B | A | E | C | A |
| Herero | Ab1:2 | A | A | C | B | A | F | B | A |
| Mbundu | Ab5:203 | A | A | A | B | A | G | B | A |
| **West Central Bantu (6)** | | | | | | | | | |
| Chokwe | Ac12:698 | B | A | B | A | A | K | B | A |
| Dzing | Ac22:736 | A | C | B | A | C | D? | B | B? |
| Luchazi | Ac27:741 | B | A | D | A | C | C | B | A |
| Ndembu | Ac6:206 | B | A | A | B | A | G | D | A |
| Pende | Ac2:5 | B | A | A | B | A | F | E | D |

| Society | Code | 1 | 2 | 3 | 4 | 5 | 6 | 7 | 8 |
|---|---|---|---|---|---|---|---|---|---|
| **East Central Bantu (7)** | | | | | | | | | |
| Chewa | Ac10:637 | B | B | F | A | B | A | A | M |
| Ila | Ac1:4 | N | B | Ha | A | E | C | A | B |
| Lamba | Ac5:205 | A | B | G | A | B | A | A | A |
| Shila | Ac35:749 | A | B | K | A | B | A | A | B |
| Yao | Ac7:304 | A | B | S | A | B | C | A | B |
| **Interior Tanzania (9)** | | | | | | | | | |
| Bena | Ad11:638 | A | B | C | A | B | A | A | M |
| Fipa | Ad19:761 | A | B | K | A | B | A | A | A |
| Nyakyusa | Ad6:208 | C | B | F | A | B | A | A | B |
| Nyamwezi | Ad20:762 | K | B | F | A | A | B | A | M |
| Turu | Ad26:768 | Aa | A | E | A | E | C | A | A |
| **Rift (10)** | | | | | | | | | |
| Gogo | Ad24:766 | · | B | · | A | A | A | A | A |
| Mbugwe | Ad5:207 | · | E | E | A | D | C | A | A |
| Sandawe | Aa6:301 | · | Ka | H | A | M | N | A | A |
| **Northeast Coastal Bantu (11)** | | | | | | | | | |
| Bajun | Ad1:6 | A | F | E | C | M | N | A | A |
| Giryama | Ad32:774 | · | K | E | F | E | C | A | A |
| Hadimu | Ad29:771 | A | A | D | A | E | C | A | A |
| Luguru | Ad14:704 | · | E | · | C | E | A | A | A |
| **Kenya Highland Bantu (12)** | | | | | | | | | |
| Kikuyu | Ad4:108 | C | D | B | A | C | C | D | Ba |
| Shambala | Ad10:629 | · | A | Oa | F | A | C | A | A |
| Teita | Ad37:779 | · | D | E | A | B | A | C | S |
| **Lacustrine Bantu (13)** | | | | | | | | | |
| Ganda | Ad7:306 | · | B | K | A | A | B | A | C |
| Haya | Ad42:786 | A | D | B | A | A | B | A | A |
| Hunde | Ae15:794 | E | B | G | B | A | A | A | A |
| Nyoro | Ad2:7 | A | B | O | A | A | B | A | A |
| Ruanda | Ae10:641 | Ab | B | G | A | A | B | A | A |

APPENDIX *Continued*

| Province & Society | Atlas Number | GrPa | GrCh | PaBr | PaSi | SbCh | SibI | CrCo | Sb-il |
|---|---|---|---|---|---|---|---|---|---|
| *South Equatorial Bantu* (14) | | | | | | | | | |
| Nkundo Mongo | Ae4:100 | B | A | A | B | A | F | E | A |
| Rega | Ae17:796 | A | A | C | K | K | C | B | J |
| Songola | Ae11:670 | B | A | B | D | . | F? | A | A |
| Yeke | Ae19:798 | B | A | A | B | A | Fb | B | B |
| *North Equatorial Bantu* (16) | | | | | | | | | |
| Amba | Ae1:8 | B | A | A | B | A | E | D | L |
| Kumu | Ae32:811 | . | K | A | B | A | C | A | . |
| *Cameroon Bantu* (17) | | | | | | | | | |
| Bubi | Ae44:823 | A | A | D | C | . | B | A | . |
| Duala | Ae12:699 | B | A | A | A | . | N | B | . |
| Kpe | Ae2:9 | B | A | A | D | A | E | . | A |
| *Southeast Nigeria* (18) | | | | | | | | | |
| Efik | Af19:919 | C | A | B | A | F | E | F | A |
| Ezinihite Ibo | Af10:643 | C | A | R | T | A | E | D | A |
| Ndoro | Ah26:1013 | A | A | A | D | A | C | A | . |
| Tiv | Ah3:116 | A | Ca | A | B | F | E | K? | A |
| Yako | Af10:643 | C | A | A | A | F | E | B | J |
| *Slave Coast* (19) | | | | | | | | | |
| Fon | Af1:10 | C | A | B | A | . | B | F | A |
| Glidyi Ewe | Af36:936 | A | L | A | B | A | A | C? | . |
| Oyo Yoruba | Af6:212 | A | A | E | D | F | C | A | Ac |
| *Akan* (20) | | | | | | | | | |
| Akyem | Af12:671 | B | C | A | B | A | E | E | A |
| Ashanti | Af3:111 | B | C | A | B | C | E | Ec | Aa |
| Ga | Af43:934 | A? | B | D | C | . | B | A | . |
| *Grain Coast* (21) | | | | | | | | | |
| Bete | Af7:310 | C | . | B | A | F | E | A | A |

| Society | Code | | | | | | | | |
|---|---|---|---|---|---|---|---|---|---|
| Mende | Af5:211 | A | A | B | D | F | E | A | O |
| Sherbro | Af14:700 | A | A | A | D | F | H | A | A |
| Vai | Af58:958 | A | A | A | D | A | A | Da | Ea |
| *Senegambians* (22) | | | | | | | | | |
| Wolof | Cb2:21 | B | A | A | B | C | C | A | · |
| *Nuclear Mande* (24) | | | | | | | | | |
| Bambara | Ag1:12 | A | L | B | A | A | A | B | B |
| Malinke | Ag9:645 | A | A | B | A | A | A | B | Y |
| Susu | Ag26:971 | A | · | A | B | A | A | B | S |
| *Habe-Senufo* (26) | | | | | | | | | |
| Dogon | Ag3:113 | C | D | C | A | X | P | B | · |
| *Upper Volta* (27) | | | | | | | | | |
| Bisa | Ag53:1171 | A | A? | K | S | F | P | A | · |
| Konkomba | Ag10:673 | A | A | C | E | L | P | Da | · |
| Lobi | Ag11:674 | A | A | B | A | L | B | E | · |
| Mossi | Ag47:992 | B | A | C | E | L | Q? | B | · |
| Tallensi | Ag4:114 | A | A | C | B | K | F | A | K |
| *Niger Bend* (25) | | | | | | | | | |
| Songhai | Cb3:122 | B | A | C | E | F | A | B | S |
| Zerma | Cb20:878 | A | A | · | C | · | P | C | A |
| *Fulani* (23) | | | | | | | | | |
| Djafun | Cb21:1079 | B | A | B | A | A | C | B | N? |
| Futajalonke | Ag6:214 | A | A | B | B | A | A | B | S |
| Wodaabe | Cb24:1082 | B | A | B | A | C | C | B | Na |
| *Hausa* (28) | | | | | | | | | |
| Dera | Cb28:1086 | B | A | A | D | A | B | A | B |
| Karekare | Cb10:683 | A | B | C | B | F | Q | A | Ea |
| Maguzawa | Cb1:20 | B | A | E | D | M | A | A | · |
| Zazzagawa | Cb26:1084 | B | A | A | B | · | A | B | · |

APPENDIX *Continued*

| Province & Society | Atlas Number | GrPa | GrCh | PaBr | PaSi | SbCh | Sibl | CrCo | Sb-il |
|---|---|---|---|---|---|---|---|---|---|
| *Jos Plateau* (29) | | | | | | | | | |
| Birom | Ah17:1004 | N | A | A | D | F | B | D? | Ab |
| Chawai | Ah10:701 | W | V | E | D | F | E | A | Aa? |
| Gure | Ah6:314 | R | C | A | . | . | B | A | C |
| Katab | Ah1:14 | A | A | A | D | A | E | B | Q |
| Kurama | Ah21:1088 | A | A | E | D | F | A | B | X |
| *Adamawa* (30) | | | | | | | | | |
| Daka | Ah29:1016 | A | A | C | K | G | B | A | A |
| Longuda | Ah30:1017 | B | A | B | D | C | F | E | A? |
| Yungur | Ah33:1020 | A | M | A | D | A | G | A | A |
| *Chad* (31) | | | | | | | | | |
| Bachama | Cb27:1085 | A | B | C | L | G | A | A | P |
| Buduma | Cb5:321 | A | . | C | E | . | C | B | A |
| Hona | Ah37:1024 | A | L | A | D | A | E | A | S? |
| Massa | Ai9:646 | A | A | B | A | . | B | A | . |
| *Wadai and Darfur* (32) | | | | | | | | | |
| Fur | Cb17:875 | B | A | A | A | C | Ma | Ka | V |
| Maba | Cb (new) | A | A | B | C | . | B | F | . |
| *North Equatoria* (33) | | | | | | | | | |
| Azande | Ai3:117 | B | A | A | B | . | C | K | . |
| Banda | Ai1:15 | B | A | A | B | . | H | D | L |
| Ngbandi | Ai26:1041 | A | A | C | B | K? | B | D | Aa |
| *Central Sudanic Peoples* (34) | | | | | | | | | |
| Mangbetu | Ai11:702 | A | . | A | B | D | E | A | . |
| *Nuba* (35) | | | | | | | | | |
| Koalib | Ai37:1052 | A | D | A | D | L | E | A | A |
| Lafofa | Ai (new) | A | A | A | D | A | E | A | Aa |
| Mesakin | Ai39:1054 | B | A | A | B | A | E | B | Q |
| Nyaro | Ai2:16 | A | K? | A | D | C | E | A | . |

| | | | | | | | | | |
|---|---|---|---|---|---|---|---|---|---|
| **Prenilotes (36)** | | | | | | | | | |
| Ingassana | Ai4:118 | A | A | A | B | A | B | B | Y |
| **Northern Nilotes (37)** | | | | | | | | | |
| Bari | Aj8:354 | A | A | A | B | A | E | D | X |
| Lotuko | Aj12:678 | B | K | B | A | . | B | B | . |
| Nuer | Aj3:120 | A | D | B | A | G | B | F | . |
| Shilluk | Ai6:218 | A | A | A | A | G | B | K | . |
| **Southern Nilotes (38)** | | | | | | | | | |
| Dorobo | Aa2:101 | A | A | M | Ba | A | E | Dc | O |
| Kipsigis | Aj9:648 | A | B | A | B | A | E | B | W |
| Lango | Aj4:219 | A | B | B | B | G | B | Dc | W |
| Teso | Aj1:17 | A | B | A | C | G | B | A | X |
| Turkana | Aj5:220 | A | T | A | C | A | B | F | Ma |
| **Western Cushites (39)** | | | | | | | | | |
| Kafa | Ca30:860 | C | D | B | A | G | B | C | B |
| **Galla-Konso (40)** | | | | | | | | | |
| Arusi | Ca11:841 | A | B? | B | C | G | B | F | A |
| Konso | Ca1:18 | A | B | A | B | B | H | F | . |
| **Horn (41)** | | | | | | | | | |
| Afar | Ca6:649 | A | B | B | A | C | B | F? | B |
| **Ethiopian Semites (42)** | | | | | | | | | |
| Amhara | Ca7:679 | A | A | D | C | C | Ad | F | O |
| Gurage | Ca8:707 | A | A | B | A | N | B | D | . |
| Tigrinya | Ca3:121 | A | D | B | A | C? | B | F | . |
| **Central and Northern Cushites (43)** | | | | | | | | | |
| Bogo or Bilen | Ca37:867 | A | A | B | A | C | B | . | . |
| Kemant | Ca (new) | A | A | B | . | D? | B | . | B |
| **Nubians (44)** | | | | | | | | | |
| Dilling | Ai8:317 | A | A | B | A | C | E | F | B |

APPENDIX *Continued*

| Province & Society | Atlas Number | GrPa | GrCh | PaBr | PaSi | SbCh | Sibl | CrCo | Sb-il |
|---|---|---|---|---|---|---|---|---|---|
| *Central Sahara (45)* | | | | | | | | | |
| Teda | Cc2:23 | A | B | B | A | C | D | B | A |
| *Tuareg (46)* | | | | | | | | | |
| Ahaggaren | Cc9:881 | A | K | A | B | B | A | B | . |
| *Oasis Berbers (47)* | | | | | | | | | |
| Siwans | Cc3:123 | C | D? | L | C | . | B | F | . |
| *Mountain Berbers (48)* | | | | | | | | | |
| Semlal Shluh | Cd5:322 | C | B | B | A | G | B | Dc | . |
| Snus Zekara | Cd10:896 | A | B | B | A | G | B | F | . |
| *Arabs of North Africa (49)* | | | | | | | | | |
| Berabish | Cc7:684 | A | . | B | A | F | B | F | S |
| Egyptians | Cd2:124 | A | D | B | A | G | B | F | B |
| *Jews (51)* | | | | | | | | | |
| Ancient Hebrews | Cj3:230 | A | D | B | A? | G | B | C | B |
| Polish Jews | Ch (new) | A | D | D | C | E | B | C | B |
| *Arabs of Southwest Asia (52)* | | | | | | | | | |
| Rwala Bedouin | Cj2:132 | A | M | B | A | G | B | F | Pa |
| *Turkey (54)* | | | | | | | | | |
| Anatolian Turks | Cl5:653 | A | B | B | A | G | B | F | Pa |
| *Southeast Europe (55)* | | | | | | | | | |
| Gheg Albanians | Ce1:25 | A? | . | B | A | E | B | C | B |
| Periclean Athenians | Ce (new) | N | D | D | C | E | B | C | B |
| Romanians | Ch (new) | A | B | D | C | E | B | C | B |
| Serbs | Ch1:30 | A | B | B | C | G | B | K | J |
| *Southwest Europe (56)* | | | | | | | | | |
| French Canadians | Cf5:1133 | A | B | D | C | E | B | C | B |

| | Code | | | | | | | | |
|---|---|---|---|---|---|---|---|---|---|
| Imperial Romans | Ce3:126 | A | B | B | A | G | B | K | · |
| Sicilians | Ce (new) | A | A | D | C | D | B | C | B |
| Spanish Basques | Ce (new) | A | B | D | C | D | H | C | · |
| *Northwest Europe (57)* | | | | | | | | | |
| Icelanders | Cg2:29 | A | D | B | A | G | B | F | B |
| Irish | Cg3:128 | A | B | B | A | E | B | C | B |
| Tristan da Cunha | Cf3:226 | A | B | D | C | E | B | C | Ea |
| *Finnic Peoples (58)* | | | | | | | | | |
| Lapps | Cg4:129 | A | L | C | E | K | B | C | D |
| *Northeast Europe (59)* | | | | | | | | | |
| Czechs | Ch3:338 | A | B | D | C | E | B | C | B |
| Hutsul | Ch2:130 | A | B | B | A | E | B | C | B |
| *Caucasus (60)* | | | | | | | | | |
| Cherkess | Ci4:229 | A | A | D? | C? | D | B | C | B |
| Georgians | Ci8:910 | A | D | B | A | C | B | F | J |
| *Armenia and Azerbaijan (61)* | | | | | | | | | |
| Armenians | Ci10:912 | A | A | B | A | · | B | B | · |
| *North Iran (62)* | | | | | | | | | |
| Iranians | Ea9:1135 | A | A | B | A | C | B | F | M |
| Kurd | Ci11:913 | A | A | B | C | C | B | K | M |
| *South Iran (63)* | | | | | | | | | |
| Basseri | Ea6:358 | A | Ca | B | A | C | B | · | J |
| Marri Baluch | Ea10:1175 | C | B | B | A | C | B | F | P |
| *Indus Valley (64)* | | | | | | | | | |
| Sindhi | Ea1:34 | C | D | B | A | G | B | K | K |
| *Southwest India (65)* | | | | | | | | | |
| Kerala | Eg6:243 | C | A | C | E | · | M | B | · |
| Toda | Eg4:143 | A | D | A | B | B | D | B | Pb |

APPENDIX *Continued*

| Province & Society | Atlas Number | GrPa | GrCh | PaBr | PaSi | SbCh | Sibl | CrCo | Sb-il |
|---|---|---|---|---|---|---|---|---|---|
| *Ceylon* (66) | | | | | | | | | |
| Sinhalese | Eh6:245 | A | B | C | E | G | A | B | B |
| Vedda | Eh4:145 | L | B | C | E | L | A | B | B |
| *Southeast India* (67) | | | | | | | | | |
| Chenchu | Eg1:43 | A | B | C | E | B | A | B | K |
| Coorg | Eg5:242 | A | B | B | A | G | A | B | Ba |
| Maria Gond | Eg3:142 | C | D | C | E | N | A | B | K |
| Reddi | Eg (new) | N | A | C | E | . | B | B | O |
| Telugu | Eg10:688 | K | B | C | E | B | A | B | O |
| *Munda* (68) | | | | | | | | | |
| Baiga | Eg9:654 | C | D | C | E | G | A | B | K |
| Hill Bhuiya | Eg7:329 | A | B | C | E | X | A | A | K |
| Kol | Eg8:363 | . | B | C | E | D | B | A | K |
| Santal | Ef1:42 | . | . | C | E | G | Ha | K | K |
| *Ganges Valley* (69) | | | | | | | | | |
| Bengali | Ef2:141 | C | B | C | A | G | A | F | K |
| Bhilala | Ef (new) | A | B | C | E | K | A? | C | K |
| Bihari | Ef (new) | C? | . | C | B | G | B | F | K |
| Chakma | Ei10:418 | M | A | M | A | G | A | F | K |
| Indo-Aryans | Ef3:240 | C | D | A | A | B | B | F | J |
| *Dardistan and Kashmir* (70) | | | | | | | | | |
| Burusho | Ee2:139 | A | B? | A | B | A | N | A | R |
| Dard | Ee5:327 | A | B | C | E | C | B | F | . |
| Kashmiri | Ef8:1082 | A | D | B | A | G | B | K | J |
| *Afghanistan* (71) | | | | | | | | | |
| Hazara | Ea3:231 | A | B | B | A | C | B | K | . |
| Pathan | Ea2:133 | A | B | B | A | G | B | B | Ma |

| People | Code | | | | | | | | |
|---|---|---|---|---|---|---|---|---|---|
| ***Turkestan (72)*** | | | | | | | | | |
| Kazak | Eb1:35 | C | N? | C | A | C | Ac | D | P |
| Uzbeg | Eb (new) | K | U | C | A | V | A | D | Aa |
| ***Ostyak and Samoyed (73)*** | | | | | | | | | |
| Yurak Samoyed | Ec4:136 | A | . | D | C | F | A | C | . |
| ***Northern Turks (74)*** | | | | | | | | | |
| Yakut | Ec2:32 | A | D | C | L | . | La | K | K |
| ***Mongols (82)*** | | | | | | | | | |
| Buryat | Eb6:359 | C | B | B | A | C | D | K | J |
| Dagor Mongols | Eb4:233 | C | A | K | L | C | D | B | J |
| Khalka | Eb3:135 | C | M | B | A | C | D | D | J |
| Monguor | Eb2:36 | A | A | C | A | B | H | . | . |
| ***Southwest China (84)*** | | | | | | | | | |
| Akha | Ej7:330 | A | B | K | E | . | A | K | . |
| Lisu | Ed (new) | C | B | K | L | . | A | F | . |
| Lolo | Ed2:40 | C | D | B | A | G | A | F | . |
| Magpie Miao | Ed4:138 | C | B | C | E | G | M | B | K |
| Minchia | Ed8:361 | C | B | C | E | E | A | F | J |
| ***Tibet (85)*** | | | | | | | | | |
| Lepcha | Ee3:140 | A | A | C | K | D | D | A | Ma |
| Nepali | Ec (new) | A | B | C | E | . | A | . | K |
| Sherpa | Ec6:630 | A | B | B | A | L | A | D | P |
| ***Garo-Khasi (86)*** | | | | | | | | | |
| Garo | Ei1:47 | A | A | C | E | B | A | B | E |
| Khasi | Ei8:365 | K | A | C | E | C | A | B | . |
| ***Naga-Kachin (87)*** | | | | | | | | | |
| Angami | Ei13:421 | A | B | C | B | O | M | Dc | K |
| Ao | Ei14:422 | A | A | A | E | B | D | D | E |
| Kachin | Ei5:243 | A | B | C | B | A | D | Db | C |
| Lhota | Ei2:48 | N | Ca | A | E | B | Ab | D | R |
| Sema | Ei16:424 | | | | B | K | A | D | . |

APPENDIX *Continued*

| Province & Society | Atlas Number | GrPa | GrCh | PaBr | PaSi | SbCh | Sibl | CrCo | Sb-il |
|---|---|---|---|---|---|---|---|---|---|
| *Kuki-Chin* (88) | | | | | | | | | |
| Aimol | Ei11:419 | A | B | A | B | F | C? | D | W |
| Haka Chin | Ei19:711 | A | M? | A | B | B? | Fa | D | . |
| Lakher | Ei4:147 | A | B | A | B | B | Ha | Da | Ea |
| Purum | Ei6:419 | A | . | C | A | M | A | D | E |
| *South Burma* (89) | | | | | | | | | |
| Burmese | Ei3:146 | A | A | L | K | E | La | A | J |
| Karen | Ei7:364 | A | A | D | C | . | C | C | A |
| *Andaman Islands* (92) | | | | | | | | | |
| Andamanese | Eh1:45 | A | A | D | C | D | C | C | . |
| *Nicobar Islands* (93) | | | | | | | | | |
| Nicobarese | Eh5:244 | A | . | . | . | D | G | C | . |
| *Thai* (91) | | | | | | | | | |
| Lao | Ej (new) | N | A | L | K | . | A | C? | . |
| Siamese | Ej9:367 | C | A | L | K | D | C | A | . |
| *Palaung-Wa* (90) | | | | | | | | | |
| Lamet | Ej1:49 | A | A | A | B | B | . | B | . |
| *Vietnam and Hainan* (97) | | | | | | | | | |
| Vietnamese | Ej4:149 | A | A | C | A | D | D | A | K |
| *Montagnards* (96) | | | | | | | | | |
| Jarai | Ej (new) | A | A | L | K | . | A | C | . |
| Mnong Gar | Ej2:50 | B | A | K | K | Ac | G | Ea | . |
| *Cambodia* (95) | | | | | | | | | |
| Cambodians | Ej5:245 | A | A | L | K | D | C | C | . |
| *Semang-Sakai* (94) | | | | | | | | | |
| Semang | Ej3:146 | A | A | L | K | F | C | C | . |

| | Reference | | | | | | | | |
|---|---|---|---|---|---|---|---|---|---|
| ***Malaya and Sumatra (102)*** | | | | | | | | | |
| Batak | Ib4:153 | B | A | C | E | A | F | Kb | E |
| Malays | Ej8:366 | A | A | E | D | D | C | A | A |
| Mentaweians | Ib7:369 | B | A | B | A | C | K | B? | Ab |
| Minangkabau | Ib6:252 | B | A | A | B | A | K | A | A |
| ***Madagascar (8)*** | | | | | | | | | |
| Merina | Eh2:46 | A | A | E | D | F | N | A | L |
| Tanala | Eh3:144 | A | A | B | A | F | N | A | L |
| ***Java (103)*** | | | | | | | | | |
| Javanese | Ib2:54 | B | A | D | L | D | D | C | A |
| ***Western Lesser Sundas (104)*** | | | | | | | | | |
| Balinese | Ib3:152 | A | A | L | D | . | D | A | A |
| Kodi (Sumba) | Ib (new) | B | K | A | B | A | H | B | . |
| ***Borneo (101)*** | | | | | | | | | |
| Iban | Ib1:54 | A | A | L | K | D | C | C | A |
| Punan | Ib (new) | B | A | D | C | D | C | A | A |
| ***Sea Gypsies (100)*** | | | | | | | | | |
| Selung | Ej6:249 | A | A | L | K | E | A | C | . |
| Tawi-Tawi | Ia13:1099 | B | A | D | C | D | E | C | A |
| ***Celebes (105)*** | | | | | | | | | |
| Macassarese | Ic1:55 | B | A | D | C | D | B | C | . |
| Toradja | Ic5:254 | A | A | D | D | D | C | A | A |
| ***Southeast Indonesia (107)*** | | | | | | | | | |
| Alorese | Ic2:154 | B | A | D | C | F? | C | A | . |
| Belu (Timor) | Ic3:155 | B | A | A | B | F | D | A | M? |
| Pantara (Flores) | Ic (new) | B | A | C | B | Ab | | . | . |
| Rotinese | Ic4:253 | A | A | B | A | C | G | Ba | . |
| Tanimbarese | Ic6:332 | B | C | A | B | B | K | A | M |
| ***Tropical Australia (108)*** | | | | | | | | | |
| Groote Eylandt | Id11:1205 | C | Y | A | B | B | A | D | E |
| Murngin | Id6:333 | C | Nb | A | B | A | D | K | E |

APPENDIX Continued

| Province & Society | Atlas Number | GrPa | GrCh | PaBr | PaSi | SbCh | Sibl | CrCo | Sb-il |
|---|---|---|---|---|---|---|---|---|---|
| Tiwi | Id3:157 | C | N | A | B | B | A | B | E |
| Wikmunkan | Id6:333 | Ca | C | Ka | Ea | Lb | A | B | E |
| *Temperate Australia* (109) | | | | | | | | | |
| Aranda | Id1:56 | C | C | A | B | C | N | B | D |
| Dieri | Id4:25 | C | C | A | B | A | D | B | E |
| Kariera | Id5:256 | C | C | A | Ba | B | A | B | E |
| Murinbata | Id7:370 | C | C | A | B | B | B | B | E |
| *Southeast New Guinea* (111) | | | | | | | | | |
| Komba | Ie (new) | A | L | B | B | C | Aa | B | Q |
| Kutubu | Ie16:691 | A | A | A | A | A | O | B | W |
| Mailu | Ie21:1144 | B | A | A | B | F | D | Ka | R |
| Orokaiva | Ie9:457 | B | C | A | B | A | P | B | . |
| Wantoat | Ie2:58 | A | A | A | B | N | G | B | . |
| *Southern New Guinea* (112) | | | | | | | | | |
| Keraki | Ie5:257 | B | C | C | A | K | A | B | . |
| Kimam | Ie18:1101 | B | Ca | E | D | F | D | A | Nc |
| Kiwai | Ie13:656 | B | C | C | L | B | A | B | X |
| Marindanim | Ie19:1119 | M | A | A | B | B | B | B | K |
| Miriam | Ie14:657 | B | A | A | D | A | B? | B | Q |
| *Northeast New Guinea* (113) | | | | | | | | | |
| Abelam | Ie15:690 | M | M | A | B | A | G | B | C |
| Kewa | Ie (new) | A | . | B | A | F | O | B | W |
| Kwoma | Ie12:655 | A | B | C | E | A | G | D | Ea |
| Manam | Ie29:1151 | B | C | A | B | . | C | A | . |
| Siane | Ie17:713 | B | A | A | B | A | K | B | . |
| *Northwest New Guinea* (114) | | | | | | | | | |
| Bgu | Ie34:1207 | B | C | A | D | F | C | A | A |
| Kapauku | Ie1:57 | B | C | A | B | A | F | B | L |
| Muju | Ie23:1146 | B | A | A | B | A | D | D | . |

| | | | | | | | | | |
|---|---|---|---|---|---|---|---|---|---|
| Samarokena | Ie36:1209 | V | A | C | L | F | D | B | J |
| Waropen | Ie6:258 | B | C | A | B | B | G | B | A |
| **Admiralty and Western Islands (120)** | | | | | | | | | |
| Manus | Ig9:373 | A | A | C | E | K | T | Eb? | · |
| **New Britain and New Ireland (121)** | | | | | | | | | |
| Bakovi | Ig15:1211 | B | C | A | B | Ab | F | B | · |
| Lesu | Ig4:163 | B | C | A | B | B | O | B | L |
| **Massim (122)** | | | | | | | | | |
| Bwaidoga | Ig16:1212 | B? | · | A | D | F | K | A | · |
| Dobuans | Ig5:261 | B | C | A | B | A | K | B | L |
| Molima | Ig19:1215 | B | C | A | A | D | Q | B | Y |
| Rossel | Ig11:693 | A | A | A? | B? | C | B | E | D |
| Trobrianders | Ig2:62 | B | C | A | B | A | F | E | · |
| **Solomon Islands (123)** | | | | | | | | | |
| Choiseulese | Ig12:1102 | A | A | A | D | A | C | A | Ac |
| Kaoka | Ig (new) | B | C | E | D | Aa | Q | B | · |
| Kurtatchi | Ig3:162 | B | A | A | D | A | K | B | L |
| Siuai | Ig1:61 | Cb | Ca | A | B | B | T | Ba | Ea |
| Ulawans | Ig6:262 | A | B | A | D | A | K | A | N? |
| **Polynesian Outliers (124)** | | | | | | | | | |
| Kapingamarangi | Ii7:1103 | La | A | E | D | F | E | A | L |
| Ontong Java | Ii5:265 | B | A | A | D | A | K | A | D |
| Rennel | Ii10:1122 | B | A | C | A | C | F | Cb | · |
| Tikopia | Ii2:66 | B | A | A | B | A | K | B | D |
| **Santa Cruz and Banks Islands (125)** | | | | | | | | | |
| Cape Mendaña | Ih (new) | U | R | A | D | B | H | A | Ea |
| Graciosa Bay | Ih (new) | N | K | A | Ba | A | F | A | K |
| Mota | Ih1:63 | B | C | A | B | A | H | E | C |
| Nakaenga | Ih9:1156 | A | B | A | B | A | H | B | · |
| **New Hebrides (126)** | | | | | | | | | |
| Efate (Nguna) | Ih (new) | C | A | A | B | A | B | E | Ca |
| Epi | Ih11:1216 | B | C | A | B | A | H | D | E |

## APPENDIX  *Continued*

| Province & Society | Atlas Number | GrPa | GrCh | PaBr | PaSi | SbCh | Sibl | CrCo | Sb-il |
|---|---|---|---|---|---|---|---|---|---|
| Eromangans | Ih12:1217 | A | A | A | B | A | N | B | Y |
| Ranon | Ih13:1218 | Bc | Aa | A | B | A | N | K | E |
| Seniang | Ih2:64 | B | A | C | E | A | M | E | M |
| *New Caledonia and Loyalty Islands* (127) | | | | | | | | | |
| Ajie | Ih4:263 | A | B | A | B | A | F | B | . |
| Lifu | Ih7:274 | A | A? | A | B | E | . | A | J |
| *Fiji and Rotuma* (128) | | | | | | | | | |
| Mbau Fijians | Ih (new) | R | A | C | E | A | F | B | D |
| Rotumans | Ih6:337 | A | K | E | D | F | N | A | L |
| Vanua Levu | Ih8:694 | B | A | C | D | A | F | B | A |
| *Southern Polynesia* (130) | | | | | | | | | |
| Maori | Ij2:167 | A | A | E | D | F | G | A | X |
| *Eastern Polynesia* (131) | | | | | | | | | |
| Easter Islanders | Ij9:1126 | B | A | D | C | Da | B? | A | . |
| Mangaians | Ij1:67 | B | A | E | D | D | G | A | A |
| Mangarevans | Ij7:658 | B | A | L | K | D | G | A | A |
| Marquesans | Ij3:168 | B | B | C | E | A | B | A | A |
| Rarotongans | Ij (new) | A | B | E | D | E | G | A | . |
| *Western Polynesia* (129) | | | | | | | | | |
| Ellice Islanders | Ii4:264 | B | A | A | D | A | K | A | L |
| Pukapukans | Ii3:166 | B | B | E | D | F | N | Ca | L |
| Samoans | Ii1:65 | L | K | E | B | D | N | A | Ea |
| Tokelau | Ii6:375 | B | A | A | B | A | O | D | . |
| Tongans | Ii12:1124 | B | A | A | B | A | | A | L |
| *Gilbert Islands* (119) | | | | | | | | | |
| Makin | If14:633 | B | C | E | D | F | K | A | L |
| *Marshall Islands and Nauru* (118) | | | | | | | | | |
| Majuro | If3:160 | A | A | A | D | A | P | Ba | Ea |
| Nauruans | If13:432 | B | C | A | D | A | C | B | D |

### Eastern and Central Carolines (117)

| Society | Ref. | | | | | | | | |
|---|---|---|---|---|---|---|---|---|---|
| Ifaluk | I14:161 | C | A | A | D | A | K | A | . |
| Lamotrek | I16:1181 | A | A | E | D | A | K | A | . |
| Ponapeans | I5:259 | L | K | L | D | A | B | E | B |
| Trukese | I2:60 | L | K | E | D | F | K | E | A |
| Ulithians | I19:428 | L | K | E | D | F | K | A | L |

### Yap (116)

| Society | Ref. | | | | | | | | |
|---|---|---|---|---|---|---|---|---|---|
| Yapese | I6:260 | A | A | A | D | A | C | E | D? |

### Palau and Marianas (115)

| Society | Ref. | | | | | | | | |
|---|---|---|---|---|---|---|---|---|---|
| Chamorro | I8:427 | A | M | D | C | E | E | C | B |
| Palauans | I1:59 | C | N | B | D | N | Ad | A | . |

### Philippines (99)

| Society | Ref. | | | | | | | | |
|---|---|---|---|---|---|---|---|---|---|
| Bisayan | Ia18:1204 | A | A | E | D | B | C | A | A |
| Hanunoo | Ia5:250 | A | C | D | C | D | C | C | A |
| Ifugao | Ia3:150 | B | C | E | C | F | E | A | A |
| Manobo | Ia15:1113 | B | C | D | C | D | H | A | L |
| Subanun | Ia4:151 | B | C | E | D | D | E | A | Ab |

### Formosa (98)

| Society | Ref. | | | | | | | | |
|---|---|---|---|---|---|---|---|---|---|
| Ami | Ia9:1095 | A | K | E | D | F | C | A | A |
| Atayal | Ia1:51 | A | K | D | C | F | F | A | Y |
| Bunun | Ia10:1096 | A | K | D | C | D | E | C | . |
| Puyuma | Ia11:1097 | B | C | E | D | F | E | C | s |
| Yami | Ia14:1100 | A | A | D | C | F | C | . | . |

### Han Chinese (83)

| Society | Ref. | | | | | | | | |
|---|---|---|---|---|---|---|---|---|---|
| Shantung | Ed10:1110 | C | D | C | A | G | A | F | J |

### Manchuria (81)

| Society | Ref. | | | | | | | | |
|---|---|---|---|---|---|---|---|---|---|
| Manchu | Ed3:137 | C | D | C | T | G | A | B | Ma |

### Korea (80)

| Society | Ref. | | | | | | | | |
|---|---|---|---|---|---|---|---|---|---|
| Koreans | Ed1:39 | C | D | D | C | E | A | A | J |

APPENDIX *Continued*

| Province & Society | Atlas Number | GrPa | GrCh | PaBr | PaSi | SbCh | Sibl | CrCo | Sb-il |
|---|---|---|---|---|---|---|---|---|---|
| *Japan and Ryukyus (79)* | | | | | | | | | |
| Japanese | Ed5:237 | A | A | D | C | E | A | C | Ea |
| Miyakans | Ed (new) | A | A | L | K | D | P | C | Ea |
| Okinawans | Ed7:326 | A | A | D | C | B | A | C | A |
| *Ainu (78)* | | | | | | | | | |
| Saru Ainu | Ec7:325 | A | A | D | C | D | E | F | U |
| *Lower Amur (77)* | | | | | | | | | |
| Gilyak | Ec1:37 | A | B | A | B | B | D | B | . |
| *Siberian Hunters (75)* | | | | | | | | | |
| Yukaghir | Ec6:236 | A | B | K | L | S | D | A | O |
| *Paleo-Siberians (76)* | | | | | | | | | |
| Chukchee | Ec3:135 | A | B | C | E | E | U | C | B |
| *Western Eskimo (132)* | | | | | | | | | |
| Aleut | Na9:458 | A | A | B | A | A | G | B | Ca |
| Nunivak | Na6:269 | A | B | B | A | C | D | B | J |
| Sivokakmeit | Na11:460 | A | A | B | A | C | P | B | . |
| Tareumiut | Na2:69 | A | A | D | C | D | A | B | Na |
| *Central and Eastern Eskimo (133)* | | | | | | | | | |
| Caribou Eskimo | Na21:484 | A | A | D | C | D | M | C | D |
| Iglulik | Na22:485 | A | A | D | C | D | A | Ba | Da |
| Nunamiut | Na12:461 | A | A | D | C | D | D | C | N |
| Polar Eskimo | Na14:463 | A | A | B | A | C | X | C | Na |
| Taqagmiut | Na44:715 | A | A | B | A | C | E | C | Da |
| *Cree-Montagnais (151)* | | | | | | | | | |
| Attawapiskat | Na7:338 | A | A | B | A | G | D | B | D |
| Escoumains | Na (new) | A | A | B | A | E | D | C | J |
| Naskapi | Na5:268 | A | A | B | A | M? | B | B | D |
| Plains Cree | Ne19:626 | A | A | B | A | | D | B | B? |

| | Reference | 1 | 2 | 3 | 4 | 5 | 6 | 7 | 8 |
|---|---|---|---|---|---|---|---|---|---|
| *Maritime Algonkians (152)* | | | | | | | | | |
| Abnaki | Ng (new) | A | A | B | A | E | D | C | L |
| Malecite | Ng (new) | A | A | B | A | G | D | C | Ca |
| Micmac | Na41:504 | A | A | B | A | E | A | C | B |
| Penobscot | Ng4:181 | A | A | B | A | G | D | A? | L |
| *Ojibwa (153)* | | | | | | | | | |
| Bungi | Na (new) | B | B | B | B | B | A | B | . |
| Chippewa | Na36:499 | A | A | A | A | G | T | B | D |
| Eastern Ojibwa | Na39:502 | A | A | B | M | S | D | C | C |
| *Northeastern Athapaskans (134)* | | | | | | | | | |
| Beaver | Na29:492 | A | D | B | A | A | A | B | E |
| Chipewyan | Na30:493 | A | B | D | C | . | A | A | Y |
| Dogrib | Na15:464 | A | A | D | C | D | A | A | A |
| Sarsi | Ne7:381 | A | L | D | B | F? | A | A | D |
| Sekani | Na28:491 | A | A | B | A | A | A | A | A |
| *Yukon (135)* | | | | | | | | | |
| Ingalik | Na8:377 | A | A | D | C | D | A | C | . |
| Kutchin | Na20:469 | A | T | B | A | F | A | A | Ab |
| *South Central Alaska (136)* | | | | | | | | | |
| Eyak | Nb5:270 | C | N | A | M | K | Ma | B | R |
| Nabesna | Na1:68 | A | B | B | B | A | A | B | . |
| Tanaina | Na26:489 | A | A | D | C | A | A | B | D |
| *Carrier-Nahani (138)* | | | | | | | | | |
| Alkatcho | Nb10:472 | A | D | D | C | D | A | A | A |
| Carrier | Na19:468 | K | A | D | C | C | A | B | A |
| Kaska | Na4:170 | A | A | B | B | Aa | A | Ec | . |
| *Northern Northwest Coast (137)* | | | | | | | | | |
| Haida | Nb1:70 | A | A | B | B | C | G | E | D |
| Haisla | Nb8:470 | A | B | A | B | A | C | B | Ab |
| Tlingit | Nb22:505 | B | A | B | B | C | G | Ec | R |

## APPENDIX Continued

| Province & Society | Atlas Number | GrPa | GrCh | PaBr | PaSi | SbCh | Sibl | CrCo | Sb-il |
|---|---|---|---|---|---|---|---|---|---|
| *Wakashan-Bellacoola* (139) | | | | | | | | | |
| Bellabella | Nb23:506 | A | B | B | A | . | L | A | B |
| Bellacoola | Nb9:471 | A | A | D | C | D | C | A | Ab |
| Kwakiutl | Nb3:171 | B | A | D | C | E | F | A | D |
| Nootka | Nb11:473 | B | A | D | C | E | C | A | Q |
| *Coast Salish* (140) | | | | | | | | | |
| Comox | Nb14:476 | B | A | D | C | D | Q | A | Da |
| Klallam | Nb16:478 | B | A | K | L | U | C | A | . |
| Puyallup | Nb17:479 | A | A | D | C | D | F | A | B |
| Quinault | Nb25:508 | A | A | D | C | D | C | A | C |
| Twana | Nb2:271 | A | A | D | C | D | A | A | Ab |
| *Southern Northwest Coast* (141) | | | | | | | | | |
| Hupa | Nb35:518 | C | S | B | A | M | A | A | O |
| Karok | Nb34:517 | U | Ca | B | A | M | A | A | D |
| Tolowa | Nb6:271 | C | M | B | A | M | A | B | C |
| Wiyot | Nb36:519 | A | R | B | A | E | E | C | . |
| Yurok | Nb4:172 | A | A | D | C | E | H | A | Ab |
| *Northeast California* (142) | | | | | | | | | |
| Atsugewi | Nc4:272 | C | C | B | A | C | N | C | D |
| Klamath | Nc8:523 | C | C | B | A | C | W | A | D |
| Shasta | Nc32:515 | C | C | B | A | C | R | B | D |
| Washo | Nd6:340 | C | C | B | A | C | A | A | Y |
| Yahi | Nc (new) | C | C | A | B | A | M | B | Da |
| *Central California* (143) | | | | | | | | | |
| Eastern Pomo | Nc18:533 | C | C | B | E | A | D | D | Nc |
| Maidu | Nc12:527 | C | B | B | A | D | A | B | D |
| Patwin | Nc22:537 | A | A | B | A | C | D | D | Na |
| Southern Pomo | Nc19:534 | C | B | C | E | V | D | E | M |
| Yuki | Nc7:377 | C | D | B | A | M | Q | A | Ea |

| | | | | | | | | | |
|---|---|---|---|---|---|---|---|---|---|
| ***Southern California (144)*** | | | | | | | | | |
| Luiseno | Nc33:548 | Aa | B | A | C | E | C | Ca | U |
| Miwok | Nc5:273 | Mb | D | A | B | E | A | A | A |
| Serrano | Nc30:545 | D | B | Ma | K | E | C | C | U |
| Tubatulabal | Nc2:173 | M | A | A | A | E | C | C | C |
| Yokuts | Nc3:174 | Y | A | A | N | A | B | C | K |
| ***Yumans (145)*** | | | | | | | | | |
| Cocopa | Nh19:443 | X | B | A | X | E | C | D | C |
| Diegueno | Nc6:339 | X | B | D | K | E | C | M | C |
| Keweyipaya | Nh23:628 | B | B | Q | V | E | C | M | C |
| Kiliwa | Nc34:549 | B | B | A | K | E | C | N | C |
| Yuma | Nh22:446 | X | B | Q | Ka | E | C | M | C |
| ***Western Great Basin (146)*** | | | | | | | | | |
| Eastern Mono | Nd30:572 | C | A | A | N | A | B | C | C |
| Hukundika | Nd5:274 | C | A | A | A | B | C | C | C |
| Kidutokado | Nd24:566 | Ca | A | A | C | A | B | C | C |
| Shivwits | Nd52:594 | O | A | A | . | U | K | C | C |
| ***Eastern Great Basin (147)*** | | | | | | | | | |
| Southern Ute | Nd2:74 | B | A | A | L | E | K | C | C |
| Uintah | Nd58:600 | Ab | A | A | L | E | C | C | C |
| Wind River | Nd64:606 | O | A | P | N | B | A | C | C |
| ***Southern Plateau (148)*** | | | | | | | | | |
| Tenino | Nd1:73 | D | A | La | C | A | B | C | C |
| Wishram | Nd18:560 | C | A | A | G | C | D | Y | C |
| ***Northern Plateau (149)*** | | | | | | | | | |
| Flathead | Nd12:554 | D | A | L | C | A | B | C | C |
| Kutenai | Nd7:380 | Ma | A | A | C | M | B | C | Bb |
| Lillooet | Nd9:551 | B? | A | D | D | C | D | A | A |
| Shuswap | Nd11:553 | . | A | H | E | O | M | A | A |
| Sinkaietk | Nd15:557 | D | A | A | D | A | B | C | C |
| ***Northern and Central Plains (150)*** | | | | | | | | | |
| Assiniboin | Ne11:618 | C | B | L | A | B | A | A | A |

## APPENDIX *Continued*

| Province & Society | Atlas Number | GrPa | GrCh | PaBr | PaSi | SbCh | Sibl | CrCo | Sb-il |
|---|---|---|---|---|---|---|---|---|---|
| Gros Ventre | Ne1:75 | A | A | A | B | B | D | A | D |
| Piegan | Ne18:625 | B | B | B | B | T | Af | A | J |
| Teton | Ne8:382 | A | A | A | B | B | D | B | B |
| *Upper Missouri* (154) | | | | | | | | | |
| Arikara | Ne10:617 | A | A | A | D | M | Pb | E | O? |
| Crow | Ne4:178 | Aa | A | M | B | G | La | E | Q |
| Hidatsa | Ne15:662 | A | A | M | B | B | L | E | C |
| Mandan | Ne6:341 | A | L | A | B | A | Mb | E | Ma |
| *Prairie* (155) | | | | | | | | | |
| Miami | Nf4:276 | A | A | A | B | B | A | D | Da |
| Omaha | Nf3:179 | A | A | A | B | B | Aa | D | C |
| Potawatomi | Na42:660 | A | A | B | A | B | D | D | D |
| Shawnee | Nf13:1158 | A | B | A | B | B | D | D | Ca |
| Winnebago | Nf2:78 | A | | B | A | B | La | D | C |
| *Northeastern Woodlands* (156) | | | | | | | | | |
| Delaware | Ng6:269 | A | A | B | C | G | D | A | . |
| Seneca Iroquois | Ng11:664 | A | B | A | B | B | A | B | Mc |
| *Southeastern Woodlands* (157) | | | | | | | | | |
| Catawba | Ng9:662 | A | A | B | C | E | B | C | B |
| Cherokee | Ng5:278 | Aa | A | A | B | B | Oa | E | A |
| Choctaw | Ng12:1159 | A | B | A | B | B | G | E | M |
| Creek | Ng3:180 | A | A | B | A | B | G | E | Ab |
| Yuchi | Ng11:664 | A | A | D | A | . | B | E | . |
| *Lower Mississippi* (158) | | | | | | | | | |
| Biloxi | Ng (new) | A | D | R | T? | B | L | . | T |
| Chitimacha | Ng (new) | B | . | B | C | D | P | C | . |
| Natchez | Ng7:385 | A | A | B | A | A | Ha | Ea | . |

| Group | Reference | 1 | 2 | 3 | 4 | 5 | 6 | 7 | 8 |
|---|---|---|---|---|---|---|---|---|---|
| ***Caddoans* (159)** | | | | | | | | | |
| Caddo | Nf (new) | A | B | M | A | B | A | L | A |
| Hasinai | Nf8:384 | A | A | M | A | E | C | L | A |
| Pawnee | Nf6:342 | Ca | E | Ba | A | D | A | A | A |
| Wichita | Nf5:277 | Q | A | H | B | K | C | A | B |
| ***Gulf Coast and Southern Plains* (160)** | | | | | | | | | |
| Coahuilteco | Ne (new) | Nb | C | L | La | L | K | W | C |
| Comanche | Ne3:177 | Q | A | A | A | B | A | C | C |
| Kiowa | Ne17:624 | · | A | O | A | B | A | · | A |
| Kiowa-Apache | Ne2:76 | L | A | A | A | B | A | C | L |
| ***Apache-Tanoan* (161)** | | | | | | | | | |
| Chiricahua | Nh1:81 | N | A | B | C | A | B | C | C |
| Isleta | Nh10:434 | A | A | A | D | A | D | A | K |
| Jicarilla | Nh16:440 | | B | Ha | C | B | A | A | A |
| Taos | Nh6:281 | J | C | A | D | C | D | Ca | K |
| Tewa | Nh11:436 | Na | C | C | D | C | D | | A |
| ***Pueblo-Navaho* (162)** | | | | | | | | | |
| Cochiti | Nh7:343 | A | A | O | Aa | D | A | C | T |
| Hano | Nh2:82 | P | E | D | A | E | A | C | K |
| Hopi | Nh18:442 | · | E | Ae | A | B | A | A | A |
| Western Apache | Nh17:441 | A | B | Na | C | A | B | C | M |
| Zuni | Nh4:183 | · | E | Ab | A | B | A | B | K |
| ***Northwest Mexico* (163)** | | | | | | | | | |
| Mayo | Ni (new) | · | A | V | R | U | L | C | C |
| Opata | Ni (new) | B | C | A | L | L | K | C | C |
| Pima | Ni6:1160 | · | B | C | W | L | K | Ca | C |
| Seri | Ni4:283 | K | A | La | K | E | C | Ca | C |
| Tarahumara | Ni1:83 | A | A | A | L | L | K | C | C |
| ***Western Mexico* (164)** | | | | | | | | | |
| Cora | Ni (new) | · | A | D | E | C | D | C | A |
| Huichol | Ni3:282 | D | A | D | D | C | D | C | Aa |
| Tepehuan | Ni (new) | C | A | C | L | E | K | Ca | C |

APPENDIX *Continued*

| Province & Society | Atlas Number | GrPa | GrCh | PaBr | PaSi | SbCh | Sibl | CrCo | Sb-il |
|---|---|---|---|---|---|---|---|---|---|
| *Central Mexico (165)* | | | | | | | | | |
| Aztec | Nj2:185 | A | B | D | C | E | A | A | D? |
| Chichimec | Ni5:717 | A | L | D | C | D | Pa | A | . |
| Huastec | Nj (new) | A | A | B | A | A | H | A | D |
| Otomi | Nj13:1231 | A | A | B | A | E | La | C | C |
| Totonac | Nj4:285 | A | A | D | C | E | Ca | C | B |
| *Tehuantepec (166)* | | | | | | | | | |
| Huave | Nj6:1105 | A | A | E | D | F | C | A | A |
| Mazatec | Nj5:344 | A | A | D | C | E | B | A | B |
| Mixtec | Nj12:1230 | A | A | D | C | E | H | A | S |
| Popoluca | Nj3:284 | A | A | D | C | D | D | A | D |
| Tequistlatec | Nj14:1232 | A | K | Da | O | F | E | A | C |
| *Mayans (167)* | | | | | | | | | |
| Cakchiquel | Sa12:1125 | A | L | D | C | E | G | A | D |
| Chorti | Sa3:186 | A | A | D | D | D | C | A | Ea |
| Jacaltec | Sa (new) | A | A | E | D | F | A | C | A |
| Tzeltal | Sa2:86 | A | L | B | A | C | D | D | D |
| Yucatec Maya | Sa2:86 | X | Na | B | A | A | Af | C | D |
| *Honduras and Nicaragua (168)* | | | | | | | | | |
| Black Carib | Sa7:388 | A | A | B | A | M | A | B | C |
| Miskito | Sa9:390 | A | . | B | C | E? | K | B | . |
| *Costa Rica (169)* | | | | | | | | | |
| Bribri | Sa5:287 | K | L | B | A | D | K | B | D |
| Guaymi | Sa (new) | A | B | A | B | A? | K | A | Q |
| *Panama (170)* | | | | | | | | | |
| Choco | Sa4:286 | A | A | D | D? | E | E | A | A |
| Cuna | Sa1:85 | A | B | D | C | E | G | A | Ca |
| *Highland Colombia and Ecuador (171)* | | | | | | | | | |
| Cayapa | Sf3:194 | A | A | B | A | G | Q | B | . |

| Group | Ref | | | | | | | | |
|---|---|---|---|---|---|---|---|---|---|
| Chibcha | Sf6:395 | A | B | B | A | D | A | C | . |
| Paez | Sf5:348 | A | A | B | A | F | M | A | D |
| Tunebo | Sf4:294 | A | B | B | C | E | F | A | B |
| **Northern Colombia and Venezuela (172)** | | | | | | | | | |
| Cagaba | Sb2:187 | A | A | D | C | F | Ag | A | Q |
| Carinya | Sb4:288 | A | A | B | A | B | L | B | D |
| Goajiro | Sb6:391 | A | B | A | A | E | A | E | C |
| Motilon | Sb3:188 | A | A | A | A | G | L | B | C |
| Paraujano | Sb5:389 | A | A | D | C | D | F | A | B |
| **Caribbean Negroes (174)** | | | | | | | | | |
| Haitians | Sb9:1237 | A | A | D | C | E | B | C | B |
| Jamaicans | Sb (new) | A | B | D | C | D | B | C | Pb |
| **Antillean Indigenes (173)** | | | | | | | | | |
| Callinago | Sb1:87 | W | A | A | B | A | L | Ba | D? |
| **Lower Orinoco (176)** | | | | | | | | | |
| Warrau | Sc1:88 | A | C | C | E | F | M | A | C |
| **Llanos (175)** | | | | | | | | | |
| Curipaco | Sc9:448 | A | B | D | C | F | A | A | Ca |
| Guahibo | Sc4:290 | A | B | D | A | E | A | B | T |
| Piapoco | Sc17:719 | A | A | D | C | E | A | A | T |
| **Southeast Venezuela (177)** | | | | | | | | | |
| Makiritare | Sc16:455 | A | A | A | B | M | Aa | Kb | E |
| Panare | Sc13:452 | A | A | A | B | C | B | B | B |
| Piaroa | Sc18:447 | A | B | A | B | B | A | B | B |
| Shiriana | Sd6:721 | A | A | A | B | A | B | B | R |
| Yabarana | Sc7:393 | A | A | A | B | B | La | B | E |
| **Guiana (178)** | | | | | | | | | |
| Camaracoto | Sc11:450 | A | A | N | M | B | L | B | C |
| Carib | Sc3:189 | A | A | N | A | B | X | B | C |
| Macusi | Sc12:451 | A | A | B | M? | G | L | B | C |
| Wapishana | Sc5:291 | A | A | N | | M | O? | B | . |
| **Bush Negroes (179)** | | | | | | | | | |
| Saramacca | Sc6:392 | B | C | A | B | E | A | C | A |

## APPENDIX *Continued*

| Province & Society | Atlas Number | GrPa | GrCh | PaBr | PaSi | SbCh | Sibl | CrCo | Sb-il |
|---|---|---|---|---|---|---|---|---|---|
| *Lower Amazon (180)* | | | | | | | | | |
| Mundurucu | Sd1:90 | K | A | A | B | A | P | B? | E |
| Palikur | Sd3:292 | A | A | A | B | B | C | B | C |
| Waiwai | Sd7:722 | A | A | A | B | E | G? | B | . |
| *Upper Amazon (181)* | | | | | | | | | |
| Tucuna | Se2:92 | La | A | B | C | C | B | B | B |
| *Northwest Amazonia (182)* | | | | | | | | | |
| Cubeo | Se5:293 | A | B | B | B | E | A | B | Ca |
| Tucano | Se (new) | A | B | Na | A | O | A | K | . |
| Witoto | Se6:347 | La | K | B | A | G | H | . | B |
| *Eastern Ecuador (183)* | | | | | | | | | |
| Jivaro | Se3:191 | A | A | A | D | E | O | B | X |
| *Montaña (184)* | | | | | | | | | |
| Piro | Sf8:1239 | A | B | B | A | B | A | B? | C |
| *Highland Peru (185)* | | | | | | | | | |
| Inca | Sf1:93 | A | A | A | B | A | H | A | C? |
| *Highland Bolivia (186)* | | | | | | | | | |
| Aymara | Sf2:193 | C | A | K | L | A | A | A | Mb |
| Chipaya | Sf (new) | A | A | C | A | G | M? | C | . |
| Uru | Sf9:1240 | C | D | B | C | G | A | C | Ab |
| *Lowland Bolivia (187)* | | | | | | | | | |
| Siriono | Se1:91 | A | A | A | B | B | E | Eb | Da |
| *Western Mato Grosso (188)* | | | | | | | | | |
| Bororo | Si9:97 | C | K | M | Ba | B | G? | E | . |
| Guato | Si6:350 | A | B | A | B | A | B | B | . |
| Nambicuara | Si4:198 | A | A | A | B | B | . | B | C |
| *Upper Xingu (189)* | | | | | | | | | |
| Bacairi | Si3:197 | A | A | A | B | B | M | B | Ca |
| Camayura | Si5:298 | A | L | B | A | B | La | B | J |

| Group | Ref | | | | | | | | |
|---|---|---|---|---|---|---|---|---|---|
| Trumai | Si2:98 | A | A | B | A | G | Cb | B | Ca |
| Umotina | Si8:1169 | A | K | E | D | F | A | A | Ca |
| Waura | Si (new) | A | B | A | B | B | A | B | W |
| **Northern Ge (190)** | | | | | | | | | |
| Apinaye | Sj7:399 | C | M | A | B | A | H | · | Ca |
| Northern Cayapo | Sj9:725 | A | A | A | B | M | B | D | Ca |
| Timbira | Sj4:200 | N | B | A | B | B | C | E | · |
| **Tupi (191)** | | | | | | | | | |
| Tenetehara | Sj6:300 | A | L | B | A | B | M | A | K |
| Tupinamba | Sj8:400 | A | L | B | A | G | C | F | K |
| **Upper Araguaya and Tocantins (193)** | | | | | | | | | |
| Caraja | Sj1:99 | A | K | C | E | C | A | A | · |
| Shavante | Sj11:1184 | B | A | C | E | C | C | D | M |
| Sherente | Sj2:100 | B | A | A | B | N | C | D | Ca |
| **Caingang (194)** | | | | | | | | | |
| Aweikoma | Sj3:199 | L | K | E | D | F | C | A | A |
| **Guarani (195)** | | | | | | | | | |
| Cayua | Sj10:1170 | A | A | B | A | B | Ha | A | · |
| **Paraguayan Chaco (196)** | | | | | | | | | |
| Caduveo | Sh4:296 | A | B | A | B | B | N | A | B |
| Chulupi | Sh (new) | A | V | D | C | E | A | A | P |
| Terena | Sh2:96 | A | A | A | A | A | F | A | · |
| **Argentine Chaco (197)** | | | | | | | | | |
| Mataco | Sh1:95 | A | B | D | C | E | A | A | A |
| Toba | Sh8:724 | A | A | D | C | E | A | A | Na |
| **Araucanians (198)** | | | | | | | | | |
| Mapuche | Sg2:195 | C | C | B | A | A | O | D | · |
| **Patagonians (199)** | | | | | | | | | |
| Ona | Sg3:295 | A | A | B | A | B | A | C | · |
| **Fuegians (200)** | | | | | | | | | |
| Yahgan | Sg1:94 | A | B | B | C | G | B | C | B |

# 15

## Cross-Sex Patterns of Kin Behavior[1]

*George Peter Murdock*

Mother-in-law avoidance, compulsory joking between cross-cousins, and comparable stereotyped patterns of behavior toward other kinsmen, especially of opposite sex, have challenged attempts at explanation from many eminent anthropologists, including Tylor (1889), Lowie (1920), Radcliffe-Brown (1940), and Eggan (1937). Twenty years ago the author (Murdock 1949: 268-283) assembled information on such patterned behavior for a sample of 250 of the world's societies and interpreted the evidence along lines partially anticipated by his predecessors but also largely suggested by John Dollard, Clark Hull, Neal E. Miller, Earl Zinn, and other former colleagues at the Institute of Human Relations, Yale University. Since that time so much new ethnographic information has accumulated, and so many refinements in cross-cultural methodology have developed, that a further examination of the subject seems called for.

The relevant ethnographic data have been compiled and published elsewhere (Murdock 1965-66), though without interpretation, from a survey of the source materials on some 1,200 societies in all parts of the world and at all levels of cultural complexity. In contrast to the 1949 study, the present paper draws selectively from this mass of information on the basis of modern criteria of cross-cultural research. To achieve maximal independence of cases it uses a greatly improved sample, consisting of only one society—invariably the one with fullest data on kin behavior—from any of the 200 "sampling provinces" into which the world has been divided (Murdock 1968). To achieve maximal reliability it deals only with the nine pairs of relatives of opposite sex for which data are most widely reported. And to achieve maximal comparability it includes only societies for which information on patterned behavior is available on at least half of these pairs. The application of these criteria has produced a sample of 89 societies from as many "sampling provinces," distributed geographically as follows:

- 21 from Sub-Saharan Africa,
-  7 from the Circum-Mediterranean region (North Africa, Europe, the Near East),
- 12 from East Eurasia (from Iran and Turkestan to the Pacific),
- 20 from the Insular Pacific (including Indonesia and the Philippines),
- 22 from aboriginal North America,
-  7 from South America (including Central America and the Antilles).

This distribution reflects very closely the quantity and quality of ethnographic field work in the several regions.

The nine pairs of relatives, selected as the only ones for which the literature provides information on patterned behavior for 60 per cent or more of the societies of the sample, are the following:

Wife's mother and daughter's husband (84 societies out of 89),
Son's wife and husband's father (66 societies),
Sister and brother (74 societies),
Mother's brother's daughter and father's sister's son (60 societies),
Father's sister's daughter and mother's brother's son (58 societies),
Elder brother's wife and husband's younger brother (80 societies),
Younger brother's wife and husband's elder brother (78 societies),
Wife's elder sister and younger sister's husband (75 societies),
Wife's younger sister and elder sister's husband (77 societies).

The patterns of behavior recorded for these relatives fall into five categories along a continuum from a strict avoidance of sex and physical contact at one extreme to privileged sex relations at the other as follows:

A Avoidance—the observance of a strict taboo against sex relations and against all but the most restricted physical and social contact.
R Respect—the observance of a taboo against sex relations and of cultural restraints which, though they do not entirely prevent social interaction, inject a definite element of formality into the relationship.
I Informality—the absence both of avoidance and respect restraints and of prescribed joking, coupled in nearly all instances with a prohibition of sex relations.
J Joking—the observance of a pattern of prescribed or obligatory joking when not reported to be accompanied by privileged sex relations.
L License—the observance of a pattern of social interaction in which sex relations prior to or outside of marriage are either fully or conditionally approved, i.e., do not incur the social sanctions customary in other relationships. Associated with license in nearly all reported instances is a pattern of prescribed joking, especially of "heavy joking" or sexual horseplay.

The distinctions between joking and license, and between avoidance and respect, are not always entirely clear in the literature, and a handful of cases may have been misclassified, but both ends of the continuum are always distinguishable from each other and also from the intermediate pattern of informality.

The data to be analyzed are presented in Table 1, where the first column indicates the geographical region (A for Africa, C for Circum-Mediterranean, etc.) and the number of the sampling province (cf. Murdock 1968).

The incidence of the several behavior patterns is far from random, as is shown in Table 2, where they are summarized for the nine pairs of relatives in the order of the descending frequency of avoidance. In most societies a

TABLE 1

Patterns of Kin Behavior in a World Sample of 89 Societies

| Region | Province | Name of Society | WiMo DaHu | SoWi HuFa | Si Br | MoBrDa FaSiSo | FaSiDa MoBrSo | ElBrWi HuYoBr | YoBrWi HuElBr | WiElSi YoSiHu | WiYoSi ElSiHu |
|---|---|---|---|---|---|---|---|---|---|---|---|
| A | 1 | Nama Hottentot | R | · | R | L | L | · | · | L | L |
| A | 2 | Kung Bushmen | A | A | R | J | J | J | J | J | J |
| A | 3 | Zezuru Shona | A | A | I | R | I | · | · | J | L |
| A | 4 | Lozi or Barotse | A | R | R | · | · | L | L | J | L |
| A | 6 | Pende | A | · | R | J | J | L | L | L | L |
| A | 7 | Yao | A | · | R | L | L | R | R | R | R |
| A | 8 | Hehe | R | A | R | · | · | R | R | R | R |
| A | 10 | Luguru | A | · | I | J | J | J | J | J | J |
| A | 12 | Nyoro or Kitara | A | R | I | J | J | L | L | J | J |
| A | 17 | Kpe or Kwiri | A | A | A | · | · | L | L | J | J |
| A | 19 | Igbira | · | I | · | · | · | A | A | A | A |
| A | 20 | Akyem | A | A | J | · | · | J | J | · | J |
| A | 23 | Futajalonke | A | R | · | J | J | J | J | J | J |
| A | 24 | Malinke | R | · | · | J | J | J | J | · | J |
| A | 25 | Songhai | R | R | · | J | J | J | R | R | J |
| C | 26 | Dogon | R | · | R | · | · | · | · | · | · |
| A | 27 | Tallensi | R | I | I | · | J | J | R | R | J |
| C | 28 | Zazzagawa Hausa | A | A | · | J | J | A | A | J | L |
| A | 29 | Katab | A | A | I | · | J | J | A | J | J |
| A | 30 | Jukun | · | R | R | I | I | J | J | A | · |
| A | 35 | Otoro Nuba | A | A | R | I | I | R | R | · | J |
| A | 37 | Shilluk | A | R | I | I | I | R | R | R | · |
| A | 38 | Dorobo | A | R | I | I | I | R | R | · | I |
| C | 42 | Amhara | R | · | I | J | J | R | R | I | R |
| C | 46 | Antessar Tuareg | A | A | · | A | A | R | R | R | R |
| C | 49 | Kababish | A | R | I | I | I | · | · | J | J |
| C | 54 | Anatolian Turks | I | · | I | I | I | R | R | · | · |
| C | 59 | Ukrainians | R | i | I | I | I | R | I | · | J |
| E | 65 | Toda | R | R | R | I | I | I | I | I | I |

## TABLE 1 Continued

| Region & Province | No. | Name of Society | WiMo DaHu | SoWi HuFa | Si Br | MoBrDa FaSiSo | FaSiDa MoBrSo | ElBrWi HuYoBr | YoBrWi HuElBr | WiElSi YoSiHu | WiYoSi ElSiHu |
|---|---|---|---|---|---|---|---|---|---|---|---|
| E | 66 | Vedda | A | I | R | . | . | A | A | A | A |
| E | 67 | Koya | A | . | I | L | L | L | . | . | . |
| E | 69 | Bengali | R | . | I | . | . | J | J | J | J |
| E | 77 | Gilyak | I | A | A | . | . | L | A | L | L |
| E | 82 | Chahar Mongols | . | R | R | . | R | J | R | L | . |
| E | 84 | Lolo | A | A | R | L | L | . | A | A | . |
| E | 85 | Lepcha | A | A | A | . | . | L | A | A | L |
| E | 86 | Garo | A | R | I | I | I | I | I | I | J |
| E | 88 | Purum | R | R | I | I | I | I | I | J | J |
| E | 89 | Burmese | L | L | I | J | I | I | I | R | J |
| E | 92 | Andamanese | R | A | I | I | I | I | A | . | I |
| I | 99 | Sagada Igorot | R | R | R | I | I | I | I | A | J |
| I | 102 | Batak | A | A | A | J | A | J | I | A | J |
| I | 103 | Javanese | R | R | I | I | I | J | J | J | I |
| I | 107 | Tanimbarese | R | R | R | I | I | J | J | J | L |
| I | 108 | Murngin | A | I | A | J | J | R | L | L | L |
| I | 109 | Aranda | A | . | A | L | . | L | L | L | L |
| I | 112 | Keraki | R | . | R | R | R | R | I | R | R |
| I | 113 | Kwoma | R | A | J | I | I | L | R | L | L |
| I | 117 | Trukese | I | A | A | A | I | R | L | L | L |
| I | 118 | Marshallese | R | R | R | L | L | L | L | L | L |
| I | 119 | Gilbertese | . | L | R | L | L | L | L | L | L |
| I | 120 | Manus | A | A | R | J | J | R | A | A | J |
| I | 121 | Lesu | A | . | I | A | A | I | I | I | I |
| I | 122 | Dobuans | I | i | R | . | . | R | R | R | R |
| I | 123 | Kurtatchi | A | R | R | A | A | A | A | A | A |
| I | 124 | Ontong-Javanese | R | R | A | R | R | I | I | I | I |
| I | 125 | Mota | R | A | I | . | . | I | J | I | I |
| I | 126 | Seniang | A | A | I | . | . | J | J | J | J |
| I | 128 | Lau Fijians | R | R | A | I | I | I | R | . | . |

TABLE 1 *Continued*

| Region & Province | | Name of Society | WiMo DaHu | SoWi HuFa | Si Br | MoBrDa FaSiSo | FaSiDa MoBrSo | ElBrWi HuYoBr | YoBrWi HuElBr | WiElSi YoSiHu | WiYoSi ElSiHu |
|---|---|---|---|---|---|---|---|---|---|---|---|
| I | 129 | Samoans | R | . | A | A | A | R | R | R | R |
| N | 136 | Eyak | A | A | A | . | . | J | J | J | . |
| N | 137 | Haida | A | J | R | L | L | L | L | L | L |
| N | 138 | Kaska | A | . | R | J | . | . | . | . | I |
| N | 142 | Atsugewi | A | A | R | R | R | J | J | I | I |
| N | 143 | Wintu | A | A | R | R | R | . | . | I | J |
| N | 144 | Cupeno | R | R | I | I | I | . | . | R | R |
| N | 145 | Diegueno | R | R | . | J | J | J | J | . | J |
| N | 146 | Hukundika | R | . | R | . | . | J | J | J | J |
| N | 147 | Wind River | I | I | R | I | I | J | L | J | J |
| N | 148 | Tenino | I | I | R | . | . | L | L | J | J |
| N | 149 | Kutenai | A | I | . | . | . | I | I | J | J |
| N | 150 | Gros Ventre | R | A | A | A | A | I | J | L | L |
| N | 151 | Attawapiskat Cree | A | . | A | L | L | J | J | J | L |
| N | 153 | Chippewa | A | I | A | L | L | J | J | J | L |
| N | 154 | Crow | A | A | A | . | R | J | J | J | J |
| N | 155 | Winnebago | R | R | R | J | J | J | J | J | J |
| N | 157 | Cherokee | A | A | I | R | R | L | L | L | L |
| N | 159 | Wichita | A | A | J | J | J | L | L | L | L |
| N | 160 | Kiowa-Apache | A | A | R | R | R | R | L | R | R |
| N | 161 | Jicarilla | L | I | R | J | J | I | R | R | R |
| N | 162 | Hopi | R | I | I | . | J | L | I | I | I |
| N | 163 | Tarahumara | A | R | R | R | R | L | L | L | L |
| S | 175 | Guahibo | R | A | . | L | L | L | L | L | L |
| S | 187 | Siriono | A | . | R | L | . | . | . | I | L |
| S | 189 | Trumai | A | . | . | . | J | I | I | J | J |
| S | 190 | Apinaye | A | . | A | . | . | I | I | J | J |
| S | 193 | Sherente | A | A | . | L | . | L | L | I | I |
| S | 194 | Aweikoma | . | R | . | L | L | . | . | L | L |
| S | 198 | Araucanians | A | . | I | . | I | . | . | . | . |

TABLE 2
Behavior Patterns for Nine Pairs of Cross-Sex Kinsmen

| Relatives | Avoidance | Respect | Informality | Joking | License | Total |
|---|---|---|---|---|---|---|
| WiMo-DaHu | 46 | 30 | 8 | 0 | 0 | 84 |
| SoWi-HuFa | 28 | 25 | 11 | 1 | 1 | 66 |
| Si-Br | 15 | 34 | 22 | 3 | 0 | 74 |
| YoBrWi-HuElBr | 10 | 16 | 14 | 22 | 16 | 78 |
| WiElSi-YoSiHu | 7 | 12 | 11 | 27 | 18 | 75 |
| FaSiDa-MoBrSo | 6 | 9 | 15 | 18 | 10 | 58 |
| MoBrDa-FaSiSo | 6 | 8 | 13 | 20 | 13 | 60 |
| ElBrWi-HuYoBr | 4 | 15 | 14 | 29 | 18 | 80 |
| WiYoSi-ElSiHu | 3 | 9 | 9 | 34 | 22 | 77 |

man tends to avoid his mother-in-law and daughter-in-law, respect his sister, and joke with his cross-cousins and sisters-in-law.

These findings accord closely with those of a previous study (Murdock 1949: 277), which offered scattering evidence on behavior patterns for 30 pairs of relatives of opposite sex on the basis of a far less adequate sample. Presented herewith for the first time, however, is an additional body of factual data equally relevant for an interpretation of the phenomena. This is the geographical distribution of the behavior patterns in question, as shown in Table 3. The nearly identical distribution of the behavior patterns for each of the nine pairs of relatives in all the world regions is remarkable. It is such that the incidence of the several patterns for each pair of relatives in each region might well have resulted from a purely random selection of the same number of cases from the world total for the pair in question. Deviations from chance expectancies are few and slight.

Such a geographical distribution is unique. Other cultural elements invariably differ widely in their incidence in different regions, as a few illustrations will demonstrate. More than half of all the known societies which depend for subsistence exclusively on hunting, fishing, and gathering are located in aboriginal North America. Pastoral economies are confined almost exclusively to Eurasia and Africa. Root-crop agriculture is mainly limited to the tropics of both hemispheres. Complex states are found, with few exceptions, only in Africa, the Circum-Mediterranean, and East Eurasia, and the redemptive religions, such as Buddhism, Christianity, and Islam, are concentrated in the last two of these regions. Patrilineal descent predominates strongly in Africa and Asia, bilateral descent in the New World. Circumcision and related forms of genital mutilations have not been reliably reported for any society in North or South America, being confined to three historically distinct areas of distribution in the Old World. Language families, art styles, folklore themes, and traits of material culture such as house types are characterized by even more circumscribed distributions. Indeed, the author knows of no other set of cultural traits which even remotely approaches patterns of kin behavior in the uniformity of their incidence throughout the world.

This fact has important implications for theory. It means, for example,

TABLE 3
Regional Distribution of Cross-Sex Patterns of Kin Behavior

| Relative | Africa | | | | | Circum-Medit. | | | | | East Eurasia | | | | | Ins. Pacific | | | | | North America | | | | | South America | | | | |
|---|---|---|---|---|---|---|---|---|---|---|---|---|---|---|---|---|---|---|---|---|---|---|---|---|---|---|---|---|---|---|
| | A | R | I | J | L | A | R | I | J | L | A | R | I | J | L | A | R | I | J | L | A | R | I | J | L | A | R | I | J | L |
| WiMo | 13 | 6 | 0 | 0 | 0 | 3 | 3 | 1 | 0 | 0 | 5 | 4 | 2 | 0 | 0 | 7 | 10 | 2 | 0 | 0 | 13 | 6 | 3 | 0 | 0 | 5 | 1 | 0 | 0 | 0 |
| SoWi | 7 | 6 | 2 | 0 | 0 | 3 | 2 | 1 | 0 | 0 | 4 | 4 | 2 | 0 | 0 | 4 | 7 | 2 | 0 | 1 | 8 | 5 | 4 | 1 | 0 | 2 | 1 | 0 | 0 | 0 |
| Si | 1 | 9 | 5 | 1 | 0 | 0 | 0 | 4 | 0 | 0 | 2 | 4 | 6 | 0 | 0 | 6 | 9 | 3 | 1 | 0 | 5 | 11 | 3 | 1 | 0 | 1 | 1 | 1 | 0 | 0 |
| YoBrWi | 2 | 7 | 0 | 8 | 2 | 1 | 2 | 2 | 1 | 0 | 4 | 2 | 2 | 1 | 0 | 3 | 4 | 5 | 2 | 5 | 0 | 1 | 2 | 10 | 7 | 0 | 3 | 0 | 3 | 2 |
| WiElSi | 1 | 5 | 1 | 8 | 2 | 1 | 1 | 0 | 2 | 0 | 2 | 1 | 2 | 2 | 1 | 3 | 3 | 4 | 2 | 6 | 0 | 2 | 2 | 12 | 6 | 0 | 0 | 2 | 1 | 3 |
| FaSiDa | 0 | 0 | 2 | 7 | 2 | 1 | 0 | 3 | 3 | 0 | 0 | 1 | 3 | 0 | 2 | 4 | 2 | 4 | 2 | 1 | 1 | 6 | 2 | 5 | 3 | 0 | 0 | 1 | 1 | 2 |
| MoBrDa | 0 | 1 | 1 | 7 | 2 | 1 | 0 | 2 | 3 | 0 | 0 | 0 | 4 | 1 | 2 | 4 | 2 | 4 | 3 | 2 | 1 | 5 | 2 | 5 | 3 | 0 | 0 | 0 | 1 | 4 |
| ElBrWi | 2 | 5 | 0 | 11 | 2 | 0 | 3 | 1 | 3 | 0 | 1 | 0 | 3 | 2 | 3 | 1 | 6 | 5 | 3 | 4 | 0 | 1 | 2 | 10 | 7 | 0 | 0 | 3 | 0 | 2 |
| WiYoSi | 1 | 3 | 1 | 10 | 4 | 0 | 1 | 1 | 4 | 0 | 1 | 0 | 0 | 4 | 2 | 1 | 3 | 4 | 4 | 6 | 0 | 2 | 2 | 11 | 6 | 0 | 0 | 1 | 1 | 4 |

that patterns of kin behavior are not to be accounted for in the usual manner of historical anthropology—in terms of centers of innovation and areas of diffusion—for these processes yield only irregular distributions. Nor are they susceptible to explanation in the usual manner of functional anthropology— as independent parallel adjustments to similar structural features such as types of kin groups or rules of descent or postmarital residence—for these too are strikingly regional in their geographical distribution. One example will suffice to demonstrate this point. Tylor (1889) advanced the plausible hypothesis that mother-in-law avoidance should be highly correlated with matrilocal residence since this brings a married man into spatial propinquity with his wife's mother and might logically be expected to generate a pattern of avoidance to reinforce the normal sexual taboo between these relatives. Yet the data from our sample, presented in Table 4, actually reveal a slightly lower (but not statistically significant) incidence of mother-in-law avoidance in the societies which practice matrilocal residence than in those following other rules of postmarital residence.

TABLE 4

Correlation of Mother-in-Law Avoidance with Matrilocal Residence

| Residence | Avoidance | Respect | Informality | Joking or License |
|---|---|---|---|---|
| Permanently matrilocal | 10 | 5 | 3 | 0 |
| Initially matrilocal | 10 | 5 | 0 | 0 |
| Optionally matrilocal | 1 | 5 | 1 | 0 |
| Non-matrilocal | 25 | 15 | 3 | 0 |

Given the unsuitability of both the historical and the usual functional-structural modes of interpretation, where can one turn for an alternative explanation of the incidence of patterns of kin behavior? The logical answer is that, since the phenomena to be explained are distributed evenly over the earth, the causal factors must likewise be universal or nearly so. One obviously universal factor is the basic psychological principles of learning and personality development, which are the same for all mankind. Another is the nuclear family, the outstanding example of a universal feature of human social organization. The same psychological principles, operating everywhere in an essentially identical social setting, might reasonably be expected to give rise to certain similar cultural manifestations in regions otherwise differing widely in geographical environment, economy, language, and less basic features of social structure. One notable example is the universality of intra-family incest taboos (Murdock 1949: 12-13). It is here postulated that cross-sex patterns of kin behavior are to be accounted for in similar fashion.

There are, to be sure, differences between societies, though rarely between regions, in the incidence of behavior patterns for each of the nine pairs of relatives here considered. This variance is presumably attributable to supplemental factors. Some of these bear no necessary relationship to geography, e.g., differences in the relative intensity and effectiveness of the internalization of sex taboos during the socialization process. Others appear to be functional, reflecting, for example, the diverse local rules governing permitted and prohibited marriages. The author has discussed elsewhere (Murdock 1949: 268-283) the probable reasons for the differential incidence of the several behavior patterns for various pairs of relatives of opposite sex, and it is only necessary here, by way of conclusion, to summarize his interpretations concerning the nine pairs of relatives for which new information has been assembled.

The relationship between sister and brother is universally characterized by a primary incest taboo. It is here postulated that the associated pattern of respect or restraint serves as a reinforcement of this taboo, and that the pattern is likely to be intensified to one of avoidance where the taboo is only weakly internalized during the socialization process and relaxed to one of informality where, as in our own society, the taboo is early, strongly, and effectively inculcated.

The relationship between mother-in-law and son-in-law lacks the support of a primary incest taboo. Nevertheless, for a man to have sex relations with his mother-in-law would inject into his wife's family of orientation the very kind of sexual rivalry which all societies have found it necessary to prevent by incest taboos. Avoidance in this relationship is to be understood as a social device to reinforce a secondary and derivative sex taboo. For a minority of societies a pattern of respect suffices to accomplish this purpose. Only in rare cases, in societies with strongly internalized sexual ethics, does informality prevail, and in no case in our sample is either joking or license permitted.

In the relationship between daughter-in-law and father-in-law the incidence of behavior patterns is similar, though slightly less extreme, and the same reasons presumably obtain.

In the several relationships between sisters-in-law and brothers-in-law, behavior patterns run the gamut from avoidance to license, with joking as the preponderant pattern in all cases. This lends support to the view of Brant (1948: 161) that "the joking relationship tends to obtain between relatives standing in a potential sexual relationship to each other." A heavy majority of all societies adhere to the levirate and sororate rules for secondary marriages, according to which brothers-in-law and sisters-in-law are preferred spouses upon the death of the first husband or wife and often for polygamous secondary marriages as well. The surprisingly high incidence of privileged sex relationships with these same relatives may be interpreted as "anticipatory responses." Moreover, since a wife's sister is likely to resemble the wife, and a husband's brother the husband, in most personal and social characteristics, one might expect "stimulus generalization" (cf. Hull 1943: 266) to produce toward them some approximation to the behavior normally exhibited toward the spouse.

In the relationships between siblings-in-law of opposite sex it is the occasional appearance of patterns of avoidance and respect that requires consideration. These exceptions mainly occur where marriage rules tend to equate particular siblings-in-law with parents-in-law or children-in-law of opposite sex, with the result that the patterns obtaining toward the latter are generalized to the former. The so-called "junior levirate" and "junior sororate" provide good examples. Where these rules prevail, preferential secondary marriages pertain only to the husband's elder brother or the wife's younger sister, so that the wife's elder sister, for example, is assimilated as it were to the wife's mother as a prohibited spouse and is correspondingly reacted to with avoidance or respect rather than joking or license.

The incidence of behavior patterns for cross-cousins of opposite sex reflects even more clearly their eligibility as marriage partners. Where they are potential spouses, the behavior patterns exhibited toward them are predominantly those of joking or license, but where marriage with them is prohibited the patterns are similar to, and presumably generalized from, those prevailing between sister and brother. Table 5 presents the relevant information for a mother's brother's daughter and father's sister's son in the 50 societies of our sample for which data on cross-cousin marriage are also available. The incidence of the several patterns is almost identical for the other pair of cross-cousins, a father's sister's daughter and mother's brother's son.

TABLE 5

Marriage Rules and Behavior Patterns Relating to a Mother's Brother's Daughter and Father's Sister's Son in 50 Societies

| Marriage | Avoidance | Respect | Informality | Joking | License |
|----------|-----------|---------|-------------|--------|---------|
| Preferred | 0 | 0 | 3 | 9 | 8 |
| Permitted | 1 | 0 | 3 | 4 | 5 |
| Prohibited | 5 | 8 | 7 | 7 | 0 |
| Total | 6 | 8 | 13 | 20 | 13 |

The highly exceptional, if not unique, geographical distribution of cross-sex patterns of kin behavior, eluding alike the usual historical and functional modes of interpretation, presents a sharp challenge to theoretical anthropology. Hopefully other scholars may be able to cite parallel or supplementary case materials or offer alternative explanations.

NOTE

1. This paper was prepared several years ago as a contribution to a proposed *Festschrift* in honor of John Dollard. Since plans to publish the volume have lapsed, the intended recipient has kindly consented to the publication of the paper in this journal. The author is deeply indebted to John Dollard, along with other former associates at the Institute of Human Relations, for providing him with the psychological sophistication which has enabled him to develop a relatively novel interpretation of a particularly interesting body of behavioral science data.

BIBLIOGRAPHY

Brant, C. S. 1948. On Joking Relationships. American Anthropologist 50: 160-162.
Eggan, F. 1937. Social Anthropology of North American Tribes. Chicago.
Hull, C. L. 1943. Principles of Behavior. New York.
Lowie, R. H. 1920. Primitive Society. New York.
Murdock, G. P. 1949. Social Structure. New York.
——— 1965-66. Ethnographic Atlas. Ethnology 4: 242-248, 451; 5: 444.
——— 1968. World Sampling Provinces. Ethnology 7: 305-326.
Radcliffe-Brown, A. R. 1940. On Joking Relationships. Africa 13: 195-210.
Tylor, E. B. 1889. On a Method of Investigating the Development of Institutions. Journal of the Royal Anthropological Institute 18: 245-269.

Appendix

# Appendix
# Studies Using the Standard
# Cross-Cultural Sample
*Herbert Barry III*

This appendix identifies and classifies publications, through 1978, that have referred to the reports of the Standard Cross-Cultural Sample or its codes. The reference list contains 128 articles or books that cite at least one of the twelve articles on the standard sample reprinted in Part I. In addition to being a useful reference tool, this list permits assessment of the initial scientific impact of the articles reprinted here.

## LOCATING THE PUBLICATIONS

Most of the citations in this appendix are articles listed in the *Social Sciences Citation Index,* an annual compilation of the items in the reference lists of all the articles published in a large number of journals. This bibliographical tool, which first appeared in 1969, is published by the Institute for Scientific Information in Philadelphia. A few of the articles were obtained from the *Science Citation Index* and the *Art and Humanities Citation Index,* published by the same institute.

Since the *American Ethnologist* is not included in these indexes, I have located the citations in that journal. I have also found the citations in books, since most of the *Social Sciences Citation Index* coverage consists of periodicals. Some of the books were found because their authors also published articles included in one of the indexes. Several colleagues, who were sent a preliminary version of the list, contributed other references not included in these indexes.

I have read each of the articles and books listed here. This was necessary to provide the complete, exact titles since the *Social Sciences Citation Index* truncates long names and omits such words as "and," "a," and "the." A more important purpose for reading these publications was to classify the reasons why they cited the articles reprinted in Part I.

## FIVE CATEGORIES OF PUBLICATIONS

Each of the 128 publications in this reference list is classified on the basis of five reasons for citing the article reprinted in this book: A, new codes on the same societies; B, analyses of the new codes; C, methodological comments; D, literature reviews; and E, residual citations.

A. *New codes on the same societies.* Following the initial article by Murdock and White (chapter 1), each of the eleven subsequent articles reprinted in Part I reports on a different set of codes applied to the same sample. Therefore, the most direct extension of this work consists of further publications that likewise report on new sets of codes on the same societies.

The list of publications includes a new set of codes on theories of illness applied to most of the societies in the standard sample (Murdock et al. 1978). A book by Murdock, giving more extensive discussion and data analysis, is scheduled for publication by the University of Pittsburgh Press in 1980.

Another new code, applied to all 186 societies in the standard sample, is on the presence or absence of belief in the evil eye (Roberts 1976). This chapter includes a report on relationships of this new measure with many of the codes reported in this book.

New codes on grief and mourning (Rosenblatt et al. 1972, 1976) and on responses of married couples to childlessness (Rosenblatt et al. 1973) have been reported on seventy-eight of the societies. Koch and Sodergren (1976) report six codes on modes of conflict management in fifty of the societies.

Two reports of new codes on large portions of the standard sample do not include the codes on the individual societies. There are several measures of closeness of supervision in 122 of the societies (Ellis et al. 1978) and measures of deference toward elderly men and women in ninety-five of the societies (Maxwell and Silverman 1978).

Other new codes are based on the same standard sample but are applied to fewer than sixty of the 186 societies. Silverman and Maxwell (1978) show codes on deference toward elderly men and women in thirty-four societies. Divale (1977b) presents new codes on marital residence in fifty-seven of the societies.

Several other new codes are not limited to the standard sample but include many of the same societies. Greenbaum (1973) studies possession trance, which has been coded in a world sample of 488 societies. Driver and Coffin (1975) report many codes on various aspects of technology in a large sample of North American Indian societies. In other studies the sample size is sixty or fewer but a large proportion of the societies are in the standard sample. Pryor (1976, 1977a, 1977b) codes a wide variety of measures of money and other attributes of the economy. Ayres (1974) codes the presence or absence of bride theft and raiding for wives; Witucki (1971), a linguistic variable; Divale and Zipin (1977), the presence or absence of nonverbal sign language; and Rosenblatt and Skoogberg (1974), the differential status as a function of birth order.

The reports on the new codes include relationships with some other variables in the same sample of societies. In many cases these other variables were introduced in the articles reprinted in this book.

Several of the articles report new information on a single society in the standard sample. Abbot and Arcury (1977), on the Kikuyu, study a sample of students and summarize the comparison of this society with the rest of the standard sample, using the codes reported in the article reprinted in chapter 7 ("Traits Inculcated in Childhood: Cross-Cultural Codes 5"). Kilbride and Kilbride (1975) study a sample of Ganda infants. Schwartz (1978) surveys the acculturation of the Tupinamba Indians.

B. *Analyses of the new codes.* The articles reprinted in Part I contribute new codes on the standard sample of 186 societies for the purpose of relating these new measures to other attributes of culture. Some of these articles include correlations or frequency cross-tabulations with other variables, but these constitute only a few examples of the relationships that could be tested. Several publications citing these articles have analyzed relationships of the new codes with various other cultural measures.

Some of the publications constitute further analyses of the data by the same authors of articles reprinted here (Barry 1976; Barry and Roberts 1972; Broude 1976; Greene 1978; Whyte 1978a). These works refer readers to the codes on the individual societies, available only in the articles reprinted in this book.

Several publications report further analyses of the codes on infancy and early childhood in chapter 6, "Infancy and Early Childhood: Cross-Cultural Codes 2." One of the authors relates new codes with prior codes on frequency of drunkenness (Barry 1976) and on games of chance (Barry and Roberts 1972). Age at the start of supplemental feeding of infants is related to female contributions to the subsistence economy (Nerlove 1974); leniency of socialization, to measures of residence and kinship (Farber 1975). Assignment of older siblings as caretakers of infants and young children is analyzed by Weisner and Gallimore (1977). Comparison of maternal with paternal contributions to infant and child caretaking is studied by Crano and Aronoff (1978). Non-maternal care is related to attributes of the subsistence economy by Konner (1976). A high degree of bodily contact of the infant with any caretakers is associated with low adult physical violence by Prescott (1976).

Sexual division of labor (chapter 10) is another topic that has attracted further analyses of the data. Nerlove (1974) relates these codes to leniency of socialization. Burton et al. (1977) and White et al. (1977) analyze the codes on sexual division of labor in terms of entailment theory. Sex differentiation is also emphasized by Whyte in the code on the status of women reprinted as chapter 12 and in the analyses of the data in a book by the same author (Whyte 1978b). Sex differences are included by Broude and Greene in the code on sexual attitudes and practices in chapter 11 and in further analyses of the data by the authors (Broude 1976; Greene 1978). Sex differences are also included in the recently published codes on childhood by Barry et al. (chapters 7 and 8) and on adolescent initiation ceremonies by Schlegel and Barry (chapter 9). Roberts and Barry (1976) relate types of competitive games to new codes on childhood separately for boys and girls (see chapters 7 and 8 by Barry et al.).

The recently published codes on sexual attitudes and practices by Broude and Greene (chapter 11) have already been subjected to further analyses. In addition to two articles by Broude (1976) and Greene (1978), Carroll (1978) relates the code on homosexuality with other variables, and Welch and Kartub (1978) relate the code on impotence with other measures.

The new codes on social organization by Murdock and Wilson in chapter 3 are used by Alessio (1978) to compare family with nonfamily agents for controlling the individual. Other articles have used portions of the standard sample of societies for reporting relationships among measures of subsistence economy or social organization (Bourguignon and Evascu 1977; Divale 1975; Erickson 1972; Goody et al. 1971; a comment by Divale in Kressel 1977). These measures have generally consisted of codes in the Ethnographic Atlas, which includes most of the societies in the standard sample. Zern (1976) uses a measure of interaction of infant with nurturer available in a portion of the sample (see Barry et al. 1967, cited by Barry and Paxson in chapter 6).

The new codes include improved and expanded versions of most of the measures in the Ethnographic Atlas. For example, this book reprints a set of thirteen codes on political organization (see chapter 4). Only two of the codes, level of political integration and selection of subordinate officials, were included in the Ethnographic Atlas. It is evident that only a small proportion of the new codes have thus far been analyzed by tests of their relationships with one another and with other codes available on many of the 186 societies in the standard sample.

C. *Methodological comments.*   Many of the publications cite one or more of the articles reprinted in Part I for the purpose of documenting a methodological discussion. In particular, many of the early publications, from 1970 to 1974, discuss the contribution of Murdock and White's article (chapter 1) to the techniques for selecting a world sample of societies.

The focus of many methodological discussions is Galton's problem, that a sample of societies fails to fulfill the statistical assumption that each society is independent of the others. Loftin and Hill (1974a) apply the alignment arcs used by Murdock and White to the much larger sample in the Ethnographic Atlas. Loftin et al. (1976) report the use and some revisions of this alignment. Bourguignon and Evascu (1977) and Divale et al. (1976) have used this information in their studies. Other discussions of Galton's problem among this list of publications are by Chaney (1976), Erickson (1974), Loftin (1972, 1975), Loftin and Hill (1974b), Naroll (1971, 1973a, 1976), Schaefer (1971), Simonton (1975), Strauss and Orans (1975), and Witkowski (1974).

Other problems concerning selection of a sample are discussed by some of the publications. Buckley and Goody (1974) recommend using the large Ethnographic Atlas sample. Greenbaum (1970) suggests using random rather than stratified samples. Otterbein (1976) evaluates the procedures for selecting several samples including the one specified by Murdock and White.

Sources of error in cross-cultural data are pointed out in some publications. Witkowski (1978) studies effects of variations in quality of field work. Schaefer and Evascu (1976) analyze systematic biases in the data. Whyte (1978a) investigates possible biasing effects resulting from the sex of the ethnographer and coder.

Only a few of the methodological discussions have focused on coding techniques. Pryor (1977b) reports using the method of Murdock and Provost (chapter 5) for measuring cultural complexity. Erchak (1976) criticizes the definitions of some of the traits inculcated in childhood (Barry et al., chapter 7) and also reports, contrary to the findings of Barry and Paxson (chapter 6), the ability to detect sex differences during infancy.

Other publications dealing with methodology include an extensive discussion (Human Relations Area Files, 1970) and briefer but general discussions by Divale (1976) and Hoon (1974). Levinson (1977b) has contributed a five-volume assessment and summary of tests and hypotheses based on relationships between variables in world samples of societies.

D. *Literature reviews.* This category contains the fewest publications. The articles reprinted in Part I may be too recent to be included in many bibliographies and reviews.

Bibliographies of cross-cultural studies have been published by O'Leary (1971, 1973), Naroll (1973b), and Levinson (1977b). Larger, more general bibliographies of social science methodology have been published by Essyad (1971, 1975).

Naroll (1970) and Levinson (1977a) have evaluated the contributions of cross-cultural studies. Erickson (1977), in a review of cultural evolution, comments that the new codes by Murdock and Morrow on subsistence economy (chapter 2) could be used to study exchange media and systems. More specific topics are covered in other reviews; these include personality differences (Witkin and Berry 1975), women's status (Quinn 1977), agricultural practices (Netting 1974), and slavery (Patterson 1977).

In addition to the publications classified as bibliographies or reviews, there are others that include extensive reviews of pertinent literature. Because these usually contain a large number of references, they are especially valuable to readers who wish to identify other publications on the topics covered. (The number of references in each publication in the list is given in brackets at the end of the publishing information.)

E. *Residual citations.* The majority of the publications citing one or more of the articles in Part I have been assigned to one of the preceding categories. The largest single category, however, is characterized as residual. In other words, the article is cited briefly, often as one of several references, without any detailed explanation of how it pertains to the new publication.

In spite of the meager documentation, many publications in this category are important references for people who are interested in the cited article. The citation expresses the author's opinion that the article is important and pertinent to the new work.

Some of these publications report new codes or analyze relationships among codes in a sample of societies. Therefore, they provide information of the same general type as the articles reprinted in this book, although they apply different codes to a different sample of societies. Blumberg and Winch (1972) analyze relationships among several measures of social organization. Lomax and Arensberg (1977) and Chaney (1973) present taxonomies of cultural types on the basis of measures of subsistence economy. Driver et al. (1972) present a typology of North American societies. Aronoff and Crano (1975) analyze women's economic activity. Dahlberg (1976) relates a new measure of average fertility of women with the percentage of women's contribution to the subsistence economy in a sample of nine African societies. Divale (1974, 1977a) relates frequency of warfare with residence and migration. Sipes (1973) relates frequency of warfare with new codes on combative sports in a sample of twenty societies. Schaefer (1976) relates measures of alcohol drinking with various attributes of social organization in a sample of fifty-seven societies. Berry (1976a, 1976b) relates cultural complexity with measures of the behavior of individual males and females in a sample of seventeen societies. Berry (1977) intercorrelates various measures in samples of ten and twenty-one societies.

Isaac (1977) reanalyzes the ethnographic information on the Siriono. Bolton (1978) describes child-holding patterns among the Yanomamo. Since these societies are included in the standard sample, the information should be interesting and important to users of that sample. Chisholm (1978) studies effects of the use of cradleboards on Navaho infants. Bolton et al. (1976) compares an agricultural with a pastoral community in South America.

Several of the residual citations are in books, which provide a broad, general coverage of the topic. These are Berry (1976a), Bourguignon and Greenbaum (1973), Munroe and Munroe (1975), Whiting and Whiting (1975), and Winch (1977). In addition, White (1973) constitutes a chapter in a book that provides a broad coverage of methodology in cross-cultural research.

Specific topics of other publications may be of special interest to some readers. Brown (1975) and Siskind (1978) discuss the role of women in the subsistence economy. This is the topic of one of the new sets of codes (Murdock and Provost, chapter 10). Prescott (1977) discusses early personality development. Fry (1975) compares children from the United States and India. Crano and Aronoff (1976) discuss the methodology of coding procedures. Smith and Fuhrer (1976) mention the availability of the new codes as data sets for statistical analyses with the aid of computer programs.

One of the publications is an extensive report on the Human Relations Area Files (Ford 1970). Two others consist of historical surveys of cross-cultural research (Schaefer 1977a, 1977b). One publication proposes that societies can be classified according to their structural tightness or looseness (Boldt 1978). Others are general discussions of method or theory in cross-cultural research (Berry 1975, 1978; Berry and Annis 1974; Chaney 1978; Malik 1975; Moles 1977; Schweizer and Schweizer 1978; Sipes 1972; Smith 1977; Triandis 1977, 1978; Udy 1973; Vermeulen and deRuijter 1975).

GENERAL ATTRIBUTES OF THE CITATIONS

Of the 128 publications in this list, sixty-four (50 percent) are in anthropology journals, eighteen (14 percent) in psychology journals, and eight (6 percent) in sociology journals. Of the remaining thirty-eight publications (30 percent), seven are in other specialty fields, such as economics or political science, eleven in general social science journals, and twenty are books or chapters in books.

Thus anthropology journals are most predominant in this list. The journal with the largest number of citations (thirty-three) is *Behavior Science Research,* including ten in *Behavior Science Notes,* the name of the same journal prior to 1974. There are twelve citations in *Current Anthropology,* six in *Ethnology,* and five in the *American Anthropologist.*

Psychology journals are second to anthropology. Of these the *Journal of Cross-Cultural Psychology* has the largest number of citations (five).

The list of publications shows no one author as the preponderant contributor. There are eight citations by Divale (including a comment in the article by Kressel), seven citations by Berry (including Witkin and Berry), and six by Naroll (including Loftin et al.).

During the span of nine years, 1970–1978, the frequency of citations was highest in the last three years; seventy-two (56 percent) were in 1976–1978. The frequency of citations of a 1969 article would normally be diminishing after 1975, but most of the citations include Murdock and White's original report of 1969 (chapter 1), even when the principal purpose is to refer to one of the subsequent articles. The accumulation of a set of codes on the same standard sample undoubtedly has resulted in more references to the articles than would have been made to any single article. Since five of the articles reprinted in Part I were published in 1976 or later, most of the citations of them will occur after 1978, the latest year included in this list.

CONCLUSIONS

Searches of the scientific literature must seek a balance between maximal comprehensiveness and maximal selectivity. The literature is so large that it is impossible to review all of it. Inspection of all the items in broad topical categories is wasteful because only some of them are pertinent and important for a specific purpose. Narrow definition of the topic imposes excessive selectivity, however, so that many important items are missed. This problem is especially serious in an interdisciplinary field such as cross-cultural research.

The citation indexes provide unique advantages for selecting references that include a wide range of topics and also a large proportion of useful items. The selection is based on the author's decision that a particular article is sufficiently pertinent and important to justify citation. Thus the search is independent of topical categories and disciplinary definitions. The search can be broadened by expanding the list of publications whose subsequent citations are identified. The citation indexes thereby help scientists to avoid being overwhelmed by the explosive growth of information. Use of this resource is facilitated by the availability on magnetic tape for computer-aided search and by five-year compilations of the Science Citation Index bringing together five years of citations of each key reference.

The citation indexes are especially useful when the key references consist of a group of closely related publications. The articles reprinted in Part I of this book fulfill this criterion. Each of them contributes new information on cultural attributes in the same world sample of societies. Most people who are interested in one of these articles will probably find useful a high proportion of the subsequent publications that cite any of them. These 128 publications constitute a manageable number for literature searches.

A remarkably high proportion of the publications have been in *Behavior Science Research*. This journal thereby appears to be the focal publication medium for the type of research represented by the group of articles published in *Ethnology* and reprinted in Part I of this book.

The following list of citing publications indicates that the articles reprinted in Part I of this book have become well established as important materials for cross-cultural research. As time elapses and other articles intervene, their influence will continue to expand, although future publications may not trace the credit back through intervening publications to these original sources. Whether they do or not, this is how knowledge accumulates.

## LIST OF PUBLICATIONS

Each of the following publications cites one or more of the twelve articles reprinted in Part I, "The Standard Cross-Cultural Sample and Its Codes." The figure enclosed in brackets at the end of each publication identifies the number of bibliographical references in the article or book; at least one of these is to an article reprinted in Part I. The final letter (A–E) identifies the category to which the publication contributed: A, new codes on the same societies; B, analyses of the new codes; C, methodological comments; D, literature reviews; E, residual citations.

Abbott, S., and T. Arcury. 1977. Continuity with Tradition: Male and Female in Gikuyu Culture. Youth and Society 8: 329–358. [27] A.
Alessio, J. C. 1978. Family Structure and Social Control: A Cross-Cultural Study. Internat. J. Sociol. Family 8: 1–18. [20] B.
Aronoff, J., and W. D. Crano. 1975. A Re-Examination of the Cross-Cultural Principles of Task Segregation and Sex Role Differentiation in the Family. Amer. Sociol. Rev. 40: 12–20. [27] E.
Ayres, B. 1974. Bride Theft and Raiding for Wives in Cross-Cultural Perspective. Anthropol. Quart. 47: 238–252. [12] A.
Barry, H., III. 1976. Cross-Cultural Evidence That Dependency Conflict Motivates Drunkenness. Cross-Cultural Approaches to the Study of Alcohol: An Interdisciplinary Perspective, eds., M. W. Everett, J. O. Waddell, and D. B. Heath, pp. 249–263. The Hague. [25] B.
Barry, H., III, and J. M. Roberts. 1972. Infant Socialization and Games of Chance. Ethnology 11: 296–308. [23] B.
Berry, J. W. 1975. An Ecological Approach to Cross-Cultural Psychology. Nederlands tijdschrift voor de psychologie 30: 51–84. [66] E.
———. 1976a. Human Ecology and Cognitive Style: Comparative Studies in Cultural and Psychological Adaptation. New York. [303] E.
———. 1976b. Sex Differences in Behaviour and Cultural Complexity. Indian J. Psychol. 51: 89–97. [21] E.
———. 1977. A Dynamic Model of Relationships Among Ecology, Culture and Behavior. Ann. N. Y. Acad. Sci. 285: 19–31. [26] E.
———. 1978. Social Psychology; Comparative Societal and Universal. Canad. Psychol. Rev. 19: 93–104. [91] E.
Berry, J. W., and R. C. Annis. 1974. Ecology, Culture and Psychological Differentiation. Internat. J. Psychol. 9: 173–193. [46] E.
Blumberg, R. L., and R. F. Winch. 1972. Societal Complexity and Familial Complexity: Evidence for the Curvilinear Hypothesis. Amer. J. Sociol. 77: 898–920. [23] E.

Boldt, E. D. 1978. Structural Tightness and Cross-Cultural Research. J. Cross-Cultural Psychol. 9: 151–165. [40] E.

Bolton, C., R. Bolton, L. Gross, A. Koel, C. Michelson, R. L. Munroe, and R. H. Munroe. 1976. Pastoralism and Personality: An Andean Replication. Ethos 4: 463–481. [38] E.

Bolton, R. 1978. Child-Holding Patterns. Current Anthropol. 19: 134–135. [15] E.

Bourguignon, E., and T. L. Evascu. 1977. Altered States of Consciousness Within a General Evolutionary Perspective: Holocultural Analysis. Behav. Sci. Res. 12: 197–216. [39] B, C.

Bourguignon, E., and L. S. Greenbaum. 1973. Diversity and Homogeneity in World Societies. New Haven. [48] E.

Broude, G. J. 1976. Cross-Cultural Patterning of Some Sexual Attitudes and Practices. Behav. Sci. Res. 11: 227–262. [22] B.

Brown, J. K. 1975. A Reconsideration of Ida Hahn's "Dauernahrung und Frauenarbeit." Current Anthropol. 16: 447–449. [18] E.

Buckley, J., and J. Goody. 1974. Problems Involved in Sample Selection. Behav. Sci. Res. 9: 21–22. [4] C.

Burton, M. L., L. A. Brudner, and D. R. White. 1977. A Model of the Sexual Division of Labor. Amer. Ethnologist 4: 227–251. [16] B.

Carroll, M. P. 1978. Freud on Homosexuality and the Super-Ego: Some Cross-Cultural Tests. Behav. Sci. Res. 13: 255–271. [22] B.

Chaney, R. P. 1973. Comparative Analysis and Retroductive Reasoning or
  ' Conclusions in Search of a Premise. Amer. Anthropologist 75: 1358–1375. [92] E.

———. 1976. On Z Factors. Current Anthropol. 17: 749–756. [45] C.

———. 1978. Polythematic Expansion: Remarks on Needham's Polythetic Classification. Current Anthropol. 19: 139–143. [60] E.

Chisholm, J. S. 1978. Swaddling, Cradleboards and Development of Children. Early Humann Development 2: 255–275. [38] E.

Crano, W. D., and J. Aronoff. 1976. On Aronoff and Crano's Re-Examination of the Cross-Cultural Principles of Task Segregation and Sex Role Differentiation in the Nuclear Family (Comment on Aronoff and Crano, ASR February, 1975): Reply to Carroll. Amer. Sociol. Rev. 41: 1072–1074. [6] E.

———. 1978. A Cross-Cultural Study of Expressive and Instrumental Role Complementarity in the Family. Amer. Sociol. Rev. 43: 463–471. [16] B.

Dahlberg, F. 1976. More on Mechanisms of Population Growth. Current Anthropol. 17: 164–166. [20] E.

Divale, W. T. 1974. Migration, External Warfare, and Matrilocal Residence. Behav. Sci. Res. 9: 75–133. [172] E.

———. 1975. Temporal Focus and Random Error in Cross-Cultural Hypothesis Tests. Behav. Sci. Res. 10: 19–36. [28] B.

———. 1976. Using Date of European Contact for Time-Lagged Variables in Cross-Cultural Surveys. Behav. Sci. Res. 11: 39–55. [40] C.

———. 1977a. From Correlations to Causes: A New and Simple Method for Causal Analysis in Cross-Cultural Research. Ann. N.Y. Acad. Sci. 285: 66–74. [34] E.

———. 1977b. Living Floor Area and Marital Residence: A Replication. Behav. Sci. Res. 12: 109–115. [15] A.

Divale, W. T., F. Chamberis, and D. Gangloff. 1976. War, Peace, and Marital Residence in Pre-Industrial Societies. J. Conflict Resolution 20: 57–78. [31] C.

Divale, W. T., and C. Zipin. 1977. Hunting and the Development of Sign Language: A Cross-Cultural Test. J. Anthropol. Res. 33: 185–201. [43] A.

Driver, H. E., and J. L. Coffin. 1975. Classification and Development of North American Indian Cultures: A Statistical Analysis of the Driver-Massey Sample. Trans. Amer. Philosophical Soc. 65: 5–120. [540] A.

Driver, H. E., J. A. Kenny, H. C. Hudson, and O. M. Engle. 1972. Statistical Classification of North American Indian Ethnic Units. Ethnology 11: 311–339 [31] E.

Ellis, G. J., G. R. Lee, and L. R. Petersen. 1978. Supervision and Conformity: A Cross-Cultural Analysis of Parental Socialization Values. Amer. J. Sociol. 84: 386–403. [44] A.

Erchak, G. M. 1976. The Nonsocial Behavior of Young Kpelle Children and the Acquisition of Sex Roles. J. Cross-Cultural Psychol. 7: 223–234. [23] C.

Erickson, E. E. 1972. Other Cultural Dimensions: Selective Rotations of Sawyer and LeVine's Factor Analysis of the World Ethnographic Sample. Behav. Sci. Notes 7: 95–156. [34] B.

———. 1974. Galton's Worst: Further Note on Ember's Reflection. Behav. Sci. Res. 9: 7–11. [7] C.

———. 1977. Cultural Evolution. Amer. Behav. Scientist 20: 669–680. [82] D.

Essyad, M.-F. 1971. Social Science Methodology: A Bibliography of Studies Published in 1969–1970. Social Science Information 10 (5): 133–161. [459] D.

———. 1975. Social Science Methodology: A Bibliography of Studies Published in 1973–1974. Social Science Information 14 (5): 181–207. [319] D.

Farber, B. 1975. Bilateral Kinship: Centripetal and Centrifugal Types of Organization. J. Marriage and Family 37: 871–888. [75] B.

Ford, C. S. 1970. Human Relations Area Files: 1949–1969; A Twenty-Year Report. Behav. Sci. Notes 5: 1–61. [15] E.

Fry, P. S. 1975. The Resistance to Temptation: Inhibitory and Disinhibitory Effects of Models on Children from India and the United States. J. Cross-Cultural Psychol. 6: 189–202. [18] E.

Goody, J., B. Irving, and N. Tahany. 1971. Causal Inferences Concerning Inheritance and Property. Human Relations 24: 295–314. [39] B.

Greenbaum, L. 1970. Evaluation of a Stratified Versus an Unstratified Universe of Cultures in Comparative Research. Behav. Sci. Notes 5: 251–289. [22] C.

———. 1973. Societal Correlates of Possession Trance in Sub-Saharan Africa. Religion, Altered States of Consciousness, and Social Change, ed. E. Bourguignon, pp. 39–57. Columbus, Ohio. [30] A.

Greene, P. J. 1978. Promiscuity, Paternity, and Culture. Amer. Ethnologist 5: 151–159. [15] B.

Hoon, P. W. 1974. Polynesian Relationships: Initial Correlation and Factor Analysis of Cultural Data. Ethnology. 13: 83–103. [45] C.

Human Relations Area Files. 1970. Second HRAF Cross-Cultural Research Conference. Behav. Sci. Notes 5: 141–193. [13] C.

Isaac, B. L. 1977. The Siriono of Eastern Bolivia: A Reexamination. Human Ecology 5: 137–154. [42] E.

Kilbride, J. E., and P. L. Kilbride. 1975. Sitting and Smiling Behavior of Baganda Infants: The Influence of Culturally Constituted Experience. J. Cross-Cultural Psychol. 6: 88–107. [45] A.

Koch, K.-F., and J. A. Sodergren. 1976. Political and Psychological Correlates of Conflict Management: A Cross-Cultural Study. Law and Society Rev. 10: 443–466. [63] A.

Konner, M. J. 1976. Relations Among Infants and Juveniles in Comparative Perspective. Social Science Information 15: 371–402. [111] B.

Kressel, G. M. 1977. Bride-Price Reconsidered. Current Anthropol. 18: 441–458. [72] B.

Levinson, D. 1977a. What Have We Learned from Cross-Cultural Surveys? Amer. Behav. Scientist 20: 757–792. [199] D.

———. 1977b. A Guide to Social Theory: Worldwide Cross-Cultural Tests. Vol. 1, Introduction. New Haven. [333] C, D.

Loftin, C. 1972. Galton's Problem as Spatial Autocorrelation: Comments on Ember's Empirical Test. Ethnology 11: 425–435. [20] C.

———. 1975. Partial Correlation as an Adjustment Procedure for Galton's Problem. Behav. Sci. Res. 10: 131–141. [12] C.

Loftin, C., and R. H. Hill. 1974a. A Comparison of Alignment Procedures for Tests of Galton's Problem. Studies in Cultural Diffusion: Galton's Problem, Vol. 1, ed. J. M. Schaefer, pp. 25–61. New Haven. [17] C.

———. 1974b. A Comparison of Alignment Procedures for Tests of Galton's Problem. Behav. Sci. Res. 9: 4–6. [5] C.

Loftin, C., R. H. Hill, R. Naroll, and E. Margolis. 1976. Murdock-White Interdependence Alignment of Ethnographic Atlas Culture Clusters. Behav. Sci. Res. 11: 213–226. [12] C.

Lomax, A., and C. M. Arensberg. 1977. A Worldwide Evolutionary Classification of Cultures by Subsistence Systems. Current Anthropol. 18: 659–708. [67] E.

Malik, S. C. 1975. Prehistoric Archeology as a Social Science in India. Man in India 55: 204–226. [212] E.

Maxwell, R. J., and P. Silverman. 1978. The Nature of Deference. Current Anthropol. 19: 151. [3] A.

Moles, J. A. 1977. Standardization and Measurement in Cultural Anthropology: A Neglected Area. Current Anthropol. 18: 235–257. [119] E.

Munroe, R. L., and R. H. Munroe. 1975. Cross-Cultural Human Development. Monterey, Calif. [479] E.

Murdock, G. P., S. F. Wilson, and V. Frederick. 1978. World Distribution of Theories of Illness. Ethnology 17: 449–470. [7] A.

Naroll, R. 1970. What Have We Learned from Cross-Cultural Surveys? Amer. Anthropologist 72: 1227–1288. [283] D.

——. 1971. The Double Language Boundary in Cross-Cultural Surveys. Behav. Sci. Notes 6: 95–102. [15] C.

——. 1973a. Galton's Problem. A Handbook of Method in Cultural Anthropology, eds. R. Naroll and R. Cohen, pp. 974–989. New York. [37] C.

——. 1973b. Holocultural Theory Testing. Main Currents in Cultural Anthropology, eds. R. Naroll and F. Naroll, pp. 309–353. New York. [455] D.

——. 1976. Galton's Problem and HRAFLIB. Behav. Sci. Res. 11: 123–148. [39] C.

Nerlove, S. B. 1974. Women's Workload and Infant Feeding Practices: Relationship with Demographic Implications. Ethnology 13: 207–214. [40] B.

Netting, R. M. C. 1974. Agrarian Ecology. Ann. Rev. Anthropol. 3: 21–56. [295] D.

O'Leary, T. J. 1971. Bibliography of Cross-Cultural Studies: Supplement I. Behav. Sci. Notes 6: 191–203. [158] D.

——. 1973. Bibliography of Cross-Cultural Studies: Supplement II. Behav. Sci. Notes 8: 123–134. [140] D.

Otterbein, K. F. 1976. Sampling and Samples in Cross-Cultural Studies. Behav. Sci. Res. 11: 107–121. [27] C.

Patterson, O. 1977. Slavery. Ann. Rev. Sociol. 3: 407–449. [363] D.

Prescott, J. W. 1976. Somatosensory Deprivation and Its Relationship to the Blind. The Effects of Blindness and Other Impairments on Early Development, ed. Z. S. Jastrzembska, pp. 65–121. New York. [286] B.

——. 1977. Phylogenetic and Ontogenetic Aspects of Human Affectional Development. Proceedings of the 1976 International Congress of Sexology, eds. R. Gemme and C. C. Wheeler, pp. 431–457. New York. [95] E.

Pryor, F. L. 1976. The Friedman-Savage Utility Function in Cross-Cultural Perspective. J. Political Economy 84: 821–834. [13] A.

——. 1977a. The Origins of the Economy: A Comparative Study of Distribution in Primitive and Peasant Economies. New York. [260] A.

——. 1977b. Origins of Money. J. Money, Credit and Banking 9: 391–409. [25] A, C.

Quinn, N. 1977. Anthropological Studies on Women's Status. Ann. Rev. Anthropol. 6: 181–225. [88] D.

Roberts, J. M. 1976. Belief in the Evil Eye in World Perspective. The Evil Eye, ed. C. Maloney, pp. 223–278. New York. [36] A.

Roberts, J. M., and H. Barry III. 1976. Inculcated Traits and Game-Type Combinations: A Cross-Cultural View. The Humanistic and Mental Health Aspects of Sports, Exercise and Recreation, ed. T. T. Craig, pp. 5–11. Chicago. [12] B.

Rosenblatt, P. C., D. A. Jackson, and R. P. Walsh. 1972. Coping with Anger and Aggression in Mourning. Omega. 3: 271–284. [63] A.

Rosenblatt, P. C., P. Peterson, J. Portner, M. Cleveland, A. Mykkanen, R. Foster, G. Holm, B. Joel, H. Reisch, C. Kreuscher, and R. Phillips. 1973. A Cross-Cultural Study of Responses to Childlessness. Behav. Sci. Notes 8: 221–231. [14] A.

Rosenblatt, P. C., and E. L. Skoogberg. 1974. Birth Order in Cross-Cultural Perspective. Developmental Psychol. 10: 48–54. [9] A.

Rosenblatt, P. C., R. P. Walsh, and D. A. Jackson. 1976. Grief and Mourning in Cross-Cultural Perspective. New Haven. [297] A.

Schaefer, J. M. 1971. Sampling Methods, Functional Associations, and Galton's Problem: A Replicative Assessment; Reply to Comments by McNett and Greenbaum. Behav. Sci. Notes 6: 266–274. [20] C.

———. 1976. Drunkenness and Culture Stress: A Holocultural Test. Cross-Cultural Approaches to the Study of Alcohol: An Interdisciplinary Perspective, eds. M. W. Everett, J. O. Waddell, and D. B. Heath, pp. 287–321. The Hague. [106] E.

———. 1977a. Growth and Development of Hologeistic Cross-Cultural Research. Ann. N.Y. Acad. Sci. 285: 75–88. [114] E.

———. 1977b. Growth of Hologeistic Studies: 1889–1975. Behav. Sci. Res. 12: 71–108. [120] E.

Schaefer, J. M., and T. L. Evascu. 1976. Data Quality and Modes of Marriage: Some Holocultural Evidence of Systematic Errors. Behav. Sci. Res. 11: 25–37. [26] C.

Schwartz, S. B. 1978. Indian Labor and New World Plantations: European Demands and Indian Responses in Northeastern Brazil. Amer. Historical Rev. 83: 43–79. [123] A.

Schweizer, T., and G. E. Schweizer. 1978. Statistische Gesetse und statistische Argumentation in der Ethnologie. Anthropos 73: 337–366. [33] E.

Silverman, P., and R. J. Maxwell. 1978. How Do I Respect Thee? Let Me Count the Ways: Deference Towards Elderly Men and Women. Behav. Sci. Res. 13: 91–108. [24] A.

Simonton, D. K. 1975. Galton's Problem, Autocorrelation, and Diffusion Coefficients. Behav. Sci. Res. 10: 239–248. [32] C.

Sipes, R. G. 1972. Rating Hologeistic Method. Behav. Sci. Notes 7: 157–198. [78] E.

———. 1973. War, Sports and Aggression: Empirical Test of Two Rival Theories. Amer. Anthropologist 75: 64–86. [143] E.

Siskind, J. 1978. Kinship and Mode of Production. Amer. Anthropologist 80: 860–872. [35] E.

Smith, B. D. 1977. Archeological Inference and Inductive Confirmation. Amer. Anthropologist 79: 598–617. [56] E.

Smith, C., and D. Fuhrer. 1976. Computer-Assisted Instruction Using Cross-Cultural Data. Behav. Sci. Res. 11: 1–18. [29] E.

Strauss, D. J., and M. Orans. 1975. Mighty Sifts: A Critical Appraisal of Solutions to Galton's Problem and a Partial Solution. Current Anthropol. 16: 573–594. [59] C.

Triandis, H. C. 1977. Cross-Cultural Social and Personality Psychology. Personality and Social Psychol. Bull. 3: 143–158. [74] E.

———. 1978. Some Universals of Social Behavior. Personality and Social Psychol. Bull. 4: 1–16. [58] E.

Udy, S. H., Jr. 1973. Cross-Cultural Analysis: Methods and Scope. Ann. Rev. Anthropol. 2: 253–270. [47] E.

Vermeulen, C. J., and A. deRuijter. 1975. Dominant Epistemological Presuppositions in the Use of the Cross-Cultural Survey Method. Current Anthropol. 16: 29–52. [172] E.

Weisner, T. S., and R. Gallimore. 1977. My Brother's Keeper: Child and Sibling Caretaking. Current Anthropol. 18: 169–190. [107] B.

Welch, M. R., and P. Kartub. 1978. Socio-Cultural Correlates of Incidence of Impotence: A Cross-Cultural Study. J. Sex Res. 14: 218–230. [22] B.

White, D. R. 1973. Societal Research Archives System: Retrieval, Quality Control and Analysis of Comparative Data. A Handbook of Method in Cultural Anthropology, eds. R. Naroll and R. Cohen, pp. 678–685. New York. [28] E.

White, D. R., M. L. Burton, and L. A. Brudner. 1977. Entailment Theory and Method: A Cross-Cultural Analysis of Sexual Division of Labor. Behav. Sci. Res. 12: 1–24. [15] B.

Whiting, B. B., and J. W. M. Whiting. 1975. Children of Six Cultures: A Psycho-Cultural Analysis. Cambridge, Mass. [91] E.

Whyte, M. K. 1978a. Cross-Cultural Studies of Women and the Male Bias Problem. Behav. Sci. Res. 13: 65–80. [18] B, C.

———. 1978b. The Status of Women in Pre-Industrial Societies. Princeton. [109] B.

Winch, R. F. 1977. Familial Organization: A Quest for Determinants. New York. [391] E.

Witkin, H. A., and J. W. Berry. 1975. Psychological Differentiation in Cross-Cultural Perspective. J. Cross-Cultural Psychol. 6: 4–87. [176] D.

Witkowski, S. R. 1974. Galton's Opportunity: The Hologeistic Study of Historical Processes. Behav. Sci. Res. 9: 11–15. [10] C.

———. 1978. Ethnographic Field Work: Optimal Versus Non-Optimal Conditions. Behav. Sci. Res. 13: 245–253. [13] C.

Witucki, J. 1971. A Language Pattern Co-Occurring with Violence-Permissiveness. Behav. Science 16: 531–537. [10] A.

Zern, D. 1976. Further Evidence Supporting the Relationship Between Nurturer/Infant Contact and Later Differentiation of Social Environment. J. Genet. Psychol. 129: 169–170. [4] B.